PAPER OF WRECKAGE

AN ORAL HISTORY OF THE *NEW YORK POST*, 1976–2024

The Rogues, Renegades, Wiseguys, Wankers, and Relentless Reporters Who Redefined American Media

---

Susan Mulcahy

and

Frank DiGiacomo

ATRIA BOOKS

New York • London • Toronto • Sydney • New Delhi

ATRIA
BOOKS

An Imprint of Simon & Schuster, LLC
1230 Avenue of the Americas
New York, NY 10020

Copyright © 2024 by Frank DiGiacomo and Susan Mulcahy

First Atria Books hardcover edition October 2024

ATRIA BOOKS and colophon are trademarks of Simon & Schuster, LLC

Simon & Schuster: Celebrating 100 Years of Publishing in 2024

For information about special discounts for bulk purchases, please contact Simon &
Schuster Special Sales at 1-866-506-1949 or business@simonandschuster.com.

The Simon & Schuster Speakers Bureau can bring authors to your live event. For
more information or to book an event, contact the Simon & Schuster Speakers
Bureau at 1-866-248-3049 or visit our website at www.simonspeakers.com.

Interior design by Dana Sloan

Manufactured in the United States of America

1 3 5 7 9 10 8 6 4 2

Library of Congress Cataloging-in-Publication Data is available.

ISBN 978-1-9821-6483-6
ISBN 978-1-9821-6485-0 (ebook)

For Myron Rushetzky, whose Post Nation
captures the paper's spirit

CONTENTS

PART IV: **1993–2024, MURDOCH 2.0**

INTRODUCTION

Editorial meetings at the *New York Post* could be raucous, testy, entertaining, politically incorrect, toadying, tense, or even somber, depending on the participants and the nature of the news on a given day. By the early days of the twenty-first century, Rupert Murdoch rarely attended the meetings anymore, but as several of the *Post*'s top editors made their way into the conference room on the tenth floor of 1211 Sixth Avenue in April 2001, there he was, jowly and dour, for the second day in a row. The tabloid's editor, Xana Antunes, sat at the head of a long table, and Murdoch occupied the seat to her immediate right. Antunes represented a sea change at the paper. She had joined the *Post* in 1995 as the deputy business editor and had so impressed her bosses with the buzzy section she produced—a section that was of prime importance to the man sitting next to her—that in 1999 she was promoted to the top job, the first woman to hold the position during the years that Murdoch had owned the paper. The *Post* was the foundation of Murdoch's American media empire, and though another of his properties, Fox News, reached millions more people (and unlike the *Post*, was immensely profitable), the tabloid remained important to him. As Antunes began going through a list of planned stories, he demonstrated in chilling fashion just how important.

Murdoch began to pepper Antunes with questions: *Why aren't you doing this? Why haven't you planned for that? I don't see any mention of this, which is really important. It's not even part of your plan.*

"You could tell he was deeply unhappy," says Gregg Birnbaum, who was the

Post's political editor then, and present at the meeting. "It was very clear that this was an intentional move."

Antunes looked surprised by Murdoch's inquisition and offered up a polite defense. "We're definitely planning on covering that, Mr. Murdoch," Birnbaum remembers her saying. "Her office was just fifty feet away. If he had issues, he could have raised them privately with her. But he was sending a message to the entire staff, that he had lost confidence in Xana."

The other editors sat in silence. "It was very painful to me, and I'm sure the other editors, to watch her be eviscerated like that. And she was all alone. Nobody could help in that circumstance. It was a conversation only between her and Rupert." Antunes was forced out soon after that meeting.

Rupert Murdoch is a newspaperman at heart, but that heart can be inhospitably cold. Wayne Darwen, an assistant managing editor at the *Post* in the 1980s, and later a producer at what was essentially the TV version of the tabloid, *A Current Affair*, admiringly describes Murdoch as "the most intimidating presence I've ever encountered," a man "with a good measure of ruthlessness, who does not give a fuck what anyone says or thinks, who's not intimidated by anybody—politicians, prime ministers, or presidents. People often say he's political, but the bottom line is, his god is his business. And nothing gets in the way of business."

When Murdoch took full control of the *Post* at the beginning of 1977, he refashioned the paper in his own image—an approach to journalism best characterized by Adam Scull, a photographer for the *Post* in the late 1970s and '80s: "We're the *New York Post*. Fuck you and your rules. We make our own rules."

Though the tabloid's weekday print and digital circulation of just over 510,000 is a fraction of Murdoch's right-wing cable TV behemoth, Fox News (average daily viewership: over 2 million in prime time in the first quarter of 2024), and it does not possess the global reach of the conservative *Wall Street Journal*, the *Post* is Murdoch's pugnacious street brawler devoted to settling scores, kneecapping the self-important, exposing hypocrisy, and bedeviling liberal politicians whose platforms don't jibe with his agenda. As onetime Gambino crime family underboss Sammy "The Bull" Gravano says, the *Post* has "balls."

A staff of rogues, reprobates, freaks, geeks, secret geniuses—many of them with Australian or British accents—and a smattering of organized crime figures pursued that agenda in the final decades of the twentieth century, creating the tabloid's multiple daily editions in a dingy, smoke-filled, cigarette butt—

and coffee cup–strewn newsroom at 210 South Street, situated on a desolate strip beneath the FDR Drive and between the Manhattan and Brooklyn bridges. By definition half the size of a broadsheet like the *New York Times*, a tabloid typically prioritizes crime, sex, scandal, sports, and gossip. In that regard, the *Post* is typical. But compared to other American newspapers, it is anything but.

Newsrooms depicted in serious films about journalism like *All the President's Men* and *Spotlight* portray reporters and editors as stone-faced, conscience-stricken men and women; shirtsleeves rolled, ties and hair askew, pounding their fists on conference tables and arguing passionately about getting the facts right. The *Post* during the South Street years was more like *Fear and Loathing in Las Vegas*: one editor wore devil horns and sent panties to female staffers through interoffice mail. A brilliant headline writer strode through the office—and atop newsroom desks—barefoot, chucking trash cans across the newsroom when he was angry, muttering, "The revolution is coming." The same man engaged in tumultuous and sometimes violent affairs with female staffers. Fistfights broke out over stories. Alcohol flowed openly, and cocaine dealing almost resulted in a police raid of the newsroom. Sex took place in the building's stairwells, vacant offices, and at bars (in full view of colleagues and other patrons). A Christmas party became so debauched, Murdoch moved it to the social hall of a Catholic church the following year. Reporters and photographers broke into apartments to record the lairs of killers and snuck into hospitals and sanitariums to interview crime victims. The pied piper of this nervy crew, Australian tabloid legend Steve Dunleavy, impersonated a grief counselor to get an exclusive from the mother of the final victim of serial killer David Berkowitz (the "Son of Sam") and may have had an affair with her. A sports reporter was slammed headfirst into a locker by a New York Jets quarterback he had enraged with his columns. Mobbed-up employees ran gambling operations; one was murdered, and a raid by the district attorney's office led to charges of loan sharking, illegal gun sales, and extortion. Reporters' stories were rewritten, sometimes with invented quotes, to match clever headlines ginned up earlier in the day, or to fit the paper's political bent. The *Post* was not a newspaper of record. Among its reporters and editors, it was called, only half-jokingly, "the paper of wreckage."

The tabloid's angry, in-your-face tone expresses a viewpoint long thought characteristic of New York, particularly during the city's near bankruptcy in the 1970s and its recession and crack-fueled decline in the 1990s. But in the wake of the COVID pandemic, the migration and homeless crises, the never-ending conflicts over reproductive rights and gun ownership, and the debates over "wokeness," cancel culture, and affirmative action, that type of anger has spread more broadly throughout the country. Fingers are often pointed at Fox News and Donald Trump's presidency as prime catalysts of this national divisiveness, but neither would have attained the power and influence they wield today without the *New York Post*. Whether you admire or despise Murdoch and Trump, the *Post* gave them both national standing. Murdoch used his to build a multimedia empire through which he seeded an alarmist tabloid sensibility that is now found on even staunchly liberal media ventures like MSNBC.

Working at the *Post* was never boring, and many staffers who hustled through its city room—even some who were fired or lost their jobs when Murdoch broke the Newspaper Guild in 1993—recall their time there as among the most exciting and significant of their careers.

There's this, too. Since the mid-1970s, when Murdoch bought the *Post*, the paper published—and continues to publish—plenty of insightful, hard-hitting journalism by reporters and editors whose own ethical compasses enabled them to learn from the Fleet Street–inspired circus taking place around them without succumbing to it. Many of its reporters have gone on to stellar careers at more conventional journalistic outlets, and some—such as the *New York Times*' Maggie Haberman, *Washington Post* reporter Devlin Barrett, and Randy Smith, formerly of the *Wall Street Journal*—have been part of groups that won Pulitzer Prizes. While critics of the paper are loath to admit it, the *Post* excels in many areas: crime coverage, state and local politics, business reporting, gossip, and sports. Ingenuity, intrepidness, and being first with a story were seared into the brains of those who worked there—occasionally through screaming, yelling, and humiliation. If a rival had already broken a story, the objective became finding a new angle that would hijack the news cycle.

The paper's politics, which grew increasingly incendiary (some would say bonkers) with the election of Donald Trump, have tended to eclipse the fact that there was a *Post* before Rupert Murdoch owned it, and that it was not always a tabloid or editorially right-wing. It is, in fact, the oldest continuously published daily newspaper in the country, founded in 1801 by Alexander Hamilton, the revolutionary and Founding Father, who, in 2015, ascended to pop cultural stardom in Lin-Manuel Miranda's hip-hop musical *Hamilton*.

Hamilton might not have approved of much of what appears in Murdoch's *New York Post*, but he would have understood the impetus for its never-be-boring tone and point of view. "Has it not been found," Hamilton asked in Number 6 of the Federalist Papers, that man's "momentary passions" have a "more active and imperious control over human conduct than general or remote considerations of policy, utility or justice?" In other words, doesn't a headline like HEADLESS BODY IN TOPLESS BAR—arguably the paper's most memorable—have a more visceral appeal than, say, SENATE APPROVES BUDGET BILL?

The *Post*'s early years would have made great fodder for the paper it has become. Its first editor, William Coleman, killed someone in a duel not long before Aaron Burr killed Hamilton. An angry story subject later thrashed Coleman so badly he never fully recovered. But as the nineteenth century took hold, the paper's politics shifted from its early conservatism to more socially progressive views, particularly under editor William Cullen Bryant.

Mostly remembered today as a poet and the namesake of Bryant Park in midtown Manhattan, Bryant wielded tremendous influence in his fifty years at what was then known as the *Evening Post*. An early supporter of Abraham Lincoln, Bryant was a dedicated abolitionist and an advocate for organized labor whose reach extended far beyond the city's borders. Other liberal editors would follow, though the *Post*'s politics shifted from left to right and back in the decades to come, depending on who owned the paper at a given time.

In 1939, the *Post* settled into a lengthy liberal period when Dorothy Schiff came into the picture. Though the Schiff *Post* paid attention to crime, celebrities, and other tabloid staples, it also featured high-minded liberal columnists like Max Lerner and Murray Kempton. Born in New York City in 1903, just over a hundred years after the *Post* was founded, Schiff was a granddaughter of Jacob Schiff, a powerful banker and leading figure in New York's German Jewish aristocracy. Her grandfather observed Jewish traditions and supported Jewish causes, but Dorothy's upbringing was more secular. As a result, she had conflicted feelings about her Jewish heritage. Still, the flavor and character of the *Post* when she owned it led one editor to describe it as the Jewish mother of newspapers: many of its writers and editors were Jewish; its editorials leaned left; news out of Israel received major play, as did stories about Jewish celebrities like Leonard Bernstein and Saul Bellow; and the *Post*'s food pages, particularly in the run-up to holidays, were stuffed with recipes for Jewish specialties and ads for Jewish products—or products eager to attract a Jewish audience. ("Guess who's coming to Seder!" proclaimed an ad in 1968. "Canada Dry.") Not surprisingly, most of the *Post*'s readers were Jewish.

As Schiff's first marriage was ending in 1931, an affair with Max Aitken, better known as Lord Beaverbrook, the British press magnate, stimulated her interest in newspapers and politics. Schiff purchased the money-losing *Post* in 1939 in large part to save from extinction an important supporter of the Democratic Party. Her second husband, George Backer, became the paper's publisher, while Schiff eventually granted herself the titles of vice president and treasurer. Neither their working relationship nor their marriage lasted. Ted Thackrey took over as editor and replaced Backer as Schiff's husband, but that marriage crumbled, too, as would, eventually, Schiff's fourth marriage, to Rudolf Sonneborn, who was not a newspaperman.

The journalistic golden age of Schiff's thirty-seven-year ownership of the *Post* took place in the 1950s, when progressive icon James Wechsler ran the paper and oversaw groundbreaking investigations of FBI director J. Edgar Hoover, Senator Joseph McCarthy, urban developer Robert Moses, powerful gossip columnist Walter Winchell, and others. (The Schiff/Wechsler *Post* plays a prominent role in *The Power Broker*, Robert Caro's biography of Moses.)

That era ended in 1961 when Schiff demoted Wechsler, who had been the paper's head editor, to running only the editorial page and writing a column. Schiff then gave Paul Sann, the paper's swaggering foul-mouthed executive editor, complete control of the newsroom, and in 1962, declared herself editor in chief. From that point on, Schiff had more influence over the *Post*'s content. In a scathing 1975 essay for *Esquire*, Nora Ephron, who worked at the *Post* for five years beginning in 1963 (and years later would trade journalism for filmmaking), wrote that after replacing Wechsler with Sann, Schiff "had changed the focus of the paper from hard-hitting, investigative, and liberal to frothy, gossipy, and woman oriented."

Schiff barely had time to put her imprint on the paper before the New York Typographical Union went on strike in December 1962, protesting low wages and the advent of automated printing presses. The walkout lasted for 114 days and led the Hearst Corporation to fold its tabloid, the *New York Daily Mirror*. Given the *Post*'s anemic circulation at the time, it almost certainly would have closed, too, but perturbed by what she viewed as a lack of respect for the *Post* (and for her) from the other publishers, all men, Schiff made the decision to leave the Publishers Association of New York City during the strike and agree to abide by whatever agreement was eventually brokered. (Murdoch would employ a similar winning strategy in 1978.) Though the members of the Publishers Association competed in selling newspapers, they traditionally presented a united front in dealing with the unions. While other papers sat on the sidelines, the *Post* returned to newsstands. When the *World Journal Tribune*, a merger of three New York papers forced by another strike, ceased publication in 1967, the *Post* became the city's only afternoon newspaper and its circulation increased by more than fifty percent. But Schiff did not drop the penny-pinching ways she had adopted when competition was fierce. She continued to cut resources, eliminated jobs where she could, and paid staff as little as possible. Landmark stories that would come to define the 1960s and '70s were passed over or relegated to wire copy because Schiff refused to loosen her purse strings.

Yet storied journalists, including Pete Hamill and Jimmy Breslin, continued to work there in the 1960s. It wasn't that the afternoon daily lost lots of money, but, after a slow year or two, Schiff feared it might. She was heir to a banking fortune, but even banking fortunes can run dry. Television was whittling away the *Post*'s circulation, as was an exodus of readers to the suburbs. The paper's late-sixties circulation high—about 700,000—had slipped to 500,000 by the mid-1970s. The New York *Daily News*, the *Post*'s primary competition and a morning paper, had also seen its numbers drop, but at two million papers a day it still outsold the *Post* by a wide margin. The *Post*'s advertising lineage had declined as well.

Like Dorothy Schiff, Keith Rupert Murdoch grew up privileged, but the early days of his newspaper career were more tumultuous. His father, a powerful figure in Australian media, died in 1952, when Murdoch was twenty-one and a student at Oxford. Murdoch flirted with socialism in his student years, but left-wing politics ultimately did not correspond to his business ambitions. After graduating the following year, and briefly working at a London paper, the *Daily Express* (owned, coincidentally, by Dorothy Schiff's mentor, Lord Beaverbrook), he returned to Australia to take over the family media business— immediately fending off competitors eager to see him fail before he'd even begun. Though forced to sell some assets, Murdoch inherited a controlling interest in News Limited, a small concern at the time, which he expanded with acquisitions. Eventually his acquisitive nature took him to England, where in 1969 he bought *The Sun*, then a high-minded London broadsheet struggling to stay alive. In a preview of his takeover of the *New York Post*, Murdoch turned *The Sun* into a tabloid and doused it with his signature cocktail of mayhem, scandal, and sex, exemplified by its topless Page 3 girls. *The Sun*'s circulation soared, leaving the competition aghast at how precisely—and quickly— Murdoch had figured out what the people wanted.

His businesses in the United Kingdom and Australia would continue to expand—in some cases, explode—in the decades to come, but he would not be content until he had made it in America.

In 1973, Murdoch bought two papers in Texas, the *San Antonio News* and the *Express*, which shared a newsroom and printing press. He turned the former into a broadsheet with a tabloid attitude (and later merged the two papers). The *News* achieved national attention with the headline KILLER BEES MOVE NORTH, which would inspire a series of *Saturday Night Live* skits. In 1974, he started a supermarket tabloid, the *National Star*, to compete with the *National Enquirer*. Those were baby steps. One paper in Texas and a supermarket tabloid did not mean real power. Murdoch set his sights on America's media capital, New York, and soon determined that the fading *Post* was ripe for the plucking.

Murdoch's *New York Post* was hardly the first American daily to lure readers with exaggerated stories, bold graphics, and lurid headlines—in the late nineteenth century, the battle between Joseph Pulitzer's *New York World* and William Randolph Hearst's *New York Journal* birthed the term "yellow journalism"—but as the twentieth century reached its final quarter, most daily newspapers in cities across the United States—even the tabloids—projected a serious tone, partly because of Watergate. Everyone wanted to be Woodward and Bernstein.

Not Murdoch. Over the four-plus decades that he has owned the tabloid—interrupted by a five-year hiatus during which the paper was owned by a real estate developer and later briefly operated by two men who would serve prison sentences—the paper's bold red-and-black logo and brazen, darkly comic front-page headlines and photos have become instantly recognizable emblems of outrage, sensational crime, and scandal. And the name of its gossip column, Page Six, remains the top trademark of its craft, akin to Chanel or Prada, even though the web and social media have stolen much of its thunder. (In January 2024, the paper launched a Page Six video studio at its midtown offices—part of its efforts to establish the gossip trademark as a multiplatform, standalone brand.) The *Post*'s coverage can be schizophrenic—aimed at both blue- and white-collar readers, through a mix of stories about outer borough crime, celebrity escapism, sports, and "rich people inconvenienced," as one former reporter put it. The tabloid has inspired artists Andy Warhol and Keith Haring, novelist Tom Wolfe's *The Bonfire of the Vanities*, and Public Enemy's rap song "A Letter to the New York Post," as well as numerous film and TV scenes, and internet memes.

According to the *New York Times*, President Joe Biden in 2021 called Rupert Murdoch "the most dangerous man in the world." That same year, Robert Thomson, CEO of the *Post*'s parent company, News Corp, revealed on a call with analysts that, after losing tens of millions of dollars for decades, the paper had reported the "first profit in modern times, at the very least." The announcement was met with disbelief in the media world, but whether the tabloid is profitable, and whether it will outlive Rupert Murdoch, who in 2023 stepped down as chairman of News Corp in favor of his son Lachlan, is beside the point. His *Post* shoved its way into a clubby, unwelcoming media landscape, and after establishing itself as a new—some would say virulent—strain of journalism and political thought, instigated a paradigm shift among its competitors. The way news and culture are covered, packaged, and presented by the American media today is the result of that shift. The pages that follow will show—through the words and anecdotes of those who were there—how Murdoch, his editors, and his reporters managed such an extraordinary feat.

METHODOLOGY AND GLOSSARY

To compile this unauthorized portrait of the *Post*, we interviewed more than 240 former and current staffers, story subjects, competitors, and astute observers of the media who have watched the paper evolve from the last years of Dorothy Schiff's ownership through current times. "We" are two former *Post* employees: Susan Mulcahy worked on Page Six from 1978 to 1985, including three years as editor, before moving to *New York Newsday* to write a rival column. She has written for the *New Yorker* and the *New York Times* and published three books, including a memoir about the *Post*. She also created and led the entertainment division at Starwave, Microsoft co-founder Paul Allen's early internet venture; and is responsible for reviving the recordings of Ruth Draper, the great monologue artist, whose biography she is writing. Frank DiGiacomo worked as a Page Six freelancer in the late 1980s and became an editor of the column from 1991 to 1993. He has since worked as a writer and editor, covering media and the entertainment business, for *Vanity Fair*, the *Hollywood Reporter*, the *New York Observer*, and the New York *Daily News*, among others. He is currently an executive editor at *Billboard*.

Because there are so many stories about the *New York Post*, we could have continued our research indefinitely. For this book, we used the memories shared by our interview subjects, as well as our own as former editors at the paper, to highlight the people and the stories that best illustrate what the *New York Post* once was, what it has become, and why it is so significant.

This oral history, encompassing nearly fifty years at the paper beginning in the mid-1970s, should not be considered comprehensive. Many significant news events and newsworthy figures from that time span do not appear in these pages, nor does every development in Rupert Murdoch's empire. Given the broad scope and reach of his businesses, that would be a very different book—one that in our estimation has already been attempted multiple times. The developments we have touched on are those that spread the *Post*'s brand of journalism throughout American media.

When memories shared in this book involved a story that appeared in the *Post*, we made every effort to locate it and compare the reporting to what we had been told. That was not always possible, however, because, at the height of Murdoch's initial ownership of the paper, eight editions appeared every day, and stories were often updated or replaced from one edition to another. But just one, the final edition, can be found on microfilm at the New York Public Library, one of the few repositories for copies of the paper from the pre-digital era. (The *Post* microfilm has been digitized, but as we conducted our research, the database that carries it was not widely available.) Also, some local editions of the *Post*, targeted at specific boroughs, were short-lived and not captured on microfilm.

In the case of *New York Post* employees, some of whom held many different jobs over the years, we have identified them by only their most senior or recognizable positions, along with the total number of years they worked full-time at the paper. We have identified outsiders—those who did not work at the *Post*—by their most relevant credit. In the case of a competitor who worked for several different news outlets, for example, a position at the New York *Daily News*—the *Post*'s biggest rival—would be the label of choice. The first time someone appears in a chapter, his or her identifying information is repeated.

The interviews for this book were conducted between 2020 and 2024, with some exceptions; in 2004, Frank DiGiacomo compiled an oral history of Page Six for *Vanity Fair*. A small portion of the interviews excerpted here derive from that research, including conversations with people who have died in the interim (James Brady, Claudia Cohen, Steve Dunleavy, Sy Presten, and Bobby Zarem). Most of the more recent interviews were conducted by phone or Zoom, some in person, and a few through email. Excerpts of interviews have been edited for length and clarity. Also, Jane Perlez, who worked at the *Post* during the Dorothy Schiff era and went on to a long career at the *New York*

Times, allowed us to quote from notes she took during the transition to Murdoch's ownership.

Anyone who has worked at a newspaper has tales to tell, but we focused on the editorial process. We spoke to a few people in other areas, including circulation and the composing room, but the bulk of our interviews involved the creation of stories in the *Post*, which is how the Murdoch ethos is disseminated. We located many of our interview subjects through Post Nation, a large email community that keeps former staffers informed of the milestones and deaths of past colleagues, created and maintained by Myron Rushetzky, a former head city desk assistant at the *Post*. Most interview subjects were happy to talk about their experiences, but we could not interview everyone, and not everyone would speak to us: some current staffers feared for their jobs; a number of ex–*Post* employees signed NDAs that preclude them from discussing the paper; and still others decided to keep their stories to themselves. We hope they see their experience reflected in the narrative nonetheless. We were fortunate to capture the voices of a number of former *Post* employees who have since passed away: Dave Banks, Guy Hawtin, Steve Hoffenberg, Warren Hoge, Ray Kerrison, Marsha Kranes, Dominick Marrano, Tim McDarrah, and Stephen Silverman. Also, Sally Kempton, whose father, Murray, was an important columnist at the *Post*.

Finally, the newspaper business has its own language. Some terms that originated in the era of lead type and Linotype operators are still in use today, though many have been forgotten. Here is a brief glossary:

Agate: The smallest type size that can be printed legibly on newsprint. It is commonly used for index boxes, statistical data, and legal and death notices.

Book: Three pieces of paper, separated by carbon and bound at the top, that allowed a writer to create an original and two duplicates for different editorial and production needs.

Cold type: The composition process that eliminated the use of hot metal and introduced computerization to newspaper printing.

Composing room: The room where typesetting is done.

Compositor: The person who arranges type into pages.

Graf: Paragraph.

Hed: Journalism jargon for a headline.

Hot type: A typesetting process used by newspapers from the late nineteenth century until the mid- to late twentieth century that involved injecting molten metal, usually lead, into molds that were used to press ink onto paper in order to produce newsprint. When computers were introduced, it was said the newspapers had switched to cold type.

Lede: The first sentence or paragraph in a news story, which is meant to grab the reader's attention and provide a basic outline for what follows. The spelling came about as a way of preventing confusion with the lead used in the days of hot type.

Linotype: Refers to the Linotype machine, used to set type in the hot-type era.

Lobster shift: A reference to a newspaper's overnight shift. Its origins are unclear. Some say it stems from the British word "lob," slang for a stupid or naive person, or in the realm of the newsroom, a neophyte, who was often assigned to work the overnight hours while learning the ropes. Others say it is so named because lobster fishermen work at night. At times, reporters and editors who have run afoul of their superiors might be assigned to lobster as punishment or to avoid further conflict. But at an afternoon paper, like the *Post* when Murdoch first acquired it, it was the shift during which the next day's paper was assembled and therefore, arguably, the most important.

Makeup: To arrange articles, photos, and ads on a page prior to printing, and in some cases, cut to fit the allotted space.

Pagination: Digital process of laying out newspaper pages.

Paste up: The pre-digital method for laying out a publication's pages.

Rim: A horseshoe-shaped desk around which copy editors sat, writing headlines and editing copy. The chief copy editor, who sat inside the horseshoe, a.k.a "the slot," was known as the slot man.

Slug: A short identifying title—as brief as a single word—given to an article during the editorial process, for tracking purposes. The slug can also contain code words that, for example, would indicate the edition in which the story is running, or an updated or corrected article.

Spike: Stories or wire copy that would not appear in the paper would be impaled on a metal spike that sat on the news or copy desk. "Spiked" remains a figurative term for killing copy.

Stereotype (also known as a stereoplate or simply stereo): A thin piece of curvable metal, cast from the mold of composed type. The stereo was clipped around the rotating cylinder of a printing press and sped up the printing process significantly. Multiple plates could be created from one typesetting—that's why they were called stereos—enabling multiple printing presses to run simultaneously.

Takeout: An in-depth article or series of articles, usually with sidebars and graphics.

Wood: A tabloid's front-page headline. In the pre-computer era, the type font in lead only went up to a certain point size, therefore the larger page-one heds had to be made using wooden type.

-30-: Used by reporters to indicate the end of a story. Its origins are not entirely clear, though it may be connected to the days of telegraph transmission.

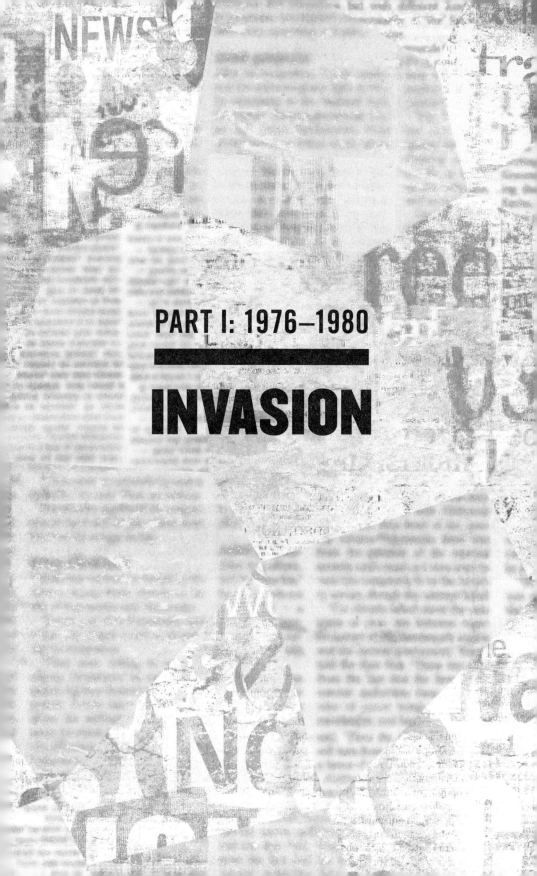

PART I: 1976–1980

INVASION

1 | GOODBYE, DOLLY

Schiff Gives Up the Ship

As the 1970s passed their midpoint, two formidable women were running newspapers in America's centers of power, but their fortunes were diverging. Katharine Graham, the publisher of the *Washington Post*, was lionized as a First Amendment hero because of her paper's investigation of the Watergate cover-up, which led to President Richard Nixon's resignation and inspired the bestselling book *All the President's Men* by *Washington Post* journalists Bob Woodward and Carl Bernstein (later a hit film). Dorothy Schiff, the owner, publisher, and editor in chief of the *New York Post*, was grappling with financial losses at the tabloid she had owned for thirty-seven years, along with criticism that the paper's once hard-hitting journalism had given way to fluff.

In the 1950s, during what was widely considered the paper's twentieth-century heyday, Schiff's *New York Post* epitomized the kind of investigative journalism that the *Washington Post* was being lauded for two decades later, and Schiff herself was not afraid to wield her political clout. In the New York gubernatorial race of 1958, the paper initially endorsed the incumbent, Averell Harriman, a Democrat and a power broker with whom Schiff years earlier had had a "brief flirtation," according to Schiff biographer Marilyn Nissenson. But, the week before the election, Harriman made remarks that Schiff felt unfairly labeled his Republican opponent, Nelson Rockefeller, as anti-Israel. Schiff, who had been ambivalent about the candidates despite the *Post*'s endorsement of Harriman, pulled a front-page story (HEIRESS TRIES SUICIDE) and insisted her editors run an appeal she had written in favor of Rockefeller. Her action may have helped push him to victory in the race for governor.

By 1976, however, the biggest question being asked about Schiff's political ties was whether she had slept with President Franklin Delano Roosevelt, as was intimated in an authorized Schiff biography published that year.

The editors and reporters who worked for Schiff knew that she had a near obsession with keeping costs low, but they did not know that the *Post* was losing money for the first time in almost three decades. Schiff had been talking about selling the paper for years. Many felt that the time had arrived.

WARREN HOGE, metropolitan editor, 1966–1976: No one called her Dolly. She was always Mrs. Schiff, this grande dame living on East 64th Street—by the way, in the same building where Bernie Madoff eventually lived, 133 East 64th Street, on the corner of Lexington Avenue. Mrs. Schiff lived in a penthouse and so did he.

ROBERTA BRANDES GRATZ, reporter, 1963–1978: It was so hypocritical of her to be known as Mrs. Dorothy Schiff. She was *never* Mrs. Schiff. She was *Miss* Schiff, married [four] times but took the privilege of calling herself Mrs. Schiff.

CALVIN TRILLIN, staff writer, *The New Yorker*: I never met Mrs. Schiff, but she was noted for keeping her name no matter who she was married to. Somebody told me she was known as the "Don't-give-up-the-Schiff Schiff."

ANDY SOLTIS, rewrite, editor, 1967–2014: She was known in those days as "The Lady Upstairs."

TONY SCHWARTZ, gossip columnist, 1976–1977: Her office on South Street was this giant room, decorated like a living room, with fluffy pillows and a couch. And her dog was there.

JOYCE WADLER, feature writer, 1974–1977: She had a nude portrait in her office. Whether or not it was her, how many publishers have a nude resembling themselves hanging in the office?

DAVID ROSENTHAL, reporter, desk editor, 1974–1977: There was apparently some sort of very vague threat that Cuban freedom fighters, anti-Castro, were going to target the *Post* building from across the East River, or something like that. Whatever was the immediate cause, Dolly put in windows, at least on her floor facing the East River, that by all accounts were bulletproof.

TONY MANCINI, reporter, 1958–1978: Whenever she appeared in the newsroom, she would be followed by her chauffeur [Everette Lawson], carrying her toy dog. It was like an event when she arrived.

DAVID ROSENTHAL: Everette was this ubiquitous personality in the building. It sounds racist, but he looked a bit like a character out of *Amos 'n' Andy*. He was so loyal to her. It seemed even odd to me in those days that a woman of obvious wealth and privilege would have this Black chauffeur. Plus, she made a point of letting everybody know that she had a Black chauffeur. I think she did that because Mrs. Schiff wanted to own the *New York Post*, but she did not want to be identified with the *Post* in some ways—that everything on the floors below her was sort of the great unwashed.

RICHARD GOODING, metropolitan editor, 1976–1993: The first day I came to work at 210 South Street, the doors to the second elevator were open. I walked in and there were two people in the elevator, Dolly Schiff, who was holding a little dog, and a guy who was clearly her chauffeur. I got off on the fourth floor. I swear, the second I got into the newsroom, somebody said to me, "You're wanted in [Executive Editor] Paul Sann's office." I got to Paul's office, and he said, "The first rule of work at the *New York Post* is you do not ride the elevator with Dolly Schiff. Nobody rides the elevator with Dolly Schiff, except her chauffeur." She must have gotten to her office, immediately called downstairs, and said, "Who was the tall, skinny bearded hippie in the elevator with me? This is not acceptable." [Though her staff was not aware of it, Schiff had a phobia of elevators.]

MARSHA KRANES, rewrite, editor, 1974–2005: The *Post* didn't pay for our Christmas party then. We all chipped in for it. We used to have a hot dog wagon or something, and we'd set up a little bar. As it was being prepared, she would come in with her mink coat over her shoulders, or maybe it was ermine. Her secretary and Everette accompanied her. One carried a bottle of scotch or some other liquor, and the other carried her little dog, Suzy Q. As she neared the part of the room where people were gathered, she lifted her shoulders so her coat would fall off. She knew somebody would dive and catch it. Remember the TV series *Lou Grant*, where the owner of the paper was a very aristocratic woman? [Mrs. Pynchon, played by Nancy Marchand, who later portrayed Tony Soprano's mother.] She reminded me of Dorothy Schiff. [The character was said to have been partly based on Schiff.] So did Meryl Streep in *The Devil Wears Prada*.

AIDA ALVAREZ, reporter, 1973–1977: During my four years at the *Post*, the one and only time that I saw Mrs. Schiff in the newsroom, she told a story about how she wore her fur coat to Harlem. She said, "That's what the people in Harlem expect of me." I remember thinking: it's probably kind of a sign of respect for people, because they have an expectation. And she's showing up as she is. She's not dressing down to go to Harlem. I didn't take offense to that. But I thought it was interesting that that was her insight, and that she felt compelled to tell that story.

FRANK RICH, film critic, 1975–1977: I saw almost nothing of Dolly Schiff, but after I had been working there for two or three months, [Managing Editor] Bob Spitzler tells me she knows my writing and wants to go to dinner with me. He said, "It will be the three of us." The dinner was at Parioli Romanissimo, a notoriously, hilariously expensive Italian restaurant on the Upper East Side. I was very nervous. It was not my scene, and Spitzler, a very nice guy, said, "Don't worry, I'll handle everything." I don't remember a single thing that Schiff said, but she had a very, very long cigarette holder. I was a smoker, so I was very aware of it. She was also a chain-smoker, and every time she butted out a cigarette and put a new one in the holder, without breaking the conversation and continuing to look at me and Bob, she would flick her hand back with the cigarette holder and know, without looking back, that someone would have lit it. And they had.

JOYCE WADLER: Al Ellenberg told me about his entry interview with Dorothy Schiff, who said to him, "I understand you're Jewish." Al said, "Yes, I am." She said, "I'm Jewish, too. In fact, I'm the last person in my family who's Jewish. When I die, I'm going to be cremated and buried in a Jewish cemetery." Jewish law says you can't be cremated. Al said, "No, you're not." She said, "Yes, I am." "No, you're not." "Yes, I am, because I bought the cemetery."

TONY MANCINI: At one point, my then-wife, the mother of my daughter, was having trouble getting pregnant. I wanted a leave of absence to have a baby—you know, work at it!—and to write my first novel. But Mrs. Schiff wanted to speak to me before granting it. She wanted to know my motives, so she invited me to a tea or a lunch in her office. I told her why I wanted [the leave], and she, having had children herself, sort of sighed and said, "I don't know why anybody would want to have children."

In 1961, when Executive Editor Paul Sann assumed full control of the *Post*'s news pages from James Wechsler, Schiff became increasingly involved in what was published beyond the editorial pages. After that, the paper's reporting became more subject to her whims, which included gossip, rent regulation, and women's maiden names.

CLYDE HABERMAN, reporter, 1966–1977: If she liked something, you covered it. The notes would come down. Paul Sann tried to avoid saying it came from Schiff, but sometimes he slipped.

ROBERTA BRANDES GRATZ: Schiff was famous for writing memos on yellow parchment paper. I remember coming back from an interview I did for a Woman in the News feature. Paul Sann gave me one of Schiff's yellow memos asking if [the story subject] was still dating a particular man. I said, "Why are you giving this to me now? I just came back from the interview." He said, "Call her." It was so embarrassing. I had to call the woman I'd just interviewed and ask her, because Dolly was interested in this man herself. It was Bishop Paul Moore, of St. John the Divine.

JOYCE WADLER: The old *Post* had things they held very dear, like rent control. When we went to do a Daily Close-up, Dorothy Schiff required that we always include a married woman's maiden name, and whether the interview subject's apartment was rent controlled or rent stabilized.

ANDY SOLTIS: Just before Mrs. Schiff sold the paper, she would invite two or three reporters at a time up to her office. One Friday afternoon, I was invited up along with Joyce Purnick and Bob Bazell, just before he quit to work for NBC. He became the chief science and health correspondent for NBC News. Our chaperone was Al Ellenberg, who I guess was there to make sure we didn't say anything wrong. This was my first contact with Mrs. Schiff. At one point, she said, "Do you think we can find out who Deep Throat is?" The movie *All the President's Men* had just come out, and she was fascinated by the identity of Woodward and Bernstein's source. Bazell looked at me strangely, like *What?* This conversation went on for about ten minutes, and then Bazell said, "If we printed what we found, we're betraying a journalist." Mrs. Schiff just smiled. I thought that was revealing. I think she just wanted to know who this was so that she could use it for social conversation. She loved the gossip that she picked up from the city room.

JOYCE PURNICK, political reporter, 1970–1978: I don't know if people even know what an afternoon newspaper is anymore, but it doesn't break news so much as analyze and featurize the news that's already been made because it doesn't come out in the morning.

BILL BRADLEY, former New York Knick; former US senator: The *Post* was a strong liberal paper that I respected. I respected its editorial page. I respected its sports page. The owner was a woman, right? I felt she had an attitude toward the paper as a public service. I read it that way. So I paid attention to what was written. The quality of the writing was always excellent. The *New York Times* was a bigger paper, meaning they had more reporters covering more things. But for what the *Post* did, they did it very well.

DANNY FIELDS, former rock journalist, manager of The Ramones: It was news for Jews.

DAVID ROSENTHAL: The two greatest things Mrs. Schiff did for liberalism were: She ran Mary McGrory [Pulitzer Prize–winning syndicated columnist]. We also had the [Washington Post–Los Angeles Times News Service], which was a big, big deal, because that's how the *New York Post* covered Watergate. We had the Woodward-Bernstein stories every day. Nobody else did in New York.

TONY MANCINI: Schiff's *Post* was a tabloid in the classic sense. Celebrity news was high on the list and so was crime—the if-it-bleeds-it-leads kind of thing. But there was a serious side to it. It had a sterling group of columnists, including Max Lerner and Mary McGrory, who were serious pundits and mostly on the left side. And we had muckrakers like Joe Kahn and Ed Katcher, Bill Haddad, who uncovered a lot of municipal corruption.

JOYCE WADLER: We were the friend of the working class. I loved this.

In the late 1950s, Victor Navasky, who eventually become editor and publisher of *The Nation*, founded a satirical magazine called *Monocle*. In the early 1960s, *Monocle* published parodies of New York newspapers, including the *Post*.

A headline suggested for the spoof of the *Post* circulated through word of mouth, in many different versions. It was thought to sum up the Schiff era and the paper's liberal, pro-Jewish political perspective at the time.

CHARLIE CARILLO, reporter, columnist, 1978–1993: The joke headline about Schiff's *Post* was "World Ends. Blacks and Jews Suffer Most."

CALVIN TRILLIN: I mostly worked on *Monocle*'s *Daily News* parody, but I suggested a front-page headline for the *Post* to indicate the Schiff-era politics, which was "Cold Snap Hits Our Town, Jews, Negroes Suffer Most." Victor rejected it. He said there wasn't any story to go with it. But I thought that was part of the parody. That is all I did on what we called the *New York Pest*. Some of the people who worked on the parody were then hired by Mrs. Schiff: Nora Ephron, who had done a Leonard Lyons parody [Lyons wrote a gossip column], and, I think, Sidney Zion, who did a Murray Kempton parody.

As the owner of an influential media property, Dorothy Schiff hosted many VIPs, first in her penthouse office on the fifteenth floor of 75 West Street, where the *Post* was housed until 1970, and then in her sixth-floor suite at 210 South Street, the former headquarters of Hearst's defunct *Journal-American*, a building she acquired in 1967. She would order lunch for her guests from the *Post* cafeteria—always, famously, a sandwich. Memories of what type of sandwich differ. According to a 1973 Gail Sheehy profile in *New York* magazine, Schiff divided "all the world into three sandwiches. Corned beef for Jews, tuna fish for Catholics, and roast beef for Prods." Once Schiff's secretary "has recorded your sandwich," wrote Sheehy, "nothing short of religious conversion can change it." But Nora Ephron, in her 1975 essay about Schiff in *Esquire*, wrote that "Everyone who had lunch with [Schiff] got a roast beef sandwich. Lyndon Johnson, Bobby Kennedy, and me, to name a few." Pete Hamill reported that Schiff insulted Brooklyn political leader Meade Esposito by serving a meatball sandwich. And when Katharine Graham of the *Washington Post* paid a visit, she had what Schiff was having, a BLT.

CAROLE LEE, assistant to James Wechsler, photo syndication editor, 1963–1993: Schiff used to have these luncheons, where people like [labor leader and founder of New York's Liberal Party] David Dubinsky and other people would come, and they all got the same exact thing: a BLT with or without mayonnaise. That was your only choice. When Dubinsky's office called to say, "He's Jewish and doesn't eat pork," they were told, "Does he want mayonnaise or not?" She wouldn't change it for anything.

ERIC FETTMANN, associate editorial page editor, columnist, 1976–1991, 1993–2019: Dolly was a big believer in the *Post* cafeteria. When the political bigwigs came for lunch, like Lyndon Johnson—this was back on West Street—he was offered his choice of a tuna fish or roast beef sandwich from the cafeteria. Dolly would order and Maxie [who worked in the mailroom] was dispatched to bring it up to the sixth floor. What she didn't know, and nobody had the heart to tell her, is that he had his own set routine. And just before he went upstairs, Maxie would eat his own lunch in the men's room. Nobody ever remembered seeing him wash his hands.

> The sandwiches Schiff served her guests were just one example of her extraordinary thriftiness, which affected the *Post*'s news gathering as well. It's a trait she may have inherited from her immensely wealthy grandfather, Jacob, who saved string.

JOYCE WADLER: Dorothy Schiff was so cheap there were never quite enough chairs for the staff. The first thing I had to do when I came in in the morning was find a chair or steal one. If you wanted a notebook, there was a guy on the desk who kept them under lock and key.

WARREN HOGE: Seymour Hersh [then a freelance journalist] and David Obst, who was his best friend, had an office in the National Press Building in Washington, which is where my *New York Post* bureau office was [before Hoge became an editor in New York]. Hersh came to me one day and said, "We've uncovered this amazing thing about My Lai." He told me about the My Lai massacre in Vietnam. Obst [then in charge of Dispatch News Service, the small news agency that released the My Lai story] offered the story to the *Post*. I can't remember the amount, but it was pretty paltry. I was unable to get an agreement from the *Post* to publish a story that won the Pulitzer Prize that year.

CLYDE HABERMAN: They practically had to fight to send somebody to Dallas when President Kennedy was killed. I believe the same thing happened when Bobby Kennedy was killed. She just wasn't going to spend money on essential travel. I covered Attica even though they didn't want to spend the money to send me there. It wasn't Bali. It wasn't Tokyo. It was a huge story—the biggest prison uprising probably in American history, in Attica, New York. It was almost in our backyard, and they didn't want to spend the money.

DAVID ROSENTHAL: We had a motto, which was: the *New York Times* has a reporter in every city in the world, a bureau in every capital—we have the telephone. This was a newspaper where you had to get permission to take the train to New Jersey to cover something.

ANDY SOLTIS: We could not take cab rides. That was absolutely forbidden. And Annie Aquilina [a head desk assistant for many years] told me that when a letter to the *Post* came in and there was an uncanceled stamp on it, they were supposed to steam it off to use again.

ERIC FETTMANN: Roberta Gratz told me she had a couple of sources over for dinner rather than going to a restaurant, figuring that, among other things, it would be cheaper. Her twenty-dollar expense report came back with a note from Paul Sann: "She's going to want to know who got the extra coffee."

ROBERTA BRANDES GRATZ: Reimbursement denied.

Despite the low pay and limited resources that resulted from Schiff's frugality, the paper was staffed with a strong group of editors and writers in the '70s, many of whose names today are equated with journalistic excellence. The upper tier of editors were all men, though not all cut from the same cloth. James Wechsler remained a force at the paper, but only in the opinion section. Executive Editor Paul Sann, who had joined the *Post* in 1931 as a seventeen-year-old copyboy, ran news, with assistance from Managing Editor Bob Spitzler, Metropolitan Editor Warren Hoge, City Editor Andy Porte, and Al Ellenberg, an assistant managing editor. Joe Rabinovich, known as Joe Rab, oversaw features.

WARREN HOGE: Jimmy Wechsler was a genuine old lefty intellectual; Paul Sann was a real tough, funny tabloid journalist who wrote about the mob and was proud of being raised in the Bronx, and never let you forget it. Paul was very compact. He always wore cowboy boots and string ties. I don't know why. There was nothing Western about him. He was completely urban New York. He was so different from Wechsler. When Wechsler was editor of the *Post*, with his columnists and all that, it wasn't intellectual, but it was a really thoughtful paper. It was not a hard-hitting tabloid. Sann turned it into a hard-hitting tabloid.

JOE BERGER, investigative reporter, 1971–1978: Sann had a persona like Sam Spade in *The Maltese Falcon*. It was the way he walked around the newsroom, the way he talked—he had a kind of clipped speech—the way he smoked cigarettes. He was a very straight-shooting editor.

WARREN HOGE: Sann would go into the composing room—it's hard to say these days, with how sensitive we've become—but he would go in and abuse the workers there, and they loved it. Some compositor—one of those guys with the funny hats—let's say his name was Santarelli or something Italian, Paul would say, "You dago fuck, get out of my way." The guy would beam, blessed by being recognized by Sann. By the way, women had no role on the composing room floor. They were terrified of going there. I can laugh about that period, but it wasn't funny for women at all.

ANNA QUINDLEN, reporter, 1974–1977: I'm from a lace-curtain Irish background. I learned from nuns to put my hands together on my desk very early on, and to be in this atmosphere was like a dream come true. The thing I remember most about Sann was the profanity. Also, he would come up with spectacular wood headlines. The one that I clasp close to my breast always—even though I don't know if it was an actual headline—was one about Gloria Swanson being let out of the hospital: SICK GLORIA IN TRANSIT MONDAY.

SUSAN WELCHMAN, photo editor, 1977–1979: Oh my god, [Managing Editor] Bob Spitzler was such a wonderful editor. He always wore these gorgeous scarves, and he was Ichabod Crane-y. He had long hair. He had long fingers. He was always going to the opera.

ANNA QUINDLEN: [Spitzler] was kind of high-handed. He had an urbane, almost British personal manner. He was a great foil to Paul Sann, who was like an actor playing the executive editor of a tabloid.

DICK BELSKY, metropolitan editor, 1970–1989: Everybody liked [Metro Editor] Warren Hoge. Like Spitzler, he made it look easy. He never stressed out. And he was good-looking—Mr. Cool. He dated Candice Bergen. He dated Sally Quinn [*Washington Post* reporter who later married that paper's legendary editor Ben Bradlee]. We had a folder on the news desk that, if you had anything you wanted to remind yourself of for that day, you put it in there. But Warren also used the folder for personal reminders. You'd be going through, seeing "City Hall press conference at 10"; "Police chief at duh-duh-duh"; "Drinks with Candice Bergen at the Plaza at 7."

LINDSY VAN GELDER, feature writer, 1968–1977: I thought [Features Editor] Joe Rab [Rabinovich] was a strange and troubled man. He was one of the guys who, in that era, we would have referred to as having had his genitalia snipped. Sometimes, if you asked him a question, he would point to the penthouse [Dorothy Schiff's office]. That was all the explanation you would get. I believe he came from a family of Holocaust survivors, and he would make this creepy, bizarre reference that was a metaphor for his job. He would say, "There you are, and you're digging your grave, and the Nazis are standing there with guns pointing at you, but as long as you have the spade in your hand, you know you're still alive."

WARREN HOGE: I found Joe a sad figure only because he was so bright, so good at what he did—and yet so underappreciated by the management.

MARSHA KRANES: [Assistant Managing Editor] Al Ellenberg was a genius. He really got to the point of things. You'd be at a press conference, come back and think you had everything covered. Then he'd ask you one more question that no one had thought to ask. You'd make that phone call, ask the question, and end up with the wood. He was a brilliant person, though a little erratic and crazy.

CLYDE HABERMAN: Al had every vice known to man. He womanized more than was wise, drank more than was wise, gambled more than was wise, probably did a few controlled substances more than was wise. One time I was talking to him, and I saw that he was not even looking at me. He was looking over my shoulder. I turned, and coming out of the composing room was a guy built like a refrigerator with a head on top heading in our direction. I turned to look at Ellenberg, and there's an empty chair. Clearly, he owed this guy money. There were loan sharks or bookies of some type—I never dealt with them—who worked in the composing room.

PETER MOSES, reporter, 1984–1993: Ellenberg once told me that he could never fully trust me because I didn't womanize, drink, or gamble.

> Getting hired at the *Post*—which typically began with work as a copyboy or copy-girl, the newspaper equivalent of a go-fer—often required knowing someone who already worked there—an uncle, a classmate, a friend of your mother. There were exceptions. One reporter was a draft dodger recently back from Canada, another had just been fired by the *New York Times*, and another had experience at two distinctly different publications—*Screw* and *Seventeen*.

ANNA QUINDLEN: I was being interviewed by Bob Spitzler for a summer job between my junior and senior years at Barnard in 1973. I felt like my interview was pretty disastrous. I told Spitzler he should hire me because he needed more women, and he took me to the door of his office, gestured out, and said, "More than fifty percent of my staff are women." When he asked me how much I expected to make, I told him I would do the job for free. He said that was the stupidest thing he'd ever heard, and I should never say that again. In desperation, when I got back to my dorm room, I did in fact take a brown paper bag and cut out letters that said, "Hire Anna Quindlen or you sleep with the fishes." I sent it to him, and he hired me on the basis of that note.

DAVID ROSENTHAL: I was working for Al Blumenthal, who was running against Abe Beame in the '73 mayoral race. I had been feeding negative research to various people at the *Post.* I believe it was Ralph Blumenfeld who said, "Why don't you come work at the *Post*?" I worked in the New York City morgue for a year before politics—as an identification clerk officially, which means I took the families of the newly homicided, suicided, et cetera to see the remains and made sure we had a legal identification. I had to interview all these people who were under extreme duress, which I guess was a plus for being a new tabloid reporter. Also, I had this wonderful talent for getting people's suicide notes for the *Post* to read. Not that I would do a thing like that, of course. But sometimes if things dropped into your hands on an interesting suicide, you would show it to your editor, and they'd be impressed with the quality of your work.

CAROLE LEE: I was looking for a job and I got tired of people telling me, "Oh, yeah, we'll call you." I knew they weren't calling me because of the color of my skin. So I went to a Black-owned agency. That same day they sent me to the

Post to interview with Jimmy Wechsler. He had interviewed eighteen people for the job, and he kept asking personnel why he hadn't seen any minorities. He or a secretary called this Black agency, they sent me out, and I got the job. The reason I got the job wasn't because I'm Black, by the way. It was because I liked baseball and could talk to him about sports.

JANE PERLEZ, reporter, 1972–1977: My first job as a journalist was at *The Australian*, which was an upmarket national daily newspaper that Rupert [Murdoch] founded in Australia—a blend of the *Washington Post* and *The Guardian.* I was straight out of university, and I worked there for three years under a very—small *l*—liberal editor Adrian Deamer, the most famous editor in Australia, who was against the Vietnam War. Rupert fired him in 1971, because the paper was not making as much money as he wanted, and brought in some conservative from London. Deamer was a national treasure. He was only in his forties when Rupert fired him. He went to law school and became a First Amendment lawyer at the opposing newspaper company, Fairfax. I could see what was happening, so I left and came to New York. Warren Hoge gave me a job on the *New York Post.*

MIKE PEARL, reporter, Manhattan Criminal Court, 1967–1998: I had worked for newspapers since 1952. I started off at the *Daily Mirror.* I was there for almost ten years, and they folded. I went to the *Journal-American* and they folded and merged with the *World Telegram* and the *Herald Tribune.* They called it the Widget. I worked there for nine months, then they went out of business in 1967. Then I came to the *Post.* I worked there for more than thirty years. I always felt like the *Post* was about to fold. I felt like I was on the *Titanic.*

CHARLIE CARILLO: Every time something went slightly wrong at the *Post*, Mike [Pearl] was convinced it was over. He'd come to me and say, "Did you see the new bathroom, Charlie? They stopped laying tile." I'd say, "What are you talking about?" "That's a bad sign—we're going under." "Mike, it's their day off." He was convinced he was the canary in the coal mine because he'd folded three papers. They used to call Mike the Walter B. Cooke of journalism because he just kept burying newspapers. [Cooke had funeral homes in every borough of New York.]

TONY SCHWARTZ: I ended up going out for a drink with Bob Spitzler. Bob was drinking pretty continuously. I was not that kind of drinker, but I was trying to be like Bob, who was potentially going to hire me, so I got progressively drunk. So did he. At some point during that conversation, he said to me, "We don't have a reporter's job, but what would you think about taking over Leonard Lyons's column?" [Lyons, longtime Broadway gossip columnist, retired in 1974.] My first reaction was: "That's not my ambition. I don't know any gossip and I wouldn't be good at it." I felt we came to an agreement that this wasn't something I ought to do or wanted to do. The next morning, he called and said, "Why don't you write three sample columns?" I wrote the columns based on either stuff I made up, or more likely stuff I found and adapted in places I thought nobody at the *Post* would read, like the *National Enquirer*. Months went by. Then Bob wanted me to have a conversation with Dolly Schiff. Dolly was doddering by that time. She didn't seem the slightest bit interested in me. I went down to Bob in the newsroom and said, "I don't think it went very well." The phone rang. It was Dolly and, if memory serves me, she said, "He's cold, but smart. Hire him." My first column was the story of my failure to find gossip in the weeks leading up to the first column. If I had had a column full of Cindy Adams or Liz Smith kind of items, I would have run them. The tone that I adopted in the first column became my voice. It was not out of intention; it was simply that doing a gossip column wasn't possible for me. I thought it would be more of a column about being out and around in New York with those kinds of people when you're not one of those people. Bob Spitzler liked it. But Paul Sann hated me for no apparent reason almost immediately.

Ted Poston, one of the first African American reporters to work for a major newspaper, joined the *Post* in the 1930s, retiring in 1972. Because Schiff's *Post* over the years employed other Black reporters, and published Black columnists like Jackie Robinson and Roy Wilkins, it could be considered diverse compared to other newspapers of the era, though not according to today's standards.

WARREN HOGE: "Diversity" was not a term bandied about in those days. Beyond Ted [Poston], the *Post* was not diverse at all. I mean, diversity for the *Post* was having Christians because it was so heavily Jewish. Part of my role was to be a sort of WASP piñata. I embraced it. I could utter things in Yiddish, and it would bring the house down because they knew my background.

ROBERTA BRANDES GRATZ: We were all copyboys. I answered to "copyboy"; I answered to "boy." Then we got our first Black copyboy and it became "copy." The way we were addressed didn't change because of our gender. It changed because of the color of someone's skin. It was an amusing little episode at the time: you weren't treated much better as the girl than you were as the Black boy.

AIDA ALVAREZ: I do think being Hispanic was part of why they hired me. I don't want to undermine myself. I was a good reporter. I don't think I would have gotten the Front Page Award if I hadn't been. [Alvarez received the award, from the Newswomen's Club of New York, for a series on New York's Latinos.] But I think they made an affirmative effort to hire me. When I went to interview, the first person I spoke to was Warren Hoge. He had my résumé in front of him, which showed that I had graduated from Harvard with honors in English literature. He asked me if I was having any trouble with English. The next person I talked to was Al Ellenberg. The first question out of his mouth was "Why do Puerto Ricans throw garbage out their window?" I said, "I don't know what you're talking about. I've never thrown any garbage out of my window." So it was not exactly a friendly environment for me.

WARREN HOGE: I do not remember that. I remember very much hiring Aida and being very proud of finding her.

JOYCE WADLER: Once I was sent to the police shack [the press room at NYPD headquarters] and the direction they gave me was: if it's above 96th Street, forget it. They were looking for rich and white, that was what was crime. That was the old *Post*.

AIDA ALVAREZ: One of the things that was interesting at the *Post* was the women were all Ivy League–type graduates. They went to Barnard, they went to Mount Holyoke, I went to Harvard. Some of the men were lucky if they had a high school degree.

LINDSY VAN GELDER: Joyce Wadler and I have had conversations over the years about how, although we totally support the #MeToo movement, our orientation back then was so different. Granted, we had [union] protection, and we were on a level playing field with everybody. I later heard that some copygirls were abused, but for us—people would say horrible sexist things to us, and we would say horrible sexist things back to them. The wiseguy quotient of the city room was your currency. I never felt remotely oppressed. The guys in that era were constantly passing notice on what we were wearing and making completely gross jokes, so we decided to turn the tables. We had a Mr. Sexy contest. All the women at the *Post* could vote, and [police reporter] Carl Pelleck won. I think Tony Mancini came in second. They could not deal with it. It was hilarious. They didn't know whether to be jealous or relieved at being a sex object. Pelleck was a sexy guy. He wasn't the best-looking, but he was sexy.

TONY MANCINI: It's true that the women [at the Schiff *Post*], for the most part, didn't push back in the sense that they said, "Leave us alone. How dare you?" They gave as well as they took.

JOYCE WADLER: Looking around the newsroom then, it was half women, and women had great assignments. You had Helen Dudar, Judy Michaelson, Joyce Purnick, Jane Perlez. There were some very competent women, and the men knew it. So if somebody was going to joke about your boobs, the women gave it right back.

LINDSY VAN GELDER: One of the reasons I went there from UPI was I knew I wanted to have kids at some point. The *Post* had the best maternity leave anywhere. And they had the most women on staff, they had a woman publisher.

ROBERTA BRANDES GRATZ: Lindsy Van Gelder and I led a fight that we lost as much because of the union as the management. As young mothers, we wanted to share a job and split the workweek. The union resisted that because they would lose a job, and [Schiff] resisted. A group of us went up to meet with her, and she had the audacity to say things like, "I raised children and had a job." This was a let-them-eat-cake kind of thing. She had a governess, a chauffeur, and a cook, and we were talking about regular working women.

DICK BELSKY: One thing people forget about the early '70s is that there were not many women covering hard, breaking news. Back then, women would be hired to work in features, or the food section, or something. The *Post* was one of the first papers to have a lot of really talented women doing all sorts of things, covering news, politics, everything.

JANE PERLEZ: I had the best, absolutely amazing time. I was really interested in politics and covered the 1976 primaries. I covered the coming of the Democratic convention to New York City. The *New York Times* didn't cover the coming of the convention in such detail as the *Post* allowed me to do and I developed very good sources. At the same time, I could do literary interviews. I loved the dance. I did profiles of Mikhail Baryshnikov, Gelsey Kirkland, the whole New York City Ballet. I interviewed the artist Francis Bacon. I did everything. I loved it.

LINDSY VAN GELDER: For anybody who's worked at a newspaper, the memos between Paul Sann and Dolly Schiff are an interesting look into the dynamic between them. In the file [at Boston University], you see Sann complaining to Dolly about me, and Dolly saying things like, "Wait a minute, you mean that women cannot be in the press box at Yankee Stadium? Why are we allowing that?" It's kind of fun to watch her say feminist things and him get completely bent out of shape by it.

By the 1970s, the *Post* was one of just three New York City dailies (not counting *Newsday* on Long Island). Its status as the only afternoon paper presented challenges, especially for a tabloid that despite gaining tens of thousands of readers as its competition fell away, still had the lowest circulation of its rivals, approximately 500,000.

DAVID ROSENTHAL: We were running ahead of everybody in a couple of limited areas. We covered sports really well, although it was a matter of taste whether you liked the *Daily News* or *Post* sports sections; the *Times* didn't even really matter. On a good local murder story, we certainly did more than credibly. And we had great second-day features [stories that expand upon the previous day's news] on funky stuff that nobody had thought of because we had people like Joyce Wadler, Lew Grossberger, Lindsy Van Gelder, and Al Ellenberg cooking up a lot of this shit. We were constantly being used by local TV—they would rip us off blind.

ROBERTA BRANDES GRATZ: I did two series that were game changers. One was on abortion, and one was on rape. I'll never forget that after the rape series ran, Sann stood in front of my desk and basically told me it was fabulous and really made him think about the subject. That was a lot coming from a male chauvinist pig editor. There was a lot of male bravado about Paul. That was the thing about the *Post*'s editors then: they read what you wrote. They were interested in what you wrote. They weren't just thinking about whether the publisher cares, or whether some politician cares. If you did something interesting, they gave you full rein, and they trusted your instincts. You can't ask for more than that.

ANNA QUINDLEN: We'd do a story better than the *Washington Post* or the *Times* version and there wouldn't be any acknowledgment. But it was unequivocally a New York newspaper. It was a subway read. Half of the people on the subway would be reading the *Post* and the other half would be reading the *Daily News*.

ERIC FETTMANN: The main attraction then for Wall Street was that the *Post* was the only afternoon paper and it had the stock prices, particularly the Wall Street final, the closing prices.

DAVID ROSENTHAL: I was the chief guy on New York City going bankrupt in the mid-'70s. I happened to know a lot about that because of my contacts in city politics before joining the *Post*. I got one story after another and kept writing explanatory pieces that ended up as the wood, "Better watch out, city's going broke," that kind of thing. I know Mrs. Schiff and Paul Sann took a lot of heat from people in Albany—that our scare tactics were leading a lot of people to disinvest in the bond market in New York. To their credit, they let me go with it. We always felt that we were running ahead of the *Times* there. For a while we were kicking the shit out of them. We became a tag team, me in the city, Josh Friedman up in Albany. And George Arzt at City Hall.

ROBERTA BRANDES GRATZ: The *Post* covered this city in a fine-grained way that the other papers did not.

DAVID ROSENTHAL: When I was new, one of my proudest moments was when a piece I did was shown on the *CBS Evening News* with Walter Cronkite. According to the powers that be, it was the first time Cronkite had ever shown a front page of the *New York Post* and credited the paper by name. I had the first, albeit brief, interview with Patty Hearst's mother after Patty was kidnapped. The Hearst PR guy told all the reporters who were staked out at the Hearst building on Eighth Avenue that in fact the Hearsts had left there and had gone to their suite at the Essex House. Everybody walked over—cameras didn't go, but the pencil press went—figuring maybe they would show. We're all sitting there in a small lobby, biding our time. The PR guy comes down and says, "They've got nothing to say, they're not coming down." Everybody packs up. Because I'm new, I'm scared shitless that if I don't come back with something, I'm going to get fired; I was still on probation and I spent an awful lot of time on a stakeout getting nada. I went to a house phone, in the lobby or off the lobby, and called the hotel operator. I said, "Could you please connect me to the Hearsts' room? It's an emergency." Something that sounded very urgent. Incredibly, she did it, and somebody answered the phone, I think it was like a maid or an assistant. I started my rap. I said my name, I know exactly what [Patty] must be feeling right now, I'm a young person, too, I know how weird things happen and so forth. I said, "I promised my editor I would get to talk with Mrs. Hearst, I'm afraid I'll get fired." I went through the whole thing. She said, "Hold on." I'm on hold for about four minutes. Mrs. Hearst gets on the phone and I do my rap again. Sure enough, in what I would describe now as a clearly sedated voice because she was speaking quite slowly, she told me, and the quotes were in the piece: "I think Patty's dead, my husband says otherwise," or whatever the fuck she said. I'm on with her for three, four minutes. I write the quotes in my notebook, and I call the desk. I get Larry Nathanson. I said, "Larry, I got the Hearst stuff." He said, "Come back to the office." I said, "You don't understand. I've got an interview with Mrs. Hearst." He said, "Okay, then come back." I said, "Nobody else got an interview with Mrs. Hearst." He went, "How the fuck did that happen?" I tell him. He put me on hold for a second. He puts Paul Sann on, who I've met maybe once or twice at that point, other than, you know, waving to him in the hallway. He says, "Take me through this." It did strike me as I was doing this: how did I know that was actually Mrs. Hearst? But then, it had to be, because the PR people never objected to it. For the second or maybe third edition, we went to the front page with it: MRS. HEARST LOSING HOPE. It was huge. It was picked up everywhere. They couldn't fucking fire me after that.

Crime stories are one of the strands of a tabloid's DNA, and two of the *Post*'s crime specialists, police reporter Carl Pelleck and night rewrite man Cy Egan, both from an earlier era of newspapering, were as hard-boiled and colorful as some of the criminals they covered.

JOE BERGER: Cy Egan was a skeletal figure—tall and thin. Not very communicative, but he wrote well. He was a real old-fashioned afternoon tabloid newspaperman. He once wrote about someone who had died, in a way that seemed as if he had interviewed the guy after his death. From what I remember, Cy indicated that the guy had either died or was murdered, then wrote that if he had lived, he would've said, blah blah blah. The headline was "Voice from the Grave."

GEORGE ARZT, City Hall bureau chief, 1968–1986: One day, Carl Pelleck, me, and Rita Delfiner are having drinks in a bar, and we run into some mob guy Carl knew. I remember this guy because the lining of his coat was unbelievable. It was so colorful, greatly designed. The guy had run afoul of his crime family, and he said, "Carl, it's goodbye." He left. I said, "What was that about?" Carl said, "They're gonna knock him off." And they did. But they took care of his family. It was stunning to know that the mob really was the mob.

NICK PILEGGI, author, screenwriter, former *New York* magazine writer: When I was a police reporter [for the Associated Press], most police reporters were almost more cops than reporters. It was another age, before being a reporter was even thought of as a reasonable profession. Carl Pelleck, though he wasn't that old, was from that era. Artie Rosenfeld was from that era. They were *Post* guys. The police reporters in those days were really good because they had such an intimate connection with the police. Back then, a lot of the reporters I worked with, they hadn't been to college or anything. It was a blue-collar job. It was Watergate in the '70s that really turned journalism into a kind of a fancy job. Suddenly the kind of reporter you had was socially and economically from a different class. I always felt that you lost that local connection and that was because of the unbelievable Watergate coverage. It changed the employment status of newspapers. You'd wind up getting to a scene of a crime or something, an airplane crash, and [the younger reporters] didn't know one person there. Before, I remember going to scenes of crimes with these guys and they knew everybody. They had brothers who were detectives, for god's sake. They weren't covering cops and firemen as an alien culture.

JERRY CAPECI, reporter, organized crime, 1966–1986: My first big story came in 1976, when I covered the funeral of Carlo Gambino. I was still working in the police shack. I got a call and I think it was Larry Nathanson on the desk. They told me, "There's a funeral mass in Brooklyn for Carlo Gambino, and we want you to cover it." I put on my only suit, a three-piece suit, a corduroy suit as a matter of fact. The funeral was in Bensonhurst. It was in my old neighborhood. Mine was Gravesend, but it was Brooklyn. I knew the neighborhood. I went to a Catholic grammar school, and I went to church. I knew what the churches were all about. I get to the back, and there's guys with big necks asking you who you're with. They were letting people in who knew the appropriate family guys, or whatever. I was with the *New York Post*; I wasn't getting in the back of [the church]. I went around to the side door and walked in. I knew my way around. I walked behind the altar into the sacristy, and I met the priest. I took my notebook out of my pocket. I told him that I was going to cover the funeral and I wanted to get the correct spelling of his name. He gave it to me. It escapes me now. He was a *paisan*. I wrote it in my book. I thanked him very much, and I had him walk me into the side door of the church, right by the altar. I got into the first empty seat, and I covered the funeral of Carlo Gambino. I didn't take my notebook out. I remembered what was happening. If I took my notebook out, I knew I would get thrown out. I just watched and listened. As I'm walking out and down the steps, a TV reporter I knew says, "Jerry, you got into the church!" I said, "Yeah." She said, "Can I put you on the news?" I said, "As long as you identify me as Jerry Capeci of the *New York Post*." And that was how I became, quote, a mafia expert. Not because I knew a thing about the mafia, but because I ran around the side door, got into the church, and got into the funeral of Carlo Gambino. It was a front-page story. Which caused me a whole lot of trouble and grief. I'm Italian American, my name ends in a vowel. People at the *Post* wanted to know how I got in. I told them the story. Some people would say, "Come on, you knew somebody. That's how you got in." It became a thing.

ERIC FETTMANN: Jerry was the only reporter to get into one of the big funerals. I asked him how he did it and he said, "You know what? You know how to get into a synagogue when they're trying to keep people out? I know how to get into a mob funeral."

The one news subject where Schiff was willing to relax her tight fists was politics.

CLYDE HABERMAN: Mrs. Schiff could squeeze a penny until Lincoln's face turned blue, but if she was interested in a political person—almost always guys—she was willing to spring for it. And she was interested in Carter. My last full year at the *Post* was 1976, in which the whole year was spent covering Jimmy Carter's presidential campaign.

WARREN HOGE: We covered Democratic politics much more closely than Republican politics, which, in those days, were people like [US senators] Ken Keating and [Jacob] Javits. Jack Javits was a big friend of Dorothy Schiff's. Somebody I got to know very well, too. The Republican Party was a very different animal than it is now. It wasn't this desperate competition in which you malign the opposition and accuse them of being treasonous and betraying American values. There was a different kind of political debate in America—and between the papers also. The *New York Post* probably was the most liberal paper in the country, but that just meant its editorials were liberal. Its choice of subjects, the things that I covered as the Washington correspondent, tended to be things that we really cared about, like the creation of a consumer protection bureau.

ANNA QUINDLEN: At the time, the *Post* was a much more liberal newspaper than the *Times*. The first summer I worked [at the *Post*], I would be interviewing someone, and they would say disparagingly, "Oh, that pink newspaper." Eventually I realized that they meant we were communist, which was terribly exciting to me.

JOYCE PURNICK: There was no problem covering politics and campaigns when Schiff was the editor in chief and publisher. I did whatever you do to cover the story and that was that. She had her political interests, but they were pretty much confined—in fact totally confined—to the editorials. I never had any intrusion or involvement by editors, directly or indirectly.

CLYDE HABERMAN: I never got a note on political coverage.

During the Schiff era, photography was not a top priority at the *Post*. The paper published photos, of course, but not in the same volume or size as the *Daily News*, which billed itself as "New York's Picture Newspaper." Nevertheless, the *Post* employed one of the city's most vaunted tabloid photographers, Louis Liotta, who had apprenticed with legendary photojournalist Weegee. Liotta, who joined the paper in 1946, always wore his press card in the band of his fedora. *Post* photographers often referred to their work as "making pictures"—in some cases because they did much more than operate cameras.

JOYCE WADLER: I loved Louis. I remember going on assignment with him up Eighth Avenue as he's yelling, "Out of my way, shit birds!"

MARSHA KRANES: Louis was very clever. He and I would be staked out on a story somewhere, and he'd cut a hole in a newspaper and have his camera lens aimed right in the middle of that hole as he waited to take his picture.

JERRY CAPECI: For the first feature story I wrote, Louis went with me to an apartment in the Bronx where we were doing a story about a building with no heat. It was a couple of days before Christmas or maybe early December, but as it turned out, it wasn't very cold that day. But we're doing a story about a building with no heat, so Louis had the mother and her kids get dressed up in hats and scarves and huddle around the stove, clapping their hands with a pot of boiling water. It was hot as hell in there, but he said to them, "Do you want to get the story in the paper?" He took this picture and helped me ask the questions, too. I wrote this story about this poor family that was without heat. It made the paper, and people who read the story and felt bad for them sent me checks. It was over $100—and this was 1969. I ended up bringing them to the woman.

JOYCE WADLER: Louis traveled with props in the trunk of his car, like a crucifix and a doll.

LINDSY VAN GELDER: [Photographer] Arty Pomerantz had good news judgment. If we were on a story and anything happened while I was away, making a phone call or using the bathroom, he would cover. He also made a deep impression on me one day when—I can't remember what the assignment was, but he was taking a lot of pictures that I knew were not going to be used for the story. They were artsy pictures. They were more poetic and intellectual. He told me that that was how he kept [the *Post*] from completely cutting his balls off—that if he always did his best work, even if it never saw the light of day, he was going to survive.

JOYCE WADLER: Frank Leonardo was one of the best-read photographers I ever worked with. Once I went to Brooklyn to interview either the director or star of some crazy, avant-garde production. I hated every bit of it and had maybe two questions—probably, "When will it close?" and "You couldn't make it sooner?"—but Frank jumped in and started asking questions. Usually when he did this it drove me nuts, but Frank actually knew this guy's work and naturally, faced with an admirer, the director/star opened up. Frank saved my ass. All I had to do was sit back and take notes.

Augusta Passarella—known simply as Miss Gerry (pronounced with a hard "G")—
was both a leader of the Newspaper Guild, the union representing editorial, advertising, circulation, and other employees, and the purchasing agent for the *Post*,
responsible for supplies and equipment. Tall and squarely built, with thick black hair,
she was a formidable and powerful figure who suffered no fools. Her partner, Chuck
Caruso, helped run the composing room at the *Post*, where the paper was put together,
and was far more affable.

TONY MANCINI: I wish we had union leaders like Miss Gerry nowadays. I served
on the negotiating committee for the [Newspaper] Guild with her and Chuck
Caruso. They were stand-up guys from Brooklyn. They had your back. Chuck
and Gerry were colleagues in the union and on the staff for many years before
they became an item. It was very, very unusual. It was a flowering of their relationship, where it became romantic.

DOMINICK MARRANO, chief paginator, 1971–2008: Miss Gerry was the union rep for
a long time. Once she got into a spat with . . . I think it was a photographer. It
had something to do with a Newspaper Guild job. I forget whose office she was
standing in front of, but I happened to look up and, bam, she punched this
guy right in the face. She had a mouth like a truck driver, but she was a sharp,
bright woman. She was kind of like everybody's buddy-buddy fixer. You had
anything wrong, you went to her, and she tried to fix it.

FRANK LoMONTE, compositor, 1966–2009: She was a wonderful lady, but she took
no shit. They were breaking her balls at a Newspaper Guild meeting once, and
she took a jar of Vaseline, put it on the table, and said, "If you're going to fuck
me, at least use this."

KENNY MORAN, sportswriter, outdoor sports and skiing, 1972–2013: Chuck Caruso,
who was the head of makeup [arranging articles, photos, and ads on a page
prior to printing] during the day, was Jerry Capeci's uncle. He had gotten a
couple of people jobs. Jerry went to Chuck, and Chuck went to Miss Gerry. Miss
Gerry is in Paul Sann's office, and he says, "We got to find somebody else for the
lobster shift. We keep losing them." Miss Gerry says, "I got somebody looking
for a job." Sann says, "If it's another one of your fucking guinea friends, to hell
with them." She said, "Fuck you, he's Irish." That's how I got the job. My mother's
Sicilian, but what the hell?

GEORGE ARZT: Miss Gerry's cousin was named Mike DeMarco, and he was a city councilman. I used to do the city council and congressional endorsements with Dick Montague [who worked with James Wechsler]. We're running down a list, and we don't endorse Mike DeMarco. At the time, we did not know he was Miss Gerry's cousin. The next year, there was a redistricting and DeMarco is up again. We come to his name, and Dick Montague says, "We're endorsing DeMarco." I said, "Why?" He said, "Because last time Miss Gerry took all the furniture out of my office."

The *Post*'s 210 South Street headquarters would become as much of a character in the paper's history as some of its most colorful reporters and editors—especially after years of cigarette smoke, spilled beer, office fights, and romances seeped into its walls and battered linoleum. The East River was just yards away and traffic on the FDR Drive rumbled outside the tall windows of the six-story building. The neighborhood was a no-man's-land, particularly in the years before South Street Seaport was developed for the tourist trade.

JOYCE WADLER: We had a very good view of the Brooklyn Bridge. Late one afternoon, I saw what looked like a guy who was going to jump, and I dragged Al Ellenberg to the window. I said, "Look! It's a jumper!" He said, "Eh, it's after three. Let the *News* have it."

ROBERTA BRANDES GRATZ: It was a real newsroom. There were dirty coffee cups, cigarette butts, and all kinds of crap. It was filthy. But it was a little bit like *The Front Page* [the 1928 play by Ben Hecht and Charles MacArthur, adapted to the screen numerous times, about hard-boiled, wisecracking police reporters]. The romance of being at a newspaper overcame the negativity about the physical space.

CHERYL BENTSEN, feature writer, 1976–1977: I vaguely remember that there was a nice ladies room at South Street, but the rest of the place was a dump. Maybe that had to do with Dorothy Schiff.

PETER TOCCO, sports makeup, 1970–2013: When people wanted to know if the presses were running, up on the fourth floor you put your hand on the wall and you could feel the vibration. As opposed to being downstairs, where it was just insane. The building would vibrate.

MYRON RUSHETZKY, head city desk assistant, 1974–1989, 1991–2013: If it was my turn to go get the edition, I used to go down early because I would not go straight to the mailroom. I liked to follow the path of the paper being printed. I would go down into stereo, where they made the plates. I would then go down into the press room to watch them put the plates on and watch the pressman press the button to start the press. As the papers came out through the sorter and cutter, and up through the conveyor system, I used to race the papers into the mailroom.

JOYCE WADLER: When I walked into 210 South Street for the first time and looked around the newsroom, I thought, I could be friends with everybody in here. There was a feeling of coming home.

TONY SCHWARTZ: I had two reactions. First, this is cool. This is the real deal. I want to be a journalist, and this is the kind of place where it really happens. The other feeling was this is pretty trashy. The typewriters looked like they were falling apart. There were coffee cups and cigarettes all over, and it was staffed by a motley crew. It didn't look like the *New York Times* newsroom, where people were more dressed up and looked like they'd gone to college.

ANDY SOLTIS: The *Post* didn't have TVs in the city room. Part of the reason was Mrs. Schiff thought television was a competitor with newspapers and downplayed it.

PHIL MUSHNICK, columnist, television sports, 1973–current: I used to get upset if my copy had been messed with. Ralph Blumenfeld would always sit there and look straight ahead, look over his glasses, and say [affects gravelly voice], "It's only a tabloid. It's only a tabloid."

ANNA QUINDLEN: Murray Kempton used to say all the time that he remembered covering a press conference where I was wearing hot pants and platform shoes. I do not myself remember that, but Murray was a pretty reliable source.

DAVID SEIFMAN: Mel Juffe was a rewrite guy. I'm a copyboy, making whatever it is, twenty dollars, thirty dollars a night, and midnight to eight, not much is happening. I'm talking to Mel about how hard it is to live your life working midnight to eight. I ask him, "How do you go out on dates?" He was single at the time. He said, "I think I found the secret." I said, "What's that?" He said, "The Playboy [Club] Bunnies, they get off at four a.m." He was dating a Playboy Bunny, and he's giving this advice to me, a twenty-year-old, twenty-one-year-old copyboy: you've got to be with a Playboy Bunny because who are you going to date at nine a.m.?

AIDA ALVAREZ: Josh Friedman was the star Albany reporter covering the fiscal crisis in New York, and he was the nicest man. One day I went over to Josh, looking really upset. I said, "Al Ellenberg says I'm not going to make it. I'm not tough enough." He said, "Do you ask hard questions?" I said I thought I was asking hard questions. He said, "Aida, look around here. You're too polite." I realized it was a rough-and-tumble newsroom. There were a lot of F-words flying around, right? And I thought, okay, I get it. I'm not fitting in because I'm not joining in the fun. I went back to my typewriter and it was defective. I slammed the roller really loud and I let out a big f-you. It was the beginning of my reeducation. I had gone to Catholic school for twelve years. I needed to undo that.

JERRY CAPECI: Remember spikes? When Fred McMorrow was news editor, he once put his right hand right through the fucking news spike, like Jesus Christ. It went through his hand and out the other side. That's the legend of Fred McMorrow.

DAVID ROSENTHAL: Ralph Blumenfeld had a sideline, which he made no attempt to hide. He wrote a football and basketball betting newsletter, which went to many customers, where he would do the betting line. The amount of betting in the newsroom, at least when I was there, was extraordinary. The horse races were being run out of the composing room. Other games were being bet throughout the building, and you had various people, like Al Ellenberg and John Gruber, who were either making hundreds of dollars or getting wiped out on any given day. It was scary because people suddenly would literally not have car fare to go home because they'd lost a shitload on the eighth race at Belmont.

JOHN GRUBER, copy editor, 1971–1978, 1980–1985: There were two kinds of betting—horses and sports. I bet both for close to ten years. The wire room was right next to the news copydesk, where I worked. We could hear when the racing wire would come at around one in the afternoon. Then we'd all run in to see which horses had won. Horse bets were placed in either the mailroom or the composing room, but you had to phone in your bets on sports. There was a guy who came to the paper once a week to collect or pay out the sports bets. In my case, he mostly collected.

GEORGE ARZT: When we had the hot type, you could go back [to the composing room] and you could get bonds, you could get stocks, you could arrange for abortions when they were not legal. And there were bookies so you could place bets.

> Gambling was hardly the only vice practiced at the *Post*. Before and after Dorothy Schiff, alcohol fueled the often outrageous, sometimes feckless antics of its seen-it-all staff. Until the late 1970s, one of the nearest, and therefore most popular, bars was Mutchie's, which had been typecast in the 1971 film *The French Connection* as a seedy dive—one that Popeye Doyle (Gene Hackman) stumbles out of early one morning.

ANNA QUINDLEN: In the newspaper business back then, there were three types of people. There were raging alcoholics, there were recovering alcoholics, and there were people who didn't really drink that much. The third group was the smallest group.

AIDA ALVAREZ: There was a lot of divorce. And there was a lot of drinking. I always felt, particularly the way we worked at the *Post*, where you had to constantly put out a new headline and a new headline and a new headline, you had to be addicted to an adrenaline high. You had to get your energy up each time for the next version, next version, next version, and do it all under deadline. It was pretty stressful. I mean, I enjoyed it. I was young, I enjoyed the excitement of it, but by the time you were done, at the end of the day, you really needed to drink.

KENNY MORAN: The people who came to Mutchie's were mostly neighborhood people and *Post* people, especially the guys who worked in the composing room, the printers, the pressmen, the drivers. Once there was a scene, I can't give you names, but two people at the *Post*—a man and a woman—were having, let's just say, a sexual encounter on the back table, not even worrying about going into a room or anything. Right on the table. I think somebody applauded.

DAVID ROSENTHAL: We used to play pool there. And there was a tie line between Mutchie's and the city desk. The city desk could call Mutchie's and talk to any of us.

KENNY MORAN: Mutchie would have food brought out. He was blind. Or he had really bad eyesight. When you'd drink vodka or gin or rye, he would put the bottle in front of you and mark with a crayon how much was in the bottle. You got a bucket of ice, and you poured your own booze. When you were ready to go, he measured how much you drank in the bottle and charged you—he charged you by the inch or whatever. I remember him having food at the bar. I would never get anything out of that kitchen. It looked terrible. He would be sitting at the end and, say somebody else came in, he'd take his teeth out and put it on top of the food. I guess so no one else would eat it or touch it. That was Mutchie.

> Another hangout for reporters and writers of all stripes, including Norman Mailer, Lanford Wilson, and Frank McCourt, was the Lion's Head on Christopher Street in the West Village.

ANNA QUINDLEN: The Lion's Head is where I learned to drink—because again, I was a twenty-year-old girl trying to fit in with these guys. I drank a lot of boilermakers just to make it seem like I was part of the crowd.

AIDA ALVAREZ: I was a few months into my quote, unquote, probation period when Al Ellenberg asked me if I wanted to go out and have a drink with him. Al was known for his drinking. We went to the Lion's Head. We sat at the bar and Al ordered a double boilermaker. I had no idea what the heck that was, but he ordered one for me, too. I was a kid—twenty-three, twenty-four—hardly a drinker. He barely said a word. He just kept drinking. I nursed the drink until they were getting ready to close the bar. He said, "Time to go home." I grabbed a cab. The next day or so, Jan Hodenfield came over to me and said, "Have you been out drinking with Al yet?" I said, "Actually, I just went out with Al." Jan said, "That means you're in." That's how I knew that I had passed my probation.

> Mrs. Schiff cared a great deal about her appearance and craved confirmation that she was still attractive, especially to younger men. She was particularly fond of the good-looking, WASP variety. Members of her family had worked at the *Post* at various times, but ultimately she did not expect one of her children to take over the paper. So she regularly discussed finding the right young man to succeed her. She auditioned several, often giving them titles such as assistant to the publisher, or associate publisher.

ANNA QUINDLEN: The person who was Dorothy adjacent and loomed rather large was a guy named Billy Woodward [William Woodward III]. His family were real Park Avenue types. His father, William Woodward Jr., was an heir to the Manufacturers Hanover banking fortune and his mother was a showgirl. She shot Billy's father because she said someone came into the apartment in the middle of the night, and she thought it was an intruder. Truman Capote fictionalized it in *Answered Prayers* and Dominick Dunne did the same in *The Two Mrs. Grenvilles.* Billy was part of Mrs. Schiff's circle and a reporter there. Dorothy allegedly loved him, and for a while, the operative rumor in the newsroom was that Mrs. Schiff was going to sell the paper or leave the paper to Bill Woodward. He was one of the handsome young men that she was interested in, along with, by the way, Warren Hoge. When the powers that be in the newsroom thought that Bill Woodward might be taking over the paper, they decided that the way to safeguard the institution was for me to marry him. So every time Bill Woodward was in the newsroom, someone would say, "Bill, have you met Anna Quindlen?" About the fifth or sixth time, he said, "Yes, *many times.*" Meanwhile, I was thinking, I don't see how this is going to work out. But they were always very concerned that somehow the paper would fall into the wrong hands. I was one idea of a backstop. It was like that all the time. There's no rumor mill like a newsroom. If we printed the things that passed among the desks, our readership would grow exponentially.

> Another attractive man, Jeffrey Potter, was Schiff's authorized biographer. *Men, Money & Magic: The Story of Dorothy Schiff*, written by Potter with Schiff's cooperation and approval, was scheduled to be published in October 1976. Long passages of the book were taken directly from interviews with Schiff, who was remarkably frank about her marriages and her affairs.

PAT SULLIVAN, reporter, night editor, 1972–1980: In those days, before the internet, everybody wanted to know what the *New York Times* had. Almost everybody, even overseas [media], would send people to Times Square when the *Times* came up, and would run it back to their offices. In one of those situations, we were working at night, and it was kind of quiet. All of a sudden the phone started ringing like crazy. It's the London *Times*, it's this paper, and that paper. Dolly had written her autobiography, and instead of leaking it to her own paper, she leaked it to the *New York Times.* And the *Times* put it on page one. Why did they put the book there? In it, she'd had sex with FDR. That was the angle. She got the publicity she wanted.

ANDY SOLTIS: The *Times* had a front-page story about how Dorothy Schiff had an affair with Franklin Roosevelt. This was coming from her autobiography, which was actually written by somebody else. But the book didn't actually say that she had had an affair. It was implied, and Schiff complained and threatened to sue. Then the *Times* interviewed the writer of the book. It turned out that, despite the extensive interviews he did with Schiff, he never asked her whether she'd had an affair with Roosevelt. [Potter said he asked if she'd gone to bed with FDR, and she gave a coy response.] They intentionally left it vague that this was something that might have happened. [The *Times* altered the story in later editions to include Schiff's denial that her friendship with FDR had been romantic.]

> The publication of Schiff's semi-autobiography and her waning attention to the details of running the *Post* were signs that, after years of rumors and lots of discussions with potential suitors, Schiff might actually sell the tabloid. Even those who loved working at the *Post* acknowledged that change was in order. In her caustic 1975 essay for *Esquire*, Nora Ephron stated as much and blamed Schiff for the paper's decline.

CLYDE HABERMAN: I'm not suggesting that the era when I was at the *Post* was the age of Pericles. We were a tabloid with all its flaws. But stories were allowed to be somewhat longer, so it was more rewarding for writers. Rupert Murdoch's complaint about American journalism being a little flabby was overstated, but I think the *Post* did get more staid and less gutsy in Dorothy Schiff's last year or two. And it was beginning to hemorrhage money that last year. It was painfully thin compared to the *Daily News*, for sure, and *Newsday*, which was fatter than an encyclopedia back then. It was worrisome, because there were no ads. There was an air of decay.

DAVID SEIFMAN: The *Post* had some spectacular writers and reporters, but if you picked it up, you saw a sea of gray type; its formula hadn't changed in decades. It needed a shot of adrenaline.

KEN CHANDLER, editor in chief, publisher, 1978–1986, 1993–2002: I did read [the Schiff *Post*] back then. I thought it was sleepy and boring, and it was crammed full of syndicated columns. It had a couple of good sports columnists, but it was a pretty dull product. If anybody had told me that that paper was still going to be around in the year 2021, I would've laughed.

Given the media industry's obsession with gossip, it's amazing that Schiff's negotiations to sell the *Post* to Rupert Murdoch stayed secret, although a few of her most senior editors were aware something was afoot. Murdoch had achieved great success and political influence with his papers in England and Australia, but the lurid content in his London tabloid, *The Sun*, especially its topless "Page 3 Girls," had earned him the nickname "the dirty digger" from the British satirical magazine *Private Eye*. While *Post* staffers debated the pros and cons of what the *Post* was and what it could become, Warren Hoge decided he was not going to wait around.

WARREN HOGE: Dorothy Schiff confided to me that the *Post* was about to lose money the next year. She was talking about 1976. She said she had always promised her banker brother, John Schiff, that if the *Post* was not making money, she would sell it. She said she was looking around for people who might be able to keep it going. She was telling me this in the guise of "I don't want you to worry." She probably said to Paul [Sann] and Bob [Spitzler], too—something like, "The three of you have a future here." She said that one of the people she'd been talking to was Rupert Murdoch. Now, this was a name nobody had heard in New York at this point. But I had been to Australia the summer before. I had an apartment on Riverside Drive. On the walls of that apartment, I had put framed headlines from the Australian press—from Murdoch papers—which were risible and funny. And I suddenly heard Dorothy Schiff confiding in me that the man who produced that kind of journalism might buy the *New York Post*. I decided to take [Executive Editor] Abe Rosenthal up on his feeler about going to the *New York Times*. Dorothy Schiff asked me to stay for a few months, for a transition. I did, but I went to the *Times* in '76.

ERIC FETTMANN: We didn't find out until later that 1976 was the first time in almost thirty years that she ended up losing money. It's one of the reasons she sold the paper. She lost half a million dollars and panicked. She bought the paper in '39 and lost money for the first ten years. The peak year for newspapers in New York in general was 1949. That was the year the *Post* finally turned around, and it kept making a profit, though nothing really great, until 1976. We never considered the *Post* to be a thriving paper. We were marginally successful. We were always decrying the fact that she ran it like a mom-and-pop store and refused to invest money into it.

ROBERTA BRANDES GRATZ: There was a lot of personal whim involved in the paper. It was the subject of a lot of either chortling or complaints on our part. Whoever expected somebody to buy the paper and make her look good?

In the latter half of 1976, James Brady, a former Marine officer who'd gone to work for Rupert Murdoch after serving as the publisher of *Women's Wear Daily* and as a columnist for *New York* magazine, dined at the World Trade Center's Windows on the World with a group that included his boss and Murdoch's wife, Anna. It was there that he learned of Murdoch's next move.

JAMES BRADY, creator of Page Six, 1977; Page Six editor, 1980–1982: We were talking about Dolly Schiff, and I said, "God, there's this new biography of [her] coming out. The *Times* has asked me to review it, and it's going to kill her. It makes her seem to be a terrible person, a fool, a social climber." Rupert called me aside at one point during the dinner and said, "I have a favor to ask of you. I'm negotiating with Dolly Schiff to buy the *Post*. No one knows about it. This might embarrass me if you do this. Can you possibly get out of it?" I said, "Yeah, absolutely." It was announced sometime later that Rupert Murdoch had agreed with Dolly Schiff to buy the *New York Post*.

2 | SID VICIOUS TAKES OVER THE PHILHARMONIC

Murdoch Arrives, Mayhem Ensues

On Friday, November 19, 1976, seventy-three-year-old Dorothy Schiff announced that she had sold the *New York Post* to the forty-five-year-old Australian publisher Rupert Murdoch. He agreed to pay $31 million. The next day, news of the sale rated prime placement on the front page of the *New York Times*. Describing Murdoch as "a man of strong commitment to the spirit of independent, progressive journalism," Schiff said she felt sure "he will carry on vigorously in the tradition I value so deeply." The staff of her newspaper hoped their soon-to-be-former owner spoke the truth.

ROBERTA BRANDES GRATZ, reporter, 1963–1978: Dolly Schiff was very removed from reality, whereas Murdoch is very involved in reality—trying to change it.

ERIC FETTMANN, associate editorial page editor, columnist, 1976–1991, 1993–2019: I was out of the office doing a Daily Close-up in the late morning and early afternoon. When I got back, people knew something was up. First, Jimmy Wechsler was in Paul Sann's office talking to him. That was something that no one had seen for fifteen years. Late that morning, Bob Spitzler let out a huge shriek after he heard something on the phone but refused to talk about it. Then, when I was sitting at my desk typing up my story, a shell-shocked Barbara Yuncker [the *Post*'s medical and science reporter and a Newspaper Guild representative] walked into the newsroom having just returned from Dolly's office and said, "She sold the paper."

ANNA QUINDLEN, reporter, 1974–1977: When it was finally announced that Murdoch had bought it, the mood in the newsroom, between the time the sale was announced and the time the Aussies actually arrived, was almost identical to the mood among my friends and I between the time that Donald Trump won the election and the moment he actually took office. There were months of us saying, "Oh, come on, it's not going to be as bad as we think. Murdoch owns some really good papers. It'll be fine. It might even be better. He might put some money into it."

DAVID ROSENTHAL, reporter, desk editor, 1974–1977: At first I thought, at least we're not going to go out of business. And maybe there'll be money to spend on train fare to New Jersey.

MARSHA KRANES, rewrite, editor, 1974–2005: The day Murdoch bought the paper, I was covering the Bronfman kidnap trial in White Plains [New York]. I usually dealt with Al Ellenberg. Toward the end of the day, I'd call and tell him what the story was. But someone was filling in for him that day. I think it was Steve Lawrence. He said, "It doesn't matter. All we want is T and A." I said, "What?" He said, "Murdoch bought the paper, T and A." I said, "What's T and A?" He goes, "Tits and ass." I'd never heard that expression before.

DICK BELSKY, metropolitan editor, 1970–1989: On November 17, 1976, I was named city editor. I had previously been acting city editor, and in order to take this new title, I had to leave the union, because I was now considered management. Two days later, we got the announcement that Dolly Schiff had sold the paper to Rupert Murdoch. Nobody had any clue this was in the works. It had been kept completely secret. That night, I went out with about a half dozen editors, and they were all saying things like, "Murdoch will come in and fire everybody. All of us will be gone." I'm sitting there thinking, just two days earlier, I had union protection! But I was pretty much the only one who survived. And Joe Rab.

TONY MANCINI, reporter, 1958–1978: There's a wide-angle photo of Murdoch addressing the staff in the city room about the takeover. As I recall, it was "You're a wonderful staff, this is a great newspaper, nothing's going to change," that kind of thing. He's on one side of the photo—and I'm on the other with my arms akimbo, glaring at him. Everyone there was attentive, some skeptical, because by that time, we had done some research on his reputation. A lot of people were hopeful. They thought, "Mrs. Schiff has had her run, she's getting on in years, we might need some new blood in here—a boost of energy." So there was a feeling that it might be okay. We soon learned otherwise.

JOE BERGER, investigative reporter, 1971–1978: He was very convincing. People said, "Hmm, maybe he's not going to be what we had heard"—in terms of what he had done with the San Antonio papers.

As part of the sale, Schiff continued for five years to have an office at 210 South Street, but her diminished status became clear on December 30, 1976, Murdoch's first official day in charge.

JANE PERLEZ, reporter, 1972–1977: (*from notes taken during the Murdoch transition*) In the afternoon, Everette, [Schiff's] faithful chauffeur, who had taken her around in the black-bottomed, white-topped Cadillac, was seen circling the building for a parking space. Dolly's front space had been preempted by Rupert's bullet gray, five times bigger though squat Cadillac. Rupert apparently went down to the cafeteria to have a BLT sandwich. He was with some of his people and paid. For the next cafeteria order, he sent Dolly's copyboy down and didn't pay.

CALVIN TRILLIN, staff writer, *The New Yorker*: What was the great [A. J.] Liebling phrase? "Freedom of the press is guaranteed only to those who own one"? The Schiff paper was known to be—in those days the right-wing cliché for the left was "knee-jerk liberal"—and all it took was some cash to change hands and it was Murdoch's right-wing paper.

CHARLIE CARILLO, reporter, columnist, 1978–1993: Murdoch came in and said, I'm not going to change anything. Then he changed everything. It was sort of like Sid Vicious taking over the Philharmonic.

ERIC FETTMANN: Nobody had heard the name Rupert Murdoch before—except for Jane Perlez, who's Australian. She immediately said, "I'm not going to be working here for much longer." She was the only one who knew what Murdoch was all about. Somebody immediately called for the clips, but of course they were signed out to Dolly. [The *Post*'s library, the Google of its day, clipped and filed articles from numerous publications, including the *Post*.] We found out he was the owner of the *National Star*. Somebody found a copy of the latest issue. The headline was "Claudine Longet's Love Diary." Remember her? [Crooner] Andy Williams's ex-wife who shot her boyfriend, skier Spider Sabich? That didn't help. Judy Michaelson, one of the chief political reporters, sat there singing "Waltzing Matilda" to anyone who walked by.

FRANK RICH, film critic, 1975–1977: I really reflected the views of everyone—oh my god, this is fantastic. A benevolent sugar daddy has come to rescue this paper from the incredible minginess of Dolly Schiff. That was soon to be proven wrong. Jane Perlez was the first hint of that.

ROBERTA BRANDES GRATZ: Jane Perlez sat next to me in the newsroom. I thought she was going to be apoplectic. I don't remember whether she told me, or others did, but she basically came to America to get away from Murdoch. And here he was standing right in front of us.

JANE PERLEZ: I felt very badly for my colleagues because though Rupert had a reputation, which they were not that familiar with, they felt that he was rich, he was the new man in town, and he was going to reinvigorate the paper—make it great again, to use today's language. He wanted to make his way in New York, and he could see a perfect vehicle, for which he paid thirty-one million bucks, which was way over what the *Post* was worth. As soon as Murdoch walked in, I knew the game was over. But at first, I was very diplomatic, because [my colleagues] were all so excited. So, I said things like, he's smart, he's intelligent, he's young. It couldn't be worse because by that stage, the *Post* barely had a penny to its name. The end days of Dorothy Schiff's *Post* were very sad.

DICK BELSKY: For the first edition, we'd figure out page one at five or six a.m. and we'd go to press around seven or eight. I was sitting in Paul Sann's office the day Murdoch was supposed to take over. There were five or six of us editors there on the overnight shift. It's dark outside, and we're all saying, "When Rupert comes in at nine o'clock, I wonder what he's going to do." The door bursts open and Rupert walks in. He's got his three lieutenants with him: Jim Brady, Neal Travis, and Peter Michelmore. Immediately Murdoch rips up the front page, and Michelmore sits next to me while I'm editing the front-page story. It was like, wow, now we see what this is going to be.

On January 3, 1977, the first wood of the Murdoch era—MOB WAR SHAPES UP OVER DRUGS—was written by Jerry Capeci. The story could have, and probably would have, also led in the Schiff era.

JERRY CAPECI, reporter, organized crime, 1966–1986: After ten years of [working for] Dolly Schiff, I had a wood about two mob bosses, Carmine Galante and Aniello Dellacroce, which I think was the first front-page story of the Murdoch-era *New York Post*. Which kind of cemented me with the new breed of editors that Murdoch brought in. The story was that Galante was out and about—he had gotten out of jail—and he and Dellacroce were the main contenders to be the so-called boss of bosses, the main mobster in the city of New York. As it turns out, it wasn't the case. They were both major players, but Dellacroce got passed over and Galante ended up getting killed a couple of years later. But the story certainly got me creds, if that's the right word, with the new editors Murdoch brought in.

Murdoch had a coterie of Australian loyalists who had been with him for years, some of whom became fixtures at the *Post*. Murdoch also hired a slate of new editors, including several Americans. But he did not replace the names on Schiff's masthead. Instead, he had the new guard work alongside the old.

LINDSY VAN GELDER, feature writer, 1968–1977: The word was that Murdoch was installing doppelgängers. I can't remember exactly the cast of characters, but there was somebody who was competing with Spitzler for his job, and somebody was competing with Sann. These people had murky duties. It was being set up as a kind of Hunger Games for editors.

ERIC FETTMANN: Editors were brought in without official titles at first, so everything got a bit complicated.

ANDY SOLTIS, rewrite, editor, 1967–2014: Murdoch went through a bunch of changes when he took over the *Post*. He tried things, and if it didn't work, he tried something else. He hired several new editors. Only a couple were Australian. The thing was, they were one level of seniority ahead of the existing Dolly Schiff editors. Paul Sann had carried the title of executive editor for twenty years, and suddenly there was a new guy named Edwin Bolwell who came from *Time* magazine and held the title of editor. He was in charge. Our sports editor Ike Gellis had been in that job since Joe DiMaggio was on the back page, and now Jerry Lisker was on top of him. That was the case in a lot of departments.

JAMES BRADY, creator of Page Six, 1977; Page Six editor, 1980–1982: [Rupert Murdoch] ran a very thin executive suite. He was always in shirtsleeves. He was always trying to help you make up a front page or scale a picture. He knew all that stuff. He knew type sizes. He knew everything. When I went to work running the *Star*, he said, "Look, I only have a couple of suggestions for you: Wherever you go drinking, don't go drinking where your reporters go drinking. That's trouble. You'll get into fistfights. You'll lose their respect. You'll get beaten up. Don't do that."

Dorothy Schiff had always found room in her paper for multiple gossip columnists, but as of the mid-1970s, the three men writing that sort of column for the *Post* were long in the tooth and the milieus they covered were changing with the times. Earl Wilson, a chronicler of New York nightlife since the 1940s, continued making his rounds of the city's nightclubs and parties, but both Sidney Skolsky and Leonard Lyons, who'd been churning out items for even longer, retired. And Murdoch was not a fan of Tony Schwartz, who'd taken over Lyons's column. The *Post*'s new owner envisioned a more dynamic and nervy gossip column, and even before he closed the deal with Schiff he tasked James Brady with its creation. Brady, who took on several roles during the nine years he worked for the Australian press lord and was eventually named vice chairman of the American arm of Murdoch's News Corp, had been involved in the creation of two other such columns, The Eye in *Women's Wear Daily*, which launched during that paper's heyday, when Brady was publisher, and The Intelligencer in *New York* magazine. According to Brady, Murdoch wanted the *Post*'s new gossip page to be fashioned after William Hickey, a column in London written and edited by a changing cast of characters.

The *Post*'s new page would work on a similar premise: a group of reporters would gather and write brief, pithy stories about the powerful and famous and file them to the column's editor, who would imbue them with a unifying voice. Murdoch wanted the column ready to roll when he officially took control of the *Post*, so in the final weeks of 1976 Brady set about pulling together a group of reporters and stringers to work out the kinks via a series of dummy columns.

JAMES BRADY: From the beginning there was an argument: what should we call it? It had been decided that [the column] would be anchored on page six; that after the first five pages—the front page and then four pages of hard news—we'd have this real change of pace. We'd come to page six and it would be a knockout gossip column with a cartoon. I was the one who said, "We continually talk about 'page six.' Let's just call it Page Six."

RANDY SMITH, reporter, 1977–1980: It supposedly was not just the position in the paper, but it was supposed to have echoes of a Pier Six, which was like a brawl. It's supposed to be scrappy and brawling and kind of an upstart working-class take on [things].

Neal Travis, a New Zealand–born Murdoch acolyte, was not part of the team that put together the early versions of Page Six. He joined Brady's special forces when they arrived at 210 South Street.

RANDY SMITH: The day came that we went down to the *Post*, practically like storming the building. We all piled into this car, and we go down the FDR Drive. We're going under all these bridges—the Williamsburg, the Manhattan. We take the South Street exit, and we pull over near the Brooklyn Bridge. I was like, what is this place? We go into this odd-looking, long industrial building and up to the sixth floor, where Murdoch's office is located. There's this big space that was probably Dorothy Schiff's office, but it's kind of bare. There's a bank of gray, industrial newsroom desks piled together—two rows of people facing each other. Neal Travis was there, Bruce Rothwell [an Australian who eventually became editorial page editor], and Peter Michelmore, who was Australian and had white hair and a saucy way of talking. Off in a corner was Murdoch's secretary [Dot Wyndoe]. Murdoch was in the next room.

ANNA QUINDLEN: The first day the Australians were in the newsroom, Neal Travis came to me and said, "Have we got an assignment for you! We're going to do a whole page every day of notable items, and we're going to call it Page Six. We want you to write it." Neal was like an overgrown leprechaun. He had this vivid quality—a kind of crazy enthusiasm for everything. He walked me through the kind of thing that he was thinking of, and then he gave me like four or five different items he had. I remember one was about Liza Minnelli, although I can't remember specifically what. Two days later, he came to me and said, "Sweetheart, where's the Liza item?" I said, "I haven't been able to nail it down." He said, "Oh, you don't have to report it. You just have to write it." I thought, I am screwed. It was becoming clearer day by day that what I was being asked to do was a gossip column. That was not how I saw my future unspooling, and I especially didn't see it unspooling as a gossip columnist who didn't confirm anything.

STEVE CUOZZO, executive editor, columnist, 1972–current: At the point that Page Six was created, gossip columns were an entirely lost art. Not only was Walter Winchell long gone, the infamous demagogue with his power, but so were the Hollywood columnists like Hedda Hopper and Louella Parsons. The only columns that were left were running on their last legs, like Earl Wilson in the *Post*. I think there was still some sort of a weak Ed Sullivan column in the *Daily News* and Liz Smith, but hers was primarily a Hollywood and celebrity column. It didn't pretend to be a gossip column. Page Six reanimated the genre by introducing the public to the idea that gossip columns would not only be about show business and celebrities, but about the corridors of power and Wall Street and the nonprofits and the arts and a smattering of society. Another thing that made Page Six very electric at the time it came on the scene had to do with the precise circumstances of New York City then. This was 1977. The city was barely trying to recover from the near bankruptcy of 1975, when New York was in such dire straits that it had to be bailed out by the state. Morale was very low, and Page Six came along and kind of reminded people just how dynamic the city was.

MELANIE SHORIN, Page Six reporter, 1977: I got condolence notes from people at my college because my goal was to become the first female network news anchor. Somehow I ended up being a gossip columnist with Jim [Brady], which actually was so much fun and sent me on a whole new career.

STEVE CUOZZO: For some reason, when Page Six was created, it was regarded as such a secretive and dangerous mission that it was actually edited entirely on the sixth floor, which was the publisher's floor. None of us ever saw the material. At some time, late in the day, it came down and entered the composing room, and that was it.

RANDY SMITH: I remember Murdoch saying two things about Page Six. He used the phrase "substantial stories." He didn't want them to be piffle. It was meant to be inside stuff, true—truly good gossip. I remember Murdoch banning the use of the word "reportedly." You couldn't say "reportedly." It was either true or it wasn't true.

ERIC FETTMANN: Brady was at Page Six and also functioning as sort of a consigliere type—introducing Murdoch to New York society, to the movers and shakers he didn't really know. Now that Murdoch had the *Post*, people started coming to him. They didn't turn their backs. But he needed a crash course in who runs the city. Jim was one of the people who guided him.

> Page Six debuted on January 3, 1977, the first edition with the Murdoch stamp. The column's lead story—about CBS chairman William Paley talking to former secretary of state Henry Kissinger about taking the reins of what was then known as the Tiffany Network—was teased at the top of the wood. On Page Six itself, a photo of the smiling Paley separated the lead story from a small item about Paul Lynde getting into an argument at an "all-male" bar called Cowboy, where, according to the column, he "defended his honor" by tossing a plate of French fries at a young ankle biter. That item featured the debut of a phrase that became part of the page's lexicon: "Paul's companions wanted to take the heckler outside but *cooler heads prevailed*." Mentions of Jacqueline Onassis and John F. Kennedy Jr. set similar precedents.

MELANIE SHORIN: I remember following Jackie O around, hailing a cab and saying, "I only have $3.50, so follow that car as far as you can go."

> Just days after Murdoch took over the *Post*, he won a legal battle to purchase the New York Magazine Company, publisher of *New York*, the temple to New Journalism co-founded by Clay Felker; *New West*, its California equivalent; and the *Village Voice*, New York City's alternative weekly. Felker was president, and owned about ten percent, of the New York Magazine Company, but other directors of the company sold Murdoch a controlling number of shares.

JAMES BRADY: Murdoch was avaricious for properties at that point. He was thinking, America's the place I'm going to make my fortune. So he went for it.

> Particularly distraught about the prospect of losing *New York*, the weekly glossy that he had founded in 1964 as a Sunday supplement in the *New York Herald Tribune*,

Felker went to court to try to stop the sale. On January 17, 1977, an image of Murdoch as King Kong straddling the World Trade Center towers while holding copies of his newly purchased publications appeared on the cover of *Time* magazine. Its faux tabloid headline screamed: EXTRA!! AUSSIE PRESS LORD TERRIFIES GOTHAM.

JAMES BRADY: I was in Rupert's office one day when Kay Graham [owner of the *Washington Post*] called him on behalf of Clay Felker. She said, "Rupert, do not do this to this boy. You'll destroy this boy. You don't know what *New York* magazine means to him. It's his heart and soul." Rupert said, "Well, Kay, I'm going to talk to Clay, too. I want him to stay with us if I get it." He hung up and said, "She kept saying, 'Don't destroy this boy.' This boy is six years older than I am."

JANE PERLEZ: I had to cover this story, and as a reporter at the *Post*, also now owned by Murdoch, the spirit of revolt at *New York* magazine was almost impossible to convey in stories. I can recall being impressed with the determination to stand up to Murdoch and wondering how it was going to end up.

JAMES BRADY: Rupert did try to keep Clay there, and Clay said to him, "Rupert, it will never work. You'll want to be the boss, and I'll want to be the boss." Rupert said later, "Clay was absolutely right." I said, "Who the hell is going to edit it?" He said, "You are."

ALAN PATRICOF, former chairman of the board, New York Magazine Company: Because the writers had been so vocal, Murdoch knew that they were going to walk out. He put in Jim Brady to run it virtually simultaneously with buying it. And the writers did walk out.

The most senior of Murdoch's new hires at the *Post*, Australia-born Edwin "Ted" Bolwell, was a disaster from day one. His second-in-command in the Hunger Games hierarchy—Ron Martin, an American from Baltimore, who became co–managing editor with Bob Spitzler—did not fare much better. Peter Michelmore, who had worked previously for the Murdoch organization and who eventually became the *Post*'s metropolitan editor, proved to be one of the few editors brought in early on who earned respect from the Schiff-era staff.

FRANK RICH: Bolwell was this truculent, arrogant, surly Australian who had been at *Time*. I had friends at *Time*, and no one seemed to quite remember him.

JANE PERLEZ: Red-faced, ghastly guy. Terrible. He was a Rupert henchman. That's what Rupert liked.

GEORGE ARZT, City Hall bureau chief, 1968–1986: Bolwell had an unbelievable temper—you'd hear him screaming and yelling—and Murdoch told me what a brilliant editor he was. I didn't want to tell Murdoch, the guy's *nuts*.

CHERYL BENTSEN, feature writer, 1976–1977: He wore platform shoes, which everybody found hilarious. I'm five eight and a half and I towered over him. He had a curly perm. The funniest thing about the Australians who were around the *New York Post* newsroom is they all had these silly white-man afros. This was, I guess, an Aussie look.

DAVID ROSENTHAL: At least at first, I was willing to give Murdoch the benefit of the doubt. Then I met Ted Bolwell, and I was no longer willing to give him the benefit of the doubt. He was vile, he was a crazy person. He was a fucking idiot, as were many of the people Murdoch brought in. Ron Martin's nickname was Memo Man, because all he did all day was write memos. He wouldn't talk to reporters or editors face-to-face; he could only write memos. You would get these two-page, single-spaced memos from him about some story that nobody gave a shit about.

DOMINICK MARRANO, chief paginator, 1971–2008: On South Street, the editors used to have offices that looked out over the highway to the East River, but their desks faced the city room. After Murdoch bought the paper, Ron Martin came in as managing editor. The most memorable thing he did was turn his desk around so that he had his back to the city room. We called him Major Major, like that character in *Catch-22* who would only see people when he wasn't in the office.

TONY MANCINI: Bolwell was a piece of work. He was lazy, and seemed interested only in going out at night, and preening around social gatherings as the new editor in chief of the paper. I thought Peter Michelmore was one of the better Fleet Street guys. He was decent. He was not underhanded. There was a lot of backstabbing in those days.

MARSHA KRANES: Basically, Bolwell's job was to get people to leave—and he got a lot of people to leave.

GEORGE ARZT: The Schiff era was a very dull paper staffed by very good newspaper people. You had a rewrite bank with people like Helen Dudar, who was a superb reporter and writer. One day, Bolwell came over and told Helen that he didn't like the way she wrote a story. I remember sitting there stunned, thinking, "You're talking to Helen Dudar! *Helen Dudar!*" She turned around and said, "Goodbye." I said, "Where you going?" She said, "It's my last day." I said, "Did you tell anybody?" "I just told you."

CLYDE HABERMAN, reporter, 1966–1977: I left the *Post* the first week, at most the second week of 1977, and went back to the *Times*. When I told Paul Sann I was leaving, he was hurt. He said, "So you're going to MetLife." He always called the *Times* MetLife. He saw it as nothing but an insurance company with a bunch of drudges sitting at desks.

FRANK RICH: Bolwell brought in a new [managing] editor. I don't remember his name, Ron something. He was American. He called a meeting of a couple dozen writers and editors. I remember it vividly because it was the day that *Annie Hall* opened. This new editor said a bunch of bland things and then, "From now on, when we are writing our reviews and features, we want to be sure to keep our advertisers in mind," which I read immediately—and I think correctly—as, we don't want to write reviews that might drive advertisers away. I was out of there shortly after that.

ANNA QUINDLEN: While we were all bucking each other up that [Murdoch's acquisition] was not going to be as disastrous as we thought, I was in a weird position. Warren [Hoge] had already left the *Post* and gone to the *Times*, and the *Times* was trying to meet the terms of a class action suit that it had settled with the women at the paper. One of the terms of the suit was that they were supposed to hire a whole lot more women. Warren had said to the various senior editors there, "You should talk to Anna Quindlen at the *Post*." I was in the middle of conversations with the *Times*, which are glacially slow, at the time that Murdoch bought the paper. When his people took over, I still hadn't had the big interview with [*Times* executive editor] Abe Rosenthal.

Ted Bolwell delivered lectures on beginning stories in a snappier way; slower, feature-style ledes—something the *Post* had been known for—were out. For many, the change was shocking.

DAVID ROSENTHAL: What we all learned that first year was we didn't understand the meaning of tabloid newspaper. The tabloids Murdoch and the rest of his crowd had been running in London and Australia were the 1930s, 1920s [Hearst-style] tabloids—not like the *Daily News* or the *Post* or *Newsday* or the *Chicago Sun-Times*. The *Post* was a responsible newspaper. It had some good political coverage; it had some thoughtful opinion people. We had a movie critic; we had a classical music critic. Some of them might have been burnout cases, but we had them, and there was some care put into it. Suddenly, the paper was like nothing I had seen.

FRANK RICH: The *Post* under Schiff and her editors really did have airs and a slightly literary bent—and that was all being thrown out the window. Copy was being butchered. There was a kind of Hitler marching into Poland atmosphere.

MARSHA KRANES: Everything became much shorter. The whole philosophy of planning the paper changed. It was a writers' paper when I arrived. As much as you wrote usually got in—they found the space. But when Murdoch came in, they planned the space and you had to write to fit. If you didn't, the story was cut to fit the space. We were used to writing fully developed stories.

BILL BIGELOW, city desk assistant, 1975–1979: In '75, I'm working in the city room, controlling the flow of reporters to editors. We're all smoking cigarettes like crazy and tossing them on the linoleum floor, where they would burn out. People were hungover, but it was a raucous, very intelligent, fun crowd. There was a bad snow-storm, and Bob Spitzler, the managing editor, turns to Ralph Blumenfeld, who was a rewrite guy, and says, "Is this a blizzard?" It was a hell of a storm. You could barely see. But it turns out that there are three conditions that have to be met for a snowstorm to be considered a blizzard by the National Weather Service. You have to have wind gusts of thirty-five miles an hour, visibility has to be less than a quarter of a mile due to snow, and those conditions have to persist for three hours or more. Blumenfeld and Spitzler are going back and forth. Blumenfeld is on the phone with the National Weather Service, and Spitzler's yelling, "We don't have confirmation for the thirty-five-mile-an-hour wind gust." Finally, Blumenfeld says, "It was thirty-seven miles an hour at La Guardia." "Great! Print it." The wood was a photograph of Times Square covered in snow and a one-word wood, BLIZZARD!, with an exclamation point. Cut to maybe a couple of years later, and there's an-other snowstorm. It's not a terrible storm. It's just a storm, and Peter Michelmore turns to Ralph Blumenfeld, and goes, "I want you to do a story on the blizzard outside." Blumenfeld says, "That's not a blizzard. There are conditions that need to be met." He tells him the three conditions. Michelmore says, "Come here, Ralph." He takes him over to the window, then points out the window at the East River and goes, "See out there? That's a goddamned blizzard. Write it." We print the story. It's a blizzard because the Australian said it was a blizzard. What that led to was a very cavalier sense of what the truth is and what you could publish.

CHERYL BENTSEN: It was total trauma from day one—just the shits. And there was this article in *Newsweek* where Bolwell said he despised the preening feature writers who were going after some artistic effect. He disparaged all these incredible feature writers who went on to have great careers.

ROBERTA BRANDES GRATZ: I had a major exposé almost ready to go about one of the museums in the city. It was killed because they insisted I tell them who my sources were. I refused. Paul Sann and Bob Spitzler might have asked questions about the sources, just to make sure they were reliable, but they would never ask for names. That's a cardinal sin in journalism. Murdoch did a very good job of befriending the right people when he came to New York, and one of the key offenders in my story was now a friend of his. That was the end of it.

JOYCE WADLER, feature writer, 1974–1977: I remember sitting in the stairwell crying, talking to Bob Spitzler because I felt they had ruined the paper. I was very happy until Murdoch came in. I could see that the stuff I held dear, which was respect for writers, respect for facts, was going. They were chopping up stories and rewriting them, and they were uglifying the universe.

ERIC FETTMANN: I signed a petition against Paul Rigby [Australian cartoonist heavily hyped by Murdoch whose work became a fixture on Page Six]. He had done a cartoon showing a scene in the jungle with your stereotypical white hunter in full Safari outfit. The hunter comes across a group of Black Africans with pointed hair and the Ubangi lips, right? Actually, it was two hunters, one saying something like: "It's the Haleys. They're doing some family research." This is at the time when [the adaptation of Alex Haley's novel] *Roots* was on TV and was a huge sensation. We all got incensed. We were sensitive snowflakes before people knew from sensitive snowflakes and we signed a petition protesting this blatantly stereotypical racial image.

DICK BELSKY: British journalism standards are a lot different from American standards. They just are. But there's a difference between a story that's made up and a story that is pushed to the limits—and I do remember a lot of stories that we pushed. We pushed them during both regimes, but in different ways. There's this classic feeling that the *Post* was a very serious, important paper, and then Murdoch came over and turned it into this sensationalistic rag. It's just not that simple. There are a lot of gray areas there. At the *Post*, in the early '70s, there was a police reporter, who, if there was a murder, might call a cop and say, "What's going on?" The cop might say, "We don't have any leads." The reporter would say, "Are you ruling out a gay angle?" The cop would say, "We don't rule out anything. We're still investigating everything." Then the guy would write a lede, like "Police are investigating a potential gay angle."

AIDA ALVAREZ, reporter, 1973–1977: Before Murdoch took over, we had a fair amount of diversity in the newsroom—not Black or Hispanic, but [other nationalities and women]. Suddenly, there were all these Australian guys parading around the office. It was clear to me that they had contempt for the city. I had never in my life given a second thought to Australians, because they were never part of my neighborhood, my life, or my education. Suddenly, it was like a foreign country had invaded.

ROBERTA BRANDES GRATZ: The first month, they didn't know their asses from their elbows.

CLYDE HABERMAN: In that first year after Murdoch took over the *Post*, it was almost as if he was standing at the arrival gate of every Qantas flight, handing out green cards. These guys were reporting on New York with a very alien ear. I vividly remember one of those standard crime-running-amok stories out of Brooklyn, maybe Flatbush, and there was a woman with a stereotypically Jewish name—something like Sadie Moskowitz—saying, "I'm afraid to even go out in the evening to the corner kiosk to buy a newspaper." Have you ever known a New Yorker who bought a newspaper at a kiosk? Did you ever know a mum—in a headline—who killed three tots? Tots, yes, but mum—no. Did you ever know of a mafioso who was found dead in the boot of a car?

ROBERTA BRANDES GRATZ: It was quite amusing. We had to tell them to de-Australianize the language—we don't take lifts, we take elevators.

ERIC FETTMANN: At one point, somebody actually had to put together a guide for the alien copy editor that translated Britishisms into Americanisms.

JANE PERLEZ: Looking back on it, I feel so badly because I think many of my colleagues really thought that the *Post* would become a better version of what it had been—that it would be rejuvenated. But Murdoch had such a supercilious view of American journalists. He thought American journalists were effete, wordy, beat around the bush, didn't know what sold newspapers. I think he thought the *New York Post* was the epitome of that. It was basically his mission to clean the place out of the people who had been there. And he succeeded.

> In remaking the *Post*, Murdoch had imported a stark tabloid template that worked in Britain and Australia. It was a formula that hastened the exit of Schiff-era staffers and others crucial to the paper's sense of itself.

ERIC FETTMANN: Murdoch made a miscalculation. He thought he would be able to do what had been successful in Britain but had never been done here: build a paper that was successful solely on mass circulation without the need to be dependent on advertising. Something like his papers in London, *The Sun* or *News of the World*, with a four or five million circulation.

KEN CHANDLER, editor in chief, publisher, 1978–1986, 1993–2002: I don't have any inside knowledge about Rupert's original plan, but it sounds pretty plausible.

ERIC FETTMANN: To get that audience, he wanted to replicate the old *Daily News* formula. He wanted to get that white middle-class Irish and Italian Catholic readership. What he didn't understand—because he didn't know the city—is that that readership had largely left the city for Long Island and New Jersey. At that point, the *Daily News* was increasingly becoming the working-class paper, which meant Black and Hispanic readers. Murdoch's formula of high crime and sensationalism, and the paper's increasingly conservative bent, scared away the middle-class Jewish readership that was the base of the *Post* circulation. He did not understand that that was precisely the readership that the department stores—which were the bread and butter of newspaper advertising—wanted.

JANE PERLEZ: (*from notes taken during the Murdoch transition*) Yesterday Rupert stopped by my desk. He talks about changes at the *Post* not being enough yet.

I say we need to keep our credibility. He says yes, "but not our dullness." . . . Spitzler came in late. He looks like he takes a bottle of Valium a day.

One of the first departures stunned Schiff-era staffers: Executive Editor Paul Sann, a forty-year veteran of the *Post*, whose resignation was announced on February 1, a month into the Murdoch regime.

DICK BELSKY: The thing that pushed Sann over the edge was [Freddie] Prinze's suicide. He was a New Yorker apart from everything else, and it was a great story. Sann threw himself into it, and ["CHICO" STAR TRIES SUICIDE] was the wood for the early editions [on January 28, 1977]. But at some point during the day, Ted Bolwell came out to the city desk and started talking about putting something else on page one. I don't remember what, but it was no comparison to the Prinze story. I was on the desk and called Sann over: "You know Bolwell said we have to take Freddie Prinze off page one." Sann went nuts. He had this confrontation with Bolwell in his office, and when he came back out, he said, "Keep Freddie Prinze on page one." Very soon after, I think it was the next morning, Paul was in the composing room, and he said, "I want you to know that I'm leaving, I'm retiring." I said, "Why?" He said, "The Freddie Prinze thing, I won that battle, but I won't win the next one." At one point, he said, "Here I am on the phone with circulation, telling them to up the press run, because we're selling so many papers, and this guy wants to take it off page one." He was so frustrated. It wasn't that Bolwell didn't like the story. My guess is that he didn't understand why it was such a big deal. Or maybe he wanted to show his authority. Who knows?

ERIC FETTMANN: The irony was that Paul was one of the great tabloid reporters and editors, and he could have fit in very well with the Murdoch people.

TONY MANCINI: I don't think he could have worked long-term at the Murdoch *Post*. He tried for a while, but fundamentally, Sann had an ethical side. He would not go as far as they would want him to go.

JANE PERLEZ: (*from notes taken during the Murdoch transition*) Bolwell left at around 8:30—complaining of laryngitis and nausea. After lunch we learned his doctor put him in Stamford [Connecticut] hospital where he'll be for the rest of the week. Everybody is hoping for the worst.

Bolwell survived his hospitalization and came back to irritate the *Post*'s staff even more. In March of 1977, the Hanafi siege, a hostage crisis in Washington, DC, led to a series of stories and an infamous front page that, for many of the old guard, felt like the point of no return.

CHERYL BENTSEN: I was in Washington to do another story, and while I was there—this was March 9, 1977—a radical Islamist group took over three buildings, including B'nai B'rith headquarters. They killed two people and took more than a hundred hostages and held them for a couple of days. Bolwell told me to cover it. I went over, but there was no way I was getting anything. I did what I could, phoning in whatever information I could get. The next day, a story appeared in the *Post* with my byline—a story that I didn't write. It was filled with all kinds of made-up interviews as if I had gotten some hot scoop and had interviewed hostages and nurses. I was absolutely stunned. I immediately took the train back to New York, went into Bolwell's office, and quit. I said I would rather work in Woolworth's than work at the *New York Post.*

DAVID ROSENTHAL: The turning point, when we all knew things were different, was when those hostages were taken in Washington. Murdoch came in himself at about 3:30 in the morning. We were all doing rewrites of wire stories and making calls. It was a scary situation. He ripped up every piece of copy and rewrote the front-page story himself. He also wrote this inflammatory headline [WE'LL BEHEAD THEM]. He sat there at the desk, jacket off, with his suspenders, his tie loosened, banging out take after take on an old Underwood. We were all wondering, "What the fuck is he writing?" It wasn't Kansas anymore. Everybody realized it by the next morning.

JIM FARBER, former New York *Daily News* music critic: I grew up just outside New York, in Westchester. My parents read the *Post* when it was the liberal afternoon columnist newspaper. They read Harriet Van Horne and all the others and quoted them religiously. When Murdoch took over, he killed all that. My first memory of the Murdochized *Post* was its coverage of the Hanafi Movement's siege in Washington. It was a Black Muslim group that took over B'nai B'rith and threatened to blow up the building and behead people if their demands were not met. The *Post*'s coverage was so brilliant. I can see it like it was yesterday. The headline was WE'LL BEHEAD THEM in giant letters. I'd never seen anything like that in the United States. Everything was pure shock and outrage. I remember thinking that the design of the paper was ugly in every single way that it could be. I was very into John Waters movies, and Waters refers to his "ugly experts," who ensure that the makeup and clothing is designed to make everyone look as repulsive as they possibly can. It was as if ugly experts had taken over the design of the paper. My parents were appalled, I was thrilled.

ERIC FETTMANN: The pre-Murdoch design of the *Post* was done [in the 1940s] by Norman Bel Geddes, a well-known theater designer. In that design, you had a lot of what you see in the *Times*, which is headlines and sub-headlines in different fonts. The Murdoch redesign got rid of that. It was all one font. It made things a lot simpler. You used things like boldfacing and italicizing, and since the emphasis was more on photos, the text became less important.

> Another Australian who joined the *Post* early on was dapper reporter Steve "Mr. Blood and Guts" Dunleavy, who since the 1960s had worked in New York for various Murdoch publications, and who became, for better or worse, a living symbol of the new hyperbolic *New York Post*.

RICHARD GOODING, metropolitan editor, 1976–1993: The first reporter Murdoch brought in, maybe a few months after he took over, was Steve Dunleavy. Dunleavy couldn't write his way out of a bag then. To his credit, over the years, he learned how to write reasonably well. But back then, he couldn't even write a simple news story. We had to write them for him. But he was a good reporter and obviously charming. He was impossible not to like.

JANE PERLEZ: Dunleavy was Rupert's ideal of a reporter. Which means, be fearless, knock down doors, get the dirt, give it to the establishment—the establishment figure, business, or institution that Rupert doesn't like at the moment. Do Rupert's bidding.

AIDA ALVAREZ: [Steve Dunleavy] was one of the roosters parading around the newsroom with the Elvis Presley hairdo. I think he sort of fancied himself. He thought he was really special. Not that he ever said a single word to me, but it's just the way he strutted around. It was really uncomfortable.

BILL BIGELOW: In that era, people wore wide ties and bell-bottom pants. Steve Dunleavy never wore bell-bottoms. He had stovepipe pants that went narrower at the ankle. I had a couple of suits with giant bell bottoms, and I'd say to him,

"What are you doing, Steve? Nobody's wearing stovepipe pants." He'd go, "This is more flattering to the male figure. Trust me. You guys wearing bell-bottoms are idiots. It doesn't look good." You know what? He was right.

DAVID ROSENTHAL: You talk about people who came in and nobody knew what they were doing, Dunleavy was one of those. Suddenly, this guy who all of us had heard about, because he had this extraordinary reputation, of drinking and all this shit, situated himself in the city room, the last row, the last desk. He's turning out lots of copy. And he's turning out copy that none of us had assigned.

ERIC FETTMANN: One of the first pieces that we ran of his was an interview with [fugitive financier] Robert Vesco [in Costa Rica]. It was written in typical Dunleavy style—purple prose. I remember Roberta Gratz asking Peter Michelmore, who became the metro editor, "Peter, please don't tell me this is what you're expecting." He kind of hemmed and hawed because he didn't want to say "Obviously it is."

GEORGE ARZT: I didn't know what to make of Dunleavy. As I watched him write headlines, I realized that the guy was all about blood and guts. The headlines had nothing to do with the story.

JANE PERLEZ: (*from notes taken during the Murdoch transition*) [Al] Ellenberg as I was leaving tonight determined not to run a Dunleavy piece of shit about Jackie Susann's husband. Second-grade English, first-grade ideas.

TONY MANCINI: Dunleavy would bad-mouth the old *Post* staff behind our backs—saying we were lazy and all that nonsense. We had a different view, obviously. It was a tale of two cities: the old staffers and the new ones.

DICK BELSKY: Everybody hated Dunleavy because he was a sensationalist, and all the old *Post* people were like, "We can't have this guy at the paper." He went on a local morning show [*The Stanley Siegel Show*] and said something to the effect of, "There are all these people who sit around all day and drink coffee and talk about journalism, but they don't actually do anything." There was a huge furor, but there was some truth to what he said. With the old *Post*, there was a lot of pontificating about journalism. With Steve, it was, there's a story, get it. I don't want to talk about it, just do it.

TONY MANCINI: Lindsy Van Gelder, Joyce Purnick, some other members of the staff, and I went on *The Stanley Siegel Show* after Dunleavy appeared on it. We were very vociferous about how we didn't approve of the way Murdoch was running the newspaper. I wasn't in a vulnerable position because I had already published a novel or two and was thinking of moving on anyhow. I can't remember specifics but [the Australians] weren't happy.

PAT SMITH, night city editor, 1977–1989: I came in naively. I get a job offer in New York, *New York Post*, hey, I'm going. I came in [from the *Philadelphia Daily News*] and there was some resentment against me. I was one of the Murdoch people, the new people. There were tensions in the newsroom. I always thought of it as kind of like a high school clique. Not to disparage people, but I mean: I had a wife and kids and a mortgage and I was a grown-up doing a job. There were factions in the newsroom. There was that big Italian faction, Dom Marrano, Paul Pucciarelli, the guys who came out of Miss Gerry's crew. They had nothing to do with the West Village–type old Posties. I found them more welcoming, more down-to-earth. We used to go to Sheepshead Bay and go fishing.

STEPHEN SILVERMAN, entertainment writer, 1977–1988: I went to see Bob Spitzler about a job. He was about eight feet tall and wore the same sweater Boris Karloff wears in *Son of Frankenstein*. I kid you not. He was very droll, and he was basically sounding me out. I was quick on my feet. He said, "You fit in here." But, he said, "the place is falling apart." He tried to dissuade me. He really made it clear that there were divisions, which I didn't understand because I didn't know who Dolly Schiff was. I didn't know anything. There was a whole features department and they instantly hated me. They said backbiting remarks about my writing. I was the new young blood. They treated me like shit. In time, I worked my ass off and I got the goods and they left me alone.

> Some new employees adapted more easily, having arrived at 210 South Street as the result of an early strategic move by Murdoch.

NED STEELE, reporter, rewrite, 1977–1980: I came from the *Long Island Press*, which was a Newhouse newspaper that covered Nassau, Suffolk, and Queens counties. It was like the seventh or eighth biggest paper in the country, but invisible in the New York area because of all the other major dailies around it. Murdoch swooped in and acquired the [paper's] assets when the Newhouse family decided to put it out of its misery. I don't know what the inside story is, but the end result was that Murdoch bought out the entire home delivery route system, infrastructure, and salespeople of the *Long Island Press*, which had a circulation of [approximately 175,000] in Queens, so it was an immediate huge bump up in the *Post* circulation very early in the Murdoch days. He basically bought any assets that were worth holding on to, plus eight or ten of us reporters and desk people. The *Press* folded on a Friday afternoon. Sunday night several of us were in the *Post* city room working. It happened immediately. [The title has been revived by different owners in recent years; the current *Long Island Press* is a monthly.]

> Understanding that visuals are part of what sells a newspaper, especially a tabloid, Murdoch's people for the first time hired a real photo editor for the *Post*.

JERRY ENGEL, photographer, 1958–1993: When I started, it wasn't traditional, like the *Daily News* or any of the other papers, that all had a separate photo editor. At our place, we were just like a big happy family. This guy did that, this guy did this.

SUSAN WELCHMAN, photo editor, 1977–1979: I was a photo editor at the *Philadelphia Daily News*, and they went on strike. I did not want to walk around that smoky barrel [with the picketers]. So a friend of mine said, "This guy just bought the *New York Post*. Why don't you go up there?" Someone from the paper had gone to work at the *Post* and I called him. He said, "Come up for an interview." I had a friend that wrote the *News*' car column, and he had a little Lotus Europa. I said, "I've got to be in New York in two hours." He said, "No problem." We got in the car. He must have gone a hundred miles [an hour] the whole way from Philadelphia to New York. I got the job, and it changed my life. When Dolly Schiff owned the paper, there was really nobody on the photo side. She didn't really like photographs—they were very small when they ran—and the copy desk picked them. Sports picked theirs. There was not a central situation. Then they said I could hire some photographers. I hired a woman. I definitely wanted a woman, so Marty Cooper came to work for me.

MARTHA COOPER, photographer, 1977–1980: My goal was to work for *National Geographic*. I had interned there and heard that you were supposed to work for a newspaper if you wanted a job there. Someone knew Susan and told me she wanted to hire a woman. People are always saying, "Was it hard being a woman photographer then?" No, it really helped me. It was the time of my life in a way. You'd go out, and you didn't know what you were going to do that day. It could be wonderful or not so wonderful, but by the afternoon it might even be in the paper. I would pass by the newsstand and there it was.

JOE DE MARIA, photographer, 1977–1993: Susan was fantastic. She knew what the photographers were capable of. When you did a good job, she made sure she told you that. I was probably the first overnight [photographer] hire that they had. Everything was breaking news. In fact, the editors were astounded that they were getting front pages, like almost every night, of breaking news stories from photos that they never had before.

JOE BERGER: I spoke a little Hebrew, I had covered the '73 war, so I was sent to Cairo to cover the 1977 meeting between Anwar Sadat and Menachem Begin. The minute I landed in Cairo, I got a telex from the *Post* telling me, "We want you to get up in the morning and a photographer is going to meet you at the pyramids. We want him to take your picture riding a camel." I telexed back that I was happy to go interview people at the pyramids, but I was not going to ride a camel. That's a stunt, and I'm not here to do stunts. I am here to be a professional reporter. It seemed to me that this was not what I had signed up for, but they kept arguing back and forth, back and forth. Apparently, they already knew what the headline was going to be, without a single piece of reporting— OUR MAN IN CAIRO—with a picture of me on a camel to go with this front-page headline. The photo editor, who was newly brought in by Murdoch as I remember, kept telexing me. I think we ended up talking on the telephone. Ultimately, I didn't do it. It was a disappointing way to start off a great assignment.

SUSAN WELCHMAN: Joe Berger? A camel? I probably did. I did anything for Rupert. I mean, the guy was a fantastic editor because he stopped at nothing. He really revolutionized that paper. He was constantly changing the front page. He was always at the morning news meeting. I felt like I worked for him. Oh, I loved it. I thought I'd died and gone to heaven. When I was at the *Philadelphia Daily News*, I had maybe eight people working for me. When I got to New York, I had maybe twenty. I ran all the photographers constantly on the street on radios. At first, the photographers would soup [develop] their pictures themselves, but then I put people in the lab to do it for them, and the photographers would go right back out. It was a great system. I would look at the film by holding it up to the window and punch holes near the film perforations of the shots I wanted. Then the copyboy would run it back to the lab. We looked at everything wet. We didn't bother to dry them. It was quick. Every single thing we did was fast. We were always screaming at each other. Everything was completely out in the open. There wasn't any time. "What is this terrible photograph? Can't you do better than this piece of shit?" They would yell back, "I couldn't get there. There was no parking." We were constantly back and forth. The radios were crackly. Oh my god. I just loved it. Trying to make a great photograph out of nothing. Tell a story. Make a story.

> Even some of the old guard saw positive aspects to the Murdochian tornado blasting through the *Post*, including their new owner's energetic involvement in its content.

DOMINICK MARRANO: When Murdoch started changing things, it became more fun. I was a little more stuffed shirt about the double entendre stuff, like, trying to get "sheet" to sound like "shit" in a headline. But it certainly was a duller paper when Dorothy Schiff was there. It was a much, much smaller operation then. In a lot of ways, you saw the paper growing.

DICK BELSKY: Because it was such a huge change, everybody [from the Schiff era] had to decide whether to adapt. I jumped in with both feet. Then I was blown away by so many talented people that Rupert brought in. Dunleavy had huge pluses and minuses, but he was one of the greatest people I've ever worked with—just full of energy. The Murdoch people liked energy. A lot of the old *Post* people were very cool and laid back.

BILL BIGELOW: The Australians brought this kind of madness of beer and booze, let's do [multiple] editions a day and stay up all night, have some laughs, and who cares what the facts are. It was colorful, it was fun, and though I wasn't there a terribly long time, it's in my heart in a way.

DICK BELSKY: One of my first exchanges with Murdoch was in an editors' meeting. Murdoch said something having to do with the Grammys—and it was incorrect because Murdoch did not know an awful lot about America then. He would say, "Do the subways run at night?" and things like that. I corrected him. He snapped at me, "That's not true." I said something back, and suddenly, I'm in an argument with Rupert Murdoch. I'm screaming at him; he's screaming at me. Everybody's staring at us. Then he threw up his hands and sat down. The meeting is over, I walk out thinking what the fuck did I do? I just ended my career. Either Michelmore or Travis came out of the meeting and grabbed me. I'm thinking, okay, this is it. He says, "Rupert really likes you. He was very impressed by what you did in there." I said, "Really?" He said, "Yeah, he likes people with energy and passion who stand up for their beliefs."

RICHARD GOODING: That first year, when Bolwell took vacation, Murdoch came in and played editor. Bolwell never came out of his office. He never talked to people. Murdoch spent all of his time out on the news desk, writing headlines, laying out pages, sitting around telling stories. I hated his politics, and the op-ed pages we ran, but he was impossible not to like. He was interesting, charming, funny. When I worked the night city desk later on, he'd call every night from wherever he was in the world—he was in Israel a lot—and say, "What's going on?" The rule was *never* to say, "Nothing is going on." You had to come up with something: "We're working on this great one. We don't quite have it yet, but we're working on it." You had to like that about him.

NED STEELE: Midge Costanza, an aide to Jimmy Carter, comes out to Queens one night to speak at some Democratic function. She gives the usual boring standard traditional political speech. I had to phone it in to the city desk. I'm pretty sure it was Bill Condie who was on. I gave him a run-through of what she had said. Then I said, "Oh, then she made some crack about her boobs and her cleavage." There was a minute of silence. Then Condie said, "Ned, that's our freaking lede. Go write it." I thought, "Welcome to the world of tabloid journalism." It was a big splash in the paper the next day, page five or three or something. I kind of enjoyed that, because I knew that would not have happened at the *Long Island Press*, or at most other newspapers. I thought, this can be fun.

Aware that he had a lot to learn about his newly adopted city, Murdoch went about creating his own crash course, a sort of New York 101.

NICK PILEGGI, author, screenwriter, former *New York* magazine writer: I was quite impressed with how much of a journalist he was. Because of the nature of the stuff I had been writing [at *New York* magazine], he wanted to know more about that—the mob, corrupt politicians in New York—he wanted to know how the city really worked. Once a week, for maybe nine months, a year, he would come up to the office at *New York* magazine, and he and I would go into the dining room, and we would talk about New York City politics, about this one and that one, and who the mobsters were. A lot of this was not known. Or if it was known, it couldn't be printed because we didn't have the proof. He wanted to know the stuff that couldn't be published. I mean he's the only publisher of a New York newspaper I ever met who was interested enough to sit down with a police reporter. Corruption, that's what he was talking to me about. What was the comptroller's job? Where was the payoff there? How did it work? He was encyclopedic in his absorption of all that knowledge. He was a throwback, from another age. He was a newspaper guy. I had no idea what his politics were and I didn't care.

ERIC FETTMANN: When Murdoch bought the paper, Pete Hamill, who wanted to be editor of the *Post* before he turned on Murdoch, wrote a piece for the *Village Voice*: "Memo to Murdoch: What to do to the *New York Post*"—most of which was to turn it into a Wechsler-style paper. One was rehire Murray Kempton and pay him what he's worth. And Murdoch did. [A highly regarded former *Post* columnist, Kempton was known for his often-byzantine prose, his support of the underdog, and his habit of riding his bicycle all over the city.]

DAVID ROSENTHAL: I handled Murray's copy for a number of months. The great line that Murray always had—people would say, "Murray, you're one of the greatest writers in the world. You're one of the greatest newspapermen. Why, oh, why are you still working at the *New York Post*?" To which he said, "To preserve my sense of privacy?"

MARTY MCLAUGHLIN, public relations and political consultant: Murray Kempton had nothing to do with the news coverage. That was all influenced by Murdoch. Hiring Murray Kempton was just a good business decision and the ability to say, "How can you say that about me? I have Murray Kempton as a columnist."

DAVID ROSENTHAL: Murdoch was very harsh with all the editors. He went around to every editor, whatever your purview was, and made you recite what your lineup was for the next day. He really wanted to get down into the weeds. I mean, what was your tenth or eleventh story that you had for the next day? I have a very firm recollection, because it shook me up, of going through the whole lineup, which was fairly standard, it was not a very busy day. I came down to the bottom of the list, I said, "Oh, yeah, we have the shooting of a bodega owner in Brooklyn. It turns out, it looked like a drug deal gone bad with the owner of the store or some shit like that." I just then went on to the next thing. He said, "Wait a minute, go back for a moment. Tell me more about the bodega murder." I told him what little I knew. He said, "This is what we want to do. We want to get a reporter and a photographer out to the wake tonight. And we want to hire a priest to say some prayers, 'Brooklyn mourns,' that kind of thing. And we want to make a picture of that." You could have heard a pin drop in the room. I actually said, "We don't really do that." He said, "Oh, yes, you do." I said, "I don't remember ever doing that"—because I'm a fool, you know, I know nothing. He says, "You're going to do it. Otherwise," he said, "when I'm stuck for a wood at 4:30 in the morning, I'm going to call you at home and ask, 'What do you suggest?' Do you understand?" I said of course I understood. I went out of the meeting very shook. I went to Aida Alvarez, I think these were Latino bodega owners. I said, "Aida, you've got to call these people. You got to find out something." I forgot which photographer it must have been. I said, "You've got to get out to Brooklyn. I'm sorry. This is like a bullshit story. But it's now a big bullshit story." Aida got me some copy, from what I remember. What would have been two graphs turned into two books or something like that. I don't think we ever did get the priest. Then we worked the cops on it. It was nothing. It wasn't even a sympathy story because it was a drug deal that went bad, as I recall. It wasn't the typical crying heart story. It was a fuckup story. I don't think they played it as wood but they played it big the next day.

MIKE PEARL, reporter, Manhattan Criminal Court, 1967–1998: I had just come from working at Hearst papers for many years. Someone like Murdoch didn't frighten me.

ANNA QUINDLEN: People assume that, with great joy, I said goodbye to the *New York Post* and went to the *New York Times*. That could not be further from the truth. It was really hard for me to make that decision before the Australians showed up, because I loved it there so much, and I loved my colleagues. I had never been one of those people who always wanted to work at the *Times*. I am so glad that I worked at the *Post* before I went to the *Times*; I learned so much, I had amazing colleagues, and it was so much fun. The *New York Times* is many things, but it often is not much fun, because of how seriously it takes itself, quite correctly. The blessing of working at a tabloid is that you understand that today's news is tomorrow's fish wrapping.

CHERYL BENTSEN: I quit because [Bolwell] used fake news. I was the first victim at the *New York Post* of fake news—my name slapped on a story with quotes from people I didn't interview or know anything about.

ANNA QUINDLEN: When I had the interview with Abe Rosenthal and told the *Post* I was leaving for the *Times*, Neal [Travis] said, "You are making the biggest mistake of your life. You will sink like a stone there, and you could have been a star here."

ERIC FETTMANN: Those who could get jobs right away did. Judy Michaelson very quickly went to the *Los Angeles Times*. Al Ellenberg was fired early on by Bolwell and he went to edit the *Soho Weekly News* and he brought [Jane] Perlez over.

JANE PERLEZ: When Al Ellenberg went to the *Soho Weekly News*, I could see that he was making a really interesting paper out of it. He was giving the *Village Voice* a run for its money because the *Voice* was an alternative newspaper, but it was an establishment alternative newspaper. I called and said, "Can I come?" He said, "Sure." I covered a lot of politics. And because I was the only person in town who knew about Murdoch, I started a column called Mixed Media. It could have been called the Murdoch Column. It was basically about his antics.

ANNA QUINDLEN: One of the things I found very difficult my first couple of weeks at the *New York Times* was that people who wouldn't return my calls the week before now would return my calls with alacrity. That made me furious because I was the same reporter I'd been before. It was just that I had a different prepositional phrase after my name, and it bespoke a way people thought about the *New York Post* that was completely inaccurate because of how good the staff was there.

JANE PERLEZ: I don't remember this, but my husband [investigative journalist Raymond Bonner] says that soon after I left the *Post*, I ran into Murdoch at a cocktail party, something with a lot of people around. Murdoch said, "That wasn't a very nice thing you did. You left very quickly. That sent a message." I said, "Yeah, I left quickly. I wanted to send a message."

3 | SUMMER FROM HELL

The Blackout, Son of Sam, Steve Dunleavy

Wednesday, July 13, 1977, was a typically surly summer day in the city of New York. It would turn out to be the first of a nine-day heat wave, with highs that would average more than ninety-seven degrees as the week wore on. No local story had enough sizzle for the front page of the *Post*'s final edition, so the wood, 2 NURSES GUILTY IN POISON PLOT, was out of Detroit. Page Six led with a report on the cancellation of a star-studded fundraiser for Bella Abzug, the flamboyant hat-wearing congresswoman from Manhattan's Upper West Side who was running for mayor. The big news at 210 South Street wasn't happening on the tabloid's pages anyway. It was in its city room. The day before, Rupert Murdoch had conducted an editorial bloodletting, firing Ted Bolwell. Some of the other editors Murdoch had hired upon taking control of the *Post* would be gone soon as well.

ANDY SOLTIS, rewrite, editor, 1967–2014: With one or two exceptions. Murdoch cleaned house because he didn't like what was happening. The paper was not changing sufficiently.

PAT SMITH, night city editor, 1977–1989: On July 13, I come to work at noon, and there's an odd mood in the newsroom. I'm fairly new to this because I'd been working lobster shift, and now I'm on the day shift. I find out that Murdoch has fired Bolwell.

DICK BELSKY, metropolitan editor, 1970–1989: Bolwell didn't have good news sense. He was totally the wrong guy in the wrong place. He might have been good at other things, but he was totally wrong for the *Post*.

If Bolwell had lasted one more day, he would have had a huge story to cover. A few hours before July 13 wound to a close, lightning hit a power line north of the city.

MYRON RUSHETZKY, head city desk assistant, 1974–1989, 1991–2013: We had a few minutes' warning. It hit about 9:37, 9:38. We started getting phone calls from people where the blackout had started—it was like dominoes. The entire city didn't go out at once. We had a couple of minutes' warning and then the lights went out. Pat Smith was on the desk.

PAT SMITH: That afternoon, I went to the editors' meeting to present what I had for the next day. Murdoch is sitting at the editor's desk, and I make my presentation. I survive, get out with a little bit of blood on me and proceed. At about nine o'clock that night, we are hearing on the police radio monitor about a blackout in Westchester. Then we hear about blackouts in the Bronx. It was rolling north to south—Upper Manhattan, Midtown. Myron Rushetzky is on the desk and alerts the composing room foreman, because if you're going to lose power, you want to get the lead out of the Linotype machines, so it doesn't harden in them. All of a sudden, the newsroom goes black. People are yelling, but no one's panicking because we know this blackout is coming. I am trying to bluff my way through. I say, "Quiet! Does anyone have any kind of light—a flashlight in their car, any source of light?" I believe it was Myron who said that the Catholic church—San Giuseppe over on Catherine Slip—might. Someone starts talking to me, about six feet from my left ear, and I look in that direction in the darkness, and say, "Please! I need quiet. I need quiet." I say, "Myron, next door to the church will be the rectory, and there'll be a priest. You tell him that Mr. Murdoch is a very generous person, and we can settle up tomorrow. But tonight I need every candle they can give me." God knows how many minutes it was, but the boxes of votive candles show up. So the *New York Post* newsroom looked like the inside of a church, with candles on every desk.

MYRON RUSHETZKY: Somebody was dispatched and they came back with a few cases of candles from the church.

PAT SMITH: I ask for the candles and now the talking is in my left ear again. Suddenly, there is a Bic lighter three inches from my nose, being held by this big side of beef chauffeur/bodyguard. Six inches from my nose is Rupert Murdoch's nose. I had just told the man to shut up. He says, "It's Pat, right?" I say, "Yes, sir." He says, "You're doing fine, Pat. When you have a minute, stop in my office." We went back to trying to organize the newsroom.

MILTON GOLDSTEIN, copy editor, 1974–current: I was seeing my shrink that night. My regular appointment was at ten p.m. He accommodated me because he knew I worked the midnight-to-seven shift. I was on the 59th Street Bridge heading into the city—my shrink was on West 79th Street—and suddenly I see whole swaths of Manhattan going dark. I got off the bridge and all the lights were out. I made it to my shrink's office, but his buzzer wasn't working, and I couldn't knock on the door. So I headed to the *Post* on 210 South Street. There was no power in the building. They were making arrangements to get power. It was surreal. There were candles on the steps going up to the fourth floor since obviously the elevators weren't working. The phones were though—copper wire phones have their own circuitry.

MYRON RUSHETZKY: At the city desk, we had those old manual call directors— big phones with all these buttons. Normally with an incoming call, the phone would ring and a button indicating which line it was would flash. Now there were no lights and no ringing. I ended up pressing each button and saying, "Hello, hello?" If someone was on the line, you could talk to them. The other thing is that the hold feature did not work. If I put someone on hold, they got disconnected. I had to stay on the line and hold down the button for that line, until someone on the desk picked up. This meant I couldn't answer any other calls while I waited.

SUSAN WELCHMAN, photo editor, 1977–1979: I remember dark pictures of nothing— buildings and skyline shots with no lights. I remember photographers telling me, "We can't shoot when it's dark." I said, "Of course you can shoot something."

PAT SMITH: The reporters rose to the challenge. People called from home and said, "Where do you want me to go?" Jared Kopel was a guy who covered the New York City fiscal crisis. Whenever I edited a Jared Kopel story, I needed someone to translate—"'program to eliminate the GAAP,' you know, generally accepted accounting principles"—that kind of thing. Well, Jared ended up running around Harlem like he was a combat reporter. We were doing a great job for a newspaper that is never going to see the light of day. We worked through the night, gathering stories, writing stories that just sat in the pile because we did not even have a composing room. We had no newspaper on [July] 14.

JARED KOPEL, reporter, 1973–1978: I don't recall being in Harlem. I don't know how I would have gotten up there. Besides, the riots were in Hell's Kitchen, on the West Side. I used to live near Sheridan Square. I made my way over to Sixth Avenue, and I could see that all the lights were out, even on the Empire State Building. I called the office, and they told me to just go out and cover what I saw. I don't remember how I made it to Hell's Kitchen, but I was afraid for my life. I definitely don't want to portray myself as a hero; I stuck to the outside of what was going on because people were smashing windows; they were throwing paving stones off the roofs of buildings down at the cops who were arresting looters. It was frightening. I think I wore my press badge around my neck, but who's going to see that in the dark? I stayed there for about three hours and then they said I could go home. I went into a bar or a restaurant, and someone who worked there drove me home. I remember going down Fifth Avenue, and drivers were stopping at the intersections to yield to cars crossing their path because the traffic lights were out. I thought, well, at least there's order in part of this city.

KENNY MORAN, sportswriter, outdoor sports and skiing, 1972–2013: I was home and the desk calls me. I go to one of the real bad neighborhoods, Sunset Park. I was living in Bay Ridge and Sunset Park is like the next neighborhood over. It was scary, and listen, you're talking to somebody who was in Vietnam. I'm driving through this, and at times, I was questioning: should I even get out of the car? Because with NYP plates, if they thought it was press, they might come after the car, or maybe think it was a cop. I remember the burning of some of the stores and the backing up of cars or pickups. They would take chains and attach them to the storefronts and pull off the gates and whip open the doors. I was nervous, watching my back. I did get out and I tried to talk to people. Nobody would talk. They didn't want to be implicated.

PETER FREIBERG, reporter, 1971–1978: I lived in an apartment at 50th and First Avenue, on the East Side, and a lot of the old *Post*, pre-Murdoch reporters lived on the West Side. As soon as I realized it's a blackout, I was wondering, well, what can I do here? I walked over to the Waldorf Astoria and immediately as you entered, there was some luxury shop, it may have been a jewelry shop. The owner was sitting outside the door with a gun. He was quite frightened or at least was very anxious to guard his store.

ERIC FETTMANN, associate editorial page editor, columnist, 1976–1991, 1993–2019: When the lights went out, I was in the Lion's Head with Al Ellenberg and Denise Martin, who worked with him at the *Soho Weekly News*. Ellenberg was smart about this. After a few minutes, when we got word that the blackout was not localized—it was all over the city—he said, "This is not going to be like the last one, in '65, when everybody was cooperative and helpful and it was like the Woodstock of blackouts. This one is going to be different." And it was.

KENNY MORAN: I didn't stay that long [in Sunset Park]. Because I was coming in to work on the city desk. I'm in the office that night at the typewriter. All of a sudden who's standing in front of me but Rupert asking me what I had seen that night. He was fairly new at the time. Somebody told him I had just come from Sunset Park. I described it—they're breaking into stores, looting, burning—I told him everything I had seen. He just looked at me and, I don't remember his exact words, but he shook his head.

PAT SMITH: We all end up in Mutchie's totally defeated by the fact that we're not putting out a newspaper. [Dictationist] Madeline Nash's index finger was black-and-blue from constantly pushing that [telephone] button to say, "*New York Post, New York Post*." She's soaking it in a glass of scotch and she's bemoaning the plight of her finger. Someone said, "Madeline, instead of using your finger, you should have used a pencil to push the buttons." Whereupon Madeline threw the drink in his face.

The *Daily News* was able to publish an edition on July 14 by using the presses of *Newsday* on Long Island. Its front page announced: BLACKOUT! LIGHTNING HITS CON ED SYSTEM. The *Times* came out that day, too, in part thanks to *The Record* in New Jersey, where the pages of the *Times* were prepared. Its main front-page headline was a three-parter: POWER FAILURE BLACKS OUT NEW YORK; THOUSANDS TRAPPED IN THE SUBWAYS; LOOTERS AND VANDALS HIT SOME AREAS. But the *Post*, its entire operation contained at 210 South Street, was not able to publish until electricity returned. Not knowing when that would happen, reporters and editors kept working as though the presses could roll at any moment.

When the lights came back on the fourteenth, the newsroom prepared a multipage blackout special for July 15. With such section headlines as "A City Ravaged" and "City Under Siege," the *Post* reported on looters trashing businesses; police arresting looters; businesses losing millions of dollars; hospitals saving patients; and, on Page Six, Frank Sinatra surviving the ordeal on the thirty-eighth floor of the Waldorf by consuming the "rapidly thawing contents of the refrigerator." The front page screamed, 24 HOURS OF TERROR, a headline that quickly became more controversial than anything Murdoch's *Post* had published until then.

PAT SMITH: Murdoch had fired Ted Bolwell, so he was the editor. I would say he was very involved in deciding what page one would look like and what the wood would say. The wood was accurate. How you gonna sugarcoat it—the mayhem, the looting, the violence that happened the night of the thirteenth into the morning of the fourteenth?

Osborn Elliott, New York's deputy mayor for economic development and the former editor of *Newsweek*, denounced the *Post*'s coverage. In a letter to Rupert Murdoch, he described the way the *Post* wrote about the blackout as the real disaster, stating that "New York has suffered enough without its only evening paper pouring fuel on the flames." Ha! riposted the *Post* in an editorial: "What would Elliott have us call it? A little local difficulty?"

KENNY MORAN: I don't know why the wood was controversial. Because that's what it was, as compared to the 1965 blackout. I was working at Citibank then. I walked home from midtown, into Brooklyn over the bridge. We all stopped to drink. Everybody was so nice. Now fast-forward to the '70s. You had to be afraid to go to certain neighborhoods. In those neighborhoods, they were looting and burning. It was mayhem. I had no problem with that headline. I don't remember why they considered it controversial.

PETER FREIBERG: They put my byline on the story. I don't remember interviewing any of those people.

On July 15, Murdoch announced Ted Bolwell's replacement—Roger Wood, an Oxford-educated Fleet Street veteran who had been editing Murdoch's weekly tabloid, the *Star*. The *Star* (originally the *National Star*) had been an early part of Murdoch's American experiment. It became a farm team for the *Post*, with editors and executives moving from one to the other.

KEN CHANDLER, editor in chief, publisher, 1978–1986, 1993–2002: When *Star* magazine started, it wasn't really a magazine. It was more like a forty-eight-page newspaper. Although the audience was predominantly female, it wasn't totally female. We even had a sports section. There was definitely a lot of celebrity stuff in it, but there was also a lot of "10 ways to avoid catching the flu," "10 ways to do this . . ." A lot of advice stuff. And there was political gossip as well, because [Steve] Dunleavy had this column called This I Believe, which was a weekly rant. It was like a precursor to Fox News in a way.

DICK BELSKY: Roger Wood came in and everybody thought he was wonderful because he wasn't Ted Bolwell. Roger could be charming and everything, but I used to say to him: "Man, you had the easiest act in the world to follow."

JOE BERGER, investigative reporter, 1971–1978: Roger Wood had the facade of a dutiful bureaucrat, but you always got a sense that he was scheming and plotting as to how he was going to manipulate this staff of miscreants and dyspeptics to do what he wanted. He was kind of a gray, faceless bureaucrat—"apparatchik" is the word.

JOYCE PURNICK, political reporter, 1970–1978: Roger was a henchman, but I thought he was very human, and I think he did care for people. He had decent values. And I think he wound up being not so thrilled with Rupert. I could be wrong, but that was my impression. Don't misunderstand me—he was a Murdoch guy, but I think he was a more centrist journalist. If he was a politician, he would have been a centrist Republican, sort of like John McCain.

Even before the blackout, New Yorkers were dealing with a different kind of dread: a string of shootings of young couples in Queens, the Bronx, and eventually Brooklyn. The city's tabloids, which thrived on crime and violence, took full advantage of the situation and amped up the tension with regular front-page stories and even appeals to the shooter, who was initially dubbed the .44 Caliber Killer because of the bullets used to murder or maim his victims. Though the shootings had started the year before, it was not until 1977 that police determined a serial killer was on the loose in the city.

CARL DENARO, survivor of Son of Sam shooting, author of *The Son of Sam and Me*: I got shot in Queens on October 23 [1976]. I don't think the *Post* or the *News* covered it. I do recall a small, like, two-paragraph article in the local, I think it was the *Flushing Tribune*. You know—local guy, twenty years old, Carl Denaro was shot on 159th Street. It was very bare-bones. Of course, because there was no Son of Sam and there was no other reason for me being shot, the police kind of assumed it was a drug deal. Because I did have long hair. I did smoke pot. So they kind of jumped to that conclusion that it was a drug deal gone bad. Then on March 10 [1977], Mayor Beame and [Police] Commissioner [Michael] Codd held a press conference stating that these seemingly random shootings are not random at all, they're the work of a serial killer. March 10, that's when the proverbial shit hits the fan, if you will.

The *Daily News*, especially its star columnist Jimmy Breslin, jumped ahead in the competition to cover what turned into one of the most lurid tales in tabloid history—especially after the killer, who called himself Son of Sam, began writing to Breslin. The *Post*—particularly Steve Dunleavy—did their best to catch up. With the paper in the midst of changing editors, Murdoch himself directed much of the Son of Sam coverage.

ERIC FETTMANN: The *Post* was late to the Son of Sam story.

CARL DENARO: It's kind of hard for me to differentiate between the *News* and the *Post* because from March '77, when the police announced that it was a serial killer, for the next basically two years, both papers ran sometimes ten, twelve, fifteen pages a day on the Son of Sam. It got to the point where it was obvious they were running out of information, and they were kind of regurgitating the same story. Of course, it was a lot of guesswork; you know, reporters making assumptions.

DICK BELSKY: Murdoch takes over in January and then right after that, we suddenly have the most sensational serial killer case ever. That's something that someone like Murdoch jumps on. The timing was pretty incredible.

RICHARD GOODING, metropolitan editor, 1976–1993: I did the first *Post* story in [March] 1977 when it started to look like there was a pattern in the Son of

Sam shootings, and by the spring, Dunleavy and I were doing Son of Sam all the time.

DICK BELSKY: He was not Son of Sam until he wrote a letter [to Jimmy Breslin] referring to himself as that.

PAT SULLIVAN, reporter, night editor, 1972–1980: The cops were definitely helping out Breslin. They were more used to dealing with him. Dunleavy, even though he was making a name for himself, was not Breslin.

ROBERT KALFUS, photographer, 1977–1993, 2002–2015: I lived in Flushing at that point, and the 109th Precinct was the headquarters for the .44 Caliber Killer task force. I got comfortable with sitting up there in the second-floor detectives' area. They had a bench outside the railing. I knew the captain in charge, and they let me sit there. Whenever I could help them, I would. I once saw a bumper sticker on a car saying "Use It Again, Sam." I managed to get a picture of the license plate and gave them a print. They went out and investigated the guy, and he worked at a recycling center. The guy was not pleased. But then another time I was sitting on the bench and saw some posters on the wall in the detective squad room, which had descriptions of what they thought [the killer] looked like. I had my camera in my lap, roughly focused, and made some pictures. They were published in the paper. Press was banned from the building.

PAT SULLIVAN: Murdoch's people went nuts over Son of Sam. Dunleavy was trying to match Breslin, and he wrote a story about a cop that thought he was chasing Son of Sam. I remember talking to the cop later on, and he says, "Boy, your man has one hell of an imagination."

ERIC FETTMANN: During that summer, a call came in from someone claiming to be Son of Sam. The only person in the city room not already on the phone was Lou O'Neill, the rock music critic, so he was given the call. But it was quickly obvious that he had no idea what to say to the guy. Rupert was there and he just grabbed the phone out of O'Neill's hand and started interviewing the guy himself. [The caller was an imposter.]

DAVID ROSENTHAL: Murdoch could not stand the fact that the killer was writing to Jimmy Breslin and not to us. There was pressure not only on Dunleavy but on all of us. We needed to get some of Sam's attention, and anything that could be done, we would do.

More than thirty years later, when Steve Dunleavy retired, Murdoch told the *New York Times* that he had changed editors, replacing Ted Bolwell with Roger Wood, in the summer of '77, because of Dunleavy and Son of Sam. "They kept spiking his copy," said Murdoch of the way his favorite reporter had been treated, "while Breslin was leading every day. It was just killing the *Post* and killing Dunleavy. So I made a change because of that."

DAVID ROSENTHAL: That's when [Dunleavy] really came into flower, because he did a terrific job of being a tabloid inventor. I mean, the whole thing was such a terrible sordid story, but Steve knew how to handle it—in some ways better than anybody else.

ERIC FETTMANN: At one point, "Doonesbury" did a week's worth of strips lampooning Breslin's Son of Sam coverage, with Breslin getting a series of phone calls from a killer calling himself "the son of Arnold and Mary Lieberman." The *Daily News* had "Doonesbury" then and they refused to run it. So, the *Post* ran the strips on Page Six. [After a couple of days, the *Post* reported that the *News* had leaned on the syndicate that represented "Doonesbury" to send a "cease and desist" letter to the *Post*. Page Six began describing what was in the strips instead.]

CARL DENARO: Certainly from June of '77 on, the *News* might have been worse than the *Post* as far as keeping the story going and sensationalizing the story. That mostly can be attributed to Jimmy Breslin. I can understand Jimmy Breslin's excitement, being the guy that received the letter from Son of Sam. But I think he really screwed up a lot of the investigation. Even though the cops told him—don't release the letter—he couldn't help himself.

CURTIS SLIWA, founder, the Guardian Angels: Before Dunleavy, I never read the *Post*. Only Jewish liberal people read the *New York Post*—it wasn't even an afterthought. When Dunleavy comes over and the Son of Sam [emerges], I'm comparing the *Daily News* and Breslin to Dunleavy and the *Post*, and I'm saying, wow, street cred, I never knew the *Post* could be that. I started reading it religiously thereafter. It became the new street paper.

ERIC FETTMANN: Jimmy Breslin may have owned the Son of Sam story, but Dunleavy owned the last shooting—Stacy Moskowitz. Steve made friends with a lot of cops. He did what reporters do—he hung out with them, he drank with them. The *Post* was becoming a force, so there was no reason why he shouldn't have gotten a favor from the cops.

> According to Dunleavy, Timothy Dowd, the detective who led the search for the Son of Sam, tipped him off about the Moskowitz shooting, which took place on July 31, 1977. Stacy Moskowitz and Robert Violante, both twenty years old, had been making out in Violante's car as it was parked on a street in Bath Beach, Brooklyn, when Son of Sam approached and shot them both in the head. Violante survived but was left legally blind. Moskowitz died the next day.

JOE DE MARIA, photographer, 1977–1993: We were staking out different areas. Every time he hit, we wanted to be close by. The last one, Stacy Moskowitz, we were all sitting in Queens, thinking it was gonna happen somewhere in Queens. Then we ran to Brooklyn and got to the scene and then went to the hospital. I had called Steve Dunleavy and told him where I was at the hospital. I was able to get him to the hospital front door and I pointed him to where the Moskowitz parents were.

RICHARD GOODING: It was late Saturday night or early Sunday morning, and I got a call at like two in the morning to get to Kings County Hospital, which I did. At some point in the middle of the night, I was roaming the halls of the hospital trying to find people to talk to, and I passed a rather large room with windows. Through the windows, I could see Dunleavy with this woman, who turned out to be Stacy Moskowitz's mother, Neysa. They were alone. It turned out that Dunleavy had passed himself off as a grief counselor and was talking to her. The next day, when he wrote her story, she knew she'd been tricked, but she didn't care. She'd been so charmed by this guy. He sent her flowers. He'd send cars to take her places, to bring her to lunch. He was her personal chronicler throughout. She didn't care that she had been conned. But you talk about this change in the way of doing journalism. That's when it really hit home that the Brits and the Aussies did things differently—and they did things we wouldn't do. It never would have crossed my mind to do what Dunleavy did, and if it had crossed my mind, I would have never done it. We had lines we wouldn't cross. They had no lines.

ERIC FETTMANN: I don't know at what point they realized he was from the *Post*, but by the time he finally told them, they had already grown to trust him. Everything the Moskowitzes said was all over the *Post*. One headline was something like, "I Want to Scratch His Eyes Out."

JOE DE MARIA: Because they knew I had a gun carry permit, Dunleavy wanted to do a setup to get [Son of Sam] to shoot at us. Dunleavy was going to put a blonde wig on somebody, and have another reporter next to him, like they're making love, with me hiding in the back seat [with gun and camera]. And hope that [Son of Sam] would show up so we could get him. With Steve, I said, "Whatever you want me to do, I'll do." He was my hero. When I was young, I never thought about [getting killed]. It's like, whatever I have to do to get the picture, I'll do. I was going to shoot him, and then take the picture of him laying there. Steve was setting this whole thing up. It was being kept quiet, but it never happened because I think that was probably right before Stacy Moskowitz. I think he was gonna use two guys because he didn't want to use female reporters and get them hurt.

The already intense manhunt took on new urgency. Days after the death of Moskowitz, the *Post*'s front page carried "An Open Letter to Son of Sam" by Dunleavy, in which he pleaded with the killer to give himself up. Ultimately the police traced a parking ticket on a car spotted near the site of the Moskowitz-Violante shootings to twenty-four-year-old David Berkowitz. He was arrested in Yonkers, New York, on August 10, 1977.

MYRON RUSHETZKY: That night, a few of the reporters who got off at midnight got a slide, which is permission to leave early. At five of midnight, [Carl] Pelleck called. He said, "Get me [Metropolitan Editor] Andy [Porte] quick." Pelleck told Andy they had caught Son of Sam.

PAT SMITH: Instead of my normal shift of midnight to eight, I was working noon to midnight and Andy Porte would come on at midnight. He had just come to the desk, and we were having our change-of-shift conversation. Myron says, "Pelleck's on the phone." Carl Pelleck, ace police reporter, totally plugged in, totally wired. Andy starts to wave him off for a second, and Myron says, "They got Sam." Andy takes the call from Pelleck. The shift is changing, and there are people getting up to leave. The midnight shift is coming in. I call out to the newsroom: "Everyone, please stay where you are. If you need to move your desks, do." Because remember, in the newsroom, you don't own your desk. You have your desk for eight hours, and then someone else gets it for eight hours. But I wanted to keep everyone there. The fact that it happened at almost exactly midnight means we had twice the number of reporters.

MYRON RUSHETZKY: My instruction was to find Dunleavy. There were no cell phones, very few beepers. I knew he was out and about, and Gloria [his wife] was with him. I started calling every single bar, restaurant that I could think of that Steve might be at. I am running in overdrive. I'm calling places like Elaine's, Costello's. But I had to be very conscious that I couldn't tell anyone why I was looking for Steve. I couldn't call Elaine's and say, "I'm looking for Steve Dunleavy because they caught Son of Sam." There might be other journalists there.

PAT SMITH: Pelleck called every couple of minutes with a new detail. One of the phone calls said he's in Yonkers. We end up sending three teams to three different points in Yonkers, so that by the time we get an address, we can be first there. Then Dunleavy showed up. Milton drove Dunleavy and Marc Kalech.

MILTON GOLDSTEIN: It was a hot, sweaty summer night, and I came in to relieve Myron. But he actually stayed the whole night because they grabbed me and said: Take Dunleavy and Kalech up to Yonkers. I drove them in my VW Rabbit. Dunleavy was drunk, of course.

PAT SMITH: Kalech walks into the lobby of this apartment building. There is embossed tape of names on the different mailboxes. The one that says "D. Berkowitz," Kalech peeled it off and stuck it in his pocket. A, he wanted it as a souvenir, and B, he did not want anyone else to find Berkowitz's apartment. He was trying to burn the trail. Marc has passed on, but I bet he had that souvenir till the end.

MILTON GOLDSTEIN: In the city room, when they found out [Son of Sam's] name was Berkowitz, I remember a copygirl saying, "Uh-oh, he's Jewish." Then it turned out he had been adopted. Alan Whitney started musing about a headline that we would never write: NOT REALLY JEWISH.

PAT SMITH: Dunleavy and Kalech now somehow come upon Sam [Carr]. There is a person named Sam who lives around the corner. He has a dog. The dog barks in the backyard all the time. David Berkowitz worked a midnight shift at the post office and was trying to sleep through the day and the dog kept him awake. That was the whole thing about the Son of Sam, about someone talking to him, giving him messages and all that. They end up knocking on Sam [Carr]'s door at perhaps three or four o'clock in the morning. From the other side of the door, they hear an ominous click, which Dunleavy recognized as someone racking a .45 automatic. Dunleavy pushes Kalech from the door and he gets back, too, because a bullet might come through the door in any minute. He says, "This is the *New York Post* reporting here. Just want to talk to you about one of your neighbors." The guy finally opened the door. Yes, he had the automatic in his hand. But they had a very interesting conversation.

DICK BELSKY: It was a very unusual page one for the *Post* [on August 11, 1977]. It was one word, but in red ink. CAUGHT. I'm not sure they had really ever done that before. A color headline as opposed to just black.

PAT SULLIVAN: When Son of Sam was arrested, it was DEFCON 1. Rosenthal was on the desk, and I was saying, "Give me a piece of it, give me a piece of it." Finally, he said, "Okay, go on up to the 109th Precinct"—that was the headquarters. I lucked out, ran into cops I knew pretty well. They had debriefed Son of Sam. Late, late in the day, way past deadline, I called in and said, "Hey, I have his confession. I know nobody's got it." I guess they ran into the afternoon meeting and all of a sudden I get a panicked call: "We want you to do it NOW." Poor Tommy Topor was going to have to take it in [on rewrite]. They put out an extra, which surprised the hell out of everybody. I still have it on my wall—it was one of the few times, apparently, that the *Post* went over a million [circulation] and it's on my byline.

JOE BERGER: The ethics of the workplace began to change. Some of the reporters that were brought in had a kind of cutthroat competitiveness. I mean, journalists are all fairly competitive, but there are boundaries. When you work for the same paper, there's a certain amount of cooperation. The day they caught David Berkowitz, I was sent to the home of the last victim, Stacy Moskowitz, to interview her mother [Neysa]. When she came out, I said, "My name is Joe Berger. I'm a reporter for the *New York Post*. Can I have a few minutes to ask you about your reaction to the arrest of David Berkowitz?" She said, "I can't talk to you. I promised Steve Dunleavy, who I'm talking to right now, I wouldn't talk to other reporters." I said, "But I'm from the *New York Post*. I'm with the same newspaper." She said, "He especially told me, 'Don't talk to any reporters from the *New York Post*.'"

The headline on the August 11 extra edition was SON OF SAM'S OWN STORY "Killing was my job . . ." As the paper was selling out at newsstands, the *Post*—and every other news outlet—sought other angles on the story.

MYRON RUSHETZKY: That morning, Pat Smith had to go to Mutchie's to throw Carl [Pelleck] and Steve [Dunleavy] out of there—they were celebrating—because he had to remind them: we have to do it again today.

DAVID C. BERLINER, former New York correspondent for *The Washington Post*: I woke up early that morning and heard on the radio that the police had captured the prime suspect in the Son of Sam case. They said he lived in Yonkers, so I called down to the national desk, but since it's a morning paper they don't get in until later in the morning. My instincts told me to get dressed, get in my car, and head up there. There were some curious people milling around, but I was way ahead of everybody else from the press. Periodically a detective would come out with a box of evidence, and I asked one of them could I go up to the apartment. He said, "When we're done taking out evidence." At that point, I knew I would have a few hours to kill, so I did exactly what you see and read when a murderer or serial killer is arrested. I went to the nearby delicatessen and other stores, and I talked to people on the street. To a one they said, "Oh, he was such a lovely boy. He was a very nice young man." I was taking notes and thinking if I was writing this as a novel, it would be so trite that my editor would just X it out.

ROBERT KALFUS: I thought, while everyone's standing around, I'll take a look around the building. What I'm telling you is absolutely, totally true. I walked down the long driveway. It was a seven-story building with more than a hundred apartments. I was twenty-five at the time. Just then the garage door rumbled open. I thought, *okay*, and walked in. The garage door closed behind me. I was scared. I'm telling myself, calm down. I let my eyes adjust to the darkness and saw that there was a door. I walked up the steps to the first floor. I was at the lobby. I continued up, and at each floor I would look out. I didn't see anything unusual until the top floor. I opened the door and off to my left, there's a police officer sitting in a chair outside the apartment. I thought, that's it. I walked up to the cop and said, "Excuse me, Officer. I'm Robert Kalfus with the *New York Post*. The officers downstairs said they're finished. Can I get some pictures looking inside?" He said, "What are you crazy? Get out of here!" I went back to the stairwell and walked up to the roof. I went down the fire escape and in front of me was a top-floor window and there were three or four police hats lined up against the edge of the window. There was no one inside, so I pressed my camera against the glass and took pictures looking inside the apartment. After about two minutes, I went back up the fire escape, and back down the seven flights to the lobby. I nodded hello to the cop on duty behind the concierge desk. When I walked out of the building, my photographer buddies said, "Did you get pictures?" I said, "I know where the apartment is. Do you want to go in with me?"

DAVID C. BERLINER: As I'm going into the building, I see three guys and one of them was Kalfus. They said, "Are you going upstairs?" I was not happy to see them because I didn't know that they were all photographers; I didn't want another reporter coming up. This was a worldwide exclusive, and I wanted the story. I said, "Yeah." We went upstairs, and there was no cop there. There was yellow police tape across the door. I recall that Bob Kalfus said he was going to go out on the fire escape, open the window, and then open the door.

ROBERT KALFUS: Four of us went into the building—Lenny Dietrick, from the *News*; Ted Cowell, who was working for *Time*; and David Berliner, from the *Washington Post*. The cop in the lobby said, "Where are you going?" Once more, I said, "The cops told us they're all finished and we can go up." He didn't do anything, so we pushed the elevator button and went up to the seventh floor. Outside Berkowitz's apartment, the chair was still there, but the cop was gone. We tried the door. It was locked. I said, "Guys, I think I know how we can get in." Ted Cowell and I went up to the roof. We crossed over to the fire escape. Cowell [said] I should lean out— seven stories up—and push the window open while he held my belt. I didn't trust him to not lose his grip. I held his belt and he pushed the window open. We went inside, and we let the other photographers in. We were in wonderland.

DAVID C. BERLINER: I went across the narrow hall to the door directly across from Berkowitz's. A woman lived there whose apartment wrapped around to his, and Berkowitz had punched a huge hole through the wall into this woman's home. I interviewed her with my back to Berkowitz's door, and when I turned around the door to his apartment was open. Lenny Dietrick, who was with me in the hallway, went in, and I stood at the precipice, debating whether I should walk into the biggest story certainly in the country. It would be a real coup being the only reporter. Or do I not go in, because of journalistic ethics. The *Washington Post* was very strict about that. The *New York Post* couldn't give a damn. I decided I'm going in.

ROBERT KALFUS: I got at least two rolls of film documenting everything inside the apartment: Berkowitz's bed, which was a mattress on the floor; the damage he'd done to the walls and the slogans he'd scrawled. The inside of his refrigerator and his cabinets. Everything. While I'm taking pictures, the batteries for my flash died. I asked if someone would let me use their flash or had spare batteries. They all said, "No!" "But I got you in here!" Everything I shot from then on was using available light.

DAVID C. BERLINER: The walls of the apartment were covered with all sorts of crazy wording and stuff about Satan and Sam the Dog. It was all in red paint. It was terrifying. It looked like some kind of witch's coven. The whole apartment was a mess. I doubt it was neat before, but the cops came in and they probably tore everything apart. The photographers were taking pictures, and each of them is picking up souvenirs, like greeting cards and stuff, and shoving them into their pants. I said, "Guys, we got in here under questionable circumstances. You don't want to be caught taking any evidence, anything out of this apartment." A couple of them mused about that and, as far as I knew, put the stuff back.

ROBERT KALFUS: That's incorrect. Lenny Dietrick and I were making photographs. Cowell told us he was working for *Time*, but we did not see him make any photographs. We did see him take Berkowitz's army web belt, which said "Berkowitz" on it, and a letter from Berkowitz's grandmother, among other items.

DAVID C. BERLINER: Then I found something that totally shocked me—a manual for the .44-caliber gun. I go, "Oh my god, how could they have missed this?" I was really thinking about taking that, but then I realized not only would it be unethical, it would make the cops look really bad, and I might be followed for the rest of my life. I left it.

ROBERT KALFUS: We stayed there far too long and made too much noise. We were shouting, "Look at this! Look at this!" We found out later that a neighbor on the floor below had called the police.

DAVID C. BERLINER: I'm writing notes furiously and there's a knock on the door. We asked, "Who is it?" "Police." So someone said, "What are we going to do?" I said, "Don't do anything. It's not the cops." "How do you know?" One of my first jobs on a daily newspaper was as a night police reporter with the *Newark Evening News* in New Jersey. I rode with them during the 1967 riots. I told the guys, "I know how cops act, and these are not cops." I opened the door a little bit and there was some guy there. I said, "You've got to get out of here. Otherwise I'm calling down." I let him infer that I was a cop. He left. A little while later, there's more banging. Again, the photographers said, "Oh shit, it's the cops!" Again, I said, "That's not the cops." I went to the door and opened it. The guy on the other side said, "I want to come in. I know there are reporters in there." I said, "No, there's not. You've got to go away or I'm going to call downstairs." I had this police radio, and I turned the squelch control to the part where it went totally staticky and I said, "This is Williams," or whatever name I gave. I said, "I may need a couple of guys from patrol to come up here." The guy left like the Green Hornet. Sometime later, there's this huge banging on the door and somebody yelling, "Open up the fucking door! Open up the fucking door!" I said, "*That's* the cops." At that point everybody is scrambling. Bob was saying, "Oh my god, I got the film in my camera. What am I going to do?" So, I told him, "Take the roll out. Take out a new roll of film. Put the exposed roll in the box and then pretend that you're taking out the new roll from the camera. That way they'll think the new roll is the exposed roll." That's what he did. I didn't see Bob as competition because, A, the *Washington Post* is not in competition with the *New York Post*; and B, he was a photographer, and I was a reporter.

ROBERT KALFUS: Four Yonkers cops showed up. We let them in and told them we had found the apartment open. Before we opened the door, I took my two rolls of exposed film and put them in one pocket. I figured we would be searched. One of the first things I was told when I started working for the *Post* was when you are out in the field you have to be in constant communication with the office. We were given two-way radios, but the *Daily News* monitored our frequency, and we monitored theirs. And *Newsday* shared our frequency, so we wouldn't put out important information over the radio. We used pay phones, which were a dime then. I always carried a whole roll of dimes. I broke it open, emptied them over the film, then blew my nose into a tissue and put that on top of the dimes. In my other pocket, I put several rolls of blank film.

DAVID C. BERLINER: Remember that show *Kojak*—the bald detective with the lollipops and that saying, "Who loves you, baby?" The arrest was like *Kojak* on a rampage. These cops came charging in and I got slammed against the wall face-first. I'm lucky I didn't break my nose. I thought they were going to pull my arms out of their sockets when they handcuffed me. The lead cop was red-faced, and they were furious. The reason was that Berkowitz, who had been committing all these murders in New York City, lived in Yonkers. And it was the New York City cops who found him. They had nothing to do with the arrest other than to come in and arrest the newspeople. Years later, I spoke to a Yonkers cop—he had retired, I think—and he basically said it was one of the worst days the Yonkers Police Department ever had. I think they took it out on us because we weren't dangerous.

ROBERT KALFUS: We were taken to their precinct and handcuffed to these little schoolroom desks. We were made to feel very small. Lenny Dietrick asked to use the bathroom, and they made him drag the school desk with him to go pee. At one point while he was sitting there, he crossed his legs and one of the cops noticed a bulge coming from his ankle. I remember hearing, "Sergeant, look at this." The sergeant looked at Lenny and said, "What do we have here?" He rolls down Lenny's sock and sees the roll of film. The cop pulls the film all the way out, holds one side up to the light and then the other, then rolls it back up. He says, "Here, Sonny, have this back." At that point, I had the only pictures. David Berliner was a reporter. He took notes. When the cops told me, "Empty your pockets," I pointed out that I was still handcuffed. The cop confiscated the rolls of film in my one pocket. Then he put his hand into the other pocket and pulled out the tissue—*eccch.* He put it down, reached back in, and pulled out a whole bunch of dimes. He said, "We have to voucher all of your equipment." He wrote down my name and "money." I said, "Hey, I want all that back. You have to count it." So he counted it. I said, "You made a mistake." Instead of counting it again, he put it back in my pocket, and I thought, this could work out okay.

DAVID C. BERLINER: Once our mug shots were taken and we were fingerprinted, we were allowed to leave. I got on the pay phone at the police station and called the national desk. I told them I had the story and that I had been arrested. I didn't tell them how I got into the apartment. More and more editors got on the line. [*Washington Post* editor in chief] Ben Bradlee was on the line. They're saying, "Okay, we'll get you a lawyer, but you've got to file your story."

ROBERT KALFUS: One of the photographers gave me a lift to my car, which was parked back on Pine Street. I found a phone at a gas station. I called the *Post*. "Get in here, get in here," they told me. I park on South Street, and there's Carl Pelleck, who I knew only a little bit, on the street with his porkpie hat and a big lit cigar in his mouth. He looked like Tony Soprano, with his unflappable attitude. I said, "Carl!" He said, "Hey, kid, how ya doin'?" I said, "Carl, I've just been arrested." He took the cigar out of his mouth, flicked it, and said, "First time, huh? Ahh, fuck you," and walked on.

DAVID C. BERLINER: I started searching around for a place to write the story. Then I saw the office of the weekly Yonkers newspaper. It was upstairs from a storefront. I knocked. This kid in his upper teens opens the door. I said, "Is it possible I can use a typewriter?" He said, "We're closed." I said, "I'm a reporter." He said, "Oh, yeah?" This kid was wrapping up bundles of the paper for delivery. There was nobody else there. When I told him I was with the *Washington Post*, his eyes lit up and after that there was nothing he wouldn't do for me. At that time being a reporter with the *Washington Post* or the *New York Times* had some merit. People took that seriously. I got some paper, and I sat down and wrote my lede. I pulled it out of the typewriter and said to the kid, "Would you do me a favor and dictate this to Washington?" I thought he was going to fly. I would type a page, hand it to him, and he would dictate it until the end of the story. I never got his name. After I filed, I got in my car and as I'm driving home, I turn on the radio to the news channel 1010 WINS—remember, "You give us twenty-two minutes, we'll give you the world"?—and they're talking about Berkowitz's arrest. They said four journalists were arrested today in his apartment, including David Berliner of the *Washington Post*. I almost swerved off the road.

ROBERT KALFUS: I took the elevator up to the fourth floor. Susan Welchman brought me over to Rupert Murdoch, who was sitting at a table doing layout and designing headlines. She said, "Mr. Murdoch, this is our photographer, Robert Kalfus. He got pictures inside Son of Sam's apartment." Murdoch said, "Oh, very good." We developed the film, and the next day there was a full-page picture with the headline: "Inside the Killer's Lair." The whole centerfold was my pictures.

DAVID BERLINER: My report was headlined, "Neighbors Recall Quiet Man, A Little Strange, But Nice." The *New York Post* had what they call a double-truck layout: two facing pages with pictures inside the apartment credited to Kalfus. The headline was "Inside the Killer's Lair." There was no "allegedly" or "according to the police." It just said he was the killer, which Berkowitz could have sued over if he had not been convicted. The *New York Post* and the *Washington Post* were a universe apart.

ROBERT KALFUS: The day my pictures ran, I had to be in a Yonkers court. Ira Sorkin, who later became Securities and Exchange Commission chairman in New York, was working for Murdoch's law firm. He was assigned to represent me in the Yonkers court that Friday morning. He's driving me to Yonkers, and he says, "Tell me the full story." I'm telling Ira the story, and he suddenly pulled over onto the shoulder and doubled over laughing. I said, "What are you laughing about? I got arrested." He said, "They can never let you testify as to what happened. The Yonkers cops left the apartment unguarded, and you got in and took pictures. And one of the guys took things? If they let you speak, Berkowitz can get off. He can claim it was a contaminated crime scene." He said, "Don't worry about a thing." We get to the courthouse courtroom. "How do you plead?" "Not guilty."

IRA LEE SORKIN, former partner, Squadron, Ellenoff, Plesent & Lehrer: I don't recall pulling over and laughing. What I do recall is the legal position we took—myself and another lawyer who represented the *Daily News* photographer—which was that this was private property and only the owner or the renter could grant or deny us permission to go into the apartment. No one was about to go to the jail and ask David Berkowitz if it was okay to cross the police line, and go into his apartment and take pictures because the police couldn't keep us out of it. The judge was pissed off as I recall, but I think he thought it was a novel argument and dropped the case.

DAVID C. BERLINER: When we were brought in for arraignment or at one of the hearings, Kalfus told us he'd gotten a $10,000 bonus. I caught hell with the *Washington Post*. My story ran at the top of the front page, but because I had gone into the apartment, they said I violated their [ethics] policy. It wound up turning out bad for me even though I got congratulated by every editor and reporter I knew. I was punished for that story. Because I had been charged with trespassing, the hierarchy decided that I could no longer report and write for the paper. I was blackballed. It was a decision that left me shocked, disappointed, and very, very sad.

ROBERT KALFUS: I didn't receive any bonus. I should have.

4 | IT WAS OBSCENE!
IT WAS FANTASTIC!

Koch, Koch, Koch

In the fall of 1977, Rupert Murdoch invited Rinker Buck, a writer from *MORE*, the journalism review, to his country house north of New York City. The resulting article, "Can the 'Post' Survive Rupert Murdoch?," went into detail on the many ways Murdoch had ruffled feathers in the city during his first year owning the tabloid, Murdoch answered the reporter's questions but made few apologies. He did admit that one Son of Sam story—in which letters written years earlier by David Berkowitz appeared with Berkowitz's byline and HOW I BECAME A MASS KILLER as the headline—had gone over-the-top. Other than that, Murdoch made it clear that New York would have to get used to him. Many of Buck's questions involved the race for mayor in 1977, and what some saw as the *Post*'s unfair and unbalanced coverage.

The incumbent that year was a diminutive Democrat named Abe Beame, who was running in a crowded primary field that included Mario Cuomo (then New York's secretary of state) and US representatives Ed Koch (Greenwich Village), Bella Abzug (Upper West Side), and Herman Badillo (South Bronx). Days after Murdoch bought the *Post*, in what would become a much-quoted interview with Alexander Cockburn in the *Village Voice*, Murdoch said that, beyond newspapering, "the only other thing I like is politics, and I've never let myself get into that. I think you prostitute your newspapers once you start joining political parties." But anyone who had followed Murdoch's career knew that his two loves were actually conjoined twins. Early in his career, Murdoch realized, as do many owners of media properties, that supporting a winning political candidate often leads to support for the media owner's businesses. Almost as soon as he assumed control of the *Post*, Murdoch focused on finding a favorite mayoral candidate. In the left-leaning city, the Democratic candidate, and therefore the Democratic primary, were of paramount importance.

JOYCE PURNICK, political reporter, 1970–1978: Abe Beame was judged to not have handled [New York's fiscal crisis] very well. The city came right up to the edge of bankruptcy and [Beame] was completely unqualified to handle it. Then infrastructure was put in by the governor and by business leaders to kind of run the city, sort of like a shadow government. Beame pretty much collapsed. He was in way over his head.

GEORGE ARZT, City Hall bureau chief, 1968–1986: Abe Beame hardly ever met with the press. Then, during the height of the fiscal crisis, we couldn't use the word "bankruptcy," a directive that, I believe, came from his press office. Asking a question in the Blue Room [in City Hall], I would say, "Mr. Mayor, uh, about the city's brush, with uh, uh, fiscal problems"—you'd have to go around it.

> Any idea of endorsing Beame for a second term quickly evaporated, leaving Murdoch on the hunt for another candidate worthy of his new political power.

GEORGE ARZT: There was an agreement of sorts that came out of Governor [Hugh] Carey's office, that everybody—all the papers—would support Mario Cuomo [in his run for mayor]. Cuomo was a good friend of Carey's. They had both gone to St. John's University. We were coming out of 1975, '76, when the city was in crisis. You needed a strong mayor. The idea was that the governor and mayor needed to work together. The papers were all going to endorse him around the same time, with the *Post* going first. Except one day, out of nowhere, early on in the race [July 31, 1977], the *Times* endorsed Mario Cuomo. Everyone's running around trying to find out what the hell happened. Rupert and the *Daily News* said they were no longer beholden to the deal. I always thought that Murdoch had qualms about Mario Cuomo, who did not represent his conservative values.

JOHN LoCICERO, adviser to Ed Koch and 1977 campaign manager: We understood that the three papers made a deal to endorse the same person. The *Times* broke their word, and went early, and endorsed Cuomo, which pissed off the head of the *Post*. Was Cuomo the person they all agreed to endorse? That, I can't prove. But once the *Times* endorsed Cuomo, the *News* and the *Post* backed off. They said, fuck you—well, what do I know what they actually said? But they obviously weren't ready to endorse so early. They were annoyed that the *Times* didn't tell them what they were doing. As far as I know, this had not happened before [all three papers agreeing to endorse the same candidate]. But we were coming out of the fiscal crisis. It was a terrible time. The papers wanted to have somebody they thought could run the city of New York.

MAX FRANKEL, former executive editor, *The New York Times* (and in 1977, editor of the *Times* editorial page): There never was such an agreement and there never could have been. We took pride in our independence and would never co-ordinate editorial endorsements with other newspapers or political campaigns.

ERIC FETTMANN, associate editorial page editor, columnist, 1976–1991, 1993–2019: Contrary to what most people think, the *Post* did not immediately become a conservative paper. It took several years. In fact, Murdoch's first instinct in '77 in the mayoral campaign—his first big campaign as owner—was to endorse Herman Badillo for mayor. But he was talked out of it. That's the irony. He had his editors on the ground saying we don't want Black or Puerto Rican stories, but he thought it would be a gutsy move to endorse this liberal Puerto Rican from the Bronx. And he thought Herman was smart.

JOYCE PURNICK: In New York, with some exceptions, the Democratic nomination is tantamount to election. Murdoch was kind of shopping around, looking for the right candidate to endorse. He considered Mario Cuomo, but rejected him, even though Cuomo had the support of the governor, Hugh Carey. He rejected Cuomo as too liberal. Then he considered [US representative] Herman Badillo, and he ultimately rejected him as having the wrong temperament and not really mirroring his own—Murdoch's—positions.

ERIC FETTMANN: Murdoch was talked out of [endorsing Badillo] by people he didn't realize at the time were allied with Koch. Like Alan Patricof [chairman of the New York Magazine Company], who put Murdoch and Koch together.

ALAN PATRICOF, former chairman of the board, New York Magazine Company: That's absolutely untrue. Sorry, I can't take credit for [steering him to Koch]. I mean, I was a supporter of Ed Koch. Ed Koch had the locker next to me in my sports club. It was Ed Koch on one side, and Ed Bradley [*60 Minutes* correspondent] on the other. So I did get to know Koch reasonably well, but I certainly can't take that claim to fame.

MAUREEN CONNELLY, former press secretary for Ed Koch: I would get regular calls—this was before the *Post* endorsed Ed—from Rupert himself. He wouldn't have someone else do it for him. He wanted to know the latest poll numbers. I told him they weren't great. Ed was not number one, but he was very strong as a second choice across the board.

JOYCE PURNICK: Koch, who was a congressman from Manhattan, was way down in the polls. People didn't know him very well. Mario Cuomo was considered the leading candidate. But Ed Koch had a campaign director, political director, commercial maker named David Garth, who was a kingmaker. He went to Murdoch and he said, "This guy can win. And this is how." He showed him polls. He showed him the strategy, and he persuaded Murdoch that Koch was quite centrist to conservative on a lot of issues that were important to Murdoch.

GEORGE ARZT: Murdoch felt Koch had great growth potential and a similar worldview. Koch was not pro-union, and Rupert was notoriously anti-union. Koch was for the death penalty, even though the mayor had nothing to do with the death penalty. He was someone who came closest to a conservative. Koch would call himself a liberal with sanity. Murdoch liked that.

MAUREEN CONNELLY: The big change came when the blackout happened. Even though there was no power, the Koch campaign kept going. They got this hand-cranked copying machine and they put out a plan of what should be done. Ed was out there saying, "We need to bring in the National Guard to handle the traffic." He ran through this whole program of what should have been done during the blackout. Abe Beame, the incumbent, was in a bunker or something. That was a real turning point for Ed.

ERIC FETTMANN: Abe Beame later claimed that the 24 HOURS OF TERROR headline cost him the election.

On August 19, 1977, weeks before the city's September 8 Democratic and Republican mayoral primaries, Murdoch placed his bet. The *Post* ran a front-page endorsement of Ed Koch, calling him "the best hope for a strong, effective mayor." From that point on, the *Post* was all-in for Koch, in a way few had seen before from a newspaper.

GEORGE ARZT: One day Koch was asleep and the phone rings. It's Rupert Murdoch. As Koch told it, all he could think of in his mid-awake state is: that's not a Jewish name. Rupert then tells him that he is going to support him and Koch tells Rupert, "You won't be disappointed."

CLYDE HABERMAN, reporter, 1966–1977: Koch said that when Murdoch called him up to say he was going to throw his support behind him, "That's when I knew I was going to be the next mayor." And indeed, Murdoch gave the huge headlines to him, while there would be pictures of [rival candidate] Bella Abzug that made her look like this big fat dumpy broad.

JOHN LoCICERO: [The *Post*'s coverage of Koch] was obscene! It was fantastic! The day the *Post* endorsed him, Koch, a guy named Ed Gold, and I bought several papers and walked down the street, flashing the front page. What happened then made all the difference in the world. The *Post* and the Citizens Union endorsed Koch on a Friday, and the *Daily News* endorsed him five days later. All of a sudden the other candidates, who didn't think Koch was a threat, woke up and said, oh my god, now we have to worry about him.

JOYCE PURNICK: Suddenly the news pages of the *Post*, which, under Dolly Schiff, had been free of influence from the publisher, were chockablock with Koch articles. Some of [the issues important to Murdoch] were racial issues. He was opposed to any kind of quota—racial quotas, affirmative action. At the time there was a big issue about integrating public housing. Murdoch was opposed to that. Koch was opposed to the way it was done—not the concept of integrating public housing. Those were the main issues. Everywhere you looked, there was a Koch article, including on Page Six, which then was a really politically influential page. You could track Rupert Murdoch's interest in various candidates that year by looking at Page Six, because at first it was loaded with items about Cuomo, then it was loaded with items about Herman Badillo, and then suddenly Koch, Koch, Koch.

JOE BERGER, investigative reporter, 1971–1978: The way Koch was elected said a lot about the warping of coverage to favor a particular candidate. Murdoch started putting [Koch] on the front page repeatedly: Koch attacks this; Koch assails that. He minimized Abe Beame. He'd run a picture of Beame on the front page with a microphone in front of his face, so he looked silly. And he emphasized his shortness. Koch ended up winning the runoff [and the general election].

JOYCE PURNICK: One of Murdoch's editors came up to me and said, "Here's this poll that shows Koch doing very, very well. Would you please write it up." I asked him questions that any political reporter would ask to see if a poll is legitimate: How many people were polled? What questions were asked? How were various ethnic and racial groups weighed? What is the name of the polling organization and what is their background? In other words, is this a legitimate poll? He couldn't answer any of the questions. I said, "I'd rather not do this piece because I really don't think we should write about it. I don't think this is a legitimate poll." It was pretty clear it was a skewed, put-up job. He said, "Okay, if you don't want to do it, that's all right." I went and did some other story, and the next day there was a big headline about this poll showing Koch way up that another reporter wrote, someone who had nothing to do with political coverage. My legitimate piece about whatever was going on in the campaign at the time was in the paper, buried somewhere. This phony or exaggerated poll got a big headline—it was blasted on page one or two or three. That's how it worked, and it was troubling.

JOHN LoCICERO: It had never been done before, that a newspaper would use the front page like that to endorse a candidate. Not that I remember. The endorsement was usually on the editorial page.

HAROLD HOLZER, former press secretary for Bella Abzug: There was an inevitable moment, when something was gonna happen. Something did: the blackout, and the street demonstrations following the blackout. That's when the *Post* began doing page-one editorials, which had never happened in the city before. Pro-Koch, page-one editorials not only about safety issues, but about this fake issue of the right to strike, which Koch made a major issue with the *Post*'s support, or at least gave it lots of coverage. The idea was that Bella would not prevent the police and uniformed services from striking. She tried to clarify her position—no one can force labor in this country, since the Emancipation

ༀ

Proclamation and the Thirteenth Amendment—but it didn't resonate. She was pounded from that day until the primary by the *Post*. My guess is, and I've never confirmed this, is that the *Post* felt that the *Times* had a mayoral candidate in Mario Cuomo, and they wanted a mayoral candidate. It wasn't going to be Bella. She was too left for the Murdoch group. It was very tough from then on to get a news story that means anything if page one is going to be a pro-Koch, anti-Bella editorial. I think the first one was not even marked "editorial" until the jump. I remember raising furious objections to that.

CLYDE HABERMAN: Murdoch did something that we hadn't seen since the days of the press barons. He decided, "I'm going to make this guy mayor."

JOYCE PURNICK: Murdoch resurrected a kind of political coverage—and politically skewed coverage—that the city had seen in the past, but with only three or four newspapers left, it was like the old days, but on steroids. And it was a departure from what anyone who came along in the '60s and '70s had ever seen. If you look at yellow journalism, look at Hearst; it's not exactly new, but it was a new take on an old approach.

> The final stages of the mayoral election were the most cutthroat. Koch, who was gay but remained in the closet for the entirety of his political career, had been showing up at events with Bess Myerson, a former beauty queen and, under Mayor John Lindsay, the first commissioner of New York City's Department of Consumer Affairs. Koch's campaign did not deny speculation that he and Myerson were a couple, but rumors of Koch's sexuality made the rounds, and signs emblazoned with "Vote for Cuomo, not the homo" reportedly appeared in Queens. Certain Koch supporters countered with a sound truck that drove through the city's Jewish neighborhoods blaring false claims that Cuomo was endorsed by the mafia. For its part, the *Post* relentlessly pushed Koch as the most viable candidate.

GEORGE ARZT: Don't forget there were three elections that year. It was a seven-person race in the Democratic primary. Then a run-off between Koch and Cuomo [which Koch won]. And then Cuomo ran on the Liberal Party line, so it was Koch and Cuomo again [vying for left-wing votes] for the general election. [Roy Goodman ran on the Republican ticket.] By the end of this, the anti-Cuomo stuff [in the *Post*] became vituperative. It started making all of us rather uncomfortable.

JOYCE PURNICK: It was not honest journalism, and I believe that the only thing that keeps us free as a society is honest, straight journalism. It's a critical part of our democracy. I hate to get on my high horse, but I felt that Murdoch was polluting our journalism.

> Koch won the general election on November 8—the day after yet another *Post* front-page editorial in his favor. For many *Post* reporters, the coverage was so over-the-top, they organized an official protest.

JOYCE PURNICK: Reporters at the *Post* who were very troubled by the coverage put together a petition complaining about the coverage. I signed even though I was one of the main people covering the campaign. They weren't criticizing my coverage; they were criticizing the general coverage.

PETER FREIBERG, reporter, 1971–1978: I signed. Absolutely. I couldn't care what Murdoch did in editorials because I disagreed with a fair number of the old *Post* editorials. But the Koch coverage was so slanted.

JOYCE PURNICK: As one of the two lead political reporters covering that campaign, my copy was not touched, but it was surrounded by, in effect, Koch propaganda. Murdoch could always say, "Ask Joyce. Ask her if I ever influenced, touched, or changed her copy." He never said it in those words, but that was the implication. And the truth is he didn't—but it didn't matter. It was like being on a little island surrounded by polluted waters.

GEORGE ARZT: The coverage *was* overdone, they were right.

JOYCE PURNICK: At the time of the petition, Koch was coming in [to the *Post*'s office] that day, I think for lunch with Murdoch. I either was there or I briefly said hello to Koch in Murdoch's presence. Murdoch turned to Koch and said, "Joyce is one of the people who signed a petition saying our coverage was unfair and was too positive and too favorable toward you." I remember Koch saying, "Gee, I thought the coverage was fair," or something like that. He played dumb. He knew exactly what was going on. Of course, he benefited tremendously from it. And he benefited from Murdoch once he became mayor because Murdoch was on his side.

RAVAGING BEASTS

"Sam Sleeps," Page Six,
Roy Cohn, Studio 54

Murdoch may have offered a mea culpa to *MORE*, the journalism review, regarding some of the *Post*'s more outrageous Son of Sam coverage, but he didn't pump the brakes. Beginning in December 1977, Steve Dunleavy, photo editor Susan Welchman, and Murdoch lieutenant Peter Michelmore, who in November had become the *Post*'s metropolitan editor, found themselves embroiled in a scandal involving Son of Sam David Berkowitz. It was the kind of story that the *Post* and Page Six would have played big—were a number of the paper's top editors not on the hot seat. James Mitteager, a cop-turned-freelance-reporter interested in landing a job at the paper, told the *Post*'s editors he had contacts inside Kings County Hospital, where David Berkowitz was being held in the psychiatric unit. Over a period of months, Mitteager provided the *Post* with information on Berkowitz's life in captivity. Then, with money and a small spy camera provided by the tabloid, he arranged for a prison guard to take photos of Berkowitz in his cell.

SUSAN WELCHMAN, photo editor, 1977–1979: I showed Mitteager how to put [the camera] on the guard. It was a Minox that belonged to a woman I lived with. It was the cutest little camera. I taped the f-stop so it wouldn't move, and gave him a cable release for the guard to put down his sleeve. The lens was under his tie. He got just a couple of frames, maybe three, of Berkowitz on the bed. The wood was SAM SLEEPS. Dunleavy must have paid the guard. He knew everybody, and he knew somebody who knew somebody.

DICK BELSKY, metropolitan editor, 1970–1989: I remember Bob Spitzler coming to me on like a Friday, saying we have this great story for Monday, and this great headline. He writes it down and shows me: "Sam Sleeps." He's like, "Oh, yeah. It's great. We've got these pictures of him on his cot, it's exclusive stuff." Everybody was excited. Of course, it turned into a shitstorm because there was an investigation, and a lot of people turned against the *Post*, saying, "This is why the *Post* is too sensational." It was that one moment where everybody had taken it a little too far. All Bob had done was write the headline. Peter Michelmore had arranged the rest.

> Not long after the pictures were published on December 5, 1977, the *Post* landed in legal trouble. Mitteager was arrested on charges that he had bribed a corrections officer to get the photos.

SUSAN WELCHMAN: After that photo ran, they tried to prosecute us, and we had to go to court. I thought, oh shit, my number's up. I'm going to jail. But Rupert had very good lawyers at that time. I remember Ira Sorkin saying, "The most important thing is don't answer what they don't ask you. Answer only what they ask you." When I got to the stand, I was so nervous. I remember exactly what I had on—this blue-green skirt and top that belonged to my roommate. It was really expensive. I had high heels on, and my hair was kind of short. I acted like the femme fatale that I wasn't. I thought that might help me. But in our heart of hearts, I think everybody involved knew nothing was really going to happen to us. Because if you get next to Rupert, Big Daddy's going to take care of it.

IRA LEE SORKIN, former partner, Squadron, Ellenoff, Plesent & Lehrer, the law firm that represented Murdoch: I have no recollection of that, to be honest with you. Zero.

> Executives from the *Post*, including Welchman and Michelmore, testified in a pretrial hearing that the *Post* had no idea the camera and cash given to Mitteager would be used to commit a crime. Even Murdoch appeared, testifying that he was out of the country when the photo shoot was arranged. Steve Dunleavy said he would appear in court but was nowhere to be found when it came time to serve him with a subpoena. The *Post* employees escaped prosecution, and the trial, which didn't take place until November 1979, led to Mitteager's acquittal. One juror told the *New York Times* that part of the reason for the verdict was "the

wrong defendant was on trial—the feeling was that the *Post* should have been on trial." The *Post* did not report on the court proceedings.

Around this time, Steve Dunleavy was hospitalized with a broken ankle. The story of how the injury occurred became legend—one of many tales associated with the hard-drinking, hard-living, hard-loving Dunleavy. His former *Post* colleague Jane Perlez had an account of the incident in her *Soho Weekly News* column, Mixed Media.

One snowy evening, Dunleavy and two women were drinking at Elaine's, the Upper East Side hangout popular with writers and celebrities. After closing the place, they were waiting for a cab when a van came by and clipped them. It was "driven by a colored boy," Dunleavy told Perlez from his hospital bed, where his leg was in a cast: "The poor bastard looked terrified." Later versions said Dunleavy had been having sex in a snow drift with one of the women—possibly both—when a city snowplow ran over his foot. "I hope it's not his writing foot," Pete Hamill remarked when he heard the news.

WAYNE DARWEN, assistant managing editor, 1983–1987: Dunleavy is notorious for screwing my then-fiancée in the snow outside Elaine's. I found out about it from Liz Smith, who woke me up early in the morning to ask what I thought about Dunleavy and my girlfriend getting hit by a snowplow outside Elaine's while they were screwing in the snow. I think I might have said, "I have to get back to you on that one." It was like, okay, it's among mates, and Dunleavy's Dunleavy. I probably would have done the same thing to him. We had a bit of a laugh about it, and life went on.

STEVE DUNLEAVY, reporter, 1977–1986, 1993–2008: Actually, Liz Smith spiked the story. Wayne Darwen was screwing this bird. We met at Costello's, and I don't know that he's screwing her, because I would never screw a mate's girl. When I say never. Never. Never. Never. We go to Elaine's. It's got to be 1978, during a blizzard. I turn her on for the boys. I did not fuck her. That's true. Because in my mind, she was my friend's bird. Never ever screw a bird of my friend. But I did go across the road to a place that was then called The Viking. Jesus Christ, it's cold, and a couple of guys are saying, "Yeah, yeah, you're a tough guy." "No, I'm not. I don't want to fight." Two chicks come up and one says, "I'll bet you can't get it up in the snowbank." "Yeah, I can." I stood up. I have an overcoat on. And we got hit. The snowplow threw me up, then this Black guy in a Volkswagen— like a van—with no snow tires hits me and I take off like a ski. The van ran over my leg and broke it in seventeen places. This poor fucking Black guy's going, shit, that's all I need. I just killed a white guy. He's shitting his pants. Actually, he was a very very decent, quiet man. I wiggled my toes, wiggled my fingers. My leg was broken everywhere, but I was all right. When some lawyer came and said, "Sue him for his house," I said, "You sue him, and I'll cut your ears off." Whose fault was it? Mine.

WAYNE DARWEN: Well. He was there. I wasn't. Ha! But he seems to contradict himself about whether he knew she was my girl—my fiancée, actually. On one hand he says he didn't know; on the other, he says he wouldn't have done it because we were mates. Pick a hand. All snow under the plow now, you might say.

DAVE BANKS, night managing editor, 1979–1981: In Dunleavy, Rupert sees the youth he never had himself—the larrikinism. In Australian terms, a "larrikin" is a hoodlum—a bit of a semi-criminal but almost a lovable semi-criminal. I think Rupert loved that side of Australia that he never experienced because he came from a rather upper-class family. He came from the land-owning, wealthy people of Australia, the upper classes—Dame Elisabeth, Sir Keith—his parents. They were very grand people.

ERIC FETTMANN, associate editorial page editor, 1976–1991, 1993–2019: Murdoch's an Australian. You do know the history of Australia? And who they are all descended from?

> Speaking at a luncheon for the Overseas Press Club in January 1978, Murdoch said the only problem with the *Post* was that it had not changed enough. His goal, he said, was not "senile survival" but an "animated, diverse, and controversial paper that could never be accused of being boring." A glance at copies of the *Post* from early 1978 proves Murdoch's point. Plenty of content could have been published in the Schiff era, including front pages on Mideast peace talks and Soviet satellites, both generated by Associated Press wire copy. Page Six, a Murdoch-era original brand, was an exception, and arguably the tabloid's principal mischief-maker. The column continued to gain traction and audience, its cheeky tone set by its editor, Neal Travis.

STEVE DUNLEAVY: Rupert Murdoch had a great affection for Neal's, I won't say arrogance, but the very fact that Neal would always say, "Ah, mate, that's the headline." And walk away. Not arrogant but assertive.

CLAUDIA COHEN, Page Six editor, 1977–1980: Neal used to say that it hadn't been a good day if he hadn't pissed off at least one person he was writing about.

COL ALLAN, editor in chief, 2001–2016; editorial adviser, 2019–2021: In those days, Neal had written a very successful book, *Manhattan*, and he'd become one of the rich folks. And he started doing a little bit of coke. He wouldn't mind me telling this story because it's all true. He was at Elaine's one night and he went into the bathroom, which is a very small place. Keith Richards is standing there taking a leak. Neal, who at this stage figured he was one of the stars, not just somebody who watched the stars, pulled out a foil thing loaded with his coke and said to Keith: "You want to do a line?" Keith Richards famously replied: "I don't do street shit." Neal Travis never forgot him for the insult. For years, if he could find anything bad about Keith Richards, he wrote it.

When Travis departed in 1978, his deputy, Claudia Cohen, took over the column.

DAVID ROSENTHAL, reporter, desk editor, 1974–1977: It was thought widely that Claudia was working at the *Post* because Rupert was wooing her family. Her main calling card and credential was Hudson News [the largest distributor of newspapers and magazines on the East Coast, owned by Robert Cohen, Claudia's father]. I don't think she was taken kindly to for that reason.

CLAUDIA COHEN: I think my tone differed significantly from Neal. I took the position that a gossip column had to have a real point of view. I didn't want it to be full of pats on the back to various Hollywood celebrities who were always written about in the most adoring way possible. I extended that to all celebrities. Therefore, the tone of my column was provocative—some thought highly provocative—and as irreverent as I could possibly make it.

STEVE CUOZZO, executive editor, columnist, 1972–current: Fred Silverman was the NBC programmer who became, in a lot of ways, the first media superstar. He had worked for Paley at CBS, and then he went to NBC and became president of NBC. So, in 1979, '80, maybe, the city's attention was focused on this guy. There was nothing charismatic about him—he was a schlub. But, because there was so much expectation about his programming genius, everybody was watching to see if his lineup of shows on NBC would do well. It was a phenomenon at the time, and a lot of that phenomenon was chronicled on Page Six.

One of Claudia's most famous stories was about how fat Fred Silverman was, standing around the pool at the Beverly Hills Hotel. That was important, because the New York media, and thus the public, was once again conscious of the possibility of its executive corps as celebrities.

CLAUDIA COHEN: I used to say that when you were reading Page Six, you should feel as if you were tiptoeing down the corridors of power and listening in at the doors. We used to write about corporate leaders almost as if they were movie stars.

CHARLIE CARILLO, reporter, columnist, 1978–1993: You'd walk by Page Six, and she'd be doing her eyebrows or eyelashes in the inverted mirror. I had to answer the phones for her one day, and she kept saying, "I'm not here. I'm not here." She had a way on the phone of saying loudly, "Are you *kidding*?" She had to get everybody's attention with whatever she was doing. I don't remember her as a terribly likable person, but she was a force there, at least for a while.

SUSAN MULCAHY, Page Six editor, 1978–1985: She would become obsessed by some minor thing someone had done or said to her, and then go after them in the column. Like, she had it in for Maureen Connelly, who worked for Ed Koch.

MAUREEN CONNELLY, former press secretary for Ed Koch: Some reporter at the *Post* told me, "Claudia Cohen screams out about you in the newsroom, 'Maureen Connelly is an anti-Semite.'" When they told me that, I said, "Frankly, the only thing I like about her is her religion." Let's just say I practiced social distancing with Claudia. I never wanted to be within six miles of her.

> One Page Six source tiptoeing down the corridors of power and phoning in what he saw was none other than Joe McCarthy's shine-headed henchman, Roy Cohn. Once scorned in the pages of Dorothy Schiff's *Post*, he had become a regular presence in the tabloid's pages and hallways.

CLAUDIA COHEN: One of my best sources was Roy Cohn. I had started writing about the parties that Roy Cohn gave, and I would list the names of all the judges who were there. Many lawyers might have been embarrassed by such a thing, but not Roy. He loved it and started inviting me to cover every single party he had. And then he started having these huge parties at Studio 54 with all the power brokers around town. He was grist for great stories because of his parties and because he loved seeing his name on the Page so much that he would also become a source for great stories. Nobody knew where more bodies were buried in New York City than Roy Cohn. I would go so far as to say that he was my number one source while I was writing the column. He could tell you what was going on in the judiciary, in politics, in the world of celebrities, in the world of lawsuits. He knew everything.

DICK BELSKY: The first time I went out with Claudia, we sat in Roy Cohn's box at Yankee Stadium.

CINDY ADAMS, gossip columnist, 1981–current: One night, Roy was giving a dinner in one of the houses of one of the people who had suddenly gone to the can [prison]. Everyone with Roy went to the can. The house was in Queens. It was a small party of twenty-five to thirty people, and there were little round tables of five. I'm sitting at one of the tables, and this big guy is sitting next to me and on the other side of him is a blonde whose neckline ended here. Nobody knows anybody. I said, "Who are you?" He said, "My name is Donald Trump." I said, "What's a Donald Trump?" I'd never heard of Donald, and I didn't know who he was. Roy was standing behind Donald and heard me say it. He said, "One day, this kid is going to own New York." Remember that story.

FRANK RICH, film critic, 1975–1977: The chicken-and-egg question between Trump, Murdoch, and Roy Cohn is absolutely fascinating. Roy Cohn saw something in Donald Trump, who, after all, was a somewhat empty vessel. He didn't exist as the Donald Trump we know now. Cohn saw this hustler from Queens who had a chip on his shoulder and who also had money—at least purported to have money. Which is what Cohn cared about. At the same time, Cohn and Murdoch had a connection. Cohn frequently used the *Post* to plug clients, air grievances, attack other people, and he would be very valuable to someone like Murdoch who, after all, was a foreigner in New York and needed those connections. It's kind of a perfect storm that they came together. In some ways it seems to me happenstance, if we are to believe the story that Trump met Cohn basically hobnobbing around at East Side clubs, and then, of course, Murdoch and Cohn would have found each other in a second because their interests were identical—not just politically, but power, fixing things, all the rest of it. And yes, it had an influence on larger journalism. Although we can't forget that even pre-Murdoch, the *Times* ran that incredible profile of Trump that was full of complete my-thology on every single subject, none of it challenged by the *Times*. He was Swedish. He talked about millions of dollars of real estate holdings he didn't have. The other thing I learned doing a *New York* magazine piece [on Trump and Cohn] is that Roy Cohn was very connected to Abe Rosenthal, the tyranni-cal editor of the *Times*, whose reign overlapped Murdoch's rise. Cohn was also, from childhood and high school, a friend of [Condé Nast owner] Si Newhouse's. What's fascinating is the *Times*, including Abe Rosenthal, openly disdained the *Post* and looked down on it as scum, and publications in Newhouse's stable—notably the *New Yorker*—would never approve of Murdoch. But the fact is, that, at that level of power and fixing and trying to gain influence in New York, they were all in that same pool with some overlapping interests.

From the moment Steve Rubell and Ian Schrager opened Studio 54 in 1977, the nightclub would become the short-lived social equivalent of Page Six: the nightclub where the rich, the powerful, the beautiful, and the freaky came together—often in the biblical sense. It was a voyeur's paradise and a petri dish for the new society that would rule New York in the '80s and '90s. The Page Sixers were all over the scene, as Steve Dunleavy used to say, "like tinsel," as were other *Post* reporters and photographers. Studio 54 fed the *Post* and the *Post* returned the favor.

JAMI BERNARD, chief movie critic, 1978–1993: I was already home from a full day's work, it was after two a.m. The news desk called me and said, "Get to Studio 54." In those days, we never said no. I never said, "I don't know what I'm doing." I never said, "I don't want to" or "I have school in the morning." You just did it. They threw you in the deep end, which was in fact a good thing. That was how we learned. Because no one sat us down and said, "Oh, this is how you do it, honey." It was "Get your ass to Studio 54."

SUSAN MULCAHY: The first time I realized the power of Page Six, I was rejected getting into Studio 54. I was supposed to go to a party there and it was my first time. Rubell and Schrager were still running it. Claudia calls and gets my name on the list. I got there, stood around like a pathetic little dweeb, and, guess what, I didn't get in! I come in the next morning and Claudia's like, "So, how was your first visit to Studio 54?" I said, "Actually I didn't get in." She said "*What?*" She called up Rubell, she called [54 doorman] Marc Benecke. I got so many flowers that day my desk looked like a funeral parlor. After that, I never had a problem.

JAMI BERNARD: For a short time, I was the Studio 54 beat reporter because I loved to dance. My big story was the night [Prime Minister] Pierre Trudeau was losing the elections in Canada. And Maggie—those are the parents of Justin Trudeau—Maggie was a little nuts, or maybe just unmedicated. I think it turned out she was bipolar. So that night that [her husband] was losing the election for prime minister, she was expected at Studio 54. They sent me there. A whole bunch of reporters from the other papers were there, and she arrives surrounded by bodyguards. I asked Don Singleton from the *News* to hold my purse, and I went over to her and asked her to dance. Part of it was to get her away from the other reporters so I could have a scoop. And part of it was because I wanted to dance. She enveloped me with the bodyguards in this weird sort of big group hug. She said, "You are one of us." We danced. The famous picture of her in white? I was dancing with her. Of course, they cut me out of the picture.

ADAM SCULL, photographer, 1978–1981, 1985–1988: I was a ravaging beast. Nothing else in life mattered than getting my photos into the *New York Post*. It was the Holy Grail for me as a freelance photographer. I did everything. I was right up a chick's pussy. I'm not ashamed to admit it. It was the greatest job in the universe. Every night was an anecdote. Robert De Niro busting the camera of one of the paparazzi because he was so full of piss and vinegar. Bianca Jagger coming in on her white horse. The daughter of [a US Senator] boogieing topless out by the DJ booth. When it came to other photographers, I said, screw everybody. I was hungry, and I wanted to make money. I would go to Studio 54, get page one or page three the next day, and [the other photographers] would be fuming. The competition between UPI, the *Post*, and the *News* was ferocious.

6 | SEVERANCE

Editorial Exodus, Modernization, a Strike, Kelvin

As Murdoch's methods took root, the departures of Schiff-era staffers escalated. The Newspaper Guild's agreement with the tabloid shielded most of them from being fired for all but egregious offenses, so they could have stayed as long as those protections remained in place. But many left because they refused to capitulate to the *Post*'s new direction.

JOYCE WADLER, feature writer, 1974–1977: That fall, which was '77, I started freelancing for the *Washington Post*'s Style section. And my rent was $325 a month. I took a leave of absence and thought I could survive as a freelancer. I was about to be thirty. By that time, it was like I was one of the last few out of Poland.

LINDSY VAN GELDER, feature writer, 1968–1977: Murdoch drove me out, though he liked me. When he came in, I had a reputation of doing fairly grandstanding reportorial things. I did a number of undercover stories. One time I disguised myself as a high school student. This was when there was a lot of ferment in the public schools, and I went to class for a few weeks and reported that drugs were sold, and teachers were racist—things that were a bigger deal than they would be now. Another time I got a tip that somebody in—I think it was a presidential campaign—was actually running a massage parlor, and I went and applied for a job as a masseuse. Murdoch thought I was one of his people. He told me he loved my stuff, and he thought we had a great future together. But we really didn't, because I soon began getting assignments that were really troubling. I think now a lot of newspapers have rules that reporters cannot take a political stand on anything. Under the Dolly Schiff *Post*, the rule was, you disqualify yourself if you take sides. For instance, there was a point where I ceased to be somebody who reported on the feminist movement. I became an active feminist and so I couldn't cover those stories anymore. I think it was completely reasonable. [After Murdoch took over] I got an assignment to write a big profile of Carol Bellamy, who was running for city council president. I went to the editors and said, "You know, I really can't do this, I've donated to her campaign." They quickly let me know that this would not be a problem. I did the story, but I didn't feel right about it. The next one was even more creepy. They wanted me to write a puff piece about Merit cigarettes. I think I smoked them at one point when I was still a smoker. They were supposed to be better for you than Marlboro. It was clearly some completely naked pitch for advertising. There were a few others like that, and at some point, I just felt I had to leave. I got three part-time jobs and left in November of '77.

AIDA ALVAREZ, reporter, 1973–1977: I quit the paper because of what they did to a story I wrote. They changed the facts and turned it into a sensational lede that had nothing to do with reality. I wasn't about to write fiction for the *Post* [and] it was the last story I ever wrote for them. I said, the only thing I have is my reputation. And if people that I interviewed see what's happened to the story, nobody's going to want to talk to me.

Perhaps with the goal of creating (as he'd told the Overseas Press Club) an "animated, diverse, and controversial paper," Murdoch decided to lay off or buy out a large group of Newspaper Guild members. In April of 1978, Peter Michelmore called staffers, one by one, into his office to offer them buyouts. Some who took the money portrayed their departures as self-orchestrated, but the fact was, Murdoch wanted to trim the workforce. If unhappy journalists were among those heading out the door, all the better.

TONY MANCINI, reporter, 1958–1978: I'd been under the Murdoch regime for just about a year when one of my friends, Jan Hodenfield, went into Peter Michelmore's office and announced that he couldn't stand it anymore: could he have severance? They said, "Sure." And then the floodgates opened. I was the next one. As far as I know, it wasn't [an idea initiated by the Murdoch people]. But they were happy to get rid of us.

JOE BERGER, investigative reporter, 1971–1978: This was a union shop, so our jobs were protected, but we said we'd be willing to leave if they gave us severance. When I quit, I told Peter Michelmore—and he was a nice guy to deal with—you guys had a chance here to produce a worthy newspaper and it's very, very upsetting to see the kinds of things you're doing with the paper we love. He just nodded.

JOYCE PURNICK, political reporter, 1970–1978: When Joe and the others left, I said, "I want out." There was a period when they had to want you to go in order for you to get a little bit of financial cushion. They didn't want me to go. I had a good reputation. I was considered a straight reporter and whatever else was going on with the paper, they wanted to be able to say, "Read Joyce Purnick. We're not doing anything to her copy." They would not give me the severance. I went to Roger Wood. He said, "Stay for three months, and if at the end of the three months, you feel that this is not the place for you, we will give you what we're giving to the others." I said, "I want it in writing"—something I'd never done in my life. He put it in writing and I stayed the three months and then I got the severance.

A month later, another group was fired outright.

ERIC FETTMANN, associate editorial page editor, columnist, 1976–1991, 1993–2019: In the spring of '78, management decided to trim the staff by laying off people who'd been there less than two years—which was allowed under an appendix to the Newspaper Guild contract that said that they could reduce the workforce in the case of economic necessity. I got a call from Joy Cook [Newspaper Guild rep] at home. She said, "They exercised [the appendix in the contract] and this is your two-week notice that you're gone." So that night I called in sick. Back then, you had to give them a reason. I said, "Tell 'em it's my appendix." [Fettmann was rehired later that year.]

Guild members whose names appeared on the "voluntary resignation" list but declined to accept the buyout found themselves assigned to less appealing beats or new schedules—for example, being moved from days to the lobster shift. Those without union protection who weren't valued by the new regime were simply shown the door. New employees were also sought.

NICK PILEGGI, author, screenwriter, former *New York* magazine writer: As I said, I would talk to Murdoch once a week when he came by *New York* magazine's offices. At a certain point, he said, "Magazines are for sissies. Come on down to the *Post*. I pull up my sleeves every morning, I get in there. You've got ink in your blood. You've got to come." It was a great sales pitch. But I didn't go.

Of the many Schiff-era staffers who stayed at the *Post*, some were young and just starting out and saw opportunity. Others felt they had no choice.

DAVID SEIFMAN, City Hall bureau chief and political editor, 1973–2019: I was one of the wait-and-sees because [Murdoch] obviously had a reputation, but remember, I was just becoming a reporter. I was thrilled at the chance to do this. I was just starting out.

JOYCE PURNICK: Joe Rab had aged out. He wasn't going to get hired anywhere else at that stage of his career. He had to support himself and his wife. I was in a great position, Joe Berger was in a great position, Josh Friedman, who won a Pulitzer subsequently at *Newsday*—we were in great positions. We were young, our careers were just starting, we had good reputations. We were going to land on our feet. Joe Rab, I don't know how old he was at the time that Murdoch came, but his career was starting to wind down, same with Jerry Tallmer. It was very sad. They had great standards, they were very talented, and they just had to hang on by their fingernails.

JOANNE WASSERMAN, reporter, 1977–1986: Richard Gooding was angry because he'd only been recruited right before Murdoch bought the paper. He showed me clips. He wrote this amazing story for the old *Post* about this old Jewish couple in the Bronx, in some changing neighborhood, who were so freaked out by what was happening and all the violence and the crime, that they put out the clothes they wanted to be buried in and they killed themselves. He had this amazing story written in the old *Post* style, where you don't really find out until the fourth or fifth graph what this is about. He had shown me that story. As if to say, "This is why I came here. These are the sorts of stories about New York I thought I was going to be able to write." He was furious.

RICHARD GOODING, metropolitan editor, 1976–1993: I have no recollection of telling her that. It *was* a tense time, with so much of the great talent at the *Post* working on exit strategies. But I was too new—no way out.

> The departure of the old guard led to a drastic culture shift; it was almost as though the *Post* had converted to a new religion.

ERIC FETTMANN: The *Post* always specialized in street-smart reporters, but it was a different type of street-smart under Dolly than you had under Murdoch. [Schiff's] *Post* was a different kind of mentality—more intellectual without being pompous intellectual. Under Dolly, everyone was Jewish, even the people who weren't Jewish. With Murdoch, everybody was Irish, even the people who weren't.

ADAM SCULL, photographer, 1978–1981, 1985–1988: Rupert has the entire South Street newsroom refurbished to look like Mutual of Omaha except he stops dead in his tracks at the darkroom. No renovation, beige paint peeling off the walls. Everybody else had these new VDTs [video display terminals]. We had old Royal typewriters [to type descriptions of photo subjects] with ink ribbons that were so dried out we couldn't even use them. It was like a darkroom from the nineteenth century. We got treated like shit.

PAT SULLIVAN, reporter, night editor, 1972–1980: When Murdoch came in, he said, clean this place up. So they brought in contractors—nothing major, but they fixed it up a bit. And of course, typical newsroom, within two days, it's a shithole. I remember Murdoch coming back one time from an overnight flight from LA and walking through the place about four, five, six in the morning. It's a shithole again. He's walking through and he's picking up coffee cups and looking at us, going, "Fucking journalists," in his Australian accent.

> No one event defined the end of the transition from the old *Post* to the new, though the departure of managing editor Bob Spitzler in the spring of 1978 served as a potent symbol. Spitzler tried to assimilate, and some of his actions were in sync with the Murdoch style, but in the end, he, too, was forced out.

ERIC FETTMANN: Spitzler wanted to keep his job, so he tried to be as good a friend as possible. At one point [Pete] Hamill had written this piece about Murdoch, describing him as the drunk uncle who throws up all over the table. Of course, anytime somebody high-profile took a knock at the *Post* or Murdoch, they immediately had to get even. Spitzler pulled something out of his desk that he had been keeping for years. It was a column Hamill had written when Jackie Kennedy married [Greek shipping magnate Aristotle] Onassis. It was a hysterical rant about how she had disgraced the memory of our greatest president, in typical over-the-top Hamill form. He had written the column for the *Post*, and they decided it was *too* over-the-top and spiked it. But Spitzler had kept the hard copy. At the time, Hamill and Jackie were a couple. The *Post* ran excerpts every day on Page Six [for a week] with the headline "Who wrote this?" Then, on the last day, they revealed it to be Pete Hamill.

DICK BELSKY, metropolitan editor, 1970–1989: Bob tried to make it work, and he had a relationship with Rupert. One day, he got a call from Murdoch to go see him on the sixth floor. When he came back, he had this look of shock on his face. He said, "I just got fired." I don't think he ever really knew why. He's supposed to [leave] immediately. He goes home and gets a call from somebody in *Post* management saying, "We know you're fired. But we don't have anybody to put the paper out tomorrow. Would you mind coming in one more day and putting out the paper?" Bob, being Bob, said, "Oh, sure, okay." He hangs up, thinks about it, calls them back, and says, "Screw you." Bob's firing was kind of inevitable and had a lot to do with his strengths. Bob was very popular and respected with a lot of the old *Post* people. [He was fired] during the period where they were starting to offer severance to people and trying to get some of the old *Post* people to leave. A lot of people looked to Bob—like, Bob's a good guy, so as long as he's here . . . I think the idea was, well, if he goes, then a lot of these other people that we want to go will leave, too. It was a culture change. Bob kind of got caught in the middle of that.

When Murdoch bought the *Post*, he had to agree to honor existing union contracts, though the function of many unions was becoming increasingly obsolete in the face of new technologies. But union leaders—especially of the craft unions, which included typesetters, mailers, and pressmen—had done their best to keep the future at bay. Video display terminals would replace most of the typewriters in the newsroom in 1978, and the entire printing process was well along the road to automation, but many workers whose duties had disappeared still had lifetime job guarantees thanks to agreements ironed out in the years following the 1962–1963 strike.

PAT SMITH, night city editor, 1977–1989: There was no big impact in the newsroom [moving from hot type to cold]. Issues around that had been settled some time before and the printers got lifetime job guarantees. So if you're working there, and you maybe had ten years in and had achieved some level of tenure, you had that job for life, even if you're no longer going to work at a Linotype machine and you're going to have to learn how to use an X-Acto blade to cut the copy and lay it out on a page.

CHARLIE CARILLO, reporter, columnist, 1978–1993: Everything had changed—the VDTs had come in, but some people, like Bernie Bard, insisted on writing on his typewriter with his cigarette in a holder—that clack, clack, clack. Trying to get into the future—it wasn't so easy for some of them.

PAT SMITH: I was there when they switched from hot type to cold type and reporters had to start working on computers. I remember coming into work one night and if you walked around the newsroom, what you heard was "tap-a-tap-a-tap-a, WAP, *shit*. Tap-a-tap-a-tap-a, WAP, *shit.*" What was happening was, as people typed on a computer, when the cursor came to the end of the line, instinctively, the left hand went up to throw the carriage. It was muscle memory. It took reporters who had been doing this for their entire lives several days to make their left hand stop doing that, because when they went to throw the carriage, what they were hitting was the side of the computer console and stinging their fingers. Every computer console had one, two, or three fingerprints on it, depending on the reporter's preference, how they threw the carriage.

DOMINICK MARRANO, chief paginator, 1971–2008: The compositors, who were part of the typographical union—a lot of those guys were deaf. The composing room, way back in the day when it was Linotype machines, was a pretty loud place to work. Those machines are always clicking and banging, so being deaf wasn't a handicap, it was almost an improvement. This was a trade deaf people learned, and they could work in a composing room because the noise didn't bother them as much. At one time the *Post* had probably close to a hundred people who were hearing-impaired, when it was a twenty-four-hour operation. When I worked makeup, I worked with those people. I knew a little sign language and everyone could read lips. They trusted me. Somehow or another I was accepted into this crew. They used to call me an honorary dummy.

KEN CHANDLER, editor in chief, publisher, 1978–1986, 1993–2002: They did their job better than the people who weren't disabled. One of them showed me some sign language, and I was later told that it meant "fuck off."

JIM WILLSE, former editor and publisher, New York *Daily News*: It used to be that [members of the mailers' union] tied the bundles of papers together and then carried them out to the truck. That's what a mailer was. But technology meant that the bundles of papers got tied automatically, put on conveyor belts, and fed into the trucks. The mailers, they probably had some work to do, but mostly what they did was stand there. As the bundles went by, they would touch them and that was known as bundle blessing. They were the bundle blessers.

CLYDE HABERMAN, reporter, 1966–1977: There were ten or eleven unions that the publisher had to sign contracts with. One by one, they each became a diminished influence as computers came into our lives. The only people you needed were the drivers. You still had to get the damn papers to the newsstands or to home delivery or whatever. You certainly did not need the [Newspaper] Guild.

In theory, the Newspaper Guild, the union representing editorial, advertising, circulation, and other departments, should have protected its members from discriminatory and arbitrary work practices, but as the power of unions faded, there was only so much union reps—in the '80s, Joy Cook and Barbara Yuncker—could do in a newsroom culture where a particularly cruel form of natural selection often prevailed. And, as some Guild members discovered, their protectors sometimes behaved more like adversaries than allies.

RAMONA GARNES, copy editor, 1978–1990, 2000–2004: I once got really upset with Joy [Cook] because I heard her say in the middle of the newsroom—I think to Ken Chandler: "Give Ramona a promotion because she's Black." I hit the ceiling and I started screaming: "Don't give me a promotion because I'm Black. Give me a promotion because I'm good." I had no love for the *New York Post* chapter of the Newspaper Guild.

HAL GOLDENBERG, photographer, 1979–1986: It's a Friday night. It's around midnight, and I'm about to get off work. There's a fire at a church in the East Village. I get a pretty decent picture of the priest standing in front of the building. I set it up, of course. In the background there's this church roaring away. I said, "Could you look upset?" He put his hand to his face and had a horrified look. Okay, that's page one, but there was no reporter. I call down to South Street and make Al Fayette—I used to call him Uncle Al—aware of the story. He said, "You need to start gathering information." I said, "Why?" He said, "Because

I ain't got nobody." I always kept a reporter's notebook in my camera bag for such occasions. I would gather information for a reporter who was late. I saved their asses a bunch of times. Al calls me on the radio and says, "You want to get in here soon because I'm holding this last edition for you." I said, "I'm on my way." There's nobody there except me and Al, so I had to develop my own film. I bring out three pictures and, of course, the one I set up was the one. Al put my name under the picture and gave me the byline. Boy, did I get shit from the union. If you're a photographer, you can't write stories and get a byline, and if you were a reporter, you couldn't take pictures and get a credit. Joy Cook called me. We were never friends to begin with because I'm anti-union. I grew up watching one newspaper after the other go out of business because the unions are greedy, and they greedy themselves out of business. Joy Cook called me and gave me a rash of shit. "You can't do that," she said. I said, "I understand I can't do that, but the boss told me to do it. Deal with him." I hung up on her.

GEORGE ARZT, City Hall bureau chief, 1968–1986: Roger [Wood] took me out of the union. He made my job, City Hall bureau chief, a supervisory job. Joy Cook and others attacked me, like I didn't want to be in the union. I'm not going to go along with Murdoch? What does she think I'm going to do? There was a trial, they ruled that it was a supervisory job. It was a horrendous period. Wayne Barrett [in the *Village Voice*] wrote about me, said I was fighting the union. I told him it was management. He said, "You still could have fought." I said, "Yeah, right, it's really in my blood to be a martyr."

JAMI BERNARD, chief movie critic, 1978–1993: I remember the Guild fighting for things like having our birthday off. It seems, in retrospect, so naive, you know? We had very good health insurance. I remember Barbara Yuncker yelling: "You don't realize how good you have it!" When I was twenty-eight, I had my gall-bladder out. Ten days in the hospital. I don't think I paid a dime.

JERRY CAPECI, reporter, organized crime, 1966–1986: I was a union guy, always, and I always wanted to get paid for the overtime I worked. One of the editors, Peter Michelmore, made sure that you either took time off or you didn't get paid. I said, "I'm not working." He put me on the lobster shift. I'd just had my third kid, and he put me on ten at night till five in the morning. I said, "Fuck you and the horse you came in on." I wrote stuff for *New York* magazine. I wrote a lot of mob stories. I broke a story about Funzi Tieri [a major figure in the Genovese crime family].

Eventually, Steve Dunleavy got me back on days. Whether I was allowed or not [to freelance for *New York* magazine], I did it. I was lucky because *New York* was owned by Rupert Murdoch. They were pissed off at me, but nothing happened.

DAN AQUILANTE, chief music critic, 1980–2012: There were a couple times we had slow-downs that weren't quite walkouts, where we were honoring another union's dispute. Nobody's working, but nobody's left the building, either. We were told not to leave. Just off the lobby, where the elevators were, there was an old horseshoe slot [known as the rim]. The slot man used to sit inside [the *U*] of this desk passing copy to people on the other side. So, someone pulls out a deck of cards and this hours-long game of acey-deucey began. If you don't know the game, you are dealt two cards, and the object is to be dealt a third card that's in between the other two. Amy Pagnozzi was just fucking killing it. Winning, winning, winning. That was when [being a union member] was kind of fun and games. It became very serious later.

> As financial losses at the *Post* mounted, Murdoch hinted that he might play hard-ball when union contracts came due at the end of March 1978, and in his public comments seemed almost eager for a strike. In his speech to the Overseas Press Club early that year, he declared that New York's three daily newspapers each employed twice as many workers as necessary. With many readers moving to the suburbs, where papers were mostly non-union, something had to give. Issues with the pressmen's union triggered the strike, which began on August 9, 1978. The other unions followed in support. It hit all three daily papers and lasted eighty-eight days. Non-union staffers—mostly editors—had to cross the picket line.

STEPHEN SILVERMAN, entertainment writer, 1977–1988: When the strike was announced and we had to clear the building, three of us grabbed our Rolodexes— me, Randy Smith, and Claudia [Cohen], who was sort of civil for once. We took a cab and went to Trader Vic's [at the Plaza Hotel]. Randy and I were concerned about the old paycheck. Claudia is gushing about how she *loves* the fact that she's gonna have all this free time: "Do you realize now I can go to lunch? Do you know how *long* it's been since I have been able to go to lunch?"

SUSAN MULCAHY, Page Six editor, 1978–1985: When picketing got boring, we'd go into the Post Mortem, the bar right next to the *Post*, or get sandwiches from Pete's. We left a lookout in case TV cameras showed up. Then we'd run out and start picketing again.

PHIL MUSHNICK, columnist, television sports, 1973–current: I still can't lose the weight I gained eating at Pete the Hero King's during the 1978 newspaper strike.

MARSHA KRANES, rewrite, editor, 1974–2005: I don't know that I should admit this, but I designed the T-shirt we wore during the strike—"Don't Waltz with Matilda."

DICK BELSKY: I don't think I ever had any issues but there were certain people, and Claudia [Cohen] was one, who would run into issues coming into the building through the pickets. The story I heard, maybe she told me, was about Joy Cook, who didn't like Claudia and vice versa, and who was a union leader at the time. Joy yelled at Claudia: "Hey, Claudia, how does it feel to be a scab." She yelled back, "I don't know, Joy. How does it feel to be fat?" I always thought that was perfect Claudia, you know.

RICHARD JOHNSON, Page Six editor, 1978–1990, 1993–2019: I got there in '78. I was hired as an editor [on the city desk]. They knew that a strike was coming and I came in as sort of a scab. I ended up crossing picket lines for several months. [I was] vaguely aware [of Page Six], but I wasn't planning on being a gossip columnist at that point. I was a hard news guy. I was probably dreaming of being the next Bob Woodward. Actually, he writes a lot of gossip.

> The strike allowed Murdoch to experiment. Right before it began in August, he printed a dummy paper without any input from union workers. For editorial staff, he borrowed non-union people from the *Post*, including Steve Dunleavy; he brought in employees from Australia and Great Britain; and he also imported talent from his other American properties, including the newspapers in San Antonio and *Star* magazine.

KEN CHANDLER: I think they had the idea that maybe they could keep publishing the *Post*, because they'd just installed computers. So they transferred me and a couple of other people over from *Star* to be copy editors at the *Post* in 1978. Of course, it didn't work, they couldn't produce the newspaper. For the first, maybe, three months, I sat around the office playing cards, and drinking with Dunleavy in the afternoon. It wasn't a bad life.

DICK BELSKY: That's when Claudia and I started hanging out, during the strike. That's when we started going out. We had to show up for work every day. We would basically sit around.

KELVIN MACKENZIE, night managing editor, 1978–1979: I don't know how long [Belsky] went out with her—for about half an hour, I think.

DICK BELSKY: In those days, most people lived paycheck to paycheck. When Claudia and I started going out, it was a whole other world. The first time I went over to her place, there was some kind of little table in the living room. There was this whole stack of envelopes on it. Like thirty envelopes, or whatever. I said, "What's that?" She's like, "That's all my paychecks. I gotta cash them at some point." She never even bothered to cash her paychecks! She didn't need them. When I was looking for an apartment, I said, "I found this place, but it's more than I can afford." She said, "You should take it anyway. You should move some of your money from your stocks to wherever." I said, "I don't have those things! I only have my paycheck!" She never understood that most people didn't live like she did. She just took that all for granted. It was kind of adorable. She didn't do it arrogantly or anything. Another time, she was packing to go to Palm Beach. I said, "What's all that?" She said, "I need fourteen bathing suits." I said, "Why do you need fourteen?" She said, "I'm going to be there for two weeks and I wouldn't wear the same bathing suit twice."

ERIC FETTMANN: Everybody thought it was bizarre [that Belsky was dating Claudia]. Nobody understood it. But then again, she went out with some eclectic guys. Remember her and Chuck Schumer?

JOE CONASON, former reporter, *The Village Voice*: Wayne Barrett [*Village Voice* columnist] died the day before Trump's inaugural in 2017. It was like he couldn't live in a world in which Trump was president. But that's not the point of this story. Even though Wayne was always going after politicians in the *Voice*, a lot of them came to the funeral and spoke, including Chuck Schumer, who got a big laugh telling the story of how he met Wayne. Schumer had been dating this "fancy" woman and she asked if he wanted to go to a birthday party at the "21" Club. Schumer was a New York State assemblyman then. I think he called himself a simple boy from Brooklyn. He's excited to go to the "21" Club. When he and his date get there, this reporter standing outside—who turned out to be Wayne—practically tackles him, asking why he's at this particular party. The fancy woman was Claudia Cohen, and the party turned out to be for her pal Roy Cohn. Schumer said it took a long time to convince Wayne he was *not* Roy Cohn's spy in the state assembly. After that, Schumer said he never again dated a fancy woman.

All three papers were off the streets until October, when Murdoch employed a similar strategy to the one Dolly Schiff had used during the 1963 strike and broke away from the other publishers by brokering a "me too" deal with the pressmen's union—agreeing to abide by the eventual deal they would make with the *Times* and the *Daily News*. This allowed him to start printing again, and for a month, the *Post* had the city's newspaper audience all to itself. "Monopoly is a terrible thing—until you have it," Murdoch told the *New Yorker* as he reveled in advertising and circulation gains, not only at the *Post* but at the *Village Voice* and *New York* magazine. He also invested in the *Daily Metro*, one of several strike papers. But when the journalists producing it (some of them striking *New York Times* employees) discovered his involvement, and his interest in buying the *Daily Metro* when the strike ended, perhaps to turn it into a non-union paper to replace the *Post*, many walked off the job. Seizing every opportunity, Murdoch started a Sunday paper as well—though it did not last once the *News* and the *Times* returned to newsstands in November—and he put together the infrastructure for a new morning paper, the *Daily Sun*.

ERIC FETTMANN: When the *Daily Metro* died, Murdoch tried to start another morning paper. They hired people—mostly Aussies and Brits—and they announced plans for a paper called the *Daily Sun* that would have been a morning paper. Frankly, the *Post* would not have survived or they would have merged. But the unions ended up blocking it. Murdoch wanted it to be a non-union paper.

HARVEY ARATON, sportswriter, basketball, 1977–1982: When we all got back to work before the *Daily News* and the *Times*, there was this whole other staff getting ready to publish a morning paper that he was going to use to eventually, or hopefully, challenge the *Daily News*. It never got off the ground because he couldn't reach deals with, I think, the drivers' or the pressmen's unions. All of a sudden, all those people just disappeared overnight.

BOB YOUNG, photo editor, 1978–1986: The new paper never got on the streets. Rupert announced to Neal Travis on the phone, when we were all in Costello's having a drink, that he wasn't going to go ahead with it. Then he got on the plane and went to London, which was a typical Rupert move. He didn't want to face everybody.

One strike romance did not last.

DICK BELSKY: One night we went out to dinner, and it was not pleasant. Right after that Claudia had this Page Six item about some member of the Kennedy family. She had been in a restaurant, and she overheard a conversation about somebody doing something like having a romance or cheating or something like that. She went back and did this item. Based on the facts, I said to somebody on the desk, "We can't run this. It's hearsay." Whoever was on the desk agreed, so I killed the item. She got furious and screamed at me in the middle of the newsroom. She brought up the dinner that had gone badly—because we were kind of ending the relationship—and said that I'd done this because I was mad at her. After that, she refused to speak to me. About a month after I broke up with her, I was with somebody else on a date and she said: "Should we go to Elaine's?" We went and stood at the bar where the poor people stand. Claudia was there with Neal Travis. The woman I'm with says, "That woman over at that table is glaring at you." I walk over and say, "This is crazy. Can we just drop this?" She's like, "Yeah, I know." While I'm talking to her, one of those bodyguards they had to prevent people from bothering the celebrities says, "Excuse me, sir, you're not allowed to talk to the people at this table." I'm like, "It's okay. I know them." He goes, "Sir, you're not allowed to talk to them." He grabs me by the arm and says, "I'm gonna have to ask you to leave." I said, "No, no. Ask her. She knows me." Claudia looks at the guy and says, "Never saw him before in my life. Throw him out." Then she starts laughing.

> Some of the non-union staffers that Murdoch imported during the strike stayed on after a settlement was reached, and one had a profound impact on the paper: the outrageously outspoken and politically incorrect Kelvin MacKenzie.

KELVIN MACKENZIE: I'm working with the London *Sun* and I meet Rupert. He's quite friendly and basically says, "There's a job." He doesn't explain what the job particularly is but says there's a job at the *New York Post*. Nor did he indicate that there were issues in relation to how the *New York Post* was doing. It was something that you discovered afterward. This was considered a big opportunity. I didn't know anything about the *New York Post*. Myself and family headed out for the summer of '78, and it was when I started meeting colleagues that I began to understand what the scale of the issue was—that the dominant provider of circulation was the *Daily News*. And the dominant provider of content was the *New York Times*. Yes, it's true, the *New York Post* was the afternoon paper, but there wasn't a lot of space for the *New York Post*. It had difficulty creating its own personality and, therefore, its own audience. I arrived during the strike. It was pretty much a nightmare kind of introduction. Going to work, sitting around and doing nothing all day or all evening, was a really strange feeling. But an interesting factor I think was that the atmosphere between the American journalists working for the *New York Post* and the interlopers, i.e., the Brits and Aussies, wasn't strained. Personally, I got on great with Dick Belsky and those guys. They were very funny people.

DICK BELSKY: Michelmore was one of [Murdoch's] very top lieutenants in the beginning. He came in and supplanted the [Schiff-era] metropolitan editor, Andy Porte. Andy decided to leave, and Michelmore was named metropolitan editor. We got along really well most of the time. But then they bring in Kelvin Mac-Kenzie about a year or so later, during the strike. Kelvin is take-no-prisoners. He and I became and still are friends. I love Kelvin, but I don't think he could work in a newsroom today. He was just so politically incorrect and screaming at people and calling people names and making references to their physical [appearance]—I mean, he was just unbelievable. He went after Michelmore and there was this whole power play. I wound up being on Kelvin's side, and so Michelmore and I had a falling out. Kelvin got the power and Michelmore did not. Michelmore left and eventually Steve Dunleavy replaced him [as metropolitan editor].

MILTON GOLDSTEIN, copy editor, 1974–current: [Kelvin] sizzled up the *Post*. A lot of the [Dolly Schiff] people were aghast. More of them left. Some stayed. Belsky stayed. He thrived.

MARTHA COOPER, photographer, 1977–1980: We always had to look for people crying. Encourage sadness. Jumper on the bridge.

KELVIN MACKENZIE: If you carried on down the [Dorothy] Schiff route, there wouldn't have been a *New York Post*. It would've gone bust.

DICK BELSKY: You can't overestimate Kelvin's impact on the paper. He made the *Post* what it was. Before Kelvin, the *Post* was weirdly hesitant of what it was going to be. We would do some sensational story and then it would be like, "I think Rupert wants more serious stuff. So let's do stories about Queens or the Bronx or something." Then they would do these boring stories about something that was very borough-conscious. The *Post* didn't really have its identity yet. People would do stuff thinking, "I think Murdoch wants this," without

Murdoch saying it, but they were trying to please him. Kelvin wasn't like that. Kelvin was like, "This is what I want to do." Boom, boom, boom. He was that self-confident. He had this vision of an in-your-face tabloid and having Dunleavy working with him, that was the perfect combination. Everything that the *Post* became in the '80s, all of that was set up by Kelvin. He's one of the most important people, maybe *the* most important person other than Rupert.

RICHARD GOODING: Kelvin was totally insane. And basically, Roger Wood was scared of him because Kelvin had a direct line to Murdoch. Roger would purposely not even look at what this guy was putting in the paper or on the front page because he knew he couldn't fight it.

DICK BELSKY: Roger Wood was the most brilliant editor ever, because he saw what he had in Kelvin and what he had in Dunleavy and he let them do their thing.

AMY PAGNOZZI, reporter, columnist, 1979–1993: Kelvin was a complete wild man. He was hysterically funny, but he would take these arbitrary dislikes to people and just harass them out of existence. There was this woman—I can't remember if she was an editor or what—she was a little bit overweight. He kept calling her a sad cow. He was very, very cruel sometimes. So it was really hard. I mean, he liked me, but he had quite arbitrary whipping boys.

KELVIN MACKENZIE: They are entitled to their view.

PHILIP MESSING, reporter, 1978–1991, 1994–2016: Kelvin used to intimidate the hell out of everybody because he had this vile Britishism he used to invoke. He used to call people a bloody toe rag.

KELVIN MACKENZIE: A bloody toe rag is somebody who's completely f-ing useless.

GEORGE ARZT: Kelvin MacKenzie wrote headlines, like in a British tabloid, that had nothing to do with the story. For people they didn't like in politics, they would put up pictures of people's faces in an unfavorable manner. For people they liked, they gave a nice headshot.

KELVIN MACKENZIE: When I got there, I didn't think the paper was interesting enough. I mean, a paper doesn't have to be tabloid to be interesting, but it does have to have interesting stuff and interesting views in it. I never talked to Murdoch about this, but I think he felt happier with something slightly closer to the edge than everybody just turning up for work every day.

DAVE BANKS, night managing editor, 1979–1981: Kelvin and Dunleavy—both have the same cavalier grasp of the truth, lovable though they both were or are. Kelvin once wrote a headline—there were twenty people killed in some incident. I can't remember whether it was a bus crash or an automobile crash but we knew that twenty were dead. It was a huge story. The wood—the wood blocks for the front page—was immovable. You couldn't squeeze the type, and Kelvin could not get "20 Dead" to fit. He said to me, "Why don't we make it '19 Dead'?" Because the [number one] was only half a character wide, and a two is a big, wide character. I said, "There's twenty dead, to say nineteen is wrong, it's deceitful." He said, "No, there are *at least* nineteen dead. We know there are twenty but nineteen fits." His argument prevailed, to my great discomfort. We went with the headline "19 Dead," which was still a big number, but it wasn't true. We knew it wasn't the truth, but it fit.

KELVIN MACKENZIE: I don't [recall that], he's sitting there making it up.

DAVE BANKS: Kelvin and I continued throughout our careers, even when we worked together at *The Sun* [in London], and against one another while I was editing the *Mirror* [also in London], we continued to have huge debates about truth and honesty, and ethical integrity. I used to say that Kelvin believed that ethics was a county in England, to the right-hand side of the M11.

KELVIN MACKENZIE: What I liked about Dick [Belsky] is that he's a confident guy, and when I was heading down the British route in relation to the *New York Post*, he did have to keep reminding me, "We're in Manhattan," we weren't in London.

DICK BELSKY: My role was basically to rein him in—you know, "Kelvin, I think you might have gone a little too far there."

JOANNE WASSERMAN: I certainly saw Kelvin lose his temper and treat people badly. I was on the receiving end of that from some other people, but not him. He was okay with me. But I had a thing going on with Belsky. Looking back now, I realize he wasn't going to scream at the city editor's girlfriend.

ADAM SCULL: Early in my time there, I was assigned to cover the Al Smith dinner at the Waldorf Astoria's Grand Ballroom. All the Catholics in the universe were getting together, and I'm the new Jewish boy in the room. I got all my pictures during the cocktail hour and was sitting outside of the ballroom because photographers weren't allowed into the dinner. Dunleavy walks over to me, sits down, and says, "Get in there." I said, "What are you talking about? We're not allowed in." Without so much as a word, he picks me up with two hands and throws me with all my camera equipment at the doors of the Grand Ballroom and says, "Get your fucking ass in there, shoot the cardinal, and don't worry about them saying you're not allowed to be in there." I did and I got the shot. That's where I learned a valuable lesson: "We're from the *Post*. Fuck you and your rules. We make our own rules."

JOANNE WASSERMAN: I have this very strong memory of [Kelvin] sitting there, designing page one, talking out loud. It was a story about Teddy Kennedy and he was going to use the word "romp" in the headline. TEDDY ROMP, something like that. How *not* the old Dolly Schiff *Post* can you get? Where they fucking found some pictures of Teddy with some twenty-five-year-old blonde kind of thing. He was loudly talking about it. I think it was sort of his way of saying, "I'm here, I'm doing this, we're changing the paper." Until then, they'd encountered a lot of resistance. He was a prick.

KELVIN MACKENZIE: That sounds right. Well, I'd be proud of that. Today, a story like that would be leading all the news websites.

DAVE BANKS: Rupert loved those two men [Kelvin MacKenzie and Steve Dunleavy] in a way that—while he, I think, had some regard for me, it wasn't the same. It wasn't the same with even Roger Wood. Rupert loved Steve Dunleavy and Kelvin MacKenzie like the illegitimate twins he never had. He would have loved it if they'd been his sons, I think. I really do.

ERIC FETTMANN: Kelvin was the guy who really created what became known as the Murdoch *Post*. He created the huge page ones and the stories that were not necessarily true. He was the one who said, we're going to change this all in one fell swoop. It wasn't just the look of the paper—it was also the attitude of the paper.

7 | WE WROTE FOR THE FANS

Blackie, Billy, Reggie, George

At the time of the Australian invasion, the *Post*'s sports section had plenty of stars and a loyal following, with writers known for taking a ruminative look at the city's athletes and their triumphs and failures. Despite Rupert Murdoch's seeming lack of interest in sports, he immediately began shaking up the status quo with the assistance of a flamboyant new editor.

GREG GALLO, executive sports editor, 1977–1989, 1994–2009: What sport did Murdoch follow? I don't know. Yachting?

HENRY HECHT, sportswriter, baseball, 1969–1984: When I got to the *Post*, there was this incredible sports staff. Vic Ziegel was my mentor and a dear friend. What a great journalist he was—in baseball and in boxing. He was part of the Muhammad Ali road show. There was Paul Zimmerman, who had played football for Columbia in the early to mid-'50s, and he was the best football writer I ever read. They had Larry Merchant, who was the best columnist I ever read; Milton Gross, who was not a great wordsmith, but a terrific hard-hitting tabloid writer. Sometimes when we got out at 8:30 a.m., Vic and I would go for breakfast at Yonah Schimmel's on Houston Street, the knish place. Our breakfast would be a knish and a bottle of Pepsi.

HARVEY ARATON, sportswriter, basketball, 1977–1982: I had grown up worshipping the *Post* sports section back in the Dorothy Schiff days, in large part because as an afternoon paper, the guys who covered the various beats had all night to write their stories, so as a result they were much more creative than the guys at the *Daily News* or the *Times* who were writing on ridiculous deadlines.

JILL ABRAMSON, former executive editor, *The New York Times*: I read the *Post* very fitfully during college [Abramson graduated from Harvard-Radcliffe in 1976] because I would only see it when I was home, but I was a very passionate New York Yankees fan, so whenever I could get my hands on a physical copy of the *Post*, I would because I recognized that their sports coverage was superior.

The sports department's longtime leader, seventy-year-old Ike Gellis, had joined the paper in 1928.

PHIL MUSHNICK, columnist, television sports, 1973–current: Ike would send me down to the composing room two, three times an afternoon, to place his bets at the racetrack with the bookies downstairs. There were probably three of them down there. I'd give the ten dollars wrapped up in a piece of paper, and across the sheet was his win bet or an exacta or win-place-show or a reverse bet. That was one of my steady duties—to be Ike's runner.

CLYDE HABERMAN, reporter, 1966–1977: I think Ike was basically prehensile. I'm not even sure Ike knew how to spell.

PHIL MUSHNICK: They had a night clerk in sports. He lived in the Knickerbocker projects across the way. His name was Joe. He worked per diem—on voucher—meaning he wasn't vested in anything. He didn't have days off; he didn't have medical benefits. Nothing. We kept imploring him to get on staff. He shows up one morning and he waits for Ike to get there. Ike is short, glasses. He looked like a cross between Edward G. Robinson and a frog. Joe is a big big guy and he stands over Ike's desk and says, "Ike, I've been on voucher for two years. I want to be put on full-time." Ike pulls his glasses down over the front of his nose, looks up, and says, "Who the fuck are you?"

BILL BRADLEY, former New York Knick; former US senator: When you're a basketball team, unlike a baseball team or a football team, you have twelve players, a coach, a trainer. Then we had four members of the press. We were fewer than twenty people. Traveling together, you get thrown into very tight settings every day for months. You get to know someone. I didn't see negative aspects to it. I got to know [Knicks beat writer] Leonard Lewin; his wife, Phoebe; and his son, John. It's all part of the same group. If you stunk up the court, he wrote you stunk up the court. He was a reporter. He was not an opinion person. He was telling people who read the *Post* what happened, and what somebody said about it or whatever. He was a good journalist, he asked the right questions, good questions. He was fair. He was not sensational. He told the truth. There was not this gossip stuff that goes on now with people thinking they're covering Watergate when they're covering the Knicks.

Murdoch initiated a slow-building wave of change, first by bringing in a group from the *Star*, led by Executive Sports Editor Jerry "Blackie" Lisker, who had previously worked for the *Daily News*, and his deputy, Greg Gallo, the son of Bill Gallo, legendary *Daily News* sports cartoonist.

HARVEY ARATON: Ike Gellis had been the sports editor for years under Dorothy Schiff. When Rupert bought the paper, he started bringing in his own people. For a while, they kind of coexisted. Ike Gellis still had a desk and was still technically the sports editor. But Jerry and then Greg Gallo, who was his assistant, were already working, kind of like a shadow staff.

GREG GALLO: Look, they had a good sports department before we got there. It was a different kind of sports department. In comparison, it was good writing, but it was slow to get to the point. The pieces were longer and inside the paper, and their presentation was not what I would call powerful or snappy.

RAY KERRISON, turf writer, city columnist, 1977–2013: I was editor of the *Star* when one day I had lunch with Rupert, and he said something that stunned me and changed my life. "I'm in the process of buying the *New York Post*," he said. "How would you like to go down there as a racing writer?" "You mean you will pay me to go to the track?" We shook hands on the deal. Rupert knew of my passion for racing because we had shared joint ownership in a horse in Australia.

HARVEY ARATON: The Murdoch people were coming in and they were looking to move the veteran folks out as quickly as possible. And I don't know how it was in the city room, but in sports, they had the Murdoch style; every quote had to be "told the *Post*," or "the *Post* has learned," and a lot of the veteran guys, Gene Roswell, Lenny Lewin, they were pretty resistant to this. This was kind of an affront to them—"the *Post* has learned" on every little factoid that essentially was given at a news conference. So the *Post* wasn't really learning it; it was just very much that Murdochian style. The Schiff style was a much more conventional, featurized form of reporting and writing, the heavy emphasis being on the fact that they had so many hours to file their stories. They didn't focus on a lot of game detail; it was more writing about personalities and issues. But the *Post* style was clearly very much hard-core, grab the reader by the collar. In my first couple years there, Greg Gallo, every time he would call to check in about what you were doing, it was always: write for the back page.

GREG GALLO: Ike Gellis left shortly after I got there. It was a whole changing of the guard, and those were uncomfortable times for, I guess, everybody.

PETER VECSEY, columnist, basketball, 1977–1991, 1994–2012: I covered the Knicks for a while with the *Daily News* when Red Holzman was the coach. He would say, "This is the deal. We take all the writers out after the game, to dinner and drinks. And we talk about basketball, but everything is off the record." I said, "No, thanks." Then things started to change. I think I had something to do with that. I wouldn't play that game. They had a whole gang mentality. They would share quotes. So everybody's story the next day was basically the same. After a big game, I'm not giving you the quotes I got. Are you out of your mind? That's why I never went to those press conferences. I would find guys in the locker room alone and get my stories that way.

STEVE SERBY, sports columnist, 1972–1993, 1994–current: Some of these players and coaches have no concept of what it means to be a reporter or columnist. Too many of them think that reporters should be extensions of the team. Don't get me wrong. There are many stand-up guys who understand that if I'm going to write that they stink, they're going to grin and bear it. But other guys will freeze you out. Other guys will try to poison the locker room because they don't understand how this whole thing works. To them it's a rude awakening. But we don't write for the players or the coaches. We write for the fans.

GEOFF REISS, former senior vice president, ESPN: Just as Murdoch is taking over the *Post* in 1977, sports was about to go through a significant change. While the *Post* may have helped speed that change, it also very much benefited from it. Sports started being a lot more about the strength of personalities. It's always been a personality-driven business to some extent—look at Babe Ruth and Joe DiMaggio—but the fact is, we went from the one-dimensional, stargazing, deification of these guys to presenting these big personalities in a much more multidimensional way. In the old days, sportswriters would nod and wink at the unsavory side of different sports stars' personalities. This was an amazing convergence, of a change in the way we look at sports and Murdoch showing up at the exact right time, to both benefit from that evolution and to help propel it.

> New hires like Vecsey took on major roles, and some of the junior sports staffers moved up the ranks.

PHIL MUSHNICK: After Murdoch and Jerry Lisker came in, just by blind luck, Jerry hired or promoted a lot of younger guys. He made some bad hires, but he made some good hires and good promotions. He didn't know what the hell he was doing, but he did it.

PETER VECSEY: Jerry Lisker hired me at the *Post* to be the NBA columnist. I became the first—or close to the first—national columnist to cover a single sport.

GREG GALLO: Phil Mushnick was a clerk way back, as Steve Serby was, under [Ike] Gellis. We put Mushnick on the Cosmos, and he covered the Nets. Serby did general assignment for a while, then he covered football, and then we got him in as a columnist.

PHIL MUSHNICK: In '77, I got my first beat. The New York Cosmos soccer team. A guy named Joe Marcus died. He covered but he didn't get much space. When Ike said, "Who knows anything about soccer?" I lied and said, "Me." So he sent me out to Giants Stadium on weekends. The Cosmos had Pelé, Giorgio Chinaglia, Franz Beckenbauer, and all these international stars. Because we were an afternoon paper, I wasn't writing just the score and play-by-play. I was writing opinion. I was writing a player's quotes, some of the injuries that were going on within that team. The next thing I know is—that team began to draw, draw, draw. They were selling out Giants Stadium. I really stepped in it. For a kid, I think I did a good job. I always came back with something.

JOE FAVORITO, sports marketing consultant; former head of PR for New York Knicks and other teams: The way Phil covered the Cosmos in the '70s and the early '80s—he had access to Pelé and all that stuff when nobody else was covering a sport that was coming up. The *Post* made soccer a spectacle in this country because of the way Phil covered the Cosmos.

PETER VECSEY: Within weeks of getting [to the *Post*], I wanted to go to Denver. This was the first year of the merger between the NBA and the ABA, and I knew all the Nuggets from covering the ABA extensively. I wanted to do a story on the Nuggets because I heard there were problems even though they were leading the league. I told Jerry, and he said, "Go." I spent maybe a week out there and broke a really big story about the team, which got about four guys traded at the end of the year. Because I did this column, everybody was killing [then–Nuggets coach] Larry Brown. I've known Larry since high school. I watched him play in high school. I come back to New York and he calls me. He's irate because he gave me carte blanche while I was there. He's yelling and screaming, and then he winds up killing two of the stars on the team to me on the phone. Now I have column number two: Dan Issel and David Thompson, who are both in the Hall of Fame—he called them soft and said, "You can't win with these guys." Meanwhile, they were leading the league. But they didn't win with them. They never did win a championship. So now I have a second column with Larry Brown knocking these two guys. The GM calls me the next day—his name was Carl Scheer—and accused me of yellow journalism. Now I have my third column. Right out of the box. Jerry was like, "Whoa, okay!" The beauty of [the Denver trip] was I assigned myself there. That's how Jerry worked. He did it with others, too, with Mike Marley and boxing. He did it with the guys he trusted. To this day, Larry Brown and I have a love-hate relationship.

HARVEY ARATON: Lisker told me to come in. I put on a suit and had all my clips and combed my hair. I showed up at his desk and he never looked up. He just said, "You're Philly Mushnick's friend." "Yeah, right." "Can you type?" "Yeah." I lied, actually. I typed with two fingers. He said, "Do you know sports?" I said, "Yeah." He said, "Come in tonight at eight." I showed up about 7:45, and I was the only one in the department. In those days, the sports department had a glass enclosure around it. About fifteen minutes later, another guy comes in, says to me, "Are you Harvey?" "Yeah." He puts out his hand and says, "I'm Bob Drury. Tonight's my first night, Jerry Lisker told me to ask for you." We had no clue what we were doing.

The freewheeling, perma-tanned Lisker usually looked as though he was on his way to a fight in Vegas, and often he was. He liked to brag that he had once sparred with Muhammad Ali.

GREG GALLO: Jerry loved boxing and he boxed. He boxed in college. He sparred with Muhammad Ali back when we were at the *Star* together. He went out and did the story, went to Deer Lake [Ali's Pennsylvania training camp] and got in the ring with Ali.

DOMINICK MARRANO, chief paginator, 1971–2008: Lisker was the ultimate. He was a bullshitter half the time and a liar the other half. He was always telling stories. He lived on this reputation that he was an amateur boxer and that's how he got to know Muhammad Ali. And he did know him pretty well. He lived on a reputation nobody could ever really put together.

PHIL MUSHNICK: Jerry was always throwing punches, shadowboxing. He always had that left hook. I'm sure it was a gag. Ali was about six-two-and-a-half. Jerry was about five-eight. There's no logical reason that they had a legitimate sparring session. It wouldn't have helped either person.

DAVID ROSENTHAL, reporter, desk editor, 1974–1977: Jerry was practically a thug.

PHIL MUSHNICK: Jerry was part of the Murdoch curse and blessing—there can't be a more loyal guy to work for than Murdoch. I mean, Jerry had no business being a sports editor. First, he was rarely there. Second, he should have been, you know, the head counselor at a boys' camp, especially one for troubled boys. But he made it work. Ike was great to me. But Jerry was spectacular to me. Jerry let me do what I wanted and encouraged it. Not that he ever read a goddamn thing I wrote. Jerry once put up a note on the board to the staff about filing earlier for the first edition and spelled "edition" "A-D-D-I-T-I-O-N."

HARVEY ARATON: Boxing was not my thing necessarily, but I went to a couple of fights at Madison Square Garden and that was Jerry's thing. He was big in the boxing world, and he would show up, dressed in all black, his shirt unbuttoned halfway down his chest. He had these gold chains on, and he was sort of mysterious. He didn't seem to fit the image of a sports editor. He looked like a character out of a Tarantino film.

PHIL MUSHNICK: He always walked like a locomotive—an angry locomotive.

DOMINICK MARRANO: Lisker walked into the office one Monday morning just as I was leaving. I had worked the night shift. He has on this black mink coat, and he was tanned, like he'd just come back from the Caribbean. I said, "Jerry, you look terrific. You been in the sun?" "Yeah," he says, "I was in London." He was always full of shit; he always had a story to tell you.

RAY NEGRON, New York Yankees executive (who started as a batboy in 1973): After Murdoch took over, I thought the coverage got stronger, to be honest with you. I thought that the writers had more freedom to kick ass.

GREG GALLO: What we wanted was—put your own take on what you just saw rather than straight reporting. We could get straight reporting from the wires. We didn't want that. Columnists are going to write that way anyway because that's what we hired them to do—but we wanted the beat guys to shout what they saw—say it in bold terms. We used to say, "Be loud and be proud. Do your beat, be out there." That was the push that we made with anybody that we hired. It wasn't a directive from above, but it was assumed that we were taking no prisoners and that's how we wanted to cast ourselves.

HARVEY ARATON: The *Post* was the first, I think, to really go full speed on gambling. It had to be '77 or '78 that they started the NFL betting guide. They were promoting the hell out of it. I was a clerk then, and I was sent to proofread the page, to make sure it looked good. With hot type, you're reading backwards, and I couldn't make hell or high water of this stuff. I looked at it and I just said, "It looks good to me." When the first copies came out, the pick box was just an empty spot. They hadn't put it in, and I had okayed it. They had to stop the press. I was lucky I didn't get fired right then and there.

GREG GALLO: When we started doing the football picks page, which still is there—everybody reads that stuff because everybody is in an office pool and they play the point spreads—the NFL came to us and said, "What are you doing with these point spreads?" They were complaining, they didn't want that. I said, "You don't want it? Why wouldn't you want it?" The office pools are much bigger today than they used to be, but then people still wanted to know who's favored by what. We had conversations with Joe Brown, who was the head of media relations at the NFL, probably at Marie's [social club]. So, we had our spaghetti and meatballs and red wine and we worked it out to where they understood that. We said, "We're trying to sell papers. You guys are trying to sell your league. Everybody's going to win from this." After that, everybody was doing it. Now, point spreads and lines are in most every paper.

HARVEY ARATON: The young guys—I have to say with some remorse—we were willing to do anything. I was twenty-four years old and went from working [at the *Staten Island Advance*], which was a good daily, but a newspaper that wasn't considered prominent in New York, to suddenly getting a byline in the *New York Post*. A lot of us—I'm thinking myself, Mushnick, Drury and Serby, Larry Brooks—were more willing to bend to that stuff. So, all of a sudden, the older guys were being moved off the beats and the younger guys moved on.

PHIL MUSHNICK: I think [the Schiff-era sportswriters who left soon after Murdoch took over] jumped the gun. You know what? Murdoch was smart enough to leave us alone. He let the sports section be divorced from the rest of the paper.

In 1977, the *Post* lavished coverage on Major League Baseball and the New York Yankees. By the end of the previous season, the city had become the red-hot center of America's favorite pastime when the Yankees won the American League East pennant—their first since 1964—and though the Cincinnati Reds swept them in the World Series, they led the league in home attendance and were the only team to draw at least two million fans for the 1976 season. Three other developments would ensure that coverage of the Yankees 1977 season would sell papers at a time when the city's other Major League team, the Mets, as well as its pro football and basketball teams, the Jets, Giants, and Knicks, were floundering. In a year when the crumbling, arson-plagued borough of the Bronx symbolized the financial straits that the city was navigating, a newly renovated Yankee Stadium reopened after undergoing a $100 million facelift. Free agency entered the picture, enabling the Yanks to hire pivotal stars (and personalities). The year 1977 also saw the emergence of George Steinbrenner as the outspoken face of Yankees management. Although the Cleveland shipbuilder and a group of investors had purchased the Yankees in 1973, Steinbrenner was indicted the following year on fourteen felony charges mostly related to his donations to the reelection campaign of President Richard Nixon. Later that year, Steinbrenner would negotiate a plea deal to avoid prison time but he could not avoid a two-year suspension from day-to-day team operations, courtesy of MLB commissioner Bowie Kuhn. Upon his return to the league, Steinbrenner asserted himself within the Yankees clubhouse and the media, and the Boss, as the tabloids dubbed him, quickly recognized that the back cover of the city's tabloids, which were devoted to sports, kept his team top-of-mind among the city's sports fans.

HARVEY ARATON: At the time, baseball was the bread and butter of any sports section. The NFL was not as big a deal. The NBA was a mom-and-pop league. It really didn't become super popular until the '80s, with Larry Bird and Magic Johnson, and then Michael Jordan. Baseball was the story day in, day out in New York sports journalism.

RAY NEGRON: If a Yankees story got the back page, the Boss used to say: "This is a million dollars' worth of free publicity." Positive or negative, it was major publicity that would turn into money. It was a scenario of getting the Yankees out there. That's what's made the Yankees brand the biggest brand in all of sports around the world, and maybe in all business.

HARVEY ARATON: Steinbrenner saw that the *Post* under Murdoch was relishing the outrageous. He was drawing a lot of attention, even before Rupert bought the *Post*. But about the time George hired Billy Martin to be the manager and free agency was coming into baseball, Rupert bought the paper. Martin was a walking headline, and then Steinbrenner brought in Reggie Jackson as a free agent. That combination of Steinbrenner, Martin, and Jackson was a dream come true for someone like Rupert Murdoch wanting to sell papers. I think Steinbrenner clearly operated in those days with the back page of the *Post* in mind.

GEOFF REISS: The Yankees had been humiliated in 1976 by the Cincinnati Reds, who swept them in four games. Steinbrenner was determined to not have that happen again. When Reggie Jackson signed with the Yankees as a free agent, it was George Steinbrenner's second big free agent signing after Catfish Hunter.

HENRY HECHT: Billy Martin and I were always at war. He was a sad, twisted, bitterly unhappy person and a raging alcoholic. Steinbrenner and I were fine. He would piss you off at times, and you would piss him off at times. Then he wouldn't talk to you until you got out of purgatory. So in '76 or '77—I can't remember—the Yankees had had a lot of bad outcomes with injured players. I did a deep dive into it and wrote a story that was very critical of their medical staff. Steinbrenner knew I was doing it, and I wanted to interview him. Basically, he threatened me. "I'll never talk to you again," ra, ra, ra, ra, ra, ra! I wrote the story, and it was like it never happened. If you stood up to Steinbrenner, that was fine.

> The Mets had begun a losing streak that would last through 1983. But as the team that replaced the Brooklyn Dodgers and New York Giants when they moved to Los Angeles and San Francisco, respectively, the Amazins (as the team was nicknamed at its 1962 debut) enjoyed a fervent following as the city's baseball underdogs. They also had pitcher Tom Seaver, dubbed "Tom Terrific" by the media, who was tangling with the team's owners.

GEOFF REISS: Anticipating the free agent era about to hit, Tom Seaver wanted to start getting paid in a way that was consistent with being the best pitcher in Major League Baseball. There was a real plantation mentality among team owners in all sports back then. They thought their players should be grateful for what they get. They should know their place. So the Mets ownership started working in concert with [influential sports reporter] Dick Young at the *Daily News* to do a PR war on Tom Seaver.

HENRY HECHT: In '76, I'm with the Mets in spring training when Tom Seaver's dispute with M. Donald Grant began. It was a year-and-a-half, two-year thing. I looked at it; I talked to people, and I decided that the Mets were one hundred percent wrong. So I wrote a column defending him. I said, "Seaver can be condescending, and he can be arrogant, but that's not the point here." The Yankees were playing the Pirates in Bradenton, Florida, where the Pirates were training. I'm wandering down the foul line where the players congregate to warm up, and Seaver comes up to me and says, "Thank you. My wife says the same thing about me." After that, we were good.

DICK BELSKY, metropolitan editor, 1970–1989: The Seaver story became part of the tabloid wars that summer. There was no sports radio, there was no ESPN. The only way people would get this is because they would be reading the *Post* and the *News* back pages.

HENRY HECHT: Dick Young was a great sportswriter, but at the end [of his career] he was a bad guy. He was a villain in Tom Seaver's contract dispute with the Mets. He went in the tank for Mets chairman [and minority owner] M. Donald Grant because he had a son-in-law who was able to get a job with the team. Young was highly critical of Seaver in his *Daily News* columns. He wrote that part of the problem Seaver had with the Mets was that [pitcher and former Met] Nolan Ryan [who had moved to the California Angels] was making more money, and he and his wife, who were friends with Ryan's wife, were upset about it. It was the most nonsensical thing in the world. That's when Seaver said, "I'm out of here." And he forced his trade [to the Cincinnati Reds]. It was the all-time bad trade.

DICK BELSKY: The *Post* was on the right side in the Seaver story. They were very pro-Seaver and anti–Donald Grant. Maybe it was because Dick Young was the opposition. Maury Allen, longtime *Post* sportswriter, was a leader in this. There's a piece that he wrote on the day of the trade or the day after, and it says, Dick Young drove Tom Seaver out of town. Dick Young was a very forceful guy, very powerful. He used to do this thing called My America: in my America, everybody works, nobody takes handouts. There was an Archie Bunker quality to him. But you couldn't necessarily pigeonhole him. He apparently was one of the strongest advocates for women sportswriters. But he was very anti baseball players making lots of money, free agents, and all that.

The trade of Tom Terrific, which took place on June 15, would have been *the* story of any other New York baseball season, but 1977 had much more in store for fans.

RAY NEGRON: The Yankees became a soap opera. It became very show business oriented. You picked up the [*Post*] to read about the Bronx Zoo.

HENRY HECHT: I got a lot of problems with Murdoch, for a lot of good reasons, and I had lots of battles with Greg Gallo. I don't want to get into them. Let's just say I'm a man of strong opinions, and we battled. But they forced me to become a better reporter. They wanted to know what was going on inside the Yankees, because that was the time of the Bronx Zoo, with Billy Martin, Reggie Jackson, and Thurman Munson. Crazy things were happening, and it was my job to report them.

RAY NEGRON: The players generally didn't [feed reporters information]. But the most media-savvy guy on the team was Reggie. Reggie was building his brand. Reggie was Michael Jordan before Michael Jordan. He understood that. I don't know that leaking is the right word for what Jackson did. It's more like he talked to all the writers. You come by, he was going to talk to you.

HENRY HECHT: Billy Martin and Reggie Jackson start their feud in Boston. The Yankees were getting their asses whipped by the Red Sox. Jim Rice hits a bloop that Reggie couldn't have caught even if he dived for it. So he sort of la-di-da'd, but a million guys do that. Martin, to embarrass him, sent out a substitute. Jackson goes into the dugout. He and Billy have to be separated. This goes on and on and on over the next few days until it's finally settled. A truce. The Yankees go to the World Series [against the Los Angeles Dodgers] and Reggie, in the last game, hits the three home runs. It's one of the greatest, perhaps the greatest one-game World Series performance as a batter. After the game, Reggie and Billy are best friends and they're sharing Champagne.

GEOFF REISS: To bring the whole New York moment to *Seinfeld*-like perfection—tying up all the loose ends—one of the guest broadcasters in the ABC booth for that World Series was Tom Seaver.

RAY NEGRON: Steinbrenner got mad that Reggie and Billy weren't getting along, because he loved Billy with a passion. He wanted Billy to do well, but he knew Billy had his demons. He knew Reggie had his ego, so these things would upset him, but at the same time, we're dominating the papers. He knew what that meant for the brand. He loved the publicity. He always was ahead of the game. He understood.

8 | WHAT THE BOSS WANTS

Dogs, Bikinis, Dead Mobsters

The *Post* had morphed into a tabloid juggernaut, and Murdoch clearly determined its course. When he occasionally ran the newsroom in the early days of his takeover, he made it clear what he did and did not want covered—and how it should be written.

BARBARA ROSS, political reporter, 1978–1985: In those days, Murdoch came in, in August, for a couple of weeks when Roger went on vacation and did Roger's job. So he was in the newsroom, hands-on, which was an interesting experience; the level of tension was high.

GUY HAWTIN, investigations editor, 1979–1989: Murdoch is the only newspaper proprietor I have ever worked for who knows how to run a newspaper. The people who owned *The Guardian* didn't know their asses from their elbows when it came to running a newspaper. It was run by the editorial department. The same thing at *The Times* of London when I was there—the Thomson organization owned it, and they were absolutely hopeless.

WAYNE DARWEN, assistant managing editor, 1983–1987: He knew what a story was, and he knew how to tell it and how to sell it. And those who worked for him, who became loyal Murdochians, developed that same attitude. It didn't matter if it was Ted Kennedy or Richard Nixon. If there was a scandal, it's going out there, and you're going to show no mercy. Don't let anything get in the way of a good story. Don't let the facts get in the way of a good story.

PAT SULLIVAN, reporter, night editor, 1972–1980: Phil Bunton and I were on lobster when Murdoch came in at like six in the morning. Abscam [the FBI sting that led to the convictions of seven members of Congress for bribery and corruption] was breaking. He just took over. He asked Phil, "Who's taking on this congressman? Who's taking on that congressman?" And we weren't. He was pissed. So, suddenly, it's DEFCON whatever—get guys out, wake 'em up, get moving on this. He was yelling at Phil more than me.

KELVIN MACKENZIE, night managing editor, 1978–1979: Strangely, what he would go most mad about is if we'd gone too far. His view, actually, I don't blame him for this—he wanted the *Post* to be a bold and brash kind of paper, but he wanted it at the same time to have some kind of weight. He wanted it to have some, not quite intellectual dynamic to it, but he didn't want it to be all down-market nonsense. He had *Star* magazine for that kind of stuff.

GEORGE ARZT, City Hall bureau chief, 1968–1986: At the beginning, Murdoch would be over my shoulder all the time. I'd be writing on the—what did they call those things? VDTs? I'd be writing, turn my head, and say, "Oh my god, he's in back of me." He'd question me about the story as I was writing. He would do that quite frequently. At first, it was scary, but then it was okay. Sometimes we had forums with mayoral candidates, or aspirants, and one year he came. We're all in an elevator together with him, the reporters—myself, Steve Marcus, other people—and he turns to us and says, "Look how many mouths I have to feed." There was dead silence in response.

BARBARA ROSS: During one of those two-week periods [when Murdoch ran the paper], I had an experience that gave me such insight into Rupert. I grew up not knowing a heck of a lot about sports, except knowing that if you were in my grandmother's house, you had to root for the Dodgers. Mickey Mantle had gotten into trouble. Peter Michelmore said, "I want you to write a sidebar about 'Mickey the Mouth'—how his mouth has always gotten him into difficulty." They gave me a shoe box full of clips. I read every single one and then wrote the story. It took all day. At the end of the day, Peter comes over and he says, "Sorry, Ross, the boss spiked it." "What do you mean, he spiked it?" "He took one look at the story, and he said, 'Our readers like Mickey Mantle.' He spiked it." I realized that, as good an editor as he might be on some level, Murdoch was really into marketing. That was a marketing decision, not an editorial decision. It epitomizes what he's done to journalism. It's what politicians have done with an overdependence on polls. If you can't stand on your own and say "This is the right thing," and you are totally interested in what your readers or your voters are going to say and give them what they want, you're a walking, talking algorithm. That's what the algorithms are doing on Facebook and Google and the rest.

PETER FEARON, reporter, 1980–1987: Murdoch occasionally turned up in the newsroom to bark at Steve [Dunleavy]. He once pointed at Mel Juffe, who was reading the *Times* with his feet on his desk, and said, "How much am I paying that bastard with his feet up?"

BOB YOUNG, photo editor, 1978–1986: We would be arguing how we should go about something. Rupert would say, "Just fucking do it." And then leave the room. It says so much about him.

BARBARA ROSS: There were certain things that Rupert liked. In the British papers it was, excuse me, a semi-naked broad on page three. In New York, he knew that wasn't going to play as well. Maybe later on that changed, but he was always interested in animal stories, a story involving a kid or something light. There was a great emphasis on animal stories.

AMY PAGNOZZI, reporter, columnist, 1979–1993: It was a slow day. I called Marge Stein, who was the publicist for the North Shore Animal League [shelter]. She said, "We have this dog. We call him Hoover because he can't stop eating. He's hungry all the time. He has this thing with his stomach where calories don't build up and he'll just waste away and starve to death." I do the story about Hoover, who obviously is shitting as much as he's eating, and we end up with like a thousand people who want to adopt Hoover. Well, the dog ended up biting off the nose of the person who adopted him. This never appeared in the paper. I would never do that to Marge! She was feeding us animal stories 24/7.

CHARLIE CARILLO, reporter, columnist, 1978–1993: I wrote a lot of animal stories. I got known for—you know, please adopt this dog or they'll turn on the gas. That kind of thing. There was no gas chamber, but what do the people know? It worked. The dogs got adopted. When I took vacations, I felt guilty about all the animals that would die in my absence.

MARSHA KRANES, rewrite, editor, 1974–2005: There was one week when all the other editors were on vacation, and I reported to [Murdoch]. He was very friendly and asked me at the end of the week what I thought about the way things were running. Was there anything I would change? I said, "I have the feeling if you indicate a dislike for something, it immediately becomes a rule in the office that we can't write about that anymore." He said, "Like what?" I said, "We had a story about an old man, and you said, 'I don't like stories about old men or old people,' and every time a story like that was offered up by somebody, we were told, 'No, no, Murdoch doesn't like that.'" He said, "That's very interesting. I'll do something about that." Of course, nothing was done.

LESLIE GEVIRTZ, reporter, rewrite, 1978–1988: There were certain tropes you followed. Every co-ed was pretty. Every cop was a hero. Every bad guy was a bad guy whether they were a bad guy or not. There was not a list per se, but you would read each other's copy and pick up words, the appropriate adjective or noun. You wanted lively verbs. You did not want too many adjectives. Dunleavy hated adjectives. He wanted the right noun and a lively verb.

MIKE PEARL, reporter, Criminal Court, 1968–1998: The first question I would ask at a press conference was "Was she a blonde?" When there was a woman involved, either the victim or the perpetrator, I would say, "Was she a blonde?" Because it's a good tabloid word, "blonde."

RICHARD ESPOSITO, reporter, 1982–1985: When I later went to a reputable newspaper, *Newsday*, sometimes I would put in my story that something was a tragedy. Then the editor would say, "We don't do that here. You can't just call things a tragedy." I said, "Then how are you gonna have a miracle?"

CHARLIE CARILLO: Someone like Barbara Ross, sweetest person in the world, she files a story. This was when I was working the desk. The next morning, she phones in and says, "Can you just read me the lede?" I read the lede. She says, "Oh my god. Could you read the second paragraph?" I read the second paragraph. By this time, she's sobbing, "Let me talk to Steve [Dunleavy]." Because it's clearly nothing like what she wrote. They just wanted to grab you by the la-

pels with every story. They didn't believe anybody had an attention span, especially their own readers, the new breed of readers, which was really confusing
to a lot of people because the older liberal Jewish population still bought the
Post after Murdoch bought it. I remember Lou Colasuonno saying to me once,
"The old readers still buy it. And they say, 'It seems different somehow.'" Yeah, a
little bit! Overnight, you go from police brutality to hero cop. Vroom!

> In 1979, Murdoch took another shot at hiring American editors: Craig Ammerman
> and John Van Doorn.

NED STEELE, reporter, rewrite, 1977–1980: I know that the folks running the place
liked the idea of creative tension and building in a couple of people to compete against each other. At some point, Craig Ammerman and John Van Doorn
appear, and they are as mainstream and as establishment as you can get. Van
Doorn had been at *New York* magazine and at the *New York Times*, and Ammerman comes in from the AP at a fairly high level. Suddenly there are these two
guys who are completely of a different culture than the people coming in from
Australia and from the UK. Even though Ammerman came out of a traditional
background at the AP, he understood intuitively the fun of working for a tabloid like the *New York Post*. I think he was enjoying the chance to loosen up a
little bit and have some fun while still being a responsible, serious journalist.
He was very helpful to me. I would want to understand, how do you take this
new culture and work within it when you come out of a traditional journalism
background? How do you meld the two and do it well, and so you're comfortable with it? He helped me see that it was possible to be a good serious journalist and still be the wild and crazy *New York Post*. Van Doorn was similar, but I
think he was even less of a fit there.

KEN CHANDLER, editor in chief, publisher, 1978–1986, 1993–2002: When the *Post*
was just an afternoon newspaper and the bulk of the editing was done overnight on the lobster shift, John Van Doorn was joint [managing editor] with
Craig Ammerman. They took turns staying until about midnight to super-
vise the story selection and layouts for the next day's paper. Kelvin couldn't
stand Van Doorn, Roger Wood wasn't a fan, either. He was way too serious
a journalist for the Murdoch *Post*, and I think Roger may have seen him as
a potential rival. On the nights Van Doorn was on duty, Kelvin would call
the editorial meeting at about 10:30 p.m. in Roger's office—Roger was home

asleep by then, or in some bar—and lock the door so Van Doorn couldn't get in. Sometimes Van Doorn would stand outside knocking on the door, and we would pretend not to hear him. In addition, Kelvin initiated the "Phony Layout Scam." When editors like myself were designing news pages, we would draw two separate layouts—one very subdued and serious layout marked "PLS" to show to Van Doorn, and another, much more exciting layout, that we would actually send to the composing room. Kelvin would do the same with page one. Van Doorn would go ballistic the next day when the paper didn't look anything like the one he had approved the night before. When he complained, Roger would just shrug and say, "Dear boy, you should have stayed later."

One night when he stayed at least until midnight, Van Doorn brought in a special guest.

MARSHA KRANES: Rosemary Clooney welcomed in the New Year with us. She was dating John Van Doorn and he was working. She came up early, before we finished putting out the paper, and she chatted with us. Then when the New Year came, she stood on a desk and sang "Auld Lang Syne" to us.

The summer of 1979 saw two key departures, one from the *Post*, the other from the highest echelons of organized crime. Shortly before James Mitteager went on trial in Brooklyn for bribing a corrections guard to take the *Post*'s famous SAM SLEEPS photograph, photo editor Susan Welchman was fired. The media and some of her colleagues speculated that she was sacrificed because of her involvement in procuring the image, but Welchman says the reason had to do with her resistance to a more frivolous editorial call.

SUSAN WELCHMAN, photo editor, 1977–1979: I got fired because I thought I was going to teach Rupert a lesson about women. The AP would send photographers to Bondi Beach [in Australia], and every day, I had to get a girl from Bondi Beach in a bikini. It made me sick. I thought, "Why? Why?" Well, for obvious reasons—but at that time, I hated it. I said, "Okay, you want women in bikinis? We're going to have local women in bikinis." I sent all the photographers to the beach. I took them all off the street in New York and told them, "Go get all the women in bikinis." I thought: I'm going to show them. Women deliver.

BILL BIGELOW, city desk assistant, 1975–1979: Murdoch decides we're going to do the equivalent of the London *Sun*'s Page 3 girls, but the women aren't going to be topless. We're doing girls in bikinis. And my recollection is Susan was reluctant to do that but did it for a while.

SUSAN WELCHMAN: Craig Ammerman, who was the managing editor then, fired me. Oh my god, such a slob. He'd go around the newsroom in bare feet. I'm sure it came from Rupert, but it was him. I would never have left the *Post*, and they took away what I loved. I was banished. They thought I was uppity and being feminist and all that, and they didn't get any of that. They were right. I learned a lesson for a lifetime. It wasn't my newspaper, it was theirs.

Welchman was replaced at the *Post* by a Brit, Bob Young.

JERRY ENGEL, photographer, 1958–1993: Bob Young was a dictator.

KEN CHANDLER: Bob Young ran a tight ship and did a good job. Not everybody liked him.

JOE DE MARIA, photographer, 1977–1993: He was a nasty little son of a bitch. For some reason, he didn't like me. When Susan left, a lot of the photographers were very unhappy.

DICK BELSKY, metropolitan editor, 1970–1989: Bob was more than just a photo editor, he was a newsman. We worked together seamlessly. I'm sure if you talk to photographers, some might not like him because he could be abrasive, he could rub people the wrong way, but all the good ones do.

On July 12, 1979, Carmine Galante, the acting boss of the Bonanno crime family, was shot dead as he finished lunch on the patio of the Joe & Mary Italian-American Restaurant in Bushwick, Brooklyn.

CYNTHIA FAGEN, reporter, 1976–1986: When Galante was killed, they sent me to the hospital because the son of the restaurant owner had also been shot. I went to the emergency room. I saw a kid come in on a stretcher. There were plainclothes cops talking to him and they went behind, I think it was double doors. I was able to put my ear through like the opening and write down the account of this kid who had witnessed the shooting, what he was telling the cops. I overheard the conversation.

HAL GOLDENBERG, photographer, 1979–1986: The restaurant was on the first floor of a three-story frame building, and the whole block was like that. So we know he's in the backyard. I go to the second building before the end of the block, and people are looking out the window. One of them was this old Italian mama, who could have been my grandma. I look up and I smile and wave. She waves at me. So, I point to myself, and I point to her with a motion, like, can I come up? I said, "Can I talk to you in the hall?" She buzzes the door. I go inside. I'm like, listen, mama, here's ten bucks, can I go up on the roof. "You no have to give me no money. Go ahead." I go up on the roof, and there's five million cops a few buildings down, where this happened. I'm ducking and crawling around flat on the roof like I'm under fire in a war or something. I put my camera bag over my back so that it wasn't dragging. I'm waiting for that "Hey!" that would be the end of it. These buildings are attached but they're not flat from building to building, so, like a snake, I slither over to the next building, and then I do it again and again because the restaurant is like five buildings down. Two buildings before, a cop eyes me. I smile, wave, and I hold up my press card so he can see it. He gives me a nod. I'm like, oh shit, this guy's not going to say nothing. I can see the backyard, but I still don't want to make my presence known—maybe his boss is up there and he'd freak out. I'm still kind of slithering around. I go to the edge of the building. I look in the backyard. I see five thousand cops in the backyard, and there's Carmine, with his cigar in his mouth and his eye blown out. I start making pictures. At this point, I figure I've got the only pictures of this. It's far away, but it's the only picture. I stand up and nobody says anything. I'm freaking out. There's a media circus beyond belief down on the street, and I'm the only member of the media up here. Why are these cops cool? It's really weird. I take more pictures. Then I get a pair of grapefruit balls and walk over to the building where it happened. And nobody's saying nothing. I lay flat down on my stomach, I put the camera over the edge and start making pictures. I get on the radio and ask for a messenger immediately. Dunleavy's not stupid. He knows why I'm saying it. By the time the messenger showed up to get my film, the entire media circus was up on the roof. They let everybody up. I was, like, shit! So my exclusive picture turned out to be the same thing everybody else had. Arty Pomerantz's picture got used on page one, which was part of a wraparound. My picture was on the back page.

A mob rubout of that magnitude meant several days of stories with contributions from multiple reporters and photographers—the kind of exposure that organized crime abhors. They let their displeasure be known. According to the *Post*, a reporter was "jostled and menaced" at the cemetery, one photographer was punched outside the funeral home, and another was decked when he and a reporter were sent to greet an out-of-town mourner at JFK airport.

CYNTHIA FAGEN: One of the wise guys was flying in for the funeral. Jerry Engel and I were sent out to JFK to basically ambush him and ask him questions about the funeral, what he was doing in town, whatever. We were at the gate as he was coming off the plane. I go up to the guy. Jerry has like three cameras strung around his neck and he starts to take pictures and the guy goes wild, picks him up and shoves him against the wall and breaks his finger.

JERRY ENGEL: Next thing I know I'm on the floor. My camera is on my hand. And on top of the camera is the guy's foot.

CYNTHIA FAGEN: The guy walks off. I say to Jerry, "This is a great story." He's bleeding. We go to a bar. I order something for us to drink, and I start to clean his finger. I go, "I'm going to take a picture of your finger, we can put it in the *Post*."

JERRY ENGEL: The picture never ran.

While Murdoch's editorial authority over the *Post* was absolute, he had a more difficult time exerting control over another of his New York media properties. He fired *Village Voice* head editor Marianne Partridge, but the staff rose up in protest, and she finished out her contract. It would have been foolish to tamper too drastically with the *Voice* because the alternative weekly had something the *Post* lacked.

DAVID SCHNEIDERMAN, former editor in chief, publisher, CEO, *The Village Voice*: I joined the *Voice* in December 1978 as editor in chief. One of the big concerns was that Rupert had said to the publisher of the *Voice* that he wanted to replace Victor Kovner, our attorney, who did our First Amendment and libel review, with his guy, Howard Squadron [who handled the *Post*'s business]. When I got to the *Voice*, people said, that's a really bad thing because then Rupert will have access to our copy before it's published. I made it clear to Rupert that I wouldn't take the job if Kovner was canned. Squadron said, "It's not important to me."

About two months into the job, I got a call from Don Kummerfeld [former New York City budget director and first deputy mayor, whom Murdoch hired to run his American holding company]. He said, "David, we're going to replace Kovner with Howard Squadron." I said, "That's not what we agreed to. Rupert said he wouldn't do that." I said, "I gave my word to the staff. If you do that, I have to quit." I wasn't being heroic. My word is shot if that happens. He backed off. It turned out Howard Squadron was pushing for the job. Rupert didn't really care.

JOE CONASON, former reporter, *The Village Voice*: The problem for the Murdoch people was that [the *Voice*] made a profit—a large profit for the time, about $5 million a year [by the 1980s]. So they didn't want to mess with us too much. We were subsidizing the *Post*, which lost a lot of money. At the *Voice*, we resented it.

DAVID SCHNEIDERMAN: Yes, the [*Voice*] earnings each week were cycled into the *New York Post* bank account.

9 | CRIMINAL INTENT
Guns, Cops, Race

In February of 1981, the NYPD announced that 1980 had been the worst year for crime in city history. In the years that followed, Gotham would continue to serve up a grisly feast of murder, rape, robbery, and other violence for the *Post* to splash across its pages. The danger and the gore appealed to some reporters and photographers. Others recoiled.

PHILIP MESSING, reporter, 1978–1991, 1994–2016: People don't realize it, but as late as '92, the city had 2,200 murders a year. Now, they go crazy when there's 400. [In the '80s] you could not literally keep up with the bloodshed.

GREGG MORRIS, reporter, 1984–1988: The thing that helped me get that job was I was really into police reporting—like going into dangerous neighborhoods. I was really crazy about this stuff. I would hook up with Joe D [De Maria], who went anywhere. Joe D was carrying a gun, he was licensed to carry a concealed weapon. And he wasn't afraid of anybody. I didn't really know the city then. I didn't understand the city. So I didn't mind going into the neighborhoods, because at that time I was crazy. We were in East New York and Brownsville a lot. We went where the stuff was going on. Sometimes it was just to get a caption or whatever we could grab.

JOE DE MARIA, photographer, 1977–1993: One of the editors—I don't remember who it was—didn't approve of me having a gun carry permit that I had had since working at the *Long Island Press*. This editor said originally, "We don't really want you carrying a gun when you work." I said, "Whatever you want, I'll do." A month or so after I get hired, Steve Dunleavy came over to me and said, "If you have the gun carry permit, and it's legal, I want you to carry it, so you can go into places where you won't get hurt." Steve went out on a lot of stories with me.

JAMI BERNARD, chief movie critic, 1978–1993: I didn't like being a reporter. The last story I reported [before becoming a copy editor] involved a little girl, she was like ten, in Staten Island, who had been missing. I had talked on the phone with her mother earlier in the day. That night they found her. She'd been murdered and they found her beaten body stuffed in a crawl space at a train station. I went with a photographer. It was a really foggy night. It was surreal. The family's house was around the corner. They were dragging her body out when I was there. This is why I hated being a reporter: I knew I had to go knock on the door. I had to go re-interview [the mother] and I didn't want to do it. I saw a priest walking toward the house. I stopped him. I thought, I'll interview him. That'll be good enough, he must know the family. I said, "Hi, I'm Jami Bernard, from the *New York Post*." He whirled around and slapped me in the face. I didn't react, but I think he did it because I was from the *Post*. The *New York Post* had a terrible reputation.

ERIC FETTMANN, associate editorial page editor, columnist, 1976–1991, 1993–2019: A woman was found in an SRO, killed and mutilated. Joe [Nicholson] was sent to the crime scene and Jim Norman was taking the notes on rewrite. Nothing fazed Joe. He was going to give you all the details. He starts talking about how the woman was in bed, her breasts had been sliced off and placed on the shelf above the bed. He wants to keep going, and Jim said, "That's enough. I don't need any more." Joe said, "No, no. I gotta give you everything—the breasts were placed on the shelf, nipples up." Jim started calling Joe "Nipples Up."

LESLIE GEVIRTZ, reporter, rewrite, 1978–1988: I think my first assignment was a homicide, in Whitestone [Queens]. It was a kid who was shot in the back of the head. He was about the same age as me. I was okay—it was my first dead body—but when I saw the ME [medical examiner] put his finger in the bullet hole, I just went "ohhhh" and walked away very quickly. I thought to myself: I don't know if I really want to do this.

JAMI BERNARD: Not everyone is meant to be a news reporter or a *Post* news reporter, which was a particular kind of thing. I admired people like Cynthia

Fagen where—that Staten Island thing? She would have gotten in the house and had tea with the mother. No one would have slapped her. I didn't know how to do that.

LESLIE GEVIRTZ: When there were beepers, you'd get beeped, and you'd have to run for a phone booth. They were much more plentiful then, except, of course, in the neighborhoods where they sent me. If it was a poor neighborhood, if it was a Black neighborhood, the odds of a pay phone out in the street? Slim. I got mugged once while I was phoning in. I don't remember the year but it was Fifth Avenue at 98th Street or 99th Street. I had my little Honda Civic. It was a standard transmission, which was great because it turned out car thieves in New York City can't drive standard transmission. The *Post* sent me to check out something further north. I was coming back on Fifth Avenue and I found a pay phone. I call the desk and as I'm calling, these two guys come over, they're Latino, and one of them claims to have a knife. At first, I thought they just wanted to use the phone, and I say, "Just five minutes, guys." They're like, "Hey, lady," and they show me the knife. Whoever I'm talking to is not picking up on anything, until I finally say, "I'm getting robbed. Could you call the cops?" They called DCPI [NYPD Public Information office]. They didn't call 911. They called DCPI, which was really embarrassing for someone who had to deal with DCPI. Anyway, they made off with some money. But when they tried to steal the car— one of them slipped into it and said, "Oh, shit, it's a stick. How can you drive this, lady?" I was like, "Because I know how?"

KENNY MORAN, sportswriter, outdoor sports and skiing, 1972–2013: The one thing the Murdoch regime did was put all police on a high pedestal. If you were a cop, you could do no wrong.

PAUL THARP, reporter, columnist, 1982–2014: Dunleavy built this great rapport with the police department. They loved him. If you got in trouble, you'd say, "I'm with the *Post*," and the cop would say, "Oh, yeah, how's Steve doin'?" "He's fine." I got out of so many traffic violations that way, it's unbelievable.

PHILIP MESSING: There was no doubt that there was a filter of protectionism for the police department as a whole that made its way into the paper. I had an exposé about somebody and they killed the story because [veteran police reporter] Carl Pelleck asked Dunleavy to kill it. He says, "This is bad for my sources in the police union, and it's bad for me personally, and it'll be bad for the *Post*." They said, "Fine, we're not going to run your story, Philip." I had a really slam-bang story. It got out two years later, but it was sort of disappointing that things like that happened. I don't suppose it's any different at the *News* or even at the *Times*. Everybody has their sacred cows. It's just that they're a little bit more prevalent, I think, and a little bit more obvious at the *Post* than they are elsewhere.

PAUL THARP: If you talk to some of the photographers, they were really tight with the police. A policeman would fall down and they would report, "Hero Cop Falls While Shooting Black Kid." They did that. Dunleavy did that.

HAL GOLDENBERG, photographer, 1979–1986: I knew a lot of cops because when I was at a job, I would take pictures, and if there's a cop in the picture—even just a patrol cop, any schmuck—I would make prints. Say the cop is guarding the body of a dead guy laying in the street. I'd shoot circles around the scene, and this one cop that's guarding the body, he'd be in different poses. I'd make ten prints, and I'd bring them back to the precinct and go up to the desk. "Who's this guy?" "Oh, that's PO so-and-so. He's working today." "Could you have him 10-2," which means return to the precinct. I'd wait, and the guy would come back, and I'd say, "Is this you?" He'd say, "Oh, yeah, thanks. Wow." You do that enough and you're going to make friends. Now they have a picture of themselves they can share with their kids, their wife.

REV. DR. C. VERNON MASON, civil rights activist: In September 1983, we had congressional hearings on police brutality here in New York. I don't remember a single case that Alton Maddox and I were involved in, in terms of police brutality, where the *New York Post* ever questioned what the police did. There was case after case after case, in all boroughs, where the system looked the other way. The *Post*, not only would they not be talking about what had happened to the victims, they would be attacking us for daring to question what the police said about this.

The *Post*'s tight-knit relationship with the cops didn't keep one photographer, an African American woman, from being arrested for doing her job.

LENORE DAVIS, photographer, 1980–1993: I was going on vacation and I get a call from Frank Leonardo: there's a female officer shot on Park Place in the subway. I'm packing to leave, but I had to rush down. I get there kind of late. And the cops won't let me take any photographs even though all the other photographers had taken them. I went to take a picture and the sergeant had a Black officer arrest me. This was July 2, 1982. He was trying to push me up the staircase. I had all my equipment on me. I said, "I'm working!" I had my credentials. He's pushing me. All these cops were there because it would have been the first female officer shot in the subway. It turned out not to be a cop and it was an accident—the woman actually shot herself—but it seemed like hundreds of cops showed up. When they pushed me up the staircase, he ripped my blouse open, so I was totally exposed. Only one cop said, "Let her close her blouse." Then they slammed me up against a wall. Phil Messing was the reporter with me. This cop was slamming the cuffs on me so hard that I was all bruised. As I'm being taken out, I said to Phil—he was totally in shock—"Get my equipment. Get my cameras." A photographer from the *Daily News*, Bill LaForce, was upstairs. He had already put his equipment away. He's looking at me like, "Oh my god, what's happening?" I said, "Take my picture," but he didn't have any equipment. I told Phil to throw him my camera. He got in trouble because one of the photographs he took got into my paper, not his. I made [the *Post*] give him credit. They took me to the precinct. Ken Chandler [then a managing editor] showed up. He walked into the precinct and basically said: stop everything. Everybody was stunned. He was so big. He just took me out. Why wouldn't they let me take pictures? I don't know! I can only suspect. That Black officer was the only Black man there. After that incident Black cops scorned me and accused me of getting that Black cop in trouble.

The paper was also the first to shine a light on a new breed of crime fighters.

CURTIS SLIWA, founder, Guardian Angels: The city was completely falling apart, because they had cut back funding [due to the city's financial crisis]. Koch comes in, he's slashing cops, firefighters, social workers, teachers. He had no choice. Out of that, I decided to fill the void by creating what everyone now knows as the Guardian Angels [originally called the Magnificent 13]. I'll never forget it. Unbeknownst to me, Steve Dunleavy, who was, I guess, the managing editor or the desk editor, said to Sam Rosensohn, who was a brand-new reporter, "Here is a bunch of guys up in the Bronx patrolling. They work at McDonald's. Go up there, see what the hell they're doing." The guy shows up at the Mickey D's where I'm the night manager and he's got on a Kevlar vest. He's shaking like a leaf. He says, "I understand you go out and patrol the trains at night. After the store closes." I say, "We're practicing right now." Sam Rosensohn comes with us. It's at a time where there were no transit cops because they had cut the transit police force at night. Gangs were roaming the trains, shooting people in the kneecaps, and then robbing them—your money or your life. He does two nights. Then, one night, I'm doing a run of Big Macs, and the house phone rings at McDonalds. It's Steve Dunleavy, who says, "Tomorrow it's going to be in the paper." February 8, 1979. He goes, "Kid, get ready for the ride of your life. Because you are going to get slammed like you never got slammed before. Good luck, mate." Right there I think, he's clearly not an American. Then the phone clicked and the rest was history. [The *Post* portrayed Sliwa as a local hero—attention that soon made him a national media figure.]

Although diversity and inclusion were not among the hallmarks of twentieth-century tabloid journalism in general, some staffers contend that race played a disproportionately large role in determining the *Post*'s crime coverage.

AMY PAGNOZZI, reporter, columnist, 1979–1993: One thing that used to bother me a lot is how little play murders would get if the victim was a Black person.

ERIC FETTMANN: Color meant down-market. Dunleavy, when he heard there'd been a murder, over the police radio or a call from the police shack, he would use something that was standard at the *Daily News* back in the '50s. If the murder was in Harlem, he'd ask: "Bongo or banjo?"

PHILIP MESSING: There's no doubt that the tabloids as a rule were not terribly sensitive to the racial issues going on at the time. I don't think it was unique to the *Post*.

REV. DR. C. VERNON MASON: Over the years, the general sentiment about the *New York Post* in the Black community was that it was the worst in terms of news coverage of Black people, of any of the media outlets. People knew what their content would be, their bias would be, and how they would cover the Black community. Basically, the general sentiment was that they would sensationalize crime.

JOANNE WASSERMAN, reporter, 1977–1986: The Brits and the Aussies weren't comfortable with people who weren't like them. You could see it. They were uncomfortable with people of color. They were uncomfortable with stories about people of color. Also, they were going for what I believe was now a kind of nonexistent, or at least dying, demographic, the white blue-collar reader in Brooklyn and parts of Queens.

AMY PAGNOZZI: The photo editor, I think it was Bob Young, told me that it was impossible to photograph Black people because they didn't come out right. I argued with him. He didn't feel like he was being racist when he said that.

BOB YOUNG, photo editor, 1978–1986: I don't remember saying that. Maybe I did. I'm not particularly proud of it in this day and age, but I'm certainly not going to dispute Amy.

DICK BELSKY, metropolitan editor, 1970–1989: I would just say it was a different time. We never really thought about covering the Black community or the Hispanic community. We just covered news.

HAL DAVIS, reporter, New York State Supreme Court, 1978–1993: I came across a story out of family court about a couple who were drug addicts. Two or three of their children had died. They were listed as crib deaths, sudden infant death syndrome. In those cases, the parents are not considered liable. The third or fourth time it happened, a trial judge said: "Something's going on here in this family. We're having trouble getting medical confirmation of why these kids died. And these people are druggies who neglected their kids—they didn't take them to the hospital. I am going to deprive them of custody of the children they still have"—there were two little babies—"because we don't want to see another baby die." This was a new application of the law. The *Daily News* gets wind of the story, too, and recognized it for what it was. At the *Daily News*, they cover the social services department. We at the *Post* did not because, you know, who cares about poor Black people. The *Daily News* [through social services sources] tracked down the kids—who were at the grandmother's home—and they hit pay dirt. They got a photograph of these two children—who were white—and put them on the front page where they belonged. I filed my story to Amy Pagnozzi on the city desk, and it was buried on, like, page sixteen. And people at the *Post* were shocked to see these bouncy cute white babies on the front page of the *Daily News*. There was this one editor at the desk who was always very curt with me. He walked over to Amy, and he said, "Hey, I thought these people were lowlifes." She says, "They *are* lowlifes. They let their kids die." He says, "You know what I mean." We knew exactly what he meant.

> The *Post*'s skewed perspective on race seeped from the news pages into other parts of the paper, leading it to miss key moments in the evolution of the city's culture—particularly when those moments did not emanate from the white and wealthy.

MARTHA COOPER, photographer, 1977–1980: The *Post* sent me to a subway station in Washington Heights because they got a tip that kids were rioting in the station. I go up there in my yellow Honda, and see that these boys, they look like they're fifteen or something and Hispanic, have been arrested in the subway. They had confiscated a gun, spray paint, and other weapons from these kids, but the cop said to me, "They weren't fighting, they were dancing. They were spinning on their heads and arguing about who had won." I'm like, spinning on their heads? This is amazing! I call the *Post* and tell them, "They weren't rioting, they were spinning on their heads." I asked the kids to come out and show me. They sent Cynthia Fagen, and she writes this story, "Jailhouse Rock." And the *Post* editors say, there is no riot, it's not a story. They don't even want the pictures. They were the first known photos of break dancing.

SUSAN WELCHMAN, photo editor, 1977–1979: The very first pictures.

MARTHA COOPER: That's classic *New York Post*. They wanted us to get these news-breaking stories, but you give them a story and they pass on it because it doesn't fit the slots they are expecting—sex, crime, and celebrity. And now break dancing is going to be an Olympic sport [at the 2024 Paris Games]. After Susan [Welchman] left, I hung on for a little while but it wasn't fun anymore. They weren't interested in doing the stories I wanted to do, so I left. I was introduced to Sally Banes, a dance writer, and we introduced break dancing to the world in the *Village Voice* in 1981.

10 | THE GOLDEN, SODDEN AGE OF DUNLEAVY

Steve's Sons, Epic Benders, Merry Fucking Christmas

Having succeeded Peter Michelmore as the *Post*'s metropolitan editor, Steve Dunleavy assembled his Murderers' Row of star reporters and instilled in them his by-any-means-necessary approach to getting the story.

DAVID NG, associate managing editor, 1980–1993: My job interview with Dunleavy consisted of four questions: (1) "Do you have any clips?" I showed him whatever stuff I had from UPI. (2) "Do you speak Chinese?" "Yes." (3) "How do you say MF in Chinese?" I'm trying to be polite. He wanted to know how to say "motherfucker" in Chinese. Luckily, I am the son of immigrants, and my father was a truck driver. The last question was "Can you start Friday?"

PHILIP MESSING, reporter, 1978–1991, 1994–2016: I became one of Dunleavy's, I guess, protégés. He favored certain people that he thought would be high energy. I don't want to get into this whole notion of primogeniture [but] the Number One Son was Sam Rosensohn. I might have been Number Two Son. There was something to suggest that he was a bit of heebephile because he seemed to like young Jewish boys—which was kind of funny because when you were in the bar with him, every other word out of his mouth was like, "This guy's a spic." "That guy was a wop." "This guy was a heeb." I don't think I ever heard him use the N-word. He was not exactly politically correct at any juncture, but he

seemed to have an affection for people that he thought were going to be inde-
fatigable. He didn't pay much attention to pedigrees because, as he told me on
a couple of occasions, he didn't finish high school. Industriousness was really
the whole metric that he measured people's worth to, the willingness to lay
down their bodies in support of not so much the *Post*, but him.

DAVID NG: He had this kind of weird paternal instinct. One night, I was at the bar,
and I happened to be smoking. And I don't smoke. I think it was a social thing
that night. Dunleavy came over and smacked the cigarette out of my hand and
said to me, "I don't ever want to see you smoking." Now this is a guy who I believe chain-smoked unfiltered Camels.

CHARLES LACHMAN, reporter, 1981–1988: I was one of Dunleavy's guys, one of his boys.
It was a fun camaraderie. We all had the same kind of skills that we brought to the
reporting game, which is a little more street than some of the old-timers, and I don't
say that with any disrespect at all, because these were people I grew up reading.

CHARLIE CARILLO, reporter, columnist, 1978–1993: I screwed something up once,
and Roger Wood was taking a piece out of me when Dunleavy stepped in and
said, "It's my fault, Roger. That was my fault." It wasn't true. It was my fault. And
at that moment, I'd have dived on a grenade for him, you know? He engendered
that kind of loyalty.

HAL DAVIS, reporter, New York State Supreme Court, 1978–1993: Dunleavy, for all his
faults, knew how to inspire his reporters. He had charisma and could be very
persuasive. He knew we were not the paper of record. He used to say loudly, "Let's
get the scam-o-matic going!" If Steve came across an American reporter who
thought he had ethics, he didn't press the reporter. He got one of his Aussie hit-
men to do the job. But there were two phenomenally good editors I've worked
with and one of them was Steve Dunleavy. He had the intensity and the charm to
pull off what he was doing. Steve was totally, totally out of that whole working-
class, tabloid, get-the-story world. He was a perfect Murdoch employee because
he lived for *the* story, whatever *the* story was that cycle. It would drive me crazy if
he had me chasing bullshit, but he knew what would work in the paper.

JERRY CAPECI, reporter, organized crime, 1966–1986: I had a big fight with Dunleavy
in the early '80s, when I was working back in the courts. There was a gangster

in prison who made an application before the judge to get a furlough to attend his granddaughter's or his grandson's prep school graduation. A furlough for one day or half a day, whatever it was. I came up with the story, and I thought it was a cute story. He got the furlough. Pete Tambone was the name of the gangster. It was the gangster's daughter's kid's graduation. Steve wanted me to put in the name of the kid. I said, "The kid's name doesn't matter. If you put the kid's name in there, you're going to have the kid ostracized as the gangster's grandson or granddaughter. The story is about the gangster. I'm going to give you his name, what he did, the case, ba, ba, ba. You don't need the [grandkid's] name." He said, "I want the name." I said, "Fuck you. I'm not going to give you the name." He said, "If you don't give me the fucking name, I'm not going to give you the story." I said, "Take the fucking story and shove it up your ass, I don't give a shit," and I hung up. I got along with Steve. He was a good boss in a lot of ways. He just said, "Fuck you," and the story did not run in the *New York Post*. The story did run in the *Daily News*. And the *Daily News* reporter, Dan Hays, did use the name of the grandson or granddaughter. I worked in a courthouse press room, where I sat one place and the *Daily News* guy sat in the same place and we had the same internal phone that we would pick up off the wall, so I could hear everything. He gets a phone call, and I can hear the mother screaming: "Why did you put the name in the goddamn, grr, grr, grr . . ." Dan had a look on his face, he wanted to crawl under the table. I was very, very happy with myself. It was easy for me because I'm an Italian, my name ends in a vowel, so I knew the stigma. I never told Steve about it. Steve, he didn't hold a grudge. He didn't give me shit about the fact that it was in the *Daily News*.

RICHARD ESPOSITO, reporter, 1982–1985: Steve was a master of tabloid journalism. Drunk or sober, he knew better than anyone how to teach a young reporter to do all the things you need to do to get the story. Some of them are ethical, some are things no one tells you—how to get a picture from a widow, or how to get a mother whose son might have killed somebody to let you in her apartment. The first thing was, always wear a shirt, tie, and jacket. Make people feel you're respecting them. Always. Some are things that a lot of reporters wouldn't think of—to bring flowers to someone's house and say, "I'm sorry you had a tragedy in your life. I'm from the *Post*." Remember Marla Hanson, the model who was slashed in the face? Steve convinced someone to get a hospital uniform and get to the hospital where she was being treated. That's completely unethical in the world of today. But in the world of tabloids, it's what you would do. Years later, I saw him at a reunion. He says, "Mate, mate, we would never, ever have done what they did in England." This was when British reporters hacked into the voicemail of the dead girl. [The hacking scandal in England—in which reporters illegally accessed information on phones belonging to celebrities and others, including a murdered thirteen-year-old girl—led Murdoch to shutter his *News of the World* in 2011.] I said, "Steve, you would have done that in a heartbeat. They just didn't have answering machines like that back then."

ERIC FETTMANN, associate editorial page editor, columnist, 1976–1991, 1993–2019: Dunleavy's strength as a journalist was his tenacity, his willingness to do anything for a story. And his weakness was his willingness to do anything for a story.

GEORGE ARZT, City Hall bureau chief, 1968–1986: The one thing you didn't want is for Steve to touch your copy because he just came up with every cliché in the world. He knew more clichés than any human being. In fact, he didn't know sentences, he only knew clichés. Although sometimes he would harden your lede, which was good.

As Murdoch's favorite larrikin, Dunleavy got away with behavior that, even in the 1980s, would not have been tolerated in others.

KELVIN MACKENZIE, night managing editor, 1978–1979: He was a one-man nuclear bloody generator, frankly. He had immense, immense energies beyond what's given to man. So he could work all the time. He could drink all the time. Belsky will tell you about the times when they were looking—this is prior to the mobile phone—they'd be trying to hunt all the bars out in New York trying to find Dunleavy, only to discover that he was, in fact, asleep under a desk in the far corner of the office.

PHILIP MESSING: The first time I met Steve, I think I had like eighteen Heinekens. I went to the bathroom a few times. I didn't see him go to the bathroom once. I said, "Where's the wooden leg? Does he have a catheter or what?"

DONNIE SUTHERLAND, city desk assistant, 1978–1988: Everybody that tried to keep up with him ended up in the gutter. Very few people could keep up. He was an alcoholic who came to work sober, in his mind anyway.

GEORGE ARZT: My proudest achievement was after an election night. We went to the mob bar on Cherry Street. The one without any windows. I drank Dunleavy under the table. I drank more Heinekens. It was six o'clock in the morning. I couldn't understand it. I was still standing but Dunleavy wasn't. I consider that the proudest achievement of my life.

PETER VECSEY, columnist, basketball, 1977–1991, 1994–2012: I was at the Post Mortem once with Lisker and Dunleavy was there. He wanted to fight me. Lisker had to step in. [Dunleavy] had a bad drinking problem. He'd get to the point where you could look at him the wrong way and he'd come at you. I tried to keep my distance from him.

MARTY McLAUGHLIN, public relations and political consultant: I'm a recovered alcoholic, but I would hang out in a bar with Steve and drink ginger ale. You had to be very careful because all of a sudden sometimes he would haul off and throw a punch.

JOE DE MARIA, photographer, 1977–1993: Steve Dunleavy had the assignment to get interviews or talk to these three characters [at a bar]. I think it was in Brooklyn. I don't know if they were mobsters or what, but he told me, "I'm gonna go in there and see what I can get from them, but we need pictures. I'm going to flush them out the back of the bar. Make sure you get a picture." I was in the back there waiting, [when] all of a sudden these three characters come running out and he's behind them. I popped three or four flashes, got pictures of them. They were about to jump me. But before I could do anything, Dunleavy ran up and cold-cocked the three of them. I'm telling you, I was like, "I'll go anyplace with you. I don't need a gun."

HAL GOLDENBERG, photographer, 1979–1986: Steve Dunleavy had a false tooth in the front that he clicked in, and he lost it. I don't know how. He swore he lost it at the Post Mortem. We were there looking for it, but we never found it.

RICHARD ESPOSITO: I had been at the *Daily News*, and then I'd been at the Philadelphia *Bulletin*, which closed. I was working for CBS Venture One [computerized "videotex" service], where they were paying like $30 a day, I'm not kidding, to write the morning news show and do investigation. I really needed another job. I called Myron [Rushetzky], who I knew for a long time. How? Myron knows everybody. He's always known everybody. I said, "I need a real job." He said, "The best way to get a job at the *Post* is through Dunleavy." I said, "How am I going to get to him?" He said, "He drinks every night at this after-hours club"—I want to say it was on Cherry Street, right around the corner from the *Post*. Myron said, "Dunleavy never has money, and he'll start borrowing from you. Just pay his bill every night. After a week, he'll realize he needs you. Then he'll hire you." I went like five days in a row. Steve would be there, drunk. He would say, "Mate, mate, do you have ten dollars?" At the end of the week, I said, "I need a job." He said, "Come in tomorrow." I started at the *Post* the next day. I was freelance. Eventually, Joy Cook in the union said, "You either have to hire this guy or let him go." I became an employee.

RAMONA GARNES, copy editor, 1978–1990, 2000–2004: Bill Feis and I are walking down Catherine Street. It's early in the morning—we might have been coming off the lobster shift—and we see this person. I look at Bill and he looks at me, and we say, "Isn't that the boss?" We were new. We didn't know much about Dunleavy then. He was lying like halfway on the sidewalk and halfway in the street, in the gutter. He was safe because Chinatown at that time of morning wasn't busy. Even in the middle of the day back then, Catherine Street was really sleepy. We go over and we're like, "Steve, Steve!" He was so still, he looked like he was dead.

DICK BELSKY, metropolitan editor, 1970–1989: [Editorial Manager] Peter Faris used to have this rule that you can drink as much as you want. But the one thing you could never do was call in sick the next day and say, "I'm hungover, I can't come in." You sucked it up and did the job. Steve did. He would sometimes stagger in at around six or seven in the morning from an all-nighter of drinking, fall asleep in one of the offices for a few hours, then clean up and go to work. There was a health club or something on the top floor of the building that had showers. One time Diane Reid [Roger Wood's assistant] went up there to get him because no one could find him. She came running down saying, "Steve's dead, Steve's dead!" because he was just lying there, not moving. Somebody else ran up and there was Steve, buck-ass naked, shaving and saying, "Hey, mate, I'll be down in a minute." He would suddenly wake up and then he would go back to work.

SUSAN MULCAHY, Page Six editor, 1978–1985: I used to swim laps every day, no matter what. One Saturday, the pool near my apartment was closed, so I went to a health club not too far from the *Post*. As I'm walking from the subway, Dunleavy stumbles out of a bar on the same block and says, "Mulcahy, you bloody cow, get in here and have a beer." He was with Peter Fearon. I said I was going swimming, but if they were still there when I came out, I'd have a beer. They were, and I did. Then I went home and took a nap because I don't usually drink at eleven a.m. They had been drinking steadily since Friday night. I heard later that Fearon dropped out at some point, but Steve kept going until early Monday, when he showed up in the newsroom and fell asleep in a chair until it was time to work.

DAVE BANKS, night managing editor, 1979–1981: When Dunleavy was stewed, it actually kept him quiet. He would never want to miss a deadline. He would work his bollocks off. In order to do that, he had to stay quiet. And he would always deliver—that was the amazing thing about him.

DICK BELSKY: There were all these stories about how nobody ever saw him eating. And, in fact, if you ate, sometimes he'd get mad at you. The other thing is, you could never pour your beer into a glass. You had to drink from the bottle. He had all these rules.

AMY PAGNOZZI, reporter, columnist, 1979–1993: I actually saw Dunleavy eat. He didn't eat a lot, but he would have to refuel once in a while. In the Post Mortem, we ate pasta with white clam sauce. I remember having a roach crawl across my plate in that place. And actually not being afraid of the roach but getting rid of it fast because I knew Geraldine [Gangi, who owned the Post Mortem with her husband, Charlie] would kill me if I saw a roach. I would have eaten the roach to avoid being caught with a roach in my food by Geraldine. And then I ate the food anyway.

DIANA MAYCHICK, entertainment writer, 1978–1989: One night I went to the Post Mortem with a bunch of people. Dunleavy was there, and Richard Johnson. Amy Pagnozzi was there, too. We get to the bar, and for some reason, Dunleavy did not want to be with Richard Johnson. So we left there in some surreptitious way and went to another bar. We were really drunk by the end, and all I know is, in the morning, in Washington Place, on my pullout bed, I wake up. And Amy's on one side of me and Dunleavy's on the other. Oh my god. Clearly nothing went on. We all passed out, I guess, but to wake between Dunleavy and Amy . . .

AMY PAGNOZZI: That's definitely possible.

LENORE DAVIS, photographer, 1980–1993: Dunleavy would say things to me like, "Do you know how far you could go if you slept with me?"—in the city room, in front of everybody. I remember Bill Condie dropping his face in his hand. Bill was such a gentleman. These other guys, all these guys were like little groupies. If [Dunleavy] shit in the corner, they'd be there to lick it up. They chased him around. When he said, "Do you know how far you could go if you slept with me?" I said, "Probably to the nearest VD clinic." The whole city room laughed, and he said, "That's why I love her. She's so quick."

DIANA MAYCHICK: I was walking to the elevator one day and Dunleavy yells— loud!—"You're the only girl I haven't slept with!"

> The tabloid frenzy personified by Dunleavy meshed nicely with one of New York's burgeoning cultural movements: the *Post* may have missed break dancing, but it did not bypass punk. The paper itself became part of the scene.

JIM FARBER, former music critic, New York *Daily News*: This was the period of punk, and the [Murdoch *Post*] was so punk. When you're a kid with a punk sensibility, you're interested in anarchy. I'm sure you probably could find pictures of Debbie Harry at CBGBs. She would dance around with copies of the *New York Post* when Blondie was playing. [She is also seen holding the *Post* in the opening seconds of the video for her hit song "Call Me."] This was like part of the act. It was just so unhinged, and so incredibly New York. At CBGBs, [the *Post*] was like mother's milk. It was so much of a piece. Because CBGBs was disgusting, the paper was disgusting, everything was disgusting. It was perfect. In terms of the level of outrage and attitude, it captured this out-of-control city of the '70s and '80s. So that was kind of a prime period [of the *Post*] for me. Even though it was copying the British tabloids' hyperventilation, it was just so New York. My friends were all like this. Everybody I knew had the same sensibility. Everybody I knew had this same gobsmacked love of the *New York Post*.

> Though Kelvin MacKenzie made an indelible mark at the *Post*, he didn't stay long. In 1979, several months before he departed, he brought in his replacement, Dave Banks, another Fleet Street veteran.

KELVIN MACKENZIE: My wife didn't like life in America and was anxious to get back to family in London, so that was the end of that. It's always a great shame to me, even though I had my doubts how long I would have survived. You can only run that very narrow line—pushing the headlines, the agenda, the content really to the breaking point in the media—for a certain amount of time, and then you fall off the other side. Something will go wrong. Murdoch was quite bad-tempered when I told him, I think mainly because that was another thing on his to-do list. It wasn't me so much as it was he had a lot on his plate, and me buggering off was unhelpful. I don't believe I really got up to speed in understanding the vagaries of New York City and its people in the time I was there—about eighteen months, maybe two years.

DICK BELSKY: The people that followed Kelvin were very much in his mold. He brought in Dave Banks, who was almost as good as Kelvin, and he was a lot nicer guy. He was the same in that he knew what he wanted. He was also very intimidating because of his size. [Banks was a robust six foot five.] He was a gentle giant, but when he would get mad and stand up—I mean, he was a huge man. Roger [Wood] could be really annoying, and he could piss people off. He came out and he criticized something Dave had done on the desk. Dave stood up, towered over Roger, and I could see Roger kind of slink back.

DAVE BANKS: Kelvin recruited me to work at the *Post*. I didn't realize he was recruiting me to replace him, because his wife was unhappy, but he left after about six months of me being there. He was always a sneaky bugger. He's a great friend and still is, but he never told me he was going to leave. I was very nervous coming to this newspaper in New York. I was a boy from Warrington, Lancashire. I knew very little of the world and I'd never traveled. I remember flying across the Atlantic with my eight-month-old daughter and my wife asleep beside me, child sleeping in a bassinet, me with a reading lamp on. I brought two paperback books that I thought would be useful. One was about the importance of trade unions in America. The other was American politics. I might as well have thrown away the trade union book, because whereas unions were very important and strong in Britain, I never got the sense that unions mattered that much in America. But the paperback on politics saw me really well-versed by the time I arrived at JFK.

One day in December 1979, as his employees celebrated the Christmas holiday in the *Post*'s fourth-floor newsroom, Rupert Murdoch stayed in his office two floors above. That was probably a good thing.

ERIC FETTMANN: It was the last Christmas party actually held in the office. What I remember about it was a certain member of the staff who took people out on the stairs going up to the composing room for a quickie and then came back and left with someone else for a quickie—oh, there must have been about half a dozen.

JAMI BERNARD, chief movie critic, 1978–1993: There was an American editor who didn't get along with the Brits—Craig Ammerman. There was a fistfight during the party, big fistfight—red faces and trying to pull their shirts off. I don't remember who he was fighting, though.

PHILIP MESSING: I took a friend to that Christmas party. He was absolutely stupefied because there was a guy named Danny [O'Donnell], who used to work in the payroll area. Danny was, I don't know, maybe about 245, 250 pounds, and he looked like a rough-and-tumble sort of fellow. He came up to the Christmas party. Craig Ammerman was the [co–managing] editor at the time. Ammerman took umbrage at the fact that this guy, Danny, was at this party that was for the editorial staff on the fourth floor when he worked in another part of the building. He said, "What are you doing here? You don't belong here. Get lost." Danny says, "I don't work for you." Ammerman says, "Fuck you." They used to say that the fastest line between two points is between Craig Ammerman and a box of doughnuts. He probably tipped in at, I would say, maybe 310 or 290 pounds. Within a matter of moments, the two of them were fighting each other in the city room like a stegosaurus and a brontosaurus in some sort of prehistoric *Jurassic Park* scenario. My friend, who was a lawyer, looked at me, incredulous. He says, "This goes on all the time? People just fight in the newsroom?" I said, "Yeah."

DONNIE SUTHERLAND: It was like something out of *Caligula*.

PETER TOCCO, sports makeup, 1970–2013: At one of the parties, Dunleavy ran across the top of the desks. He got to a point—you remember how the fire sprinklers hung down? He smacked his head right into it. He fell backwards onto the desk.

MICHAEL SHAIN, television editor, 1978–1993, 1996–2013: They never had the Christmas party in the newsroom ever again because they were worried about what was going to happen to the equipment—in those days remember we had VDTs.

SUSAN MULCAHY: I don't know what led to the fight, but I remember Ammerman stood on a desk at one point. I heard later that after the party one of them—I can't remember which—drove his car into the window of a car dealership way over on the West Side. Murdoch was upstairs as the party was going on. When he left, a drunk guy, or maybe a couple of drunks, got onto the elevator with him and gave him tips about how he could improve the paper. The next day a sign went up saying "no alcohol on the premises." Which was hilarious when you think about who was running the place.

PHILIP MESSING: So the end result was that they banned the *Post* from having parties in the newsroom, and the following year, I think it was, or a year after, they had it at the local church on the back end of the *Post*, about two or three blocks away.

CHARLIE CARILLO: It was in that church basement with the steam table and the Sternos under the sausage and peppers—Our Lady of Perpetual Guilt or whatever it was.

JAMI BERNARD: I was thrown out of two of the parties. At one, I punched Dunleavy in the gut. There was this nude photo of me that people got their hands on and showed around to everyone including all the printers. Now, at this age, I look back, I have the photo and I think, what a gorgeous photo. It was taken secretly, on a cruise. We called it the cruise to nowhere. A group of us from the newsroom went on a cruise together to the Caribbean. I was sunbathing topless, and Chris [Oliver] was up above on some deck. I didn't know. He took the photo and he showed it around. What I was trying to do was beat him up and Dunleavy stopped me. I punched Dunleavy in the gut. I also threw a drink in his face. So they made me leave. At the other party, an ex of mine showed up, and I got so mad it looked like there was going to be . . . something—so they quickly ushered me out. The Christmas party was always a place where people were getting into trouble.

PHILIP MESSING: They had a fight at the party in the church, too, and they banned us from the church.

11 | GUTTER RATS
Sports Desk Slugfests, Damned Yankees, the Back Page

The sports department that Jerry Lisker and Greg Gallo built beginning in the late 1970s reflected the take-no-prisoners attitude of Murdoch's *Post*, and yet it was a world unto itself at 210 South Street—not subject to city room rules or the whims of senior management.

GREG GALLO, executive sports editor, 1977–1989, 1994–2009: We were an island. When Jerry [Lisker] was there, we were even more of an island. He liked to have his little gutter rats. We had chips on our shoulders because Jerry was like that. We had nothing against the city room, but we felt a little bit apart from them. In those days we never even went to meetings. Eventually we did, but Roger Wood, who conducted the meetings, didn't know anything about sports. So he wasn't that interested in what we were working on unless we had a big story. Then he wanted to know about it.

HARVEY ARATON, sportswriter, basketball, 1977–1982: The sports department was a bit of a nuthouse. They used to stick your check into these little mailboxes. I remember coming in one day. I really needed it to pay my rent or something, and my check wasn't there. I got really pissed off. I was a bit of a hot head in those days, and there were these wooden spools of brown paper that used to lie around. There was an empty one sitting on the desk near the mailboxes, and I picked it up and flung it across the office. It smashed into the glass window of [managing editor] John Van Doorn's office. It didn't break the glass, but it ricocheted off the window and bounced around the floor. Van Doorn happened to be in his office and came running out, like, "What the *fuck*?" And everybody in sports—they knew who had thrown it—put their heads down, like, "I didn't see anything." I just turned my back and started stuffing something into the mailboxes. He went into his office, and nobody ever got into any trouble for it. That was the kind of stuff that went on.

DIANA MAYCHICK, entertainment writer, 1978–1989: The sports guys at night would zoom around in their chairs—really fast—and throw a basketball at each other's heads. There was no hoop. Throw it at each other's heads.

GREG GALLO: [In 1979] we had a guy who was a clerk at the time [Elli Wohlgelernter]. He went to Columbia. He was a runner and the New York Marathon was about to happen. He said, "I'm entering the marathon." We said, "How well do you run?" He gave a time. I said, "That's pretty good." In those days everybody started [the race] together. We said, let's have fun with this, as opposed to just tailing along. "How about you bolt to the lead as soon as they drop the flag, and we're going to say 'Our Guy Leads the Marathon' [the eventual headline would be '*Post* Sets the Pace']—and write it from the perspective of the few steps that you're going to be in front of all these great runners." [Wohlgelernter actually jumped out *before* the flag dropped.] We had a photographer poised, and Elli took the lead by ten yards or so—he was in front of everybody because he snuck up. We played it almost like a gag, but we had the picture to support it. We thought it was fun, and maybe some readers did. But the marathon people didn't think it was fun. They changed the rules after that. Now, the elite runners go first, and all the schleps stay in the back.

PHIL MUSHNICK, columnist, television sports, 1973–current: Lisker had one of those glass-enclosed offices. When he saw Roger Wood walking by, he'd pick up a phone and say, "Goddamn it!" and start screaming. There was no one on the other end. He just wanted to make sure Roger saw he was working his ass off. He was putting on a show.

GREG GALLO: Jerry Lisker walked into the office one day, he sits down, and his hand is all swollen. I said, "What happened to you?" He says, "I was out last night with Blue Rinse [George Viles, a top News Corp executive]. I got in a scuffle with some idiot we ran into and I just popped the guy, that's all." He comes back later in the afternoon; he's got a cast. He broke his hand. He was a roust-about, and so were his boys. And we were his boys.

HARVEY ARATON: Jerry really didn't get his hands dirty in the day-to-day opera-tion unless we were covering a fight. Then he was intimately involved. He was attractive to the Murdoch people as someone who could create a raucous, chaotic sports department.

MICHAEL KAY, sportswriter, 1982–1988: Greg Gallo worked you to the bone. But I had nothing against it. Because that's all I knew. It was like Stockholm syn-drome. That's the way I thought everybody worked. When I was doing college basketball, I went to the Final Four [1985]. It was me, Steve Serby, and Peter Finney Jr. It was in Lexington [Kentucky]. I remember Gallo telling me, "I want you to be busy. I want to see a lot of bylines." Villanova shocked the world and upset Georgetown. Because Gallo was in my head—I don't know if it's still the record, but it was the record for a while—I had thirteen bylines in the paper the next day. That was just Gallo, riding Secretariat down the stretch in the Belmont, he just kept whipping.

HARVEY ARATON: Gallo was Jerry's opposite. He was a mild-mannered-looking guy whose shoulders were always stooped. He looked like he had the weight of the world on him, day in, day out.

> The sports (and other) editors' favorite local hangout was an Italian social club located on the ground floor of Knickerbocker Village, a housing complex known at that time to be populated by organized crime figures. If you knew the right people—and only if you knew the right people—you could drink there and get a plate of pasta.

GREG GALLO: There was a place behind the *Post* when it was on South Street, Marie's, where we went routinely for lunch. I don't know if there was an official name for the place. Marie tended bar, so we called it Marie's. It was a [social] club next to Pete's deli that was closed to most people, but Jerry acted like he owned the place. It was a dive, like one little room, no windows. They'd cook spaghetti and meatballs upstairs. That's it, one meal, everybody had the same thing. Every time we had a sports celebrity show up at the *Post*, we would take them to Marie's. Jerry took Charlie Finley, the owner of the Kansas City Athletics and then the Oakland A's. Another time, there was Boom Boom Mancini, the fighter. We would sit at the bar and have these fun conversations.

CYNTHIA FAGEN, reporter, 1976–1986: It was run by a couple of guys, if you know what I mean. They were very protective. If they knew you, they would look after you.

CHARLIE CARILLO, reporter, columnist, 1978–1993: I got thrown out of the social club once. I went in there for a drink and they said, "Do we know you?" I said, "I just came for a drink." They said, "We're going to have to ask you to leave."

As professional basketball's popularity exploded, the *Post* dominated coverage in the city. And the tabloid's sharp-elbowed NBA columnist Peter Vecsey became its most feared chronicler as well as a polarizing figure among his colleagues.

DAVE CHECKETTS, former president, New York Knicks; former president and CEO, Madison Square Garden: The rest of us read Pete because we were so happy it wasn't us. That's basically how it worked. We felt bad for our friends that were getting killed, but we were just mostly glad it wasn't us.

GREG GALLO: [Peter] Vecsey had an in with the NBA and its players. He'd coached some of them, way back, in the Rucker league [Harlem's storied summer league]. He was a coach for these great athletes, including the pros that would go up there and play. He knew all these people who were in the NBA. He knew the front-office people, but he also knew the players. His columns would be loaded with these little nuggets of information that would have everybody's head spinning, whether it was a trade rumor or something management wanted kept quiet. He would get it from these guys. He was the top of the line when it came to the NBA. He was unique. He became a very popular read.

DAN KLORES, filmmaker: Vecsey was chased out of locker rooms by six-foot-nine, 250-pound guys who wanted to kill him. He'd give them nicknames and report on their personal lives. He was sarcastic and colorful and almost always right, and fearless. Man, he really didn't give a shit who he pissed off.

PETER VECSEY, columnist, basketball, 1977–1990, 1994–2012: I gave a lot of people nicknames. I knew Marvin Webster since he was a young guy. We were tight.

Then he came to the Knicks, and he bombed. I used to kill him in the paper. So that relationship went down the tubes. I did not give him the nickname "The Human Eraser." That was too positive. I think I called him the "Number Two Pencil." The one I'm most proud of is "Larry Legend" for Larry Bird. In the early Knicks days, I called Spencer Haywood, "Driftwood" or "Deadwood." Joe Barry Carroll, I called "Joe Barely Cares." And when you're known for giving people nicknames, people are going to send you nicknames. I had a referee who sent me nicknames—he was responsible for naming my column Hoop du Jour.

HARVEY ARATON: I was working dayside as a clerk, and the Knicks were playing a game in Cleveland that night. They called in Vecsey, and Peter told them, essentially, I don't do windows. I'm not a game story reporter, I'm a columnist. I'd had a lot of conversations with Peter taking his copy over the phone during the NBA finals in the spring of '77. He knew I had an interest in the game and knew the game. He pointed to me and said, "Send that guy. He knows basketball." Jerry called me over and said, "Can you get to Cleveland tonight?" It was probably eleven o'clock in the morning. I said, "I'll walk there if I have to." I ran home, drove to the airport, and hopped on a plane. I found myself in the suburbs of Cleveland covering a Knicks game before I really knew what the hell I was doing. But again, that was the kind of change that was occurring rapidly at the paper in general.

> Just a few weeks into the 1978–1979 NBA season, Araton found himself in the middle of one of the biggest pro basketball stories of the decade, involving one of the sport's legends.

HARVEY ARATON: After the newspaper strike [of 1978], the *Post* goes back first. The Knicks were on a West Coast road trip and Willis Reed, who was my boyhood hero back when he was the captain of the Knicks, was now the coach. He was said to be on shaky ground with the new president at [Madison Square] Garden, Sonny Werblin. I fly out to pick up the team in Seattle. It was the middle of the afternoon, and I'm the only reporter at practice. I ask Willis if the rumors about his job status were disconcerting, and he said matter-of-factly, "I've got a lot of young players on the team, and it creates a sense of instability. They want to know who their coach is going to be. So I kind of would like to know whether I'm in or out." I went back and wrote the story and finessed the lede a bit because he hadn't said it as an ultimatum. He'd said it as more of a plea. But the lede was rewritten, inaccurately paraphrasing Willis demanding a decision "one way or another," which was clearly not his intent. When I wrote the story in my hotel, it was like seven o'clock in New York. It was too late to call Werblin at the office to get a response. The rewritten story ran just with Willis's quotes. I called Werblin the next day to get a response, but also to let him know that the story didn't actually read the way I wrote it. I felt like I owed that to Willis. Werblin said, "Okay, I hear you." But three days later, when we got home from the West Coast trip, he called a press conference, fired Willis, and said, "Nobody gives me an ultimatum." Werblin seized on the "one way or another" rewrite to pull the plug. There I was, in my first several months on the beat, Willis Reed is my boyhood hero, and because of the way the *Post* went about its business in those days—not going with what the reporter filed, but writing the story for the headline effect—we definitely participated in the dismissal of this New York icon from the job he had coveted: to coach the team that he had captained and [in 1970 and 1973] led to win the only two championships—still—in the history of the franchise.

The combative style that Pete Vecsey brought to his column was also aimed at the competition—including Mike Lupica, then the star sportswriter for the New York *Daily News*—and sometimes bled into his behavior toward his *Post* colleagues.

PHIL MUSHNICK: Vecsey dealt in intimidation. He was a bully, and a bit of a psychopath.

PETER VECSEY: Only a *bit* of a psychopath?

MARK KRIEGEL, sports columnist, 1991–1993: Vecsey could be a terrorist if he thought you were competition. He called Mike Lupica "the little man on the wedding cake." What Vecsey did wasn't necessarily literate, but it was its own language. I played a lot of basketball and hung out in a lot of basketball parks. And Vecsey was the shit. It was like he invented punk rock. I know that Murdoch loved him.

PETER VECSEY: There were guys that I broke in that I felt were disrespectful to me afterward. So I cut them loose. Harvey Araton is one of those guys. I caught him going through my mailbox. People who had left numbers for me there. I was like, what?

HARVEY ARATON: We each have different memories of what the argument was about. I'll always say that I was eternally grateful for Peter helping me get the Knicks beat, but it could be very difficult to work with him—especially since I was the beat reporter, and he was a columnist in this sort of self-appointed policeman's role. What I recall is there was one summer where we were off-season but working our beat. I had heard that one of the Knicks players, a guy named Ray Williams, who was a free agent, might get an offer from the Cleveland Cavaliers. I was in the office one night working rewrite, and I moseyed up to Peter and I said, "I heard something about Ray Williams and Cleveland." He looked at me and said, "Yeah, I've heard something about that." That was the last I spoke to him about it. It was my beat, so I continued to work on it. I confirmed it and wrote it, and it was a back page, with the old "*Post* Exclusive" slapped on it. The day that it ran, I got a call from Mushnick saying, "I'm in the office. Vecsey's here, and he's steaming mad." I said, "About what?" "He said you stole his story." I said, "Stole his story? It's my beat." I went up to him and told him that I had heard it, and that I thought he'd be happy that one of us confirmed it. And that we beat the *Daily News* and the *Times* on it. Anyway, we had words and that was it.

GREG GALLO: Araton and Vecsey hated each other, but everybody hated Vecsey. They thought he got away with murder, because, number one, they were jealous of his contract. He had a long-term deal for a good chunk of change and the others were envious. And Peter was not easy to get along with. There was a time when I didn't talk to him for two years. And I was the guy running the department. Jerry couldn't tell Peter what to do or suggest what he could be doing, because Peter would take offense and do some silly things or say something in his column that was not appropriate. Then we'd have to kill his column. It became untenable. I said [to Jerry], "You can handle him, but I'm not. I'm hands-off at this stage." Then we had a Marie's sit-down where we were able to verbalize our thoughts and got back together again.

HARVEY ARATON: I don't [think there was resentment of Vecsey]. Actually, I think most of us—I know the other basketball writers—loved the fact that the *Post* had something that nobody else had. And that was a full-time person devoted to just covering the league. Specialty columnists now are the norm, and they are the people making the most money by and large in the sports part of the print or digital industry. Peter, I believe, was the first. He was the groundbreaker, the first insider whose only job was to produce three columns a week on the NBA. In my early years there, covering the Knicks, that was a tremendous source of pride—to be working for the paper that was considered the basketball paper.

MICHAEL KAY: Vecsey was great with me. When I was a clerk, sometimes I would take his dictation and stuff like that. He always treated me like gold and all the other clerks liked him, too. I don't know if he shot up, but he never shot down.

GREG GALLO: We wouldn't let another writer travel to a team's location without a specific reason. Vecsey had an in with the people he was trying to go see. The other guys didn't have the connections to bring back what he was going to bring back. So we would allow him certain privileges. Do I regret it? Yeah, from time to time I'd think, maybe we're a little bit too lenient with him, because it caused other frictions that didn't need to be there. But, yeah, I gave him a lot of rope. At my retirement party, he came over to me and said, "I just want to say one thing. What I appreciate the most, you let me do what I thought I could do; what I thought I could give you. And hopefully you thought it was worthwhile." I said, "I did." And it was true.

> The Yankees remained Britney Spears in pinstripes, a never-ending source of controversy and drama.

GEOFF REISS, former senior vice president, ESPN: The drama got even thicker in 1978. The team got off to a bad start when a fight between Billy Martin and Reggie Jackson broke out in the dugout at Fenway Stadium. Martin accused Jackson of not hustling. Martin gets fired. The Yankees end up winning the World Series again.

HENRY HECHT, sportswriter, baseball, 1969–1984: In the middle of the '78 season, the Yankees were struggling. Martin is doing a gaslight. He's Charles Boyer. Reggie's Ingrid Bergman—and Reggie is falling for it. They're in an extra-inning game with the Kansas City Royals, and Billy wants Reggie to make a sacrifice bunt. Well, Reggie can't bunt, and the cardinal rule of any coach/manager is, you always have to give your player the best chance to succeed. So, Reggie bunts once. Foul. Billy takes the bunt sign off. Reggie says, "Screw you." He bunts again and he strikes out. Now Billy goes berserk and suspends Reggie for five games. When Reggie's suspension is up, we're in Chicago and he has not repented. Basically, it's "Fuck you, Billy." Martin hears about it. He's not happy. He has a couple of drinks in the press room after the game.

The *New York Times*'s Murray Chass and I are the only permanent first-string league writers on the trip. We get to the airport and Billy tears Reggie a new asshole. I go to the phone and call the desk. Big story and it's still an afternoon paper, so I've got hours.

Billy comes back from the airport bar and after all these years as a player and a manager, he says, "Did you guys get your story in?" Nobody had their story in yet. Murray and I started walking with him to the gate. Billy is just raging. Then, the famous quote: "The two of them deserve each other. One's a born liar, the other's convicted." So, Reggie's the born liar and Steinbrenner was the convicted liar [a reference to Steinbrenner's illegal contributions to Nixon's campaign]. We're heading back to Kansas City. I talk to Reggie, and he unloads. I go back to my room there, call the desk, and tell them the world is blowing up. George called at one point. "Did he really say it?" he asks. I tell him the whole story, which I write. The *Post* puts it on the front page. I also wrote a column—a goodbye and good riddance about Billy. No one told me, but I knew he was gone. I went to bed at six a.m. When Billy announced his resignation under pressure, I was sleeping. I got up at two o'clock and Bob Lemon was the new manager.

DAVID SCHNEIDERMAN, former editor in chief, publisher, CEO, *The Village Voice*: Right after Billy Martin got fired by Steinbrenner in the summer of '78, I remember seeing a guy hawking the *Post* on 57th Street. He was saying, "See what happens when you piss off your boss?"

HENRY HECHT: In 1979, Yankees' spring training was still in Fort Lauderdale [Florida], but they would always take a relatively lengthy trip to the Tampa Bay area because that's where Steinbrenner owned a hotel and where his company, American Ship Building, was located. It was a way to show off his prized possession, and he eventually moved them there permanently. There was a curfew for the players, and he had security people on the long hall where they were staying. Well, the players wanted to go out and party because they were men in their twenties and thirties, loaded with testosterone, and they figure out that you could open the windows that looked onto the back of the hotel. It was just a little bit of a drop to get out, and it wasn't too hard to get back in. So a bunch of players went to a room on that side of the hall, got out, and partied. But when they came back, they got caught.

Thurman Munson, Mickey Rivers, and Jim Spencer were among them. I wrote about it, and maybe that day or a day later I was in the clubhouse. Spring training was very relaxed. At a real game, you're never in the clubhouse until the game's over. But it's spring training, I'm in the clubhouse, and Graig Nettles sees me, and calls me a "backstabbing Jew cocksucker." I wrote about that. He claimed he called me a "backstabbing Judas cocksucker." That's a lie. I may wear a hearing aid now, but I didn't wear one then.

> Thurman Munson may have enjoyed an occasional night out with the boys, but he was essentially a family man. In fact, he was learning to fly so he could more easily visit his wife and children in Ohio on days off. He piloted his last flight on August 2, 1979.

MYRON RUSHETZKY, head city desk assistant, 1974–1989, 1991–2013: Steve [Dunleavy] sometimes went to the Post Mortem during the day. One day he was down there when Roger came out of his office looking for him. He'd gotten a call saying [Yankees catcher] Thurman Munson had been killed in a plane crash. He'd probably gotten the call from Howard Rubenstein [powerful public relations executive who repped both the Yankees and the *Post*]. I knew Steve was downstairs, so I called the pay phone down there—was it 227-3344? Maybe—and he picks up the phone. I said, "Steve, get up here. Thurman Munson is dead." With Steve, I would have codes if someone called for him, with levels of urgency. If it was something really, really, really big, it was "The balloon is up." That was like it was nuclear war. Then after that, we instituted something beyond "the balloon is up." I would call and say, "Thurman Munson is dead." That became the ultimate.

> Murdoch did not devote deep attention to what transpired in sports, but he liked the approach taken by the department's reporters and editors, which matched the ferocity of the *Post*'s news and gossip pages.

GREG GALLO: [Murdoch was] always positive, always upbeat, never telling us in sports what had to be done. He was respectful of our knowledge and the way we were doing things. He would stop by the little office that Jerry and I had on South Street. Two of us sat in that tiny cubicle. After he'd go through the newsroom on his way back to the elevators, he would come through sports, duck in, and say, "How's everything going?" He always kept it upbeat: "How you doing? How you feeling? How's your wife?" Like that.

BOB DRURY, sports columnist, 1977–1984: Murdoch used to have lunches in a dining room on one of the top floors. I was up there three times for lunch. Every single time, he said the same thing to me, "Have we met before?"

> Though New York's football teams did not have an owner as outrageous and publicity mad as George Steinbrenner, they still provided plenty of red meat for the *Post* to grill.

BOB DRURY: The first year I started covering the Giants, they had a coach, Ray Perkins—"the Perk," I called him—who was a real southern redneck. He had been an All-American wide receiver at Alabama. I don't know why the Maras hired him, but he and I were oil and water. I used to ask him questions that he wasn't used to getting from sportswriters. At one point he stood up, and I could tell he wanted to fight me. I stood up, too, and a million people got between us. Back then, Wellington Mara owned the team with his nephew Tim Mara, who was a scumbag of the first order. He would beat up women. It would get covered up, but I had a cousin who was a cop. He would tell me about this. I didn't write about it. I couldn't prove it. But I knew what a scumbag he was. At some point, Tim Mara heard about this thing with me and Perkins. You'd always get to the stadium three hours before the game. So, say it's a four o'clock game, I'm sitting there at one o'clock, and Tim Mara comes up to me. He says, "I didn't like what you wrote about Ray." I said, "Tim, that's your prerogative to not like what I wrote. There are a lot of things I don't like about you, but it's my prerogative." He said, "Like what?" And I said, "Well, Tim, I could tell you, but I'm not a woman, so you probably wouldn't hit me like you hit them." He came at me. He had two guys with him who immediately pulled him off. All I could think of was "*Post* Beat Writer and Giants Owner in Press Box Fistfight." I'm sure the *Post* headline writers would have come up with something much better, but that's the kind of shit that Blackie Lisker wanted.

> Lisker and Gallo's zeal to break news sometimes led to their reporters becoming the news, and other times, the protagonist—or antagonist—of a wild tale told over too many drinks at a bar.

BOB DRURY: Mike Marley was the best boxing writer in the city, but he was fucking nuts. [In 1980], we were at the "No Más" fight, Sugar Ray Leonard vs.

Roberto Durán—"Manos de Piedra," hands of stone—in New Orleans. Do you know what running is? We had so many editions that whoever was watching the fight would be on the phone with the night editor giving a running description of what was happening: "Durán throws a right; and Sugar Ray is on his bicycle. He's walking back." That's running. Mike was supposed to do the running that night. I'm watching the undercard, and Marley's not around. Blackie comes up to me and goes, "You're doing running tonight." I said, "I thought I was down here doing sidebars." He goes, "Ahhh, last I saw Marley, he was with this fucking Colombian hooker, and I don't know where the fuck he is. So you're doing the running."

PHIL MUSHNICK: I caught Howard Cosell being given the results of boxing matches and then making believe that he guessed them right. It was a pretty big story for its time.

BOB DRURY: When the 1980 Winter Olympics up in Lake Placid [New York] came around, the *New York Times* sent, like, sixteen reporters and thirteen photographers, and even the *Daily News* had a dozen people up there. But at the *Post*, we didn't give a shit about the Winter Olympics except for this skater named Tai Babilonia, who wouldn't talk to the press. Blackie tells Marley and me, "I'm sending you to Lake Placid. You got one fucking thing to do. Get an interview with Tai Babilonia." Okay, sure. Marley and I get up there, and our first night, we decided to scale the fence into the Olympic Village to look for Tai Babilonia. It's the Cold War. The Russians are in the same Olympic Village. Within five minutes, security was on us. Spotlights. I felt like *Stalag 17* or something. We're taken to the Lake Placid police station, and for some reason, the desk sergeant or whoever was in charge says, "I gotta keep one of you guys overnight. I'm sorry. That's the rules." We get one phone call, so we call Blackie at home. It's two or three in the morning. I explained the situation to him. He says, "Okay, let me think." The Olympics were starting the next day. Blackie says, "Bobby, you're better on deadline. Tell them to keep fucking Marley." So Marley spent the night in jail.

MARTHA COOPER photographer, 1977–1980: They sent me some place in the Midwest where athletes were training for the Olympics. They told me to be sure to get cleavage, and I tried hard. I told somebody to take her top off by saying something like, I want to see your muscles, but what I really wanted was to photograph her in her sports bra because they could airbrush the cleavage in. I consider myself a feminist, but I figured if I'm going to work for this newspaper, I have to try to get them what they want.

In 1981, a sports columnist's dim view of Richard Todd, the New York Jets quarterback who succeeded Joe Namath, led to a trip to the hospital—and the *Post*'s back cover.

STEVE SERBY, sports columnist, 1972–1993, 1994–current: Richard Todd did not have the temperament to play in New York much less follow a legend like Joe Namath. We had our differences because I was partial to his backup quarterback Matt Robinson, who I thought was a more fiery leader for that team in 1978. I remember writing a column where the headline was "Jets will go nowhere with Todd at the helm." It turns out I was right, but I think that story sent him over the edge. I knew he was ticked off, and for a number of weeks I avoided him. Then one day in the locker room, November 4, 1981, we got into an exchange of f-you's. Most of the team had already left the locker room to practice, and I had a sense of impending doom when Todd was staring at me and cursing. Sure enough, he lunged at me, grabbed me around my neck with his right hand, pushed me back, and smashed my head into a locker. I slumped to the bottom of the locker and must have blacked out. When I woke up, which wasn't long afterward, I saw Mark Gastineau standing over me wondering what the hell happened. Todd had already gone out to practice. I think Gastineau said to me, although it may have been someone else, "It looks like your nose is broken," which it wasn't. Larry Weisman, who was with a Westchester newspaper, took me to the local hospital to be examined. They saw that I was very shaken up, but they weren't going to admit me overnight. I did have an abrasion on my nose, so I got a Band-Aid from someone there, and our photographer Bob Olen took a picture of me. The next day, the back page was a huge picture of me with this Band-Aid on my nose, and the headline was "Todd Assaults Our Man."

BOB DRURY: After the Todd thing, the Jets were playing Baltimore the next week. Blackie said to me and Marley—we were both fairly big guys—"I want you to go to the game and pick a fight with Richard Todd. You don't have to write anything. Just pick a fight." Okaaay. Sure. I can't be certain someone tipped them off, but they knew what Marley and I were there for, and they had put this big long, wide table in front of Todd's locker. So these two fucking thugs from the *Post* can't accidentally nudge him and turn it into a brawl.

STEVE SERBY: The *Post* filed a criminal complaint, and the Nassau County DA, I think his name was Denis Dillon, dismissed it. While that was going on, the *Post* had me not cover the Jets for two weeks. That first week, the Jets were on TV playing the Baltimore Colts, and the game was a blowout. If Richard Todd had thrown four interceptions in that game, I might have been a hero, but he had an unbelievable game. So I was villain number one in the eyes of Jets fans. During the game, Bob Costas was doing play-by-play, and former Cincinnati Bengals tight end Bob Trumpy was doing color, and they were debating the incident. Because the game was a blowout and they had nothing to talk about, they spent like ten to fifteen minutes debating my incident with Richard Todd. Costas was the voice of reason. He took my side, and Trumpy took the side of the athlete, saying that I might have provoked him or whatever. It was like *The Twilight Zone*. I couldn't believe my ears and my eyes.

> Along with becoming the center of a national debate, Serby had to endure the consequences of angering Todd's teammates and ride-or-die Jets fans.

STEVE SERBY: That was a scary time because I got a few crank calls, and somebody slashed one of my tires while my car was in its parking spot in Bayside, Queens. I remember going to the hardware store and getting this iron bar to carry with me. I became quite paranoid during that short period. When I went back to cover the Jets two weeks later, half the team wouldn't talk to me because a lot of them were buddies with Richard Todd. I respected the hell out of the guys that had the guts to talk to me. Todd and I ended up shaking hands about a month later in Cleveland, where the Jets were playing the Browns. He got traded in 1983, and then he came back to the Jets not long after that. I thought we had totally patched things up, but I must have written something else that he didn't like later on because to this day he will not answer my calls. I've given up trying to reach him. It's unfortunate. He wasn't a bad guy. He just wasn't the right quarterback at the right time for the Jets.

JOE FAVORITO, sports marketing consultant; PR for Knicks, 76ers, and other teams: The *Post* covered the [New York] Sack Exchange [a.k.a. the Jets' defensive line, which included Mark Gastineau] and Gastineau off the field, too, with his wife and all that, more than anybody else did. [Gastineau became engaged to actress Brigitte Nielsen while still married to his first wife, Lisa, who later starred in a reality show on E!] That's the beauty of the *Post*—the *Post* would give you that kind of lunatic fringe that you wouldn't get as much from the *Daily News* and certainly wouldn't get from the *Times* or *Newsday*. The *Daily News* would give you your meal, but the *Post* was dessert.

BOB DRURY: The Giants used to train at [Pace University] in Westchester, and they all lived in dorms. A bunch of writers were out there one night in '81. We were at some bar. Kamikaze shooters were big at the time, and we were all drinking them. Lawrence Taylor comes in. It's his rookie year, he's from North Carolina, and he doesn't know what he's not supposed to do in front of reporters. He says, "What do you got there?" He takes a taste and goes, "Oh, fuck that." He tells the bartender to make him a pitcher. We thought he was going to pour us all shots. Instead, he downs the pitcher. Then he stands up on the bar. I wrote about this, and he got dressed down by the Perk. The next day, he wanted to kill me.

After turning in a story, sportswriters might see a different version in the paper. Notable transformations involved the most important real estate in sports: the back page.

HARVEY ARATON: We always had to deal with [backlash over the back page]. I remember walking into a Knicks practice once after I had written a story—this was in maybe 1981—about how the Knicks had too many backcourt players coming out of training camp, and they were going to have to cut a couple or trade a couple. It was just a run-of-the-mill story about how they had too many guards and the *Post* back page was "Guards for Sale." It had photos of all the players with little dollar signs over their heads. Then it had "Call the Garden and ask for Eddie." Eddie Donovan was the GM. And it had the phone number of [Madison Square Garden]. I walked into practice, not having seen the paper. All of a sudden I was getting all these dagger looks, like these guys wanted to kill me.

For years, many of the *Post*'s most eye-catching back pages were created by night editor Pat Hannigan, a.k.a. Hondo, who took his nickname from one of his favorite NBA players, Boston Celtic John Havlicek (who himself had taken the name from the title character of a 1953 John Wayne western). Hannigan also wrote the paper's immensely popular—and initially controversial—betting column, and for his former colleagues, the phrase "tossed salad" will forever be associated with his wedding.

MIKE VACCARO, lead sports columnist, 2002–current: Hondo was king of the back page. Before I worked at the *Post*, I used to collect back pages that were unbelievably clever. I remember talking to guys when I got hired. I'm like, this one? This one? Yeah, that was Hondo, that was Hondo. The one that really sticks with me, although in this case, it's going to be sort of obscure unless your memory goes back more than two weeks. Remember the old commercials, "Nobody beats The Wiz"? [The Wiz was a popular chain of electronics stores in the Northeast.] They were everywhere. The Mets had a player named José Vizcaíno. This is probably 1994, '95, before I worked at the paper. There was a big brawl at Shea Stadium because one of the Atlanta Braves pitchers had beaned Vizcaíno. The back page was "Nobody beans the Viz." I'm like, that's Einstein-level genius.

PHIL MUSHNICK: Pat Hannigan gets married. It's an outdoor wedding. They made a tactical error. They served alcohol before the ceremony. There's a *Post* sports table. Jerry and Gallo are sitting at a main table up front. One of our writers, Steve Wilder, is eating a salad and says, "It's a tossed salad," and Mike Marley, who is shit-faced, says, "Toss salad?" And he throws his salad with dressing and hits Wilder, covering him. All of a sudden there's a brawl. Lisker comes running down, separates everyone, and says in his Providence accent, "What do you think you're on—a *bahhrge*?" This pall falls over the wedding. He goes back to the main table. Everyone's looking at him expectedly, like he's going to tell them what happened. He just says, "That's my boys."

HARVEY ARATON: Jerry was fiercely protective of us. I remember when Bernard King was traded to the Knicks before the '82–'83 season. He was a New York kid from Brooklyn, and he had a troubled past. He had some trouble with the law in Salt Lake City; he had some cocaine and alcoholism issues. He came to New York, and he did some interviews where he addressed his past initially. But then maybe half a season or a full season went by, and he became this unstoppable force. He was really worth the price of admission. When he reaches full-blown stardom, Greg says to me, "You need to do the definitive Bernard King piece." I called up his agent, Bill Pollak, out of DC, and said, "Hey, I'm doing this piece on Bernard. Can you arrange for me to have a lengthy sit-down?" He said, "Bernard likes you, he'll talk to you. But he's made it clear that he doesn't want to talk about his past, and he doesn't want it addressed." I said, "That's ridiculous, Bill. It's part of his story." He said, "I'm just telling you, if you write about Bernard's past, there's going to be problems." So I write the story and of course I have to address the A-to-Z aspect. I just happened to be in the office one afternoon and I hear the office secretary say, "It's Bill Pollak calling for Jerry." So now I'm listening—not on the extension or anything—and Pollak is clearly explaining that I had been warned not to write about this and what is the *Post* going to do about it? Jerry says, "Hold on a second." He puts Pollak on hold, turns around to me, and goes, "It's King's agent. He wants to know what I'm going to do about the fact that you wrote about his past when he warned you not to." I say, "What do you want me to do, Jerry?" He goes, "Just listen to me." He picks up the phone and says, "Listen, I've talked about it with Harvey. I guess what I can tell you is: go fuck yourself." And he slammed the phone down.

As other publications took notice of Lisker's gutter rats, the poachers came calling.

HARVEY ARATON: In 1982, Gene Williams, the sports editor of the *Daily News*, calls me and says, "Dave Sims, who's our Knicks writer, he's leaving. We would love to have you." I meet with them. By that point I had been at the [*Post*] five and a half years, and it was getting increasingly difficult to be an NBA reporter at the paper that Pete Vecsey worked at. He was not above ripping somebody at his own paper in his column if he disagreed. One thing that was fairly unique to the *Post* sports section was the fact that everybody on the staff had the privilege of writing a column. Many nights I'd come into the office, write my game story, and then Steve Bromberg would yell out, "We got room. You have anything in your notebook that you could turn into a column?" I would say, "Hell, yeah." I got my little headshot in the paper. It was a great opportunity. It meant I was going to be there until three or four in the morning, so I would load up on coffee and work all night. But the more I expressed myself, the more Peter would take issue with some of the opinions I was expressing. That created some discomfort.

So when the *Daily News* called, I felt like, they don't have any real distinguished basketball writers. I could go there and make a name for myself at a bigger newspaper; maybe I'll make a little more money. I took the offer back to Greg and Jerry. Greg calls me and says, "Meet us at Marie's tomorrow." I show up, I'm looking around the joint, like, what is this place? I had never been in there. I'd been in the Post Mortem many times, which smelled like there was a dead body in the back, but I had never been to Marie's. I'm sitting there with Greg, and Jerry comes in and he looks at me, with a scowl. He says, "I'm going to give you three reasons why you cannot go to the *Daily News*. Number one, it's going to fold in six months." So I'm thinking: if that's actually true, there's really no reason for reasons number two and three, is there? But he persists. "Number two, they hate Jews." Number three was "And Gene Williams? He's a fag." He gets up and walks out, and Greg looks at me and goes, "And there you have it." I went to the *Daily News* and absolutely hated it.

GREG GALLO: Jerry used to go to boxing matches in Vegas and bring back hires that nobody had ever interviewed. They just showed up. He would call and say, "I hired a guy, and he's coming. He lives in Chicago, but he's coming." There were good ones. Lyle Spencer was hired in Las Vegas. Mike Marley [who became the *Post*'s lead boxing writer] was hired in Las Vegas. But sometimes those hires from [boxing matches] didn't work.

HARVEY ARATON: The next guy they hired [on the Knicks beat] was Doug Blackburn. Jerry met him at a bar at a fight in New Orleans. Doug must have impressed him somehow. He didn't work out because he didn't know what he was getting into.

GREG GALLO: I said, "Jerry, we can't put him on the Knicks." We have this conversation about what I thought and what he thought. Blackburn goes on the Knicks beat, because Jerry was the executive sports editor. One night in Chicago, he's covering the Knicks–Bulls, and he wound up fighting with the mascot, the Chicago Bull, on the floor. I don't know if the Chicago Bull called him a name, or whatever he did, but Doug Blackburn took offense to it and then the two of them were rolling around at mid-court in the arena.

DOUG BLACKBURN, sportswriter, basketball, 1983: I seriously do not remember anything like a fight.

Despite its dominance in many aspects of sports coverage, the *Post* lacked something the *Daily News* had had for years: superstar sports columnist Dick Young. In 1982, the *Post* added him to the roster. Despite the presence of this legendary dinosaur, the *Post* continued to cover sports in a brash and youthful way.

HARVEY ARATON: I used to joke that I was traded not-so-even-up for Dick Young, because when I left the *Post*, it was about the time that he came over. At the *News*, I think there was a lot of relief when he left. The staff was starting to get younger at the *Daily News*, and the younger guys thought Dick Young was becoming fossilized. He had gone from being an advocate for players to being a front man for management, he was cranky, and there was a sense that Mike Lupica was the rising star columnist. Everybody thought Lupica was more in line with the way sports coverage was evolving.

PHIL MUSHNICK: Lisker was a hero to me because his neglect benefited me. He didn't know if I was any good. But I think I rewarded his ignorance. When he'd belly up at Gallagher's, and people told him what they read in the paper, it would be [Mike] Marley on boxing, me on TV and radio, that kind of thing. And that's how he formed his impression.

HARVEY ARATON: The way the *Post* operated, grabbing the reader by the collar, really forced the *Daily News* to quicken its pulse. It raised the temperature of the way sports was covered in New York City and ultimately in the country. Because no matter what you think of the *New York Post* and its sensational style, it definitely had an impact. Many of the things the *Post* did back in the mid- to late '70s, starting when Rupert bought the paper, are now common practice. In sports journalism, in journalism in general, the insertion of how reporters write their stories—"he told me," or "so and so told ESPN." A lot of the things we pioneered back then, and that were decried, are now common practice in the industry. Whether that's right or wrong, it's hard to not recognize that the *Post* had a tremendous impact on the way journalism operates in the United States.

PART II: 1981–1987

EVOLUTION

12 | IT'S ALL THEATER

An Oxford Editor, Cindy
and Joey, Cocaine Carnival

*T*he *Front Page*, the 1928 play and subsequent films about hard-bitten newspapermen, is often cited as the paradigm of twentieth-century tabloid life. A remake set at 210 South Street in the late '70s and early '80s would play like a Martin Scorsese movie—gritty, tense, darkly funny, occasionally surreal, at times violent, and stocked with unforgettable characters. They included the *Post*'s executive editor Roger Wood, whose lunches were legendarily long and liquid, his idiosyncrasies many. Although the Oxford-educated Wood proved a more serene leader than the universally loathed Ted Bolwell, the frenetic pace of the newsroom still frazzled nerves and sent adrenaline soaring. It also encouraged or at least tolerated various forms of bad behavior as a way to let off steam.

CHARLES LACHMAN, reporter, 1981–1988: Roger Wood was in a class by himself. He always wore the same perfectly cleaned white shirt and tan pants, and he had that long black knit tie. He would call everyone "Dear boy, dear boy." I thought his relationship with Dunleavy was interesting, because you had this street kid from Australia, and this erudite Oxford graduate, Roger.

KELVIN MACKENZIE, night managing editor, 1978–1979: Roger was this urbane English guy, who said to me once, right about half ten at night, he said, "I'm going now." He said, "If you want me, I'll give you a call." It took me some time to realize that "If you want me, I'll give you a call," how does that work? He was very clever. One day, Murdoch comes in early. I'm there and, mysteriously, Roger is there. This is eight, quarter past eight in the morning. What on earth he was doing there, I don't know. I was in Roger's office and we're standing behind the desk. In comes Murdoch, who starts shouting, god knows what about, starts shouting about the quality of the paper—"This is bloody rubbish. I don't like this. Why are you doing that?" All the rest of it. While he is shouting at me—because he can't be shouting right at Roger, who had no idea what was going on at the paper—I noticed Roger very slowly making his way around the desk so that he's on the same side as Rupert shouting at me. I've always thought that that was the finest piece of office politics I've ever seen in action. He was a very clever bloke, old Roger.

DAVE BANKS, night managing editor, 1979–1981: Murdoch made sure his interests were served straight through Roger. Roger was a canny operator, a very cunning, sly man. He knew where his bread was buttered. The butter was applied liberally by Rupert Murdoch and he wouldn't do anything to gainsay what Rupert thought and Rupert wanted.

SUSAN MULCAHY, Page Six editor, 1978–1985: When I would freak out about a Page Six item that might blow up and cause trouble—not the good kind of trouble— Roger would chuckle and say, "It's all theater, dear girl, it's all theater."

CHARLIE CARILLO, reporter, columnist, 1978–1993: Roger was a strange guy. When I was a driver, one of my jobs was picking him up at his place on the Upper East Side in the morning and driving him to the *Post*. He wore this cologne that made your eyes water and he would wear a cape sometimes. He was like Darth Vader.

JAMES BRADY, creator of Page Six, 1977; Page Six editor, 1980–1982: On cold days, Roger had a wool shawl that he would drape over his shoulders as he walked around the city room. Very Dickensian. He called everyone "dear boy," pulling his shawl a little tighter. He really belonged in *Great Expectations*.

HARRY BENSON, photographer: I worked with Roger in London and he offered me to be picture editor of the *Post*. Of course, I didn't take it. Roger told me this story. He had a twin. He was in London and he'd been asked to come into the *Express* [newspaper] to meet a man in charge of contracts. Roger sends his twin, who had a big-shot job at the Bank of England or something. His brother gets him a great deal. He knew how to negotiate.

STEPHEN SILVERMAN, entertainment writer, 1977–1988: Roger had a leisurely gait, he would walk through, and you never really knew what was on his mind. And of course, after lunch, after all that grappa, what *was* on his mind?

RAMONA GARNES, copy editor, 1978–1990, 2000–2004: When I was an editorial driver, often I was either driving Roger home, or picking him up from someplace. Roger liked to invite me inside to wherever he was going. "Come in, lovey, don't sit waiting in the car. I'm going to be a while. Come in. Have a drink, have a snack." I'm thinking, "Roger, I can't drink while I'm driving." My nickname was "Dressed to Thrill." I sewed my own clothes and I'd have weird outfits. Roger would like to walk into some fancy joint or meet some fancy friends with me, this six-foot-tall Black kid, with him.

STEPHEN SILVERMAN: The only time Roger called me on the carpet was for using the past imperfect tense. I got called into his office. He started sounding like Henry Higgins. I said, "Okay, I'll watch out for that."

ERIC FETTMANN, associate editorial page editor, columnist, 1976–1991, 1993–2019: I found a clip that said the *Post* had the desk belonging to William Coleman [the first editor of the *Post*, 1801–1829]. I asked around and I think it was Lucy Lambert who said, "Yeah, it's in the sixth-floor women's room." I went up with Cynthia Fagen. The chair was there with a [papier-mâché] Alexander Hamilton figure. Roger said, "Put it in my office." We did, right by the door. It used to shock people as they walked in. Mario Cuomo once jumped two feet in the air when he walked in and saw it.

DAN AQUILANTE, chief music critic, 1980–2012: They had a full-size mannequin of Alexander Hamilton sitting at the desk in a writing position. The first day I delivered a paper to Roger, the mannequin was there, and he said, "What about Alexander?" After that, I had to also put a copy on the scrivener's desk.

KEN CHANDLER, editor in chief, publisher, 1978–1986, 1993–2002: Roger Wood taught me that [no one editor symbolized the *Post*]: "Remember who owns the paper. You're just a guest."

ERIC FETTMANN: Roger brought creative tension to the *Post*. He did it in a very smooth way. At one point, he kept telling [Steve] Cuozzo, who was features editor, that he was giving too much space to Harriett Johnson, who was the classical music and opera critic. He said, "Cut her." When he did, Harriett would call Roger and explode, saying, "This is critical, it has a following, I have a following." Roger would say, "You tell Cuozzo that you're not going to stand for your pieces being cut." They would go back and forth. Roger would just sit in his office and say, "Neither one of them ever says, 'Can the three of us sit down and talk this out?'" They were totally oblivious that he was manipulating the whole thing.

CHARLIE CARILLO: The rock and roll writer Lou O'Neill Jr.—long hair, tinted glasses, a motorcycle. Steve Cuozzo fired him one day, so Lou O'Neill went into Roger's office. Roger said, "Dear boy, whatever is wrong?" He says, "I don't understand it. I have the most popular column and I get more mail than anybody else. Steve Cuozzo just fired me." "Dear boy, go back there and demand to know why he did that." He went back to Cuozzo, "Why'd you fire me?" Cuozzo said, "Roger told me to."

> Roger Wood may have been officially in charge, but those lower on the totem pole made the place run.

DONNIE SUTHERLAND, city desk assistant, 1978–1988: The city desk assistant would be asked to help with everything. Craig Ammerman had forgotten where he parked his car. He hadn't driven it home that night. Could I find his car? In New York City. I said, "Okay, I'll do my best."

CHARLIE CARILLO: Donnie Sutherland was always putting signs on people's backs. Like C. Z. Guest, the gardening columnist, would be walking through the newsroom and all of a sudden there'd be a sign on her back that said "Where have all the flowers gone?"

DAN AQUILANTE: She was one of the few people who was truly offended.

DONNIE SUTHERLAND: There's a lot of stress in the city room, you're exposed to a lot of elements of life that you weren't brought up with—murder, crime, everyday trauma. You need a sense of humor.

CHARLIE CARILLO: Somebody said the truest thing once. They said, "I really like the *Post*. They do stories about lost wallets." It's true. If a cabdriver found a wallet and he called the *Post*, he would get somebody. I used to call them "listen-to-this-guy stories." Dick Belsky used to say to me, "Listen to this guy. See if it's anything." I'd listen to the guy. I don't think it's like that at other papers. It's one of the things that made the *Post* unique. You got through to the city desk. You didn't get an automated thing.

Some city desk assistants thrived under these conditions, including Annie Aquilina and, especially, Myron Rushetzky, who worked there for decades.

DAVE BANKS: Myron knew where all the bodies were buried. Annie was hugely efficient in her own way—big, beefy, motherly. She always knew where things were, how to get things done. Myron always had a huge bunch of keys. He knew where money was. He actually was a bit of a money lender himself. He used to peel off a big wad, if Dunleavy needed thirty dollars, forty dollars. He was an operator. They were vital to the operation, auxiliary journalists in a way.

DONNIE SUTHERLAND: Myron had this little yellow piece of paper in his wallet that was full of names of people he had lent money to. People would come up to him asking Myron for money. He would pull out this piece of paper and write it down and put it back in his grimy little wallet. I found a moment where I slipped in and I got the paper from his wallet. He panicked and said, "I don't have a copy!" The amount of people on that list was unbelievable. It was probably half the folks that were at the Lion's Head after two a.m.

MYRON RUSHETZKY, head city desk assistant, 1974–1989,1991–2013: If I was on a call with a bomber or a threat, I used to keep an eraser. If I thought Steve [Dunleavy] should be overhearing this conversation, I would throw an eraser at him, and, you know, with my fingers indicate which line so he could at least listen to this bomb threat or whatever.

CHARLIE CARILLO: Myron's the original rain man. He was just amazing, what he could maintain in his mind. If you gave him a name, he'd spit back a phone number—"Nine-one-seven-four . . . And the weekend number is . . ." delivered in a monotone. He was proud of that kind of thing.

JAMI BERNARD, chief movie critic, 1978–1993: Myron did things like tracking people down at their lovers' apartments when they needed them. He knew everything. He was really good at that job.

GREGG MORRIS, reporter, 1984–1988: There was a murder or some violent thing going on in East New York. It was about two o'clock in the morning. Joe D [De Maria] was going and I was going and I didn't think it was a big deal. I had a *Post* car. And Joe D had his car. I was roaming around the neighborhood, stopping people: "Do you know anything about a shooting? Have you heard any bullets?" I couldn't find anything. Eventually I hooked up with Joe D. He says, "Let's get out of here." He left. I went back to the car and it broke down. I called Myron, who was on the desk, to let him know where the car was. I said, "The car's not working. I'm in East New York and I gotta get home." He says, "How are you getting home?" I said, "I'm just gonna hop the subway." He started shrieking through the phone: "Get out of there, they're gonna kill you, you're going to die, get a taxi." He was *frantic*. I never forgot that. I have an attachment to Myron that I can't explain. That guy, he's an amazing person. I never bad-mouth the *Post* when I'm talking to Myron! He made me see things. He showed me the complexity of things, of being a Black reporter in a place like the *New York Post*, in dealing with people.

JIM NOLAN, reporter, 1986–1993: Myron took his job very seriously. He would invoke Alexander Hamilton sometimes when people would question what the *Post* was doing. He felt a responsibility for the institutional integrity, all the way back to Hamilton.

> The duties of a city desk assistant were many and varied. The tabloid also hired "editorial drivers" to pick up food for staffers working at night; copy from writers, like nightclub columnist Earl Wilson; and the first editions of the other newspapers. Drivers also ferried editors and executives home or to bars and restaurants. Instead of town cars, a small fleet of junkers served as News Corp in-house taxis, and occasionally the boss relied on his employees for transport.

RAMONA GARNES: I drove Mr. Murdoch home maybe three times. One night, I overshot his apartment building by like half a block—he lived on Fifth Avenue. Instead of going around the block, no, no, no, no, I back up. I have Rupert Murdoch in the car. I wasn't speeding. I looked back, I turned all the way around, but I think he said, "That person is never driving me home again."

TOM KREUZER, editorial driver, 1972–1978: Ramona was a terrible driver, but such a funny free spirit. She could never find her way. When she was driving and there was merging traffic and it's you-go-I-go, back-and-forth alternate, if there was a BMW trying to cut in ahead of her, she would open the window and scream, "Company car! Company car!"—meaning, you got a lot more to lose than I do, buddy, cause I'm just going to crash into you.

HAL GOLDENBERG, photographer, 1979–1986: One night, I hear, "Yo, Goldenberg." It was Dunleavy. "You want to drive the boss and his wife somewhere?" As he's saying that, Murdoch walks into the city room with his wife. He's in a tux. They've got to go to a thing at Lincoln Center. It's in twenty minutes or something, and we're way down on South Street. I gave them a ride they'll never forget. They're in the back. As I pull out, I said, "You want to do this like you don't care what I do to get you there?" He said, "Do what you've got to do." So I put the cherry light on the roof, plug it in the cigarette lighter, turn the siren on, and make a U-turn. I get on the FDR Drive, and we go flying. Didn't get stopped. I was looking in the rearview occasionally while I was driving, and I could see them rocking back and forth as I was doing all this crazy shit—weaving in and out of traffic. I was swallowing my Adam's apple going, I hope this guy isn't going to freak out on me.

> Payday was Thursday. For immediate gratification, employees could cash their checks right in the building. An odd tradition involved showing a little extra gratitude for the service.

DOMINICK MARRANO, chief paginator, 1971–2008: They had a cashier, his name was Danny O'Donnell, and you'd get a check and you would go to him and cash it. That service was interrupted in 1971. Somebody came in and stuck the place up [and stole $180,000] because they knew they had money that they were going to use for cashing checks. Supposedly, it was somebody from the neighborhood. But nobody was ever charged.

DONNIE SUTHERLAND: Everybody who got a paycheck would give Danny a tip—the loose change, a couple of dollars. The guy cleaned up every paycheck. He had quite an ego.

DOMINICK MARRANO: I would tip anybody, but I couldn't understand why this guy needed a tip. Did you ever see the movie *The Pope of Greenwich Village*? One of the characters actually tips the token seller on the subway because you gotta tip everybody.

> Before search engines, reporters researched story subjects on paper in the *Post* library, sometimes referred to as the morgue.

BILLY HELLER, librarian, deputy features editor, 1978–1988, 2000–2020: Basically we'd sit there all day, with either straight-edge razors, or an X-Acto knife, and clip stories out of the newspapers. And also deal with a million photos coming into the library. The library was this huge space with all these mostly wooden file cabinets that probably had been around since the 1920s, filled with little manila envelopes, with clips folded up, on a billion different subjects. Say you wanted to look up Babe Ruth, you could find clips from the 1920s.

FAIGI ROSENTHAL, assistant head librarian, 1978–1986: Nothing was computerized. It was all manual, crazy manual.

GEORGE RUSH, Page Six reporter, 1986–1993: There were clips that were so old they would just crumble in your hand like papyrus when you pulled them out.

SUSAN MULCAHY: We were once threatened with a lawsuit on Page Six when we wrote that a well-known entertainment executive had been indicted for something, but we didn't mention the charges had been dropped. Kind of an important detail, but I swear that story was missing from the clips.

> Despite the staff exodus after Murdoch bought the *Post*, many reporters and editors stayed, some for decades. Some thrived, others grew increasingly churlish. A crusty collection of copy editors sat at a U-shaped desk in the newsroom, with the slot man in the center overseeing the editing of copy and the composition of headlines by those who sat on the perimeter, known as the rim.

CHARLIE CARILLO: Jeanette Wilken worked [on the rim]. She was also an actress. She took bit parts. She serves John Travolta a hamburger in *Saturday Night Fever*. She's in the movie *Fame*. She's a lunch lady with the hairnet on, dancing and swinging the big spoon. And Frank Skerratt. He was from Scotland.

Wonderful guy. Bruce Russell was a real Connecticut guy. He should have been on a horse with riding breeches somewhere on a farm. Lloyd Talmadge. He was a little shaky, and he had had some problems in the past, but the prize, I remember I filed some kind of service story, I hadn't been a reporter for long, and Lloyd said, "Did you write that?" I said, "Yeah." He said, "Man, that's clean copy." I had a surge. Coming from one of these guys who didn't say much, it really meant something.

JAMI BERNARD: When they put me on copy editing and headline writing, I thought it was such a demotion, I thought it was like being put out to pasture in my early twenties. Because the copy editors were ancient and decrepit. They were older, and a lot of them were alcoholics. They were not happy to have me around. I was the first of the young-uns to be put there. I would waltz in, thinking, "I love this, can't wait to see my pals," and this one really ancient guy, Bob Taber, who was really crotchety, would say to me, "It's like you're running for president." Because I was social. He was so crotchety that when his brother died, Myron went over to tell him, and he shooed him away because he was finishing a shift. Myron said, "Your brother died." Taber said, "Get outta here."

CHARLIE CARILLO: Cy Egan worked the lobster shift. His whole career was waking people up in the middle of the night. One time, working late, I was next to him. He phoned somebody and says, "Cy Egan from the *Post*," then, "No madam, I do *not* apologize for waking you. Your husband is a public official." Cy was a byline hound. You'd do a story and the next day you'd come in, and it would say, "By Charles Carillo and Cy Egan." He'd figure out a way to get in there. The joke was somebody was wearing a pair of designer jeans by Sergio Valente and Cy Egan.

Another veteran *Post* reporter, George Carpozi Jr., had worked with Egan at the *Journal-American*, the defunct Hearst paper that once occupied 210 South Street.

CHARLIE CARILLO: George Carpozi was a reporter with a very, very loud, very tabloid style. There was a story about a baby found in a garbage can alive and taken to a hospital. Carpozi wrote the story. The lede was something like, "The bravest little baby in New York City is doing A-OK." Marsha Kranes, who was the editor, said, "George, I'm taking that out. The baby, he's not even aware of what happened." George lunged at her, leaned over the desk, and said, "Go to that hospital. Look at that kid and tell me he's not the bravest kid in the city."

MARSHA KRANES, rewrite, editor, 1974–2005: The baby was found in the trash and George attributed certain feelings to the baby. I told him, "George, you can't do that. I mean, *it's a fetus*, the baby can't talk. It can't communicate." He says, "What do you know? You're not even married."

CHARLIE CARILLO: I filed a story once and it wasn't emotional enough. They gave it to George Carpozi to soup it up. He turned to me and said, "The thing of it is, Charlie, you gotta be able to make Hitler cry." George wrote something like a hundred books. You'd say to him, "George, what'd you do this weekend?" "I wrote a book."

> Al Ellenberg, a respected editor who left the *Post* soon after Murdoch bought it, returned to the *Post* in the '80s and eventually became metropolitan editor.

CHARLIE CARILLO: Al Ellenberg was a Jewish man who looked Italian and could drink like an Irishman—and he would've loved that description of himself. He was such a good teacher. He had a way of making you figure out the way to make the story right. He didn't just tell you. Then you had it, for good. He lived a kind of chaotic life. He would hint that maybe he spent the night on a bench in Washington Square Park. He would come to work sometimes with a suitcase because he wasn't sure which girlfriend was going to let him in that night. He was one of those guys who was a habitual offender at the *Post*. He'd work a few years, he'd leave, he'd come back—you know, the *Post* always took everybody back. It was really the Statue of Liberty of journalism. Give me your tired, your unemployed.

> Shanghai-born Tommy Ko, who started as a copyboy in 1972 and retired in 2009 as an assistant managing editor, became known for his catchphrases, including "This is a newspaper, not oldspaper!" "All men with mustache, not your father!" and "Nobody care!" Though Ko often spoke in a way that suggested he was not fluent in English, he paid close attention to detail.

CHARLIE CARILLO: Tommy Ko was dealing with a columnist once and she kept calling in with changes. Finally, Tommy yells, "This is not an all-night diner!" Bill Hoffmann did a story about a Chinese band and he threw in "wok and roll" and every Chinese pun he could think of. We were just waiting for it to reach Tommy Ko. Suddenly Tommy jumped up with his T square and runs over to Hoffmann and says, "Hoffmann, are you pulling my prick?" And Hoffmann says, "What is it, pal? What is it?" Tommy wasn't upset about the Chinese thing. There was a minor grammatical error. That's all he cared about.

One of the features Murdoch added early on to the *Post* was a joke column by Borscht Belt comic Joey Adams, then in his late sixties.

CINDY ADAMS, gossip columnist, 1981–current: Joey was never number one. He wasn't a Seinfeld or a Bob Hope. He was always number two. But he had the number-one lifestyle. First of all, he was the [self-described] adopted son of [New York City mayor Fiorello] La Guardia. So some of the best judges money can buy were made in our living room. He knew everything that had to do with politics. Secondly, by his first wife, he was the brother-in-law of Walter Winchell. [Adams's first wife, Mary Magee, was the sister of Winchell's second wife, Elizabeth June Magee.] Therefore, as a kid, he was sitting in the Stork Club having dinner with Frank Sinatra and all the rest of them. Third, he was president of the [American Guild of Variety Artists]. Therefore, he had this huge lifestyle. He lived at the Waldorf Astoria. He had made money from investments. He knew every celebrity because of Walter Winchell. He knew every politician because of Mayor LaGuardia. He knew the phone numbers and addresses of everybody. So I married into an enormous potpourri of what I suddenly adopted or adapted. I was a model who wasn't great. I was okay. I tried to be a little bit of a singer, but I wasn't. I wasn't anything.

Born Cindy Sugar to a single mother, and later adopting the surname of her stepfather to become Cindy Heller, the future Mrs. Adams was a late 1940s beauty queen whose titles included Miss Brooklyn Dodgers of 1947, the Girl Disc Jockeys Would Most Like to Spin Around, Miss Upswept Hairdo of 1948, Miss Bazooka Bubble Gum of 1948 (at one photo shoot, Cindy was supposed to teach the New York Giants how to blow), Miss Coaxial Cable of 1949, Miss Manischewitz Wine of 1949, and Miss Airfoam Rubber Cushion of 1949. She worked clubs as a comic, too. When she was dropped from one gig in 1948, Lenny Bruce replaced her.

ERIC FETTMANN: She started out as an ingénue, a model, who was discovered by Joey in 1949, I think it was. She was entering all kinds of pageants and beauty contests. Joey, as the saying goes, took her under his wing. Somebody found a photo in the clips, a photo of her posing with one of her titles—Miss Brighton Beach Bagel 1949. The photo later disappeared.

CINDY ADAMS: I was a good writer. Before I was ever on the *Post*, I was getting $200 an article from *TV Guide* and publications like that. I would help Joey with jokes. Then Rupert came in. Joey's column was in the *Long Island Press* at that point. Rupert knew that if you're coming into New York, you need to have a smart-ass Jewish comic. How he knew this, or why he knew this, I don't know. So, he co-opted Joey Adams, who he didn't know from a hole in the wall. He bought [the *Long Island Press*] subscription list, and he bought Joey. With Joey, you get me. When the first editors were running around, they had the great ideas, but they didn't have the Rolodex. They would come to us because Joey and I knew everything. He had all the connections, and I understood what they wanted. We would have dinner with Roger Wood. Bit by bit, they began to need what we had.

AMY PAGNOZZI, reporter, columnist, 1979–1993: I used to take Joey Adams's dictation sometimes. I could never really understand why he had a column. I never thought it was very funny. But there was a lot of material in the *Post* that I didn't really understand why it was there.

KEN CHANDLER: Joey's column was already there when I arrived. It was pretty awful. I used to dread having to edit it.

CHARLIE CARILLO: Somebody on the desk once said to me, talk to Joey Adams. He went to an inner-city neighborhood, he entertained the kids. Joey gets on the phone and he says to me, "I told these kids, you don't have to take drugs or anything like that; you can become a comedian. That way you won't become hookers and prostitutes." I remember thinking, isn't that the same thing? We didn't use that quote.

CINDY ADAMS: In the early 1960s, President Kennedy sent Joey to head a cultural exchange unit to Southeast Asia. For four and a half months, the troupe traveled to Laos, Afghanistan, Cambodia, Indonesia, the Philippines, and because I looked like I looked fifty years ago, and I had a New York attitude, [Indonesian president] Sukarno said, "What is that?" He loved me, and the Shah of Iran loved me. These big shahs and kings, I treated them like a New Yorker. They weren't used to that. I had nothing to lose because I wasn't anybody. This is how I got on the *Post*. Not that I wanted it, not that I asked for it. It all started with the Shah, when he was at New York Hospital, and he was dying.

LESLIE GEVIRTZ, reporter, rewrite, 1978–1988: The Shah of Iran was at New York Hospital for like six weeks [from October to December 1979]. Every night, you would [stake out] a fixed place. Sometimes you would be at this entrance, sometimes you'd be at that entrance. Once there was a rumor that a plane was coming in that would somehow whisk the Shah off. And Joe D, a photographer, and I sat and watched the flag fly at the Marine Air Terminal. There was nothing landing or taking off. Meanwhile, we all made tremendous amounts of overtime—reporters at the *Times*, the *News*, us, even the TV folks—and at one point, there was talk of, when Christmas comes, we should buy the guy a case of Champagne. He can't be *that* sick. But he left New York before Christmas.

JOE DE MARIA, photographer, 1977–1993: We tried all different ways of getting into the hospital. One thing was, at the '64 World's Fair, I had worked as a dispatcher for a company called Moses Vehicles [executive cars and limos]. I had taken the Shah into the World's Fair to wherever he wanted to go, drove him around for the day. He told me, "If you're ever in my country, and you want to have special treatment, just tell them who you are. I'll remember you, and I'll take good care of you." I said, "Okay, thank you so much." When he was in the hospital, dying, I wrote a letter, which the hospital gave to his wife. I wrote down the story and I said, "I would appreciate it if I can come up and just get a photo of the Shah," or with you, or whatever. She actually sent me back an answer, saying, "I would really love to do that for you, but I can't because of what's going on." But she did answer it. We never really got in there.

CINDY ADAMS: It's a long story why the Shah and I would have a friendship, but we did. His twin sister, Princess Ashraf, who then lived on Beekman Place, called me and said, "His Majesty has requested you come to the hospital." The New York press corps was not allowed anywhere near the hospital, and he's asking for me to come because I always made him laugh. I was fun, you see. I go up to the hospital room. I am there for two hours, alone with His Majesty. That night, I was supposed to have dinner with Joey and Roger Wood. I had to call and say, "Roger, I can't make dinner. I'm seeing the Shah." There's a thud at the other end. He said, "What are you talking about, darling?" I said, "Listen, I can't explain it. I'm a friend of the Shah, and I'm going up." He said, "Uh, do you expect perhaps, dear one, you might give us an article about it after your visit?" I said, "I don't know. I gotta go." I went to the hospital. I'm two hours alone with the Shah. He had two rooms, and across the two rooms was a banner that had been taped or glued up on the wall. It was a picture of a gorilla with his fangs bared, saliva coming out, and claws. The legend under it said, "Cheer up. Things have got to get better." You have to understand, the Shah had lost his kingdom. He'd lost his health. He'd lost his title. And now, he was dying. So I understood that I had some sort of a weird story, with the Shah sitting on the edge of his bed in his little white silk pajamas, his slippers falling off his feet. I didn't know what to do with myself. I came home. Roger Wood called me and he said, "Well, darling, tell me." I told him the story, and he said, "Can you write this?" I said, "Yeah, I can write it." It was the wood. It said *New York Post* Exclusive," and it went around the world. They never paid me for the story. They sent me a bunch of flowers that were so cheap they looked like soup greens.

As the *Post* ratcheted up its outrageousness, legendary columnist Murray Kempton remained an island of liberal calm, until he wasn't.

DOMINICK MARRANO: Murray used to ride his bike to work through these terribly nasty, drug-infested areas and nothing ever happened to him. He was oblivious to it. Murray was looked up to by most people. He was also kind of an egghead, more intellectual than a lot of people. Everybody was sad when he left because, even in spite of the reputation that the *Post* might have had at that time, he was acknowledged as a real good writer.

ERIC FETTMANN: Under Kelvin MacKenzie, with Belsky as the hatchet man, Murray's columns, which ran up front, started getting chopped. You don't blue pencil Murray Kempton. Belsky was the guy who had to do all the dirty work. Murray never forgave him.

DICK BELSKY, metropolitan editor, 1970–1989: Every encounter I had with Murray was an unpleasant one. Everybody talks about him as this legendary guy. I never thought his writing was particularly good. He was the kind of guy that would use eleven big words when one simple word would do. At one point in the '70s, it was the whole period of the Weather Underground. There was so much crazy stuff going on with bombings and all that. There was some big Weather Underground person on the run. Because Murray was this liberal icon, this person called the *Post* to talk to Murray. We're sitting there thinking, "My god, Murray's on the phone with him right now, what a great story. It could be page one." Murray gets off the phone. We're like, "What did he say?" He goes, "Oh, just a few things. I don't think I'll write anything about it." I can't remember if in the end [Bob] Spitzler convinced him to write something, but Murray didn't want to be bothered, even though he'd gotten this giant exclusive because of who he was. I remember thinking, "Are you crazy? The whole world is looking for this guy!" It wasn't like he didn't want to write it; he didn't think it was worth writing about. It wasn't like Murray said, "I have a moral obligation, I promised him this or that." He just puffed on his pipe. He always had this attitude that he was above it all.

CALVIN TRILLIN, staff writer, *The New Yorker*: Murray Kempton—maybe "hero" was a strong word, but I definitely looked up to him. I loved reading his column. That is the one thing that I did read in the [Murdoch] *Post*.

HAL DAVIS, reporter, New York State Supreme Court, 1978–1993: He was revered among the people I dealt with. He had a very uncomfortable tenure under Murdoch because Murdoch didn't believe columnists' space was sacred. I once looked at an early issue of the *Post*, and there was a Murray column that was more opaque than usual. You had to make giant leaps between paragraphs in order to get the transitions. It was very unlike Murray. Sure enough, by the end of the day, Murray's column had been restored to its original length—it had been cut severely. I think Murray decided after a while, this was not the way to proceed. He knew how to write eight hundred words perfectly, every word in perfect sequence to the next.

DICK BELSKY: Steve Dunleavy and Murray Kempton had this incredible relationship, which was weird. They would go out drinking together. Murray would ride his bike and meet Dunleavy for a drink. One day, I'm talking to Steve and he says, "Murray doesn't like you." I said, "Yeah, and I don't like Murray." He said, "No, he *really* doesn't like you." I'm like, "I know." Dunleavy says, "Mate, you don't get what I'm saying. If he could figure out a way to put a bullet in your head, he would do it. That's how much he does not like you." I said, "Okay! I guess he does not like me!" I had no use for him. He had no use for me. Fortunately, I didn't really *have* to have use for Murray because he really did not play that big a role in the paper.

SALLY KEMPTON, teacher of meditation and spirituality; daughter of Murray Kempton: Murray used to refer to his time with Murdoch as having been difficult and, at a certain point, unsustainable.

MILTON GOLDSTEIN, copy editor, 1974–current: After he's hired away by *Newsday* [Kempton left the *Post* in 1981], Murray won a Pulitzer for his writing. The Pulitzer committee would never give a Pulitzer to the *Post* for anything.

ERIC FETTMANN: When he won the Pulitzer Prize at *Newsday*, Roger sent over two bottles of Champagne. Murray sent back a handwritten note, which Roger posted on the board. What it said roughly—I should have kept a copy—was "If I could, I would take this prize and lay it at Rupert Murdoch's feet because when everyone in the whole journalistic world was saying, 'Hire Murray Kempton, hire Murray Kempton,' Rupert Murdoch was the only one who did. He gave me a job and he gave me an outlet and he rejuvenated my career."

In the Murdoch regime, the viewpoint of another icon of progressive journalism, editorial page editor James Wechsler, who had worked at the paper for nearly forty years, became increasingly irrelevant.

ERIC FETTMANN: Before Murdoch, Jimmy Wechsler and Dolly Schiff would do political endorsements. [Bruce] Rothwell was brought in as [Wechsler's] deputy under Murdoch.

CHARLIE CARILLO: They used to call him Frothwell because he really got his teeth into whatever he was writing. Rothwell came into the newsroom once when something had happened in the Middle East. He had his pipe and this white whale look in his eye. I didn't know him really, and he turned to me and said, "Now is the time. Bomb them! Bomb them! Now's the time." I said, "Okay, Bruce, I'll see you later."

ERIC FETTMANN: The [endorsement and editorial] positions would be decided in a conference with Wechsler, Rothwell, and Roger Wood. Jimmy would always get outvoted two to one. He finally said, "I can't have my name as editorial page editor on a page that comes out with positions that I don't hold." They agreed to let him write his column and made Rothwell the editorial page editor. Jimmy's final years at the paper were not pleasant.

CAROLE LEE, assistant to James Wechsler, photo syndication editor, 1963–1993: One of my duties was to make sure that Wechsler always had alcohol. I had to buy two quarts of whatever a week. That's a lot of booze. It was not bourbon. It wasn't Jack Daniel's. It was whiskey and it was rotgut. And at 12:15—not 12:10 or 12:20—12:15, he'd have to have a glass and a bucket of ice on his desk.

ERIC FETTMANN: Jimmy was my hero. I used to go back and talk with him. Nobody else paid him much attention in the city room anymore. I think he was grateful for anybody who knew who he was.

> Of the photographers employed by the *Post* in the '80s, Hal Goldenberg became known for doing whatever it took to get the job done, including in at least one instance putting his life, and that of the reporter assigned to work with him, on the line.

HAL GOLDENBERG: I won the Humanitarian Award from the National Press Photographers Association in 1985. I'm with my friend Doug, and we go into the office to pick up my paycheck. On the way home, we're on the Brooklyn Bridge. I'm driving behind my friend's car. We had walkie-talkies to talk to each other. We're starting to decide how to spend my money. Maybe we'll go get drunk in the afternoon. I look to the right, and I see a guy sitting on the ironwork on the bridge. I said to Doug, "Get off at Cadman Plaza and pull over by the water." I put the long lens on my camera, and son of a bitch, there's a guy with his legs hanging over the end. Nothing was on the police radio, so nobody else had seen it and called it in. I call it in, emergency service gets there. Doug wasn't a gung-ho freelance photographer, but he knew how to shoot a camera. He didn't have his cameras with him that day, so I gave him mine. The guy jumped, and he got a couple of frames with him in midair. The guy hits the water headfirst. He actually cut the water, which is difficult to do. As long as you cut the water, you're not going to break your neck or do a belly flop. He lives. We see the current taking the guy, and him putting his hands up in the air, like, help help, as he's bobbing up and down. We're by the River Café, and there's a guy with a tugboat. He's got a mop and he's swabbing the deck. He was a waiter. I said, "Some guy just jumped off the bridge, and we see him in the water. You want to go get him?" Because I got balls. I do crazy shit. He's like, "Yeah, okay." Doug and I get on the boat, and we get out to where the guy is. I throw on a life vest. I put my arm through a donut. I give my buddy my cameras, and I'm like, "If I don't come back, keep them." I jump in the water and save the guy's life. My buddy's taking pictures of me doing this. The PD launch boat comes, puts a ramp down, and drags us up on the ramp. Turns out the guy jumped because his girlfriend told him, go fuck yourself. While he was on the stretcher, a reporter from Channel Five asked him, "Do you have any regrets?" And the guy goes, "Yeah, I regret that I didn't succeed at killing myself." When the reporter told me that, I was like, thanks a lot, guy. Next time I'll let you fucking drown. The *Daily News* made pictures of me looking like a drowned water rat. I was page one in the *Post* and the *Daily News* on May 25, 1985.

LESLIE GEVIRTZ: Hal Goldenberg is the only man I ever rode with that drove north on Fifth Avenue because he didn't want to miss a shot. The other thing is, he almost got me killed. There used to be a supermarket like six blocks from the office. There was a hostage situation. I jump into Hal's car, he's got all his radios playing, and it looks like a police car. [Retired cop cars were Goldenberg's vehicle of choice.] We pull up right at the front of the grocery store. I'm going, this can't be right, there are no cops here. As I'm saying that, a SWAT team pulls up on the other side. So now we're between the SWAT people and the hostage situation. We have a radio that we can call, but the *Daily News* and other people are monitoring that frequency. Hal's solution was not to move the car, but for us to just stay down below the window. I said, "Hal, we're gonna get killed. Get us the fuck out of here." "No, no, no, this will be a great shot." I said, "Yeah, in my head!"

HAL GOLDENBERG: What was that Dunleavy goof? "Horror! Terror!" And the old media saying, "If it bleeds, it leads." I saw a lot of shit like that, and what happens is, after a while you get what I call body shock. After seeing so many dead bodies—what's left of somebody after a collision, what's left of somebody after they get fifty holes blown in them, however they die—it becomes the same old shit. You can't let things like that bother you, or you can't do the job. When I'd had enough of body shock, I asked the photo editor to take me off the breaking news horror-terror stuff, and asked, could I do some of the paparazzi shit? Studio 54; Xenon; New York, New York; Magique. Every paparazzi had a club that was their club. They hung out there and would always get tips about who's shown up. The *Post* sent me to Magique the day they converted it from a Cadillac showroom into a club. There's three people there: Some English multimillionaire in a Bentley, who's most of the money behind the club. The other two are Steve Rogers [who was one of Magique's owners] and his brother Gary Rogers—two guys who graduated from high school with me. So that became Hal's club. That led to rubbing elbows with the rich and famous and winding up with their hobby. That's how I wound up a drug addict.

JAMI BERNARD: The photographers—and I don't really remember which ones—but they would do lots of drugs. They would snort coke off the light tables. So if you went into the darkroom through those clunky revolving doors—they were like turning canisters—there'd be people just snorting coke.

HAL GOLDENBERG: [At the *Post*] if you did cocaine, you would go up to one of the people you knew did it, and be like, "Yo, you got anything?" If someone asked me, I'd say, "Yeah, take a walk in ten minutes." I'd go into the color darkroom because it wasn't used, lay some lines, and put something on top of it so that it wasn't laying out in the open. The next time you saw that person in the city room, you give him a knowing nod. The next time, when I asked, "You got anything?" they'd reciprocate.

MYRON RUSHETZKY: I heard years later about some drug activity, that back in the darkroom, in the photo studio, they weren't just developing photos. Decades later I heard that the police wanted to make a raid because they thought there was a couple of people in the photo department who were dealing. I think these people were told by management: cut it out.

HAL GOLDENBERG: I started out as a weekend warrior, and then I started doing it while I was working. On 10th Street off Second Avenue, there were walkups. The Colombians worked out of the second walkup after the 2nd Avenue Deli. If the girl that sold wasn't on the street and there was nobody around, I'd double park my car and stand with my back up against the building, smoking a cigarette. I'd look around, being a little bit cautious, put my hand over my head, and knock lightly on the window behind me. Then I'd take a step forward and turn around so they could see my face. They didn't give discounts, but I got to know them so well that I'd pay for three grams and get one free.

You didn't have to be a detective to put two and two together. Here's a car with NYP plates [which identified members of the press and allowed them to park in otherwise illegal spots] going up the stairs of the drug place, coming back down, getting back in the car, and leaving. Run the plate. Oh, Hal Goldenberg from the *New York Post*. Back and forth, back and forth, back and forth. I don't know the intricacies, but word filtered down from Manhattan South to Dunleavy for us to cease and desist so that they didn't take us out of the city room in cuffs.

JAMI BERNARD: I was at Xenon with a photographer. We're dancing. He put a popper under my nose. I don't remember what a popper is—amyl nitrate? I had never had one before. That's the last I remember because when I woke up, I had been dragged off the dance floor. I fainted. I guess we were on some kind of story. The photographer said that the people who worked there were so annoyed. Like, "Get her out of here." I also had my first Quaalude from one of the photographers. I couldn't wait to take it. I took it on the subway on the way home. You're supposed to go out and party with it. But, OMG, I loved it. It was a real one. Yeah, there were people into drugs. But it was mostly cocaine. I had to stop because I had a lot of allergies and stuff and I was using Neo-Synephrine. I was ruining my nose. It was bleeding. I had to stop. Otherwise, I probably would have had a problem. It was just $100 a gram. I used to score some under the FDR Drive, from a dealer who met me there.

RAMONA GARNES: One day I get it into my head I'm gonna smoke a joint before I go to work. I got to work and I get on the computer. I was like, "Oh, no, no, no, no." You can't edit, you can't take dictation, you can't write—not in this newsroom—when you smoke weed. I get up, pack up my pocketbook, and I go to Myron and say, "I'm sick. I really feel horrible. I need to go home right now." I never got high at work again. Now, the minute I stepped out the door, that was a whole other thing.

HAL GOLDENBERG: I was in rehab half a dozen times. I walked out of every one of them after a few days and went right back to the block to get something. Then one day, I ran out of money. When my mother died, I inherited $101,281.17, and I got high on every penny of it. When there was ten bucks left in the ATM, I said, "Am I going to be one of these lunatics who's going to start robbing stores and people, or am I going to call it a day with this shit?" I put it down and never went back. It's been more than twenty years since I did anything besides aspirin or stuff that was prescribed for me.

For most reporters and editors, alcohol maintained its position as the most popular substance to abuse, both inside the office and beyond.

DAVE BANKS: John Cotter [then day city editor] sometimes would go on the lam for two or three nights, not go home. I remember getting him home once. It was winter. Deep snow. Cotter begged me to come to the Bridge [the Bridge Cafe, another watering hole popular with *Post* employees]. I think he'd quit. He was always quitting. I got a message saying he was absolutely paralyzed. I told them to stop giving him drink. He came on the phone and begged me to come down. It was a night Ken Chandler and his wife were coming to dinner at my house in White Plains. I had to help my wife set up and get the booze on the way home. I told Cotter I'd have one drink, but he had to promise to leave then. I go around the Bridge and we have three or four drinks of course. I get him in the car. The snow is coming down. We have to drive to Connecticut, to drop him. I helped him out of the car. The door opened. His wife threw a pan at me. She said, "You've kept him out for two nights." I was blamed. You always were blamed if you were out with Cotter. Then I got blamed by *my* wife for forgetting the booze. The Chandlers had been there for half an hour.

KEN CHANDLER: I vaguely remember that Banks was completely shit-faced when he showed up, and his wife was furious. He did bring the alcohol home, it was just inside his stomach.

AMY PAGNOZZI: I hated going to the Lion's Head. People at the Lion's Head would start out drinking and be really happy but they always ended up maudlin.

JAMI BERNARD: We used to go to after-hours clubs after the Lion's Head closed. There was one they called the Candy Store, because that's what it was during the day. At night, it was this club. It wasn't a dancing club. Everyone was smoking indoors back then. I felt sick, because of the closeness of the air and everything. It was almost dawn. I went out on the street to get some air and Dunleavy came out to see if I'm okay. He advised me to throw up because I would feel better. I say, "I can't just throw up." He said, "It's easy. Just put your finger down your throat." I tried; it didn't work. I said, "You show me." He put his finger down his throat and he threw up into the street, and I said, "Oh, well, I feel better now just watching." It was dawn and children were coming along to buy their Skittles because it was a candy store during the day.

WAYNE DARWEN, assistant managing editor, 1983–1987: It was always how far could you push the envelope before you broke it. It was very daring, and it was fun— and exciting. You were with your mates. It was almost like it was a party. A lot of dudes with beer and other intoxicants in their desks. I remember those late shifts when you're putting out those editions. There'd be six-packs of beer popped out. Everyone would come back from a break half-trashed or fully trashed. Normally, you'd get fired for it. There, you were more likely to get pro- moted, and if you didn't do it, you might get fired. Now, you'd be canceled for the rest of your life. Some of the stuff was close to criminal by today's stan- dards. Bad behavior was pretty much a badge of honor.

JAMI BERNARD: Everything was tolerated. The weirder the better. From sex to drugs to people. Weird people worked at the *Post*.

13 | A GOOD MEASURE OF RUTHLESSNESS

Kicking Kennedy, Roy Cohn's Cons, Gubernatorial Follies

n June of 1980, *Sweeney Todd*, one of Stephen Sondheim's musical master-pieces, ended its initial Broadway run. "City on Fire," a song from the show, refers to nineteenth-century London, where the tale of the vengeful and mur-derous barber is set, but it could have applied to New York as the 1980s took hold. Fueled by Reaganomics, a greed-is-good mania consumed the city, eras-ing the last vestiges of the gentler postwar metropolis. Rupert Murdoch found much to like in Ronald Reagan and his policies.

ANDY SOLTIS, rewrite, editor, 1967–2014: During the summer of '79, the *Post* seemed to be competing with the *Daily News* as to who could be more pro–Ted Kennedy. For example, the *Post* ran a story saying, "[House Speaker] Tip O'Neill says Ted Kennedy can get the Democratic nomination just by asking for it." Of course, we had an incumbent Democratic president [Jimmy Carter] who was not going to allow that to happen. Then the *News* countered with some-thing that was even more pro-Kennedy. This continued until the Iranian hos-tage crisis. One day, Ted Kennedy said something about the Shah of Iran that was very critical; something to the effect that "We wouldn't be in this mess if it weren't for the Shah." It got a big positive reaction among the students who were holding the American hostages. The *Post* wood the next day was

TEDDY'S THE TOAST OF TEHRAN! I've heard people say that Murdoch wrote this or that the headline was ordered by him. The person who actually came up with it, I believe, was [Michael] Hechtman, who was the most apolitical person I've ever met. The *Post* then became very pro-Carter and anti-Kennedy.

DICK BELSKY, metropolitan editor, 1970–1989: We did that headline, and Rupert got in trouble. People were saying, "You're going after Kennedy?" and Rupert didn't even know anything about it. Supposedly, he told somebody, "My boys sometimes get a little over-the-top."

BARBARA ROSS, political reporter, 1978–1985: I recall meetings with [potential] presidential candidates, but not being invited to the table. I was allowed to escort Joan Kennedy to the ladies' room. The boys dealt with the boys. There was a bit of a hullabaloo before [the Kennedys] arrived because we had all those front pages on the wall, across from the elevator. I think somebody had the common sense to take the TEDDY'S THE TOAST OF TEHRAN! wood off the wall before he showed up.

DAVE BANKS, night managing editor, 1979–1981: I remember Rupert coming to the *Post* one night. He'd been out to dinner with Ronald Reagan. He was kind of appalled that Reagan was going to run for president. He said, "Nice enough guy, affable, but he's an old guy. He can't hear. I'm not sure that he's all there." If those were not his exact words, it was the tenor of his words. We were amused by this, but a bit gobsmacked. Then he put his full weight behind Reagan, even though he had these private misgivings.

GEORGE ARZT, City Hall bureau chief, 1968–1986: Dunleavy believed I knew more than I knew. One day, Ronald Reagan was in the office. Dunleavy had awakened me after a long night and he said, "Where are you? Murdoch is here." I said, "Where am I supposed to be?" "You're supposed to be in Murdoch's office." I grabbed anything I could and ran down. He said, "Where's your jacket?" He got a jacket off a really skinny guy. I'm struggling to get into this jacket and then all of a sudden we go into the meeting with Reagan. I say hello and I'm thinking, "God, I hope I don't fall asleep." I have my tape recorder going and soon Murdoch looks at me, and says, "What's that on your shirt?" I look down and there's this big Rorschach ink blot going across my shirt. I think, "This is going to be a hell of a day." Then he said, "What's on your head? You look like you came off a wedding cake." It's shaving cream. Suddenly, I raised my hand to ask a question and the whole sleeve rips. Dunleavy got me out of there immediately after the meeting and got me some coffee to sober up. He said, "Except for the fright of having the boss there, that was hilarious."

ANDY SOLTIS: In the spring of 1980, the *Post* endorsed Carter in the Democratic primary in New York. The fall comes around. I'm backing up Steve Dunleavy on the city desk. It's the night of the Al Smith dinner in the Grand Ballroom of the Waldorf Astoria, the big political and Catholic charities dinner of the year. Both Carter and Reagan were there. [*Post* political reporter] Deborah Orin calls in and says, "There's a crazy rumor going around the room. Is it possible the *Post* is going to endorse Reagan tomorrow?" I laughed. I said, "Debbie, Murdoch has owned the *Post* for four years and the *Post* has not endorsed a single Republican for any significant office. Why would he suddenly do that now?" She said, "You got me, but the Republicans are being coy. I need to know, is this happening?" I said to Dunleavy, "Debbie wants to know, are we endorsing Reagan?" Dunleavy said, "Yes, mate. Tomorrow." That absolutely shocked me. People are going to say, "Well, the *Post* endorsed Koch, and Koch was right wing." That's nonsense. Koch often had a one hundred percent rating from the Americans for Democratic Action, which was the litmus test in those days. He was about as pure a liberal as you could be at that time. Four years into Murdoch's ownership, the *Post* had swung around and changed politics.

ERIC FETTMANN, associate editorial page editor, columnist, 1976–1991; 1993–2019: The factor that I think more than anything else did it was Jimmy Carter: Murdoch thought Carter was god-awful.

SUSAN MULCAHY, Page Six editor, 1978–1985: At Madison Square Garden during the 1980 Democratic convention, I remember curtains separating the headquarters of different news organizations. One night Carl Bernstein lifted the curtain in front of the *Post*'s booth. He didn't say hello or introduce himself. He was with somebody else and said to that person, in a disgusted voice, "This is the *New York Post*." It was like he was pointing out animals in a zoo. Which was clear to everybody working that night. A couple of people started jumping around, scratching under their arms and making ape noises.

ROGER STONE, Republican consultant: I don't think Rupert Murdoch is a conservative. I think he's a believer in free enterprise, and a strong capitalist. He wants what's best for him and his business. He's not afraid to think outside the box. He and the *Post* had not only played a major role in Koch's election as mayor, but also his reelection. The *Post* actually ran full-page ads urging the Republicans to endorse Koch, and indeed, in his reelection run, Koch was the nominee of the Republican and Democratic parties, having won both party primaries. In any event, going into the 1980 presidential campaign, Murdoch uses Koch and the *Post* to torture Jimmy Carter. Koch never actually endorsed Carter. He certainly never endorsed Reagan, either, but on a clockwork basis, he criticized Carter regarding Israel in the closing weeks of the campaign, which did real damage to Carter among Jewish voters. Koch was saying, look, I'm a Democrat and I'm supporting Carter, but he's completely bungling the situation in Israel. He was killing Carter with love.

MAUREEN CONNELLY, former press secretary for Ed Koch: I wouldn't trust anything Roger Stone had to say.

WAYNE DARWEN, assistant managing editor, 1983–1987: Murdoch is remarkable, whether you like his politics, you like him, or you don't. He's a remarkable dude. I don't know what sort of character it takes to be that fricking strong, with a good measure of ruthlessness, and not giving a fuck what anyone says. He is not intimidated by anybody: by politicians, by prime ministers, by presidents. He didn't give a shit what they thought. People often say he's political, but I've seen him support left and support right. The bottom line is, his god is his business. And nothing gets in the way of business. Politics is not going to get in the way of it. He's successful because he's single-minded. I'm going to make a fortune, and I'm going to build an empire, and no one is going to stop me. And I don't give a fuck what anybody says.

BOB DRURY, sports columnist, 1977–1984: During the '80 presidential race, Murdoch came to Jerry Lisker and said, "Let's cover this like we would cover a sporting event. Pick two of your guys." Jerry picked me and [sportswriter Mike] Marley. Marley was going to travel with Reagan. Reagan's people said, "Sure. No problem." I was supposed to travel with Carter, but Carter's people wouldn't let me. So, that idea, which, for the time, was a good Murdoch idea, went down the tubes.

ROGER STONE: There's an instance a few weeks before the election where, during a speech Hamilton Jordan—who you may recall, was always referred to by [then–Speaker of the US House of Representatives] Tip O'Neill as "Hannibal Jerkin"—says Carter can win without New York State. His remark becomes a huge front page: CARTER'S MAN SAYS IT: 'WE DON'T NEED NEW YORK!' I have it framed somewhere. Remember that in 1980, the Liberal Party had endorsed John Anderson, and the Conservatives and the Republicans had endorsed Reagan. There was no Working Families party then, so Carter had only the Democratic nomination. That's why Reagan carried the state with forty-six percent of the vote in a three-way race. Murdoch was very much a part of that strategy. After Reagan was elected, Murdoch presented me with the plate for the front page of the *Post* with the headline REAGAN WINS. I still have it. It's very cool.

> The road to Reagan had been at least partly paved by Roy Cohn, whose power at the paper grew despite unease among reporters and editors who had either experienced the McCarthy era or knew the history.

ROGER STONE: When I first went to New York for Governor Reagan's presidential campaign in '79, I was introduced to Sheila Mosler, a socialite whose divorce Roy had handled. She introduced me to Roy, who had been a friend of Ronnie and Nancy Reagan in the '50s, because of the whole McCarthy period. It was Roy who introduced me to Rupert Murdoch. Murdoch was in Roy's stable of clients-slash-friends, who included [George] Steinbrenner, Donald Trump, that great gadfly [well-connected limousine and transportation mogul] Bill Fugazy, the archbishop, and two or three other standards.

ERIC FETTMANN: Roger Wood became enamored of Roy Cohn at one point.

GEORGE ARZT: I don't think anyone at the *Post* was enamored of Roy Cohn. It's just that he had access to the owner. I think everyone knew that he was a BS artist. Why was Murdoch chummy with him? I think because he could get him into circles that he needed to get in. Republican circles.

ROGER STONE: Roy, myself, and Rupert were at lunch at the "21" Club. In those days, you ate on the second floor. We were at Roy's table and right next to us was a two-top with these two society ladies. We sit down and Rupert says, "Roy, who is Mildred Hilson?" Roy says, "She's a big, fat nobody. Why?" Rupert says,

"We just got an invitation for Anna [Murdoch] and me to go to a reception at the Waldorf Towers for George and Barbara Bush." Roy says, "I wouldn't be caught dead with that group of stiffs." We are proceeding with our meal, and Roy has this habit, which he did everywhere, of reaching into other people's plates. Roy never ordered food because he—quote, unquote—wasn't hungry, then ate half of yours with his fingers. He reaches over to the next table and takes a piece of lettuce out of this woman's salad and pops it in his mouth. He does this almost unconsciously—he's talking the whole time. The woman screams; the maître d' comes over and this woman is irate. "This man! This man put his fingers in my plate." Roy looks at her, and he says, "Lady, you're drunk. When did you start drinking—about ten o'clock this morning? You're loaded. I can smell it. Why don't you mind your own business?" She's like, "I demand that you move these gentlemen's table." The maître d' says, "I can't. But I can move you to another table." She moves to another table. We finish our meal. Then Roy says, "Bring me three of [political power broker] Jerry Finkelstein's finest cigars." The waiter brings us cigars. Roy is blowing smoke at this woman, who's like three tables away. When she gets up to leave, she comes by the table, shoots Roy a dirty look, sticks out her hand, and says, "Mr. Murdoch, I'm Mildred Hilson. I'm so delighted you'll be joining us for our little party for Poppy and Bar." Murdoch found Roy very entertaining.

MICHAEL SHAIN, television editor, 1978–1993, 1996–2013: I was still a schlubby reporter, but I remember Roy Cohn striding into the newsroom and going straight to Roger Wood's office and they would close the door. I grew up in a postwar Jewish family in suburban Philadelphia. Roy Cohn was the closest thing you could come to the devil incarnate. I would think: if my mother could see me now, she would kill me. She would disown me that Roy Cohn walks back and forth in my newsroom and I don't say anything or do anything.

CLAUDIA COHEN, Page Six editor, 1977–1980: There's only one thing worse than someone who double plants [the same item in a competing column], and that is someone who gives you a bad story. That happened to me in a very significant way. I had such success with Roy [Cohn] that it got to the point where he would say, "You can just go with this. This is solid." I trusted him enough to do that. These stories always were totally solid until the dreaded day. There had just been a rough piece written about the Studio 54 case [the owners of the disco eventually pled guilty to charges of tax evasion] by someone at *New York* magazine. It created a lot of waves. Roy called me, or maybe I called him and said, "What's the reaction to this piece?" He said, "Listen, tomorrow morning, I am filing a libel suit. I'm charging twenty-five different things against the magazine, against the author. By the time the paper comes out tomorrow, this suit will have been filed." I said, "This is absolutely solid?" He said, "You can go to the bank on this one." I ran the item. Not only did Roy never file the suit, Roy never intended to file. It was one of the darkest days I ever had in journalism. I was mortified. I banned Roy Cohn from Page Six. After a couple of weeks, he started calling and calling and calling.

SUSAN MULCAHY: I can't remember why Claudia and Roy Cohn had an argument, but they did because Roy suddenly started calling me with stories. I had been too lowly to deal with until then. I would make this face—an "eeeewww-ick" face—and signal to Claudia when it was Roy on the phone. She thought this was very funny. Claudia wanted to teach Roy a lesson by refusing to take his calls, but she didn't want to lose a good story so I had to talk to him. When I hung up, I wanted to take a bath. Roy represented pure evil to me, but as time went on, I came to appreciate his value as a source. I won't go so far as to say I grew to like him, but I did come to appreciate him.

Roy Cohn reestablished his relationship with Claudia Cohen by planting racy but questionable stories involving Studio 54. The disco's owners, Steve Rubell and Ian Schrager, had been charged with obstruction of justice and conspiracy, in addition to tax evasion. Cohn represented Rubell. In a bid to reduce their sentences, and on the advice of their attorneys, Rubell and Schrager said that Hamilton Jordan, Jimmy Carter's chief of staff, had been seen snorting cocaine at Studio 54, an accusation that a special prosecutor later determined had no merit. The obstruction of justice and conspiracy charges were dropped when the two pled guilty to tax evasion and spent nearly a year of their three-and-a-half-year sentences in a federal prison camp in Alabama. (Rubell died in 1989 and President Barack Obama pardoned Schrager in 2017.)

NED STEELE, reporter, rewrite, 1977–1980: When I was filling in for Claudia on Page Six, I was aware of political agendas occasionally swirling around in the background. I'm not going to remember all the details, but I remember Cabell [then–Page Six reporter A. Cabell Bruce III] was really bent on developing some stories involving shenanigans at Studio 54 with Carter aides, including,

I believe, Hamilton Jordan. I wasn't satisfied that it was nailed down and I didn't let it run. I think it ultimately did run later, but not on Page Six.

PETER HONERKAMP, Page Six reporter, 1979–1980: Roy Cohn was trying to put pressure on the Carter administration to get a better deal for Rubell and Schrager. One of the ways he was pressuring it was through negative publicity that was coming out on Ham Jordan allegedly doing cocaine in the basement of Studio 54. It was a setup. No credible journalist would have touched that story. The *Post* headline read something to the effect of "Ham Did Coke in Studio 54, Top P.R. Agent Says." Well, the top PR guy was in with the guy who's defending him [Cohn]. I was becoming disillusioned about what the paper was doing. Around that time came the famous Ham Jordan blowjob story [which appeared in the *Post*'s news pages with a Claudia Cohen byline]. Allegedly a friend of Hamilton Jordan's got a blowjob in a limousine outside Studio 54 while Ham Jordan was inside. [According to Cohen's story, the intimate encounter took place outside the Essex House, where Hamilton Jordan had been dropped off following the Studio 54 visit.] It was just: *Who cares?* It was totally meaningless. It was like: a friend of Peter Honerkamp's got laid last night.

CLAUDIA COHEN: Roy was thinking very strategically. Rather than give items about himself, he started to give Susan Mulcahy the most fabulous stories, asking her to pass them on to me because I wouldn't even talk to him. The items were worthy of page-one consideration. I think he gave me two in a row. Just because I was mad at him and wasn't putting his name on Page Six, it didn't mean that I wouldn't use the information that he gave me. However, these tips were thoroughly one hundred percent reported and checked out. Both ended up on page one. That was how Roy wormed his way back onto Page Six.

HAL DAVIS, reporter, New York State Supreme Court, 1978–1993: One day I'm talking to Dunleavy and he pauses to take another phone call. He says, "Uh huh, okay, thank you." He hangs up, gets back on the phone, and says, "Is there a judge named Edward J. Greenfield in your courthouse?" I say, "Yeah." He says, "What's he like?" I say, "He's the William F. Buckley of the courthouse. He crafts elegant conservative opinions. The knock on him is he sometimes takes too long to decide a case." He goes, "Is he a crook?" I say, "There's never been a question about his integrity." He says, "I just heard that three lawyers testified before a grand jury that Greenfield is on the take. Go talk to him about it." I say, "Whoa, whoa. Slow down. Let me see what I can find out." I know there's a grand jury in Kings County [Brooklyn] looking into crooked judges. I ask the two *Post* reporters covering it, "Any New York County judges mentioned?" Nope, they say. I called Dunleavy back and said, "I need more information." Dunleavy says, "I know this may sound strange, but this information comes from Roy Cohn, and his information is always unimpeachable." I say, "I'll see what I can find out."

It's already late and the courthouse is closed up tight. I come back the next morning and the first decision out of the box, dated the previous day, which means the lawyers clearly knew about it then, was Judge Edward J. Greenfield dismissing a lawsuit by Donald Trump against the Bank of New York for a supposedly failed real estate deal on Wall Street. Trump had no case. Now I know what's going on. Obviously, Greenfield's office had notified the lawyers what the decision was, and now, by some sheer coincidence, we have Roy Cohn, who is the lawyer for Donald Trump, calling Dunleavy and giving him supposed dirt on Greenfield? I go to Greenfield's chambers and suggest his law secretary not be part of the meeting. I explain to him exactly what's going on. Greenfield says, "But I've already issued my decision. How does this help [Cohn]?" I say, "Oh, he doesn't care about the decision. What he wants is to influence the *reporting* of the decision so that if we decide to go big on it—as in 'Trump, Cohn Lose Wall Street Case,' the next column will say, 'Greenfield named corrupt by three lawyers.'" Greenfield was shocked and stunned. But I think he was educated about how Roy Cohn conducted his business. I don't believe the case was ever appealed and we didn't write anything. It was a bullshit suit by Trump, who was then just a real estate guy who brought a lot of lawsuits.

GEORGE ARZT: Roger [Wood] was very funny, because he would call up and say, "I heard from a very unreliable source." I always knew who the unreliable source was: Roy Cohn. He knew that Roy Cohn was not a person of honor and was not trustworthy. Roy Cohn was full of shit most of the time and would hear something and decide that he would call it in to Roger. I would say maybe there was a grain of truth in about one third of them. Roger basically was saying, "Check it out just in case there's something there."

ROGER STONE: Roy hooked Cindy [Adams] up with the Reagans. I mean, Joey knew the Reagans in the '50s, but Roy is the one who made sure that Cindy was at Reagan's table.

CINDY ADAMS, gossip columnist, 1981–current: Roy Cohn was not my friend. I meant nothing to Roy. He loved Joey, and he loved Joey for a reason. Roy Cohn always was pseudo-political. If a monsignor became a bishop, and there was a dinner in his honor, Roy was there. And Joey was the emcee, the toastmaster general. For Roy, Joey was useful. As a result, Roy gave Joey's birthday party every year. We were in Hong Kong many times, because I was doing the Sukarno book [the autobiography of the first president of Indonesia, "as told to Cindy Adams"] and Roy once flew all the way to Hong Kong just to have dinner with Joey. I inherited Roy, but I was nobody, and he didn't care about me at all. Until I got the column.

MARTY McLAUGHLIN, public relations and political consultant: Cohn's office was in a brownstone on East 68th Street. I'd go there to see [Cohn's law partner] Stanley [Friedman]. Stanley's office looked like a political pro's office: phones, papers strewn all over the place. Roy had an office upstairs. I remember going up there and Roy would be in a white bathing suit with oil, laying out on a chaise lounge with two of his boys. Roy was very gay though he never let anybody know about it. There was a terrace. He's laying out there and taking the sun. He had two muscle-bound guys in pink jumpsuits standing by.

SUSAN MULCAHY: Roger Wood decides two days before the [first Reagan] inaugural [in 1981] that I should go cover for Page Six. I had no Secret Service clearance. I had no press pass. One call to Roy, I was in the White House. I could have been a terrorist. *No problem.* I was very apprehensive about taking his help, but guess what? He had the best party at the Reagan inaugural. Richard Johnson was a city desk reporter then, and they sent the two of us. Roy's connection to Trump is what everyone talks about now, but he was a major fixer for the Reagan White House, too.

> Roy Cohn's influence at the paper infuriated James Wechsler. In the early 1950s, when Wechsler was editor, the *Post* had aggressively attacked Senator Joseph McCarthy, Roy Cohn's then-boss and mentor. And in 1953 Wechsler himself had been hauled in front of McCarthy's communist witch-hunting Senate subcommittee. Cohn had been one of his inquisitors.

GEORGE ARZT: After Murdoch took over the paper, he was having lunch with Roy Cohn, and he said to me, "Go downstairs and tell Jimmy Wechsler to join us." I thought, "Oh my god." I went downstairs. I said, "Jimmy, Murdoch wants you to come up to lunch, but Roy Cohn's there." He turned around to me and said, "I'm not going." Then he opened up the bottom drawer, took out a pint of something, and took a swig. When I went back upstairs, Murdoch laughed. My stomach was jumping. [Wechsler died of cancer in 1983. He was sixty-seven.]

> Cohn essentially worked for himself. A more likable and equally well-connected power broker appeared on the Murdoch payroll—Howard Rubenstein, a lawyer and public relations executive whose firm represented Murdoch along with the *Post* and such other New York institutions as George Steinbrenner and his New York Yankees, Columbia University, the Metropolitan Opera, and Donald Trump.

BILL KNAPP, political consultant: Lobbying firms have reputations. You want to get to this guy? You hire this lobbying firm. Want to get to that guy? You hire that lobbying firm. That's a big piece of the business [in DC]. In New York, you want to get to the *Post*, you hire Howard Rubenstein. In the early days anyway. He was thought to be Murdoch's guy.

JOANNE WASSERMAN, reporter, 1977–1986: Tony Alvarado had just been named schools chancellor. He was this charismatic, fiery, young, good-looking guy, who had all these big ideas, like setting up full-day kindergarten. This story breaks in the middle of the night—always in the middle of the night—about this guy they arrest named John Chin, who's waving a gun around. The girlfriend called the cops. He's got a safe. They open the safe, and inside is a note from Tony Alvarado saying, "I owe you ten grand." It turns out Tony Alvarado had borrowed close to a hundred grand from people who worked for him. This is the biggest story I have ever been on. Alvarado hires Tom Puccio, a big-deal criminal defense attorney. Puccio is tight with Howard Rubenstein—and Murdoch had this relationship with, and the *Post* was a client of, Howard Rubenstein. Rubenstein starts to get Rupert to kill my stories. I get a story about how the Alvarados bought a house in Park Slope and they used part-time Board of Ed workers to paint the house. They killed the story. They also said, suddenly, "You can't have anonymous sources." I said, "Are you kidding me? This is the *New York Post*." Every day was a nightmare. There's Dunleavy screaming at me, Ellenberg screaming at me. Meanwhile, they know, they had to know, the stories are being killed. But they're still demanding the stories!

BARBARA ROSS: When Liz Holtzman was running for Brooklyn DA, I was covering the race. I'd file a story, and it would be re-topped every day with, like, a press release from the Republican candidate. I got so upset when I realized what was happening: Dunleavy was getting a call from Howard Rubenstein's folks who were representing somebody running against Liz. She was anti-organization. They were part of the organization [the Brooklyn political machine]. Dunleavy would get the press release [from Rubenstein]. The Holtzman people got angrier and angrier. I got so upset, I got shingles. What I did—oh, man, I got into such trouble for this—I called Rubenstein and I said, "Howard, what are you doing?" I said, "I write the story and you guys call up and you get your press release put on top of it. Now, I understand that you're representing a client, but I'm the reporter. You should be talking to me. By the way, doesn't this represent a conflict of interest? You represent the *New York Post*. You are trying to persuade Bloomingdale's that our readers are not their shoplifters. You are trying to say that we're a credible news organization. And here you are undermining that credibility by slanting the coverage of a political race." Howard being Howard was very skillful in deflecting my criticism. But maybe an hour later, I got George Arzt coming at me with, "Are you out of your mind? You called the biggest public relations guy in the city, a guy who talks to Murdoch on a regular basis, and told him he had a conflict of interest. Are you crazy?" Howard called Roger Wood and Roger called George saying, "What is she doing now?"

GEORGE ARZT: I would never do that.

> Murdoch's empire-building led him to demand that reporters toss aside old habits, like honoring gentlemen's agreements with other newspapers and local government.

GEORGE ARZT: Murdoch called me to his office. He said, "Look at that budget story the *Daily News* has. How come you didn't have that?" I said, "Because they broke the embargo." He said, "Next time you break the embargo." I soon learned that this was a different game. All norms are out, he just wants you to get the story first. Everybody had worked this way for years. You didn't have to worry about another paper beating you. From the administration's point of view, they get everything out, and everyone gets the same story. At this point, I started hunting for stories. I became extremely aggressive both on political and governmental stories, and we became the dominant political paper in the city.

JOANNE WASSERMAN: In Room Nine [the press room] at City Hall, Joyce Purnick was there for the *Times* and Clyde Haberman, too [Purnick and Haberman both left the *Post* after Murdoch bought it], and [Mike] Oreskes for the *Daily News*. The *Post* was very much in the tank for Koch, so I think they kind of looked down on George. But he scooped them all the time. Compared to how things play out at the *Post* today—disgusting stuff like what they did with Hunter Biden—what George got were actual scoops, real stories that [the other City Hall reporters] then had to follow.

CLYDE HABERMAN, reporter, 1966–1977: I was always in terror of George, because when I was at City Hall [for the *Times*], George was plugged in in a way that I could not possibly have matched. We had different audiences and different needs and saw different types of stories, but George always knew infinitely more than appeared in the paper. Sometimes it was hard to tell—did he really know? Or did he say that he knew? George is one of those guys who if you ever said, "I heard blah-blah-blah," he would say, "I already knew that. John LoCicero [adviser to Mayor Ed Koch] told me that weeks ago." I would say, "I didn't see it in the paper, George." "I didn't think it was worth very much." There was a little bit of, are you for real? Or do you just simply say you know everything?

DAVID SEIFMAN, City Hall bureau chief, political editor, 1973–2019: When we were still an afternoon paper, another reporter in Room Nine coined the term that Koch was "unavoidable for comment." Meaning, if you were walking in the hallway and Koch was walking in the hallway, he would stop and answer your questions. You could ask him anything, right? Today, everything's so tightly scripted and [former governor Andrew] Cuomo wouldn't even allow the press into a press conference. One day I'm in the hallway, and there was tension with Iran. We're an afternoon paper. Must have been, I don't know, noon-ish? I see Koch, so I figure, what the hell, I'll ask him a question. I asked him about tensions with Iran, Israel. I forgot the precise nature of the conflict at that point but he says, "The US should bomb Iran." I said, "Oh, okay." Mayor of New York says bomb Iran. It's on the front page in the afternoon edition. This is a happenstance meeting in the hallway, which says more about Koch than it says about the *Post*. But it gives you a better feel for the times. You couldn't get near the mayor today without pre-clearance.

RANDY SMITH, reporter, 1977–1980: I started writing these stories about gimmicks in the city budget—it was something critical of how the city was doing the budget to make it look better or whatever—and I was pulled out of City Hall. Later, I was told by somebody that I had been Kummerfelded. The *Post* didn't want stories critiquing the city budget because they wanted to be supportive. [Donald Kummerfeld, former budget director and first deputy mayor in the Abe Beame administration, and an adviser to other mayors on fiscal matters, had been hired by Murdoch.]

LESLIE GEVIRTZ, reporter, rewrite, 1978–1988: I tried very hard to stay out of the political beat. I made the mistake once. It was the '80s, crime was high. Koch was going up to Harlem to address tenants in a public housing project. They were asking for more police protection. I thought it was a little bit ironic that as I looked up from [Mayor Koch's] motorcade, there were sharpshooters on the roof. Three or four buildings had sharpshooters on them. Because he was a controversial figure. I'd never seen that before. I just sort of wrote the story—people demanding police protection were very well protected; last night, there were sharpshooters on the roof as the mayor walked in. The mayor did not like that very much. And complained. Not to [then–City Hall bureau chief] George Arzt but to Rupert. Rupert told Arzt to take care of it. Arzt called me. He said, "They want an apology." I'm like, "What is there to apologize for? There were sharpshooters." Arzt just shook his head in total disbelief. I said, "There's nothing wrong with the story." I was like, "I'm not going to apologize." I don't know what Arzt did. But whatever it was, I never heard about it again. By the same token, I never covered City Hall.

GEORGE ARZT: I have no recollection of that.

> Contrary to Murdoch's current notoriety as a conservative kingmaker, Ed Koch wasn't the only Democrat backed by the *Post*. The paper also endorsed and threw its weight behind Governor Hugh Carey when he ran for reelection in 1978. At the Inner Circle dinner in Manhattan, an annual charity event where members of New York's media establishment roast local and state politicians in musical skits, Carey got a taste of the *Post*'s pugnacious office culture.

DAVE BANKS: A bunch of us went to the Inner Circle. There's so much free booze at those things, and afterward, Rupert had taken a private suite upstairs in the

Hilton to entertain political guests. I remember Governor Carey and Rupert being closeted at one end of the room. Dunleavy and I got into a fight. My great friend at the *Post* was John Cotter, a great journalist in my view, but probably a great Democrat more than a great journalist. Dunleavy and I were arguing over whether Belsky or Cotter should head up the afternoon editions that I now ran as managing editor. We both loved Belsky, but Cotter and I had this wonderful relationship, which was seeing us get hit after hit after hit. Our woods were spectacular. Dunleavy wanted to put Belsky into that role. We got very drunk arguing about this and gradually the argument got more and more serious. I can remember the crump of gin and tonic glasses sliding through our fingers—icy, perspiration-laden—they were just falling, shattering on the floor. Then we were throwing punches and missing. We were so drunk we couldn't land a hit, and people were trying to separate us. My wife fled weeping from the room. Rupert escorted Governor Carey out. I woke up the next morning in the Hilton, where we had taken a room for the night, with a huge hangover, and said to my wife, "I had a terrible dream that Dunleavy and I fought." She said, "It was no dream." With that she went home. We had left our child for the first time with a babysitter to have a special night at the Hilton and I'd ruined it by brawling in public with Steve Dunleavy. It was awful, but those are the sort of incidents that you could get into at the *Post.*

DICK BELSKY: They were standing face-to-face threatening to punch each other out. Dave was a huge guy. And Dunleavy, nobody ever wanted to take him on, pound for pound, in a fistfight. Dave kept turning to me and saying, "This isn't about you." It was a real, real tense scene. I have a feeling it might have been Ken Chandler who broke it up because it's the kind of thing he did.

KEN CHANDLER, editor in chief, publisher, 1978–1986, 1993–2002: I don't think I did that, but it's a good story so I won't deny it.

DICK BELSKY: Monday morning, I come to work at like six o'clock and Dave's there. He grabs me and says, "What did I do Saturday night? My wife wouldn't talk to me for the entire weekend." I said, "Did you ask her?" He said, "Every time I asked her, she says, 'You know what you did.'" I tell him the whole thing and he's like, "Oh my god." He thinks he's gonna be fired. Dunleavy was a powerful guy. Steve comes striding in it at noon or whenever, "Hey, mate, how are you?" Dave starts to try to apologize. All Steve says is, "Oh, mate, good night.

Good night. What do we got going on?" It was nothing to Steve. This was the kind of thing he did all the time. It's a lot of that old Aussie, I guess, tradition of journalism: drinking and fighting.

Despite the *Post*'s support for Carey, he did not have immunity from less desirable attention.

CHARLES LACHMAN, reporter, 1981–1988: Hugh Carey was a widower with a lot of kids, and he and his wife had had an apparently great marriage. [Several years after his wife's death], he started dating this socialite figure from Chicago [Evangeline "Engie" Gouletas]. That was a big story for the *Post* and any other newspaper in New York. I was assigned to help on the story. The *Chicago Tribune* did this long, long feature on Evangeline. She was a very interesting character. I'm reading and reading and reading and reading. I got like eighty paragraphs down and see that she had been married more times than she'd said. I say, "Whoa, that's a story." Of course, at the *Post*, you think about headlines. You really think about the story arc. Those were the key skills learned. Evangeline Carey said she'd been married twice before, but it was three times. I wrote the story. It was a big headline and Carey was really upset about it. I remember getting a call from the *Chicago Tribune* writer who wrote the story. He started screaming at me for stealing his scoop. I said, "Well, buddy, you shouldn't have put it eighty paragraphs down. That was your lede." Then we went crazy on getting into her as a personality.

One of Murdoch's Australian imports won the contest for most scintillating life story—financial editor Maxwell Newton, who became an enthusiastic proponent of Reaganomics. In Australia, Newton had been an editor, a publisher, and an owner of brothels and a sex shop. After moving to New York and joining the *Post*, he was said to have married a former prostitute who had advertised in one of the papers he ran in Australia.

KEN CHANDLER: We didn't see a lot of [Newton] in the newsroom. When he did come through, he was very loud, and had a booming voice. He was a little bit of an intimidating character. In retrospect, I'm not sure why anybody would be intimidated by him. He seemed to have Rupert's ear. Most of the columns were an attack on the Federal Reserve policies. Max Newton was obsessed with the Fed, and how their policies would lead the country into ruin. I think that

Murdoch probably thought there was some truth to it, although he probably thought Max went too far sometimes.

MARSHA KRANES, rewrite, editor, 1974–2005: I was once invited to a lunch in a dining room that Murdoch had upstairs, somewhere on the sixth floor. It was around Easter, and Hugh Carey and his Greek wife, Evangeline Gouletas, and a couple of other reporters were there. And Maxwell Newton. He was married to a woman who supposedly was a madame in an Australian brothel. The conversation got around to Greek culture or something. Newton, who was a little drunk, said, "How come you're dark-haired? The ancient Greeks were blond and blue-eyed. I think it was the conquering Turkish hordes." She got up. She was insulted. Murdoch—and everybody—looked at Newton. She stormed out and Hugh Carey stormed out after her. That was the end of lunch.

KEN CHANDLER: I wasn't there, but I heard about it. Max couldn't keep his mouth shut. Max was always saying the stuff that in today's world would have been totally non-PC. But even in those days it was a little non-PC, to give you an idea of how bad he was.

EVANGELINE GOULETAS, former wife of New York governor Hugh Carey: I don't recall that at all. First of all, I would not get insulted if somebody says I'm dark-haired because I love my dark hair. I think there is a misquote because I never ever would leave a board meeting. I believe that is a made-up situation. That was my first and, I think, only encounter with Mr. Murdoch. He was extremely polite to me, a very fine gentleman at that meeting.

> After Murdoch had given Americans Craig Ammerman and John Van Doorn a shot at the co–managing editor positions, he installed two with Commonwealth accents. In 1981, Ken Chandler and John Canning took over as co–managing editors.

DICK BELSKY: Ken was a voice of sanity in the newsroom.

ERIC FETTMANN: John Canning was about as sweet a person and as un-Murdochian a person as you could think of. And he was a layout and design genius. He's the guy who invented these magazine-style front pages for newspapers, which frankly I hate, but he started it.

As the '80s began, the *Post* endorsed both Democrats and Republicans in local races, based on their politics, connections, and potential usefulness to the paper and to Murdoch's expanding empire. But there was one candidate, Liz Holtzman, whose brief interaction with the *Post*'s owner initiated a barrage of negative coverage by the tabloid, an early example of his weaponization of political coverage in the US. It began with the 1980 Senate race, in which she won the primary but lost the general election; then on to her successful campaign to become Brooklyn district attorney in 1981; and later included her winning race to take over the New York City comptroller's office in 1990; and her second losing bid for the Senate in 1992. No matter her goal, Liz Holtzman remained perennially in the *Post*'s crosshairs. Though the paper's aim at times failed, Murdoch's troops kept on shooting.

GEORGE ARZT: One day, Liz Holtzman comes to the *Post* to see Murdoch. As she came out of the meeting, I said, "How did you do, Liz?" She said, "I think we got along really fine." Maybe a few minutes later, a red-faced Rupert comes out and says, "She used the L-word! And she used the P-word!" I said, "I know what the L-word is. What's the P-word?" "Progressive!" I said to myself, "How could Liz think she did well in that meeting?" After that, it was downhill. How could she not have done her homework? Yes, of course she was liberal, but did she have to say it?

BILL KNAPP: The *Post* was totally in the tank for Bess Myerson [one of Holtzman's opponents in the 1980 Democratic primary]. I was the office manager and the assistant press person for Holtzman during the 1980 Senate race. There was another press assistant in our campaign, this little-known woman named Elena Kagan [now a US Supreme Court Justice]. The *Post* was always a burr in our side. When the *Post* doesn't like you, they don't like you. At the time, I believe it was George Arzt who drove coverage. The political chattering class paid attention to his assessment of a race. And to Page Six.

CHARLIE CARILLO, reporter, columnist, 1978–1993: At one point Elizabeth Holtzman was running against some guy—I think he was in the Queens DA office—and the *Post* hated Elizabeth Holtzman. What they would do is have the campaign headquarters for the other guy call up with some ridiculous accusation and then I'd have to call the Holtzman people and they'd try and cobble something together. I tried to do as decent a job as possible. Once, I gave the story to Dunleavy. He punched it up on his screen and said, "Tut, tut, mate, you're trying to be fair." He rewrote the lede. You have to take the bullet once in a while like that.

NED STEELE, reporter, rewrite, 1977–1980: I went to work for Liz Holtzman when she became the DA of Brooklyn. I really jumped at the chance to get on the inside of the criminal justice system, having covered it on the outside. At one point we brought her into the editorial board at the *Post*. I don't recall if she was up for reelection, or if they were doing something on her first year in office. She sat down with all the editors and ran through her spiel, talking about all the wonderful work she'd been doing. Her presentation was very statistical in its orientation. When she finished, there was a bit of a pause and Steve Dunleavy said, "Miss Holtzman, that's all very good, but statistics are like bikinis: what they reveal is interesting, but what they conceal is crucial." It was a wonderful line and delivered the right way to somebody who was very statistically driven. That kind of got the conversation off to a rough start, but we got past that.

BILL KNAPP: The other thing that the *Post* does—that they're famous for, in my view—is, what's the expression? Dog with a bone? When they decide to go after something, they go after it. When Liz was comptroller and ran for re-election [in 1993], and she had this—quote—scandal over a loan she took out during the Senate race the year before, they pounded that and pounded it and pounded it. [Holtzman took a campaign loan from a bank connected to a company seeking city bond business; she denied a conflict of interest but apologized for poor judgment.] The attack was unfair, and in my mind total bull, but the *Post* clearly had an influence. Frankly, I think it influenced the *New York Times* editorial board, it influenced television coverage, and it put us on the defensive. When the *Post* decides to do something, their front page can drive a lot. That's the number one thing about the *Post* over the years—their ability to use that front cover is just unparalleled.

> After Ed Koch's reelection to City Hall in 1981, Murdoch and the *Post* decided to play kingmaker again by putting its muscle behind him for a 1982 gubernatorial run.

GEORGE ARZT: I get a call from Roger Wood to meet him for lunch at Nicola Paone, a restaurant on 34th Street. I had written stories about rumors that Koch was thinking of running for governor. Roger said, "We're going to have a contest." I said, "Oh?" "Yes, it's gonna be a write-in contest. It will ask, 'Do you want Ed Koch to run for governor?' Then it's going to have a tear-out that will say 'yes.'" I said, "Is there a 'no'?" "No." He held out the best part—that it was only for Koch—until we had already left the restaurant.

DAVID SEIFMAN: It was like a communist vote. "Should Koch run?" "Yes."

> The ersatz straw poll drew heat from the *Village Voice*, which despite being owned by Murdoch rarely missed a chance to tweak the *Post*. In fact, the *Voice* published its own coupons, exhorting readers to mail them in to "Impeach Governor Koch." Then the real fun started.

CHARLIE CARILLO: In the early '80s, the *Post* had a very strange campaign: let's draft Ed Koch for governor. There were coupons in the paper you'd fill out and mail them in. Richard Johnson and I wrote the story, and a guy named Joe Conason at the *Village Voice* made fun of it. He said the story was brought to you by "Wingo specialist Charles Carillo and the unreliable Richard Johnson." [Wingo was a circulation-building game in the *Post*.] Johnson went to the *Voice* that day and went up to Conason. Conason said, "What is it?" Richard said, "Well, I'm here," and Conason says, "I'm not going to throw the first punch." Richard said, "Then I will." He decked him. He came back to the office and said, "Charlie, I avenged our honor." I said, "Are you crazy?" Dunleavy was so proud of him. Then he said to me, "Mate, now you must go and take a pop at Joe Conason." I said, "Steve, I *am* a Wingo specialist."

JOE CONASON, former reporter, *The Village Voice*: Richard called me up and started cursing me out. I basically said, "Fuck you, too." He was like, "I'm gonna kick your ass, blah, blah blah." The next thing I know, I get a call from the front desk at the *Voice* saying that Richard Johnson is here. I thought, "Oh, fuck." Richard was about twice as big as me. I go out to the front desk. I said, "Come back to my office, let's talk about this. Because I'm not gonna fight you." We're walking back. The next thing I know, he slugs me from behind, punches me like in the right ear. I turned and *then* I was ready to fight. But two other people grabbed us, they held us for a second, and then Richard broke free and ran out of the building. Next thing I know, he's gotten the hero's welcome at the *Post*, because he told them that he coldcocked me; he had knocked me out. His punch wasn't really that impressive, to be honest. Although I'm sure he could have kicked my ass. Time goes on, eventually the hatchet was buried. I would run into him around town, and he was always friendly. I remember calling him up once or twice and asking him to do something for me on Page Six, and he always did. We developed this weird, friendly relationship.

RICHARD JOHNSON, Page Six editor, 1978–1990, 1993–2019: We were facing each other. I took the first swing. That's not a sucker punch. A sucker punch is when the guy isn't expecting it and doesn't see it coming. If it was a sucker punch, I would have landed a better shot. When I got back to the office, Roger Wood calls me into the office. I was worried that I'd done something wrong. Then Roger called Marty Singerman, who was then the publisher of [the *Voice*]. Roger Wood was obviously having a very good time, needling Marty. He was like, "My guy just hit your guy, and I'm happy about it." But I became friends with Joe Conason.

DAVID SCHNEIDERMAN, former editor in chief, publisher, CEO, *The Village Voice*: We had been attacking the *Post*, mostly Murdoch and a little bit of Richard Johnson, almost every week, I think partly because Rupert owned the [*Voice*] at the time, so part of the fun was: what can we do? From my point of view as the editor, I was fine with it, but every time I came into work on Wednesday—we published Wednesday—I thought, this could be my last day. Who knows at what point Rupert is gonna get fed up? That's when [former *Village Voice* VP] Jack Berkowitz made that great comment, that we're Poland and Rupert is Russia. The only question is, when will he invade?

JOE CONASON: It was like kids running around with testosterone, and craziness, egged on by assholes like Steve Dunleavy, God rest his drunken soul, Roger Wood, Rupert himself—you know what those guys were like—they were all drunken, screwed up, super macho. If they could pick on the faggots at the *Village Voice*— as I'm sure they thought we all were, you'll excuse the expression—they would.

> As suspect as the *Post*'s efforts in support of Koch were, they seemed to convince one crucial person that the mayor had a shot at becoming governor.

MAUREEN CONNELLY: There was a meeting at Gracie Mansion in, I believe, December 1981. Allen Schwartz [New York City corporation counsel] and a number of people were there to talk about Koch's second term. He comes in and he's late—and Ed was never late. He says, "Sorry, I just finished my interview with *Playboy* magazine." I say, "Excuse me?" He says, "Don't worry, little lady, I didn't say anything controversial." I said, "You had how many hours of interview with *Playboy* magazine? And you didn't say anything controversial?" "Absolutely not." For some reason, Allen Schwartz is predicting that the city is going to have another financial crisis, and [Koch] should run for governor. He was really pushing this. I said, "Why would you do this? You were just [reelected] mayor and you're going to turn around and run for governor?" Then Ed took this trip to Europe, and while he was away the *Post* decided to have this campaign to urge him to run for governor. It was enticing, I guess, and the numbers looked great. But I said, "Why? You'd be miserable. What happens if you win? You'd have to be in Albany. You don't like Albany. You don't like to go north of the Bronx."

CLYDE HABERMAN: I was covering City Hall [for the *New York Times*]. This was 1982. Murdoch decided he was going to push Koch for governor. He had a big front-page headline, RUN ED RUN. Murdoch later did the same thing with Bloomberg—RUN MIKE RUN—to give Bloomberg his third term. Koch was coming back from wherever he was on vacation, and all of us who covered City Hall ran out to the airport to meet him to see what he was going to do. There was a mini press conference, and, being a wiseass, I said, "Mr. Mayor, you told us that when you were running for mayor, and you went to Israel and the Western Wall, that you put a prayer in the cracks asking God that if he would only allow you to become mayor you would never seek higher office." It was the only time Koch got really angry at me. He blew up. He jabbed his finger at me and said, "That was between me and God, not between me and you." I said, "But you told us."

GEORGE ARZT: I meet Koch at the airport along with all the other reporters who want to ask the same question. At the airport, he takes me aside and says, "How long is this charade gonna go on? I'm not gonna run." I said, "I don't know." He said, "Okay." He gave a nonanswer to reporters. Then a while later, Koch calls me in and says, "I'm gonna run." I said, "What happened to this equivocation at the beginning?" He said, "I thought about it. I'm gonna run."

MAUREEN CONNELLY: After [Koch] announced, he said to me "to stay behind." When he would use an infinitive like that—say, if my phone rang at City Hall and he said "to come into my office now," not "please come in," but "*to* come in"—that was an alarm bell. That was always a sign that someone was being fired. So I stay behind, and he says, "I got an advance copy of *Playboy*." He starts to read. It was so bad, both of us were hysterical laughing. He's talking about how hokey [upstate New York] was, the suburbs are sterile, and more like that. We are in hysterics because [we knew then] his campaign is over. I was relieved because he would have been miserable in Albany.

CLYDE HABERMAN: It all came unglued after he gave an interview to *Playboy* in which he dumped on upstate New York and talked about small-town living in their Sears, Roebuck dresses and that kind of killed him. But if Murdoch had not been beating the drum, would he have run? I don't know.

Regardless of his comments in *Playboy*, Koch had said he was running, and he did. The *Post* sponsored the first of the debates with his competitor in the Democratic primary, his former adversary for mayor, Mario Cuomo.

CHARLES LACHMAN: I didn't cover politics, but I did cover the first of the big debates between Ed Koch and Mario Cuomo. I was there to do a color story. It was really a crystallization, to me, of the power of Rupert Murdoch. The debate was at, I think it was the Sheraton on Seventh Avenue—he had the whole ballroom, and it was packed with hundreds and hundreds of people at tables, and all these power brokers. It was like covering a boxing event. In fact, that's how Dunleavy told me to write it. I asked Cuomo what he had for breakfast, as he made his way through the crowd.

ERIC FETTMANN: When we sponsored debates or had forums, we would publish stories about them the afternoon they happened—this is when we still had afternoon editions. We would hire a court reporter to produce a transcript. My job was to go through the transcript, compare it to the tapes, and write the stories. With the debate between Koch and Cuomo that the *Post* sponsored, we were running a long transcript, and this is one where Cuomo won hands down. I've got the transcript, we're upstairs in the composing room going over it, and Dunleavy is not happy. Because I was for Cuomo then, in addition to editing it pretty much the way it was, I made sure Cuomo's good lines got in. Dunleavy is upset by the fact that this thing reads really well for Cuomo. It was one of the few times I saw him in his cups on edition. He's saying, "Mate, is there any way you can, you know, get in hills and valleys—hills and valleys!" I said, "Look at the transcript. This is what happened." Steve knew better than to tell me to change it. He asked me, he begged me, but he never ordered me. I always talk about that because in 2016, at the editorial page, columns were killed and edited to take out anti-Trump stuff. It never used to be like that.

Mario Cuomo did not hold back when he did not like a story.

GEORGE ARZT: One day during the Koch-Cuomo campaign, I'm in City Hall. I ask somebody what's on the calendar that day with the Board of Estimate and I'm told that Charlie Raffa is. He's Mario Cuomo's father-in-law and he's trying to get back a piece of property that he lost for nonpayment of taxes. I write a straightforward story. The day it appears, I get a call in Room Nine from Mario Cuomo—how could I write a story about a poor Italian immigrant, why didn't I write about this person, or that person? He went on this rant. But the first thing he said was, "The sewer runs to your desk." I had never heard that phrase before or since. Because I had this weird disease, which later became known as Epstein-Barr, I taped my interviews. Because of my ailment, his was on tape. I was shaken. I played it for the other reporters in Room Nine, who were astounded that Mario would have said that to me. Andy Logan, of the *New Yorker* magazine, went up to Mario Cuomo at some function, and said, "You have no right to do that with a well-respected reporter." He did not apologize. He started bumbling and saying, "Well, I was upset, it was in the heat of the campaign," and that kind of thing. I never forgot her for doing that. By the way, Andrew Cuomo, a very young Andrew Cuomo, saw me later at an event and said, "My father was just upset that day and he said those things. He didn't mean it." I never forgot that, either.

> To enhance the *Post*'s coverage of state politics, the editors replaced Arthur Greenspan, the paper's Albany bureau chief, with a reporter known for a more aggressive style.

FRED DICKER, Albany bureau chief, 1982–2016: I was the Albany *Times-Union*'s state government reporter. I had come up with some very important stories, and one day at a Governor Hugh Carey press conference, Barbara Ross, who was there maybe filling in for Arthur Greenspan, took me aside and said that the *Post* was looking for someone in Albany, and would I be interested? I grew up in the Bronx. While the *Post* had an obviously controversial reputation back then, it wasn't one that offended me. I thought that working for a New York City paper would be just great, especially on the beat that I was on already. Over the course of four or five months, I had the sense that they were jerking me around. I was interviewed by Steve Dunleavy and Ken Chandler. I was interviewed by Peter Faris. I was interviewed by Bruce Rothwell, who was the editorial page editor. I liked them all. I kept calling up asking, "Are you going to hire me or not?" The pièce de résistance was the final interview with Dunleavy. I think it was right before the November 1982 gubernatorial election. It's the fourth or fifth time I'm down there. It was a little chilly, and I was wearing this long, three-quarter-length leather coat. It was a dress jacket, very smart, European kind of looking. I used to wear shades a lot. I see Dunleavy at the city desk. He goes, "You're like a storm trooper." He escorts me into a closed office, and he says, "Listen, mate, I've told people that you are Hunter Thompson. A guy here, Phil Messing, is going to come in and interview you in about five minutes. He thinks you're Hunter Thompson." I remember thinking, "Only at the *New York Post* do I have to pull off a goddamn scam to get hired." I opened the desk drawer, and there are packets of Sweet'N Low there. I quickly opened them up, and lay them out on the desk like lines of coke. I still have my shades on. This young police reporter comes in. He sits down, and he does a fifteen-minute interview with me as Hunter Thompson. I offer him lines of coke. He says he doesn't want them. He goes out. Five minutes later, Dunleavy and Ken Chandler come in, laughing their heads off, saying, "You got away with it!" I said, "Am I hired?" Dunleavy says, "Yeah, yeah. We're going to hire you." I always felt terrible because I don't think Phil Messing ever forgave me. I had to do it to get the job, but I didn't do it willingly.

PHILIP MESSING, reporter, 1978–1991, 1994–2016: They thought I was like the dumbest guy in history. They thought it was hilarious. I only saw [Thompson] on his book jacket. I knew later that he was much taller than Dicker, but he does bear some resemblance to him. He offered me sugar on a plate as cocaine; I said, "No, no, I don't do that." Nah, that's not really true [that he never forgave Dicker]. He was in a bind because it was his interview process.

FRED DICKER: At [the Albany *Times-Union*], I had written many critical stories about Mario Cuomo, which the *Post* liked. So Mario associated me with his two opponents, Koch and [GOP candidate Lewis] Lehrman. He was making his first visit to the *Post* after having been elected. I had just come to the *Post*. I'm down at 210 South Street, and they have a contingent to meet him— Rupert Murdoch, Roger Wood, Dunleavy, and Ken Chandler. They invited me, of course. The elevator doors open, and there's Mario Cuomo. He comes out, he shakes Rupert's hand, a few others, and then he points at me while looking at Rupert and the others and says, "So is he my punishment?"

14 | THE PAGE

Staff Shuffle, Bodacious Ta-Tas, Paul Newman's Dressing-down

Murdoch's instincts in having Jim Brady create a new kind of gossip column had been spot-on. Items on politicians and corporate tycoons, along with celebrities and socialites in conflict, in love, in a talkative mood, and in flagrante delicto made Page Six one of the tabloid's most-read features.

KELVIN MACKENZIE, night managing editor, 1978–1979: Page Six has been a great brand, hasn't it, for the *New York Post*? I think if Rupert had his way, Page Six, that aspect of it being both popular and deep at the same time, that would have been the perfect *New York Post*.

GRAYDON CARTER, former editor, *Vanity Fair*; founder and co-editor, Air Mail: The *New York Times* told you about the world, and the *New York Post* and Page Six, especially in those days, told you about your world. I first came to the city in 1978, and Page Six was very valuable to me as I tried to figure out and put together the jigsaw puzzle of New York.

> As the column's power grew, and Claudia Cohen's power grew with it, she was not afraid to flex some muscle.

BOBBY ZAREM, publicist: Claudia Cohen barred me from the Page because I wouldn't pass a note to Kirk Douglas, with whom I was having lunch at the Russian Tea Room. I didn't know that they'd had a prior relationship. I was having lunch with him and a few other people. Claudia sent me a note to give to Kirk. I put it under the plate. Then she sent me another one saying that unless I gave it to him immediately, I was going to be barred from Page Six. I ripped them both up for her to see. I was barred from Page Six. Her column went to shit because she barred the single most resourceful person with information that there was.

CLAUDIA COHEN, Page Six editor, 1977–1980: Bobby refused to give him the note. But I don't remember banning Bobby as a result. I don't remember ever banning Bobby. At that time, it would have been impossible to ban Bobby from Page Six. I saw Bobby almost every night of my life at Elaine's.

PETER HONERKAMP, Page Six reporter, 1979–1980: An editor on the desk that night came in at like ten o'clock and told me, "I'm sick of reading about *Cruising* [a controversial Al Pacino movie about an undercover cop in the gay S&M world]. I'm killing this [story on Page Six]." He said, "You're a reporter. I'm your fucking boss. Write something." This was before cell phones. I didn't know how to get ahold of Claudia. I knew a couple of cop flacks, and I called up one PR guy, got him in bed with his wife. I said, "Just give me anything." I'm petrified. He goes, "I don't know, Peter. I don't have anything." Then he said, "I was on a bumpy flight today with Muhammad Ali." I said, "Well, what is that?" He goes, "I don't know. Call Muhammad Ali up and ask him if he was scared." I said, "How the fuck do I get Muhammad Ali?" He said, "He stays at the Waldorf." I called the Waldorf and said, "Could I have Muhammad Ali?" Who picks up the fucking phone? Muhammad Ali. I go, "Look, I'm twenty-five-years old, I'm in a lot of trouble. I know you're the most famous man in the world. I beg you to talk to me about anything for five minutes." He was eating chicken. He goes, "Okay, you got me for as much time as you want." I remember him telling me he would only give me an interview if I promised to send him a picture of myself, which I did. He gave me this great thing about how he was going to come back [out of retirement] and fight [Larry] Holmes, which he hadn't announced at the time. He said, what was he going to do—go fishing with Howard Cosell? He told me he was going to save the world. The heading of the story went, "Ali has a plan to save the world."

The column's focus on the rich, powerful, and famous created the perception that no one was exempt from the tabloid's scrutiny—not even the family members of a *Post* employee.

ADAM SCULL, photographer, 1978–1981, 1985–1988: My parents [art collectors and taxi fleet millionaires Ethel and Robert Scull] were going through this major, major, very public divorce that was covered by Page Six, and Roger Wood would call me into his office when I came in from an assignment. He would point to the column and say, "Dear boy, look at this with your parents." I'd say, "Roger, it's my parents' divorce. I work for you and the *Post*. Let me just be and do my job." They didn't give a flying fuck about me and what I thought.

PETER HONERKAMP: Claudia knew I'd gotten disillusioned with the Page. I didn't like writing about people's personal lives. One day I was asked to write a story about Bess Myerson, who was running for the Democratic nomination for senator. The story was supposed to be about how she was carrying on her Senate campaign even though her parents were very ill in a nursing home. It was going to be a fluff piece that complimented her, actually. But I called her up, and she said, "My father is still mentally together, but if he reads this story that his illness and my mother's are in any way impeding my campaign, it will break his heart. Please don't write it." I said, "I'm not writing this story." Claudia was pissed off. In front of the features room, she yelled at me. She said, "Woodward and Bernstein would have written this story." I said, "No, they wouldn't have." I said, "If it's so important, you write it." That was it. I was out of there. She never wrote the story.

SUSAN MULCAHY, Page Six editor, 1978–1985: After two years as Claudia's lackey, I lost it one day. We had a huge fight and were barely speaking. Peter Honerkamp had quit. Cyndi Stivers came in from the city desk but didn't stay long. Claudia left for the *News*. I was the last one standing.

> Cohen bolted to the *Daily News* when it started an afternoon edition in 1980, giving up her powerful pulpit for a similar column to be called I, Claudia, a riff on a popular 1976 BBC series, *I, Claudius*, that aired on PBS.

CLAUDIA COHEN: I put the page to bed that night, picked up my Rolodex, and headed straight for Elaine's. I sat down to dinner with my Rolodex—my most prized possession—right next to me.

STEPHEN SILVERMAN, entertainment writer, 1977–1988: Jerry Tallmer [arts critic and editor] became my friend and teacher, but at first he didn't speak to me. Until one day, we were standing at the elevator, waiting, and he looked at me and smiled and said, "Yes, I heard." The news was: Claudia was leaving to go to the *Daily News*.

YVONNE DUNLEAVY, author (*The Happy Hooker*), first wife of Steve Dunleavy: Claudia Cohen was my housemate at my Sagaponack property one summer. I remember her saying, this was when she was on Page Six, I really wish I was doing something more substantial, something more meaningful. When Claudia left the paper, Murdoch ordered her banned from the premises immediately.

NED STEELE, reporter, rewrite, 1977–1980: Roger Wood called me at home and said, "We want you to do Page Six." That was the evening of the day when I shook hands on the deal to go to the *Daily News*. I had been planning to come in the next morning and hand in my resignation. I said, "Roger, I thank you for the opportunity. But I've decided to move to the *Daily News*." Silence on the other end, then, "Goodbye, Ned." I didn't regret not taking the [Page Six] job. I enjoyed doing it as a vacation fill-in, but it was not my goal in life to do that long-term.

> James Brady, who had created Page Six, agreed to run the column for a few months until the *Post* could figure out a long-term plan. He ended up staying for more than two years, with Susan Mulcahy as his deputy. Brady's editorship of the column marked the only time Page Six regularly broke from its detached point of view. Brady often wrote in the first-person singular, and virtually every column carried an item at the bottom of the page called "Brady's Bunch," his take on the news or on some boldfaced name. As with everything that he wrote, it was composed with a two-fingered peck on a typewriter.

JAMES BRADY, creator of Page Six, 1977; Page Six editor, 1980–1982: I went to Roger Wood at the Democratic convention [in 1980]. I said, "Roger, you've got a real problem here." I said, "I will take over Page Six if you want me to and I'll find the people to run it for you because I don't want it to die." He said, "If you do that, old boy, that would be great."

SUSAN MULCAHY: They were so thrilled when Jim agreed to come back that Miss Gerry painted one corner of our office—a huge filthy windowless room we shared with some of the entertainment and features writers—but just that one corner where Brady sat. Everything else stayed filthy.

BOB MERRILL, Page Six assistant, 1981–1982: Brady would look at all his notes. Then he would put his head back and close his eyes for a minute. He had this old typewriter. He probably had it in the Korean War. And then, *bang*, he would type it out, and he would hand me the page, which I had to then put into the computer. He'd maybe make one little typo, but his copy was clean and concise, and it was an item. It was a perfect item, a one-take-Charlie kind of thing.

SUSAN MULCAHY: On Fridays, Jim would wait until I was going to the ladies' room or something, and then he'd say, "We're in reasonably good shape, I think I'll head out to East Hampton." Then I'd come back and someone would say, "Susan, we told him not to leave, and he left!" I would quickly call the people at the newsstand [in the *Post*'s lobby] and tell them to cut him off at the pass while I ran down and made him come back upstairs.

BOB MERRILL: Brady would say, "Bobster, I'll be in chapel from five to six." Or at lunchtime he'd say, "I'm going up to the chapel. I'll be back at two." I remember saying, "Man, this guy, he must be a really devout Catholic." Then, of course, I met him at "the chapel" once. It was a bar called St. John's, on 49th Street and First Avenue, near his house, where he used to hang out with his cronies.

SUSAN MULCAHY: Jim got along well with almost everyone, but Joe Rab [Rabinovich] drove him crazy. Joe was the last pair of eyes on Page Six, a final edit. He might have questions on items, so we had to tell him where we would be after we left the office. When you work at Page Six, you are out every night. Jim was often at Elaine's, but he made sure Tommy the bartender, who answered the phone, knew to say he wasn't there.

DIANA MAYCHICK, entertainment writer, 1978–1989: The first day I got there [as Page Six assistant], Jim said, "Welcome aboard. You're the only brunette I've ever hired." I know he was kidding, but I thought, "Geez. I'm not going to go far." I really liked him. He was so debonair compared to the other men.

Page Six played a major role in the *Post*'s political coverage. The editors and reporters who worked on the column found that political consultants like Roger Ailes, who later created and ran Fox News, and Bob Squier, a prominent Democrat whose clients included Bill Clinton and Al Gore, made just as good, if not better, copy than the pols they worked for.

BILL KNAPP, political consultant: Page Six covered the [political consulting] business the way it had never been covered before. Like the *Hollywood Reporter* covers Hollywood. They covered politics like a blood sport and a personality sport. A person's name was always in bold letters, right? That drove the celebrity of consultants and the celebrity of politics for sure.

GEORGE ARZT, City Hall bureau chief, 1968–1986: Murdoch said, "I want political news on Page Six." When we were at conventions, Jim Brady would always come in with booze for us. Bottles of booze and stick it on the table. I thought that was brilliant. And we fed him stories!

SUSAN MULCAHY: It was daunting when I realized how much influence Page Six had with politicians and their advisers. These people are running the city, or the state, or the country, and they care about some little item? Oh, yeah.

JAMES BRADY: Rupert was a great source. And, unlike most press lords, Rupert can really write a story and scale a picture and write a headline. Rupert would delight in it—he'd say, "I have a great one. A great one!" And he'd give it to you. "Call so-and-so and just check this out." He'd pass the stuff right on.

After Brady left the *Post* in early 1983, Mulcahy took over Page Six. A few months later, Richard Johnson moved from the city desk to become the reporter on the column.

SUSAN MULCAHY: No one told me I was on probation, but I know some of the executives were wary of me running the column. I was twenty-six years old. Whenever Bruce Rothwell [editorial page editor] wanted to tell me something, he'd march into our office and say, "Little girl, come here."

HAL DAVIS, reporter, New York State Supreme Court, 1978–1993: My dealings with Page Six were heavenly. Page Six would publish stories I could not get into the rest of the paper. Because Page Six was such a prominent permanent display part of the paper, I sometimes would favor Page Six more than shoving a story into the randomness of Metro. As I recall, every contributor to Page Six got paid a pittance [twenty-five dollars per item]. It was added to my paycheck. It was nice. From what I could tell, the two most litigious industries in New York were showbiz and the rag trade. So a lot of really fine stories were perfect for Page Six, and I would file them and they'd use them. Then there was a decision not to pay anymore, and I understand that Page Six lost a bit of volume in staff submissions. But if I had a great story, I wasn't going to sit on it, so I kept filing.

SUSAN MULCAHY: Hal really understood what worked on Page Six. He took notes on his hands and arms so when he was giving you a story, he'd be checking his wrists to make sure he got all the details.

HAL DAVIS: I would occasionally take notes on the back of my hand—page numbers, case numbers, phone numbers. I had a notebook, but occasionally a notebook wasn't reachable, and so the hand became a very useful place to put down a couple of notes.

MARSHA KRANES, rewrite, editor, 1974–2005: Hal is the only reporter I know who lived up to the "ink-stained" title.

MAURA MOYNIHAN, Page Six assistant, 1981–1983: [Another thing] I always loved about Page Six were the anonymous tipsters. They were wild and you never quite knew what to believe. And there was this one guy who used to call up and say, *"Who was the man that Betsy Bloomingdale was with on the night her husband died?"* I'd say, "I don't know." "I am that man. *I am that man."* He'd go on and on about Betsy Bloomingdale, then he'd hang up.

RICHARD JOHNSON, Page Six editor, 1978–1990, 1993–2019: We had a mole at the *Wall Street Journal* who sent us a list of all the salaries of the executives over there, which caused a huge uproar. There's nothing more subversive you can do to an organization than reveal what they're getting paid. It was funny because our source at the *Journal* actually would call up and introduce himself as Mr. Mole: "Hello, this is Mr. Mole."

NORMAN PEARLSTINE, former executive editor, *The Wall Street Journal*: I thought Page Six was more careful than many publications I read. I thought it had a lot of credibility. I tended to believe what I read on Page Six. While it did deal in anonymous sources to a high degree, that only works if it's accurate. Because otherwise, you get burned enough and just stop reading it or don't care. But Page Six, to the degree that I knew any of the stories, I thought was accurate, I thought it worked hard to be accurate.

SUSAN MULCAHY: Someone who'd given us stuff before called and said that JFK Jr. had rented *Bodacious Ta-Tas*—which is a film that I'm not familiar with—from this Upper East Side video store and hadn't returned it. He'd apparently taken it out with *Broadway Danny Rose*. We ran the item, and Kennedy called us the next day. He was a nice guy. He was very young, very young, when I was the editor of Page Six, but his mother had trained him in dealing with the press. He was not rude. He was cooperative to a point. He said that he had not rented *Bodacious Ta-Tas*, but that he had rented the Woody Allen movie, and he said that he had rented it with his AmEx card, so why would he be stupid enough to rent something called *Bodacious Ta-Tas* with his AmEx card? But I think that's actually how we knew. Anyway, we ran his denial. So, we got two items out of that.

STEVEN GAINES, author and friend of Page Six: I spent years in therapy talking to my psychiatrist about my compulsion to call Page Six. My psychiatrist interpreted this to mean that I felt unimportant and that by giving items to Page Six and seeing them appear instantly the next day I felt important. Except that nobody else knew. I couldn't tell anybody that I was doing this. It had to kind of be my thing.

SUSAN MULCAHY: Murdoch never called me with items himself, and, in fact, barely knew my name. His cronies—and by this I mostly mean people on staff—were always telling me he wanted certain things in the column, and though I would always listen to ideas from those guys, I never ran the items without thoroughly checking that they were actual stories, and much of the time they were not and never appeared. Occasionally someone would try and foist an item on me that was all about somebody's political agenda. Most of the time I would just ignore it, but there was this phase where there was too much of it going on. One night, Roger [Wood] killed my lead at, like, six o'clock. Everybody else was gone. I'm trying to come up with another lead story and Howard Squadron [Murdoch's lawyer] calls me. There was a battle between two companies, including the phone company, to get the rights to advertise on those small phone booths. Howard represented the company that was not the phone company. But he called me up with this item that was so biased and so ridiculous, and I just thought, I give up. I'll run his item. I called the phone company PR guy in the office, even though I knew he wouldn't be there. This was the one and only time I've ever done anything this lazy, irresponsible, and unethical as far as I'm concerned. The item appears in the paper, totally biased in favor of the company that was not the phone company. The phone company calls the next morning and threatens to pull, like, $2 million worth of ads out of the paper. Well, I'm not there, because I'm at a funeral. I come back and Richard [Johnson, then a reporter on Page Six] goes, "You're *so* lucky you weren't here yesterday. Murdoch came down with steam coming out of his ears looking for the, quote, 'Page Six girl.'" Richard said, "If you had been here, you would have been totally fired." It was one of my biggest errors, and for years afterward, whenever I'd see Howard Squadron lionized in the press in New York, I'd think, he's not so fucking great.

> Publicists pitched stories about their clients to reporters in all departments of the *Post*, but the Page Six staff had a special fondness for the hardy survivors of the golden age of flackery, who'd been slipping columnists items since the days of Walter Winchell and Dorothy Kilgallen.

CHARLIE CARILLO, reporter, columnist, 1978–1993: Sy Presten was always calling with tickets to *Oh! Calcutta*. Twenty years after the last person saw *Oh! Calcutta*, he had tickets.

MAURA MOYNIHAN: I became an invaluable member of the staff because I *loved* talking to flacks. I could do it all day long. I had a really deep, intimate relationship with Sy Presten the whole time I was at Page Six. He had three clients: *Penthouse* magazine, Chock full o'Nuts, and Morgan Fairchild. He'd go: "Morgan Fairchild walked into Chock full o'Nuts with a copy of *Penthouse* under her arm."

SY PRESTEN, legendary press agent: She got two out of three. I represented *Penthouse* and I represented Chock full o'Nuts, but I never represented Morgan Fairchild. William Black, who founded Chock full o'Nuts, was a conservative guy, so I would *never* have linked *Penthouse* with his company. Are you kidding? I would have lost the account.

SUSAN MULCAHY: I was at a party and Christopher Reeve was [there]. It was a dinner, and I was seated next to him. He said, "Let me ask you a question. What is this in these columns where somebody will say, 'Christopher Reeve said to Moses over dinner at—fill in the name of the restaurant—that he's going to be starring in—[fill in the name of the movie]?'" He said, "It's some restaurant I've never been in." I said, "That is the restaurant plant." I explained to him about how a press agent had a little nugget of information that that press agent wanted to pass on to the columnist but he needed to get a client in there. So they slipped in the restaurant name. Those were the only stories I would run that I knew had a large error factor in them, because you knew that no one had ever been inside that restaurant.

> Real-estate-developer-on-the-rise Donald Trump liked seeing his boldfaced name in the column, although his penchant for prevarication reduced his appearances for a time.

SUSAN MULCAHY: Trump lied so regularly I became wary of items involving him. A source phoned once and said Trump had had a long meeting with Richard Nixon at Trump's office. Okay, that seemed item-worthy. I called to check. Trump said the meeting didn't take place. Nixon's office confirmed that it had happened. Given Trump's track record, I believed Nixon.

JAMES BRADY: Donald and Ivana Trump had rented [in East Hampton] one summer, and they had wangled a temporary membership at the Maidstone Club, which I don't think was too difficult to do. One of my friends who is a trustee said, "The Trumps really liked the club. They liked it so much that they're going to put in for a permanent membership, but the word has been discreetly passed: 'Don't embarrass yourselves or us by doing that, because you'll be blackballed.'" Of course, I put that right into Page Six the next day. The phone rang and it was Donald Trump. He was cursing me with every four-letter word. "You SOB. You bleeping this. You bleeping that. I'm going to sue you. I'm going to sue the *Post*. I'm going to sue Murdoch. I'm going to sue everyone." I'm holding the phone out here, and I said, "Oh yes, Donald, oh yes." I had no sooner hung up on this one-way conversation when the phone rang again and it was Roy Cohn. Roy said, "Now, Jim, I'm Donald's lawyer." I said, "Wait a minute, I don't mind fighting with Donald Trump. He's a civilian, I'm a civilian. You're a lawyer. I'm not going to get into a discussion with a lawyer. You better call

Howard Squadron," who was Murdoch's lawyer. I always remember what Cohn said: "Jim, Jim, Jim. There's going to be no lawsuit. It's very good for Donald to let off steam. That's just Donald. We encourage that kind of thing, but no one's going to sue anybody. I'm just telling you that there will be no lawsuit." And there was no lawsuit.

SUSAN MULCAHY: In 1983, a source told me Trump was going to get involved in or might even buy Lincoln West, the largest piece of undeveloped property in Manhattan, about fifteen blocks on the West Side. Trump denied it, emphatically. I hesitated. My source kept saying, "What the hell? When are you going to run the story?" Eventually I ran it, but small. My source was annoyed that I had not made it a lead. It turned out to be true, of course, as did everything Trump denied. A year or so later, Richard Johnson, who was then the reporter on Page Six, was planning to go up to Trump Tower to talk to Trump about his latest scheme—he'd offered to negotiate an arms deal with the Soviets—and I ended up going with him. I asked Trump about Lincoln West. He said nothing was happening but he'd keep me posted. The next day there's a story on the front page—the front page!—of the *Times*, "Trump Set to Buy Lincoln West Site." Roger Wood knew we had talked to Trump the day before and he was pissed: how had we missed this? Trump had some lame excuse, like, he had made a deal with the *Times*. So don't do an interview with the *Post* the day before! I killed the arms negotiating story. Trump wanted NBC to move to the Lincoln West site, but he needed tax abatements. He got into a major pissing match with Koch over it.

GEORGE ARZT: They were hoping to get NBC over there and Alair Townsend, former budget director for Koch, then deputy mayor, said the famous line, "I wouldn't believe Donald Trump if his tongue was notarized." People say it's Koch's line. It's not. It's Alair Townsend's. [The city] gave a big abatement, big benefits, for NBC to stay at Rock Center. Trump went nuts. That was the end of Television City on the West Side. Koch always hated Trump. I think he felt Trump was a greedy, selfish person without any redeeming qualities. To know that Trump was elected president? It probably would have killed him.

There was one celebrity whose name could not appear on Page Six, or on any page in the *Post*. Paul Newman was unofficially banned after he went on the warpath against the tabloid. In 1983 he told *Rolling Stone* magazine that his 1981 movie

Absence of Malice, a drama about an irresponsible journalist, was a "direct attack on the *New York Post*." Instead of retaliating, the paper did its best to ignore Newman's existence.

SUSAN MULCAHY: There was definitely a shitlist at the *Post*. And I'm sure it was broader than even I knew. There were certain people, like Paul Newman, who were not allowed to be mentioned in the paper *at all*. They were not even allowed to mention him in the television listings. If *Hud* was playing, they would write "*Hud*, starring Patricia Neal."

JIM MONES, drama editor, 1980–1987: Things got filtered down to you. How it came down the ladder, I don't really remember, but basically, we were told not to put Paul Newman's name in the paper. We'd say "blue-eyed actor" or something like that in a review. Jerry Tallmer was a stickler and at times no-nonsense. When he saw, I guess, maybe a page proof of a review without Paul Newman's name, I remember him saying, "I'm not going to call this unprofessional, which it is. I'm not going to call it disrespectful, which it is. And I'm not going to call it petty, which it is. But I will call it silly. It's just silly."

15 | KILL THE COMPETITION
The *Post* vs. the *Daily News*

Long before Rupert Murdoch appeared on the scene, all of New York's afternoon papers, except the *Post*, had died off. Ever since, the *Post* had viewed the city's other surviving tabloid, the New York *Daily News*, as its chief rival. The *News* had always had more readers than the *Post*—in early 1980, weekday circulation figures exceeded 1.5 million—but its numbers were slipping, in part because city residents continued to relocate to the suburbs, but also because of interest in the revamped and revitalized *Post*. The *Post*'s average weekday circulation, which had fallen to just over 505,000 during Dolly Schiff's final days, grew to more than 621,000 during Murdoch's first year of ownership, and by 1983 had cracked 961,000. As the '80s began, the *News* and its owners, the Chicago Tribune Company, went to war with the *Post*.

MILTON GOLDSTEIN, copy editor, 1974–current: In 1980, the *Daily News* announced they were starting an afternoon paper and were going to put the *Post* out of business. They started *Daily News Tonight* and hired Clay Felker as editor. If you know Murdoch's history, you know he bought *New York* magazine out from under Felker, and Felker wanted to get back at him. The *News* technically became an all-day paper. Murdoch said, then we're starting a morning paper.

PAT SULLIVAN, reporter, night editor, 1972–1980: The Murdoch influence started to bother me, so I jumped to the *Daily News Tonight* edition. Dunleavy and everything—I had fun with all those guys. But it was time to go. It was getting way too Australian and too tabloidy.

NED STEELE, reporter, rewrite, 1977–1980: Patrick Sullivan and I had become good friends. He moved over [to the *Tonight* edition] and encouraged me to make the move. He said, it's going to be really exciting, it's going to be all the fun of starting a new paper from the ground up.

GEORGE ARZT, City Hall bureau chief, 1968–1986: While we geared up for it, I don't think there was a strong feeling that they were really competition. We were established and had become a twenty-four-hour paper at that point. They were tabloid reporters, but they were old style. Murdoch can out-tabloid them any day of the week.

> Even after poaching several *Post* staffers, the *Tonight* edition, which debuted in September 1980, failed to slay its South Street competitor. During the year that it lasted, however, the *Post* took the challenge seriously, Murdoch included.

PAT SULLIVAN: Clay Felker didn't quite understand what a tabloid was. He wanted it to be much more upscale, because we were going to deal with people in the afternoon, commuting home, or whatever, and it would attract business-people. But he had a lot to learn. I pointed out to him in the first or second meeting that if you're going to have an afternoon paper, you really have to have an overnight shift, which they hadn't planned on. Then guess who got stuck running the overnight shift?

HARVEY ARATON, sportswriter, basketball, 1977–1982: When the *Post* was going from being an afternoon paper to a virtually twenty-four-hour operation, Jerry Lisker took us all out to some Italian place on the Upper East Side and gave us this pep talk. And the pep talk pretty much amounted to this: "We're going to bomb [Felker] in the morning. We're going to bomb him in the afternoon. We're going to beat the living shit out of the *Daily News*." Then he said, "You're going to be writing early stories and running stories and p.m. stories and we're going to kick their ass." That was pretty much the extent of it. When somebody raised a hand and said, "Jerry, are we going to get paid more?," he said, "I'll take care of all of you." Then he left it all to Greg [Gallo] and of course, we didn't get a dime more. One day, I'm stuck in traffic with Phil Mushnick. He's riling me up saying, "Jerry's not giving us any money. We're going to write twice as much for this whole season, and we're not getting a dime [extra]." We walk into the office and Jerry's sitting at his desk and I say to him, "Jerry, are we getting raises or *what?*" I grew up in the projects in Staten Island and this was the projects kid in me coming out. Jerry bolted out of his chair and grabbed me by the shirt and pinned me up against the wall and said, "Don't you ever give me that street bullshit again." He literally pinned me up against the wall, but the guy was kind of lovable in his own way. The next time I came into the office, he probably felt guilty about it. He sees me out of the corner of his eye—he used to call me "Hah-vey" because he had that Providence accent—so he goes, "Hah-vey, that was a great fucking piece today." I go, "Thank you, Jerry." The problem was, I hadn't written anything that day.

CYNTHIA FAGEN, reporter, 1976–1986: We had to be the last people to leave the scene. Never leave before the competition. It was understood that as long as the *Daily News* was there, we would have to be there. That was very smart. Because sometimes their reporter would say, "I got enough" and leave, and then we would score this great interview.

DAVE BANKS, night managing editor, 1979–1981: It was late afternoon, while I was just wrapping up for the day. It would have been [John] Cotter and I finishing. It was when we were going up against the *Daily News* in the afternoon, and Rupert said, "I'm heading to Grand Central. Anyone going that way need a lift?" I said, "I wouldn't mind a lift, boss." We sat rather awkwardly in the back of his limo and we got to Grand Central. He said, "What time's your train?" I said I was only going to White Plains, so I could get any train. He said, "Do you want a drink?" I said, "Oh, yeah, that'd be nice." I was very flattered. We got the escalator up to the top floor to Charlie Brown's [Ale and Chop House, in the Pan Am Building, which was connected to Grand Central]. As we got to the top, he saw a newspaper seller struggling with armfuls of the New York *Daily News* and the *New York Post*, with a huge commuter crowd around him, and he simply couldn't cope. So Rupert snatched up a bundle of *New York Post*s—only the *Post*—and started selling them: "Thirty cents, thirty cents." I said to the guy, "It's okay. He knows what he's doing." The news vendor was very, very nervous. But Rupert eventually finished the pile on his arm, selling them: "Thirty cents, thirty cents." When he'd waved off the last commuter, he poured all these thirty cents into the guy's tin, and the guy thanked him and we continued to Charlie Brown's. The guy was a multimillionaire then—so what was he doing at the top of the staircase, selling his own newspapers? I've never, ever lost that image. But that is Rupert.

The *Tonight* edition's lifespan was brief, but its impact on the *Post* was more permanent. The *Post* kept its all-day schedule for a while, publishing eight editions a day, then gradually eliminated the afternoon editions, turning into a morning paper.

PAT SULLIVAN: [The *Tonight* edition] didn't work out. Part of it was because the regular *Daily News* guys did not like the *Tonight* guys. They were very reluctant to work with us. They wanted to hold whatever they had for the morning edition. You had almost to pull it out of them. And the *Daily News* in those times was an Irish civil service. Those guys had been there a long time and they had no competition.

NED STEELE: It was like two separate animals, side by side, trying to find a way to share the turf.

JIM FARBER, former music critic, New York *Daily News*: There was a period where the [*Post*] was putting out an incredible number of editions per day. You could walk into a subway car, and if there were eight people reading the *New York Post*, every person would have a different front-page headline. It totally individuated the experience, and it made it look like your copy of the *New York Post* had been handcrafted for you. So again, like art, brilliant.

KEN CHANDLER, editor in chief, publisher, 1978–1986, 1993–2002: We abandoned the Wall Street Final [with closing prices] because it was being delivered to newsstands too late, due to rush-hour traffic. Eventually our afternoon editions were also dropped partly because of the growing popularity of ESPN and sports radio, which undercut our appeal with sports readers. Previously, we were the only way to get post-game analysis and West Coast scores, which were too late for the morning papers.

In 1980, the *Post* and the *News* each ran a different controversial picture of a murder victim whose death shocked the world.

MARSHA KRANES, rewrite, editor, 1974–2005: Dunleavy and I were on the desk. I was like the assistant to him. He'd look at a story briefly, pass it on to me, and then I'd look at it. He hadn't changed it, there were things wrong with the story, and I would work on it. Finally, the production desk started screaming, "Where are these stories that we're expecting?" He says, "Marsha has them." Then he looks at me and says, "What are you doing?" I said, "I'm fixing these. There were all these clichés in the ledes, and they don't make sense." He says, "Leave the clichés in. That's how people know what the stories are about." He started screaming at me in front of the whole city room. I said, "I want to talk to you." He calls me into somebody's office and he just starts screaming at me. I said, "Can I just talk?" He kept screaming and screaming and screaming. He walked out first. I walked out after him and I had fists like I wanted to kill him because he didn't let me say a word. He said, "And don't you forget it!" so everybody in the room knew that he won this argument. So, I just socked him, right in the gut. But he tensed up and it was like a brick wall. My hand hurt, and I was on the verge of tears. I went into the ladies room, regained my composure, came out, and said, "I'm going home. I am not working with you anymore. I'm coming in either to quit or to have another assignment, but it's not going to be with you." I started to leave and the phone rang. Somebody handed me the phone, and it was a police reporter or somebody saying John Lennon's been shot. I sat down and I went back to work.

ERIC FETTMANN, associate editorial page editor, columnist, 1976–1991, 1993–2019: ABC was in the middle of *Monday Night Football* when Howard Cosell announced that John Lennon had been shot and was dead. [Photo assignment editor] Vern Shibla, who was watching, immediately called the desk. Back then the only television in the newsroom was an old black-and-white set in the metro editor's office that we didn't monitor. Immediately everybody goes into hyperdrive. Especially since we had maybe ten, fifteen minutes before the first edition locked up. That was a hard lockup because the first edition is the one that had to get to Grand Central and Penn Station on time, because they were sent out of town on the trains. You miss that, you missed the out-of-town distribution. We had to confirm he was dead—we couldn't just go on Cosell's say-so. Dunleavy got on the phone to Carl Pelleck. Pelleck was in "I'm not doing any more work anymore" mode. You really had to push. Dunleavy said, "This is the big one. You've got to come through. We've got to confirm that he's dead. You have like five minutes to find out." Carl worked his sources and came back a minute or so before the lockup and said: "He's dead." We had the front page. We ended up doing a replate afterward, but the first one just said, "John Lennon Shot Here." And a story with a few paragraphs at the bottom of page one. It wasn't long before the place started to explode. I've worked lobster and generally people kind of straggle in and it isn't till about two or three o'clock that everything really gets jumping, but I'd never seen the place so crowded overnight. You knew the story was going to take over the whole paper. I was assigned to write the obit. I did several versions for the various editions.

CYNTHIA FAGEN: I was in the office. One of my cop friends called and said Lennon is dead. He's been shot. And I'm thinking, really, Lenin? Ilyich? It was beyond my grasp that he was talking about John Lennon. He gave me the address, at the Dakota. I'm not sure if other people got the tip as well. But I remember running up to the news desk and telling Bob Young and Steve. They told me to get up there right away. I don't remember who I went up with, what photographer. It was freezing. I was one of the first people there. There was barely a crowd outside but people started to gather, light candles, flowers, et cetera. I stayed through the night, or I should say I froze through the night. Of course, I had to file, go to a phone booth to file. I would do that on the hour throughout the night. At one point I climbed a light pole to get a sense of the masses forming outside of the Dakota, and realizing how cold my hands were. I could barely write. There was a subway station on the corner and people were coming up, presumably going to work. The street was filled at that point, and when they saw me with my pen and pad, they would ask me what was going on. I would tell them that John Lennon had been shot. The reactions were people just breaking down and crying and screaming. They couldn't believe what I had told them. I remember feeling very affected by having to give them this sort of left-field answer. "John Lennon is dead." I couldn't even believe it. Some continued on to what they were supposed to be doing that morning. Others just stopped and stayed. I stayed through the morning, and I got very sick from being out in the cold all night. It was a very New York City story, very emotional. He was this legendary figure who represented the best of the city. He was untouchable. Then he's cut down and people really, I think, took that as something very personal.

CHARLIE CARILLO, reporter, columnist, 1978–1993: When John Lennon was shot dead, the *Daily News* had a picture of Lennon giving an autograph to Mark Chapman a few hours before he killed him. Some guy got the shot, and at the time, they said he was paid fifty grand for it, which is a lot of money in 1980. It's a lot of money now. Not to be outdone, the *Post* ran a picture of John Lennon on a slab in the morgue.

BOB YOUNG, photo editor, 1978–1986: It was taken by a mortuary assistant who sold it to Sygma, the French news agency. I had good contacts there. I think I paid $2,000 for it. Maybe less. We discussed: Should we run it? Should we not? Roger came up with a brilliant idea, of saying, "We run pictures of the pope when he's dead, and this guy is as important as the pope." An aside to that, Yoko Ono thought it was beautiful.

CHARLIE CARILLO: Supposedly Yoko loved it. But Donnie Sutherland and I had to keep track the next day—four hundred people called, outraged about this picture: "How could you do that?" One guy calls and says, "Hi, my name is James Woods. I'm an actor." And I said, "Oh, man, you were wonderful in *The Onion Field*." "Oh, thank you very much. Well, anyway, I'm really upset about that picture."

DONNIE SUTHERLAND, city desk assistant, 1978–1988: Charlie Carillo and I—our ears basically fell off from the complaints about putting that morgue shot in the paper.

> The *Post*'s unceasing efforts to build circulation were not always as morbid. In September 1981, the tabloid introduced Wingo, a game of chance that was a hybrid of bingo and a scratch-off lottery ticket. The paper mailed out 6.1 million game cards—each containing more than two dozen weekly chances to win— and then, every weekday, published four numbers. Oddly, Wingo was inspired by Zingo, a similar game that the *Daily News* had unveiled in the fall of 1980 but lasted less than a year. Murdoch recognized the potential circulation benefits of the game and imported it to his papers overseas before launching Wingo at the *Post*. When the *News* discovered Murdoch's plans, it revived Zingo, although it did not promote the game with the same Fleet Street zeal as its rival.

ERIC FETTMANN: Fairly early on, they discovered that they couldn't get that mass circulation without circulation games. They couldn't get the kind of numbers in the millions, the old *Daily News* kind of numbers, just on the content of the paper alone.

CHARLIE CARILLO: Wingo was a $50,000-a-week giveaway. Everybody in the tri-state area was mailed a Wingo card and urged to keep it. It was a huge advertising campaign for the *Post* and the winners appeared on page three, week after week. There were days circulation of the *Post* went over a million. It backfired on Murdoch in a way, because he'd had contests like this in his other papers, but he'd never had one in New York. Who plays contests? A lot of people who play are minorities. So for the first time under Murdoch, Black people without handcuffs were appearing in the pages of the *Post*, holding up their winning cards and celebrating. It was a kind of a great equalizer. I remember Roger Wood, reeking of that eye-watering cologne, calling me into his office, shaking a loose fist in the air, and proclaiming: "Now, Charles, I want you to go out there and create Wingo fever."

CHARLES LACHMAN, reporter, 1981–1988: Carillo was never really a street reporter. He was an extraordinarily talented writer. So he worked feature stories, and because of his humor, they assigned him to do the Wingo contest, which was hilarious. Only he could pull off making this ridiculous promotion effort kind of fun and amusing. That was one of his great skills, finding the humor in these situations.

CHARLIE CARILLO: I got teased quite a bit, but I could take it. Bob Young, the photo editor, sent all of his photographers out with a supply of Wingo cards and said, "Any time you photograph a celebrity, give them a card and see if they're willing to hold it." Then I'd get the photo and write a caption, publicizing whatever it was they had going, and it worked out well. It was an amazing array—Andy Warhol, almost anybody who had anything to publicize would hold up a Wingo card because it guaranteed publicity.

BOB YOUNG: [Photographer] Arty Pomerantz went to West Point. You know how the cadets throw their hats in the air? He took some friends and they threw Wingo cards in the air. The next day, I got a call from some fucking major general. He screamed at me, said I had committed sacrilege, the integrity of the American army—I really got it in the ear.

CHARLIE CARILLO: There'd be a bakery that said, "We've created the Wingo cookie," or a bar would say, "We have the Wingo stinger." It was guaranteed publicity. Everybody was on to it. We just went along with it. It wasn't journalism, but on the other hand it was part of the game.

ROBERT KALFUS, photographer, 1977–1993, 2002–2015: Bob Young told me that the Dalai Lama was giving a talk about Communist China trying to destroy

Tibetan culture. I said, "This is great. I want to go there. It's important." He said, "You can go to the press conference, but we're not interested in that. I want you to get a picture of the Dalai Lama holding the Wingo card."

CHARLIE CARILLO: The way I recall it, the plan was for me to hand the card to the Dalai Lama—but I just couldn't do it. This failure on my part shames me to this day. So Bob [Kalfus] had to do it, which cost him a precious few seconds to get set with his camera, in which time the card was ripped from the Dalai Lama's hand by one of his Lam-ettes. I recall Bob saying something like, "Your Holiness, this is for you." What a look of puzzlement on the Dalai Lama's face, in the brief time he held the card! And what great words we'd have had if I'd performed my duty and we'd gotten the shot! A Monk in the Money! It's the Dalai Lama with his favorite game of chants! It's the best way Ti-bet without betting—you have nothing to lose, and your bank account will be as enlightened as your soul! We're making the world a Buddha place with $50,000 weekly jackpots, so check those daily numbers, only in the *Post*!

ERIC FETTMANN: Every time we would do one of these circulation games, the circulation would spike. When the game was over, we couldn't hold the circulation.

DICK BELSKY, metropolitan editor, 1970–1989: To be honest, it was more fun than the Dolly Schiff days, and the other thing was: you were a winner. When you were at the Dolly Schiff paper, you were kind of like the third paper in town or whatever. When Murdoch takes over, the paper is at 500,000 copies a day. By the '80s, we sell nearly a million copies a day. It isn't even just the numbers. It's the impact the *New York Post* has on New York. I mean, everybody talked about the *Post*. "Oh my god, did you see that page one?" It's hard for people today to understand one publication having that kind of impact because obviously it's a whole different world.

NED STEELE: After leaving the *Post*, what I did miss and miss to this day was the incredible camaraderie of the city room and the wonderful, awesome people. It was the most fun I ever had on a job. I have had great jobs since then, but nothing that could match that experience or that cast of characters.

ANDY SOLTIS, rewrite, editor, 1967–2014: I have a memo that says, "Important news stories, 1977 to 1986." It basically begins when Murdoch took possession of the paper. It has the wood story, the date, and the approximate additional sales of the paper over its normal circulation. So, the day that we reported that Son of Sam was caught in August of '77, the circulation that day was over a million. That was nearly 400,000 copies more than normal. The death of John Lennon sold about 900,000. Elections were always big. When Reagan was shot, that was a big deal. When Grace Kelly died, that was a big deal. Sales were over a million for that issue and the next-day follow-up.

JIM WILLSE, former editor and publisher, the New York *Daily News*: When I left New York [for California] in 1974, the *New York Post*, as I remembered it, was sort of the NPR of tabloids, this relatively gentle, liberal-leaning, unsurprising piece of New York. When I came back it was like somebody had applied electrodes to the place. It was a completely different newspaper. If you ask a room full of two hundred people, which I did, what is the classic *Daily News* headline, they will almost all say FORD TO CITY: DROP DEAD. If you're asking what was the classic *New York Post* headline, they will almost all say HEADLESS BODY IN TOPLESS BAR. The Ford headline was 1975; Headless Body was 1983. In a way, those two headlines tell the story of what the advent of Murdoch did to the *Post* and to tabloids in the city.

16 | THE LOUDEST VOICE IN THE ROOM

Headlines and the Stories That Inspired Them

Headlines came to define the *Post*—and still do—particularly the front page, or wood, which roared, brawled, and punned its way into the fabric of a city on the rebound. The period in which the *Post* began to dominate newsstands, with eight editions, six days a week, was a golden age for the Murdoch *Post*. Like it or not, the paper demanded attention.

CHARLIE CARILLO, reporter, columnist, 1978–1993: Wayne Darwen was a chain-smoking Australian who looked like he could have been in the band Spinal Tap. He had this shaggy blond hair and a growly voice. To give you an example of what Wayne was like, the Hasidic Jews in, I think it was Williamsburg, were complaining that their roads were not well paved. The New York City Marathon was coming up, and they were going to block the marathon—stand in the street and keep 20,000 runners from going through. We had a picture of a bunch of guys, with the hats and the tallit and the whole shebang. Wayne wrote a headline, "The Dukes of Hasid," which got kicked back. Then he writes, "Yidlock." Which gets kicked back. But I applauded. I said, "Wayne, at least I know how great you are." Another time, I think it was Wayne—though it might have been Roger Franklin—Joseph Bonanno, the famous Joe Bananas, after years of eluding the law, was taken into custody and the headline was "Yes, We have Joe Bananas." Those things made the day worthwhile.

WAYNE DARWEN, assistant managing editor, 1983–1987: Ah fuck! I don't remember that, and it's probably best I don't. Yeah, I was supposed to be good at writing headlines. But all the guys down there were good at that. An old buddy of mine, Dick McWilliams, was probably the best layout and rewrite man around. Vinnie Musetto was great. Drew MacKenzie [brother of Kelvin]. I picked it up from them. It was like a game. We threw them around. "What do you think of this?" It became headline by committee a lot of times.

JOHN WATERS, filmmaker: No matter what its politics were, I always think of [the *Post*] as a paper that I read for the entertainment news and great headlines.

HARRY SHEARER, humorist, actor, co-star of *This Is Spinal Tap*: The art of the tabloid front cover headline was, and still is, mastered by the *Post*. You can't take that away from them.

JAMI BERNARD, chief movie critic, 1978–1993: When I was put on the rim, I didn't know what was expected of me. No one interviewed me or [determined] whether I could do it. They simply dropped me there and gave me a short to do. The story was about how they had to stop construction on a kids' baseball field because of an endangered bird species. My headline was "Bird Keeps Diamond in the Rough."

MILTON GOLDSTEIN, copy editor, 1974–current: Fans started throwing rocks at a Rolling Stones concert in Cincinnati or something. It was a one-paragraph, one-column brief hed. "Real Rock Fans." It's bread-and-butter of what a tabloid hed is. Not every hed is a page-one screamer.

JAMI BERNARD: It's not exactly about making a pun. A pun is good and alliteration is good, but the perfect headline comes out of left field a little bit. I'm not saying "Bird Keeps Diamond in the Rough" is perfect. It's not exactly a pun. It's word play. It also has to break at the right place. The right word has to come over to the next line so that it isn't misread. The pressure was intense, and there was an unspoken competition.

DREW MACKENZIE, day news editor, 1979–1991: If you do a double entendre, it has to work twice. Sometimes it works three times.

PAT SMITH, night city editor, 1977–1989: It's like haiku. You have a very limited amount of space. Our goal was to make a big bold impact on a newsstand in New York City during the rush hour, when everyone's moving fast. People came to rely on that—the *Post* page one.

JOHN WATERS: The best headline ever was tiny, and it was inside. It was when Ike Turner died. The headline was "Ike Beats Tina to Death."

PAT SULLIVAN, reporter, night editor, 1972–1980: I go to cover a fire on Park Avenue in an office building. It's a pretty good fire—a high-rise. The fire commissioner at the time was [Augustus] Beekman. He kept coming over to the press corps and saying, "It's not the towering inferno, it's not the towering inferno." I go back and I put in the second or third graph, "It's not the towering inferno." Guess what the headline was? Roger Wood said something like, "Dear boy, they expect us to do that."

CLYDE HABERMAN, reporter, 1966–1977: An asteroid was heading uncomfortably close to Earth. Then astronomers realized there was no way it was going to come within worrisome distance of New York. The *Post* headline was "Kiss Your Asteroid Goodbye." That made me laugh even though normally I don't like this tendency to go for the cheap, winking play on body parts.

CHARLES LACHMAN, reporter, 1981–1988: BOY GULPS GAS, EXPLODES—that was my story. Dunleavy was upset there was nothing going on. They had no wood. He says, "Mate, help me out. Find something." So looking, looking, looking. AP Wire, AP Wire. And I remember an old editor of mine, Walt Jackson, would tell me that some of the best stories come in the smallest paragraphs. I saw on the AP local wire out of, as I recall, Newark, two lines about a teen who committed suicide. He stuck his—I have to double-check this—stuck his head in the oven, and then he exploded. I said, "Steve, I think I've got something." This one-liner turned into a front-page *New York Post* story with a semi-classic headline. I got a kick out of it being referenced in the *New York Times* obit on Roger Wood.

FRANK DiGIACOMO, Page Six co-editor, 1989–1993: The only time I ever made Hal Davis laugh was when he gave me a story for Page Six about a trial or proceeding being interrupted, and the case had some sort of sexual element. I used "courtus interruptus" in my lede.

WALTER BERNARD, graphic designer and co-founder of WBMG; former art director *New York* and *Time* magazines: The design premise with a tabloid was: don't make it too well designed. You had to have a kind of tackiness and quirkiness to the overall look. If you examine the *Post* after Murdoch bought it, compared to the *Daily News* and the pre-Murdoch *Post*, you'll see how conservative and straight they were in their design. I am sure [Murdoch's design] was based on his experience in Australia and the UK. Tabloids there were sensational and tacky and not as neat in typography or in layout as those in the US. They used insets, they used sexy pictures, they contrasted big headlines with small headlines, changed typefaces on the same page. It's really what a tabloid should be, a bit chaotic throughout.

> Mike Pearl, who covered Criminal Court for the *Post*, loved nothing more than seeing his byline under a spectacular wood. He papered the courthouse press room with them.

DAVID NG, associate managing editor, 1980–1993: [Mike Pearl's] nickname was The King. He owned the courthouse. Everyone looked at Mike with a mix of bewilderment, curiosity, and fright. He was a very quiet guy with this little short crop of gray hair. He could pass for an economics professor somewhere.

MIKE PEARL, reporter, Manhattan Criminal Court, 1967–1998: I was really lucky because the trials that came through the Criminal Court were some of the biggest in the country. I didn't start the Wall of Shame until after Murdoch had taken over the paper and the headlines became really racy. It became the Wall of Shame because of Columbia Journalism [School] students. Every year or two the Columbia instructors would bring students to the press rooms at City Hall and Criminal Court to show them what it was like to be a beat reporter, and the students were sure that the *Daily News* reporter had put up these headlines to shame the *Post* reporter. So they started calling it the Wall of Shame. But I had put them up. You were always looking for a story that was big enough to be on page one. I was getting so many of them. My all-time favorite was from a trial of a guy who killed a violinist and threw her off the roof of the Metropolitan Opera House. SHE WAS NICE TO ME, THEN I KICKED HER OFF THE ROOF. We wanted to do FIDDLER OFF THE ROOF. They thought that was in bad taste.

CHARLIE CARILLO: I think the wall still exists. They should laminate it.

WAYNE DARWEN: If the story didn't fit the headline, we made sure it did. With a little deft rewriting we'd line it up—put in probably what they left out. There was always that. No matter which paper, no matter which genre or media, you've always got that friendly friction between writers and editors, where writers very rarely know what editors do to their work.

MICHAEL SHAIN, television editor, 1978–1993, 1996–2013: They wanted something. Your job was simply to fill in behind it. You made the story. I had never been taught that a reporter makes a story. In my seven or eight years before the *Post*, I'd always thought that the people you talked to were the ones who made the story. But at the *Post* I learned quickly that it was your job to get what the boss wanted.

CHARLIE CARILLO: I remember you'd be told, "We want a story on this, the headline is going to be this." Which is backwards, but it's very much tabloid and it saves time, you know, if you have a destination, instead of this *New York Times* kind of thing—go out there like a wet piece of clay and absorb whatever it is—as opposed to, here's the hero, here's the villain, fill in the blanks.

> Another headline master, Vincent A. Musetto, was the *Post*'s resident beatnik. Musetto wore artsy eyeglasses, Converse sneakers, a shaggy beard, a stringy ponytail fashioned from the remaining fringe on his head, and a protuberant belly. Erratic, confrontational, and sometimes violent, Musetto was a polarizing figure in the city room and beyond.

JIM MONES, drama editor, 1980–1987: Vinnie saw a movie every day, not on TV or something. He actually went to the movies. His headlines were often inspired by films. He liked to test them out by singing them in an operatic voice. He always said the best headlines could be sung. You could hear him singing something like, "Tiny Tot Turns Cannibal"—one of our joke headlines. He's singing headlines while walking along on top of desks.

DAN AQUILANTE, chief music critic, 1980–2012: Vinnie was a volatile person. He was a phone thrower; a garbage-can kicker. One day I had to get him ice in the cafeteria because he broke his toe kicking a metal trash can full throttle.

DONNIE SUTHERLAND, city desk assistant, 1978–1988: He was a drama queen.

DICK BELSKY, metropolitan editor, 1970–1989: He had a trumpet he would blow in the newsroom. He'd throw trash cans at doors. You'd come in and there would be dents in the door, and he'd say, "I don't know how that happened." When he was really exasperated, he would scream, "I'm surrounded by idiots!" at the top of his lungs. He was the day managing editor; I was the city editor so I sat right next to him. After he screamed this, he'd turn to me and say, "Not you, Dick."

MARCY SOLTIS, copy editor, 1976–2014: [Vinnie] once attacked—or maybe just threatened—a copy editor with a spike. Do you remember those? That's where the term "spiking" a story came from. Back in the day, stories that were killed were literally skewered on metal spikes.

DAN AQUILANTE: Miss Gerry was a warlord at the *Post*. She brought in candy vending machines just outside the drama department. Vinnie went to get something from one of them, it didn't drop, and the machine didn't give him his money back. Vinnie went berserk on the candy machine and tipped it over. The glass on the front broke. All of the candy in the front was up for grabs. Now, remember, this wasn't just a candy machine; this was Miss Gerry's candy machine. I think what saved Vinnie is that he was Italian.

DICK BELSKY: Vinnie had a very tangled romantic life. Much of it involved women at the *Post*. Every relationship Vinnie had turned ugly.

AMY PAGNOZZI, reporter, columnist, 1979–1993: Vinnie had a ton of girlfriends. The thing is—he didn't mind getting shot down a hundred times. Everyone would say: How did he get such good-looking women? Because eventually he'd find the weak link. Also, he was really into foreign, esoteric films. That was his entrée into meeting girls from NYU film school. [Late in his *Post* career, Musetto reviewed films for the paper.]

JIM PRATT, copy editor, 1990–2013: He was big into Asian porn. Absolutely.

DICK BELSKY: Once he was dating somebody in features and he broke up with her. He was mad at her, so he dismantled her chair.

JAMI BERNARD: Vinnie had restraining orders against him. He was not allowed in the library. He beat up every girlfriend he had. Police pulled up one time and took him outside.

AMY PAGNOZZI: If someone slept with him, and then stopped sleeping with him, her credit or byline would disappear.

KEN CHANDLER, editor in chief, publisher, 1978–1986, 1993–2002: When I came on at night, we'd have to put the bylines back on if we were using the story for the next morning's paper.

KELVIN MACKENZIE, night managing editor, 1978–1979: If you administered any kind of reprimand to Vinnie, he used to get very, very upset. He was wearing a leather hat like Crocodile Dundee. He'd climb onto the desk, sit cross-legged with the hat on, and stare at you. I often wondered if he wasn't too well, because he had to go and see the psychiatrist after the shift. I just wondered whether we were all in danger of having some terrible ending at the *New York Post.*

DAN AQUILANTE: One time, I was paginating something, and Vinnie wanted me to do something else. I'm sorry that this ever happened, but he started yelling at me, and I started yelling back. He picked up a Manhattan phone book. He had it lifted over his head and was about to pummel me with it. I yelled back at him, "Go ahead, motherfucker! Do it, do it! You're my retirement plan." He put the phone book down, and suddenly, we were called into an editor's office together. It was a Friday, a day when I did a lot of interviews, so when I walked into the office, I put my tape recorder down and turned it on. Vinnie went berserk and ran out of the office. Vinnie was a good guy. I wish we didn't fight at the end. I wish I was closer to him when he passed on.

Vinnie's most famous headline—and the *Post*'s—almost didn't get into the paper.

WAYNE DARWEN: HEADLESS BODY was just before I got there, and there was always a dispute as to who wrote it—whether it was Vinnie Musetto or Drew MacKenzie. Probably the truth lies somewhere in the middle. I think they hated each other. I was friends with both of them, and you didn't want to get in the middle.

DREW MACKENZIE: We didn't get along, Vinnie and me. I found him batshit crazy. He was angry, a manic guy. I was working days when the story came in and I wrote, "Headless Body Found in Topless Bar." Vinnie took out the "found" and took credit for the headline.

RICHARD GOODING, metropolitan editor, 1976–1993: The thing about reporting a story is that they always change during the day. You'd hear the first flush of a story, and it would be one thing. By the end of the day, when you reported it out, it would be something else and often less exciting. But once the news desk got their teeth into it, that was it. They didn't want to hear later on that the story had changed. They'd spent the day thinking of headlines and how they were going to play a story, and that's the way it was with HEADLESS BODY. Belsky put a whole team on the story. It was not a topless dancing bar. It was a bar in Queens. But we had a dozen reporters making calls to anybody you could possibly think of who had ever been to this bar to try to back up that it was a topless bar. That was the daily problem. If you had something that looked like it would be good, you'd try to keep them from finding out about it until you knew more. Once they found out about it, they weren't going to let your facts get in the way.

DAVID NG: I was working at police headquarters [in the press room], a.k.a. the Shack. Belsky was the city editor. The beeper went off and he said, "We got this murder we're chasing down in Queens. We need to find out whether it was a strip club." I said, "Anything else?" He said, "No, we have everything else." I went upstairs to public information. I asked the question. I think they contacted someone in the local precinct. They called back: "It definitely was a strip club." I called Belsky. He said, "Thank you." Click. I had no idea why they needed to know that until I saw the headline.

CHARLIE CARILLO: When Vinnie tapped out HEADLESS BODY IN TOPLESS BAR, we were all surrounding his VDT. It's like pictures of the Declaration of Independence with everybody gathered around John Adams and Thomas Jefferson because they know it's something big. By that afternoon, it was legend. Dick Belsky worked the desk that day, and he yelled over, "Vinnie, hang on, we're checking. We're not sure it's a topless bar." Vinnie jumped on the desk and said, "It's gotta be a topless bar. This is the greatest fucking headline of my life."

The events that inspired the headline took place at Herbie's Bar in Jamaica, Queens, on the night of April 13, 1983, and into the next morning. The headline may have been amusing. The crimes involved were not.

PETER DUNNE, former Queens assistant district attorney: No one was prepared for the level of violence that occurred in the city in the '80s. We were inundated with hundreds of homicides. In five years as an ADA, I was responsible for trying fifty homicides. Now, it's one or two a year, if that. Herbie Cummings was the owner of this topless bar. Charlie Dingle comes into the bar, tells Herbie he wants to be a partner in the bar. Herbie was a big guy, very muscular. He tells Charlie to go to hell. Charlie shoots him right between the eyes. Then he throws all the customers out and locks the door. All that's left is the corpse, Herbie's wife, and a topless dancer. There may have been another woman there. That I don't recall. Charlie robs everybody and rapes the dancer. There's a knock on the door. It's Herbie's niece, who turns out to be a mortician. Charlie tells the niece to get the bullet out of the head. A couple of hours go by. Imagine that: trying to get a bullet out of the skull of your uncle. With a steak knife. Charlie finally tells her, "Cut it off, I'll take it with me." She saws off her uncle's head. With a steak knife. There's a box of decorations left from New Year's. He puts the head in the box. He decides he's going to throw it in the East River. He calls a car service, locks the driver up, and lets the dancer go. He takes the wife and mortician with him. The women are in the front seat. One is driving. He's in the back with the box. He falls asleep. They stop the car near 168th and Broadway. The wife and the mortician go to the subway and tell the token booth clerks what happened. Nobody believes them. They tell them to go to Columbus Circle, the transit police. They are referred to Fred Mack, a detective. The women tell Mack this bizarre story.

FRED MACK, retired NYC Transit Police detective: I thought I would have a quiet day. About a quarter to eight, the desk sergeant says, you better talk to these ladies. Couple of well-dressed Black ladies. One was hysterical. She drank the coffee like it was iced tea. The other one said, "I witnessed a rape, a robbery, and a homicide." Most people don't use that word "homicide." They say a killing. That was the mortician. The other one was his wife. Later they told me [the murderer] drank two bottles of rum, he did three lines of cocaine, and smoked four joints.

PETER DUNNE: Mack doesn't believe them. He calls the police precinct in Queens [where Herbie's Bar is located]. The guys in Queens say, "Do you have the head?"

The cops had gone to the bar [after the cabdriver escaped and called them] and found the headless body. Now Fred believes the women.

FRED MACK: I say, "Do you know where he is?" "He's in a car up near Columbia Presbyterian [Hospital]." I don't know how they ended up at [the transit police district office] at Columbus Circle. I would have gone into the hospital building. It was right there, and it was safe. I only took the mortician up there with me. The wife was too upset. We get up there, and I see an old beat-up Lincoln and two police cars. I had called ahead to the local precinct. The police have got someone on the ground. But it's not the guy. The mortician says, "That's not the car. It's on the other side." Exact same [white Lincoln] on the other side of the street. [Dingle] was sleeping when I opened the door, which stirred him. He reached for his gun, I reached for mine, but I left it at the office. I still managed to get his gun and used it to hold him. The head was in an Almaden wine box filled with party decorations. Somebody forgot to ID the body in the morgue. They had only IDed the head. So I had to go to the funeral home. The funeral director put the body back together. He used a piece of wood, either a two-by-four or a two-by-three, drove it down the spine, attached the head to the wood, sealed up the neck, and pulled up a turtleneck. It was an open casket.

PETER DUNNE: The case was thrown on my desk. I did not ask for it. I knew about it because of the headline. Charlie Dingle waived a jury. His case was decided by a judge. This was totally out of the ordinary. Most defendants want a jury because they think they can fool people. He had a psychiatrist testify that he was insane. One of the cornerstones of the insanity defense is you don't recognize that what you have done is wrong. I cross-examined the psychiatrist and got him to admit that, if Dingle wanted to take the head with him as a way of getting rid of the bullet [which would tie him to the crime], then he knew what he was doing. That was the end of the insanity defense. The judge determined Dingle was guilty. I don't remember any press people being there.

DAVID PATERSON, former governor of New York, 2008–2010: I have one connection with the *Post* that has nothing to do with when I was governor. I had just started working in the Queens DA's office and was part of the arraignment for a person who went to a bar, shot its owner, and had a woman there cut his head off. I saw a picture of the owner's head. I thought I was going to jump out the window. Because of the crazy things he did, we thought it was a mental health issue, and I was working in the forensic bureau, which was for mental health cases. In 1990 or '91, when I was a state senator, I asked the *Post*'s editorial board for a meeting. My staff member and I were sitting in the lobby, and he says, "Hey, look at this headline, HEADLESS BODY IN TOPLESS BAR." I said, "I was there!" I went into the editorial board meeting, and we talked more about that incident than the things I wanted to discuss with them.

DICK BELSKY: Vinnie had a lot of the great ones. There was KHADAFY GOES DAFFY and I SLEPT WITH A TRUMPET. His favorite was GRANNY EXECUTED IN HER PINK PAJAMAS.

CHARLIE CARILLO: HEADLESS BODY was the perfect perfect tabloid headline. It was on *Saturday Night Live*. Vinnie was on Letterman.

> The headline became a pop-culture touchstone and inspired a low-budget 1995 movie, but Rupert Murdoch did not congratulate his troops because he learned about it well after the headline had run, and according to those who worked for him, he remained surprisingly squeamish about the more adventurous content that ran in his flagship American publication.

KEN CHANDLER: There was a difference in headlines when Murdoch was in town. A classic example is HEADLESS BODY IN TOPLESS BAR. That story broke during the day, at a time when Vinnie Musetto was actually running the daytime edition in the paper. When I say daytime, he was working from I think six in the morning till three in the afternoon. So he would do the p.m. editions of the paper. Vinnie thought up that headline, but he didn't have the guts to put it in the paper, because Murdoch was around and he was afraid to use it.

DICK BELSKY: Murdoch was defensive about this idea that he was over-the-top.

KEN CHANDLER: When Vinnie went off at four or whenever his shift ended, we saw this headline and I said to Steve Dunleavy, "I guess the boss is still around." Dunleavy said, "I'm not sure, let's find out." We made some calls and we discovered he was getting on a plane to go to London that evening. We used the headline in the next morning's paper [April 15, 1983] when he was in London. He never objected to it. ["Cops Find Headless Body in Topless Bar" ran on the front page, but not as the wood, in the final edition on April 14. The headline on the story that accompanied it, on page eight, was "Headless Man in Topless Bar."]

MYRON RUSHETZKY, head city desk assistant, 1974–1989, 1991–2013: I was assigned to find out when his plane left the ground. Then Ken and company would use the headline. In the earlier versions, the story read better. They didn't have the [famous] headline, but the story itself read better. For the next day's paper— editions one, two, three, when they did have the headline HEADLESS BODY IN TOPLESS BAR—the bylines are different from the earlier editions. That story was a mess. Might've been bad copy editing, bad editing, maybe moving graphs around, but it didn't read as well.

KEN CHANDLER: Murdoch once called me from London yelling at me for "putting a photo of a topless woman in the paper." Apparently, the ad manager had claimed advertisers were upset. When I pointed out that the photo in question, on page seven, was a statue in Rome of a nude Venus and it was relevant to the story alongside it, and it was a nice picture, he went silent for a moment and then said: "If it was so nice, why didn't you bloody well put it on page one. You might have sold some more copies!"

When the *Post* found a story worthy of its headlines, usually involving murder, sex, scandal, or another high-profile crime, it ran updates for days, creating a narrative that was the equivalent of a tabloid telenovela, with heroes, villains, and victims, who sometimes earned clever nicknames that stuck. When the paper discovered that a woman with a classy pedigree was running a high-end Manhattan escort service, it christened her "The Mayflower Madam."

PAUL THARP, reporter, columnist, 1982–2014: It was a two-day-old story of an escort ring on the Upper West Side. We were trying to do a follow on it. The best lead came from Phil Messing. He was a street reporter. He went up to the building and the super told him there's a guy named Sidney Barrows who you call if there's a water leak or something. Then Mike Pearl calls and says, *her* name is Sydney Biddle Barrows. I said, "Biddle? She's a Biddle?" We used to have the Social Register then, the little black book. And there it is. She lived on the West Side. She grew up in central Jersey, and there was a local paper. I got out microfilm of the paper, and we found some photos of her on a vacation. That same day, somebody, I think it was her boyfriend, had sold pictures of her to Bob Young. They were the same pictures he'd taken for the local newspaper. A team of four of us put together this story. Peter Fearon was the rewrite guy.

SYDNEY BIDDLE BARROWS, former owner, Cachet escort service: None of my friends knew my middle name was Biddle. I never used it.

PHILIP MESSING, reporter, 1978–1991, 1994–2016: I can't lay claim to the discovery that Ms. Barrows was a blue blood whose ancestors arrived on the *Mayflower*. I think this tidbit was discovered by Paul Tharp or Peter Fearon. But it was a *New York Post* revelation. We were even more jazzed when we learned that the young service providers came from the ranks of the patricians they hoped to serve—supposedly they all went to elite schools.

SYDNEY BIDDLE BARROWS: Peter Fearon named me the Mayflower Madam? I remember Steve Dunleavy claiming he had dubbed me the Mayflower Madam.

PETER FEARON, reporter, 1980–1987: You know how when you write a story, you have to write a slug at the top? [The slug identifies the article as it's in production.] I used to try to write meaningful or catchy slugs so that I could get back to them. After I'd written "Mayflower Madam" for the slug, I thought, "Oh my god, that's it." That also became the first paragraph. And the headline.

SYDNEY BIDDLE BARROWS: For two weeks [in 1984], I was the cover story every day. Although they didn't publish on Sunday. It was also the cover story on the *Daily News*, except for the day Indira Gandhi got shot. That was the only thing that kicked me off the front page. I ended up being extremely fortunate in that there was that newspaper war going on between the *Post* and the *Daily News*. And fortunately, both papers figured out that what made the story interesting was the dichotomy between my background and the business I was in. They played that up to my benefit. Instead of making it a sordid story, which they usually do with people who did what I did. Instead of making me out to be a low-life villain, they made me out to be some glamorous socialite-type person, which I wasn't.

The reporters who broke news about the 1982 disappearance of Kathie Durst, wife of Robert Durst, son of a Manhattan real estate developer, had to replay their exclusives in court many years later. In 2021, Durst was tried for the murder of his friend Susan Berman, whose death had not been connected to the disappearance of Durst's wife until HBO aired *The Jinx: The Life and Deaths of Robert Durst*, which contained previously unknown and incriminating details.

MARSHA KRANES, rewrite, editor, 1974–2005: I was the first person to talk to [Robert] Durst. I found him through the reverse directory [which enabled you to find a person's phone number if you knew their address, though it did not work with unlisted numbers]. I spoke to him right after he reported his wife missing. It was a great interview. He just picked up the phone and started talking. He said an awful lot that he probably shouldn't have said. The next day, Charlie [Lachman] took over. He did a lot of stories and we did several together.

CHARLES LACHMAN: Marsha [Kranes] and I both had to testify at Durst's [2021] trial. It's interesting how something you wrote—what? four decades ago?—can come back like that. I had a couple of good scoops. I found out that Durst was having an affair with Mia Farrow's sister, so it was the perfect loop of connecting a missing, presumed dead wife, famous wealthy New York real estate family, to the sister of a famous actress. That delivered. Then I got the first sit-down interview with Robert Durst in Howard Rubenstein's offices. Rubenstein represented Murdoch, the *Post*, and all the big real estate companies. Whether that factored into Bob Durst agreeing to the interview, I don't know, but he made some really compelling admissions in the interview. It was one of those rare times that the *Post* went with that front page with all its editions. Back in the day, they tried to change the headlines of the wood to sell various editions of the paper. But this wood stayed for the duration of the day. I remember there was a buzz in the newsroom about that—and some grumbling.

On the afternoon of December 22, 1984, Bernie Goetz shot four Black teens on the number 2 subway train after, he alleged, they attempted to rob him. One of the men, Darrell Cabey, was left paraplegic and brain damaged. The case became national news, sparking a debate about whether the shooting was justifiable in a city notorious for crime. When he turned himself in, the *Post*'s wood declared "I AM DEATH WISH VIGILANTE," a reference to a 1974 movie starring Charles Bronson.

RICHARD ESPOSITO, reporter, 1982–1985: I was supposed to stake out Bernie Goetz in his apartment on 14th Street. I'm parked in front of this building and I've been there forever. I called the office and I said, "Hey, when do I get relief? I've been here like twelve hours." They're like, "We'll let you know." They meant it. Rule number one was: do the stakeout. And get us a picture of Bernie Goetz, which I did. It was the first picture. This was right after [the shooting] happened. No one knew where he was. No one had a photo. The photographer had almost no involvement and was terrified to even be a part of getting the photo, which involved sneaking past the detectives in the lobby and getting into his apartment. Bernie was not there. I flipped the lock with a credit card and got the photo from his passport. I had to take it out of the apartment for the photographer to take a picture and then put it back. After a while, the cops called up on the intercom and said, "You had enough fun. You need to get out of there now." They figured out I was up there. I did not tell anyone for a very long time because even though I only removed the passport for a little while, and then put it back, technically, it could be considered stealing a passport.

MIKE PEARL: In the Goetz case, we were going to get this confession in the lawyer's office. Dunleavy wanted me to be there. I could see he was smashed. We had the confession; it was twenty or thirty pages long. He wanted me to pick out the good quotes. But by the time I did, he was sober enough to write the thing. He wrote the story, and the story was brilliant.

RONALD L. KUBY, attorney for Darrell Cabey, former partner of activist lawyer William Kunstler: In the forty years that I've been practicing law in New York, I've had a love-hate relationship with the *Post*. Look, the lurid headlines are interesting. People like them and comment on their cleverness, and I'm among them. Back when I had more friends at the *Post*, I used to do sample headline writing for stories they were working on, just for fun, because it's kind of a brainteaser. The race-baiting though, the insistent demonization of Black youths, many who turned out to be innocent, excusing police brutality—year after year, generation after generation— and the paper's contribution to sentiment in favor of mass incarceration doesn't get washed away by cute and clever headlines. That is the most enduring legacy of the *New York Post* in those forty years. The first one [in my experience] was the vigilante shooting of four Black youths by Bernhard Goetz, none of whom threatened Goetz, none of whom displayed any weapon. Goetz just opened fire on all four of them. Every day the *Post* championed him as the hero of the white man: Mr. Charles Bronson, Mr. Average Citizen who's had enough. I've got to tell you they weren't alone. It's true the *New York Post* did things more luridly, more colorfully, and more viciously than the other newspapers, but it's not like the other papers or the citizenry were in a different place. The *New York Post* has always tried to reflect the most ugly part of their readers and give that full voice. The other papers nod and wink to it. Goetz, of course, got acquitted of all serious charges, but ultimately, I held him accountable in civil court for $43 million [in 1996]. We never collected, but the idea wasn't to collect. The idea was to dethrone him from his hero status. That's when the *New York Post* made one of its sort of rare personal attacks on me in the form of a cartoon by the great Sean Delonas. He had me in court—a big fat version of Ron Kuby—representing some horrible person; the headlines making some sick excuse. To this day, Sean remains a friend of mine. I'm not a jihadist in France. I don't hate people for their cartoons.

BOB YOUNG, photo editor, 1978–1986: Dunleavy and I were drinking one night at Marie's, the mob pub, when he got a call from the desk saying Bernie Goetz wanted to speak to him. Dunleavy called him back and invites him down to Marie's. The guys in Marie's were in awe.

> Though the *Post*'s coverage and headlines mostly focused on New York and Hollywood, it also covered national and international news as it related to its hometown readers. But other than maintaining a bureau in Washington, DC, the tabloid mostly relied on a network of stringers. The paper's pro-Israel stance was one of the few ways Murdoch's *Post* aligned with Dorothy Schiff's. Thanks to one well-connected correspondent, the *Post*'s Middle East coverage could be so inside, its stories would not be validated for years, and its knee-jerk hostility toward Israel's enemies also put at least one reporter in danger.

ANDY SOLTIS, rewrite, editor, 1967–2014: I used to work all the time with Uri Dan, who was our Israeli correspondent, and he told me that the way he got to the *Post*, in 1981, was when he called the news desk and asked to speak to Al Ellenberg, who he knew. Ellenberg had gone by that time [though he later returned to the paper], so he asked to speak with an editor. I don't know who it was, but Uri said the conversation went something like, "My name is Uri Dan. I'm an Israeli correspondent. I have a story that I can't print here because of censorship. It's pretty good story, and I'm offering it to you guys. The Israeli Air Force just destroyed Saddam Hussein's nuclear reactor." The editor said, "Well, it's not on the wires." Uri said, "It's not going to be on the wires because the Iraqis aren't going to admit that four Israeli aircraft just zoomed over central Baghdad and blew the hell out of their reactor. The Israelis aren't going to admit it, either." In fact, they didn't admit it until one of the pilots [Ilan Ramon], who had become an astronaut, died in the 2003 *Columbia* space shuttle crash. When he died, Israel identified him as one of the pilots that flew on the Iraq raid—the first official confirmation this had happened. Anyway, the *Post* ran the story based solely on Uri's report. Uri was very tight with Ariel Sharon, that was his main line of information. I'm sure he got it from Sharon. It became a big international incident.

BARBARA ROSS, political reporter, 1978–1985: My knowledge of what went on behind the scenes at the *Post* was based in part on what Carl Pelleck would tell me. He hung out with Dunleavy, so he would get information that way. Pelleck tells me Uri Dan is in the Mossad [Israeli intelligence agency], and I'm like, "Why is somebody from the Mossad showing up in the *New York Post* with a byline?" One day, I asked Al Ellenberg, "Is it true that he's in the Mossad?" Ellenberg glared at me and said, "Mind your own business." I said, "But if he's in the Mossad, isn't there a conflict?" He said, "That's it." He just shut down the conversation.

ERIC FETTMANN: Uri was not in the Mossad, and Ariel Sharon was not his main source. He was a highly respected and well-connected journalist.

CHARLIE CARILLO: Charlie Lachman was in the Middle East. He filed a story and Dunleavy got on the phone and said, "Uh, you know, mate, this is a little dry." Charlie said, "Steve, I'm exhausted. I've been up for seventy-two hours. Just be careful, whatever you do. I'm the only Jew in Lebanon."

CHARLES LACHMAN: It was like being Indiana Jones. Dunleavy sent me to Lebanon [in December 1983]. It was the civil war, and [Yasser] Arafat, head of the PLO, was being kicked out of Lebanon. There were American troops there. Bob Hope came to entertain, and there were shootings. I had to duck the fire. It was great. I think what Carillo was talking about is, I wrote this story and Dunleavy put a spin on it. I think the front-page headline was ARAFAT, YOU YELLOW RAT. [The final edition that day was ARAFAT TURNS TAIL.] My picture was in the paper. They called me "The *Post*'s Man in Beirut." I'm at the dock at the Port of Beirut covering these thousands of PLO fighters, all armed with their AK-47s, leaving the port. I get my shirt pulled up behind me by my neck. There were these guys who had a fax of the *New York Post* front page. Nothing happened, but that was wild.

With eight editions to fill, the *Post* more than lived up to its nickname, "the paper of wreckage"—a mordant play on the *New York Times*' reputation as the paper of record. But *Post* editors assigned legitimate investigations as well as the frivolous kind, though the results might be buried if they didn't jibe with the Murdochian worldview.

BARBARA ROSS: If they thought what I was writing was not in keeping with the politics of the paper, they wouldn't give the story much play. They asked me to do a series on abortion, and I knew they were anti-abortion. I researched abortion clinics in the city. I had everybody in the office peeing into a cup. Boys, too. I took them to clinics all over, pretending I was pregnant. When they would ask for a urine sample, I would give them whatever I had collected in the office. What I found was only one place misdiagnosed what was in the urine. This place on Park Avenue South said, "You're pregnant. You need an abortion." I gave them another sample, making sure it was from one of the guys in the office. They did it again. I arranged to go through with the procedure, to the point of getting up on the table. Then I said, "Stop!" The doctor says, "Don't worry about it. It's normal to be nervous." I said, "I'm not nervous. I'm a reporter for the *New York Post.*" What Murdoch wanted was more of that, but the lawyers said, because I didn't have anybody in the room with me, and you can't take a tape recorder into an operating theater, I had to write around it. I couldn't identify the clinic. I did talk to the New York City health department to ask if there were any complaints about the clinic. Long story short, I wrote a four-part series that got no promotion up front because it did not reflect what Murdoch was hoping it would—which was people were getting abortions left and right who didn't need them, and that doctors were profiteering and that this was unsafe. But truly it was only one. I must have checked with a dozen different clinics.

CHARLIE CARILLO: One Memorial Day weekend, there was nothing going on in the city. Nothing. A toy company was doing a publicity stunt about some action figure, and at the 30th Street helipad, they had a guy coming down from a helicopter on a rope with this toy. He was going to land and he was in a uniform. There were three print guys there: me, a guy from United Press International, and a guy from the *New Yorker* magazine. It hit me: the guy from the *New Yorker* is here because it's quaint Talk of the Town stuff. The guy from UPI is there because they cover everything. And I'm here in case the rope snaps.

17 | ART IMITATES *POST*
Culture, Entertainment, and a Bag of Shit

he features section of the *Post* under Murdoch—coverage of music, movies, theater, fashion, travel, lifestyle—did not rival the anarchy of the news section, yet it had its own idiosyncracies. Aussie Arnold Earnshaw ran the section for a while, working alongside Schiff-era editor Joe Rabinovich ("Joe Rab," to those who worked with him). Unlike most Australian imports, Earnshaw did not have an easy ride.

KEN CHANDLER, editor in chief, publisher, 1978–1986, 1993–2002: Old-school, pedantic, everything had to be done [Earnshaw's] way. With the Australians versus the Brits, there was a lot of back-and-forth between the two groups, and they didn't really respect each other very much. I don't think Roger [Wood] respected Arnold [Earnshaw]. Roger thought Arnold might be a potential rival. Roger was very protective of himself and made sure there weren't any rivals flourishing.

AMY PAGNOZZI, reporter, columnist, 1979–1993: I remember everybody used to be afraid of Arnold. I got along with him fine. Arnold was maybe sixty years old, very gruff. I didn't see what there was to be afraid of. He would basically ask you to do something and then grunt. He was like a troll.

STEPHEN SILVERMAN, entertainment writer, 1977–1988: Arnold was pickled most of the time. But he still wore his suit and tie and vest. A lesson I did learn from

270

him, and I do it to this day, is—Friday, you clear off your desk. You leave it with no unfinished business from the week. But these Murdoch editors really didn't say much. I just have images of them all sort of—because they'd been drinking—leaning back in their chairs.

DOMINICK MARRANO, chief paginator, 1971–2008: Arnold went on vacation. He came back, and his desk was moved from the features department. It literally was not there anymore. He was named special events editor or something.

> Other features editors succeeded Earnshaw, herding a varied group of critics and writers, several of them holdovers from the Schiff era. One longtime columnist had stopped writing just months before Murdoch bought the paper: Dr. Rose Franzblau, who applied Freudian theory to requests for advice sent in by troubled readers. Another pre-Murdoch columnist had more staying power.

CALVIN TRILLIN, staff writer, *The New Yorker*: I occasionally read Rose Franzblau's stuff. I liked it because she always attacked the person who wrote in. The person would ask some innocent question about how his mother-in-law was treating him, and she would attack him for being stupid and not understanding. I liked that part.

ANDY SOLTIS, rewrite, editor, 1967–2014: In 1972, Bobby Fischer won the World Chess Championship in a match against Boris Spassky that lasted all summer. I remember writing the wood story, which had the headline BOBBY'S THE CHAMP. Among the people in the office who were interested in chess was Al Ellenberg. I played him occasionally. He wasn't a bad player. After the match, he said, "Would you be interested in writing a chess column one day a week?" That's like asking me, "Would you like to play quarterback for the New York Giants? It'll just be one day a week." [As of April 2024, grandmaster Soltis was still writing the chess column.]

JIM MONES, drama editor, 1980–1987: In my first year at the *Post*, TV was still looked upon as the enemy. We basically had no TV coverage. You never assigned someone to cover something on TV. We had zero radio for many years. The TV thing changed maybe two or three years later, but it was odd how old-school it was, how TV was looked at as a threat.

DAN AQUILANTE, chief music critic, 1980–2012: The drama department and the features department were two separate units in those days. Drama was theater, music, television. What they called features was the women's pages—gardening, cooking, et cetera. Steve Cuozzo and then Jimmy Mones were the drama editors.

JIM MONES: We once had a story in the travel section on the Leaning Tower of Pisa with a little picture of the tower. Somebody in the composing room straightened it.

DAN AQUILANTE: You had Jerry Tallmer, one of the founders of the *Village Voice*, who was teaching me as he edited my two-inch shorts, saying, "Don't do this, do this."

Tallmer gave many young *Post* employees their first bylines and some helpful training for the future, though not everyone was a fan.

AMY PAGNOZZI: At some point, Jerry Tallmer noticed that I was writing little pieces for features and he had me doing pieces for his Week in Review section. He became a mentor for me and a lot of other people, teaching us how to write. I got to do work that I was proud of.

DIANA MAYCHICK, entertainment writer, 1978–1989: There was a place near the paper that had bagels. I'd have to go there for Jerry Tallmer. He always wanted almost half a stick of butter on one side and a pile of cream cheese on the other. I really loved him. When I found out he was one of the founding editors of the *Village Voice*, I was shocked that he was now at the *Post*. I didn't think any liberal with any conscience could work there—well, I shouldn't say that because I was there. There were a lot of liberals, I guess, but it didn't really show.

RAMONA GARNES, copy editor, 1978–1990, 2000–2004: When [Jerry Tallmer] died, Myron [Rushetzky] sent out one of his emails and people were saying what a wonderful person Jerry was. I remember calling or emailing Marcy Soltis and saying, "He was a racist piece of shit. Nastiest person I ever knew." Marcy said, "Yeah, what is all this praise people are sending? That's not the guy I knew."

MARCY SOLTIS, copy editor, 1976–2014: I agreed with Ramona that Jerry was not the nice guy people were describing, but I *did not* agree that he was a racist.

DAN AQUILANTE: Another great thing about the drama department—and it's something the *Post* lost over time—was that you also had these ancient people, like Harriett Johnson, who was the classical music critic, and Archer Winsten, a film critic and our skiing columnist. They were fixtures around New York, and there wasn't a push to, "Hey, let's get a young person in to replace Archer or Harriett, or let's get a younger person in to replace Clive Barnes." It's why, even as a twenty-three-year-old, I thought, this is a place where I can get old.

SUSAN MULCAHY, Page Six editor, 1978–1985: Archer Winsten had been there so long, if you got the *Gone with the Wind* clips out of the library, you'd find Archer's 1939 review. He also wrote about skiing. Supposedly he taught the Murdoch kids how to ski. He was in his eighties when he retired.

DIANA MAYCHICK: Harriett Johnson was an anachronism. She did not seem to be *Post*-like.

JIM MONES: The feeling was that Clive [Barnes], and the Harriett Johnsons, those people, kind of gave credence to the newspaper, offsetting stuff in the front of the paper. They were bringing some respect with their opinions.

STEPHEN SILVERMAN: Roger said, "Stephen, we depend on you to class up the paper." Because I interviewed Simon Wiesenthal. I interviewed Joseph L. Mankiewicz. I still thought of the readership as Jewish. That's what Joe Rab had instilled in me, and Jerry [Tallmer], too. That there was this core readership of older Jews, despite everything that was going on.

DAN AQUILANTE: On a nightly basis, people on the city desk would steal chairs from the drama department. Harriett Johnson was so upset by this that she went to the hardware store and bought this three-quarter-inch-thick chain—something that you could use to haul a tractor—and every morning I would have to get on my hands and knees and unlock her chair from her desk. When she left at night, I would have to relock her chain. Harriett was very good to me. She saw that I was writing about music, and she gave me some of the most valuable advice I ever got about being a critic. She said, "Don't kind of like something. Either love it or kill it. Don't leave it wounded." She said critics who found middle ground were nothing. I have to say, I took it to heart. I wrote a review of a Van Morrison concert where he looked at his watch and he looked impatient. I fucking crucified him. I did such a number on the concert that the *Irish Echo* did a full-page story about why I should be fired.

JAMI BERNARD, chief movie critic, 1978–1993: Archer Winsten was the second-string movie critic. He had been a critic for fifty years. I don't know what he was like in his heyday, but he was very elderly and he was losing it. He put a rape joke in one of his reviews that I had to take out. He said about a pretty actress: can't blame the male character for trying to force her. I didn't know if it was his age alone, or because he was from an old guard. To say that Archer was messy was an understatement. He had like old half-eaten sandwiches, buried under piles of paper—a real hoarder kind of thing.

JOHN WATERS, filmmaker: In the old days, my experience with the *Post* was the film critic Archer Winsten, who hated me. He's the one who wrote, if you see my name on the marquee, walk on the other side of the street and hold your nose. That's how I thought up *Polyester* [featuring Odorama]. We always used his negative reviews in the ads.

DAN AQUILANTE: Rex Reed was a film critic for about five years. Prissy little fuck, but he got attention. One of my jobs as desk assistant was to open the mail, including Rex's. He never came into the office. Anything of value or importance would be shipped off to him. I can't say that I'm a hundred percent sure that this was the movie in question, but my recollection is that when [David Lynch's 1986 film] *Blue Velvet* came out, Rex wrote a review saying that it was more disgusting than a John Waters movie, or something along those lines. [The review advised "Bring a barf bag."] He was revolted by this movie. It was generally accepted at the *Post* that anybody who wrote to the paper was probably crazy. So if you got a personal letter that said, "What an asshole you are. You should be fired," it was almost a badge of honor. You always read them out loud. I'm opening up the mail that day, and there's something rank going on. I get to this small box addressed to Rex. I cut it open, and inside is a hate letter and a baggie of shit. Everybody was like, oh my god. It was like the Baby Ruth in the pool scene in *Caddyshack*. Someone said, "Dan, go wash your hands," which I immediately did. Then the question was "Should we send it to Rex?" I don't really recall how the turd was gotten rid of. I know Rex was informed about it.

REX REED, film critic, 1982–1986: A prissy little fuck? It's just a silly opinion, and I don't know who this person is, so I don't know whether I should be offended by someone I admire and respect, or whether this is just some jerk. But I never received a box of anything in my career.

JIM MONES: There was this voluptuous B movie actress, Edy Williams. She called one day when I was in drama, probably early '80s, and gave me an earful about Rex Reed, who had written that her body, which was always scantily clad or completely nude, had seen better days or words to that effect. [Reed called Williams an "aging sexpot."] Edy, who had been in a lot of Russ Meyer's films [and was married to Meyer for a time], took exception to this. Though she was pushing forty, she said she still had a great body. She ended the phone call by saying, "Tell Rex Reed I'm coming over." Two hours later, a security guard calls me: Edy Williams is in the building and she's coming up. So much for security. She arrives with a guy with a boom box. I told her that Rex Reed was not in the office, that he never came into the office. It didn't matter. A button was pushed on the boom box. Burlesque music came on. The actress's clothes came off. She did a striptease for a crowd that included almost every guy in the newsroom, plus security guards—again, so much for security. She left on just enough clothing to avoid an X rating. But she made her point.

DAN AQUILANTE: Murdoch was very hands-on in those days. He would walk the composing room floor. He would be in the elevators, in the hallways, saying, "What are you doing?" He'd say it to a copykid. At some point, I started doing this column called Popcorn Panel. The idea was all Murdoch, and in retrospect was pretty smart in the way it anticipated the internet phenomenon where regular folks love being critics. I believe I got the column because, as crazy as it sounds, my mother wrote Murdoch a letter. She saw me doing all these jobs—I was a driver, I worked in the wire room, the composing room—and unbeknownst to me and to my great embarrassment when I found out, my mother wrote to Murdoch saying, "My kid works really hard, blah, blah, blah." I'm one of the children of the *Post* that didn't have a guru. I got there through Don Broderick, who was another copykid. Something in that letter must have stirred Murdoch because about a week later, he said to my boss, Jim Mones, that he had an idea for a column about a group of young people going to a movie and then giving brief feedback as to whether they liked it or not. Out of the blue, I was doing this column with my own photography and interviews with kids at movie theaters.

JIM MONES: The jazz critic during my time was Richard Sudhalter. He was an acclaimed trumpet player, bandleader, music historian. He was a very good writer, but there was never enough room for his reviews. So his stuff would get cut. He would call me and say, good-naturedly, "You slashed my review!" An opportunity to hear him play came up. My wife and I got there late and Sudhalter was already on stage. He looked up as we were being seated and, without missing a beat, said into the microphone: "It's the slasher! The slasher is here!"

DAN AQUILANTE: Sometimes when we did a Popcorn Panel on a movie that was about a profession, we'd get people from that line of work. For instance, if it was *Backdraft*, we'd invite six firefighters to comment. There was this movie called *Milk Money* that starred Melanie Griffith as a prostitute, and at an editorial meeting the suggestion was "We need a panel of prostitutes to review this." After five minutes of kicking it around, one editor said, "We can't do it. Do you know what that would cost?"

> Theater critic Clive Barnes had a prominent profile in New York, having previously been the uber-powerful critic at the *New York Times*, but some felt that early on in his tenure at the *Post*—especially before he gave up alcohol—he was phoning it in.

FRANK RICH, film critic, 1975–1977: There was a drama critic named Martin Gottfried who'd been hired, maybe around the same time as I was. He was older. He was actually someone I had read when I was in high school and college. He wrote for *Women's Wear Daily* in the days when they had arts critics. Meeting Gottfried turned out to be a disappointment. He was an arrogant, condescending guy, but I was fascinated by him. He was a drama critic, and I was interested in drama criticism. I admired his writing. When Murdoch took over, I got a phone call from Gottfried, who had never called me. He said, "I hear you're thinking of leaving." I said, "Yes." He said, "You are making an incredible mistake. He's going to pour money into the *Post*. It's going to be fantastic." It was flattering that he wanted me to stay, and he was older than I was and much more experienced. I was in my mid-twenties, and I thought, oh god, maybe he does know. But I had already made the decision to leave. Within a matter of months, when Clive Barnes, essentially for reasons of alcoholism, was stripped of being the drama critic by the *Times* and limited to dance criticism, Barnes was furious and the *Post* poached him. Martin Gottfried was fired and never had a major gig again.

AMY PAGNOZZI: Clive didn't get along with [the *Times'* executive editor] Abe Rosenthal. Clive definitely drank too much, and he also carried on outrageously. I don't think anybody would argue about this. But he also wrote really well and did really good-quality work. But Rosenthal pretty much had it in for him. [Pagnozzi married Barnes in 1985.]

RICHARD KORNBERG, theater and dance publicist: Certain people would suggest that if Clive came to a show when he was not in the greatest shape, you were happy if he went with his wife Trish [the second of Barnes's four wives; Pagnozzi was his third] or with another *New York Post* reporter, then you knew there was someone else there, if Clive was nodding out, to capture the essence of the show.

DAN AQUILANTE: Clive Barnes wrote a review of some play, the title of which I can't remember, where he killed it. Everybody I had talked to who had seen it, loved it, and I said, "Clive, why does everybody love it, and you hate it?" He said, "The public knows nothing about theater."

AMY PAGNOZZI: The *Post* started using Clive to review all kinds of things you wouldn't normally have a dance or drama critic do—current events, elections, debates, the royal wedding. Whenever they wanted something splashy, they would ask him to do it. At one point, Roger Wood told me that they were going to put him in a hang glider over some big concert, I think it was Michael Jackson. Clive gave up drinking early on in our relationship, so that's not why I was concerned. I was begging Roger every day: please don't send him, it's not going to be safe. They were pulling my leg the whole time. Clive didn't know this, either. He was going to do it! He was very old-school journalism.

JIM MONES: Clive was a machine. He could write long, he could write fast, he could write funny. He did it all. You know that Beatles song "Paperback Writer"? Write whatever you want—long, short, change it. That was Clive. Once he went on, like, a two-week vacation. He left behind a couple of columns, four off-Broadway reviews, four re-reviews of Broadway shows. It was like 205 inches of copy, give or take a yard. If you had to cut a chunk out of his story, he didn't mind. He would take the copy and use it in a magazine article he was selling in London or re-purpose it somewhere. The most efficient and fastest guy in the West.

DIANA MAYCHICK: When I became the Broadway columnist, I would have to dress up for opening night. I would have to walk through the city room to get to the stairs and everybody would look at me like, "Who the fuck does she think she is?" In the beginning, I just wore anything. But I realized if I could talk to the stars at the show, I would get more items. If I dressed in a really fabulous way, they would think we were sort of equal. I didn't have the money to really do that. I would go to Bloomingdale's, buy a dress, put the tag into the back of the dress so you couldn't see it, and return it the next day.

BARBARA CARROLL, former theater publicist: It was one of the greatest events ever—3,389, the record-breaking performance when *A Chorus Line* surpassed *Grease* as the longest-running Broadway show. It was September 29, 1983. All the companies of *Chorus Line*, including the original—more than three hundred dancers—took part. The finale—"One"—was everybody. It was spectacular. There were so many people, the stage of the Shubert had to be reinforced. It was black tie—an invited audience—and the gala party was just as amazing. They tented Shubert Alley. At the end of the party, all these trucks from the *Post* pull up and they drop off bundles of the early edition of the paper that had total coverage of the show and the party. It was a wraparound with everything about the event. Joe [Papp, founder of the Public Theater, where *A Chorus Line* originated] just loved this. He said, "Get me Roger Wood." I must have used the phone in the lobby of the Shubert. I called the main number of the *Post* and got Roger. Joe thanked him and said, "If you could just see all these *Times* editors standing in a row looking at that paper." Roger said, "Then it was all worth it."

> Nightlife columnist Earl Wilson, who began writing for the *Post* in 1942, continued to appear at Broadway and other openings. Though he no longer broke big stories, as he had in his heyday, his longevity had a retro appeal.

JOSH ELLIS, former theater publicist: I loved Earl. And I loved the fact that he made me feel like I was working in old New York—where the press agent calls the gossip columnist at like eleven o'clock at night and things that happened in the theater get out there. It was my movie version of what it was like to be a press agent.

BARBARA CARROLL: A lot of people who came backstage [at the musical *Annie*] wanted to meet the dog. Earl Wilson made Sandy a star. [PR rep] David Powers got him an interview with Sandy. He was the first non-human Earl ever interviewed.

JIM MONES: I remember asking Earl Wilson once about a blind item. It was some actor walking around drunk or something. I was curious: who's the celebrity? He said, "The answer is always in the column." If he had a blind item, he said, their name popped up somewhere else in the column. I don't know if that was always true, or sometimes true. But that's what he told me.

> Earl's legmen, Martin Burden and Tim Boxer, had filled in for him over the years, but when Earl retired in 1983, Cindy Adams landed the job. She wasn't the only one who wanted it.

TIM BOXER, assistant to Earl Wilson, TV columnist, 1966–1986: She was envious of my connection with Earl and schemed to replace me.

CINDY ADAMS, gossip columnist, 1981–current: When Earl Wilson retired, I was pushed and pushed and pushed to take the column. Roger Wood called Steve Cuozzo and said, "Go have tea with her." It was tea. We met in the lobby of the Mayfair Hotel, where Le Cirque used to be. Cuozzo laid it out for me.

STEPHEN SILVERMAN: The fix was in because I, in fact, approached Roger about [Earl's column]. I said, "Roger, I don't want you to think I'm not still an ambitious young man. I can do Earl's job." "No, no, you like what you're doing, and it's being taken care of." Next thing we knew, it was Cindy.

CINDY ADAMS: Roger Wood was a prince. He started the whole thing. He grabbed me. He loved me.

CHARLIE CARILLO: In Cindy's column, everybody from Robert Redford to Barack Obama begins every quote with "Listen."

> Cindy became known for, among other things, her devotion to her husband; her work ethic; and her appreciation of a freebie.

AMY PAGNOZZI: She was so loyal to Joey. She sang his praises from morning till night.

LESLIE GEVIRTZ, reporter, rewrite, 1978–1988: Cindy reminded me of someone's idea of an all-knowing, beautifully attired aunt. I have never ever seen Cindy wearing jeans. She was also like a Jewish mother. If she saw you were in trouble, she would reach out to you. I found her to be very generous. On the other hand, at one point, she got an award at the Newswomen's Club of New York for reporting, and I got to do the introduction. Of course, it was a very nice introduction. But later, she wants to know: "So, do I get a free membership?" I was startled by that because, usually, no, but I said I would see what I could do. I spoke to the board about it, and we gave her a free membership. She did love a freebie.

ERIC FETTMANN, associate editorial page editor, columnist, 1976–1991, 1993–2019: Cindy and Joey were always taking junkets. They took a lot of free trips in return for plugs. One was a river voyage up the Yangtze in China. One of the things that Cindy did outside of her column was, when a celebrity died, she would write a special column with all her personal reminiscences. Before she went on this thing, which may have been a monthlong cruise, she gave us five envelopes and said, "These are people who may die while I'm away. Here are my columns." Four of the five died in the order that she left—she left the envelopes one on top of the other. The only one who didn't die was Earl Wilson. The joke was: somebody call Earl and find out how he's feeling.

CINDY ADAMS: Wow. Not true. Listen, there's a lot of little stories you will hear. A lot of people are saying things about me just because I'm still here.

> Once Cindy's turf had been established, she did not want anyone else treading on it, especially *Post* reporters with similar beats.

DIANA MAYCHICK: When I was going to be given the Broadway column—Names in Lights it was called—which Roger wanted, Cindy went into Roger's office and screamed about me; she went totally nuts, really really upset, saying, "She's no good" and that kind of thing.

STEPHEN SILVERMAN: She hated me, because I got all the movie stars. Even after I had left the *Post*, I was seated next to Paul Newman at a dinner party. She was relegated elsewhere—the looks she gave me.

KEN CHANDLER, editor in chief, publisher, 1978–1986, 1993–2002: She's the most competitive person I ever met.

AMY PAGNOZZI: I saw something one night when I was with Clive, just a minor item. I called to give it to her. She said to me, "What do you want?" I go, "What do you mean?" She goes, "You must want something for it." I was like, "No, what do you mean, what do I want?" She goes, "You scratch my back. I scratch yours." I just remember being so taken aback by it. Also, I went to Earl's funeral with Clive. [Earl Wilson died in 1987.] We went because he was dead! And we knew him. Joey [Adams] walks up to me and says, "What are you doing here?" I go, "Earl died." He goes, "Cindy's here." I go, "Yeah, I know." He goes, "Cindy's covering." I go, "I'm not covering." He goes, "Then what are you doing here?" He practically made me leave! He was outraged that I should have gone to the funeral. They definitely were territorial. They had their turf. And they didn't want anybody stepping on it. They came from that era where, "I'll give you a story today, you print what I need tomorrow."

CINDY ADAMS: I don't believe I was mean and hurtful to anybody. I might have been, but I don't believe I was. That may come a little from jealousy or maybe people who don't like me or don't know why I'm still around. If you're harsh with me, I will hate you forever. I have intense loyalty. Friends from old days who were good to me, I'll never forget. If you're evil to me, I'll probably try to get you in this world or the next one. I lack fear. You can't send me back. I have nothing to lose. You can't hurt me. You don't like me? You fire me because there's a story I didn't get? I'm still going to go back to Doris Duke's apartment, which I own. If my ego was involved, and I wanted something—hey, we all do that.

> Adams's doctrine regarding friends and enemies dovetailed with the *Post*'s vindictive attitude toward critics, whether it was Paul Newman or a local media outlet.

MICHAEL SHAIN, television editor, 1978–1993, 1996–2013: Television cared to death what newspapers said about them. So I was always very welcome. I never had any trouble until, well . . . every once in a while, there would be an ordered hit. Channel Five, pre-Fox, when it was owned by Metromedia, had some story on its *10 O'Clock News* knocking down a *Post* story and doing it with great glee and gusto—that the *Post* had gotten it wrong. They went out of their way to denigrate the paper. The next morning, Roger met me coming in the door. He said, "Dear boy, I need you to find a story that will piss in Channel Five's shoe."

> The comics, games, and other content from features syndicates may have seemed trivial relative to the rest of the *Post*, but woe to the editor who changed or eliminated one of the regulars, and to those who answered the phones.

CHARLIE CARILLO: Sometimes when I was on the city desk people would call up crying if the word jumble was wrong. "I can't get five across!" And it really was not a tough jumble. It was like, "C–blank–T" and there's a picture of a cat. But if people couldn't get it . . . This is part of the reason people buy the paper and nobody seems to know that.

DONNIE SUTHERLAND, city desk assistant, 1978–1988: Without notifying anybody, someone decided to throw [long-running comic strip] "Mary Worth" out the window and put "Garfield," this cat cartoon, in. We couldn't operate for a week, the phones were ringing off the hook. "Mary Worth" people were aggressive. [Perhaps because of the ruckus, "Mary Worth" and "Garfield" shared the comics pages into 1994.]

> Along with serving as in-house newspaper for the punk music scene, the *Post* inspired downtown visual artists, too, including Keith Haring, Martin Wong, and Andy Warhol. Warhol had used tabloid images in his work for years.

PAIGE POWELL, former associate publisher, *Interview* magazine: The *Post* was a bible for Andy in a way. Both Andy and Fred Hughes [Warhol's business manager] said to me, pretty much at the beginning, when I started working at *Interview*, "You need to read the columns so you know what's going on." Andy loved gossip. And he loved the gossip in the *Post*.

SUSAN MULCAHY: Andy always wanted to know the gossip that wasn't in the paper, what we couldn't print.

VINCENT FREMONT, former vice president, Andy Warhol Enterprises: The *New York Post* came up with great headlines. And it was trashy, which was an allure for us at Andy Warhol Studio. In the 1980s, Andy revisited making headline paintings. He was always fascinated with headlines. It really goes back—there was "129 Die in Jet," that painting from 1962, it was hand-painted. And there was a *New York Post* painting from 1961—"A Boy for Meg."

Warhol created a number of paintings using Murdoch-era headlines, including a series done in collaboration with Keith Haring that built upon the *Post*'s coverage of a big Madonna story. When nude photos of the pop star surfaced in July 1985, a month before her wedding to Sean Penn, the *Post* ran a wood with her reaction.

JIM FARBER, former music critic, New York *Daily News*: This was a really great moment in Madonna's career when old [nude] photos of hers were used, this must have been in the '80s, in *Penthouse* and *Playboy*. Madonna came out and did something that was really, really smart, that people didn't do at that time, but probably would know to do now, she said: "I'm not ashamed." I believe that was the *New York Post* front page, Madonna saying "I'm not ashamed." She kind of redefined nudity.

VINCENT FREMONT: Keith Haring and Andy collaborated on [a series of] *Post* headline paintings and took them to the wedding of Madonna and Sean Penn. A whole group of people flew out. Andy did the silkscreen, and then Keith painted on top. They did six paintings, and brought out, I think it was four paintings. They finished the paintings very close to departure and gave them as wedding gifts. After Andy died, somebody came to 22 East 33rd Street [Warhol's last studio address] with one of those paintings, wanting to get it authenticated. I called the FBI because we knew it was stolen. I told the person when they came back, "Agent so-and-so would like to talk to you." The stolen painting was one of Madonna's that Andy and Keith gave her. I believe the FBI returned the painting to her. Much later, Brigid Berlin [a Warhol confidante] did needlepoint of *New York Post* and New York *Daily News* headlines, like "Bad Heir Day" [about the son of socialite and philanthropist Brooke Astor]. There's also a time capsule from 1977 [at the Warhol museum in Pittsburgh] that has a lot of *New York Post*s.

PAIGE POWELL: Andy liked quick reads. It wasn't his regular thing to read long novels. He liked really spicy quick reads. I don't necessarily mean a paragraph or two, longer than that, but I never saw him reading the *New Yorker*—not to say that he didn't—but it was luscious to him to read the *New York Post*.

18 | THE WOLVES OF SOUTH STREET

Bad Boys on Deadline

Women like News UK CEO Rebekah Brooks would eventually join the C-suites of Rupert Murdoch's news operations, but in the final decades of the twentieth century, men—all of them Caucasian—exclusively occupied the upper ranks of his organization. They oversaw a workplace often brutal in its treatment of women and minorities. Two of Murdoch's longest-running and most loyal associates were fellow Australians: Adam "Curly" Brydon, a decorated World War II flying ace, held several positions at the *Post*, including general manager and vice president for operations; and E. George "Old Blue Rinse" Viles had helped broker Murdoch's first US purchase, the *San Antonio Express-News*, and later served as publisher of *New York* magazine. At 210 South Street, both men were viewed as Murdoch enforcers with ambiguous company roles.

CHARLIE CARILLO, reporter, columnist, 1978–1993: Curly Brydon was a World War II hero. Once, there was some kind of union thing, and he came down and said, "All of you, get back to work, and I mean this minute." It was almost like the headmaster of a school. It's the only time I'd ever heard him speak. I had a feeling Murdoch liked keeping him around. He was sort of like Luca Brasi [from *The Godfather*].

JAMES BRADY, creator of Page Six, 1977; Page Six editor, 1980–1982: "Old Blue Rinse," George Viles, functioned as the general manager of the company. He was a Rupert warhorse from Australia. He had gray hair that was sort of tinted blue. Adam "Curly" Brydon had been a wing commander during the war in the Australian Air Force [and had a metal plate in his skull to show for it]. Dunleavy had a nickname, too—"Street Dog." [Within the pages of the *Post*, Dunleavy was sometimes referred to as "Mr. Blood and Guts."]

KEN CHANDLER, editor in chief, publisher, 1978–1986, 1993–2002: George was a bit of an Australian John Gotti character. Everybody was a little bit afraid of him. He lived up to that reputation. He enjoyed it. He was Rupert Murdoch's heavy when they were doing union negotiations. He'd send George in to pound his fist on the table.

GREG GALLO, executive sports editor, 1977–1989, 1994–2009: George Viles was—I don't want to say a bodyguard, but he was a protector. He was the guy who [could] get it done. Way before, he was like a lifeguard, an Adonis on the beach in Australia. Curly was more serious, almost like a silent assassin. When we were at the *Star*, Murdoch was trying to get into supermarkets, and he sent George to talk to the unions so they could sell the *Star* where it's sold today— everywhere. They were being shut out. Murdoch was a foreigner, and they were just ignoring [his attempts]. George went down there and whatever magic happened, happened. He got deals done.

MARSHA KRANES, rewrite, editor, 1974–2005: George Viles. I just loved his name. And he was. I remember Curly Brydon, too. I disliked all of them. They were just strutting pricks.

KEN CHANDLER: Curly Brydon was a pain in the neck to me, because when I was managing editor, and basically in charge of production of the paper at night for the next morning, we were always a little bit late locking up the paper, because that's what we do. Curly would come up from the press room, stand over my shoulder, and yell at me, "We can't sell fucking papers unless we print fucking papers."

CHARLIE CARILLO: For the Australians and the English, the city began at around 14th Street and ended at 96th Street. Then you have the outer boroughs where weird things happen, like baseball games and airports. These guys, they drank on the East Side. They lived on the Upper East Side, that was their whole existence. Some lived on Long Island, like Dunleavy. [And several Murdoch stalwarts lived on Roosevelt Island, off Manhattan's East Side.]

KEN CHANDLER: The Australians had been with Murdoch for much longer than the Brits because Murdoch had been in the UK for a shorter period of time. People like Neal Travis [a native of New Zealand] and Dunleavy had been with him almost since the beginning. So he was very loyal to the Australians. I don't think there was any bias against the Brits. If anything, I would say he might have been a little more willing to listen to advice from people who'd worked on Fleet Street, just because it was such a competitive place.

DAVID SCHNEIDERMAN, former editor in chief, publisher, CEO, *The Village Voice*: When I became publisher of the *Voice* the first time, I went down to the *Post* to present the budget. I got all dressed up, coat and tie. I knew the people sitting around the table waiting for Rupert to come in: [Donald] Kummerfeld and Marty [Singerman] and all those characters. Rupert comes in, and I see that three-quarters of them—all men—are wearing blue shirts with white collars, including Rupert. I said, "I didn't know there was a dress code." One of the virtues of being from the *Voice* was they expected you to be a little bit of a wise guy. Marty said, "What do you mean?" I said, "Everybody has this white-collared shirt." Rupert laughed. He thought it was really funny. Then Rupert wanted to know why we ran abortion ads in the *Voice*. I said, "Because it's legal." He said, "Do you have to run them?" I said, "Why wouldn't we run them?" Then I made up some numbers, I said, "They bring in $50,000 a year." He said, "Okay, fine, run them." Then he went off on this reminiscence about how he had hired somebody to spy on Lord Rothermere [a rival press baron in England] and his girlfriend. He went into this out of nowhere. That was the Rupert that existed I think before he came to this country. Of course, it came back to bite him with the [phone hacking by reporters in the UK]. But he was getting a huge kick out of telling stories about spying on these guys, and then he would let them know what he had found out, just to say: leave me alone, and I'll leave you alone.

Though she had no editorial clout, one female holdover from the Schiff era remained powerful at the *Post* and had Murdoch's respect.

MARSHA KRANES: Miss Gerry was the boss of the building, everybody cowered in her presence. She apparently had a relative who was a painter and he painted the building. It took him a whole year, and then he started all over. He had a lifetime job just painting and repainting the building. I don't know what she had on who, but she was something else. Then at one point I met her socially out here, in the Hamptons. And she was delightful and totally nonthreatening.

SUSAN MULCAHY, Page Six editor, 1978–1985: The story was always that Miss Gerry was the only person in the building Murdoch was afraid of.

TONY MANCINI, reporter, 1958–1978: [Miss] Gerry made the transition to the Murdoch regime very easily. And they treasured her.

CHARLIE CARILLO: Miss Gerry was like a jukebox. Big square heavy. She was in charge of a lot of things, like annoying things you'd need, requisitions for pens and whatever else. Annie Aquilina sent me to her office, and when I showed up at the door, she says, "What the fuck do you want?" Whatever I needed, she said, "You're going to have to talk to Hal," and I said, "Who's Hal?" She says, "You know who I mean. He looks like a dick." When I found Hal, he was this bald-headed guy with a turtleneck up high, and I realized, she's right—he looks like a dick. So, Miss Gerry had an unusual accuracy to her. That's how I met her. I got to like her. She lived with Chuck Caruso [chief makeup editor, who helped run the composing room], and I loved Chuck.

GREG GALLO: You'd go into her office, and she always had something for you. Cookies, raincoats. I don't know where she got this stuff. She probably got it from Chuck Caruso, but I remember, "You need a raincoat? I give it to you, twenty bucks." I said, "Okay, I'll take a raincoat." I'd take my kids down there when they were little and she'd always have stuff for them, little toys and cookies. She was as gruff as could be, but a velvet glove, she had. She was there for you when you needed it. She was a great lady.

> Some of the men who ran the *Post* lorded their power over female staffers, especially the young. It was not like the Schiff era, when the lion's share of women took no shit.

MARIANNE GOLDSTEIN, assistant city editor, 1979–1993: When I started at the *Post*, there was only one woman on the news desk. She was never promoted upwards. There were no women editors.

AMY PAGNOZZI, reporter, columnist, 1979–1993: I was called a cunt out loud in the newsroom a couple of times. I didn't really take it seriously. To me, that's not sexual harassment. That's just general bad manners.

ERIC FETTMANN, associate editorial page editor, columnist, 1976–1991, 1993–2019: Under Murdoch, it was very much a boys club except for chicks who were regular guys.

RAMONA GARNES, copy editor, 1978–1990, 2000–2004: My first week at the *Post*, Dunleavy comes over to me, all charming and bright-eyed, and he says, "So, what do you want to be when you grow up?" I go, "I want to be a reporter." He says to me, "You'll never make group 8 [the Newspaper Guild employment category that included reporters] if you don't sleep with me." That is a direct quote. I thought he was joking. Silly me.

AMY PAGNOZZI: John Van Doorn kept trying to sleep with me, but honestly, we were friends and I never felt like anything was presented to me in a quid pro quo way. Jerry Tallmer harassed me also. He put a lot of pressure on me, but I just took it as—you say no, and that's that. I was able to stick up for myself. I don't know why. But it was never presented to me in some kind of casting couch way. God forbid it ever had, I don't know what I would have done. If somebody had said to me, a year in advance of getting a column: you can have a column if you bop so and so. I mean, Jesus, if that's the path of least resistance?

JAMI BERNARD, chief movie critic, 1978–1993: One reporter was complaining about a young woman [in the newsroom] saying, "She's such a Valium." I figured out by osmosis what I was supposed to be. I was not supposed to be a downer. I had to be fun. I had to be smart and good at my job. But I also had to be sexy and kind of available. It's hard to explain to generations today. It wasn't like you had to give your body so that you would get promoted. It was more like to be accepted and to get training and to get stories, you had to be what they wanted you to be. Which, for a woman, was smart, vivacious, sexy—someone who can drink with the guys.

DIANA MAYCHICK, entertainment writer, 1978–1989: Women were sort of second-class citizens. They would commend women if they did a really good job, but in their mind, they thought it was pure luck if a woman got a good story; [they thought] if it hadn't been a woman, they would have gotten a better story.

AMY PAGNOZZI: Being sexually harassed and discriminated against, to my mind, was not as bad as being intellectually denigrated 24/7, which is the experience I had with Dunleavy.

JAMI BERNARD: Bill Hoffmann once said to me, some years later, "You have to understand. It was a candy store." He was talking about how the men looked at us. Like they could help themselves to all these young women.

AMY PAGNOZZI: Of all the fucking that went on there, I don't think it ever did any woman any good.

MARCY SOLTIS, copy editor, 1976–2014: You wouldn't have been able to find a copy-girl who had not had some sort of contact with sexual harassment in the office. It was so prevalent, a *Mad Men* sort of atmosphere.

JAMI BERNARD: I never slept with Dunleavy but most everyone else did. He was always flirtatious. I found it fun. But I also had some resentment because of the power differential. There was a wall of offices that were half glass. Once, I was in one—the one with a conference table—with Dunleavy. I don't remember why. He closed the door. I knew he was a person who cannot turn down a dare. I said, "Take it out and put it on the table and let me see it." I knew he'd have to. It was a half-glass wall [from the middle up], so anyone could have seen in, but they didn't. I was ready with my line. I said something like, "Is that all, is that it?" I [wanted to] humiliate him in a fun kind of way. He's trying to stretch it out with his thumbs. I thought that was funny. I wanted the power difference to go the other way. I wanted to be the one in control.

RAMONA GARNES: I trusted Ken [Chandler] and Roger [Wood] because neither one of them ever hit on me.

JAMI BERNARD: I wish there had been a stronger bond among the women to protect each other.

> The type of harassment experienced by women at the *Post* was not unusual for the time, but one editor's behavior stood out as close to criminal. Yet he stayed employed at the *Post* for years in a series of managerial positions. His aberrant proclivities emerged even before the paper moved to 210 South Street in 1970, though many women from the Schiff era had no idea.

MARIANNE GOLDSTEIN: Oh my god. Every time I see a #MeToo story, I think of Alan Whitney.

DAVID SEIFMAN, City Hall bureau chief and political editor, 1973–2019: That's a guy who should have gone to jail.

CHERYL BENTSEN, feature writer, 1976–1977: Alan Whitney was overweight, balding, glasses, maybe something wrong with one eye. Looking somewhere between Oliver Hardy—the fat one from Laurel and Hardy—and Winston Churchill.

KENNY MORAN, outdoor sports columnist, 1972–2013: He used to chase the copygirls all night long. He was brilliant at what he did. But he also was a deviant.

MARCY SOLTIS: He would sometimes wear these red devil horns and carry a trident.

DOMINICK MARRANO, chief paginator, 1971–2008: Whitney was a very bright guy who could talk about anything. But he was just off the fucking rails. Giving the copygirls panties. I don't know how far he actually went, but he went over the line in terms of sexual harassment. He would also sit cross-legged on his desk playing a flute. It was like he was from another world.

MILTON GOLDSTEIN, copy editor, 1974–current: He used to hang out at the Cedar Tavern, and he'd hire copygirls from there to work per diem shifts overnight. He would want to spank them. Some young women would play along with him and some not.

MARCY SOLTIS: Alan Whitney was responsible for scheduling all the nighttime and lobster shift copypeople, who were almost exclusively copygirls. He also scheduled the wire room and news clerks, dictationists, news desk assistants—

who answered the phones—makeup people for various departments; and the editorial drivers. He decided when you worked and in what department. Every one or two weeks, he posted the schedule at the entrance to the composing room above where the AP, Reuters, and UPI machines were spewing out wire photos. When he posted the schedule, all the guys who worked at night would rush over to the schedule to see which copygirls would be working which nights. When I worked there as a copyperson, there was no such thing as a copyboy on the lobster shift. There were only copygirls.

JOYCE WADLER, feature writer, 1974–1977: It wasn't until years after I left the paper that I became aware of Al Whitney spanking and terrorizing the copygirls. My experience was that the *Post* was a place that was very nurturing to writers and allowed you to be yourself. I knew that Alan Whitney was kind of a lunatic. He wore devil horns, or one night, Mickey Mouse ears. A few years ago, I wrote a story that was sort of a reaction to #MeToo. It was about my concern that it would not allow for a give-and-take in the workplace, which had been very much part of the old *New York Post*. I started poking around because I'd heard these stories [about Whitney] and it wasn't funny. He really *was* spanking copygirls on their birthday, and demanding they spank him. He'd give his name and number to women he met on the street and say, "Hey, if you want a job, come be a copygirl." If you didn't go along with him, you wouldn't get promoted, or you wouldn't get work. So, while I was having a perfectly lovely time being a feature writer and not feeling intimidated by anyone except Al Ellenberg if he didn't like my story, other women were having a terrible time. I asked Anna Quindlen if she was aware of this, and she said, "No." Lindsy Van Gelder said, "No." She said she felt terrible. She wished the girls had come to her. She knew Whitney was a loon—one day he dropped a pair of panties on her desk for her birthday, but she just knocked them off.

MARCY SOLTIS: One night, in the summer of '76, I was working in the wire room, where we often used these metal strips as straightedges to separate wire stories and bring them to the appropriate people. Alan came in, took one of these metal strips, and lightly hit me. It wasn't across my buttocks—it was on my arm or somewhere on my back. I got really upset. I said something along the lines of "I don't know what that was, but I don't want it to ever happen again." He stormed out of the wire room, and I was immediately taken off the schedule. I had not been hired full-time yet, and I thought: I may not be working here anymore. After a period of time, though, things smoothed over, and I was back.

CAROLE LEE, assistant to James Wechsler, photo syndication editor, 1963–1993: When the *Post* was on West Street, Alan and I were walking down this dark corridor, and he grabbed my behind. I slugged him. His glasses fell off and broke. I went running to Jimmy [Wechsler] crying. I knew I was going to lose my job, because how could I slug an editor? I told him what happened. He went down to see Paul Sann. They said, "It's okay. He forgives you." I was very happy that he had forgiven me, but I never talked to him or looked at him again. On my birthday for the next, at least ten years, I got a brown paper bag on my chair with a pair of lace French underwear. He always delivered them when I wasn't there.

ERIC FETTMANN: At the beginning of each shift, he put candy out. I reached for a piece once and got immediately upbraided by [Michael] Hechtman: "That's copygirls only." It is surprising that the [Newspaper] Guild didn't make more of a stink about it.

DICK BELSKY, metropolitan editor, 1970–1989: Lou Colasuonno [who eventually became editor of the *Post*] tells this story about Murdoch coming into the newsroom. I don't know if Lou had met Murdoch before. Alan Whitney was the day managing editor at the time, and Lou had the desk next to him. Rupert comes in and says something like, "Who's in charge here?" Somebody points to Whitney, who is in one of his outfits. He's got a whip or something. Rupert looks at him in just absolute horror. As Lou tells it—it was kind of a slow-motion accident. All he could think of was edging backwards because he knew that that image of Whitney was going to be frozen in Rupert's mind, and he didn't want that image to have him in the background.

TOM KREUZER, editorial driver, 1972–1978: It's about twelve o'clock at night, Alan Whitney is at the city editor's desk and Kenny Moran is the desk assistant. They get a phone call. "This is the FALN [Puerto Rican separatist organization], and we have posted a communication at 56th and Lexington Avenue, taped underneath the telephone." They're like, "Tommy, you got to go up there, and take this guy [with you]"—I forget his name, aging hippie; he was a copy editor or something. We drive up there, I'm all excited; this twenty-two-year-old kid. I find this thing [taped in the phone booth]. I feel like I'm on *NCIS* or something. We go back and they write this story. Later on, two FBI agents show up, clean-cut guys, short haircuts, they have windbreakers with "FBI" on it. How did the FBI know about [the story]? I always assumed the *Post* did its civic duty by notifying the proper authorities. They walk in and they're like, "Who's in charge?" It's now 4:30 in the morning. Kenny Moran points to Alan Whitney, who's editing copy, and has two devil horns suction-cupped to his bald forehead. These straitlaced guys are looking at this guy, who's weird-looking even without the horns. They say, "This is serious business." Kenny says, "He's in fucking charge." They go over to him and they do an investigation talking to a man with plastic devil horns coming out of his forehead.

CYNTHIA FAGEN, reporter, 1976–1986: I ignored him. It was a male-dominated place. I think he knew who to pick, the weaker ones in the flock. I think he thought he was being funny and that everybody enjoyed it. But he was not funny. And no one enjoyed it.

MARIANNE GOLDSTEIN: If you were one of Alan's "favorites," he would give you underwear for your birthday. Sadly, I never made it into that category. I think his wife went to Barnard, and I don't know that any of the Barnard grads were treated like that.

MILTON GOLDSTEIN: Ultimately it ended when a copykid who eventually became a photographer, Mary McLoughlin, complained to Lucy Lambert in HR. Lucy was aghast. They didn't fire him, but they took away scheduling the copykids. At that point, I was a full-time desk assistant. They gave that job to me.

CAROLE LEE: Mary is the one who went to human resources. She was afraid—her birthday was coming, and she was scheduled for a spanking. He was apparently quite mean to whomever decided not to be spanked. I remember one of the girls saying, "If I don't, I'm going to lose my job." He was suspended, I think for two weeks, after Mary blew the whistle. Two weeks!

MILTON GOLDSTEIN: I immediately started getting grief from copypeople who felt I was slighting them. One young woman broke into tears because I gave her two shifts one week instead of four. I said, screw it, and turned the scheduling job over to Vinnie Musetto, who was happy to take it.

AMY PAGNOZZI: The funny thing was, they put Vinnie [who also had a history of abusive behavior toward women] in Alan Whitney's place when Alan got in trouble for all the sexual harassment!

MILTON GOLDSTEIN: Alan's behavior led to his downfall eventually. He was demoted and then finally left under who knows what circumstances. He lived at 3 East 9th Street, just off Fifth. After Alan left the *Post*, one day Myron gets a call from the NYPD. Alan had died in his apartment. The neighbors complained about a stench so the police went in and they found some things from the *New York Post*. They called the city desk: "You know an Alan Whitney?" Myron said, "Of course."

Rules governing other sorts of interoffice entanglements did not exist.

DICK BELSKY: There was so much sex going on there—a lot of it, most of it, under the table. Somebody once said, "I put together a list of everybody in the office who's *not* having an affair with somebody else in the office." She said, "It's a very short list."

GEORGE ARZT, City Hall bureau chief, 1968–1986: There was a very quiet quality about the Schiff era. The Murdoch era was right out of a movie. It was *The Front Page, Deadline-USA*, it was all the tabloid movies you could ever think of. We were hard-drinking, and, though I didn't partake, there was a lot of womanizing. You open up the wrong closet and you're gonna see something you don't want to see.

DONNIE SUTHERLAND, city desk assistant, 1978–1988: I would try to connect interoffice relationships in a diagram—a Margaret Mead–type thing. I did take anthropology in school. I would diagram the female and the male symbol, and this person made it with this person who made it with that person. You got to see there were certain alpha males. Certain editors would have a bevy of connections in this diagram. People would say, "Don, you gotta get rid of that. You can't circulate that."

CHARLIE CARILLO: I was going to write a book about office relationships that break up and it was going to be called *Goodbye Forever, See You Monday*. I never got around to it 'cause the title says the whole thing. When I was answering the phones at the *Post*, I knew everybody who was involved with anybody because you'd pick up the phone and there'd be a whisper. You'd say, "Yes, he's there," and "Hey, pick up number three." At the time it was Donnie Sutherland and I writing out everything on paper and hanging on to these secrets. It's a very incestuous bunch because you have to date other journos. They're the only ones who understand why, five minutes to a date, you have to say, "I can't meet you, there's a shooting in Brooklyn," or "I can't meet you, there's a water main break in the Bronx." Relationships were people working crazy hours, breaking up, coming together, moving out. And Bernie Bard's chugging along all those years with the same wife. I said to him one time, "Bernie, how do you do it?" He took the cigarette out of his mouth and said, "The key to a long and happy marriage: do not get emotionally involved." Then he went back to writing.

AMY PAGNOZZI: That's how I met Clive [Barnes]. I used to take his dictation. Susan Friedland told me Clive was gay. We were out to lunch, and he was kind of pawing me. It took me a long time to catch on because he was supposed to be gay. I was only twenty or twenty-one when I met Clive. I kept it a secret for a long time because he was still married. He told me he [and his wife Trish] had an open marriage but I still didn't want people at the office to know that I was sleeping with a married person senior to me. Once we were living together, I became open about it.

JOANNE WASSERMAN, reporter, 1977–1986: When I went out with Belsky, nobody was cheating. But he was my boss, so we tried to keep it quiet for a while. The best thing that happened was when Amy Pagnozzi started to go out with Clive Barnes. Then it was like, nobody cared about JoAnne Wasserman and Dick Belsky because that was way more interesting.

JAMI BERNARD: There was this mentally retarded—as we said in those days— young woman, homeless, who used to hang out under the overhang of the FDR [across from 210 South Street], where the cars were parked. There was one reporter—you can't use his name—who used to go down pretty often and pay her, I don't know, five bucks for either a blowjob or handjob—something to do with his dick. I found that so disgusting and revolting, and I called him on it. He gave this smirk. He said, "We're both getting something out of it." I never looked at him the same way again. I don't know that I told anyone about it. Who are you going to tell? Everyone was doing something.

Despite the inherent challenges of tabloid romances, some traditional relationships bloomed in the *Post* newsroom as well, including one dating back to the Schiff era.

MARCY SOLTIS: Working at the *Post* was also a very personal experience because of Andy [Soltis]. We were members of the same chess club in Greenwich Village. Andy introduced me to the paper, and the only way to really start was to work on the lobster shift. After my first shift, I wanted to thank him, and asked if he wanted to go to see *All the President's Men*. We went to see the movie, and I took him to McDonald's after that. There may have been fries involved. That night changed my life. I worked lobster while Andy worked days, and he would leave these, like, love notes in my mailbox. They were usually typewritten on whatever rickety manual typewriter he was using, talking about stuff in the office, people we knew in chess, what we were planning to do the next day. I loved getting these letters. I still have a box full of them. I would leave notes for him, too. Another thing Andy would do is, there were signs with graphically raised letters outside of various rooms and departments, like sports, the restrooms, or the library, and he would leave pennies for me in the rounded letters of the signs. As I went about my job in the middle of the night, I would collect these pennies.

BILLY HELLER, librarian, deputy features editor, 1978–1988, 2000–2020: Susan Mulcahy gave me tickets to Whoopi Goldberg's one-woman show. I asked Jennifer [Shaw], who at the time was still a clerk in the business department, to go with me. There was a party afterward at Tavern on the Green. I covered it for Page Six. We ran into Joan Kennedy. I had met her when she and Ted came to the *Post*. I said, "I met you once before," blah, blah, blah. One of the *Post* freelancers took a picture of me and Joan, which I still have as a souvenir of my first date with Jennifer. In March [2022], we'll be married thirty-four years.

Though Dolly Schiff's *Post* made more of an effort at diversity than many papers, its newsroom was still not a model of inclusion. The situation did not improve when Murdoch took over.

DICK BELSKY: All newspaper staffs back then were so one-sided, though at the *Post* we did have a lot of women. But we had very few people of color. I think we were looking for somebody at one point who was Spanish-speaking. It was very piecemeal in those days, not like now, where it's very clearly on everybody's mind. The [backgrounds of] the staff affects the coverage. That's the argument for having a diversified staff. If we're a bunch of white males sitting around, we're not particularly aware of what's going on in a community that's not ours.

> The newsroom environment proved problematic for people of color, who confronted racism on a regular basis. Some left the *Post* quickly. Others found ways to deal with it.

LENORE DAVIS, photographer, 1980–1993: I made it to the *Village Voice*, which Rupert Murdoch owned. Fred [McDarrah, longtime *Voice* photographer] liked me. They would send me on stories thinking that, being Black, I knew the worst of the world. They would send me on these drug stories. I would knock on the door, like the good little girl that I was, saying, "Excuse me, can I take pictures while you're sticking yourself with a needle filled with heroin?" I got dramatic pictures. That's how I got to the *Post*. I started on August 6, 1980. When I was on tryout, some people tried to sabotage me. Everybody wanted their cousin to get the job. I was hired, but I felt like a prostitute because the *Post* was so anti-Black. Do you remember the Atlanta child killings? A bunch of [Black] children were killed in Atlanta [from 1979 to 1981] and later on, they put all the murders on one guy. I would go into the office and hear somebody say, "Oh, the great white hope has hit again."

GREGG MORRIS, reporter, 1984–1988: I got hired on a temporary basis. I wasn't looking for a job. I was looking for a paycheck. I was working part-time, like three or four days a week, and I was writing this book. I was always getting into squabbles [at the *Post*], and so I refused to have my name on stories. I just didn't like the way they were fucking over my stories. I would submit them, and they would change them and make them into something else, particularly if there was a racial element. I got tired of it. And then, there was this thing with the *Daily News* and the *Post*. The *Daily News* got hit with a big EEOC [Equal Employment Opportunity Commission] lawsuit, complaint. They were exposed for being racist, and Jimmy Breslin wrote this column. His thing was that there were no Black reporters at the *New York Post*, and the *Daily News* got hammered. [The *Daily News* reached an out-of-court settlement with four Black journalists.] Breslin was upset that the *Daily News* had more reporters and copy editors of color than the *New York Post*, and nobody was saying anything negative about the *New York Post*. I'm paraphrasing, but then he wrote: they got this Black guy over there and his byline's not showing up on his stories. Someone should investigate the *Post*. Now the *Post* was under pressure because Breslin was hammering them about this alleged Black reporter. So I had to become full-time.

RAMONA GARNES: His first day, I see Gregg coming into the newsroom. And of course, seeing a Black person walk in, we caught each other's eye, and kind of nodded to each other. Later, when we had a chance to talk, part of why we became friends is, at least back then in professional situations, if there were like one thousand white people in a room, and two Black people, a lot of times the other Black person would not speak to you. Gregg said: "You spoke to me." I said: "*You* spoke to *me*." We said, "We're on the same plane here."

GREGG MORRIS: Ramona and I talked a lot about the stuff that she had to put up with, and Lenore and I talked about it. I don't think the three of us ever talked about it together. And there was a very attractive young Black woman, very dark, who kept insisting, "I'm not Black. I'm British." She used to do it in the newsroom. It drove me crazy, but that was her thing. I kept my mouth shut.

RAMONA GARNES: I dug in my heels. If they don't want my Black eyeballs looking at or writing their copy, I'm going to make sure that that's exactly what I do. I wanted to be a general assignment reporter. Then, one night, at the Mudd Club, I was talking to [copy editor] Neil Landry, and he said, "Why would you want to be a reporter? You'll get called at four in the morning to go cover a fire in the Bronx. You should become a copy editor." That's when I said, "I want to be a copy editor."

GREGG MORRIS: A phone call would come in to the desk about a car accident or something. I would get assigned to cover it. There was a photo editor—this happened several times—he would say, "Is the victim white?" I would say, "What difference does it make?" He'd say, "Is the victim white?" I'd say, "I'm not going to tell you." I did this several times. Finally, the photo editor said, "Does this guy know where he's working? He's working at the *Post*."

RAMONA GARNES: I used to tell Gregg Morris that my attitude [in dealing with racism at the *Post*] was to become water. Water can be rough; it can absolutely destroy things. But it can also quietly and slowly carve out the Grand Canyon. My attitude at the *Post* was, be the Colorado River, just quietly and slowly make this place my Grand Canyon. To get what I wanted meant being agreeable, being friendly. It meant not pissing them off. I'm gonna piss them off by becoming a copy editor, not by hating them.

GREGG MORRIS: Dunleavy was pissed that I got hired. Even though other editors wanted to hire a Black reporter because Breslin was pounding them, Dunleavy hadn't approved it. I had told another editor—I think Roger Wood—that I had talked to Dunleavy, and he was okay with it, but I never talked to him. I was on the elevator with Ramona, and Dunleavy got on. He was in the back, and he was mumbling. I don't think he was drunk at the time. Ramona and I were talking, and all of a sudden I heard him say "nigger." I turned around. My mind went blank. A few moments later, I could hear Ramona screaming at me, "Gregg, don't! Gregg, don't!" I had cornered Dunleavy in the elevator, and I guess it looked like I was getting ready to beat the shit out of him. I backed off, and when we got down to the floor, everybody sort of did a nervous laugh. It spread the next day that Dunleavy and I had an incident.

RAMONA GARNES: I'll say this about the Brits and the Aussies: they were upfront. There was no smile in your face and stab you in the back. Like the time Dunleavy said to Gregg Morris, "There are too many niggers in the newsroom." Gregg got angry. I think I held my arm out, like to stop Gregg. I might even have said, "Don't hit him. Don't do it, Gregg."

GREGG MORRIS: There was one young Black guy who was on some kind of trial. I think he lasted a week. I remember talking to him, and he said he didn't like it there. He wasn't comfortable. He didn't know why I was able to stay there and deal with it.

ERIC FETTMANN: Did Dunleavy hate Black people? It depended. He certainly didn't hate Baz [Bamigboye, who in the 1980s was a New York correspondent for one of Murdoch's British papers]. Baz was a friend, Baz was Black. If you were one of the guys, it didn't matter what color you were, but if you were certain colors, you had to prove yourself first. You weren't given the benefit of the doubt.

CHARLIE CARILLO: Murdoch definitely was very plain about how he felt. Which is interesting 'cause he married a Chinese woman, and I think his daughter married a Black guy. So Murdoch inadvertently became the UN.

GREGG MORRIS: The whole race thing for me is, was, complicated. Murdoch and some editors there, no doubt they were racist. There were others I thought might be prejudiced, but I had a working relationship with them. I couldn't have hung on to the job as long as I did without those relationships. People with prejudices don't go out of their way to hurt you. Racists do. That is one of my mantras for surviving.

DAVID NG, associate managing editor, 1980–1993: The whole issue about diversity, and how we deal with each other in the workplace. What we did then could not exist now. The smoking in the newsroom alone would have been considered a violation of law and protocol. The thing that I've always taken to heart, and that I am very grateful for, was the intent. Dunleavy, for all his politically incorrect language, always treated me with an incredible amount of respect, and protection, and comfort.

19 | ARMPIT OF
THE WORLD

Life and Crime Around
210 South Street

Every issue of the *New York Post* was conceived of, constructed in, and printed at 210 South Street. As a result, an unusual and sometimes intimidating collection of unions, machinery, craftsmen, and subcultures operated under its roof in a neighborhood that mirrored the tabloid's often lawless attitude.

CHARLIE CARILLO, reporter, columnist, 1978–1993: One driver used to say, "If you want to be a truck driver at the *Post*, you must have a criminal record. You didn't want anybody who's clean." There was always a rumor that the truck drivers kept a tank full of piranha in the building, and if anybody was giving them a hard time, union-wise, they would just dip their arm in the tank and wait until they saw the light—lost a little bit of flesh. Total bullshit. But what a great way to look at it.

FRED DICKER, Albany bureau chief, 1982–2016: A couple of times I got rides in the [*Post*] trucks going up to Albany. I would ride with these whack-job drivers. I don't remember exactly what we talked about—certainly we didn't talk about New York State politics. Supposedly, their union was kicked out of some Teamsters Union because they were even too corrupt for the Teamsters. You remember they would sell stuff in the newsroom—stolen goods off trucks? It was really something out of a Damon Runyon story.

DOMINICK MARRANO, chief paginator, 1971–2008: 210 South Street was in the armpit of the world. There was nothing else around there.

ANDY SOLTIS, rewrite, editor, 1967–2014: South Street was isolated. When the *Post* first moved there from West Street, they tried to get the city to provide a separate bus line to pick up people. The closest mass transit stop was the East Broadway stop on the F train, and that was a bit of a hike. 210 South Street had been the *Journal-American* building. [That newspaper closed in 1966.] It still had the [Hearst Corporation's] signature eagles on it. It was a terrible neighborhood then. Cars were stolen in the parking lot.

PETER VECSEY, columnist, basketball, 1977–1991, 1994–2012: I lived on 20th Street and First Avenue, but I would take my car down and park across the street under the bridge. I had two cars stolen. It took me two cars before I said, "Okay, that's it for me, taxis from now on." One time a guy calls me up and says, "Peter Vecsey?" I say, "Yeah." He says, "Where's your car?" I say, "It's parked across the street." He says, "Nah, I'm in the Bronx and they're burning it." I say, "WHAT?" The guy found some identification in the car—he was probably one of the guys burning it. They stole it, they took it apart, took the tires, the radio, everything, and they were burning it. He called to let me know. He's like, "Hey, I know who you are!" How can you not love the *Post*?

MICHAEL SHAIN, television editor, 1978–1993, 1996–2013: When you walked along the parking lot underneath the East Side Drive, you had to make sure you didn't step into something that would drop you straight into the river. There was nothing but like a four-by-four piece of wood that went along the edge of the river that kept cars from going in. Plus, that area really wasn't solid ground, it was jacked up over the river, and it was nothing but asphalt. A couple of times a year they would pull cars out of there that had driven off, on purpose, or by accident, and they were always looking for bodies in them.

JAMI BERNARD, chief movie critic, 1978–1993: It was almost like a horror movie setting—nothing around it, except the Fulton Fish Market a few blocks down. I worked nights. There were homeless camps under the FDR Drive sometimes, and then bodies, floaters, would wash up around there.

FRANK DiGIACOMO, Page Six co-editor, 1989–1993: Once you hit midsummer, the stench of the Fulton Fish Market would mix with the body odor and cigar smoke of the Italian guys in their wifebeaters who hung out in the park next to Knickerbocker Village. God help you if you came to work with a hangover.

AMY PAGNOZZI, reporter, columnist, 1979–1993: I loved the neighborhood. I liked working late at night; getting out at three in the morning and going to bars at the South Street Seaport that would have a fish-cutting counter on one side of the bar and the other side would be a bacon-and-eggs breakfast.

CHARLIE CARILLO: It kills me to think the old offices are a Manhattan Mini Storage now. I walked through Chinatown to get to the *Post*, and the things you'd see there. I remember these live fish in tanks. There was a guy with an ax cutting a giant carp like he was chopping a log on the street.

DIANA MAYCHICK, entertainment writer, 1978–1989: If it rained, there would be flooding—rivers of water in front of the building with lots of rats swimming. I had to walk through rats to get there.

PETER TOCCO, sports makeup, 1970–2013: When there was a really heavy rain, the water came into the building with all the vestiges of the neighborhood. It smelled. It wouldn't go through the swinging doors that were in the front, I guess because there was rubber on the bottom. But you had to go out and get your car, which was parked underneath East River Drive. If it wasn't floating away.

FRANK LoMONTE, compositor, 1966–2009: There was a little Italian bakery around the side [of the *Post* building] near the church. One day, I get an urge for cannoli, so I go down there. When the lady who ran the place went back to get it, I could see there was four or five slot machines in the backroom.

MICHAEL SHAIN: When I was courting my wife, I took her to the *Post* for the first time. It was a beautiful spring day. We walked out underneath the East River Drive and we're looking at the river. It's just beautiful, and across the river is Brooklyn, and over here is the Williamsburg bank tower, and da da da. I look up the street a little and I see two cops walking, with about six kids behind them. They're walking slowly toward us, maybe a block away, and I said, "Come on, we gotta go." She goes, "Why? It's so pretty." "No, no, no, we gotta go." What had happened was, in the spring, any bodies that had fallen or been thrown into the river came up. These cops had one of those grappling hooks—a six-foot, eight-foot thing—and were waiting for a body to get close enough to hook. The kids thought this was like the greatest entertainment they'd ever had. I was trying to impress this woman that I worked in a nice place. I wasn't able to get her away in time. Some guy floated right up to the edge of the bulkhead right there on South Street.

CHARLIE CARILLO: The Post Mortem at high tide on the East River—the rug would be squelching under your feet. They had the veal Parmesan special on Wonder Bread. It was not to be missed if you were young and single and didn't know anything about food. You could eat and drink there for about five dollars. Geraldine serving, Charlie at the stick, and in the same building as the *Post*—later it became the South Street Diner. [Though it seemed part of the paper, the bar, later diner, was actually in a small building next to 210 South Street.] But when it was the Post Mortem, it was terrific and seedy, the pressman and the truck drivers.

MARSHA KRANES, rewrite, editor, 1974–2005: I once ordered a drink at the Post Mortem. I forget the name of the woman who ran it. I ordered this scotch on the rocks or something and the drink came, with this big black ice cube. I said, "Ew, this is a dirty ice cube." She said, "It's what you get." I walked out and that was the only time I was in there.

DAVE BANKS, night managing editor, 1979–1981: In the middle of the night, like two in the morning, there was no one in accounts, and Dunleavy needed cash to send someone out of town to cover a breaking story. It was very much a cash economy in those days. Credit cards were few and far between, and not everybody accepted them. If you had to get a guy to Kennedy to get on a plane to fly out of state, you needed money. The only place Dunleavy was going to pick up four or five hundred dollars to fund the reporter was the Post Mortem downstairs. He had an arrangement with Geraldine [Gangi] and her husband [Charlie] that he could borrow money, but it was at a usurious interest rate. He had to refund them the following day. If he'd borrowed $500 it would be $30 or $40 interest when the account department opened. It was very short-term cash. I think it was mob money, frankly. If Rupert had realized that he was taking advantage of mafia money to run his newspaper, he probably would have been appalled. But that was Dunleavy's way of doing it.

KEN CHANDLER, editor in chief, publisher, 1978–1986, 1993–2002: Steve would go downstairs and get whatever he needed from Geraldine. In those days, most of the business was cash, so she would have a lot of cash down there. If she was mobbed up, I don't even think [Murdoch] would think about it for a minute. Well, if he was confronted with it by the district attorney, maybe he'd bother about it, but otherwise it's just a way of doing business, right?

ED BURNS, retired NYPD sergeant, former department spokesman: The Post Mortem became an adjunct of the city room. Geraldine knew everything in that neighborhood. She helped everybody. But the police had to be careful with her because she might steer you in the wrong direction. Was she mobbed up? You could use that metaphor for the entire neighborhood. It was an old-fashioned, hardworking Italian neighborhood.

AMY PAGNOZZI: Geraldine stabbed her husband in the stomach at one point. It was this whole South Street Seaport mafioso thing.

MATHEW J. MARI, attorney (who grew up in Knickerbocker Village): Geraldine and Charlie were anything but America's most loving couple. They had many verbal arguments—like every day—and many knock-down, drag-out physical fights in the street and at the bar. Geraldine won most of those battles but Charlie fought like a man and held his own.

CYNTHIA FAGEN, reporter, 1976–1986: Remember those marks in the bar at the Post Mortem? Those were from a hammer. Geraldine used to chase Charlie with a hammer.

DOMINICK MARRANO: Oh, yeah, [Knickerbocker Village] was mobbed up. So many connected people were living there, and so many of them actually worked at the *Post*, mostly in the trade unions. I didn't know any real racketeers who worked at the *Post* on the editorial side. Back in the day, they used to have sit-down meetings in the cafeteria on Sundays—different guys who were connected. The *Post* didn't print on Sundays then, but they all had keys to the building and they used to literally have meetings in the *Post* cafeteria.

JERRY CAPECI, reporter, organized crime, 1966–1986: I knew about Knickerbocker Village being mob. I knew that the neighborhood, Monroe Street, Monroe

Place, Cherry Street—gangsters lived there—but I did not hang out at any of those joints. For the most part, they were with the Bonanno crime family, but there were others. Al D'Arco was with the Lucchese family. But primarily the Bonanno crime family guys had a lock on Knickerbocker Village.

PETER TOCCO: You remember the park that was directly outside the building? There was a basketball court there. We would just go outside and play, fool around between editions or whatever. Sometimes the people that lived in the neighborhood objected to the fact that we were playing on their basketball court. These guys would come onto the court and say, "You have to get off the court." Some of the guys that worked at the *Post* would start to argue, and either Dom Marrano or myself or other people that knew how things went would say, "This is their court." They would say, "What do you mean, it's their court?" "Trust me, it's their court. Let's leave."

CHARLIE CARILLO: Once I was running—I had a story to tell, a notebook full of notes. I was heading to the door and a guy yelled at me, "Hey, kid." He'd come right from the airport. His car was filled with boxes. He said, "I got Armani suits here. What are you, 40? 42? 42 long?" I said, "I don't want a suit." "One-fifty come on, come on." I said, "I really don't want one," but every step I took toward the paper, the price went down: "One twenty-five, fifty dollars." He had to get rid of this swag, and I really should've bought a suit. My mother would have liked that.

PETER TOCCO: I once saw a guy across the street right by the [Knickerbocker Village] buildings. There was a truck. Obviously the truck had been hijacked. He took out a pistol and blew the lock off and opened it up: 12:30 in the afternoon.

KEN CHANDLER: When I first went to the *Post* and was working the lobster shift, there were guys who had nothing to do with the *Post*, who would come through the newsroom in the evening and take orders for VCRs, stereo systems, fresh lobster, all stuff that had fallen off trucks. I remember this being about eight or nine at night. You'd say, "I want a new nineteen-inch TV," or something. When they came the following week, they'd bring the goods with them, and you'd pay them cash. Anything that you would get on Amazon now, they would bring it in. They had a menu of what was currently available, and if you asked for something that wasn't on the menu, it might take three or four weeks to get it, but they would get it. The other thing was cigarettes. Thursday night, you'd get a carton of cigarettes without paying tax on them.

SUSAN MULCAHY, Page Six editor, 1978–1985: One Sunday I came in the back entrance and right outside were two guys with a truck and a van. They were taking TVs out of the truck and putting them in the van. They looked at each other, then at me, and one says, "You want one?" I said, "No, thank you."

PHILIP MESSING, reporter, 1978–1991, 1994–2016: There was this guy. He worked as a pressman for the *Post* and the *Times*. He served serious time, I can't recall for what exactly, something with a gun. He was scary. Cynthia [Fagen] knew him.

CYNTHIA FAGEN: True. In fact, one time he had just come back from Florida and was drinking at the Post Mortem. I said, offhandedly, I wanted to kill [Al] Ellenberg because he was being such an asshole. This guy—let's call him Tom—opened up his Pan Am travel bag and showed me wads of cash and a gun on top and asked, "Do you want me to kill him?" I adamantly, but kindly, declined. Then I ran to the pay phone and called Ellenberg. "Don't ask me any questions," I told him. "Just get out of there as quick as possible and use the back entrance."

CHARLIE CARILLO: One of the drivers lived a few blocks from me. He came to me one day and says, "My daughter worked for this doctor and the doctor hasn't paid her. I feel like breaking the guy's legs. Can you maybe do a story about this guy?" I said, "I don't know if we can do a story, but I can phone them and tell them I'm with the *New York Post*, say I'm asking him about a situation. If he owes your daughter the money, he'll probably say, it just slipped my mind and she'll get the money." He said, "That'd be nice, but I think I'm going to break his legs anyway." I said, "You want to give me the number?" He says, "Sit tight, sit tight." About a week later I saw him. He said, "She got her money." I thought: oh my god, somebody's on crutches.

DAN AQUILANTE, chief music critic, 1980–2012: I was not there for this, but heard the story a number of times. A lot of guys in the composing room had mob connections. Sometimes they had no-show jobs. They did more or less what they wanted. The printers had five minutes to wash up before their shift ended, and one day, one of them went to wash up a half hour early. Supposedly, his boss says, "Where are you going? You've still got thirty minutes to go." The guy pulled out a handgun, shot the time clock, and said, "It's time to go."

FRANK LOMONTE: He told you that, that son of a bitch! Down in the press room, they had a button man. Do you know what a button man is? He's the guy who pulls the trigger. The guy who shot the clock off the wall was his brother. He was ten minutes to quitting and ready to go out the door. Foreman said, "Look at the clock. You've still got ten minutes to go." The guy pulled out a gun and shot the clock off the wall. That's the truth.

KEN CHANDLER: During the time we were producing morning and afternoon editions, I was working from two in the afternoon till eleven at night. And after we locked up the first edition at about nine, Dunleavy, myself, and some others would go to [the social club] Marie's for a beer, and come back when the paper started coming off the press at ten. The reason I stopped going there was because one night, around '84 or '85, I came downstairs to walk over to Marie's, and the street was full of police cars with flashing lights. I don't know if it was the feds or who, but somebody raided it, and they wanted to catch *Post* people in there.

> The *Post* and the mob seemed inextricably linked, and in the 1980s, a crime boss emerged who captured the glamor and grit of the era and the tabloid aesthetic that Murdoch was selling to a growing audience. Gambino crime boss John Gotti—dubbed "The Dapper Don" by the *Post*, and later the "Teflon Don"—and his glowering crew became an edgy storyline in the paper's ongoing tale of the city.

JERRY CAPECI: John Gotti jumped onto the scene in '82, '83. He became a folk hero to some, public enemy number one to others, and the real impetus for the expanded mob coverage. Then there were other things. The federal government had finally figured out how to use the RICO [Racketeer Influenced and Corrupt Organizations] statutes and they were making cases. And there was Joe Pistone [who, as Donnie Brasco, infiltrated the Bonanno crime family]. The Gotti crew was the toughest, meanest-looking crew that I covered, and in '82 and '83, Gotti's crew—not Gotti himself, but his brother Gene, John Carneglia, Angelo Ruggiero, and a bunch of other guys—were arrested on drug trafficking charges. That was before the Bail Reform Act. So, for the most part, everybody was out on bail. In the courtroom, the press—there were six or seven of us—sat in the first row. [The defendants] sat behind us and talked to each other about how would it look if bad things happened to us. Like, "If he got hit in the head with a bat, what do you think would come out of his head? Do you think he'd have any brains in there?" Not only me, but they'd talk about other reporters. It was a way of trying to intimidate us, of course. We ignored it. You had to ignore it, because you hoped they were going to abide by the rules of the mafia, which was not to go after any law enforcement people or newspaper reporters. [After two mistrials, Gene Gotti and John Carneglia were convicted on drug charges in 1989 and served twenty-nine years in federal prison. Both were released in 2018. Angelo Ruggiero was not tried a third time because of illness. He died of cancer in 1989.]

SALVATORE "SAMMY THE BULL" GRAVANO, former Gambino crime family underboss: Nobody likes to be written about, especially when, you know, they're telling the truth. Jerry Capeci is one of the best reporters that ever covered crime because he told the truth. Do you know why his sources were so good? Because he was honest and fair. The mob was glued to him. They still are. Do you know how many times I heard mob guys say, "Did you see Jerry's article?" I think Jerry's going to go down in history as a historian of the mafia.

JERRY CAPECI: John Gotti became the Dapper Don because I used the phrase in a story. I covered his first appearance in federal court after the killing of Paul Castellano in '85. Everybody and his grandmother was there covering it. That's the famous day when Gotti walks through the metal detector and the reporters follow, jump in the elevator, and follow him up to the sixth floor. He gets to the door of the courtroom with Mary Gay Taylor, a CBS [radio] reporter, opens the door with his left hand, and ushers her in with his right hand and says something like, "My mom told me to be a gentleman and open the door for ladies." It was something that everybody saw, everybody remembered, and he became like a good guy. He became like a bigger-than-life person for the people who covered it. I wrote in my story that he looked like a dapper don. The copy editor was sharp. He changed my story, the wording in my story, to dapper mobster. He used "The Dapper Don" as the headline.

SALVATORE "SAMMY THE BULL" GRAVANO: Listen, if they knew how he felt—he would have probably given them $100,000, easy, to use that label for him. He was a fucking narcissist motherfucker. He loved that fucking label, the Dapper Don. He loved Teflon Don, too. I don't know if he saved the headlines, but if I was a betting man, I wouldn't bet against it.

20 | THE EMPIRE RISES
Reagan, AIDS, Murdoch's Big Move

As the *Post*'s pugnacious profile expanded, so did Murdoch's. Though he owned media properties on three continents, his American interests thus far had been confined to print. The press lord harbored grander dreams, many of which came to fruition in the go-go '80s, in large part thanks to the *Post*. Helping to keep the right politicians and their enablers in power—and undermining those who ran counter to that agenda—was key to his strategy.

DAVE BANKS, night managing editor, 1979–1981: Murdoch does different things in different theaters of war. I edited two newspapers for him in Australia. I used to write my own editorial for the *Telegraph*, which was the leading tabloid. I was never given any running or writing instructions. But Rupert, I'm sure, having appointed me, felt comfortable that I knew pretty well what sort of newspaper I was running. [Banks ultimately worked for Murdoch on three continents.] I understood what the paper stood for, and that's important. I've always been of the opinion that journalists do have political persuasions and feelings, but I've never been a member of a political party. I don't think it's appropriate for journalists to do so. I've always believed that you only had stewardship of a newspaper—you wouldn't dream of changing its politics because you were only the editor. But somehow that worked differently in New York. The publisher had a lot more input.

HAL DAVIS, reporter, New York State Supreme Court, 1978–1993: I had two sources on the committee that was weighing the [Roy Cohn] disbarment recommendation. This was 1983. It was a committee under the supervision of the Appellate Division of the State Supreme Court in Manhattan that looked at the behavior of lawyers and recommended discipline if need be. One of my sources was a lawyer in private practice. One was a lawyer who acted as kind of a hearing officer at the courthouse. They told me what was going on. There were four cases in which Roy Cohn acted egregiously. Supposedly, in one case, with somebody on his deathbed, he takes the guy's hand and moves the hand to have the guy sign a document, things like that. I thought, great story. I alerted [Page Six] first because, though it was sourced, I didn't have any documentation at that point, except that all four cases that Cohn was involved in were public, and I had covered a few of them. So I knew about them in great detail. I passed this information about the committee to Susan Mulcahy, who told me later that Dunleavy slapped down the idea.

SUSAN MULCAHY, Page Six editor, 1978–1985: Roy Cohn was pragmatic. If it suited his interests, he would feed us negative stories about his own clients. When Hal called me about the disbarment investigation, I knew Roy would not be happy, but he'd probably give me a comment denying everything. He had never tried to actually kill a story on Page Six, and this one was going to get out eventually, right? Minutes after I got off the phone with Roy, Dunleavy calls and tells me I'm an idiot. How could I be so stupid as to even think about running such a negative story about the paper's best friend?

WAYNE DARWEN, assistant managing editor, 1983–1987: There was a story on Al D'Amato, and I just did what I normally did. I punched it up. Just the truth. I didn't change it. That was the problem, I told the truth. I got called in by [co-managing editor] John Canning after the edition came out. He said, "What the fuck are you doing? Don't you know that Al D'Amato supports Rupert Murdoch?" Well, I didn't know to what degree. What the fuck. We got into it, and I was fired. I knew John for years. He was a buddy of mine. I said, "Come on, John. Give me a break. I'm assistant managing editor here. I'm not sitting in your meetings with Murdoch every day. I just did what I always do. It's accurate." It was too accurate. That was the problem. It undermined Rupert's relationship with D'Amato. I was fired, but that only lasted twenty-four hours. I got a call from John saying, "Let's forget that. Come on back." I knew why. John realized he would have got his ass kicked if I went out and said I got fired for telling the truth on a story and not tilting it to favor Al D'Amato. He had to hire me back.

I also think John was half in the bag when he fired me. I don't mean to put the late, great John Canning down. He was a great newsman. I'm saying this affectionately. John got his ass kicked because [Murdoch was asking]—how did this end up there? He found out who did it, me, and he kicked my ass. Then he realized he'd get his ass kicked a second time for kicking my ass out the door because it looked bad. That was a memorable one. Fired for twenty-four hours.

CHARLIE CARILLO, reporter, columnist, 1978–1993: The *Post* loved Ronald Reagan. When he was running against Walter Mondale, Dunleavy sent me out to do "Man on the Street" interviews with the following "question": "Walter Mondale is a good man, but he is perceived as weak. Why do you think this is so?" That's right up there with "When did you stop beating your wife?" I wasn't in a great mood when I met with my photographer, Frank Leonardo—remember him? Sort of a hippie-ish guy with a goatee? Before we got going, I told Frank the "question" I had to ask, and how we had to hope people would fall for it. "I see," he said. "It's the morally bankrupt preying upon the intellectually bereft." What a beautiful way to put it.

> The announcement that Geraldine Ferraro, the first female vice presidential candidate for a major party, would be Mondale's running mate was a huge story. And she was local.

GEORGE ARZT, City Hall bureau chief, 1968–1986: We were in San Francisco for the [1984 Democratic] convention and Geraldine Ferraro was picked for VP. The phone rings. It's Roy Cohn. He says, "Ferraro. Within two minutes, you're going to have a dossier on your desk, read it." It's all about her husband, John Zaccaro—mob stuff, all sorts of weird stuff. Cohn calls me back and says, "Did you read it?" I said, "Yeah." "Dynamite, isn't it?" I said I was too busy to do anything with it, and I gave it to someone else. I had this unbelievably slimy feeling. I just gave it to one of the editors. I don't know what happened to it, but undoubtedly it was used.

GUY HAWTIN, investigations editor, 1979–1989: I was in Quebec with my family, and I'm watching the Democratic convention when they announced that Geraldine Ferraro was the nominee for vice president. I said to my wife, "I can't believe this." She said, "Why?" I said, "Her husband [has Mafia connections]. Everybody in New York knows that." Jeff Wells and I worked that one. We uncovered a lot about Ferraro's family, too. Roger Wood didn't want to run it because he didn't think it was good for the paper. He wanted somebody else to take the lead. Roger was not keen on us stabbing the [first] woman vice presidential candidate in the back. Jeff and I were writing this thing and Rupert Murdoch comes along. He looks over my shoulder and says, "What have you got there?" I said, "It's the story of Geraldine Ferraro." He sat down, read it, and said, "We've got to run this." He overrode Roger Wood, who wouldn't speak to me for two days. He thought I engineered it. [Zaccaro and Ferraro denied connections to the mob.]

KEN CHANDLER, editor in chief, publisher, 1978–1986, 1993–2002: Guy was a curious character. He was in charge of propaganda or something. He was considered to be a little dubious as an investigative reporter. I'm not entirely sure that's fair, but definitely people were a little bit suspicious. They felt that sometimes he would cut corners to come up with what Rupert was looking for.

> The *Post* remained largely in Reagan's corner through both of his terms, and in October 1985, when the president ordered the interception of a plane carrying Palestinian terrorists who had hijacked the Italian cruise ship *Achille Lauro* and killed an American passenger, Leon Klinghoffer, the *Post* fed the president one of his most memorable lines of rhetoric.

ERIC FETTMANN, associate editorial page editor, columnist, 1976–1991, 1993–2019: It's afternoon and they were already planning the front page. They knew it was going to be off Reagan's speech. The wood was going to be: YOU CAN RUN BUT YOU CAN'T HIDE. Dunleavy called [Washington Bureau Chief] Niles Lathem and said, "If you can get Reagan to say that in his speech, you got a fat bonus coming." Niles gets [Attorney General] Edwin Meese on the phone, tells him what the *Post* wants, and says, "By the way, this is apparently going to be worth a lot of money to me. And it happens to be a great line." Meese agreed and, sure enough, Reagan used it. We had our wood, Niles had a $5,000 bonus. His stock at the *Post* went *way* up.

EDWIN MEESE, former US attorney general: I remember the phrase very well, but I don't recall the specific circumstances of [Reagan] saying it.

HARRY SHEARER, humorist, actor, co-star of *This Is Spinal Tap*: When I came back to *Saturday Night Live* in 1984, I was trying to do Reagan pieces and looking for whatever tidbits I could find anywhere. In New York it was hard to find a lot of Reagan supporters. That was, of course, before the era of conservative talk radio and conservative television. The *Post* was really the only place you could reliably turn to for that point of view.

At times, however, the *Post* surprised the White House with unflattering stories about the administration and its players—some that made international news.

SUSAN MULCAHY: When Reagan ran for reelection, we wrote that the campaign was about to hire Jerry Della Femina, a Madison Avenue guy who was considered kind of racy, to do their ads. A week later, I found out they were *not* going to hire him. Everyone said it was related to timing, but clearly somebody had alerted the White House to an interview Della Femina had done in *Oui*, a skin magazine. The campaign spokesman told me they would have a hard time working with Page Six if I didn't "play the story right." "Is that a threat?" I asked. "Oh, no," he said. He called again and said if I handled the story as they wanted—meaning, downplay it, or kill it—Ed Rollins, the campaign manager, will "make you a hero in Mr. Murdoch's eyes." Give me a break. It was the kind of story Page Six was invented for. We ran it as a lead with plenty of detail from the article—like the sex contest in Della Femina's office. There was no blowback.

GUY HAWTIN: The interesting thing about the *Post*, whether it was in Reagan's camp or not, it never fully behaved like it. For example, Reagan names his cabinet and the head of the CIA is Bill Casey. Bill Casey was a naughty man. While he was an incredibly good CIA operative, he used the CIA to research his investment portfolio strategy. That's a no-no. We wrote about it. There's the myth of the *Post*, then the reality of the *Post*. And the reality is it was not bought in that way. Roger Wood was a very clever guy.

CHARLES LACHMAN, reporter, 1981–1988: They sent me to cover the invasion of Grenada, which was a huge, international story. The thing about the *Post* is, you just can't cover it the way the *New York Times* would. You always have to think sidebars and scoops. One of the controversial aspects of the invasion was a total news blackout. They did not allow any American reporters onto the island. All the news came from debriefs in Barbados or in Washington. There's this whole mystery about what's really going on. I flew to Barbados with Mike Norcia, a very talented photographer I had worked with before. We're down there, and the point was to get on the island.

We flew on a puddle jumper to, I think, St. Vincent Island. There we found a drug smuggler who was willing to take us by boat to Grenada. Norcia did not want to go. I don't blame him. It was a rickety old small motorboat in the open sea, choppy waters. It was definitely dangerous. I called it in and told Dunleavy what the story was. Believe me, no hesitation: "Go for it, mate." I don't like speaking ill of the dead, but the whole trip Norcia had seasickness. I took a Dramamine. He was sick to his stomach. He didn't pack his equipment very well, so very quickly they became soaked by seawater. I had packed one of his cameras in double plastic, and that was the only one that ended up working. We jump off the boat, I gash my leg on rocks. I don't even know how to swim. Got to the shore, and there we are on this island that had been invaded by US troops. We spent the night on the beach, and it was freezing. I found newspapers and stuffed them inside my shirt to keep warm. My teeth were chattering. Finally, the sun comes up, and we climb up to the nearest town. We were the first Americans they saw. They surrounded us. We were treated like conquering heroes. We got a guy to take us by car into the capital, St. George's. We're roaming around. There are American soldiers there, and they're surprised to see us.

We find out that a mental hospital had been bombed by accident by US war planes. I'm going to say forty-seven people were killed. [The *Post* reported that "as many as 50" died. The White House later confirmed the accidental hit, but said the death toll was twenty people, though some remained unaccounted for.] It was a huge, huge story, but there was no way of communicating the information to the *Post*. We had to get off the island and get back to Barbados and a phone that worked. This is before satellite phones and all that stuff. We got on a US transport plane, which was very cool. They fly us back along with a lot of other people to Barbados. We had our passports, we're Americans and they said "Sure, come on."

I call in this story to Dunleavy. It was a big Reagan policy decision to invade the island. It was obviously controversial. When I told [the *Post*] about the accidental bombing of the mental institution and all those deaths, it was like, "Uh-oh, Murdoch's not going to like this," because Murdoch had politicized the *Post*, the front page, and the endorsements [in support of Reagan]. Dunleavy did mention that the *Post* supported the invasion, but to the editors' credit, they didn't try to censor it. It was picked up all over the world. They credited me as a war correspondent, which I thought was really, really fun.

During the Grenada sojourn, Lachman and Norcia engaged in their own conflict.

CHARLES LACHMAN: Norcia and I had not had a great time together. It was a personality conflict. Again, the whole idea that he didn't pack the equipment correctly, and he didn't want to be there. We're at the airport in Barbados waiting for a flight back [to the US], and we're having dinner. It was vague as to when the flight to New York would be leaving, and I thought I heard them say it was in ten minutes. I said, "Oh my god, we got to go," and Norcia wanted to wait for the check. Because if you want your money back when you get to the *Post*, you need a receipt. I said, "What the—?" Right? "Come on, we got to go, we're going to miss the plane." So the tension was really, really high as we were making the flight, and at the gate, I'd had enough and I said, "You are such an a-hole." Fists flew. We fought at the gate. Let me tell you, some of the soldiers who were involved in that invasion, that was the most dramatic action they saw. So, we board, and we were the only ones on the plane because the whole island had been cut off. We wouldn't sit next to each other.

The presumption that the *Post*'s reporters are all right-wingers is a myth, and so is the presumption that all journalists are liberals. Some reporters and editors evolve, often as a result of their experiences on the beat and with the *Post*'s office politics.

ERIC FETTMANN: I was a moderate Democrat when I joined the paper—a *New Republic* Democrat. But eventually, I became more conservative. I never became an out-and-out flaming conservative. I tend to be a skeptic of everyone. The whole political correctness movement did a lot to change my worldview.

FRED DICKER, Albany bureau chief, 1982–2016: I headed two chapters of SDS [Students for a Democratic Society, a left-wing activist organization], one at Long Island University and one at the University of Massachusetts in Amherst. Actually, my first job as a journalist was as the editor of a radical newspaper at the University of Massachusetts called *The Mother of Voices*, one of the so-called underground press newspapers. Even though I was close to people in the Communist Party, the CP USA, and I knew serious radicals, I was never a communist, even though they wanted me to join. But in a nutshell, the more I learned about the real world as a journalist, and I love journalism for giving me that, the more I realized a lot of the stereotypes—my assumptions about businesspeople, or about what the police were like—were not accurate. I generally liked most of the people I met, didn't feel there was any kind of conspiratorial effort to suppress the working class. As I learned more, and was in unions, I wasn't exactly impressed with what I saw, especially at the Albany *Times-Union*. So over the years, I evolved.

> The *Post*'s support of the Reagan administration collided with an epidemic that would devastate New York in the 1980s and '90s, particularly the gay community. While the *Post*'s editorial pages were predictably homophobic, and its news pages radiated an anti-gay perspective, the paper also did some groundbreaking, informative reporting, thanks in large part to Joe Nicholson, who took over the medical and science beat from Barbara Yuncker. In 1980, Nicholson came out to the newsroom by volunteering to write a first-person piece in response to a deadly shooting at a gay bar in Greenwich Village. In doing so, he became the first openly gay reporter at a daily newspaper in New York City.

ERIC FETTMANN: The *Post* could have been the first paper to report the existence of AIDS. Barbara Yuncker—top-notch, well-connected medical reporter that she was—wrote stories before anybody else, probably about 1980, about this new worrisome disease that seemed to be prevalent among gays. The stories all got spiked.

PETER FREIBERG, reporter, 1971–1978: The Dorothy Schiff *Post* was not homophobic, but it was only after I left the *Post*, that summer [1978], that I decided to come out. I knew Joe [Nicholson], but neither of us was out at the time. I didn't know when I left the *Post* that he was gay.

JOANNE WASSERMAN, reporter, 1977–1986: When I first got to the *Post*, Joe Nicholson asked me out, so he wasn't out yet. It sounds like he maybe wasn't even sure. Or aware, I guess is the better way to put it.

DAVID FRANCE, reporter on tryout, 1985: Joe was this former Navy officer, pugnacious, aggressive, boundary-crossing journalist. He was very competitive—out to win—which is what you needed to be to work as a journalist at the

New York Post. He came out in 1980 in a cover story interview for the *New York Native.* It made him one of only three [openly] gay journalists in the country.

> At the same time, the *Post*'s turf writer turned out columns with a decidedly different point of view.

RAY KERRISON, turf writer, city columnist, 1977–2013: In 1985, Rupert called me up to his office. "Do you want to write about racing for the rest of your life?" he asked. "I want you to go up front of the paper." Up front I went, and immediately got a swift introduction to the perils of the column business. Civic leaders gathered in the city to welcome the first openly gay man to join the Criminal Court. They gave him a standing ovation. Next day I wrote a smart-alecky, ill-advised column on the premise that no one had ever given me a standing ovation for being straight. Next day, I picked up the *Post* and was shocked to see a blistering retort from Mayor Koch, likening me to Hitler and Castro and all the other dictators who persecuted gay people. I fired back in kind. Later, we became friends and shared a couple of lunches.

DAVID FRANCE: Ray Kerrison's columns in the front of the book were mostly harsh takes on the culture war, and he often wrote about gay folks. He was running this series into which Joe was throwing occasional articles. Often Joe's pieces were carved down to little more than sidebars, but they were a kind of ballast to what the paper was trying to do, which was to foment even more anti-LGBTQ hostilities than were already rampant in the city. It was a very dangerous time to be gay in the city, not just because AIDS was taking us by the dozens, but because the reporting on AIDS was stirring up violence mostly in the boroughs but often coming into the city. There were marauding gangs of straight white guys from Queens with bats in the Village.

CHARLIE CARILLO: In the context I knew him, Ray was a gentleman all the time. It was hard not to like him. Apparently, he was a brilliant racing writer. I don't know anything about horse racing, but he had a very engaging style. Ray had like seven or eight kids, maybe more. Every time he made love, he had a child. And he had been married forever to the same woman. He was not a classic Murdoch, Steve Dunleavy–type in that way. I think he was just a very devoted guy who believed in what he believed.

GEORGE ARZT: I loved Ray Kerrison, but his views were a little strange.

JAY BLOTCHER, activist (ACT UP), journalist: Joe Nicholson was a gift from God. Even though we were at loggerheads with the *New York Post* on every other aspect of AIDS coverage, we had a savior in Joe Nicholson. He was a great skeptic when it came to Big Pharma, and he dug deep to find out what the real story was.

SUSAN MULCAHY: At Page Six we got a bunch of calls telling us that Calvin Klein had AIDS, which was not true. They weren't all anonymous tipsters, either. One press agent I knew said his sister was a nurse who had treated Calvin Klein. We figured out later that the rumors started because Carl Rosen, whose company made Calvin Klein jeans, had cancer. He died in 1983. People heard "cancer" and "Calvin Klein" and played whisper-down-the-lane. I didn't believe in outing people, even if it had been true.

RICHARD ESPOSITO, reporter, 1982–1985: Irresponsible anonymous sex in certain clubs was spreading the disease in the homosexual community. No one really wanted to talk about it because of fear of homophobia. I was volunteered by Steve Dunleavy to spend two weeks naked in bathhouses and run back and write notes down. A photographer would wait outside and I was like: you're useless to me. JoAnne Wasserman was terrified that I was doing this, and she found a kind of very mainstream gay guy who would be my date on some of these things. He felt that no one was speaking out on behalf of the homosexual community that this was not a healthy set of practices. The Mineshaft was a rough sex club. I mean, rough sex. I'm in the Mineshaft one night, at the bar, watching things going on, and I see a neighbor of mine. He's so happy that I'm there, that I seem to be part of this. I'm like, "No, I'm working." He was also a reporter, but he wasn't working. He was there for sex. I wrote it in some overheated *New York Post* style in the second person. The story runs and all the places were closed down within two weeks. No reporter had gone in and seen firsthand what was going on. The hate mail was phenomenal. The mob sent death threats to my phone at home because a lot of the places were owned by the mob.

Coming out of the closet did not have an impact on Nicholson's career at the *Post*. Yet when he helped another gay reporter land a tryout, he warned him not to reveal his sexual orientation.

DAVID FRANCE: Joe Nicholson was a mentor of mine when I started to work at the *New York Native* in 1982. When it came time for me to find a bigger platform, he encouraged me to apply at the *New York Post*. He told me that I would only get in if I created a résumé that made me seem like little more than a typist—that if I confessed to having worked as a journalist, I would have to show my clips, which were from queer presses. I was brought in on a ninety-day try-out basis. On the ninety-first day you gained [Newspaper] Guild protection. I would take text over the phone and help render it into copy. I was doing that on the investigations desk. There was one other person who was gay. I am trying to remember his name. He just wasn't out. He was out to Joe. Joe told me and introduced us and so he was out to me as well. There was somebody else there who was very quiet. Leslie Gevirtz. I don't think she was out. Nor was she really in—she was just Leslie. I knew her because her girlfriend worked at the *New York Native*.

LESLIE GEVIRTZ, reporter, rewrite, 1978–1988: I wasn't formally out. I never said to Dunleavy, "Hey, I'm a dyke." But I have no doubt that he surmised this. The man was fairly worldly. Also, he would look after his favorites. He could be really understanding. That's why I said I would walk into wildfire for him, because he helped me.

In 1985, a group of activists founded GLAAD, the Gay and Lesbian Alliance Against Defamation, to protest what was viewed as the *Post*'s histrionic and homophobic point of view, Joe Nicholson notwithstanding.

DAVID FRANCE: GLAAD was formed as a street action organization, not the kind of Hollywood celebration it is today—and it was formed exclusively in response to the *New York Post*. I was at the founding meeting, and the organizers divided up into committees. There was one called "The swift and terrible retribution committee." They called for an organized protest in front of the *New York Post*. They called it The Rags Action—everybody was to bring a rag, like a dust rag or dirty rag—to throw at the *New York Post*, which was the rag we were protesting.

JAY BLOTCHER: I was at that first demonstration against the *Post* by GLAAD. By then, the *Post* had an ironclad reputation for being gleefully homophobic.

DAVID FRANCE: I knew I had to go to the protest. I wasn't working that day, it was a cold day in December, I recall, or late November—sleeting rain. I went in disguise because I was afraid I would be seen. The protest did cause something of a stir inside the [*Post*]. But it didn't change the coverage. Within a week or two, my editor [Guy Hawtin] calls me into his office, and there are my clips from the *Native*, and the *Voice*, all having to do with AIDS and queer subject matter. He said, "I found out you're gay," or something, with this look, like the investigative editor had finally investigated something. And that was it.

GUY HAWTIN: That would *not* have been the case at the *Post*, for crying out loud! Joe Nicholson was there, and he had no trouble whatsoever. The idea that I'd let people go because they're gay is very bizarre. That's absolute crap. If he was fired—and that's possible—he was fired because he was incompetent. Nobody would fire him because he was gay. A big problem, actually, with gay people is they come out and say, "I'm gay and I want to write about it." The truth of the matter is, it was interesting when done once, but a constant parade is ridiculous. I am also an Anglican priest, and I volunteered at St. Vincent's [hospital in Greenwich Village where many AIDS patients were treated]. I didn't make a big thing about St. Vincent's because I didn't want people to shun me while I was in the office. People were terrified of AIDS. They thought that you get it by touching people.

LESLIE GEVIRTZ: I didn't work directly with Guy, but I knew him from the newsroom and he did not strike me as homophobic.

MARY PAPENFUSS, reporter, 1984–1991: Cardinal O'Connor became my beat. Murdoch was so pro-Catholic. There was a big demonstration against the pope and we did a story on it. The editors were in the layout room, and Murdoch came up raging. He said something like, "I've been trying to change us from a Jewish to a Catholic newspaper, and you do this story!" He always highlighted Cardinal O'Connor, and I loved the beat because the stuff O'Connor said was outrageous. I think he was happy he was in the newspaper. I was there another time when the gays were having their own mass every week outside St. Patrick's Cathedral because O'Connor was raging against them. We had a lot of gay readers, and they loved to read what the cardinal was saying. I think O'Connor was happy with that stuff to get out. He was like the pope's mouthpiece then. And if it was anti-gay, he loved to see it on the front page.

GEORGE RUSH, Page Six reporter, 1986–1993: The centennial celebration of the Statue of Liberty took place in 1986, and the celebrations included a black-tie gala cruise in New York Harbor. The attendees included President Reagan, Nancy Reagan, French president François Mitterrand, General William Westmoreland, and Governor Hugh Carey. Bob Hope was part of the entertainment, and he tosses out this joke: "Hey, did you hear that the Statue of Liberty has AIDS?" Just that premise caused some wary murmuring, but then he says, "Nobody knows if she got it from the mouth of the Hudson or the Staten Island Ferry." A lot of jaws dropped and the crowd was rumbling, which Hope sensed. He started blaming his writers for handing him this bad joke when a subsequent interview with his head writer revealed that the writer had actually tried to talk Bob out of telling this joke and he refused. It immediately struck me as something worth repeating, and so we did it on Page Six. The other piece: Ronald Reagan and Nancy were laughing. I think some of the old-timers on the ship were not as offended by the insensitivity of the joke. Bob Hope, when I called and when other reporters subsequently called, said the joke was taken out of context. His excuse was there wasn't supposed to be any press there. Like that would just go unreported. It put him in such hot water—particularly with his friend Elizabeth Taylor, who was a staunch AIDS activist. She made him do some benefit performances as penance. That was the sort of mischief you could get into. I had been writing for *Esquire* and could never find anyone who had read my profile of Brian Eno, but one paragraph on Page Six could instantly rock the city.

CHARLIE CARILLO: At the height of the AIDS crisis, some huckster came up with a card people could carry around, declaring themselves clean of the disease. You got the card after you passed a blood test. I was sent out with [photographer] Don Halasy to ask people if they would want to carry around such a card. We had a hell of a time getting people to play along—who wanted their name and picture on a story about AIDS? It was frustrating, and as we wandered around the shops at the South Street Seaport, I pointed at a female mannequin and said to Halasy, "We might as well ask her if she'd want to carry one of these cards." Halasy took a picture of the mannequin, we called her Betty Blank, and when I got back to the office, I turned in the mannequin photo along with the other pictures, and here's what the mannequin had to say: "We mannequins don't have to worry about AIDS. We just give each other splinters." I stood by as Dunleavy read the words, quick to explain that it was just a joke, that I'd clear it from the story. "I'll take care of it, mate," he assured me, and when I got to work the next day, what a shitstorm. The mannequin photo and her response were in the paper, and the gay community was going crazy: how could you make fun at a time like this? They were right. It was crazy that he put the joke in the paper, but, you know, that's how things would happen at the *Post.*

Steve Dunleavy's outrageous behavior reached its peak in the mid-1980s.

MARTY MCLAUGHLIN, public relations and political consultant: Steve comes home one night—he lived on Long Island—and he's drunk and his wife is gone. He gets undressed, maybe takes a shower, throws on a robe, and flops down on the sofa. Well, it wasn't a robe. It was his wife's peignoir. The desk calls him because there's some guy out on Long Island that they're trying to track down. Steve says, "Okay, mate, I'll get him." They don't know that he's still in the bag. He goes racing out of the house to a house where he thinks this guy is. He bangs on the door. They open the door and here's this guy, naked, in a peignoir, looking for somebody. They call the cops and the cops come down. Then the cops call the *Post* and they say, "We have this guy, he doesn't have a wallet. We think he's Australian." The *Post* says, "We know who he is. We'll send a car out for him."

ERIC FETTMANN: John Canning told me what is probably the most disgusting Dunleavy story of them all. You're not going to want to use it. The two of them are in this bar, and the place is packed like a sardine can. Dunleavy is with some woman and Canning is doing most of the talking. Dunleavy and the woman are basically smiling at each other and not saying much of anything until at one point Dunleavy takes Canning's hand—I heard the story from Canning, by the way—and pulls it down to let him realize that Dunleavy and the woman are fucking standing up, he put his hand on Dunleavy's cock. Canning had once either been a seminary student, or had thought seriously about becoming a minister, so he was a fairly straitlaced kind of guy except for drinking, and he said, "My jaw literally dropped to the floor." Dunleavy loved it.

DICK BELSKY, metropolitan editor, 1970–1989: One day we got a call from that hospital in the Village, St. Vincent's. It was this confused thing. Some guy in their psych ward or their drunk tank keeps screaming that he's the metropolitan editor of the *New York Post*. I remember going, "Holy shit." I take the call and it's Dunleavy. Somebody had picked him up unconscious on the street, and they'd put him in the drunk psych tank. When that happens, they can't just let you go. He's telling everybody, "I'm the metropolitan editor of the *New York Post!*" They're all like, "Yeah, right. And I'm President Reagan." In the end, I think it was Carl Pelleck, who was the fixer in those days, who had to pull strings to get him sprung.

RAMONA GARNES, copy editor, 1978–1990, 2000–2004: One day, Ken Chandler says to me, "Ramona, you're not running copy today. Your job is to sober up Steve. Because he has an appointment to interview Mario Cuomo." Steve is sitting at the city editor's desk. He's not passed out or anything, but he's really drunk. For half the day, I'm bringing him toast and coffee. I don't remember where I got the toast. He did the interview and the story ran.

KEN CHANDLER: I think he allowed the drinking to take over.

BARBARA ROSS, political reporter, 1978–1985: Ultimately Dunleavy became more than a pain in the neck. He became a really abusive boss, and I couldn't stand it anymore. Toward the end it was so bad, I would've taken a job with the sanitation department to get out of there.

SUSAN MULCAHY: Dunleavy drove me out. He'd come around every day, telling me I had to run this item, that item. It was like he had nothing else to do. We were fighting all the time, and it was getting unbearable. One day, this was November 1985, I get to the office and see a lead story on Page Six that is new to me, even though my name is on it. It was some item about the Soviets. Completely wrong for Page Six. I'd been working on the column for more than seven years at that point, so I knew what worked. Even if it had been a decent story, I would have been pissed because no one called me. I'd had items killed, but not like this. I walked into Roger's office and quit. Without another job. He said, "Don't do anything hasty, dear girl." But he couldn't guarantee it wouldn't happen again.

KEN CHANDLER: I would say probably on balance Steve [had more power than Roger Wood], because he had a long, long, long relationship with Murdoch. Roger was just like me. We knew we were hired hands, and hired hands come and they go.

As the paper's reputation as liberal, upstanding, and Jewish disintegrated, admitting to employment at the *Post* generated a strong reaction—often for those attempting to move on from the paper. But the deluge of departures that took place during the first years of Murdoch's ownership eventually slowed. Established and new employees who questioned Murdoch-rules journalism figured out ways to make their peace with the *Post*, and rival publications began to raid the tabloid and mimic its ways because, though they were loath to admit it, Murdoch had changed the game.

JIM WILLSE, former editor and publisher, New York *Daily News*: In the first year I was [at the *Daily News*], I was sent to London, to learn the dark art of tabloid journalism. By 1985, the *News* circulation was going down, the *Post*'s circulation was going up, and it was clear that the *News* had to incorporate some of the tabloid energy that Murdoch's *Post* had. One of the weaknesses of the *Daily News* was that its look had not changed in forty years. You could look at front pages of the *News* from 1940, then pages in the early '80s, and they looked exactly the same. You had no sense of change, no sense of vitality, and one of the thoughts was that there were lessons to be learned from the British tabloids.

BARBARA ROSS: When I'd tell people I was from the *Post*, it was like I just farted.

PHILIP MESSING, reporter, 1978–1991, 1994–2016: I was covering this thing in a mosque in Queens. There was some sort of drama. All the press was there. I went into a store, and these people were stamping tuna fish cans, two for eighty-nine cents. This guy looks at my press pass, and he says to his friend, "Hey, this guy works for the *New York Post*." He started laughing. He thought it was hilarious that I worked for the *New York Post*. He's stamping items with a stamper in a supermarket, I'm working for a major New York newspaper, and he's making fun of me. It kind of stuck with me. There was such a vituperation and dislike toward the *Post* that people working menial jobs thought they were on a higher moral plane.

GREG GALLO, executive sports editor, 1977–1989, 1994–2009: When I would tell people [I worked at the *Post*], it would be, "You work at the *Post*?" And I said, "Yeah." "So where do you work?" "Sports." "Sports!" So, it went from "You work at the *Post*?"—like "How could you dare work at the *Post*!"—to "Oh, sports!" There was a change-up in delivery and reaction.

JOANNE WASSERMAN: While I was at the *Post*, somebody arranged for me to interview at *Newsday*. I went out there and I took a [news] test. Isaac Asimov's brother, Stanley, worked there in HR, and he was a prick. The first thing he said to me when I sat down was: "How can you work at the *New York Post*?" I thought, The deck is stacked.

AMY PAGNOZZI, reporter, columnist, 1979–1993: At *New York Newsday*, I got interviewed by Stanley Asimov. He made me cry so badly that I left before I could do the news test. He said to me, "I really like your writing, I like your clips. But how do I know that your character and your ethics haven't been so irretrievably ruined by the *Post* that we could ever trust you?" Normally, I'm not a weeper. But I thought, oh my god, it's the big time, maybe I'll get a job as a reporter. He punctured my balloon so deeply that I just started bawling and left.

HAL DAVIS: I didn't have to make things up. I had a courthouse full of marvelous stories. But working with people who made things up was one of the prices you paid. I found I was able to do a job that I loved, report things I wanted, and if the paper wouldn't take something, or if I had a story I knew the *Post* wouldn't be interested in, I'd pass it on to other reporters, like Murray Kempton [after he went to *Newsday*]. He'd do wonderful stuff with it. I worked often with people at the *Village Voice*—Joe Conason, Wayne Barrett, Jack Newfield. Nat Hentoff got a lot of my stuff. That's one way I was able to justify my existence at the *New York Post*. I also loved the job and I loved the stuff I *could* get into the paper because it was so varied and often the other dailies would just ignore it.

JOANNE WASSERMAN: Tom Topor, Gene Ruffini, Charlie Carillo—the *Post* was their day job. They had these creative things going on. Carillo had his novels, Topor had his plays [Barbra Streisand starred in the film version of Topor's play *Nuts*]. Gene was an actor. He was in some mob movies. All the pain that I felt about, you know, how we were portraying things, they didn't care. They came in every day. They liked each other, they had fun, exaggerating things and making jokes or getting assigned like Charlie did to cover Wingo. As Nora Ephron would say, it's all copy. It's all gonna end up somewhere somehow in something you do—a play, a novel.

GEORGE ARZT: You don't justify it. There's a deep conflict. It rips you apart inside. You're constantly saying: why don't you leave? If you have enough guts, you leave. I was in a good position at the *Post*. I had a lot of friends at the *Post* and I had a relationship with Rupert. I was one of the stars of the paper. I did not think I would be that on another publication. The *Daily News* was largely Irish; the *Times*, I would be one in a million; I was offered City Hall bureau chief at *Newsday*, but then [John] Cotter went to *Newsday*, and he and I never got along. He was always going to stab me in the back. Instead, [in 1986], I became Ed Koch's press secretary.

JAMI BERNARD, chief movie critic, 1978–1993: If you left the *Post*, you had to go through a deep cleansing. You had to launder your byline. I mean, I did get to the *Daily News*, but I knew [the *Post*] would be a stain if I ever tried to go to the *Times*.

STEPHEN SILVERMAN, entertainment writer, 1977–1988: When I met Katharine Hepburn, I was afraid to tell her I was associated with the *Post*. This was for my book on David Lean, because she wrote the introduction. At that point, I'd left the *Post* and I told her about leaving and getting severance. She looked at me and said, "Did you get the money?" I said, "I did." She said, "Good for you." That's all she cared about. People would rather have been talking to the *Times*, but whether the numbers were inflated or not, there were a million readers [of the *Post*]. I had a bit of an inferiority complex. But then, I knew people at the *Times*, and they had prestige, they were also miserable. I had fun. I was at every film festival, every opening night, every movie premiere. I did care what people thought about the *Post*, but it didn't stand in my way.

BARBARA ROSS: I got so tired of people putting their noses up, but I understood why, and I knew that if I was going to have a career, I had to get the hell out of there. I left a lot of money on the table to go to the *Daily News* in October of '85.

JERRY CAPECI, reporter, organized crime, 1966–1986: The killing of Paul Castellano is what triggered my departure from the *Post*. I wrote a big page-one story for the *Post* two days after Castellano was killed, basically saying, "Gotti did it." It was huge for me and for us at that time. I was told later by the *Daily News*, which hired me, that that was one of the things that got them to realize I would be good for them. I was pissed at [the *Post*]. I had asked for a raise, and they had never given me a raise. When I told the *Post* I was leaving, they offered me more money. I told them to shove it in their fucking hat.

JOANNE WASSERMAN: For a long time, if you were at the *Post*, it was easy to beat the *News* because they were lazy. It was a bunch of older white men who didn't work that hard. Some of them were wise, and knew a lot, but that didn't always translate into good stories. When they brought Gil Spencer from Philadelphia to edit the *News* [in 1984], they really wanted to make changes. And when the PVB [Parking Violations Bureau] scandal happened, [which resulted in the suicide of one public official and seriously marred Ed Koch's third term as mayor], the [*News*] owned that story. [Barbara] Ross pretty much broke that story, because by then she had left the *Post* and Capeci had left. I was the third one. That's what I wanted to do. I didn't have a novel. I wasn't trying to be an actor.

In 1985, when *Newsday*, the Long Island newspaper, launched a city edition, *New York Newsday*, even the paper that employed Stanley Asimov became more open to bringing in staff from the *Post*.

SUSAN MULCAHY: I had turned down a job offer from *New York Newsday*, but when Dunleavy drove me so crazy I quit in a huff, I had to go back to them. I agreed to do a column for less than I had been making at the *Post*. So, in the middle of a tabloid war, I managed to switch papers and lose money.

STEVEN ISENBERG, former publisher, *New York Newsday*: Just because somebody was at the *Post*, doesn't mean they couldn't come to your newspaper and adapt and write for you and grow in your way. We were picking up people from the *Post*. We were going to pick up talent from other places. They knew New York.

RICHARD ESPOSITO: I left the *Post* in two and a half years. I always tell people, it's a great place to be as a young person, and it's a great place to leave before it becomes exhausting, or soul destroying. As Mike Pearl used to say: "At the *News*, there are two sides to every story. At the *Times*, there are three sides to every story. At the *Post*, there's one side to every story and if we like you, we leave you out." That becomes a burden.

JIM WILLSE: The widespread perception of the *Post* was that it was, of the three [tabloids], the most down-market, but that was not correct. There was a component of the *Post* readership that both the *Daily News* and *Newsday* coveted:

white-collar, relatively well-to-do New Yorkers who would typically buy the *Post* in the afternoon to enjoy the gossip, the business coverage, including media, and the fun of it.

STEVEN ISENBERG: The *Post* was for many readers their second or third paper. There were very few people who read the *New York Post* and that was their paper. They had a kind of bipolar demographic profile, because many people who read the *Post* also read the *New York Times* and the *Wall Street Journal*. The *Post* was their tabloid pop. Few human beings could live off the information provided in the *Post* alone.

Murdoch's other New York–focused print publications, *New York* magazine and the *Village Voice*, also enjoyed increases in circulation in the mid-1980s, but communications had evolved into a digital- and satellite-transmitted world dominated by film, video, and photographs, and the Australian media baron, whose first foray into television took place in Australia in the 1950s, wanted the same diversity in his American holdings. In 1985, he bought fifty percent of the Twentieth Century Fox movie studio, and he was just getting started. Within weeks, Murdoch and Marvin Davis, who owned the other half of Twentieth Century Fox, reached an arrangement to buy a group of independent television stations owned by Metromedia, including WNEW-TV, Channel Five, in New York. Pesky details had to be ironed out: Murdoch was not a US citizen, a requirement of the acquisition; federal regulations prevented a newspaper proprietor from owning more than five percent of a broadcast property in the same market; and in the end, Marvin Davis reneged on his commitment to the Metromedia purchase. Murdoch had to buy him out and also purchased Davis's half of Fox. To make the deal, he had to raise capital, and some of his print holdings were put up for sale. Complications aside, Murdoch's vision of a mega-media conglomerate with power far beyond print had begun to crystallize.

JOE CONASON, former reporter, *The Village Voice*: I wrote a piece about a fundraiser for Koch and one person who attended was Murdoch himself. He had just gotten a big tax write-off from the city for the *Post* building at 210 South Street, so I wrote about that. I think the headline was "Fat Cats Feast." He went nuts. He told David Schneiderman to fire me.

DAVID SCHNEIDERMAN, former editor in chief, publisher, CEO, *The Village Voice*: Even though the paper aggravated [Murdoch], he instinctively knew that if you mess with the *Voice*, as in terms of what it was and what it was all about, it would be less valuable. Once he did threaten to sell the paper. I remember exactly when it was, August 3, 1983. It was four days before my daughter was born. I had this very pregnant wife and Rupert was, "Oh, how you doing, I heard your wife is pregnant, you're about to be a father, it's a great thing," all this nice social stuff, and then he completely turned and said, "If you don't fire Conason, I'm going to sell the paper"—and then he hesitated—"to someone worse than me." My first thought was, who does Rupert think is worse than him? I didn't say that. I said, "Just because you asked me to fire someone, I can't do that." He said, "You'll be a hero in New York. Everybody hates him." I said, "No, my career will be done. If I do that, why would anybody hire an editor who took an order from the owner to fire someone? I can't do that. I won't do that." He never raised his voice. It was just a conversation.

JOE CONASON: It blew over. I didn't get fired.

DAVID SCHNEIDERMAN: We did take a fair amount of shots at [Murdoch]. But he was generally good about it. A couple of incidents were what I would call close calls. Which we survived. Generally, it was fine. It was kind of ironic. Yes, because we were profitable. He once said to me, "The thing I don't understand is—why is it my Marxist newspaper is so well run, and some of my other properties aren't?" He liked to tweak me that we were Marxist. I said maybe Marxists have a good business sense.

ED KOSNER, former editor in chief and publisher, *New York* magazine: For all his reputation, Murdoch was a wonderful proprietor of *New York* magazine. The reason is that he didn't consider *New York* magazine a political property. He thought of it as a boutique, a specialty store. I worked for him for eleven years. In all that time, there were only two interventions. One was when Julie [Baumgold, *New York* magazine writer and Kosner's wife] was contemplating doing a column about Claudia Cohen. I think it was when Claudia was at the *Daily News*. Rupert called and said, "Her father is Bobby Cohen. We do not want to get on the wrong side of Bobby Cohen." [As the head of Hudson News, Cohen controlled the flow of magazines and newspapers to retailers.]

As it happened, Julie had already decided not to do the story. She didn't think there was enough there. The only other negative comment Murdoch made: Marie Brenner did a column about Cornelia Guest, who was the Deb of the Year. Remember her? I think she swung from a chandelier or something like that. Marie wrote kind of a frisky column about her. What I'd forgotten was that her mother [C. Z. Guest] was a chum of Murdoch's. The mother wrote a gardening column for the *Post*. He called up and said, "She's only eighteen years old. Maybe we should take it a little easier on her." I said, "It was a benign column, it didn't mean anything." So, in eleven years, those were the only two, not really interventions—more like questions. The rest of the time, he never intervened in anything.

DAVID SCHNEIDERMAN: He called me down to his office at the *Post* in 1985. He said, "I'm going to sell the *Voice*, but don't take it personally." I said, "I don't take it personally." He said, "I need the money to buy," I think it was the other fifty percent of Fox. Initially he had half of it. And that guy, Marvin [Davis], was the other half. I said, "Gee, I didn't know we were worth that much, that you could buy a film studio." He said, "It's not just the *Voice*, I have to ramp up money. That's part of it." I said, "Oh, okay." Like he's saying to me: "Are you naive or something? You think I'm just going to do it with the *Voice*?"

FAIGI ROSENTHAL, assistant head librarian, 1978–1986: I remember having to go upstairs to [Murdoch's] office—I'm not sure why. There were a gazillion books on television. This is way back, before he got involved in television [in the US] officially. I was like, "Oh, that's interesting."

WAYNE DARWEN: It was part of Murdoch's plan as much as his plans never had any ceiling. He was determined to build an empire, and if you were going to have a communications empire, you had to have TV.

21 BONFIRE AT 210

A New Editor, Tabloid TV, Teddy's Revenge

In 1986, Rupert Murdoch, who a year earlier had purchased a movie studio and a major television station group and was about to establish what would be the first new national television network since 1948, found himself a member of the media establishment that his print properties loved to needle. His rise to respectability coincided with changes at the *Post* meant to soften the tabloid's loud, rude, and often ethically challenged voice. The housecleaning included the eventual departure of Murdoch stalwart Steve Dunleavy and the arrival of a new executive editor, New Zealand–born Frank Devine, who had been running the *Chicago Sun-Times*, which News Corp had acquired in 1984.

DICK BELSKY, metropolitan editor, 1970–1989: Once somebody complained that the *Post* was too much like British papers, and Rupert got very defensive. Supposedly—I wasn't there, but I heard about it—he walked into an editor's office, picked up a stack of British papers, and said, "I don't want these around," and hurled them out into the newsroom. They scattered all over and the whole newsroom goes silent, because Rupert's throwing papers out of the editor's office. Then he went back into the office. Somebody said to him, "Do you have any idea what the reaction is when you do something like that?" He said, "Oh, of course I do."

ERIC FETTMANN, associate editorial page editor, columnist, 1976–1991, 1993–2019: Frank Devine was actually brought in to tone the paper down. That was a conscious decision by Rupert. Rupert would blow hot and cold. He'd want to tone the paper down, to attract advertisers. Then, if we lost readers, it would be: let's go back to the old formula. So Roger Wood was bumped upstairs and then sent to the *Star*. Frank was brought in from Chicago. They did not use the Murdoch formula in Chicago. Or if they did, it was to a very mild degree. They were more of a classic tabloid.

DICK BELSKY: In some ways, when Frank was running the *Post*, it was the best that it was. He took it upmarket somewhat, but you still had a lot of the tabloid element to it.

KEN CHANDLER, editor in chief, publisher, 1978–1986, 1993–2002: When they brought in Frank Devine to be the editor of the *Post*, I was pissed because I thought I should have got the job. I'd been Roger's number two for three or four years, and I thought everything was going fine. They were like, "Oh my god, he's upset." Then they sent me to Boston to be editor of the *Boston Herald*.

GEORGE ARZT, City Hall bureau chief, 1968–1986: I went to the *Boston Herald* to show them how to do polls and read polls. I met some guy who later became famous on Fox, Bill O'Reilly. What an opinionated asshole he was.

> While Frank Devine dialed back some of the *Post*'s more sensational tendencies, the newsroom remained largely untamed.

ERIC FETTMANN: When Roger Wood was replaced as editor, he was given an office on the sixth floor—basically his cave to dwell in. One time he came down to the fourth floor and Donnie Sutherland managed to put a sign on his back saying "Fourth floor visitor's pass."

CHARLIE CARILLO, reporter, columnist, 1978–1993: Frank Devine would come out in the newsroom and yell, "SOOEY." That's how he would call a meeting. Like a hog call. Everybody had to come in.

GEORGE ARZT: There was less structure under Frank. With Roger, I always knew what I had to do. I would talk to him every day. Frank told me about Chicago journalism and people who wrote for him at the Chicago paper. I kept scratching my head: this ain't Chicago. He was a very nice man, but I missed the heartbeat of a good tabloid, even with all the craziness of Dunleavy.

CHARLIE CARILLO: Chernobyl was terrifying. Al Ellenberg was on the desk, and we're all writing our doom-and-gloom stories. Somebody filed a story that said the poisons from Chernobyl will go into this river and that bay and the Atlantic Ocean and the Pacific Ocean and poison the world's waterways. Ellenberg looked at it and said, "Can we at least make it 'may'? So at least I can have my swordfish?" Those are the moments that broke the tension.

TIM McDARRAH, reporter, Page Six co-editor, 1985–1993: There's a photo of me chasing down Dan Rather after the "Kenneth, what's the frequency" incident. We wrote a pretty good story. The next day I got a call from him. He goes, "I don't necessarily like where you work, son, but I think you wrote a fair story." I didn't think it was Dan Rather at first because people would call up posing as famous people all the time. But the voice was familiar. He didn't become a source necessarily, but we spoke other times over the years. I'd call him whenever there was some CBS News upheaval.

CHARLIE CARILLO: When the *Challenger* exploded, I was on the rewrite bank. It was daytime and the pieces of the wreckage were still falling from the sky. David Ng and I had the astronauts' obits written as soon as—before—the wreckage hit the water. That was 1986. I remember Michael George, big Black guy who worked in the sports department. He was walking through the newsroom, shaking his head. I said, "You okay, Mike?" He turned to me and said, "I just know they're going to find a way to blame the Black astronaut."

ERIC FETTMANN: Marc Kalech was our space guy. He'd actually applied to be an astronaut when they were taking civilians and ended up with Christa McAuliffe. The day the *Challenger* exploded, Belsky said Kalech was stunned by the whole thing. He sat there moaning that now he would never get to fuck Judy Resnik, this hot Jewish astronaut who was on the flight.

DICK BELSKY: I was standing next to Marc in the newsroom when it exploded. I didn't hear him say that [about Judy Resnik] but if he did, it was said in that kind of *Post* newsroom, dark gallows type of humor. Marc immediately said, "I want to go down there." He got on a plane, got down to Cape Canaveral as soon as he could. And he did great, great work, some of the best of his career.

CHARLIE CARILLO: Coincidentally, Joey Adams had a bunch of astronaut jokes that ran the day the *Challenger* blew up, if I remember correctly. They had to be yanked. Occasionally we'd have "Fly Delta" ads next to a smoldering plane crash. Classic.

TERRY GOLWAY, sports copy editor, 1987–1992: I started in late summer or early fall of '87. I was on a two-week tryout, and the second night I was there, Dick Young dies, the top sportswriter in New York. There I am, I'm about to turn thirty-two—I'm not a kid, but I'm a little awestruck about being in the newsroom of a New York City paper. Dick Young dies. Jerry Lisker, Greg Gallo, and Frank Devine are scurrying about because I guess he died suddenly and there was no obituary prepared. I put up my hand and say, "I used to edit obituaries at the *Staten Island Advance*. If you want somebody to help out, I can do it." Amazingly, the three of them looked at me, and said, "Really? We're in the sports department, we don't deal with death." They said, "We'll take your help." They assigned the obituary to the second senior sportswriter, Maury Allen, who, in his own right, was quite famous at the time. He was the natural choice because he and Young had worked together for years—they had been competitors and later, after Dick Young came to the *Post*, colleagues. You would think he was the perfect choice. We're trying to get the obit done for the edition that went to press around 8:30. We're Dick Young's paper. We've got to get this out. The obituary comes in, and Lisker, with his gravelly voice, says, "Okay, kid, it's yours." Now, over my right shoulder is Frank Devine, the editor of the paper. On my left shoulder is Jerry Lisker. And here's the thing: Maury Allen hated Dick Young, and it showed. High up in the story, it said that Dick Young was a Hall of Fame sportswriter, renowned for years, but in his later years, he became a laughingstock. The word "laughingstock" was there. Mind you, it was true. In the mid- to late '80s, Dick Young's columns could have been written by Donald Trump or Bill O'Reilly. He used to lament what has happened to, quote, "my America." He was getting into politics and racial politics. Maury Allen maybe wasn't wrong, but perhaps he could have found a better way to phrase it. This is Dick Young's obituary—in his home newspaper! I remember saying, "We can't say this." They're like, "Yeah, right. Fix it up." I think I had ten minutes to edit before the 8:30 deadline. At that point Devine was fairly new. I'm not sure he knew who Dick Young was—but Lisker is coaching me. Suggesting words here and there. I get it done, and we all breathe a sigh of relief. I can't believe I did this, but I went to Lisker and Devine after this, and I said, "That obituary really sucked, and I would like to rewrite it completely between editions." They basically said, have at it. So, I completely rewrote Maury Allen's obituary of Dick Young. I sent him off to heaven with harps and violins—under Allen's byline, mind you. I made Maury Allen into a better writer. Then I did a sidebar—I don't know if it ever ran—of seven or eight paragraphs of vintage Dick Young—well, it wasn't even vintage Dick Young because vintage Dick Young would have been in the '60s—but memorable paragraphs he'd written. That's what went into the 11:15 edition. Some of the other sportswriters, like Phil Mushnick and Mike Marley, did pieces about him, too. My shift ended at about one o'clock. I go home. I come back the next day, and as I'm walking in, there's Frank Devine, who literally says, "Son! You've got a job!"

CHARLIE CARILLO: The 77th Precinct scandal—that was a big story. Guys like Mike McAlary [at *New York Newsday*] were all over it, big, heavy-hitting reporters. They said to me, we want to get an interview with Frank Serpico. Now Serpico at this point is still pretty much in hiding, but somebody from the drama department said, if you leave a message with [film director] Sidney Lumet, he can get through to Serpico. [Al Pacino played the whistle-blowing New York City cop in Lumet's 1973 film, *Serpico*.] I left the message because you got to cover your ass. I'm working some other story, and the phone rings. "We have a collect call from Frank Serpico. Do you accept the charges?" I clapped the phone to my chest and I mouthed to the editors, "I got Serpico." He says, "This is Frank—you looking for me?" It's this really gentle voice, and I think it helped that we were both Italian Americans. Once I primed him, he really wanted to talk—about how things never change, it's rotten to the core, we've got to do better than this. He gives me this terrific interview. I hang up the phone typing, twenty minutes to deadline. Phone rings again, collect call from Frank Serpico. He says, "I thought of another thing, Carillo." I type and say, "Thanks so much." I hang up. Now it's ten minutes to deadline. Phone rings again. Collect call from Frank. I felt like saying, "Hey, Frank, I'm on deadline here, you know what I mean?" But I didn't, of course I listened to him, finished it up, and he made me look really good that day. Front page, SERPICO SPEAKS. That's one of those sudden things, when it happens so quickly, you're in that zone. You have no time to write, but you do, you get it done.

JIM NOLAN, reporter, 1986–1993: It was right before one of Gotti's trials. They gave me this address in Howard Beach. They wanted me to do the classic—what do neighbors think about the Dapper Don going on trial? I was fairly new and they hooked me up with a new photographer, David Rentas. We're walking around and who but Mrs. Gotti, John's wife, comes out of the house in a housedress, hauling the garbage to the curb? David Rentas starts taking photos. Then we walk up to her. This is something you do when you're young and stupid. I said, "My name is Jim Nolan. I'm a reporter with the *New York Post*. I was wondering if I could talk to you about your husband going on trial," blah blah. We didn't ever expect Victoria Gotti. I knocked on a lot of doors when I worked for the *Post*, but that was the one door I was not going to knock on. But there she was. She gives me this stare and says, "After all the things you people have written about my husband, you have the nerve to come to my house, and ask me how I'm doing." I'm like, oh, this could go very badly. So I quickly said, "There's a lot being said about what he's been accused of. We just wanted to find some balance for the story, and talk to people who know him, we want to get that side of the story." She lets her guard down a little. She says, "All these people who are saying these things, they're rats, and they're squealers. But you ask anybody in this neighborhood, they'll tell you what a great man John is, he's a man all the way." We're talking for a few more minutes. Then Junior pulls up in some kind of Monte Carlo–looking car. Junior's a big guy. "Are these guys giving you trouble, Mom?" She said, "No, no, it's okay." We actually had a decent, pleasant conversation. But you could tell he would have knocked our blocks off if she had said, "Get this guy out of my face." We finish talking, and then as we're leaving, she says, "And no pictures." We didn't say anything. But I'm looking at Rentas. He's basically like every new reporter or photographer: you want to do what your boss tells you to do. We drive to a phone booth. Al Ellenberg gets on the line. He was one of my rabbis and a mentor just like [Dick] Belsky, but Ellenberg basically could have been a rabbi. Al is very deliberate and thoughtful. He's like, "You're gonna come back, then you're going to write a very careful story. Because if this woman doesn't like it, she can have your balls cut off." I write a straight story of what she said. The headline is "John's a man all the way." The first edition comes out, and it's got my story, and it's got the picture on the front page. Let's just say Mrs. Gotti had looked better. She looked like anybody looks when they're taking out the garbage. There's my name on the story. But there's no name on the photo. I called the desk, "I told you she said no photos." They're like, "Yeah, yeah, yeah." I said, "I'm the only person whose name is on this story." The next edition comes out. They took my name off. I'm like, "No!" I said, "The photographer's name should be on the picture. And my name should be on the story. My name has already been on this story. If something happened to me, I want people to know my name was on this story."

MARSHA KRANES, rewrite, editor, 1974–2005: I remember really courageous things that reporters did. There was a polar bear who killed somebody at the Prospect Park Zoo—a kid who somehow managed to get into the bear's cave or den. I assigned reporters to go to the other zoos, to see how easy it would be to get access to a cage. I get a call from the police precinct near Prospect Park, telling me, "We have a reporter of yours in custody for trying to climb into the . . ." It was Lucette Lagnado, this diminutive, frightened-looking little person; this tiny little thing . . . I mean, she would not have been even a canapé for the bear. But she said, "I was afraid I might not have my job if I didn't do it." But I didn't ask her to do it!

ANN V. BOLLINGER, national correspondent, reporter, 1986–1999: During the Iran-Contra hearings, Oliver North was testifying before Congress every day, and he was taking the Fifth. He was getting threats from different terrorist organizations because he was talking about whether or not they traded arms for hostages. He was under constant guard by special agents, and so was his family. He hadn't given any interviews whatsoever. One day, Al Ellenberg calls me into his office and says, "Ms. Bollinger"—he always called me Ms. Bollinger—"I have a special assignment for you. You're going down to the Iran-Contra hearings, and your assignment is to interview Ollie North." I go, "Is this prearranged?" He goes, "Oh, no. You have to go down and get the interview." I called it mission impossible. I was down there and the entire US and European press corps are covering the hearings. You can't even get near Ollie North because he's completely surrounded by these special agents all the time. I would go to his house—he lived in Virginia—and there were already three hundred reporters there staking him out. I was there for maybe two days trying to figure it out, and something occurred to me. I called Al and I said, "This is the plan I think we should do. I'm going to do a feature story on the agents that protect him—who they are, what they do, that they're willing to sacrifice their lives for Ollie North. We have to play it really big, lots of pictures." Al said, "Yes, yes. This is what we'll do." I went around and started interviewing the agents who were at his house. As promised, the *Post* played it big. A few days after it was in the paper, I was at the front of Ollie North's house with three hundred other reporters. It was early in the morning because we knew they were going to church. The agents come out, and they say, "Clear the way." I must have had a car phone. We had those big clunky car phones that looked like a brick. I called Al from the location and I said, "It's not working. They're just pushing me back." He's like, "Here's what you have to do, Ms. Bollinger. When the motorcade starts to leave the house, I want you to walk out into the middle of the street and block it." I'm like, "What?" He goes, "Block the motorcade. Just stand in front of it." I'm like, "Al, are you going to get me out of jail when they arrest me for blocking Ollie North's motorcade?" He's like, "Don't worry. We'll bail you out." I hang up the phone and I'm like, my god, this is ridiculous. But Al and I had this thing. He would always say, "Just trust me." So, as the motorcade is coming out of Ollie North's driveway, I stepped into the street and blocked it with my little notebook in my hand. All the other reporters are looking at me like I'm a nut. The agents there knew me because I had just done this huge story on them. They're saying, "Ann! Get out of the street. We're going to have to arrest you." I'm like, "Can I please just have a few words with Ollie." They're coming toward me like they're going to drag me away, and I hear the noise of an electric window rolling down. I look over, and Ollie North is sitting in the back seat of a car reading the *New York Post*. He said, "Did you write this story about my men?" I said, "Yes, I did." He said, "Do you know that these men would take a bullet for me?" I'm like, "Yes, that's why I wrote the story." He looks at me, looks at the *Post*, and he opens his door. He says, "Get in. You can ride with me." I got an exclusive interview. I went to church with the family and hung out with them all day long.

That Murodochian brand of bold inventiveness backfired in a big way for Hal Goldenberg when he went to extraordinary lengths to see his beloved Mets play in the World Series.

HAL GOLDENBERG, photographer, 1979–1986: I got fired because I took the press passes to the World Series. I'm not a Mets fan—I'm a lunatic. My mother took me to the first game they ever played as an organized team at the Polo Grounds in [Upper Manhattan]. If you look at the videos of when they won, I'm the second or third person to the mound in '69, and, after they won in '86, I'm the second one to jump on Jesse Orosco after he went down on his knees and crossed himself. In '86, I couldn't get tickets without spending a small fortune, so I took one of the press credentials out of the photo desk drawer. In '85, they first came out with color Xerox. I went to a color Xerox store and spent about $13 to get copies made. I threw the guy five bucks and told him, "You didn't see this." I took the two sides, pasted them together, and laminated them. Either the *Post* knew I did it and gave the people at the gate a heads-up, or the girl at the gate was sharp and noticed. They grabbed me, confiscated the credentials, and blah blah. I went into the parking lot and bought a scalped ticket anyway, and when I got back to the office, Joy Cook, the union person, was there. We didn't get along, so she didn't want to help me. I'm pretty sure they used what I did as an excuse to get rid of me because the drug thing got out of hand. It got worse afterward. Now, if a countryman got too fucked up drinking and/or doing drugs—there were Australian people in the office that did drugs, too—they would put them in a rehab and pay for it. But being that I wasn't from Australia, I got fired. It was enough. I did my seven years.

MILTON GOLDSTEIN, copy editor, 1974–current: John Waldvogel was the overnight driver for a while. John loved owls and he would go upstate or somewhere and he would take an owl from a nest—he'd say, "The mother can't count"—and he'd raise them. He fed them live rats. Plenty of rats on South Street by the water. I'm not sure how many times the owl was in the car when he drove an editor. Not that often. It wasn't his pet owl on the dashboard or anything.

AMY PAGNOZZI, reporter, columnist, 1979–1993: He was weird. And I have a huge tolerance for weirdness. Nobody would accuse me of being socially well adjusted, but even by my standards, I thought he was really weird.

BOB YOUNG, photo editor, 1978–1986: Roger [Wood] sort of fell in love with Waldvogel, not romantically. John wanted to be a photographer. He said he wanted to cover the story of how drugs were getting into the country. Much to the consternation of all of us in the photo department, where we always had trouble getting new equipment, Roger arranged for John to get a new Nikon camera set. He goes to Pakistan. One day I come into the office and a US official in Lahore calls and says, "Mr. Young, one of your photographers was found in a hotel. He was dead for three or four days. The local authorities went crazy and they buried him." We did get the cameras back, about four months later. I don't think he died of the common cold.

In 1986, the *Post* hired a new editorial page editor, thirty-year-old Eric Breindel, who, less than three years earlier, had been busted for buying heroin in Washington, DC, while on the staff of New York senator Pat Moynihan. A drug arrest would have derailed most careers, but Breindel's high-powered connections, many forged at Harvard—where he befriended various Kennedys, including Caroline and her cousin Robert Jr.—largely erased the stain of his days as a junkie. Having been raised in a liberal Jewish household in Manhattan, Breindel would have made a neat fit for the Dorothy Schiff–era *Post* had he retained that sensibility. But Breindel's politics in the mid-1980s aligned with neo-cons like *Commentary* editor in chief Norman Podhoretz, one of his mentors.

ERIC FETTMANN: Breindel was as smart as they come. He came highly recommended by people like Pat Moynihan, whom he'd worked for, and a lot of other people. Really good writer. They needed somebody who knew and understood global, national, and local politics and shared their worldview.

MARTY McLAUGHLIN, public relations and political consultant: Claudius, we called him. Eric was very smart, he was really well read. There was a brilliance about him. But he was also extremely conservative. I mean, to the right of the right.

ERIC FETTMANN: We ran Pat Buchanan's syndicated column. He wrote a series of columns on the search for Nazi war criminals, which were pretty over the line. One actually went way over the line and was out-and-out Holocaust denial. Eric Breindel called him and said, "This is really unacceptable stuff. You're wrong." Buchanan's response was, "I hear you," but he wouldn't change it. Breindel was the son of Holocaust survivors. For him it was an especially sensitive issue. But he never gave any thought to killing the column. He ran it. And he ran a long editorial criticizing and disputing the column right next to it.

JILL ABRAMSON, former executive editor, *The New York Times*: I knew Breindel really well from childhood. He went to the same elementary school I did and his sister, who's one year older than he was, is one of my really close friends. I spent a lot of time at their apartment on Gramercy Park. His politics underwent a huge change. He left [New York] to go to Exeter [prep school in New Hampshire], but we were reunited and lived in the same house at Harvard, Winthrop House. His politics there were not conservative, although people have said they were becoming more so. I didn't notice. But by the time he was doing the editorial page of the *Post*, certainly I noticed he'd gone off the deep end. He once made me truly furious. I ran into him at the White House Correspondents' Dinner in Washington. It was maybe a year after Jane Mayer and I had written the book

[*Strange Justice*] about Clarence Thomas and Anita Hill. He gave me a hug and a kiss and said, "You don't believe any of that stuff you wrote in the book." I was, like, *what?!* That was my signal that he and I no longer could transact. I vouched for him to the FBI, before he worked for Moynihan, so I stuck my neck out for him, and then he got arrested for heroin. I was really close to him. It wasn't like I officially stopped talking to him, but it seemed to me that he'd become a lunatic.

JOE CONASON, former reporter, *The Village Voice*: Breindel's politics were sickening to me—hard-core, red-baiting, right wing. And at the same time, he was this squeaky-voiced character; he had this idea of himself as kind of a jumped-up society figure, because he dated Lally Weymouth [daughter of *Washington Post* owner Katharine Graham]. He was truly horrible. And very well suited to editing the *Post* editorial page.

ERIC FETTMANN: As the years went on, and there were a lot of changes in the city, the *Post* recaptured part of the Jewish audience, which had grown more conservative. In a way the timing was right. You had people like Koch and Giuliani, who started moving the city in a more conservative direction. It has never become a conservative city but under the whole fear of crime, you did have a different attitude.

> Koch's third term, which began in 1986, was marked by scandal. Queens borough president Donald Manes, once favored by Murdoch as a potential successor to the mayor, figured prominently in one of the biggest political stories of the '80s, the Parking Violations Bureau (PVB) scandal. Right before his connection to a web of kickbacks and bribes became public, Manes attempted suicide. As indictments and convictions rained down on other city agencies and their leaders, including Brooklyn and Bronx borough presidents Meade Esposito and Stanley Friedman, respectively, Koch finished his political career under fire.

GEORGE ARZT: I called an FBI guy. I said, "Does Manes's attempted suicide have anything to do with PVB?" He said, "We can't tell you anything, but if you say something that's incorrect, we'll tell you." I said, "Okay." I went to the Green Book [a directory of New York City government]. I said, "Is this an investigation of Shafran?" Silence. "Is this an investigation of Lindenauer?" Silence. [Lester Shafran and Geoffrey Lindenauer were top PVB officials.] "Is this an investigation of Manes?" Silence. So I write my story, and the lawyers for the *Post*, one was Slade Metcalf, came back and said, "If we publish this story, Manes will own the paper." I said, "It's true." He said, "Who do you have?" I said, "I have an FBI guy." The lawyers said, "You have to have a second corroboration." The *Post* publishes the story without names, just "Three top city officials in bribe probe." The next day, there is a City Hall press conference. I tell [TV journalist] Gabe Pressman to ask who were the three top officials being investigated. Slade Metcalf had said that when I went to the press conference, I couldn't bring this up. So I asked Gabe Pressman to do it. Gabe gave some convoluted question. Joyce Purnick [then at the *New York Times*] screamed out, "What's he talking about?" [Deputy Mayor Stanley] Brezenoff said, "He's talking about Geoffrey Lindenauer." I call it in. Metcalf gets on and says, "You didn't ask that, did you?" I said, "No, Gabe Pressman did." Of course, he didn't really because no one knew what Gabe was talking about. But Brezenoff gave us Lindenauer's name. [Manes attempted suicide a second time by plunging a steak knife into his heart on March 13, 1986. He succeeded.]

The *Post*'s outsized impact on the city caught the attention of Tom Wolfe, who used the *Post* as a model for *The City Light*, a tabloid that figured prominently in his novel *The Bonfire of the Vanities*, which became a runaway bestseller and, later, a terrible movie. Peter Fallow, the novel's tabloid reporter character, was said to have been inspired by Liverpudlian Peter Fearon, one of Steve Dunleavy's favorite reporters. Although Fearon, a controversial figure in the newsroom, fit the description, the dubious distinction actually belonged to another Brit.

ED HAYES, agent, attorney who inspired defense lawyer Tommy Killian in *The Bonfire of the Vanities*: Peter Fallow wasn't based on Peter Fearon. It was another guy—upper-class English, he drank and behaved badly at parties. Anthony Haden-Guest.

PETER FEARON, reporter, 1980–1987: The original description in *Rolling Stone* [where *Bonfire* first appeared, in serial form] of Peter Fallow was—how can I put it? It was descriptive of my lifestyle at that time. Also, you have the name, Peter F., and the *New York Post*. But it was never closer than that.

ED HAYES: *The City Light* was the *Post* and the book itself is written like the *Post*. Tom was a great tabloid reporter. People don't remember that. They think, well, he's this very white-suit kind of guy. He was a great tabloid reporter. He could see a story, and the city and the criminal justice system was the story at that time. And he had it.

PHILIP MESSING, reporter, 1978–1991, 1994–2016: I've seen Peter Fearon a few times in the years since, and he seems to have mellowed out, but he was a really obnoxious person back in the day.

DONNIE SUTHERLAND, city desk assistant, 1978–1988: You're sitting very close to people every day, and you can't go through that without having a hissy fit once in a while. Peter was one of those people that would have gotten beaten up a lot in my playground. He seemed to have no problem shooting off at the mouth. But he didn't have a charm side. That was a problem. I was handling a dog story. People were always calling in with stories about a dog to be adopted. I had to brush this person off, and Peter didn't like the way I was handling it. After I hung up, he made a derogatory comment about my character. He was standing near me.

PETER FEARON: Somebody called who had had something devastating happen to her and Donnie was rude to her. After he got off the phone, I sort of remonstrated with him.

DONNIE SUTHERLAND: I just took his head and smashed it into the typewriter in front of me. His friend Dick McWilliams, a charming man, grabbed my arms. Any other job, I would be up for a lawsuit. You don't assault people. I slammed his head into my typewriter. He had a bloody nose. All the sports guys, Jerry Lisker and his staff, stood up—they saw some action like "Oh! Fight!" Everybody had deadlines, stories, but everybody stopped. [Editorial Manager] Peter Faris comes out of his office like a disciplinary father and says, "Get in my office, the two of you, right now." I figured that's the end of that job. I was apologetic right off the bat. "Peter, I'm so sorry." Fearon didn't want to hear it. He just looked up from his bloody tissue. Then Faris says, "Looks like everything's okay here. Just go back." Peter was on the desk opposite me the rest of the day. Later on, we were drinking someplace and there he was. He pretended to throw a shot right at my face. I said, "Yeah, go ahead. Tit for tat." But he pulled back. George Arzt was the one who called first and said, "Is it true? Did you hit him?" I thought, how the hell did the City Hall bureau chief find out so fast?

PHILIP MESSING: There was a no-fighting rule. They decided that they were immediately going to fire Donnie Sutherland. Donnie was well respected and well liked, and you could not say the same for Fearon. Everybody said, "We're protesting. We're not going to work. We don't want Donnie fired." The next thing you know, they did what you do in school. They said, "Okay, you apologize to him, and he'll apologize to you, and we'll pretend it never happened." I mean, this is the type of place it was.

PETER FEARON: I got suspended for a day, I think. There are worst punishments than a day off. I think Donnie had something similar.

> New Page Six editor Richard Johnson brought his own brand of pugnaciousness to the job—feuding with bellicose celebrities. Mickey Rourke was the first. Alec Baldwin and others would follow.

ED HAYES: I represented Richard [Johnson]. He really, really knew how to grab a story. He understood that one of the key things you have to do as a gossip columnist is you have to have feuds.

RICHARD JOHNSON, Page Six editor, 1978–1990, 1993–2019: It started when they didn't have a cartoon on Page Six. They were using photographs. One day, somebody pulled a photograph of Mickey Rourke with some woman who was not his wife. It had a caption basically saying that. I had nothing to do with it. Mickey got very upset. Because basically, it's like, he's cheating. He was giving an interview to somebody else, and he attacked me.

GEORGE RUSH, Page Six reporter, 1986–1993: Mickey Rourke became one of these public figures that Page Six targeted for ridicule whenever his name came up. He was always getting into some kind of trouble. So, every time there was a Mickey Rourke item, Richard would run the most unflattering picture of Mickey in character as Charles Bukowski, the alcoholic poet he played in the [1987] movie *Barfly*, and refer to him as Mickey "Barfly" Rourke. One time, Richard was on vacation, the phone rang on the desk, and I picked it up. I hear this voice, "Yo, is Richard Johnson there?" and I said, "I'm sorry, he is on vacation." I hear, "This is Mickey Rourke. You tell him that I'm going to kick his ass when he gets back. I'm tired of those lies he's writing about me, and we're going to settle this man to man." In the background, I heard some guys yelling, "You tell him, Mick! You tell him!"

RICHARD JOHNSON: It may have extended to the *Daily News* [where Johnson wrote a column in the early '90s]. Rourke had said he wanted to beat me up or something. I ran a story saying, "Any time, any place." I did a little research. I outweighed him, and I'd seen some of his fights. The guy couldn't fight worth a lick. Everybody had to agree not to hit him in the face when they fought him because I think he had so much plastic surgery that if you hit him in the face, it would explode.

GEORGE RUSH: The bout never came off but it did yield a classic Johnson line: "The only thing Mickey Rourke is fit to box is pizza."

> Another gossip gold mine for Page Six was Elaine's. When Elaine Kaufman opened her eponymous restaurant on the Upper East Side in 1963, she attracted a writing clientele, with George Plimpton, Gay Talese, and Norman Mailer among her regulars. Celebrities followed and in the mid- to late '70s, Elaine's became *the* watering hole for the performers from *Saturday Night Live*, then in the process of remaking late-night television. Some of the writing customers worked as journalists, including all of Page Six's editors over the years. An evening at Elaine's reliably produced an item or two. As the '80s neared an end, reporters often occupied more seats than stars did.

BOB DRURY, sports columnist, 1977–1984: Mike McAlary and I were in Elaine's one night, and Jerry Brown, the governor of California, walks in, and he had just broken up with Linda Ronstadt. McAlary goes up to Tommy the bartender and says, "Give me twenty-five quarters." He goes over the jukebox, and he plays Linda Ronstadt's "You're No Good" twenty-five times. Elaine, of course, knows it's us. She turns toward our table, shoots daggers, marches over to the jukebox, and pulls the plug.

KENNY MORAN, sportswriter, outdoor sports and skiing, 1972–2013: Elaine was the best. She knew how to take care of newspaper people, media people in general. She loved the guys 'cause the guys were the ones who spent money. I saw her throw out a table of women who didn't have a drink on the table. They ordered seltzers or something. I got winked at by Elizabeth Taylor. I got to kiss Sophia Loren's hand. I dated Joey Heatherton. Yeah, I did, for a while. I first walked in, and she jumped on top of me. She thought I was this hockey player from Boston, Derek Sanderson. I guess I looked like him. She looked at me, and I said, "I don't know who you think I am, but I will be him." She got all embarrassed. Later on that evening, she was just sitting by herself. I went over and started talking to her. Boom, boom, boom, she gave me her number. I want to say it went on and off for eight months or so. Then she wound up with Frank Sinatra Jr.

BOB DRURY: Elaine's went through phases. In the late '80s, when the *SNL* people stopped coming, and the celebs kind of fell off a little bit, we filled that gap. I wasn't at the *Post* then, but me, Mike McAlary, and Richie Esposito started bringing the detectives, and it became a cop place. [Police Commissioner William] Bratton loved the spotlight, so he was there a lot.

> Steve Dunleavy briefly got his wish to become part of the Page Six machinery. The machine kept churning regardless of whose name appeared on the column. His stint there was brief. Murdoch had other plans for him.

RICHARD JOHNSON: Dunleavy was working sort of secretly, but he didn't have his name on the page. Just from reading it, you would never know what he was up to. But he was definitely involved. Although I had to do all the work—he couldn't keep track of eight stories at a time. He was basically like a star reporter who would work on one story. Sometimes it would work. He left quickly to go to television [the syndicated TV program *A Current Affair*, produced by Fox's New York station]. That was probably for the best, for both of us.

> In 1986, Roy Cohn, the *Post*'s favorite political fixer in the Murdoch era, lost his livelihood, and soon after, his life.

HAL DAVIS, reporter, New York State Supreme Court, 1978–1993: As a lawyer, Roy sucked. His disbarment brought that out in rather close detail.

> Though the *Post* had killed Hal Davis's scoop on Cohn's mounting professional troubles three years earlier, it had to stop ignoring the inevitable. As Cohn came to the end of his long career as a power broker, the *Post* ran ROY COHN DISBARRED as the wood. The paper also gave Cohn space to defend himself. He claimed he "couldn't care less" about the "cheap politicians" who had brought him down: "I feel about as concerned about this as if Hellmann's had called me to say they had come out with a new brand of mayonnaise."

SUSAN MULCAHY, Page Six editor, 1978–1985: Roy died right after the disbarment. I was surprised that the *Post* ran the cause of death, complications from AIDS, which Roy had pretended he didn't have. He said it was liver cancer.

> With the Fox network and a collection of TV stations in the nation's largest markets, Murdoch ordered the creation of original programming, much of it—in front of the camera and behind—shaped by voices familiar to readers of his print properties. Steve Dunleavy and Cindy Adams both appeared on *A Current Affair* and other former and future *Post* employees produced or wrote for the program. The age of tabloid TV had begun.

KEN CHANDLER: Dunleavy left the *Post* because, one, they were starting *A Current Affair*. I think also Rupert was getting a little nervous about some of the things Dunleavy was doing at the *Post* and wanted to move him out. At some point, [before Roger Wood was kicked upstairs] there was tension between Steve and Roger, and I think Murdoch thought that Roger wasn't able to control Dunleavy, and that Dunleavy had become too much of a free agent who was doing whatever the hell he wanted to do. It was convenient, because they wanted him at *A Current Affair*.

CHARLES LACHMAN, reporter, 1981–1988: Murdoch bought the Metromedia stations and I said to myself, "Here I go." I'd always wanted to work in TV. Very quickly Dunleavy went over there, Bob Young, too, and I said, "You've got to bring me there." At that time, it was revolutionary in television in terms of its stories and its approach. I had to get there. But Murdoch was in a bit of a jam. You couldn't own a TV station and a newspaper in the same market. There was all this political turmoil about the cross ownership, and I was caught in the middle. They wouldn't bring me to Fox until I had another job, even though Bob Young and Dunleavy had gone there. They felt it was too many bodies going from the *Post* to Fox. They wanted to claim that they'd be separate editorially. I got hired by the *Daily News*, and I gave my two weeks' notice at the *Post*. On the Friday before I was supposed to start at the *Daily News*, Bob Young called and said, "Welcome to television." I called Artie Browne, the city editor of the *Daily News*, and told him I wasn't going to be coming. He was really upset and ripped me one, but, oh well. That Monday I started at *A Current Affair*. The plan was always for me to learn "television" at *A Current Affair* and then go to local news as managing editor, and that's what happened. Cynthia Fagen was there, Dunleavy was the star of the show, Maury Povich was the anchor. John Corry in the *New York Times* wrote a very strong, positive review. There's nothing like working on a hot show, and that was a hot show. It was making a TV revolution, and very controversial. No one had ever done anything like it before.

> The Murdoch machine's first entry into original TV programming became a ratings success and even more of a national headline generator than the *Post*. Dunleavy, who proved as outrageous on TV as he had been in print, became a minor star. His TV antics included wrestling a bear on camera, and in 1991, taping an interview with Michele Cassone, who was at the Kennedy family's Palm Beach estate when Senator Ted Kennedy's nephew, William Kennedy Smith, allegedly raped a woman on the beach. (Kennedy Smith was acquitted later that year.) Cassone did not claim she had witnessed the alleged crime, but she nonetheless became a frequent interview subject for the media. During her *A Current Affair* segment, Dunleavy showed Cassone a photo of her engaged in oral sex, and the interview turned physical. Before the two were separated, Cassone had elbowed Dunleavy in the gut, kneed him in the groin, and bitten his hand. Footage of the interview, which can be viewed on YouTube, shows Dunleavy smiling through all of it.

STUART MARQUES, managing editor, news, 1993–2001: I was at *A Current Affair* beginning in October 1990. Steve's personality was a perfect fit. He had a great sense of news value, and how to milk a story. I don't know about [wrestling a] bear, but are you talking about Michele Cassone? He had the picture of her giving someone a blowjob. I was there for that. They went out to lunch, and they probably had a drink or two. I see them coming back, and she's all laughing, and I said to myself, oh, you don't know what you're getting into, girl. It went from there. I don't remember how we got that picture. I think we came across it in Florida when we were talking to people who knew her. But we got it, and Steve was going to spring it on her. And that's what happened.

WAYNE DARWEN, assistant managing editor, 1983–1987: I ended up running *A Current Affair* for a while with a buddy of mine, Burt Kearns, after [the program's creator] Peter Brennan went to *Hard Copy*. I incorporated those screaming *Post*-style headlines in type on the story-opens. And we used a lot of the same devices that were used in writing a story. You hit it hard; tease the story but don't tell them everything. Let it unfold. TV hadn't been done like that. I went from *A Current Affair* to *Now It Can Be Told* with Geraldo [Rivera], and I did the same thing over there. You took that tabloid style of storytelling, and you used the same technique and devices, but you applied it to television. That, in turn, changed the way I wrote when I wrote for print, too. Because then I incorporated some of the short, half-sentence stuff into my writing. If I write now, I write with a combination of TV and print devices—not too wordy; very short, punchy, let sound work for you. I think the *New York Post* was the greatest influence of all. Those *Post* front pages. You couldn't beat them.

CHARLES LACHMAN: What I brought to television, at *A Current Affair* and Fox, and at *Inside Edition*, was the headline. The thing about the *Post*, headlines were like diamonds. They were fine-tuned, you knew instantly what the story was, and I think that is a key component of what makes the *Post* a success, and what makes what I learned in television a success, which is: think about the headline; what's the narrative? Keep it linear, keep it simple: A B C D, and most important of all, think pictures. In the *Post*, you didn't get the front page unless you had the artwork to go with it. It's stating the obvious, but in television, a lot of these stories were written as if they were being written for newspapers, and nothing is as dry as a TV story that doesn't have the images to go with it. You had to think visually, and that's something that I brought over from the *Post*. In this case it wasn't so much still shots, but video.

CYNTHIA FAGEN, reporter, 1976–1986: Working at the *Post* was like my childhood. I learned how to listen, I learned how to socialize with people of all different backgrounds. I loved the thrill of the chase. It was an adventure every day. Tabloid is shouting the story instead of whispering it. I took the skills with me and applied them as a TV producer.

STUART MARQUES: *A Current Affair* and the shows that followed it really changed news media and video magazines. Elements of tabloid TV crossed into, for lack of a better word, mainstream shows: faster cuts, wackier stories sometimes, and stories with an edge. A lot of the people who went to those other shows started out at *A Current Affair*. Peter Brennan and some of those guys went to *Hard Copy*. Charlie Lachman and others went to *Inside Edition*. It was that same mentality. But nobody could do it like Steve.

ERIC FETTMANN: Dunleavy had left *A Current Affair*. He was going to be starting a new Fox show called *The Reporters*. He had, I think, a week between shows and he had gone on the mother of all pisses. He shows up at the *Post*, not having changed his clothes in a week, unshaven, completely smashed, looking like somebody who'd wandered over from the Bowery, missing a few teeth. I think he had false teeth. He's telling the guards to let him in because he used to be the metro editor. They're saying "Move on," until Richard Johnson shows up, recognizes him, and brings him up to the city room. It was Dunleavy like you had never seen him before. He reeked. Dunleavy wanted some money so he could get something to eat. I think I finally gave him five bucks. He goes downstairs to the cafeteria, orders a plate of mashed potatoes. And immediately collapses face-first into the potatoes. I didn't see it, but somebody said, "You're not gonna believe this, but Dunleavy is asleep in a bowl of mashed potatoes." Apparently, he showed up a couple of days later at *The Reporters* like nothing had ever happened. The man had the most amazing powers of recovery.

> Murdoch's ownership of a film studio occasionally led to awkward, conflict-of-interest moments.

JIM MONES, drama editor, 1980–1987: Dan Aquilante came back to the office to do a Popcorn Panel after talking to moviegoers about a new film [from Twentieth Century Fox, Murdoch's studio]. "I have some bad news for you," Dan said. "Only three people liked it." Nobody wanted to see a Popcorn Panel slam a Murdoch movie. I said, "*Three* liked it? Great! The headline will be, 'Three cheers for the movie!'" And that's what we printed.

> Murdoch's expansion into broadcast media in the US came with a catch and, for Senator Ted Kennedy, an opportunity for payback. When Murdoch bought the Metromedia station group in 1985, he was aware of the FCC regulation precluding ownership of a television station and a newspaper in the same market, as well as the necessity of becoming a naturalized US citizen. (He became an American that same year.) Three of his new stations put him in violation of the cross-ownership regulation, including WNEW-TV in New York. Murdoch had been granted a two-year waiver to meet the FCC requirements. When the two-year grace period ended, Murdoch assumed he would be granted an exemption in New York, thereby allowing him to keep WNEW-TV and the *Post*. After all, the *Post* lost money and employed a large number of people, so keeping it alive verged on philanthropy.

MICHAEL SHAIN, television editor, 1978–1993, 1996–2013: The weirdest part was to be involved in trying to convince people to let [Murdoch] keep the paper. The

FCC and Congress could give exemptions. And the [Newspaper Guild] was very much involved in lobbying Congress to say, look, give him an exemption. The whole point was the paper wasn't making any money. We knew that he was subsidizing the whole thing. I remember going [with other Newspaper Guild reps] to see Cardinal O'Connor and trying to get him to come out for us, which he did. He was always a very pro-union Catholic clergyman. If the union wanted this, then the cardinal was saying, "Okay, I'm out for you guys."

Ted Kennedy may have been a Roman Catholic, but he apparently didn't care that a leading Catholic prelate had declared his support for Rupert Murdoch. Kennedy made certain that the press lord did not receive an exemption or anything resembling special dispensation.

WAYNE DARWEN: I don't know where Murdoch's enmity toward Kennedy came from. I can guess where Kennedy's enmity toward Murdoch might have come from. That would have gone back to Dunleavy and that [1976] book *Those Wild, Wild Kennedy Boys* [co-written with Peter Brennan], and all the Kennedy stories they did. Dunleavy, I remember, swam across [Poucha Pond, where Mary Jo Kopechne drowned] to show that Kennedy could have done it. They just fed off the Kennedys. It was always scandal. Unless it's bad news, it ain't news.

ERIC FETTMANN: It was all Ted Kennedy's doing, using Fritz Hollings of South Carolina as his straw man. They put through this rider to a three-thousand-page communications bill that would prevent anyone from cross-owning a newspaper and a broadcast property in the same city but which grandfathered in all existing arrangements. It was clearly aimed at Murdoch. Both [New York senators] Pat Moynihan and Al D'Amato did what they could, but they could not get Kennedy to reverse.

MICHAEL SHAIN: The big moment was when the union people—the Guild—went down to DC to lobby Teddy Kennedy. We knew that the Guild, especially at the *Post*, was terribly vulnerable. And that if Murdoch left, whoever came in could slice and dice. Joy Cook went with Barry Lipton, the head of the Guild in all New York. And maybe one other person. Apparently, it was one of the worst meetings of all time. Kennedy made it pretty clear that he wasn't going to go for the exemption. Murdoch having to sell the *Post* was one man's decision: Teddy Kennedy's. If Teddy had said, "Okay," Murdoch could have kept the *Post*.

PART III: 1988–1992

INTERREGNUM

22 | ENTER KALIKOW

New Owner, New Editor, Fewer Australians

For those who cared only about balance sheets, selling the *New York Post* would have been a no-brainer. According to the *Washington Post*, the paper headquartered at 210 South Street had lost more than $100 million since Murdoch acquired it for $31 million in 1976—$17 million in 1987 alone. The Fox network, on the other hand, was on its way to becoming a successful fourth television network. But money had nothing to do with Murdoch's decision to give up the *Post*; he had been forced by government regulations, one of his perennial banes, to relinquish his first important American acquisition. Now some other proprietor would have the opportunity to discover the tabloid's true value. The paper's fragile financial health undercut its appeal to potential buyers as an influential political voice and bully pulpit.

DAVID SCHNEIDERMAN, former editor in chief, publisher, CEO, *The Village Voice*: Leonard Stern owned the *Voice* [purchased from Murdoch in 1985] and he decided he'd like to buy the *New York Post*. Leonard was the kind of guy who would make quick decisions. He owned a private company [the Hartz Mountain pet supply empire]. He sent his CFO down to the *Post* and said, "This is what I want to pay for it, let me know." I'm sitting in Leonard's office, hours go by, and this guy comes back and he said, "We've got a deal to buy the *Post*." I said, "Oh, shit." Then they walk through the deal, and Leonard realized that in his quickness in making this decision, he left a few zeros off something. He'd made a mathematical miscalculation in his head. He said to this guy, "Call up Rupert's guys and say, the deal's off." That all happened in one afternoon.

ERIC FETTMANN, associate editorial page editor, columnist 1976–1991, 1993–2019: Murdoch and his people did not sell to the first bidder. People sniffed around, and there was one serious bidder—a real estate developer named Philip Pilevsky. He was a liberal, though, and he would have moved the paper to the left. They didn't sell to him partly because of that, and partly because I think they suspected he might actually be able to make a go of it. He was a real estate operator, but he'd done more than that. He'd been involved politically, too.

PHILIP PILEVSKY, chairman and CEO, Philips International: We tried to buy the *Post*. I forget the price exactly—thirty, thirty-five million? It was a long time ago. The paper was losing money, but they owned a property on South Street—that's the reason I was interested, the real estate. I would have kept it going, sure. We had a couple of ways to cut the costs down. They were wasting a lot of money. Within two years we would have broken even. Maybe we wouldn't have made any money, but we would have broken even. I wasn't worried about the unions. I'm used to dealing with unions. I was somewhat involved politically back then. I'm an independent, but I definitely would have moved [the *Post*] to the left. We had the money. We didn't know why they didn't sell to us.

ERIC FETTMANN: Everybody was surprised when they picked [Peter] Kalikow, who had done nothing but real estate and whose only political involvement was as a [financial] contributor. I remember talking to Roger Wood and saying, "I suspect that you guys picked someone who you think is not going to be able to keep the paper running without losing a ton of money, and then you'll be able to step in and take it back." Roger said, "I don't think you're entirely wrong there."

PETER KALIKOW, owner, 1988–1993: [Media executive] Peter Price said to me, "You should buy the *Post*." My answer was, "Nah, I don't want to get involved, what do I know about newspapers?" Then they started convincing me that it was a good idea. What I realized early on is that most people that wanted me to buy it didn't want me to buy it for me. They wanted me to buy it for them. Peter thought he could figure out a way to figure himself into the paper. But water under the dam, over the dam. Murdoch didn't think I was serious when I first tried to get a price, or Price tried to get it for me. But then [Reagan foreign policy adviser and then–*Post* columnist] Jeane Kirkpatrick—my guess is she said something to Murdoch like, "If you left it in his hands, he'd keep the *Post* in the same political vein as you have. It would be good for our political group in America."

A high-end real estate developer who favored suspenders and brightly colored socks, Kalikow was then one of the four hundred wealthiest Americans with an estimated worth of $500 million, according to *Forbes*. He paid $37.6 million for the *Post* in a deal that gave Murdoch first right of refusal should Kalikow ever sell the paper. Some speculated that the value of 210 South Street's waterfront property is what led Kalikow to purchase the money-losing paper. The *Washington Post* reported that Kalikow could close the paper, pay off its estimated $30 million in contract obligations, and develop the site.

PETER KALIKOW: Sometimes it's hard to make people see the truth. I would say, if I wanted to buy real estate, I could think of twenty places I'd rather have than 210 South Street. I think I started with [*Post* editorial page editor] Eric Breindel. I showed him where my properties were and said, "Why the hell would I want to come down here to this mess?" We had to have plexiglass windows on the west side of 210 South Street because of the guys shooting BBs from the projects.

A small group of employees favored by Murdoch received a special token of his appreciation for their service under his ownership.

DICK BELSKY, metropolitan editor, 1970–1989: I still have the watch, engraved from Rupert. Exact wording on the back is, "My thanks and appreciation, Rupert Murdoch." It was an expensive watch, a Tourneau, and someone—maybe [Al] Ellenberg—took it to a jeweler and found it was worth $1,000.

Kalikow took control of the paper on March 7, 1988, and named Peter Price publisher. They immediately hired George Lois, celebrated for his provocative *Esquire* magazine covers in the 1960s and early 1970s, to redesign the paper. A $500,000 ad campaign in newspapers, on TV, and on the sides of city buses and bus stop shelters also heralded the new ownership. One featured an engraving of the paper's founder, Alexander Hamilton, with the copy line "Don't worry, your paper is in good hands!" Another declared, "We're keeping the sizzle, but adding the steak." Despite Kalikow's conservative politics, he added liberal voices to the *Post*'s editorial pages. But editor Frank Devine, who replaced Roger Wood in 1986 and stayed at the paper after Murdoch bowed out, bristled at some of the new owner's directives.

PETER KALIKOW: If you ever watched the National Geographic Channel and seen how a gorilla will walk around and piss in a circle to say, this is my area, Frank Devine used to do that every once in a while. He would have a tantrum that he was the editor of the paper. The first couple of times I didn't say anything. Finally, one day I said, "Hey, Frank, you're not the editor of this paper because God came down from Sinai with a message that you're the editor of the paper. You're the editor of the paper as long as I say you are." He didn't like it.

DICK BELSKY: They set up this lunch between Pete Hamill and Frank Devine. Frank asked me to come along. I didn't really know Pete, but like most people, I was a big admirer. We went to the Water Club. Pete started making suggestions to Frank about staffing—like, I know some good people, and I could put you in touch with them. Frank went kind of nuts. He was a big guy. I got along great with him, but he could be intimidating. When he got mad, his face would get red. He goes off on Pete. It was some version of: don't you tell me how to run my paper. He tells Pete to butt out. I thought they were going to come to blows. I remember looking down at the water, thinking, oh my god, what is going to happen? The only thing I can think of is that somebody was pushing Pete Hamill on Frank, and that must have been Kalikow.

PETER KALIKOW: I told Eric Breindel, "I don't want a left-wing lunatic, but we need to have other points of view." It started with the editorial page. Someone told me I should have Hamill back as a columnist. I didn't realize that Hamill didn't work that hard, but he gave us legitimacy.

DICK BELSKY: Jerry Nachman was out of work, I guess because he had left whatever TV station he had been at. He wrote Frank [Devine] a letter in which he said something like, "I know cops. I know everything about this town. I'd like to write a column for you." Frank was so impressed with the letter that he gave Jerry a column. Eventually we set up a triumvirate, with columns by Ray Kerrison, Pete

Hamill, Jerry Nachman. They each would write a couple times a week. Every time you opened the paper you'd generally have two different columnists, and they were all so different. Ray was very conservative, but he was sort of intelligent conservative. Pete Hamill was Mr. Liberal. Jerry was in the middle. He would write funny columns.

PETER KALIKOW: Frank decided to leave. I would have kept him under my circumstances, meaning, I give you a free hand but not a free hand to tell me off.

Frank Devine agreed to help find a new editor. He then returned to Australia, where he'd worked early in his career, to take a job at another Murdoch paper, *The Australian*. Devine's replacement would be the first female editor of the *Post* (if you didn't count Dolly Schiff giving herself the title): Jane Amsterdam, a media superstar who had been editor of the *Washington Post*'s Style section and who ran the influential business magazine *Manhattan, inc.* from 1984 to 1987. Amsterdam had turned down an earlier offer to oversee the *Post*'s business coverage, but eventually came around to the opportunity to run the whole show.

PETER KALIKOW: Price and Devine both liked her. Peter thought she would vastly increase the circulation.

JANE AMSTERDAM, executive editor, 1988–1989: I was an editor at Knopf when I got a call about going to the *Post*. I had been there about six months, and I loved it. I loved [Knopf editor in chief] Sonny Mehta. I had an interview with Kalikow and his bodyguard Danny. Danny was a total sweetheart—an Irish guy with a bulge in his ankle. The next day, [then–*New York Newsday* editor in chief] Don Forst told the *New York Times* that he had turned down the job. I went back to see Kalikow, and I said, "Am I the latest jerk you've offered this job to?" Kalikow looks at Danny and goes, "This guy [Forst] is a fucking liar. Take care of it." Danny leaves the room. I went back to Knopf, and I said, "Sonny, I think they're going to kill an editor." Sonny said, "Give it three days. If the guy's still alive, take the job." He said, "You'd be the first woman editor. You don't want to go through your life regretting not going for it and taking a chance. You can always come back here." He kept saying, "If there's anything really great on Page Six, call me first, okay?" Sonny published Nobel Prize winners, and never missed a day of the *Post*. We had a really strenuous negotiation. I said that Kalikow could have the four editorial pages, but I insisted that I have completely free rein over the rest of the paper. He said, "I can't do that." I walked out of the negotiations. My lawyer said, "What are you doing?" I said, "I don't know this guy. It's my reputation, and the *New York Post* is something totally different for me." But then Kalikow called me and said, "Okay, I'll sign it."

PETER KALIKOW: Danny wasn't my bodyguard. He was my senior guy, Dan Cremins. I never had a bodyguard in my life, and I ain't starting now.

DICK BELSKY: Jane was one of the first female editors of a major daily. She decided to take the *Post* in a different direction. After having gone through all the Murdoch stuff, it was another change. The idea was, let's try and take it upscale, although Frank Devine did some of that, too. We hired some really good people, and they did a much longer form of journalism.

ERIC FETTMANN: I thought she was very much a one-trick pony. She did *Manhattan, inc.*, but at the *Post* she just kind of sat back and was amused by everything and spent her days talking to Bob Woodward on the phone. She tried to do a few things that didn't work out, and she tried to bring in liberal people to attempt to remake the city room from the Murdoch-Dunleavy culture.

DAN AQUILANTE, chief music critic, 1980–2012: When Kalikow came in, it seemed like there was some money behind him and that things might change. Small things, like the cafeteria suddenly was kind of a nice dining experience. You were able to go down there and a cook would make you an omelet per your order, right in front of you.

> While *Post* staffers interpreted Kalikow's arrival as a sign that the paper had a future, the paper's new editor reversed the idiosyncratic decrees and fast-and-loose habits of previous management. A culture clash was inevitable.

JANE AMSTERDAM: When I got there, one of the first things I heard was a photographer on the phone saying, "I have a hundred-dollar bill, and I'll tear it in half. I'll give you fifty now, and if I get the pictures, I'll give you the other fifty." I said, "We don't do that anymore. No paying for anything." He said, "Really?" I said, "Yep. A new regime." He was like, "Oh no." That, and I remember looking at the TV listings. It had *Butch Cassidy and the Sundance Kid*, starring Robert

Redford. I asked Lou Colasuonno, "What's the deal with that?" He said, "Rupert said we couldn't mention Paul Newman ever." I was like, "We can fix that one." He was Butch! Also, no one was allowed to mention Teddy Kennedy because he made Murdoch sell the *Post*. We fixed that, too. Early on, I recall [former *Post* reporter–turned–Koch spokesman] George Arzt "explaining" how things worked at the *Post*: if the mayor didn't want a story to appear, it didn't. Another Rupert Rule. I made it clear there was a new policy.

GEORGE ARZT, City Hall bureau chief, 1968–1986: That's not true. I never talked to her, and I don't remember Ed ever talking about Jane. I was already [Ed Koch's] press secretary, and I was asked by Peter Kalikow to come to his Park Avenue office. Kalikow had just bought the paper. He offered me the job of metropolitan editor of the *Post*. I said, "I've only been in the mayor's office for a year. I can't leave him now." I get a call a week later from the *Times*. They asked me all sorts of questions about conflict of interest—being the mayor's press secretary and then becoming metropolitan editor of the *Post*. I said, "It's not true. I'm with Ed, and I'm staying with him." I found out later from people that Jane was really paranoid about me.

PETER PRICE, publisher, 1988–1989: I went to Bergdorf Goodman and the leading department stores—Bloomingdale's, B. Altman, and Saks Fifth Avenue—and convinced them to advertise on page seven, opposite Page Six. I said, "Have a look at what's changing. Have a look at our new editor." They bought into the *Post*. This went on for a year. Every day, one of them would advertise. The *New York Times* even wrote an article, my god.

ELIZABETH POCHODA, Sunday book review editor, 1989: I remember Peter Price telling me, "We're going to bring Pauline Trigère [fashion designer] into the office, and she'll probably advertise." I said, "You really should be on the phone with P.C. Richard" [a chain of appliance and electronics stores]. He didn't want to hear that.

PETER KALIKOW: I was there a month or two when I said the only way this paper survives is with a Sunday edition. I didn't know anything about newspapers, but I said you can't make a living on six days a week. It's five days, really, because you don't make any money on Saturday. We had forty-eight- to fifty-two-page papers, which meant there were no ads in them.

JANE AMSTERDAM: He came to me one day and said, "I've been thinkin'." He pointed his finger to his brain. He said, "To be a real paper, you got to have a Sunday paper." Without any research or advice, he gave me like six weeks to get it together. We hired some great people. Frank Bruni was one of them.

FRANK BRUNI, reporter, rewrite, 1988–1990: I had just graduated from the J school at Columbia. One of the professors was Ken Goldstein, whose daughter Marianne worked on the metro desk at the *Post*. I didn't take a class from him, but his son was a childhood friend of mine. I was a standout at Columbia. I graduated second in the class or whatever, and I hadn't landed any of the jobs I was looking for when graduation happened. Ken Goldstein said, "You should call Marianne. They need summer help at the *Post*." Although I'd intended to go into a full-time job I said, "Okay, one more internship." I went to the *Post*, and on like my fourth or fifth week there, Dick Belsky, who was the metro editor, said, "We'd like to hire you."

JANE AMSTERDAM: When I was first in New York, I used to go out with sportswriters all the time. Mike Lupica kept asking me out, and I said, "No." We were both in our early twenties, and everybody kept saying, "Yeah, in your dreams, Lupica. Ha, ha, ha." When I got to the *Post* years later, I tried to steal him from the *Daily News*. He said, "They all said you'd never call, and I said you would." I was like, "God, I love you." Imagine waiting all those years to say that. He did not come to the *Post*.

ELIZABETH POCHODA: Jane Amsterdam hired me to run a stand-alone book review. I knew her through my friend Duncan Stalker, who she also hired. Duncan and I had worked at *Vanity Fair* together. Duncan was going to do features and I was going to do a book review, which sounded to me like fun. I had worked at *The Nation* for fifteen years. *The Nation* wasn't a lot of fun, but I learned a lot. When I decided to go to the *Post*, they were completely flabbergasted.

PAMELA NEWKIRK, reporter, 1988–1990: I was a Capitol Hill reporter at Gannett News Service when Jane Amsterdam reached out to me in 1988. She asked me to be a part of efforts to revitalize the paper. I was torn because of the paper's horrible reputation—particularly among Blacks—but [*Village Voice* investigative reporter] Wayne Barrett, one of my mentors, convinced me to take a chance.

MICHAEL KAY, sportswriter, 1982–1988: It's the opening of Mickey Mantle's restaurant, which was a big event. This was [in February] before the '88 season. Greg Gallo tells me, I want you to get into the restaurant—do whatever you can. I found out there was a side door. I went into the apartment building next door, and I gave the doorman twenty bucks, which was a lot of money in '88. He let me in the side door. I worked my way up to [Yankees manager] Billy Martin, who was there as a guest of Mickey. I introduced myself and Billy said, "What's your impression of me?" I said, "I know what I've read, but I'll judge you by how you treat me." He said, "That's all I ever wanted from anybody. You know what, kid? We'll be okay. If you just judge me without any preconceived notions, we're good." From that day forward, Billy Martin told me everything that was happening a day before it would happen. The *Post* loved it. I was on the front page more than some news reporters.

> Kay's relationship with Martin paid off later that year.

MICHAEL KAY: Billy called me into spring training that year. He said, "Let me ask you something, kid. If I give you a story, does it hurt Bill Madden?" Bill Madden was the beat writer for the *News*. I said, "Yeah." He goes, "That's all I need to know." He would call me into his office in front of all the other writers, including Bill, just to torment them. One day, in, maybe it was June, the Yankees are in a little bit of a rough patch. Billy is having problems with the umpires. I'm walking out of the building with Mike Lupica at about one in the morning after writing, and I see Billy's car, still in the parking lot. I'm exhausted, but I said to Lupica, "I gotta go back inside. Something's up if he's still here." Billy was in his office. He'd had a couple of drinks, and he told me that he was gonna quit because the umpires were screwing him, and thus screwing the Yankees. I wrote it. It was a big front-page story. The headline was something like, BILLY TO QUIT. He didn't. But that resonated with Lupica, who went to Jim Willse, the head of the *Daily News*, and said: "We need this kid. He's killing us in the *Post*." At the end of that year, they make a move to bring me aboard. The only reason I considered it was because the *Post* would not give me a raise. I was making around $40,000 at that time. I go to [the *News*] offices, and Bob Decker is their sports editor. Strangely, he's whispering, "This isn't the greatest place to work. I don't know if you should come here." I'm looking at him, like "*Wha?*" He says, "Yeah, as a friend, I'm telling you." I wasn't his friend.

BOB DECKER, sports editor, 1989–1994: Not true. I told Michael Kay, "I've been [at the *News*] fifteen years. I loved it. But it's funny you're talking to me now, because I have had preliminary talks with Jane Amsterdam." Kay said, "No wonder Gallo is walking around so pissed off." I said, "But if this gets out, I will find you and I will fucking kill you."

MICHAEL KAY: I went back to the *New York Post* offices. Jane Amsterdam calls me into her office. She goes, "If you're leaving because of Gallo"—which I wasn't— "we're gonna fire him tomorrow. We're bringing in Bob Decker." I said, "I don't want Greg Gallo fired! I'm leaving because of the money!" She goes, "We'll match the money." I ended up going to the *News*. I was twenty-seven years old, and my head was spinning because Gallo was telling me, "You can't go there. They'll misuse you. I'm the only guy who can get greatness out of you." I'm looking at him, thinking, "You're gonna get fired." I didn't say it. He *was* fired, and Bob Decker ended up being hired as sports editor at the *Post*. Decker didn't want me to go to the *News* because he thought I was an asset. There was all this palace intrigue.

BOB DECKER: They wanted to change the paper a bit, not to be as sensational. They wanted yesterday's back page—and the front page, too—to stand up the next day.

GREG GALLO, executive sports editor, 1977–1989, 1994–2009: Jane Amsterdam wanted to make a change. I had a year left on my contract. They offered to have me stay and put out a sports magazine. I said, "No, thank you," and went to work for Murdoch at the *Daily Racing Form*.

ELIZABETH POCHODA: The minute I got to the *Post* I was entranced. Duncan and I had a little office, then they moved us into a bullpen with a sort of hip-height wall between me and Richard Johnson. There was Richard, yelling at a woman on the phone, saying, "What do you mean, I ruined your life? You should have thought of that yesterday." Duncan grabbed my hand and said, "We're going to love this."

JANE AMSTERDAM: I loved Page Six. One of my favorite scoops of all time came from, I think one of the political conventions. One of our reporters was at a strip bar and saw [*New York Times* executive editor–turned–columnist] Abe Rosenthal stuffing dollar bills into wherever you stuff bills on a stripper. A reporter called Rosenthal, and I got an immediate call from him saying, "This is not news." I said, "Are you denying it?" He said, "This is not news. What's wrong with you people?"

GEORGE RUSH, Page Six reporter, 1986–1993: Richard [Johnson] had a very workmanlike approach, which was necessary to get the page out every day. He had done some carpentry earlier in his life, and I think he viewed the lumberyard of the newspaper as an extension of carpentry, since they were both derived from trees. He would type with two fingers, and often it was like he was hammering nails into the coffin of some celebrity.

ISAAC MIZRAHI, fashion designer: There was an item about me in the *Post* when I first started out, saying I was spotted at a gym in New York City wearing a leopard-printed spandex bodysuit or a thong or something like that. At that point, I went swimming at a pool but never to a gym. And when you think of me, you don't think leopard-printed spandex, you know? It made me laugh and taught me this wonderful lesson about how sometimes, you have to take [gossip columns] with a grain of salt. From then on, I've never really been too hurt by or sad about stuff reported about me in gossip columns.

JANE AMSTERDAM: We did something on Carl Bernstein, who I knew from the *Washington Post*. I don't remember what the story was, but he called me and said, "How dare you? I can ruin you." I said, "Carl, you can't ruin anybody at this point. Sorry." I was a good friend of Nora Ephron, and anybody who was a friend of Nora's wasn't thrilled with Carl at that point. [Ephron's 1983 novel, *Heartburn*, was inspired by the breakup of her marriage to Bernstein.] But again, he didn't deny it. He just said, "I'm a newsman, and you don't know what news is." That was the basic response to anything that people didn't want to see on Page Six.

GEORGE RUSH: Early on, Richard [Johnson] gives me this number and says, "Call this guy." It was the owner of a deli around the corner from the residence of Pulitzer Prize–winning Watergate reporter Carl Bernstein. I talked to the deli owner and he said that Mr. Bernstein had ordered a lot of food there and had not paid his bill in a long time, which came to several hundred dollars. I called Carl Bernstein and explained that this deli owner said he was in arrears. I discovered that Carl Bernstein, like most journalists, did not want to talk to another journalist. He says, "This is a story for you?" He goes, "Listen, I want to talk to you. I want to straighten this out. I need to call you back." I go, "Okay." Like a half hour passes and the deli owner calls back and he says, "Mr. Bernstein just came in and paid his bill." I think Carl Bernstein thought that is the end, there is no story now, but no, there was a better story: "Page Six gets action."

JOHN WATERS, filmmaker: I've been on Page Six a lot, but nothing that ever made me angry. I'm not that stupid to do things in public that I think could, you know—doesn't every person that could possibly be on Page Six worry about that? If they wrote about me, they weren't wrong. I might not have liked it, but it wasn't a lie.

In addition to Page Six, the *Post* published the Suzy society gossip column, written by Aileen Mehle, although entertainment publicist Bobby Zarem claimed that he ghostwrote it for a while. Farther back in the paper, Cindy Adams was covering Broadway, movie openings, and dining free at restaurants, which were then mentioned in her column.

SUSAN MULCAHY, Page Six editor, 1978–1985: Suzy's column was lists of people who went to society parties. It was pretty dull. Jim Revson, who wrote a much livelier society column for *Newsday*, decided to point out that a lot of the people in Suzy's lists didn't actually attend the parties. Suzy did not like this. She started trashing Jim, calling him "Rat Revson." It was funny at first, but she made it hard for him to do his job. A lot of the socialites were afraid of Suzy—what if their names did not appear in her lists! The horror!—so they stopped inviting Jim to parties. The feud, if you can call it that, became a huge deal and got tons of national publicity.

JANE AMSTERDAM: Cindy was one of the great surprises to me. What I knew of her was she was Miss Bagel 19-whatever. I was like, oh, god, do I have to meet Cindy Adams? But she was the hardest-working reporter at the paper. She never stopped working. Her stuff checked out, and every dictator and dictator's wife adored her. She'd go into hotel suite bathrooms and phone in the story. I could see why people would talk to her. She was very likable. She took a bum rap from a lot of people. Not that I would advise everybody getting friendly with dictators or being loved by dictators, but she got stories, and she didn't pull many punches. She was so devoted to Joey. She was very supportive of me as well. I kept saying, "I'm not a dictator, though!"

ISAAC MIZRAHI: We don't follow Cindy for being the greatest news breaker, but she is an incredible arbiter. She's seen it all. When she calls, you answer right away.

ELIZABETH POCHODA: Cindy took me to dinner, with Joey, someplace on Central Park South. It was a Cindy Adams experience—eat dinner, get up and leave, no money changes hands, and the next thing you know, she writes a column mentioning that restaurant, and you ask her about it, and she says, "Why do they hire people like you?"

DICK BELSKY: Cindy took me to lunch once at the Bull & Bear [restaurant in the Waldorf Astoria]. People were bowing and took us to this big circular table in the middle of the restaurant—the best table. She puts her hands in the air and starts snapping her fingers, and waiters come flying from every direction. "Yes, Miss Adams, yes, Miss Adams." We order. The food comes. I had chicken or steak or whatever. She asks, "How's your food?" I say, "Honestly, it's a little dry." She goes nuts. She calls the manager over. She summons the chef out of the kitchen. She's yelling at the chef, she's yelling at the manager, the manager's yelling at the chef. They take my food back and bring me more. She asks, "How is it this time?" I say, "It's great!" I never saw her pick up a check. I don't know how that worked. Let's just say, I didn't pay anything.

> Amsterdam's reshaping of the *Post*'s news and feature coverage—and journalistic ethics—earned her fans and detractors.

JANE AMSTERDAM: There was a lot of skepticism because I had never done anything like that. The *Washington Post* was a long way from the *New York Post*, and that was four years of newspaper experience. They thought I was a, you know, goody-goody and whatever else they called me that I didn't hear. But I said, no buying stories, no making up stories, because I'd heard all the tales—you know, there was no such thing as a bad news day; make it up. Once I said that, I was amazed at how good the reporters were. They were a pretty talented group. I think a lot of them were relieved. They wanted to be real reporters.

TERRY GOLWAY, sports copy editor 1987–1992: The sports department regarded Jane Amsterdam as a dilettante; as someone who just didn't understand tabloid journalism, which, by the way, was a pretty good argument. It had nothing to do with politics. In Jane Amsterdam's case, maybe there was a gender thing there. But ultimately, she wasn't one of them, and there were women who were. That's why I wouldn't put it down to a gender issue. It was a tabloid issue.

JANE AMSTERDAM: Koch was in Ireland, and he got into a big flap [when he said the British were not "occupying forces" in Northern Ireland]. I wrote the headline, "Eddie Go Blah." I got a call from [Koch political adviser] David Garth. He said, "Your paper is such a piece of shit that I don't even read it." I said, "Then how do you know it's a piece of shit?" He said, "You owe the mayor an apology." I said, "Are you calling on behalf of the mayor?" He said, "The mayor and I are really close." I said something like, "If you're speaking on behalf of the mayor, I think the mayor owes the *Post* an apology." We ended up having a lunch with Koch's people. All male. And me. It was the most awkward lunch I've ever been to because Ed Koch had to apologize. That was the beginning of the end of my term at the *Post* because Koch worked very hard at getting me out of there. There was a lot of pushing—a lot of talk that I just didn't get it.

GEORGE ARZT: I did attend a lunch at the *Post* but Dave Garth wasn't there, and Koch did not apologize.

RICHARD GOODING, metropolitan editor, 1976–1993: I thought the paper was pretty good under Kalikow, except for the Jane Amsterdam period, which was pretty grim. Belsky and all the middle-level editors became Jane's protectors. Jane couldn't talk to anybody without them. If you somehow got into her office and had a conversation with her, as soon as you got out you were attacked by three of the middle-level editors saying, "What did you tell her? What's she want?" They were dazzled by her. I think they thought Jane would be great at the *Post*, then go great places and take them with her. It didn't work out so well.

DICK BELSKY: Jane had her people. She had people that she loved and depended on, and I fortunately was part of that group. She would invite us into her office to have a drink or a beer after deadline, things like that. I found out after the fact that there were some reporters who felt that there were two levels of people—her people, and then the rest of them. I wished I'd been aware of that when it was happening because I would have tried to get her involved more.

JANE AMSTERDAM: I had no idea that was going on, and if it was going on, I regret that I didn't spend a lot more time walking around that newsroom and talking to everybody.

> Amsterdam's *Post* was a mix of high and low: the *Post*'s city desk and gossip stars mixed in with multipart investigative features and a well-regarded Sunday book review section.

ELIZABETH POCHODA: I wanted to edit something smart that could be read by everybody with pleasure. That's what the Sunday book review was. Everybody wanted to write for me: Barbara Ehrenreich, Francine du Plessix Gray, Joe Nocera, Walter Clemons. I would say to people like Jan Morris, "You can write whatever you want. But you're going to write for a big audience, for people that you hang out with, and for people you've never met, that you might want to reach." As I'm looking through it now, I'd forgotten how many ads it had. The *Times* wouldn't accept Barnes & Noble at that time. They thought it was beneath them. Len Riggio [executive chairman of Barnes & Noble] came to see me and he said, "I can help you really get this going. Because the *Times* won't let me advertise." He wanted the last page [of the *Post* book review for an ad], and I said, "Sure." That was significant, because other people followed.

CHARLES SENNOTT, reporter, 1988–1989: I was doing big takeouts on things like— remember that drunk captain of the *Exxon Valdez*, Joe Hazelwood? He crashed and caused a huge oil spill. We found out he lived in upstate New York. I did a huge Sunday takeout because it was this suburban New York sea captain who crashed the *Exxon Valdez*. Or I was doing a story about the crack baby unit [at a hospital] in the Bronx. Those are the kinds of big stories I was doing under Jane's direction—exactly the kind of stories that weren't driving circulation.

Amsterdam coaxed her friend Nora Ephron to write a profile of New York Yankees owner George Steinbrenner for the premier issue of the *Post*'s Sunday edition, which launched with a party at the Waldorf Astoria.

JANE AMSTERDAM: Nora really didn't want to write for the *Post* ever again, but I talked her into it. I had promised her that I would see the story through every step of the way, which I did. But once it went to the printers, we weren't allowed to touch anything because of union rules. One of the printers dropped the page and put two columns on backwards. No one said, "Oops, we dropped it. Can someone read it?" They just stuck the pieces back on.

RICHARD GOODING: I was the night city editor that night. Belsky told me, "The paper is the way we want it. Nora's story and the first few pages are exactly the way we want it. Don't do *anything*." There was a history of the night city editors coming in and saying, "This story is crap," and changing it. His message basically was, you want to change a story on page twenty, change a story on page twenty, but the front of the book is exactly the way we want it. When the proofs came up, we were busy on other stuff, and I said, "There's no sense in me even looking at Nora's stuff because it's the way they want it." But something was out of order, and I didn't catch it. It wasn't really my job—the copy desk should have caught it—and I had been told to keep my hands off it anyways, so I did. The first edition came up and was delivered with great fanfare to the party at the Waldorf. From the Waldorf, Nora called the office. Someone gave the call to me, and Nora tore me an asshole that I'd never been torn before. She was using the most creative profanities I'd ever heard. She went on for twenty minutes.

JANE AMSTERDAM: Nora wasn't at the party. She probably just went out and bought the first edition at a newsstand at ten p.m. She was quite angry with me. I begged her to forgive me for a long time. She would say, "You made me go back there!" She ended up getting back at me. I went to a dinner party she threw, and she sat me next to the most boring guest at the party—I won't tell you who. I looked at her and said, "That's for the column that was dropped, right?" She said, "Uh huh." It was the perfect back slap. Nora would not cut me out of her life. She would just make my life miserable for as long as hers was miserable.

ELIZABETH POCHODA: I did the book review by myself and it was a huge amount of work, so I went to work that first Sunday to start on the next week. The phone kept ringing. It was all women. They were saying, "Where are the coupons?" I called my husband and said, "What are they talking about?" He said, "That's what they get for hiring help like you. My mother wouldn't buy a Sunday paper if it didn't have coupons." That killed the Sunday paper.

PETER KALIKOW: I remember it clearly. The coupon company was owned by Murdoch, and he wouldn't give them to me. I don't know why. We were selling a couple hundred thousand papers on Sundays. He was [doing business] with lots of papers with way smaller circulations.

New Yorkers accused of great cruelty, sexual exploitation, bribery, and murder starred in that era's most high-profile trials. The "preppy killer" trial began in January 1988 and ended with Robert Chambers pleading guilty to first-degree manslaughter in the death of eighteen-year-old Jennifer Levin. In April, he was sentenced to fifteen years in prison. That same month, then–US attorney Rudy Giuliani indicted wealthy hoteliers Harry and Leona Helmsley—she was dubbed "the Queen of Mean" for her tyrannical treatment of staff—on tax-related and extortion charges; the *Post*'s Ransdell Pierson had broken the story in 1986 that they were illegally billing renovations on their Connecticut mansion as business expenses for their hotels. In October, lawyer Joel Steinberg stood trial—the first ever televised in New York—for the November 1987 beating death of his and Hedda Nussbaum's illegally adopted six-year-old daughter, Lisa. Another child, sixteen-month-old Mitchell, was found "urine-soaked" and "tethered to a playpen," according to the *New York Times*. Both Steinberg and Nussbaum were initially charged with second-degree murder, but charges against her were dropped when she agreed to testify against Steinberg, who, prosecutors alleged, had also abused her for more than ten years. Also in October, another legal imbroglio that began with a *Post* exclusive (on Page Six back in 1983)—the "Bess Mess," as it was dubbed by the media—landed in court.

Former Miss America and Department of Cultural Affairs commissioner Bess Myerson had hired a woman named Sukhreet Gabel to work in her office. Gabel's mother, Hortense, was a judge who happened to be presiding over the divorce of Myerson's boyfriend, Andy Capasso. Back when Page Six had first learned of it, the arrangement appeared too cozy to be a coincidence.

SUSAN MULCAHY: My original source had multiple agendas, but that didn't mean the story wasn't worth looking into. Richard Johnson did the reporting. Everybody denied any impropriety, but it sure looked fishy, so we ran it. Eventually it came out that there was lots of impropriety. Myerson had to quit her job, and she and Hortense Gabel and Capasso were indicted on various charges, like fraud and bribery. They were acquitted, though Capasso went to jail for something else. Sukhreet Gabel became a tabloid personality for a while. It always pissed me off that once the scandal became a big deal, and went to trial in 1988, the *Times*' coverage said it had originally been reported in a "small item" in the *New York Post*. The lead story on Page Six was not a small item! As Roger Wood used to tell me all the time: after the front and back pages of the tabloids, and the front page of the *Times*, Page Six was the most widely read page of newsprint in the city.

FRANK BRUNI: One would be hard-pressed to find another chapter of New York life, that 1988 to 1990 period, in which there were so many hugely newsworthy trials. That period spanned the last fumes of the preppy murder trial; the Joel Steinberg and Hedda Nussbaum trial; the Queen of Mean Leona Helmsley trial; and the trial of Hortense Gabel, Bess Myerson, and Andy Capasso. I remember that Hortense's daughter, Sukhreet Gabel, was one of the star witnesses, and she was such a sort of deliberately, affectedly kind of nutty, free-spirit eccentric. I remember her giving testimony at one point that led to the *Post* front-page headline MY MIND'S LIKE SWISS CHEESE. She became this sort of local icon.

JANE AMSTERDAM: This is straight out of a Ben Hecht screenplay. At about eight o'clock [on December 22, 1988], the jury came in from the Bess Myerson trial. There was all this scurrying. We're going to have to rip up the front page. I look across the newsroom. There was a glass office and in there was some stranger. I said, "Who is that?" Someone said, "We got one of the jurors." Our reporter Tim McDarrah had walked him out of the courthouse and brought him to the newsroom.

TIM McDARRAH, reporter, Page Six co-editor, 1985–1993: I had been in the court-room a couple of times and recognized what the jurors looked like. I saw them coming out, and I said, all right, which one can I get? I walked up to a guy and I gave him my card. I told him I worked at the *New York Post* and said, "New York is so fascinated with this case. Can I borrow you for half an hour to come to the newsroom? We can take some pictures." It worked. I did that fifty times, but it didn't work fifty times.

JANE AMSTERDAM: He said, "This juror has been taking notes, and he's writing a book called *Sukhreetions.*" We were very competitive with the *Daily News.* I can't remember if it was Lou Colasuonno or me who said, "Let's just keep him talking until the *News* closes its edition. Then take him back to the hotel." That's what we did. That was my favorite night of all nights there. It was classic *New York Post.*

FRANK BRUNI: Sukhreet ended up giving quite a lot of interviews at the height of her brief fame, and in one of them she mentioned dejectedly that she had no New Year's Eve date. The *Post* said, "Would you be willing, as a feature assignment, to ask her out for New Year's Eve?" I said, "Yes," because I thought it would be hilarious to write about, but also because she had a particular kind of camp flamboyance. She'd become an icon in the gay community. I thought, this is really simple. I'll take her to a New Year's Eve circuit party, and I'll be the belle of the damn ball. Because people would say, "Oh my god, someone brought Sukhreet Gabel." As I remember, there was garden-variety delighted gawking and some people talking to her. She lapped up the attention. It was both a sweet and sad story. Because you realized at that moment that she was living a kind of vignette that was never going to come again. It was sweet to watch, but it was also bittersweet because it was sort of dying as you were seeing it.

JANE AMSTERDAM: I was invited to Barbara Walters's home for a stuffy dinner in honor of an editor who had written a boring book. The guests were all big-time people. I was seated next to Henry Kissinger on one side, and on the other, Gianni Agnelli, who was head of Fiat at that point. They all said they didn't read the *Post.* Until Kissinger said, "I have a question for Jane: what was Sukhreet Gabel really like?" At which point, the whole party dropped down to my level, and everybody knew everything that was in the *Post.* Then Barbara Walters and I got into a big discussion about Mike Tyson. Everybody read the *Post.* Page Six had a lot to do with that.

> Joel Steinberg was eventually found guilty of first-degree manslaughter and sentenced to twenty-five years in prison—and Hedda Nussbaum entered a mental health facility. Determined to get an interview with her, the *Post* relied on two of its most intrepid staffers.

TIM McDARRAH: We found out that Hedda Nussbaum was at a place called Four Winds up in Katonah, and we snuck onto the grounds. Knowing what I know now about battered women and people's privacy, I may not have done what I did. But I did. It's a competitive environment. You want to beat the *News*. You want to beat the *Times*. And there was no bigger story in the country than this nice white upper-middle-class couple doing coke and living where Mark Twain once lived on 10th Street in the Village. Hedda was an editor at Random House. It was a huge story. Bob Kalfus and I snuck onto the grounds of Four Winds. First, he took some long shots, so we'd have something before we got chased off. Then I just fucking walked right up to her and introduced myself. She starts talking, but within, like, eleven seconds, two guards come running. "Who are you? What are you doing here?" I took out my ID and told them who I was. They said, "You have to leave!" I said, "Okay, bye." Because I'm breaking every law in the book. I got sued. The *Post* got sued. Marsha Kranes got sued. The lawsuit was dismissed, although it took a long time.

MARSHA KRANES, rewrite, editor, 1974–2005: I took info from McD and Kalfus over the phone and put the story together. Kalfus got pictures of Hedda walking on the grounds with other patients. The lawsuit partly involved another female patient whose stay at Four Winds had been kept secret until she appeared on the front page of the *Post* with Nussbaum. I don't recall being served any papers or being deposed, so the suit likely was dropped or quietly settled.

ESTHER PESSIN, reporter, rewrite, 1988–1990: I was there for the verdict. Hedda Nussbaum was an interesting figure. How you felt about her was a bit like a Rorschach test. There's no question that she suffered mightily at the hands of Joel Steinberg. But I always wondered—and I don't think anybody will ever know the truth—how much of a role she played willingly or unwillingly.

> Though Murdoch no longer owned the *Post*, the Robert Chambers story provided a perfect opportunity for synergy between the paper and his tabloid TV show.

DICK BELSKY: One of the things about being an editor at a place like the *Post* is—when there are so many murders, so many killings—recognizing the one that says, "Oh my god, this is the big story." Somebody was telling us the basics of [the preppy murder], and I remember running into Frank Devine's office and saying, "This is amazing." My first day as metropolitan editor was when Chambers was on *A Current Affair*. He was at a party and there was some video of him strangling a doll. It became a big deal. Bob Young, who had gone to *A Current Affair*, called and said, "Your first day, I got a great story for you. We have video."

Another frequent subject of coverage was Donald Trump. Although the real estate developer first appeared on the *Post*'s wood in the early 1980s, he became a page-one staple in the late 1980s—appearing on the front page more than twenty times from 1988 through 1993. Trump's status rose exponentially in 1987 after Si Newhouse, owner of the Condé Nast magazine group and book publisher Random House, and a good friend of Roy Cohn, published *Trump: The Art of the Deal*, a memoir mixed with business advice. Written with former *Post* gossip columnist Tony Schwartz, the book spent thirteen weeks at number one on the *New York Times* bestseller list and cemented Trump's national status. Newhouse's decision to publish Trump was prompted in part by what appeared to be newsstand sales of an issue of Condé Nast's *GQ* magazine that featured Trump on the cover.

GRAYDON CARTER, former editor, *Vanity Fair*; founder and co-editor, Air Mail: Art Cooper, the editor of *GQ*, called me when I was at *Life* magazine, or maybe it was *Time*. He said, "There's a guy called Donald Trump. Would you be interested in doing a story on him?" I had a vague knowledge of who he was, and I needed the money. So I said, "Sure." This was the first national exposure Trump ever had. He let me hang around with him for three weeks. I was sitting in on meetings, and I traveled around with him as much as I could escape from my job. The story came out, and Trump hated it, but had the cover framed and put on the wall of his office. It was the May 1984 issue. There were a couple of sentences that drove him crazy. One, about the size of his hands. Another about the color of his limousine and his suits. He had his staff buy up every copy they could get their hands on off New York newsstands, back when we had newsstands. Si Newhouse sees the figures the next month and thinks, this guy really sells. He goes to Bob Bernstein [chairman of Random House] and says, "We should sign Trump up for a book." That's how that got started. Maybe ten to twelve years ago, Si and I were having lunch, and Trump's name came up. I told him the story about Trump buying up the issues, and Si didn't know about that. He thought Trump had sold honestly on the newsstand, but like everything else with Trump it was a fraud.

JANE AMSTERDAM: Oh god, he was all over. At the *Post*, he mostly was a staple of Page Six. I never have met anyone who could look you in the eye and lie like Trump could. Right in your eye. You could tell he was so full of it. I remember he had this stationery with a raised gold symbol on it and that same signature that looked a lot like the COVID charts. I wanted almost nothing to do with him. But he was great copy for Page Six.

PETER KALIKOW: Donald has always been a friend of mine. Our fathers were friends, that's how long it goes back. There aren't that many big Queens builders. Donald and I are blue-collar people. I got along as well with the guys that printed the paper and the guys who delivered the paper as I did with the guys upstairs because I spent my life on construction sites. You come to understand the psyche of people that work like that—often difficult physical jobs. He was the same as me in another way in that he was born into that business. I don't think he needed the paper to help him. He loved the paper. He loved being in it. He did lots of things for us, too. Every time we had a contest, we borrowed his yacht to give away the grand prize. Stuff like that. He was very good to us, and we were good to him.

DICK BELSKY: The only time I ever met [Trump] was when they brought him in for one of those editorial lunches. It was probably six or eight of us. The one thing I was struck by, when I would see him at the debates years later, is that he was exactly the same guy. There were moments where he'd be kind of entertaining. Then there would be moments where you'd cringe. Jane hated him. She was one of those real rough-and-ready people. Nothing bothered her. Like, "I'm one of the guys, I can take it." That's how she was. Trump told some off-color joke or said some curse word. He turned to her and apologized, "Oh, I'm sorry, little lady, for offending you" or whatever. Afterward, Jane was furious—not at whatever the off-color remark was. It was "How dare he think that he had to apologize to me like that." He was just tone deaf.

MARY TRUMP, niece of Donald Trump; author of *Too Much and Never Enough: How My Family Created the World's Most Dangerous Man*: I think sometimes people don't quite understand what kind of damage papers like the *Post* did. The *Post* was his stenographer. It took everything at face value and allowed him to use them toward his own ends.

GEORGE RUSH: Trump viewed the tabloids as a public address system, and I think he felt like the *Post* was probably easier to get into because its standards were more lenient. They would accept anything he told them. In the pre-internet age, New York's tabloids were a kind of Twitter for him where he could just spout off at will, and a lot of the pugilistic circus performer skills he is famous for were developed in the tabloids.

RICHARD GOODING: There were guys who sold papers. Steinbrenner sold papers. John Gotti sold papers. Trump sold papers. And we were in the business of selling papers. When you were a tabloid and most of your sales were on the street, you had to pay attention to how that front page sold papers. It's not like we had a million home deliveries that were going to take the paper regardless. You had to appeal to the people on the street. Trump was perfect.

FRANK RICH, film critic, 1975–1977: In the early going when Trump was becoming a celebrity, the *Post* played an enormous role in making him a star in New York. It was to the making of Trump what the PT-109 incident was to the making of Kennedy. Forget about the citizenry of New York. That wasn't the important thing. The important thing was that mass media is based in New York, and those people—the bookers at NBC, ABC, and CBS and editors at national magazines—read the *Post*. The pieces, often fawning, done about Trump by Barbara Walters, Diane Sawyer, countless others, all created [a mainstream celebrity]. I'm convinced that never would have happened without the *Post*. Of course, the ultimate payoff is that Trump himself would become a television star of sorts in his own right. But the intermediate step was the *Post* building him up; selling him to what we called the mainstream big three broadcast networks before there was cable news. Let's take the *Post* out of the equation. Let's say it had no interest in him. If you had a counternarrative of history, he might have ended up being Douglas Durst or a member of the Tisch family—someone that couldn't possibly enter the national stage.

GEORGE RUSH: It's hard to convey to people born after the dawn of the internet how newspapers were so widely shared and critical and set the agenda of the rest of the media. The glossy magazines at Condé Nast would get a gossip pack, where the interns would Xerox tabloid stories, particularly the gossip columns, staple them together, and distribute that to all the editors in the morning so that the editors could steal the stories and assign think pieces based on what those grubby rags had discovered the day before.

ERIC FETTMANN: I once walked into Kalikow's office when he was on the phone with Trump. Trump was complaining about something that had been in the paper that he wanted changed. Kalikow, for all his other faults, was really good—at least at first—about not imposing things on the paper. He told him, "Donald, you don't understand. I can't tell these people what to write."

> Sports columnist Phil Mushnick took aim at Trump several times, dubbing him a "wealthy egomaniac," among other jibes. The thin-skinned real estate developer took action.

PHIL MUSHNICK, columnist, television sports, 1973–current: It was implied that [Trump] wanted me fired. The letter he sent to Jane [Amsterdam] was like two pages of absolute crap. But the funny part is—his MO has never changed. The post-script was something like: "I see Mushnick's column and he's ugly, too." Just so typical. I've known him and dealt with him personally and professionally— through boxing, the USFL [the short-lived United States Football League; Trump owned its New Jersey Generals], all of it—for thirty-five years, and he fucked up everything he touched.

> The *Post* skewed more liberal under Jane Amsterdam, but its coverage of stories involving race, especially crime, had not completely transformed.

AMY PAGNOZZI, reporter, columnist, 1979–1993: Pam Newkirk worked at the *Post* and she's now one of the leading race experts in the country. She wrote a book called *Diversity, Inc.*, which is one of the best books on race I've ever read. She's [a journalism professor] at NYU now. I remember that she and her husband lived in a beautiful brownstone in Bed-Stuy and some story broke in Bed-Stuy and one of the editors said to her, "Go out and interview the people. They'll probably be home. Nobody who lives there has jobs." Pam was like: Hello?

PAMELA NEWKIRK: I don't recall that and can't imagine anyone saying anything that blatantly racist to me, but I remember that crimes against Blacks, no matter how heinous, were not considered newsworthy. It was clear whose lives mattered.

FLO ANTHONY, Page Six co-editor, 1984–1993: There were hardly any Black staffers at the *Post*. Someone once said, "Why don't you go to the *Post*'s affirmative action person?" I said, "I *am* the head of affirmative action. I can't go to myself!" When I got them to send us all to the National Association of Black Journalists conference in LA, I told one of the guys at the *Daily News*. He said, "You all can't even fill up a taxi cab." It was Mike George, Pat Jacobs, Pamela Newkirk, and me.

PAMELA NEWKIRK: I was the only Black news reporter. Flo Anthony covered gossip but was rarely in the newsroom. I don't know if there were any Blacks in sports. Initially it was clear that some people felt awkward around me—one person told me a lot of people didn't speak to me when I joined the staff because they didn't know what to say. Over time, they relaxed. I was personally treated well but the general coverage of Blacks left a lot to be desired. That's also true of other papers, but the *Post* was probably the most notorious. I won some newsroom battles but, in the end, there was little I could do to salvage the paper's tainted reputation in Black circles. However, it was especially gratifying to receive an international reporting award from the New York Association of Black Journalists for my reporting from South Africa. At least my efforts were recognized by my African American peers.

> On the evening of April 19, 1989, a young white woman, Trisha Meili, was attacked while jogging in Central Park. The rape and beating she endured were so severe she lapsed into a coma, though ultimately survived. A city infected by fear of violent crime wanted culprits, and quickly. The media, including the *New York Post*, helped find them. Five Black and Latino teenagers— Antron McCray, Kevin Richardson, Yusef Salaam, Raymond Santana, and Korey Wise—who happened to be hanging out in the park that night, were charged and convicted of the horrific assault. After serving several years of their sentences, the Central Park Five, as they were initially known, were exonerated in 2002. In 2023, Yusef Salaam was elected to New York's City Council District 9, in Harlem.

PAMELA NEWKIRK: While I was sometimes able to offer nuanced coverage of certain issues, the *Post*, like many other papers, covered Blacks in a very sensationalized, one-dimensional way. The worst example during my time there was the coverage of the Central Park jogger case.

CHARLES SENNOTT: On my one day of reporting on the Central Park Five, I went up into the neighborhoods and in and around Schomburg Plaza [in Harlem], with the assignment that the police are saying that these youths were using this word "wilding." My job was to find out: What does that mean? Is it real? It was a triple byline, Murray Weiss, Andrea Peyser, and myself, but I did the reporting on the street. In this time of racial reckoning, it's important to go back and look at these things. The story is sort of classic *New York Post*. It's street reporting that's real, factual, and close to the ground. The young people I talked to who knew these kids said a couple of things. They said, one, wilding has nothing to do with rape. Two, wilding is about messing with people. They used a lot of street language—like "gassing people up"—about what it meant, but I distinctly remember one of them saying it's got nothing to do with rape. They also said these boys, who they knew, weren't like that. They came from good families. They had a walkthrough of each of them saying, there's no way this happened. If you dissect that story, there were some really important facts in it. But the explanation from the street contravened the machinery that was saying, "This is connected to a rampage that ends in a rape." And with all the prosecutors and police who were feeding that racist machinery, it was very hard for that *New York Post* story—with the wood being WILDING—to ever be part of tapping the brakes. But no one—not the *New York Times*, not *Newsday*, not the *Daily News* or *New York Post*—was tapping the brakes. It's one of the great shames of New York journalism, that we didn't work harder, that we didn't do what we do best, which is keep pounding the pavement and keep challenging and asking hard questions. I think all of us, anyone, even if, like me, you only reported on it one day, you have to own that now, you have to be responsible for it.

ROCCO PARASCANDOLA, reporter, 1989–2001: "Wilding" and "wolf pack" took on racial connotations. That whole case was loaded with race. Trump took out the famous ad about the death penalty. It was bad and around that time there was a woman raped in Brooklyn and thrown from a roof. She survived, and at the hospital there was a press conference. A host of ministers, I believe, had visited her and they lambasted the media for giving the attack on this woman, a Black woman, far less coverage than we had given the Central Park jogger. Actually, that might be the first time it really hit me that certain stories get played over others. Manhattan takes precedent over all the other boroughs. If it's a woman, it's a bigger play than a man. If it's a white woman, bigger play. If she's an attractive white woman—you know what I'm talking about. That was an eye-opener.

RONALD L. KUBY, attorney, former partner of activist lawyer William Kunstler: The Central Park jogger case, now called the Exonerated Five case, was day after day of the most vicious news coverage—publishing the confessions, which should never have been released. Publishing the names and addresses of the juveniles and their history, which never should have been released. Demonizing these kids to the point where there was no way on earth they were going to get a fair trial. The *Post* did that worse than anybody else, but again, they were not alone. Kunstler never thought those kids were guilty. He thought the confessions were coerced. I was still an itty-bitty baby lawyer, but I trusted Bill's instincts because his instincts were almost always right when it came to issues of race. We were two of the very few white people who raised questions about the guilt of the Central Park Five, and later, we represented Yusef Salaam on appeal. It was my honor to have actually written that brief. Unfortunately, we lost in the court of appeals, and Yusef served out his sentence. When he along with the others were completely exonerated in 2002, the *New York Post* not only didn't apologize for the role they played in the case, they continued to raise questions about whether the youths were actually innocent.

YUSEF SALAAM, New York City councilmember: Some of the most scathing comments came from the *New York Post*. After we were convicted, I read my rap poem, "I Stand Accused." I always wanted to be a rap artist. Here I was in court and I was able to say something in defense of myself, and it was in the form of hip-hop. This young woman ran to the front of the courtroom and wanted to take a picture of my song. I said, absolutely. When the story ran in the *Post* the next day, the [front-page] headline was SALAAM BALONEY. It was devastating. They talked in mocking fashion about how I was rapping in the courthouse. I was sixteen years old. I served nearly seven years. Years later, when Ken Burns's [2012] documentary on the Central Park Five was produced, and after we were exonerated and received compensation [from New York City], a lot of articles [in the *Post*] pointed at things Donald Trump said, like, now they are going to be rich rapists. The *Post* has been one of the most unforgiving in terms of its negative coverage of the Black community.

In 1988, AIDS deaths would approach 62,000; Dr. Anthony Fauci was appointed the head of the National Institutes of Health's new Office of AIDS Research, and protesters from the AIDS activist group ACT UP swarmed the FDA's headquarters in Maryland to demand it speed up the approval of drugs to combat the virus. The *Post*'s coverage was bipolar. Ray Kerrison, a conservative Catholic, used his column to rail at abortion and gay rights. Columnist Amy Pagnozzi provided a more empathetic perspective.

AMY PAGNOZZI: ACT UP was the epitome of fine, theatrical street-level activism. ACT UP did one thing and AZT [an early antiretroviral drug used to treat AIDS] suddenly became much cheaper. They were incredibly effective. The *Post* had Ray Kerrison writing, "Adam and Eve instead of Adam and Steve," that kind of thing—bilious and anti-gay. Basically, he was writing that AIDS was a plague against these immoral people. He was a huge source of protest.

JAY BLOTCHER, activist (ACT UP), journalist: There was a real schizophrenia to the *Post*. Amy Pagnozzi, like Joe Nicholson, was an unexpected blessing and a counterpoint to the thugs at the *New York Post*. Her columns were raw poetry—you could dismiss them as bleeding-heart, but they had a lot of soul to them.

ELIZABETH POCHODA: Ray Kerrison, who had been a turf writer, and then became a right-wing zealot, came in to see us in the features department. He wouldn't talk to Duncan [Stalker], probably because Duncan was gay, but he wanted to talk to me about books. Then he said, "We'll continue this conversation later, because I have to go to San Francisco. You ever been there?" I said, "Yeah." He said, "It's a great town except for all the fags." He looked at Duncan and walked out.

JIM FARBER, former music critic, New York *Daily News*: I was a member of ACT UP, taking part in actions at churches. Obviously, these events were not covered favorably by the *New York Post*. But I distinctly remember a *Post* front-page headline that made me, and my more perverse friends, scream with laughter. It read GRANNY DIES OF AIDS! In general, ACT UP found the paper's coverage of AIDS abominable. An exception was Amy Pagnozzi. I remember she even came to speak at the Gay and Lesbian Community Center, which took some guts.

In April 1989, *Post* publisher Peter Price left to help start the short-lived sports publication *The National* and was replaced by Valerie Salembier, publisher of *TV Guide*, which had been purchased the year before by Rupert Murdoch as part of his nearly $3 billion acquisition of Triangle Publications. At the *Post*, Salembier was given the title of president and a $400,000 salary, which led the money-losing tabloid's more meagerly paid staffers to dub her "Salary Valembier." The *Post* also hired Don Nizen, a former circulation executive at the *New York Times*, as vice president of circulation. Nizen brought aboard Kathy Kahng, who had worked for Gannett and the Times-Mirror Company, as his deputy. All three found a back office in serious need of modernization, a staff resistant to change, and a tabloid that did not—could not—operate by the playbook used by home-delivered newspapers.

VALERIE SALEMBIER, president, 1989–1990: Rupert hired me at *TV Guide* and eight months later, I was going to the *New York Post*, which he just lost. He was one of the best bosses I've ever had. He knew exactly what he wanted, and he was very clear about communicating that. If you did what he wanted, you were okay. I got along very well with him. When I resigned to go to the *Post*, he pulled out every stop to get me to stay. I think part of it was his ego. He didn't want to see me going to the *Post* from *TV Guide* in the headlines. But I am a Postie in my heart and soul. I grew up reading it, even though I hated the fractious nature of most of the political pieces. And I believe in taking risks. My contract lawyer from Skadden, Arps said, "Valerie, this is the first job you will ever be fired from. Can you deal with that?" Because he pretty much believed that real estate developers were, how can I say it tactfully, media fuckups. I said, "Sure, no problem."

PETER KALIKOW: I had no right to buy the paper. That I admit. Whether I was a media fuckup—whatever I was, I clearly wasn't as big a fuckup as she was.

KATHY KAHNG, assistant to the vice president of circulation, 1989–1991: I went up to the circulation department, and the highest technology they had was a copy machine followed by the coffee pot. They had manual typewriters. Okay, they had a fax machine, but there was not one single computer. Don said, "We're putting in this computer system, and I need you to manage that." The average age of the people that worked in the department was over fifty. I said, "I don't even think these people know how to use an ATM."

DON NIZEN, vice president of circulation, 1989–1991: They did have a helluva system in circulation. The routes that went out, basically in the boroughs, they called them COD routes. Cash on delivery. The driver that was a route man would go out and hit the newsstand. He knew how many papers to give the guy. He'd give him maybe ten *New York Post*s, and he would collect for it, right there and then. When he went out the next day, he'd pick up the papers that didn't sell, give the guy credit for them, and then collect for the balance [of the new editions he left]. You didn't have to send bills out; you didn't have to worry about retailers paying. If they didn't pay the drivers, they didn't get the papers.

KATHY KAHNG: I was told to teach the senior driver guy and mailer guy the new computer system. Every day at ten o'clock, we're supposed to have training. And these two guys don't give a shit. What should have taken a month of training took six months. The log-on for the computer system was "NY space Post" and it took them like five minutes to find the *N*, ten minutes to find the *Y* key, and they'd say, "Kathy, which is the space key. I don't remember." After they signed in, it was easier because it was all numbers, and they were good with numbers. They were also big guys with big fingers, and they kept breaking all the numeric keypads. It was a MicroVAX computer. The representative came in to see us, and he was like, "What are you doing with these keyboards?" I introduced him to Mickey and Tommy, and he was like, "Oh, I see the problem." They were used to a blotter. A blotter clerk has a big rubber stamp, and they stamp the paper. Then they handwrite in the number, you know, like, how many copies are in there. They were used to punching things really hard.

VALERIE SALEMBIER: My very first meeting with the whole ad sales staff was so shocking. We met in the cafeteria, the number two ad sales guy ran the meeting, and this is how it went: He pulled out a big wad of bills and said, "Okay, Louann Jones, here's five bucks because you sold three classified ads. Joe Jones, here's a hundred bucks because you sold blah blah blah." I was appalled. Trying to bring some sort of organization into a sales staff that was basically unaccountable was really quite a challenge.

KATHY KAHNG: When I first got to the *Post*, I said, "Can I get direct deposit for my paycheck?" They said, "Are you, like, uppity? Only the top executives get direct deposit." I'm thinking, it costs you less to use direct deposit than to give me a check. Also, I had been there five or six weeks, and I still hadn't gotten put on the payroll system. They said, "We'll give you a cash voucher." I said, "Can't you just give a me a check and I'll go to the bank?" They said, "Just take a voucher." They gave me one of those yellow voucher things. It was a lot of money because

I hadn't been paid in a month and a half. I go to the cashier. The guy was like, "I only got singles. Come back tomorrow after eleven, I'll have bigger bills." The next day, I had a meeting. I came back around noon. He said, "I told you to come in at eleven. I don't have any more big bills, I only got fives." I said, "Just give it to me." I had a huge stack of five-dollar bills. It was like $1,500 in fives. I ran over to the National Westminster branch in Chinatown to deposit the money. They were looking at me like, you're the strangest-looking crack dealer we've ever seen.

VALERIE SALEMBIER: Peter was a vanity buyer, and vanity buyers don't understand the business. I had been a successful newspaper executive and magazine publisher, so he thought that I would start on Monday and by Tuesday, we would have sold $10 million worth of advertising. I explained to him how ad sales works. He listened and took it all in, and I really believed that he understood. He didn't understand. Bricks and mortar was what he understood.

> By early May 1989, with two women holding the top jobs at the *Post*, the tabloid appeared to have become—to outsiders, at least—a progressive workplace, especially compared to the swaggering, male-dominated newsroom culture of the Murdoch years. The machinations of the next few weeks proved otherwise.

JANE AMSTERDAM: I think my editorial autonomy was hard on Kalikow because he needed permits for all those buildings he was building or ran. I think some of the people we were covering, like Koch, spent a lot of time talking to him, pushing him. And for a long time, he was saying, "Hey, I've signed a contract. I can't control it." But I think it really got on his nerves.

ELIZABETH POCHODA: I thought Jane was doing a great job, but Jerry Nachman and Pete Hamill were conspiring against her. I think they thought it was a boys' paper.

JANE AMSTERDAM: I totally underestimated the deviousness of Nachman and Hamill. Nachman sat in my office as my best friend every day. He was always sticking up for me, he said, and I guess, going back to Kalikow, which I didn't know at the time. God knows what he was saying. I didn't see it coming. Things started appearing in the *Village Voice*—which my husband [Jonathan Larsen] was then editing—in their version of Page Six, by Doug Ireland [who had worked at Dorothy Schiff's *Post*]. There wasn't anything either one of us could do. It turned out that Nachman was the source of all of it. Jerry was a pretty good columnist. Pete Hamill was, too, although Pete was not great when he was writing for the *Post*. We ran a front-page story about Marilyn Monroe having the affair with JFK. It was a big story for the *Post*, for everybody. Pete wrote a column attacking the *Post* and defending Jackie O. I said, "Pete, we have a whole file of pictures of you with Jackie O. I can't run your column until you put in that you dated her." He refused. I was on my way to the copy desk to say, "Hold the story," and I got a phone call from Doug Ireland asking, "Why did you kill Pete's story?" I said, "That's interesting, because I haven't killed it yet." Then Pete's lawyer called to scream, "You better run Pete's piece." I was like, "Wait a minute, how do you all know that?" I realized it had been written with full knowledge that it wasn't going to get in. That's when I figured out what was going on.

PETER KALIKOW: We had Jane and Valerie at the same time. There was this women-in-business organization, I can't remember the name of it, and they were going to give me an award because I had two women in high positions. I had somebody tell them, "Peter can't accept the award because something is going to happen that you're not going to be happy about."

JANE AMSTERDAM: Something major was happening in Israel—I can't remember the specifics—and I went to Kalikow and said, "I'm sending Jerry Nachman." He said, "You can't do that." I said, "You can't tell me I can't do that." He said, "Nachman is not going." When he said that, I was like, uh-oh, something's up. Within two days I was fired and Nachman was the editor of the paper.

PETER KALIKOW: Jane didn't ring the cash register. I spent a lot of money on stuff that she wanted done and none of it worked. If I had a managing agent in one of my buildings and he didn't rent any space, he'd be gone after a year.

JANE AMSTERDAM: It happened on a walk down to the cafeteria. He said, "I can't have you here anymore. There's nothing I can do. You made me sign that document. I'm sorry, but you're fired." He was always incredibly nice to me until that moment. They put out that I had resigned. I had never been fired, but I said, "Unh-unh, I was fired." I wouldn't have resigned. I loved that job. They did give me a going-away party, and one of the union guys, a printer, came up to me and said, "I was one of the guys who was against having a broad as editor. But for a broad, you weren't bad." I said, "I think I want that on my tombstone." Most of my memories about the *Post* are good, except for Nachman and Hamill. I was so mad that the men had beat me, because I had spent my whole life competing with guys and not losing.

DICK BELSKY: When Jane got fired and Jerry got the job, a lot of us felt that he had stabbed her in the back. They fired everybody on the masthead. It was part of a whole housecleaning. They fired Jim Fabris, who was her managing editor, and then they fired me, who was like the closest person to Jane. Nachman had done a whole power play.

JANE AMSTERDAM: About four months later, I got a call from Kalikow saying, "Can you come to my office at 101 Park Avenue [where Kalikow's real estate operations are located]? Come in and have lunch with Danny and me." We talked and then we went down to the first floor and across to some secret elevator. We went down in the elevator, and then down these locked, stark white halls with pipes that were stark white. Finally, the last key opens the door, there were like at least twenty-five Ferraris there, and a white Volkswagen Cabriolet with a big red bow on it. I used to have a white Beetle with a white interior and a white top, and I absolutely loved it. I couldn't afford a car when I had it, so I ended up having to sell it. Peter said, "I know you always wanted your white Volkswagen back, but we couldn't find the one you had. So I got you this." I said, "No, no, no, I said Ferrari." He laughed, and he gave me a car. Wow. I was like, "Why would you fire me and then give me a car?" He said, "I didn't want to fire you. We loved you. We still love you."

23 | A SCRAPPY TABLOID DOING ITS JOB

Big Scoops, Massive Debt, *Posta* Nostra

The newspaper business proved much more expensive than Peter Kalikow had imagined. The paper's average weekday circulation had dropped from just over 740,000 in 1987, Murdoch's last year of ownership, to slightly more than 535,000 in 1989; advertisers weren't biting, and a recession loomed. After the firing of Jane Amsterdam, Kalikow scaled back the *Post*'s Sunday edition and eventually killed it. With the corpulent, chain-smoking Jerry Nachman—a veteran of local television news—in charge, the *Post*'s sensationalist bite returned, and a 1990 ad campaign, "The 3 biggest lies in New York," touted its underground popularity. In a revolving list of common urban falsehoods—such as "I'm an actor, not a waiter," and "This train will be moving shortly"—the third was always, "I never read the *Post*." The paper also published some of the best investigative journalism of its late-twentieth-century period.

CHARLIE CARILLO, reporter, columnist, 1978–1993: Nachman brought attention to the paper. We were on television continuously because he was so smart and articulate.

JIM NOLAN, reporter, 1986–1993: Jerry liked attention. There was an expression in the newsroom, "Lights, camera, Nachman."

ELIZABETH POCHODA, Sunday book review editor, 1989: There was a summer camp where a bunch of kids had gotten sick. Jerry wanted an investigation. The thing that knocked me out was, we were sitting in a news meeting, and he said to Duncan [Stalker], "We're gonna really shake our tits at this one." Duncan and I had to squeeze our hands really hard because—Jerry had tits. He was a big boy.

JOANNA MOLLOY, Page Six co-editor, 1990–1993: Nachman was not a hands-on editor. He would come in at maybe three o'clock and Jimmy Lynch, Richard Gooding, and John Cotter would tell him what the front page was for the next day. Maybe editors in chief have to meet with big shots during the day. But of all the editors I've worked for, he was the most AWOL. We called him Snack Man because he had the copykids go out and get both the salty and the sweet. He had one file drawer of chocolate chip cookies, Chips Ahoy. Another drawer was full of Tostitos and that kind of thing.

FRANK DiGIACOMO, Page Six co-editor, 1990–1993: One of his nicknames was Jerry the Hutt.

AMY PAGNOZZI, reporter, columnist, 1979–1993: He didn't want anybody else getting attention besides him. At one point, I went into his office and said, "Why are you burying my copy all the time?" He said, "If you're really as good as you think you are, I wouldn't be able to bury you."

Just weeks after Nachman took over as editor in chief, the tabloid broke a story about the state's Regents exams—standardized tests that high school students must pass in order to graduate—that rocked New York State's educational system and made national headlines.

TIM MCDARRAH, reporter, Page Six co-editor, 1985–1993: My friend Tom Allon [then editing a community newspaper, the *West Side Spirit*] was teaching a journalism class at Stuyvesant High School, where we both went. He said, "Can you come in and do this one or two afternoons a week?" I said, "Sure." One of the kids in the class said, "We're getting advance copies of the answers to the Regents exam." I go, "Sure you are." He goes, "We are." It wasn't the kids in the journalism class who stole the tests, but they had been offered them. The kids told me, everybody has them. I said, "All right, let me get one." They came back and said, "They want to sell the answers to you." I said, "I can't do that. But think how great these guys will feel knowing they screwed the whole system." The kids with the test answers said, "Okay," and asked me to meet them at, like, a 7-Eleven on Union Turnpike. They were Asian kids who lived out in Queens. I drove out there and one of the kids had a manila folder. He had the answers to the chemistry, biology, physics, math, and history tests. I'm like, holy crap. I said, "Let me go to the Xerox machine." They said they couldn't give them to me. I said, "I didn't see them if you don't give them to me." I needed proof. They finally give me two: the chemistry exam and one other one. I walk into Nachman's office with [Marc] Kalech, and Kalikow is there, like, shaking. He's saying, "This is good, Jerry, isn't it?" Nachman smiles. He's like, "Oh, this shit is good."

ERIC FETTMANN, associate editorial page editor, columnist, 1976–1991, 1993–2019: Nachman says, "We're publishing the answer key on page one under the headline EASY AS PI," which of course is not chemistry, but, you know.

TIM MCDARRAH: As we're sitting in Nachman's office, he calls up [Governor Mario] Cuomo's spokesman and says, "I need the spokesman for the Department of Education. I have in front of me the answers to tomorrow's Regents exams. We're going to put them on the front page of the paper. Here's your chance to comment." He gets a call back from I don't know who it was—maybe it was education commissioner Thomas Sobol. Whoever it was was going ballistic. "You can't do that! We've spent hundreds of thousands of dollars and everything's underway. The tests are going to happen." Jerry goes, "You're on speaker. I'd like to introduce you to the publisher of the *Post*, Peter Kalikow, and the reporter who uncovered the story." The guy goes, "I don't care who I'm talking to, you can't do that." Jerry goes, "Have a nice day." Click. He gives the answer key to Kalech and says, "Page one."

ERIC FETTMANN: They ended up having to cancel the exams. We got lambasted by the Board of Regents, by everybody—parents were calling in furious, saying: you ruined our kids. It took, ironically, the *Times* to publish an editorial saying, "Nonsense. What happened here was a scrappy tabloid doing its job."

Nachman's term as editor saw the return of familiar faces from the Murdoch years. They, and a few holdovers from the Schiff era, would educate a new generation of young reporters.

FRED DICKER, Albany bureau chief, 1982–2016: I was at Fox Five [Murdoch's New York station] for maybe eight months. Ian Rae was the news director. A Murdoch guy. He was very nice to me, but I hated television. So, in late fall, I guess it was Eric Breindel who called and said Peter Kalikow would like to talk to me about possibly coming back. I thought he was great, very impressive. I had known him before, but I got to know him a little better. I quit Channel Five and went back.

PETER KALIKOW, owner, 1988–1993: Fred Dicker used to write a column on, I believe, Mondays. The first thing on my desk in the morning would be a message that Governor Cuomo called. He used to bawl me out, and I would say, "Governor, this is Fred's view. He's not a newsman, he's a columnist. I can't tell him what to write."

MARK KRIEGEL, sports columnist, 1991–1993: There were real differences going from the *Daily News* to the *Post*. With the *News* you felt connected to the old power source of the city—cops, firemen, the boroughs. When you walked into the *Post* it was much more of an oddball newsroom. You had the sense that everyone there had survived, and some of them had survived from Dolly Schiff through Murdoch through Kalikow. Everyone in that newsroom had a chip on his or her shoulder. Except Jane Furse [who worked rewrite], who was wonderful and beautiful and had a naturally patrician air to her. One day Paul Schwartzman turns to me and says, "She's like Marilyn on *The Munsters*."

SETH KAUFMAN, Page Six reporter, 1989–1993: I'm answering the phones, and a woman calls. She wants to talk to Chris Oliver. He was old guard. Sometimes when he filed stories with me, it sounded like he was in a bar. This woman wanted to talk to him. I'm giving him messages, and she keeps calling. I'm like, "Chris, this woman says you got something wrong in a story, and she wants a correction." He turns to me and says, "Tell her that's why they're called stories."

> Dorothy Schiff reappeared in the pages of the *Post* after she died on August 30, 1989. The obituary had labor negotiator Ted Kheel calling Schiff "the only publisher in New York with balls." As she predicted to Al Ellenberg in the 1970s, Schiff was indeed cremated, contrary to Jewish law. But she did not own the cemetery in which her remains were placed.

ERIC FETTMANN: After Schiff died, her cheap kids sold all her books to Argosy [Book Store]. I found them one day. The best thing I have is Dolly's annotated copy of Nora Ephron's *Scribble Scribble*, which contained her essay for *Esquire* on Dolly. It's got line-by-line responses. Most of the comments in Ephron's essay about Dolly were things like "lie," "untrue." But the best lines from Dolly did not have to do with the essay on her. Dolly went through the rest of the book and annotated everything else. In the essay on [CBS reporter] Daniel Schorr, Nora writes, "A man's character is his fate (or, put another way, the chickens always come home to roost.)" Dolly wrote: "This will happen to Nora."

RICHARD GOODING, metropolitan editor, 1976–1993: The two best editors I ever had were Al Ellenberg and John Cotter. Cotter came back as metro editor in '89. [After working as day city editor at the *Post* in the early '80s, Cotter had left for other employment.] He made everything exciting. He knew how to attack a story. I had known him from his first time at the *Post* and stayed friends with him over the years. I just liked being around him.

JOANNA MOLLOY: Cotter was very competitive. The *Daily News* actually missed the [1990] Avianca plane crash story, and every time the editor who was responsible for that walked into Maguire's [a bar at Second Avenue and 42d Street, popular with both *Daily News* and *Post* staffers], Cotter would yell, "Avianca!"

MARK KRIEGEL: I can't remember wanting to please any editor more than I wanted to please [Cotter]. Some of it was the alcohol, some of it was my ambition. He was bright, and he was profane in a way that defies easy characterization. Remember that movie *Dead Poets Society* where all the prep school kids at the end, they get up on their desks, and I think it's a Walt Whitman poem, "Captain! My captain"? He made you feel like that. You'd want to do anything for him. He made the tabloid business like a holy mission. And he was funny as shit. It was always vodka, with two olives, at Maguire's. Then he would take the vodka and bless it. He would raise it as if it were a chalice, and he'd go, "When supper was ended, he took the cup," and then he'd slurp the whole fucking thing down. Then he'd touch the nitroglycerin packet on his chest. Because he'd already been in for a heart procedure.

CHARLIE CARILLO: He had a bad heart. He was always putting nitroglycerin under his tongue. The legend about Cotter was that if somebody was annoying him, he would pull out his upper plate—he had dentures—and say, "Hold these for me, would you, pally?"

PAUL SCHWARTZMAN, reporter, 1989–1993: He was this great gale of irreverence. Very little, if anything, was sacred and that's what made him so much fun. There were a few of us who had come from broadsheets, young reporters who had ideals that included the notion that there could be great writing in a newspaper. We used to get the out-of-town papers: the Philly *Inquirer*, the LA *Times*, all these great papers. Cotter would see me reading the *Inquirer* and he'd be laughing at me. "It's all type to me, pally," he'd say. He had all these sayings—"My Jews!" he'd say when referring to a bunch of us working for him. Or he'd put his foot up on his desk, scan the half-empty newsroom, and say, with mock satisfaction, "My vast staff." For all the jokes, he appreciated great writing and great stories and loved pushing and promoting young reporters. He'd walk around, bantering with everyone, cracking jokes. He would never make it in a politically correct world. But if you were gonna go on a boat ride through tabloid hell, was there a better captain?

CHARLES SENNOTT, reporter, 1988–1989: I was reporting on crack cocaine. I kept saying to him, "We should be going to Medellín. Why are we always reporting on it here? I speak Spanish, I really want to do that kind of reporting." We were at Maguire's when one of the big shifts in the story in Colombia happened. Cotter asked me: what is this about? I said, "This country is becoming the Beirut of Latin America." That was all it took. He's looking at the TV screen, he's thinking about what I've been harping on—why are we always looking at the effects of crack cocaine from the peddlers on the streets and not looking at the international aspects and how it comes in? I went to Columbia School of Journalism and worked at the Bergen *Record*, and he's annoyed by all of that. But he gets it. He leans over to Jimmy, the bartender at Maguire's, and says, "Jimmy, give me $2,000." He hands me the $2,000 and says, "Go to Colombia." I go home, get my passport, and leave the next morning. He gives me like two weeks to go write the hell out of the surge of crack cocaine and where it originates. We got in with the Ochoa brothers [of the Medellín cartel] and it was really exciting. Cotter was challenging me, like, you got this chance, better not blow it. He was very tough. He was one of those editors you always wanted to deliver for. We made it in and then military curfew was imposed. No other reporters were allowed in. I also was stuck in a hotel where there had been a fashion show. There were all of these stunningly beautiful women trapped in the hotel. Cotter loved that. He thought: that's exactly what you should be doing, kid. At that point, I was dating the woman I would marry. The thing with the models was a fiction that

Cotter created. I never had the heart to tell him, "Actually I got a great girl-friend." I never wanted to disabuse him of it because that was no fun.

On August 23, 1989, as Manhattan borough president David Dinkins was in the thick of running against US Attorney Rudy Giuliani to become the city's first Black mayor, Yusef Hawkins, a sixteen-year-old Black teenager from Brooklyn's East New York neighborhood, was shot to death after he, his brother, and two friends were attacked by a group of white youths in the largely Italian American neighborhood of Bensonhurst in Brooklyn. Hawkins's murder sparked weeks of racial unrest and protests led by Reverend Al Sharpton.

ROCCO PARASCANDOLA, reporter, 1989–2001: I remember being out there [in Benson-hurst] ten, twelve days straight. There were marches every Saturday, and they were nasty and violent—the vitriol and the racial epithets were just awful. As someone who's Italian American, it was godawful to watch. I probably got sent there in part because I'm Italian American, which is fine. I'm from Bensonhurst originally. At the first Saturday protest, I remember Ellis Kaplan, a photographer for the *Post*, showed up wearing a helmet, and we all laughed at him. The minute the first bottle was thrown we were not laughing. The bottles were being thrown by the residents of the neighborhood and people who showed up to shout down Sharpton. None of the reporters got hurt but it was about as ugly as ugly gets.

PAMELA NEWKIRK, reporter, 1988–1990: When whites in Bensonhurst were jeering and brandishing watermelons during a protest led by Reverend Sharpton, the headline over a front-page photo of the spectacle was SHAME. I think Jerry Nachman tried to bring more balance to the coverage but it's hard to change a culture.

ROCCO PARASCANDOLA: The city was so divided then. Say what you want about Sharpton, he's always been diligent about making sure that whoever is march-ing with him doesn't fight violence with violence. Don't bring weapons, don't throw bottles back at them. The missiles were coming from the people scream-ing in anger at Sharpton and Yusef Hawkins's parents.

TIM McDARRAH: One of my main beats was Al Sharpton. He was kind of a villain and an object of ridicule when I was at the *Post*, and he's had this transfor-mation. He's thinner and he doesn't wear the tracksuit anymore, and he has achieved what he wanted to achieve. He's certainly not altruistic. There's a lot of narcissism there. But I like Sharpton. He would call me. We would talk. He saw that while I did mock him—for a trip that I took with him to Haiti, I wrote about how he kept fried chicken and Hawaiian Punch in his luggage—I'd mock him in two inches of the story, and for nine inches, I treated him seriously. He believed in what he was doing, and we see now, thirty fucking years later with Black Lives Matter, Sharpton was right. He said there was systematic racism. He said that the police treated Black kids bad. As I wrote in the Haiti story [reading], "Sharpton seemed surprised to find himself being taken so seriously." Because he wasn't always taken seriously at home.

> Every media outlet encounters stories that result in handwringing over whether to report them—the result of concerns about their veracity, highly personal nature, the agendas of the sources involved, and sometimes all the above. In the fall of 1989, the *Post* came into possession of correspondence between Mayor David Dinkins, who was married, and women who were not his wife—fodder that, in the Murdoch days, would have led to a raft of ribald front-page headlines and stories.

FRED DICKER: I was talking to people on the periphery of the Giuliani campaign, people I had known for some time, and one of them asked me if I'd be interested in seeing the love letters that were sent to Dinkins while he was borough president, indicating that he was involved in multiple relationships with various women, including, I believe, at least one who was on his staff. I said, "Sure." Eventually they were made available for me. There was a lot of fighting going on behind the scenes to try to get them made public. Dinkins's people were doing all they could along with their allies in the Democratic Party to prevent their disclosure. I absolutely thought they should run, that it was a legitimate story to pursue, especially if we could link it to anything he may have done that was inappropriate in his office—for instance, if some of the women were on the Manhattan borough president's payroll, and they weren't doing anything for the money except being in a relationship with him. I did try to find some of the women to see if it could be tied to any official actions he had taken as borough president. John Cotter was involved in threatening me and killing the story. As was Nachman.

MARTY McLAUGHLIN, public relations and political consultant: There were three days of fearsome back-and-forth—whether to run the letters or not run the letters. [Peter Kalikow and the *Post* were among McLaughlin's clients.] The Giuliani forces obviously wanted them to run. I believe the source of the letters was [New York Liberal Party boss] Ray Harding, who was then very tight with Giuliani. It was really close to the election.

DAVID SEIFMAN, City Hall bureau chief, political editor, 1973–2019: I was not involved in those [discussions]. I do recall that at one point Kirsten Danis, fabulous Kirsten [now senior editor, investigations, at the *New York Times*], was trailing—what was the girlfriend's name? Cynthia something. Kirsten was trailing her around City Hall, and I remember her calling me and saying that Cynthia had gotten into a phone booth and was hiding from her.

VALERIE SALEMBIER, president, 1989–1990: Jerry Nachman gave the letters to me to read. I read every one. They weren't lusty. They were sweet and loving. They said things like, "It was the loveliest weekend. I had no idea it would be this loving and sweet, and you really are the love of my life." Nachman gave them to me because he wanted my point of view. Ultimately I said to Jerry, what do you want to do? He said, "I've got to call Peter." To Peter's credit, he said, "Do what you want." So they called Dinkins's campaign office and said, "We have these letters. They are authentic. We are trying to decide whether or not to publish them." The campaign called back the next day and said, "If you publish these letters, we will boycott everything that Peter Kalikow has his hands on. Every building, every piece of property he owns." It was a real threat.

MARTY MCLAUGHLIN: There were some great lines in the letters. One called him "my chocolate cupcake." [One woman referred to herself as "cupcake" and another called Dinkins "my chocolate button."] That's the one that would have gone on the front page. Jerry finally said, "I don't think we should run them. We don't have it confirmed enough and it could turn the election around." I said to Peter, "It could really bite you in the ass if they are false. The Black community would be up in arms."

PETER KALIKOW: Dinkins's love letters. I kept them in my drawer. I wouldn't print them. Because I thought it was despicable. He was running for election. I said no.

RAMONA GARNES, copy editor, 1978–1990, 2000–2004: The *Post* ratcheted up racism in this city to a ridiculous degree. When David Dinkins won the election, I remember walking by the news desk, and I'm not gonna say who said it, but he was very angry. He said, "The Jews, damn it, the Jews, that's why Dinkins won." I thought to myself, yeah, because the Jews don't want a race war. Which I think the *Post* was just ginning up.

> With Cotter's guidance and not-so-gentle prodding, Charlie Sennott would break an even more controversial story that would reverberate nationally and presage a reckoning for the Catholic Church.

CHARLES SENNOTT: The desk gets a call from a kid who says that Bruce Ritter, legendary street priest, head of Covenant House, America's answer to Mother Teresa, is actually a chicken hawk in the Port Authority going after young street kids. I wouldn't say it's pedophilia, because they were teenage kids, but it's absolute predatory behavior. By a priest. Cotter knew I came from a Boston Irish Catholic family. He's looking across the newsroom. When they get the call, he looks at me and he says, "Pick up that call." That was the most complicated story I ever did at the *New York Post*. The digging that I did to try to figure out if this was true drove Cotter crazy. He kept pushing to get the story in the paper and I kept saying, "We have no idea if it's true, and I'm not doing it." I really fought with him, and he fired me. He said, "Take your fucking things and get the fuck out of here. You're insubordinate." I packed up my boxes, and I walked out. The next morning, he called me up. "Where the fuck are you?" "You fired me yesterday." He's like, "Get the fuck in here and get to work." I took my boxes back, sat down, and kept working. He was challenging me—you can be methodical, you can go after stuff, but you can also get beat. "And if we get beat, you *are* fired," he said.

CHARLIE CARILLO: A young prostitute named Kevin Kite came to the *Post*, told his story about Ritter, and they were very careful about how they broke it. Cotter worked with Sennott hand in hand the whole way.

CHARLES SENNOTT: Ritter's board of directors and other supporters included people like Peter Grace, from the Grace chemical fortune; William Simon, a former treasury secretary; and William Casey, former director of the CIA. As I'm researching the story, I start to realize this is true. This young person comes forward, and I say, "How do I know you're not lying?" He said, "There are other kids who want to tell their story." I'm like, "You better tell them to come to me. I need to hear their stories." It starts to get to four and then five kids. This is a priest who when President George H. W. Bush launched his "thousand points of light" initiative [supporting volunteerism], he did it during a visit to Covenant House. All the TV networks were there, and the cameras went right to Bruce Ritter, with his priest collar on, and his rosy cheeks and healthy demeanor. I'm saying to Cotter, "This is a huge story about power in the Church," and he's like, "Just shut up and write it." One of the young men who came forward was Kevin Kite, and he said, "Hey, I've been talking to Linda." I'm like, "Who's Linda?" "You know, at the DA's office." "Linda Fairstein?" He says, "Yeah, they set me up with the tape recorder and everything." I tell John, "This is getting real, it's serious." He says, "We have to write it." I say, "The kid could be lying. They have the lie on tape, and we've punished this priest. We've ruined this charity that helps street kids. I don't want to be part of that." Cotter is just looking at me shaking his head, like "I swear to God, if you fuck this up, I'm gonna fire you." I held in there. I forget the timeline, but maybe a week later, Kite tells the DA's office, "I'm very worried. I think these people could be violent," and they sent a truck with paperwork to pick up his things and move him to a new location. I said, "Photocopy the paperwork." He went across the street to, I think it was a pharmacy, and photocopied it. I met him, got the paper, and thought: *now* we have the story. The DA can never deny that it's investigating Father Bruce Ritter.

VALERIE SALEMBIER: I got a call from a friend of mine, a top editor at Hearst who was on the board of Covenant House, and she said, "You've got to put a stop to a story." I said, "What are you talking about?" She said, "The *Post* is doing a story about Father Ritter—that he's a pedophile. I'm on the board. I know him very well. This is absolutely false." She believed that in her heart. I called Nachman, and I say, "I think we've got a problem here." I gave him her number. I told her, "He's going to call you." He did. They had quite a fight. He continued with the story, and my friend called me so distraught and bereft because it was true.

CHARLES SENNOTT: I kept saying to Cotter, "They're not focusing on the sex, they're focusing broad." He did not want to hear that. He said to me, and this is a direct quote, "This is not fucking morality. It's the *New York Post*, pal. The story is about sex. S E X all caps."

JIM WILLSE, former editor and publisher, the New York *Daily News*: I know this is true because both Cotter and Sennott told me this. Cotter was standing over Charlie's shoulder while he's working on the Father Ritter story. Charlie's writing about how it illustrates the problem of putting certain types of public figures on pedestals, blah, blah, blah. He's being very serious and earnest. Cotter says, "Charlie, this story is about one thing—cocksucking."

Sennott's story led the paper on December 12, 1989. TIMES SQUARE PRIEST PROBED read the wood, followed by "Former male prostitute cites 'gifts.'" It is not the headline most remembered by *Post* staffers.

CHARLES SENNOTT: December 11, 1989. It was a Monday, and the story was going to run the next day—the big exclusive. We had to come up with a wood. That's when the jokes would really start in the city room. The funniest headlines were the ones you could never run. Even at the *New York Post*. Lou [Colasuonno] is moving a photo of Ritter around on the [page-one] layout, trying to see how it's going to look. "How about KINGDOM CUM?" he says.

CHARLIE CARILLO: I wrote the dirtiest headline in the history of the *Post*, which never made it in. It was a really tense thing: what's our headline here? The real story is that he's having sex with this kid and violating this kid. Kevin Kite was his name so I said, "How about OUR FATHER WHO ART IN KEVIN?" It didn't run, but I got a newsroom round of applause, which was just as good. TURN THE OTHER CHEEK was another—they didn't use that one, either.

The *Post* stood alone in its initial reporting on Father Ritter, and because of preconceived notions about the tabloid and—at the time—the Catholic Church, most of the New York media remained skeptical of Sennott's scoop.

ERIC FETTMANN: Dick Oliver [former *Daily News* reporter and editor–turned–local TV correspondent] was on Channel Five saying, "Here is the story that's gonna finally kill the *New York Post* for good," because he was a big Ritter defender. Everybody was a Ritter defender. Nobody believed it. Ritter had this reputation as a saint. It's a wonder the *Post* didn't cave. But it wasn't the Murdoch era. Certainly early on, Kalikow was really good about stuff like that.

PETER KALIKOW: For ten days, everybody had us with a rope around our neck because there was no backup on it.

CHARLES SENNOTT: The New York media came out strongly against the story. Everyone was challenging that it may not be true. We responded by stepping up coverage. We started really showing what we had. We had a photographer who nailed Ritter and the kid getting into a car. The *New York Times* began to investigate the *New York Post* story. They assigned M. A. Farber and Ralph Blumenthal, the two big investigative reporters on the metro side. I was twenty-seven, twenty-six? I was horrified. I have the *New York Times* investigating my reporting. I had been incredibly careful and documented everything, which had annoyed John Cotter to no end, but it sure did become helpful when we got challenged, and I could say, "No, I have notes on that." The *New York Times* basically confirmed my reporting.

RALPH BLUMENTHAL, investigative reporter, *The New York Times*: We weren't really investigating his reporting, rather seeing what there may be to follow up. Also we took our reporting way beyond his.

ERIC FETTMANN: It was the first high-profile accusation of pedophilia against the Catholic Church, but at the time, it was seen as an aberration.

FRANK BRUNI, rewrite, 1988–1990: Kevin Kite came into the office a few times. I was a much younger and, I guess, attractive gay man at the time, and one day I came to work and, if my slightly hazy memory is correct, Cotter said they knew the DA was going to announce whether it was bringing charges against Father Ritter and Covenant House. The *Post* didn't want any rival publications to be able to get reaction quotes from Kite, so, as Cotter peeled off a bunch of twenties that I think equaled $200, he told me that Kite had said in the newsroom that he thought I was really cute, and that my job for the day was to entertain him and keep him away from any phones except the phone that I'd use to call in every ninety minutes to see if there's been a verdict. I think he even said, winking, "I don't care how you do it." He didn't really mean it; he said it with humor. What did we do? This is where my memory totally breaks down. I think we went to a movie. By the time it ended it was early afternoon, and we were like, I guess we should get some drinks. So we had some drinks and then I was getting antsy, and we went back to my apartment and watched TV.

MILTON GOLDSTEIN, copy editor, 1974–current: The *Post* doesn't have a lot that would merit a Pulitzer over the years, but if Charlie Sennott's story on Father Ritter and Covenant House was published at any other paper, they would have gotten a Pulitzer.

CHARLES SENNOTT: The *New York Post* was not going to win a Pulitzer. I've now been a judge for the Pulitzers, and the World Room [where the Pulitzer Prizes are announced], with its stained glass, has a certain pretension to it. They would have had a hard time at that point in history, recognizing a place that had had a reputation for sin being holier than thou about a priest in a sex scandal.

> The 1990s had begun with a freneticism well suited to the *Post*'s editorial bandwidth. Continuing coverage of the Father Ritter scandal, the Central Park jogger trial, and the AIDS crisis, among other national stories with New York origins, vied with the antics of celebrities, mobsters, and the city's nouveau riche.

KENNY MORAN, sportswriter, outdoor sports and skiing, 1972–2013: I contributed a couple of headlines, but my best was, one night, walking out, I'm going by Lou Colasuonno—he was probably managing editor then—and he's got this picture. I said, "What's that?" He said, "I think it's gonna be the wood tomorrow." It was a picture of a dead wiseguy laid out. *Goodfellas* [Martin Scorsese's 1990 film] was going on, and I said, "That's a deadfella to me." I kept going, and the next day, that was the wood, DEADFELLA. Lou took credit for it, but it was me.

RICHARD JOHNSON, Page Six editor, 1978–1990, 1993–2019: Malcolm Forbes's events were pretty amazing. You'd go ballooning [in France] during the day and then they had those parties at night where you'd go bumper car riding with celebrities and socialites. When I went to the Forbes party in Morocco, they had a list [of who was rooming with whom]. All you had to do is look on the list to see who was sleeping with whom. I thought, this is the easiest Page Six item I've ever done. I had [*Daily News* gossip columnist] Liz Smith hooked up with her girlfriend. She didn't give me any grief. Not really. She was half out of the closet by then. And I think she liked the idea that somebody thought she was having sex with anyone.

MARY PAPENFUSS, reporter, 1984–1991: I used to go and listen to Cardinal O'Connor every Sunday. He always loved to make headlines, so I would sit and listen and think, what's the question I can ask him to get me the wood tomorrow? One day his whole sermon was how we can't call God the Creator. We have to call him Heavenly Father. We can only talk to him as a father. We can't call him something gender neutral. David Ng was on the desk. I loved working with him. I called him up and I said, "The Cardinal said God is a man." That was great about Sundays. There weren't a lot of people there to second-guess. Dave said, "Yeah, let's go for it." That was probably my favorite headline, GOD IS A MAN. I got a call from Joseph Zwilling [director of communications for the Archdiocese of New York] at two in the morning when the paper came out. He said, "Mary, did he really say that?" I said, "Yeah, I think he did." Peter Kalikow said, "Mary, did he really say God is a man? I don't want to get in trouble with the diocese." I said, "What can I tell you?" and I told him exactly what he said, which was essentially that mothers can't be fathers. I think Nachman was really nervous. The *New York Times* did a story about it.

FLO ANTHONY, Page Six co-editor, 1984–1993: I broke a lot of stories—front-page stories. I broke that Kim Basinger and Alec Baldwin were getting married, and by the end of the day, they had figured out who the publicist was that had given me the story. He was uninvited to the wedding. I broke when Julia Roberts left Kiefer Sutherland. I broke Nicole Kidman and Tom Cruise adopting Connor. I broke John McEnroe and Tatum O'Neal getting married. I broke Mike Tyson and Robin Givens getting married. I broke Mike Tyson and Robin Givens getting divorced. I broke Bobby Brown and Whitney Houston dating. At first their spokesperson told me no, then she called me back and said, "Bobby said you could say they're dating." I also broke that they got engaged.

FRANK DiGIACOMO, Page Six co-editor, 1989–1993: Flo's connections to the Black entertainment world were mind-blowing. She could get Michael Jackson on the phone, Spike Lee, who was not a fan of Page Six or the *Post.* She had started out doing publicity for some top boxers, so her connections were serious there, too. But when the *Post* did something racially offensive, those same celebrities and Black power brokers would call her and vent, even though she had nothing to do with the story. She was part gossip columnist, part diplomat.

> John F. Kennedy Jr. had been an object of media fascination since he saluted his father's funeral procession in 1963, but interest intensified in the '90s, when he became one of New York City's most eligible bachelors.

GARY GINSBERG, executive vice president of global marketing and corporate affairs, News Corp, 1999–2009; former senior editor and legal counsel for John F. Kennedy Jr.'s *George* **magazine:** The paper really defined [JFK Jr.] at the beginning of his professional career with THE HUNK FLUNKS [the New York bar exam]. That was an unfortunate headline for him. [The *Daily News* and the *Post* ran the same wood.] But John was a pretty playful guy. He was not a guy who held grudges, not a spiteful guy. He understood that that's the role of a tabloid. He understood that that was part of being a celebrity in a tabloid town. He handled it with incredible elegance and grace. He was the one who pushed me to take the job [with Murdoch's News Corp], for god's sake. He was really keen on me going to Rupert, it was not like: you can't go to this evil empire that humiliated me time and time again.

FRANK DiGIACOMO: We would report on the most inane things involving him. He was a big bike rider, and once he wrapped his bike chain around his waist and misplaced the key. That was a Page Six item.

TIM McDARRAH: Through [Manhattan Criminal Court reporter] Mike Pearl we had broken that Kennedy had failed the bar exam the first two times he took it in New York. Then Mike Pearl learned that he had taken it in Connecticut and passed. I'm on Page Six and he calls me, says they don't want the story on news side. He tells me to make it the lead on Page Six and says, "Make sure you spell my name right."

MIKE PEARL, reporter, Manhattan Criminal Court, 1967–1998: The first day that John-John started working in the Manhattan DA's office, I was in Forlini's, the restaurant near the courthouse. He was there. One of the DAs called me over to the table and introduced me. I said, "I want to apologize now." He says, "Why?" I said, "I'm going to be a pest." It was true. Two or three times a week, I had to call him, because the desk had gotten a hint he was going to leave the DA's office, or because he was dating such and such a woman. I had to run all this stuff by him. He was really a gentleman. He answered all my questions. Mostly "no comment," but he was polite. I had the story that he was leaving the DA's office. He called me—he wanted to know where I got it. I didn't tell him. The only other call I got from him was—I had invited him to my retirement party and he called me and told me he couldn't come because, he didn't say it in these words, but I knew it was because if he was there, I wouldn't be the center of attention.

FRANK DiGIACOMO: In 1991, Allen Grubman, an entertainment attorney who represents a slew of A-list actors and music artists, got married at the main branch of the New York Public Library. I believe it was a first. The guest list was insane. Madonna, Robert De Niro, Mariah Carey, David Geffen, Naomi Campbell. I was there to cover it for Page Six. At one point, I wander by a record label executive I knew who was talking to De Niro and he attempted to introduce us. I'm a big De Niro fan, but we've also covered him incessantly on Page Six—and not always in the most flattering light. My father's oldest sister was married to a De Niro. I figure I'll mention that. But when De Niro hears my name, he immediately says, "Where do you work?" When I reply, "Page Six," he says, "Page Six? You fucking prick."

> The *Post*'s president Valerie Salembier passed down the tip that led to what is arguably its second-most-famous headline. In February 1990, Donald Trump's fifteen-year marriage to Ivana Trump imploded because of an affair he was having with Marla Maples, a model and aspiring actress seventeen years his junior. The resulting drama would produce eight days' worth of consecutive woods and ratchet up the rivalry between the *Post* and the *Daily News* as Cindy Adams became Donald Trump's media mouthpiece and Ivana chose *Daily News* gossip columnist Liz Smith, who broke the story.

RICHARD JOHNSON: I was the first one to ever write about [Marla Maples]. I think I did an item on how she had a big-name boyfriend who I couldn't name or something. Because Donald was married at the time. You had to be pretty careful. But we all knew about it. We ran a picture of her on Page Six with an item about this hot-shit new mistress in town.

DAVID NG, associate managing editor, 1980–1993: Sunday, February 11, 1990, the editors on the night shift, Lou Colasuonno and Jim Lynch, were figuring out Monday's wood. We had just had our asses kicked by Liz Smith of the *Daily News*, who broke the news that Donald and Ivana Trump were heading for a divorce. That hurt. We had the story, or most of it, but had been sitting on the blockbuster to make sure it was airtight. Our choices were either—run our late-to-the-party, nothing-new-here Trump story or run the wire story of the day. Ultimately, Lou and Jim decided to go with the Trump story and the cliché illustration of a torn photo of the couple with The Donald on one side and Ivana on the other. [The vertical headline read: SPLIT.] That decision boosted the circulation of a tabloid that had been bleeding money. It was editorial triage, but it kept us going for a few more months. By the way, that other option, the wire story? It was Nelson Mandela being freed from prison after nearly twenty-seven years.

GEORGE RUSH, Page Six reporter, 1986–1993: Ivana Trump spilled her tale of woe to Liz Smith, who was then at the *Daily News*. In retaliation, the *Post* became Donald's organ, pardon the expression.

CINDY ADAMS, gossip columnist, 1981–current: The thing that people would love to build up was a rivalry between me and Liz Smith. I had no heartfelt upset with Liz, nor she with me. I think more with me than I with her, because she was the grande dame, and who the hell am I to come on. There was a bit of that. Then there was the fact that she broke the Donald and Marla story. Which she did. She had Ivana call her. Then it was Donald and me. I kept talking to Donald. She kept talking to Ivana.

VALERIE SALEMBIER: I was in my office. It was about 7:30 a.m., a quarter to eight. A man who had become my friend happened to be a *New York Post* advertising client. He was the CEO of a major retailer. We got to be fast friends, and it was sort of fun that he was a client. That morning, he calls me and says, "Do I have a story for you!" His trainer had a roommate named Marla Maples, and the trainer told my friend that Marla was having an affair with Donald Trump. The trainer said to my friend, "She told me it was the best sex she's ever had." I said, "I'm hanging up the phone." I called Jerry Nachman and said, "You are not going to believe this, but this is a true story." He assigned Bill Hoffmann. Bill called me. I called my friend to ask him, "Is it okay if I give a reporter your number?" He said, "Of course, but it has to be off the record." I called Hoffmann back and said, "You can call him but you can't name him—especially because he's a big advertiser." That's how the story evolved.

SETH KAUFMAN: The story that I heard from more than one person at the *Post* was that Hoffmann found someone who was in Marla's acting class. Bill was always working the phone, and he contacted this person and asked them—he is a fast-talking guy, and he was like, "So, did she talk about her sex life [with Trump]? Did she say he is like a good kisser? Did she say he's the best sex she ever had?" They were like, "Yes, I guess, kind of." In the ancient tabloid practice of not lying but not telling the truth, he pulled that quote out. It was totally not a Marla quote. She never said it.

RICHARD GOODING: Hoffmann was a wild man. You had to watch his stuff and rein him in a little bit—and he couldn't really write anything. But he was one of those guys you had to like because he had so much energy and enthusiasm.

JIM NOLAN: Bill [Hoffman] was the Trump whisperer. Trump would call Bill or Bill would call Trump. They did a lot of stories together.

> The resulting front page, published February 16, 1990, depicted Trump with a wolfish grin next to the headline, BEST SEX I EVER HAD. The story identified the source as an actress who had been in a class with Maples. The next day's wood told a much different story: MARLA RAGES! blared the headline. And beneath it: "Says jealous actress trumped up sex quotes." The *Post* wasn't worried about being sued—not on this story.

MARY TRUMP, niece of Donald Trump; author of *Too Much and Never Enough: How My Family Created the World's Most Dangerous Man*: I was in my mid-twenties when that headline was published. I wasn't naive, but, by the same token, he was my uncle. I didn't think about him like that. Why would I? People in my family were disgusted by that cover—not surprised but not pleased. The only conversation like this I had ever had, to that point, was with my aunt Maryanne [Donald's elder sister, then a federal judge]. We weren't particularly close at the time, but the cover came up, and I was just mystified because I thought, being a germaphobe, Donald would not be celibate certainly but not the kind of person who's [generating headlines like that]. So, Maryanne is like, "Oh my god, he is like the horniest person I've ever known."

CINDY ADAMS: He never told me how he felt about that headline, but he was happy when he was in the headlines. That's all he cared about.

PETER KALIKOW: He actually didn't like it.

ANNA QUINDLEN, reporter, 1974–1977: One of the things that was great about working at the *New York Post* when I did is that I learned a lot of Yiddish, like *gantse macher*, a big shot. BEST SEX I EVER HAD elevated Donald Trump in the mind of the entire country into a *gantse macher*. Everybody thinks it was the business stuff and the celebrity and *The Apprentice* and everything. But that headline—which was like, man, this guy can blow anybody else out of bed—I feel like that elevated him in the public mind in a way that made everything else plausible.

Trump and Maples's on-again, off-again relationship was off again in June 1991 when the *Post* reported that he had dumped her for the model Carla Bruni, the future wife of France's president Nicolas Sarkozy.

PATRICIA JACOBS, fashion writer, columnist, 1978–1993: One incident that made the *Post* focus on fashion a bit more was when Trump was reported to be having an affair with Carla Bruni. They had a story up front that he was dating this mystery model Carla. They didn't have her last name. When I saw the story, I knocked on the door where all the editors were meeting. I said, "The mystery model 'Carla'? That's Carla Bruni." They all looked at me like, *What?* I'm like, "I work in fashion. No one thought of asking me?"

JOANNA MOLLOY: I had heard Trump was going out with Mick Jagger's former girlfriend, Carla Bruni, who was a model at the time and future first lady of France—ironic, because look who Murdoch is with now [at the time Molloy said this, Murdoch was married to Jagger's ex Jerry Hall]. I said to Trump, "I hear you're going out with Carla Bruni." He said, "Joanna, I never kiss and tell." Then he puts his arm around me and says, "But let's just say she's got a great ass."

FRANK DiGIACOMO: There were many exhausting things about Page Six and Trump became one of them. The Marla Maples period coincided with financial difficulties he was having. He had missed a $30 million bond payment, although he was bailed out by his banks, and I couldn't help thinking that he was using his personal dramas, which made him look like a player, as a distraction from the stuff happening with his businesses. Fielding all the tips on him was like getting caught in a sandstorm. You're getting pelted. You're losing perspective. You keep asking yourself, is this news? The tabloids were so competitive then that god help you if you got scooped. Toward the end of my time at the *Post*, I remember Murray Weiss, who covered crime and the mob, and John Cassidy, who now writes for the *New Yorker* but who was at the *Post* back then, giving me shit for getting beaten on some Trump story. It messed with my head because I was totally burned out on the guy, but because I worked for Page Six and the *Post*, I could not afford to have that attitude.

Despite the wins that the editorial staff had scored, the *Post*'s financial losses far exceeded Kalikow's predictions as weekday circulation sank below 505,000 in 1990.

With the drop in numbers, Valerie Salembier's relationship with the developer and his top executives deteriorated. And that wasn't the only factor bleeding the *Post*.

PETER KALIKOW: I had bought a piece of property in London as an investment. I sold it for a $10 million profit. Literally I didn't get to see that money for more than a week. It came in and out and you know where it went? Into the *Post*.

KATHY KAHNG, assistant to the vice president of circulation, 1989–1991: Valerie had a tough time. It was an unwinnable situation. She brought a lot of energy, and she brought a lot of ideas, but that place was very calcified then. When you looked at advertising, the *Times* had the high end, and the *Daily News* the low end. The readership of the *Post* is more duplicative of the *Times*, so there were not advertising dollars left for the *Post*. It was a two-newspaper market. The *Post* was also very backstabbing. They were trying to figure out ways to bring [Valerie] down.

DON NIZEN, vice president of circulation, 1989–1991: When you start getting into circulation in New York, it was pretty dirty.

JERRY CAPECI, reporter, organized crime, 1966–1986: The drivers' union was controlled by the Bonanno crime family. They were into it big and heavy. And Al Walker [Al Embarrato, a *Post* delivery foreman] was a made guy. There were a few made guys who worked at the *Post*. Joe D'Amico was Al's nephew, and Richard "Shellackhead" Cantarella worked there, too. But there were, how should I put it, organized crime connections or ties to other unions. There were the paper handlers, the stereotypers; there was a loan shark in the place who worked for one of the other unions. I'm not giving up names, but there were several organized crime–connected guys working for the *Post*. But at that same time, there were organized crime guys working for the *Daily News*, the *New York Times*, and for the *Wall Street Journal*. It was not like the mob went after the *New York Post*. The mob was involved in unions, labor racketeering, whenever and wherever they could get involved. Doug LaChance, for Christ's sake, the most corrupt of the drivers' union presidents, worked for the *New York Times*. He was a labor leader who was indicted twice by the feds. [LaChance went to jail for racketeering and extortion.]

KATHY KAHNG: When I first came to the *Post*, I did lots of projects for [Don Nizen]. One of the first things he asked me to do was to reconcile the payroll. I reconciled the payroll, and there were, I think, twelve paychecks and only eleven foremen. I'm asking, "Who is this twelfth guy?" That was when we had, for a short time, the Sunday edition. They were like, "Oh, he works Sundays, he works Saturday night." Finally, it turns out it's Al Walker, the infamous Alfred Embarrato, who was a capo in the Bonanno family. He lived in [Knickerbocker Village] behind the *Post*. He was a fake foreman from the drivers' union. I used to call him "the Salad Maker" because the foremen used to have Saturday-night dinner together [at 210 South Street], and he used to make the salad. I had a run-in with Al Walker once. I didn't know who he was at the time. We used to have a little parking lot in the back of the building. The executives had a key. I had this little car, and I would keep it there during the week. I would drive it on the weekends, and then on Sunday nights I would drop it off. One Sunday afternoon, I was coming in, and he was there—this guy with this giant white Cadillac, with the white belt, white shoes, and a big cigar. He's like, "Who are you?" I'd been there, two months or three months. I said, "I'm allowed to park here." He was giving me a hard time, and I said, "What's your name?" He wasn't very happy about that.

VALERIE SALEMBIER: The Bonanno family controlled the trucks, the drivers, the pressmen. I loved the night operation because that's when everything happens. So I used to hang around a lot at night. And did a lot of deliveries on trucks with the delivery guys. Standing on the passenger side of the truck, throwing out newspapers. I loved it. It's how you get to know the newspaper business. I made friends with a great guy, Bobby Perrino. Bobby was the superintendent of deliveries at the *Post*.

DON NIZEN: Bobby reported to me. He was a very charming and bright guy, and he was a very effective foreman. He didn't take any BS from anybody else. I gotta tell you, he must have told me ten times, "I'm not touched. I don't belong to these guys with the crooked noses." He used to reassure me that his wife had family members who were involved, but not him.

KATHY KAHNG: Bobby was the superintendent of delivery. He was the head driver guy. When I first came to the *Post*, I was working on more administrative stuff, like counting up the number of trucks, and vans. Then we started getting into DOT [Department of Transportation] regulations. They had to take pee tests and stuff like that, so several people lost their routes. We were trying to bring things into maybe the nineteenth century. The thing with the drivers is, they were collecting a lot of cash every day. So I had a list of drivers who were a day or two behind in their receivables. I would go down and talk to Bobby and say, "This guy is three days behind. What's his story?" Bobby would say, "I'll break his fuckin' arm if he doesn't come in." I'm laughing at this. Two days later, I see that driver come in with a giant cast on his arm. I'm like, "What happened to you?" "Oh, I fell down the stairs. Here's my money." I'm like, oh my god. When people would say, "What's it like working at the *Post*?" I'd say, "Did you ever see that movie *Goodfellas*? Those are the people I'm working with."

VALERIE SALEMBIER: One day, I'm in my office, and the mail gets delivered. There is a personal and confidential handwritten letter—about eleven pages on legal-size yellow note paper—explaining that the drivers were dealing drugs in that little park next to the *Post*. I don't really know what kind of drugs. I assumed it was heroin, cocaine. I'm a nice girl from Teaneck, New Jersey. That night, I took it home with me. I had my husband read it. His opinion was that it was authentic. So, the next night, I go see Bobby Perrino, and Bobby reads it. I'm sitting in his office. He turned to me and said, "Valerie, who do you want hurt?" I started laughing. He said, "I'm serious. Who do you want hurt?" I said, "I don't want anybody hurt. What I want is for the drivers to stop selling drugs in the park next door to the *Post*." He said, "I'll take care of it." He had a conscience.

KATHY KAHNG: The *Post* was unusual because we took full copy returns. With other papers, the stores would rip off the headers—which contained the paper's name and date—and return those. The *Post* drivers would drop the unsold copies off in the return room, and the return room manager was supposed to spray those copies with red paint so they couldn't be sold again. Then they would be tossed in a tractor-trailer. But we discovered a scam where the return room manager wasn't spraying all the bundles, and the tractor-trailer guy, who was in on it, too, would drive down the road a couple of blocks and meet a bunch of drivers. They would take the unsprayed bundles, split them up, and return them a second time. It was a four- or five-million-dollar scam. The drivers who weren't in on it were upset because, while they weren't against stealing, putting in returns more than once was depressing the circulation, and they knew that the circulation total was making the place go. The guy who was the mastermind was suspended for a few weeks and that was it.

VALERIE SALEMBIER: Peter [Kalikow] was aware of the Bonanno family at the *Post*, but he looked the other way, as did all his henchmen, like Dan Cremins and Rick Nasti [*Post* vice president]. They knew something. But they decided not to do something about it.

PETER KALIKOW: I always thought there was an organized crime level, but on a really low level. It wasn't something that I thought was a big deal. Later, I was astounded at how big it was.

> By the summer of 1990, the *Post* was losing more than $27 million a year. Some higher-paid executives and editors, who were not part of the union, were either terminated or not replaced when they left, and Kalikow asked for $19 million in concessions from the paper's unions. In mid-September, after weeks of negotiations and one near-death experience, they agreed to drastic pay cuts—effectively twenty percent by Guild Members—to keep the paper open, although one shadowy employee kept his full salary.

RICHARD JOHNSON: At a certain point, it was just Frank DiGiacomo and me, and we had to do like six pages a week—just two of us. I said, this is crazy, because people would leave and then they would never replace them. You look at Page Six now and it's got like six bylines. I got a job offer from [*Lifestyles of the Rich and Famous* host] Robin Leach. I remember going into Jerry Nachman's office and saying, "Robin Leach called. He's starting a new TV show and offered me this job for $100,000." Before I could say anything else, Jerry goes, "That's great. I'm so happy for you," and walks me out of his office. I'm thinking, what just happened? I didn't even mean to quit. I was just telling him. The TV show was called *Preview: The Best of the New*, which we started calling *Preview: The Worst of the Old*. It was canceled within two months of starting. Then I went to the *New York Observer*. That lasted about six weeks.

DEVLIN BARRETT, reporter, 1992–2002: At the time when Kalikow's ownership of the paper basically falls apart, one day, I want to say it was like three or four p.m.—a time when everyone is actually doing real work—someone stands up and says, "Hey, guys, we're out of business. We're shutting down. Everybody's got to go home." All around me, people are really upset because as far as they can tell, they're losing their jobs and the paper is dead. After about half an hour of general confusion, everyone decamped to the Lion's Head. I was nineteen or twenty, definitely underage. The Lion's Head is packed to the gills, and everyone is getting rip-roaring drunk. They're having an Irish wake, basically. That was the first night I discovered that you could buy alcohol at a bar with a credit card. I started buying whiskeys, and I'm not a whiskey drinker. Not then and definitely not since. I am seven or eight drinks in, can't handle my liquor, and suddenly, I have to run into the bathroom and start puking my guts out. The bathrooms are very small, and all I remember is hugging the toilet and hearing some guy yelling through the door, "Hey, Opie's all fucked up. Ha, ha, ha." I had bright red hair and a lot of freckles and most people at the *Post* called me either Opie or Richie Cunningham. I thought, oh, man, this is terrible. Then I thought, this doesn't matter. I just got fired. I'm never going to see any of these people again. I come back out and start ordering drinks again. No one bats an eye. There was a heatwave that week. The apartment I was bumming in did not have air-conditioning and was often ninety-five degrees. I wake up in the bathtub, soaking wet. I assume I had gotten into the tub to cool myself down, but who knows. The phone is ringing, and I'm like, god, why would anyone be calling me on my first day off from this fake job? It was the *Post* and they're like, "Hey, we're back in business. They found some money. You've got to come in and get back to work." I'm like, "Do I have to?" Obviously, I'm horribly hungover. When I go back to the office, the place was stripped bare. All the VCRs were gone, any TV that wasn't bolted with at least five bolts was gone. You couldn't find a notepad, you couldn't find pens, staplers. A lot of it was just souvenir taking, but I think some of it was, I can't believe I just lost my job with no warning. I'm getting a VCR out of this. At that point, I was doing what they call the typist shift, which meant I did really lame stuff like the index—the weird agate type stuff within the news section. There are TV crews in the newsroom, and I remember watching a TV guy do a stand-up in the newsroom after the first edition goes to print. He's holding up a copy of the paper and he's like, "The *New York Post* is back." Then, I swear to god, he said something like, "The index is wrong but who cares. Everyone is happy here."

KATHY KAHNG: We were going through tremendous financial problems, and we cut back the Newspaper Guild to four days a week. We were trying to make cutbacks with the drivers, and Don [Nizen] said to the foreman: Al Embarrato has to go because he doesn't actually do anything. The foremen were so scared of Embarrato that they said, take my salary. So that's what we did. We lowered everybody else just to cover Al Embarrato.

VALERIE SALEMBIER: Every Friday, for about three months, I would get a phone call from Peter's assistant, asking me to meet at his office at five o'clock on

Friday. I knew I was about to be fired. But then every Friday at four o'clock, she would call me and cancel the meeting. That's really abusive. That went on for three months. Until one day, I was asked to go to Dan Cremins's office at five o'clock on Friday, which I did, and he said, "Valerie, you're a really good girl, and we like you, but you can't stay here." He blamed it on—I knew nothing about this—he and Peter were in renegotiations with the unions and the unions wanted a giveback. The *Post* was losing over $20 million at that point. I think I still have some financials. So, he fired me. And then, oh my god, talk about big news. The media were relentless.

PETER KALIKOW: Same as Jane, Valerie didn't ring the cash register, either. That's all I ever cared about. Circulation and ads, and who could give it to me. I didn't care who they were, but if they couldn't give it to me, I didn't want them.

> The *Post*'s decline paralleled, and was exacerbated by, the aftershocks of the 1987 stock market crash and a spike in violent crime in the city. Murders rose to a record high—up 17.8 percent from the previous year—and robberies were up 7.4 percent. On September 7, 1990, the tabloid published one of its more famous front pages. Alongside a photo of a pensive Mayor David Dinkins, who as the caption noted had "vowed to be 'the toughest mayor on crime,'" the headline blared, DAVE, DO SOMETHING!

PETER KALIKOW: I liked Dinkins. He was a nice man. But I thought he was impossible as a mayor. He was worse than [Bill] de Blasio and that's hard to say. Jerry Nachman and I used to say he was a Black [Abe] Beame, which meant a nice guy. He wasn't one of those racist lunatics, but he was incompetent. He couldn't run a city.

DAVID SEIFMAN: Dinkins should have been an ambassador or something—protocol, and proper dress, and saying the right things. When he was on the record, he famously spoke almost high English—didn't speak like you and I speak right now. One year during the Inner Circle show, in which every mayor participated, he decided he was going to give a middle finger to the press because he didn't like the coverage. He brought a donkey on stage. It was some sort of reference to the press being an ass. He got on the donkey in a pair of jeans. I found out afterward that before he got on the donkey, he had the jeans ironed. That, in some ways, captured Dinkins better than almost anything else.

On October 25, 1990, the *Post* pulled out of its nosedive when unions at the *Daily News*, which had been working without contracts for six months and were being asked to make $50 million in cuts, among other drastic changes, went out on strike. Suddenly, advertising money and some of the *News'* best reporters and columnists were pouring into 210 South Street, including the rival tabloid's swaggering marquee crime reporter and columnist, Mike McAlary.

MARK KRIEGEL: McAlary was the best police reporter I ever saw. And everything we do comes down to being a cop reporter. He wasn't an especially graceful writer, but he was relentless [in pursuing a story]. When he was good, there was no one better on a big story, especially on police corruption. He was also the closest thing I had to an older brother. Other people saw different sides of him, his ego, his ambition. But to me he was unfailingly kind. There was a lot of intramural hate directed at him in the newsroom. I get it, these papers are failing. And owners keep throwing more money at him [to switch from one to the other] but to me, he was the best.

CHARLES SENNOTT: McAlary went from the *Post* to *Newsday* to the *Daily News* to the *Post* and then back to the *Daily News*.

ED HAYES, attorney, agent: McAlary called me, and I said, "Michael, where are you?" You could hear screaming in the background. He said, "I'm in Bed-Stuy." I said, "Michael, the police won't even go there. They're having a riot out there." He says, "That's okay because I'll be on the front page tomorrow." That's when I knew this guy had potential.

MARTY MCLAUGHLIN: McAlary became a superstar because of [John] Cotter. Columnists have a tendency, especially when they start to get a little notoriety, they say, "I'm gonna sit down and write my opinion on this and that." Cotter got McAlary to focus. He'd say, "There's a good story down here. Go down to the courthouse, check this out. You've got a good column if you do it." He got McAlary to do the reporting work that's needed to be a great columnist.

MARK KRIEGEL: The *Post* was having financial problems because Kalikow did not have the pockets that Murdoch had. He was buying people out, and the worst-kept secret in the newspaper business was that the *News*, where I was at the time, was gonna go on strike. We just didn't know when. When I look back on that whole period, whether you were with the *News* or the *Post*, you were waiting for journalistic Armageddon. You had the sense that any paper, except the *Times*, could go at any moment. [The *Daily News* goes] on strike October 25. A month passes, two months pass. Like three months into the strike, I get a call from Bob Decker in the *Post*'s sports department, and I signed a two-year deal to write a sports column.

PETER KALIKOW: The only thing that gave us a profit after the Sunday edition failed was the *Daily News* strike. We were making a million dollars a week for doing nothing. Finally, we got the high-end advertisers back. We started with Bloomingdale's by offering them the page opposite Page Six. They saw that there was some content in the paper that was maybe not so reprehensible.

> The *Post*'s brighter financial picture did not soften its hard-boiled approach to the news.

SETH KAUFMAN: Kevin McLaughlin was working the morning shift the day they printed the photo of Eric Clapton's dead kid [after the four-year-old fell from the fifty-third-floor window of a Manhattan apartment building on March 20, 1991]. The phones were erupting, and Kevin was totally swamped. On the morning shift, you're helping the editors get all the reporters into where they're going for the day and who's doing what. Reporters are checking in, the phones are lighting up with complaints. Cotter walks in and says how's it going? Kevin says, "John, these people are screaming about the picture of Clapton's kid." And Cotter says, "Fuck them. Just tell them we were going to use the picture with the headline CREAMED."

CAROLE LEE, assistant to James Wechsler, photo syndication editor, 1963–1993: David Rentas is the one who took that picture, and he did not want that picture released. But it was on the roll of film that he sent in. He said, "I'm a father. I don't want to see my son like that. I don't want anything to do with that." I think he made them take his name off the picture. They published it. He was so upset about that.

PETER KALIKOW: It went out before I knew about it. After the story came out, Jerry Nachman said something to me that was really interesting. He said, "Do you have any idea of how many window guards were put on buildings in New York because of that?" It was a big number.

On March 21, 1991, the New York *Daily News* strike ended when another media baron, Robert Maxwell, acquired the languishing tabloid and began offering out-sized salaries to *New York Post* employees laboring under the twenty percent pay cuts. Although the *News'* labor strife had boosted the *Post*'s weekday circulation to almost 645,000 copies, Peter Kalikow filed for Chapter 11 bankruptcy protection in August of that year. The New York tabloid war was on again, and in this round, the *Post* was the wounded underdog.

PETER KALIKOW: The *Post* absolutely played a role in my having to file for Chapter 11. From day one until the day I left, I lost $154 million.

RICHARD GOODING: In the summer or fall of '91, Robert Maxwell had his yacht tied up on the East River, and people from the *Post* were trooping there trying to get jobs at the *Daily News*.

John Cotter was among those contemplating a move away from 210 South Street and the promise of a larger salary at the *Daily News*. He and Jerry Nachman, whom Cotter often referred to as "that fat fuck," had been feuding for months.

ERIC FETTMANN: In the beginning, Cotter deferred to Jerry because Jerry had given him a lifeline. He was fired by *Newsday* [for allegedly making a racist remark, which he denied] and nobody wanted to hire him except Jerry. So in the beginning they worked well together. At a certain point, Jerry was a lot less hands-on and Cotter and [Lou] Colasuonno drove the news coverage. But Cotter became less useful once he started drinking again. He became needlessly provocative. He would come back from lunch juiced up and walk into Jerry's office and pick a fight. Jerry was not the type to stand down.

CHARLES SENNOTT: Nachman had good instincts and was an amazing street reporter but a flawed human being. He wanted the story to be more about him than the story. For instance, Cotter drove the Bruce Ritter story, even though Nachman tried to put his arms around it, and he accepted a public service award we won for it.

JIM WILLSE: After Maxwell bought the [*Daily News*] at the end of the strike, he wanted to do all sorts of things to announce that he was now the big dog in town and the paper was going to be revivified. One of the techniques, which is really at play in London where there's an abundance of newspapers, was pirating staff and making big hires. The word was out that Maxwell was hiring and paying a pretty good buck. This brought Mike Lupica back to the paper. He had decamped and gone to *The National*, which was attempting to be the *USA Today* of sports and did not survive. Maxwell asked me, who is the best editor in New York—I should say the best tabloid editor—who's not currently at the paper? I told him John Cotter [then still at the *Post*]. Cotter and I grew up together in the news business. We were at the Associated Press in the early '70s together. I knew his work, his personality, and his bounce would fit beautifully at the *News* as it tried to inject even more energy into itself after the strike. I pitched this to Maxwell and he leapt at it. We made a deal to bring John in as managing editor. The deal included a $100,000 signing bonus. We did all the paperwork.

Another of Maxwell's high-level hires was Richard Johnson, who, given his own column, wasted no time in taking aim against the *Post* and its owner. The *Post* reciprocated via the column that Johnson had once helmed, which operated for the first time under multiple editors' bylines.

RICHARD JOHNSON: I wrote a story that Peter Kalikow had a weasel deal to get a [127]-foot pier put in at his house out in Montauk, which is, you know, against every suggested thing to do with the environment. [Kalikow eventually built a smaller dock.] So then Page Six wrote that I got a free haircut from Frédéric Fekkai, which was absolute bullshit, because I was pissed off that I had to pay a hundred dollars for it. There was nothing I could really do. If I wrote an item saying that they were wrong, that I paid a hundred dollars for my haircut, it would make me look worse. I faxed them the receipt, but too late.

RICHARD GOODING: After Cotter had gotten a huge contract from Maxwell to become the *News'* managing editor, I remember sitting around some restaurant in the fish market with him, my wife, and a couple others from the *Post*. We were basically plotting how we were all going to get rich off Maxwell.

JIM WILLSE: John was scheduled to start work on a Monday. The Thursday before, he had a heart attack at home and died. He had a history of heart disease and was not as attentive to it as he might have been. So he never came to the paper. The footnote to that is I went to Maxwell and I explained that we still owed the family, which did not have a lot of money, the $100,000 signing bonus. Maxwell said, "I don't pay for a dead horse."

CHARLES SENNOTT: He died literally a few nights before he was supposed to come into work at the *News* [where Sennott had moved]. He called me the night before he died, talking about my manuscript [Sennott's book about the Father Ritter scandal, *Broken Covenant*, was dedicated to Cotter]. It was still on his night table, and he said something like, "What do you think? Should I wear socks?" You know how he never wore socks? I'm like, "Don't wear fucking socks. I'll see you in the newsroom."

ED HAYES: Kalikow paid for Cotter's funeral and I think he gave Cotter's wife some money. He was a very decent guy.

CHARLES SENNOTT: The pallbearers were Colasuonno, McAlary, Kriegel, Paul Schwartzman, me, and Willse.

MARK KRIEGEL: I remember one of Cotter's daughters putting a paperback copy of Graham Greene's *The Comedians* in his casket.

CHARLES SENNOTT: He was the Keith Richards of the last, great New York City newspaper war.

Before the year ended, another death rocked tabloid-land. On November 5, Robert Maxwell went missing from *The Lady Ghislaine*, which was cruising off the Canary Islands. His naked body was recovered in the Atlantic, and it is speculated that the media mogul, who weighed more than three hundred pounds at the time of his death, fell overboard during his morning ritual of urinating over the side of his yacht. Maxwell's death revealed the massive debt and questionable financial transactions at the heart of his media empire.

PETER KALIKOW: Every fall there was a Parents' Day at the Brearley School, where my daughter went. I was there when Nachman called and says, "They found the body of a three-hundred-pound guy floating off the Canary Islands and being that I'm sitting here, it can't be me. So it must be Maxwell."

24 | WHO ARE THESE NUTS?

Amy Fisher, Woody Allen, the *Post* Gets Raided—and Pillaged

The events that followed Peter Kalikow's Chapter 11 filing were so outlandish, no tabloid could have invented them. It started with a shift in newsroom leaders. After months of rumors, Jerry Nachman departed the *Post* in April 1992 to, he said, write a novel, which never materialized.

ERIC FETTMANN, associate editorial page editor, columnist, 1976–1991, 1993–2019: EASY AS PI [the story about stolen Regents exam answers] was Nachman's greatest triumph. It was almost like he'd been to the top of Everest and there was nowhere else to go. From then on, he lost interest. He confessed at one point, "I've done everything in this business except get a huge severance payout."

> Lou Colasuonno took over as editor. A veteran of more than twenty years at the tabloid and a hockey enthusiast who often worked the newsroom in spandex pants, Colasuonno kept the paper's never-say-die spirit intact despite the grim reality of Kalikow's bankruptcy and the paper's circulation, which dipped beneath 471,000 in 1992.

MARSHA KRANES, rewrite, editor, 1974–2005: I liked Lou, but I was not impressed. At one point, he and [Marc] Kalech were very full of themselves. I feel uncomfortable saying that on the record. Yes, he wore his hockey tights in the office. Real tight.

Less than two months later, Maxwell's heirs relinquished their hold on the *Daily News*. Once again, the *Post*'s most serious competitor lacked an owner.

JIM WILLSE, former editor and publisher, the New York *Daily News*: Maxwell was dead and we took the *Daily News* into Chapter 11 bankruptcy. One of the things that happens in bankruptcy is, you have a list of creditors, everybody that you owe money to. I put the Cotter family at the very top of the list. They didn't get a hundred thousand, but they got pretty close to it.

The gravity of the two tabloids' respective financial troubles only intensified competition. Increasingly, it looked like only one would survive.

JIM WILLSE: The *News* was in Chapter 11 reorganization for a year. It wasn't like the bankruptcy happened and then it was over. We cleaned up the finances, some of the old contracts were abrogated—especially the printers, the rubber room that went back to the strike of '63, where there were printers on the payroll who never worked. The paper was put up for sale. Our job was to keep the place alive until we could find a new owner.

As he grew more frantic about the *Post*'s drain to his finances, Kalikow began to interfere with stories when they risked damaging his political connections or chances of selling the paper.

RICHARD STEIER, reporter, 1989–1993: There were certain people who got special treatment while Kalikow was there. One of them was Alfonse D'Amato, who was close enough with Kalikow that . . . my understanding is that when Alfonse was in the process of getting divorced, he stayed at Kalikow's apartment. [It was reported in the *Village Voice* that D'Amato used the *Post* owner's Fifth Avenue apartment as his legal address.] The other one was Andy Stein [then City Council president].

DAVID SEIFMAN, City Hall bureau chief, political editor, 1973–2019: In all my years at the *Post*, there was only one time when something I had written was pulled before it got into print, and that was under Peter Kalikow. I was City Hall bureau chief and used to write this column, Inside City Hall. I'd write it on a Friday and it would appear in Saturday's paper. I'd generally hand it in five, six p.m. I was out with some friends Friday, and I get a phone call from Richard Gooding. He

says, "Dave, we're going to have to pull your column." I said, "What?" I was flabbergasted. In the column, I had a little scoop, that Andy Stein, who was then
running for mayor, was going to pull out of the race, which is not a bad little
story. The reason: Kalikow was desperately trying to sell the paper, and a guy
named Leon Black was looking at buying it. Leon Black was friends with Andy
Stein and Stein's father, Jerry Finkelstein. Kalikow, I guess, was afraid that any
story that might be viewed as negative to Andy Stein would hurt the deal, and
they pulled the column.

PETER KALIKOW, owner, 1988–1993: No, I did it because I liked Andy.

> On May 19, 1992, seventeen-year-old Amy Fisher shot Mary Jo Buttafuoco in the
> head on the front porch of the Long Island housewife's Massapequa, New York,
> home. Buttafuoco survived and Fisher, who was having an affair with Mary Jo's
> thirty-eight-year-old husband, Joey, was convicted of attempted murder. Joey,
> who owned an auto body shop, was convicted of statutory rape. The "Long
> Island Lolita" sparked a tabloid feeding frenzy that resulted in movies, books,
> and TV segments, including an ABC film based on Amy Pagnozzi's reporting,
> in which Drew Barrymore played Amy Fisher and Harley Jane Kozak portrayed
> Pagnozzi.

AMY PAGNOZZI, reporter, columnist, 1978–1993: Amy Fisher took me out to
lunch because she wanted me to write her book. She told me a lot more
than she had ever told me at that point. It turned out that much of what I
thought about her was false, and she was actually a lot worse than I thought.
I mean, I properly reported it, but she was actually a much worse person
than I had any inkling of. She maintained that [Joey Buttafuoco] really had
told her that he would pay her if she shot Mary Jo, that he was going to give
her $3,000. My perception at the time was that she wanted to take Mary Jo's
place, and this man distorted the feelings of this teenager. Look, I do believe that she was probably sexually abused by her father, and she certainly
was raped in jail. So who knows what made her what she is? When I had
lunch with her, I hadn't really wanted to do the book, but after lunch with
her, there was no way I was gonna do it. When I first wrote about her, I
think I was right to be sympathetic. At the time, "Lolita" was being used as
shorthand for a young temptress that was breaking up this happy home.
People forget that the Nabokov book is actually about a pedophile. This guy

seduced her. He was a grown man. She was a child. So, no, I don't really regret that part of it. I didn't put words in her mouth. But she and her lawyer were concocting the quotes that she was giving me. One thing I will say for her: she was genuinely sorry that she shot Mary Jo. That part was not fake. She really had remorse for it.

Some of 1992's stories ticked all the boxes of tabloid perfection—including one that had the *Post* reporting on itself. In late June, a page-one *Daily News* headline blared, N.Y. POST GUILTY OF FRAUD. As the result of a raid of the *Post* earlier in the year, the New York district attorney's office arrested eleven employees. A ninety-nine-count racketeering indictment charged that a group of Bonanno crime family members, including Al Embarrato, Richard "Shellackhead" Cantarella, and Bobby Perrino ran criminal operations out of the *Post* that included loan-sharking, extortion, gun sales, bribery, and stealing and selling papers. (A major heroin ring that also allegedly involved the Genovese crime family was uncovered as well.) The New York Post Corp. pleaded guilty to falsifying its circulation by 50,000 phantom copies a day—eleven percent of total circulation. The falsified numbers were used to attract advertisers and charge them higher rates. The paper was fined $10,000 and agreed to provide $2.3 million in free advertising space to clients who were overcharged because of the inflated circulation numbers. The *Post*'s vice president and general manager, Rick Nasti, and vice president and controller, Steve Bumbaca, pleaded guilty to misdemeanor violations of the New York State Labor Law but kept their jobs. (Nasti's license to practice law was suspended temporarily in 1996 in connection with his guilty plea.) One Bonanno family member who wasn't arrested was Bobby Perrino. Despite his denials of being mobbed up, wiretaps revealed him to be a ringleader of the racketeering operations. But he had not shown up for work since the night before the raid.

FRANK LoMONTE, compositor, 1966–2009: There were drivers that used to . . . let me just say that if they took the paper to their designated places, they would also make drop-offs of other things for other people. They weren't always just working for the *Post*.

PAUL THARP, reporter, columnist, 1982–2014: One of my Park Avenue friends was on a grand jury, and he called me and said, "The feds have this little [radio-operated] toy truck at the *Post* that goes around up above in the ceilings, and it's bugged. They're wiretapping all the guys on the loading docks and in circulation." I said, "Oh fuck, what am I going to do with that?"

SETH KAUFMAN, reporter, 1989–1993: State troopers were in the building. They were checking everybody's ID because they had busted members of the Bonanno family; they had busted drivers for delivering heroin.

KATHY KAHNG, assistant to the vice president of circulation, 1989–1991: About four or five days after the *Daily News* strike ended, Don Nizen was recruited by Maxwell. I went there a couple of weeks after that. We were at the *News* when the raid happened. It was a RICO investigation of the drivers' union, so it was a simultaneous raid of the *News*, the *Post*, and Metropolitan News, which handled most of the *Times* deliveries. I heard through the grapevine that the night before the raid, Bobby Perrino was not at work because they raided his house. He wasn't there, either, but they found over $100,000 in cash and, I heard, books in the attic about how to dismember and disappear a body.

VALERIE SALEMBIER, president, 1989–1990: Right after I left the *Post*, Bobby Perrino disappeared. I don't know if you remember this, but around three years ago, there were two Bonanno captains who were tried and convicted. They admitted to the murder of Bobby, and the feds dug up his remains. The Bonannos thought he was turning fed because he had suddenly found religion. This is the stuff they make movies about.

By August, the circulation scandal was largely forgotten as the *Post* and *Daily News* each scrambled to right themselves financially. Canadian media magnate Conrad Black and real estate mogul and *U.S. News & World Report* owner Mort Zuckerman emerged as potential saviors of the *News*, while Kalikow had begun talks with private equity investor Leon Black, then CEO of Apollo Global Management. The possibility that either paper could shut down with little notice would loom over both newsrooms into 1993, and *Post* staffers would endure another round of pay cuts and close calls. While the *Times*, the *Washington Post*, and other papers across the nation reported on the death watch, the tabloids kept slugging it out, with the *Post* breaking a story that would reverberate well into the Harvey Weinstein #MeToo era: Woody Allen's affair with Mia Farrow's adopted daughter Soon-Yi Previn.

JOANNA MOLLOY, Page Six co-editor, 1990–1993: Woody Allen was the accidental story, really, unfortunately for him. It might never have happened. The source who first told me about it—months before we broke it—told me that they saw, quote, "Woody Allen making out with one of his Vietnamese daughters at a Knicks game back behind the seats." First of all, Soon-Yi came from Korea, and so I was like, "Get the hell out of here. Making out? Are you sure? Come on." He was taking one of Mia's daughters to a Knicks game. It's always in full view. But a series of lucky and amazing things happened, story-wise. For example, I asked photo to get me all the recent pictures of Woody and Mia and the kids. In one of those photos, Soon-Yi is carrying a bag that is obviously from a college and there was a letter—an *R*—on the bag. In the back of dictionaries then, paper dictionaries, they listed all the colleges of the United States. So I got a dictionary and looked at all the colleges. There was one that started with *R*, Rider University, in New Jersey, and then we matched the [college's logo] to what was on the bag. We sent a photographer there, and he found her. We got her picture, but she wouldn't answer any questions. He followed her to where she lived, and we had that. Another amazing thing that happened was that Mia had another one of the daughters, Lark, call up and tell us that Mia would really like to talk to Soon-Yi and where is she? If Mia was indeed the one paying Soon-Yi's tuition at Rider, she apparently was in denial that Soon-Yi would have the gall to continue living her life on campus. Mia had gotten Woody's doorman to let her into his apartment, and after snooping around, she found nude photos of Woody and Soon-Yi on his fireplace mantel. It didn't help that Ronan, then a toddler, had said, when Mia questioned him about being brought over to his father Woody's apartment by Soon-Yi, that the two adults had gone into the bedroom together and were "exchanging compliments." Sources told me that Mia was outraged, and I made her promise not to harm Soon-Yi if I revealed her whereabouts, which I never did. I said to Lark, if you come into the newsroom, I might tell you. She came in! The great Marianne Goldstein was my partner on the story at that point. I said to Lark, "I have to hear from Mia. She has to guarantee Soon-Yi's safety if we say where she is." So Lark calls Frog Hollow, Mia's estate, and we put Mia on speaker. She's like, "Oh, of course, she'll be in total safety" and hangs up. I said [to Lark], "Let me check with Soon-Yi"—as if I was always chatting with Soon-Yi. After Lark left, Marianne pressed redial on the phone, and we had Mia's home number. So we could start really bugging her for more information. Once we nailed the story, it led to a series of front pages. The Trump [divorce] story beat me, but I think I'm in second place.

The Page Six department in the 1990s consisted of four desks shoved together in an L-shaped formation. While the reporters who shuttled on and off the desk during the Kalikow years tracked the hookups and breakups of VIPs, the close quarters resulted in one lasting romance.

JOANNA MOLLOY: Frank DiGiacomo and I were the editors of Page Six, and George Rush was a freelancer. There are so many events in New York every single night, we would divide them up. We each had about three. I started to see George showing up at mine, and I'm like, "George, you were supposed to be at . . ." and he's like, "I was already there. Nothing's going on." So after a bunch of those—it went on for weeks—he said to me, "Do you think you could consider these events that we've been covering dates? Retroactively?" That's how it started. We got married on December 12, 1992, and the editors presented us with a front page that said BEST SIX THEY EVER HAD.

FRANK DiGIACOMO, Page Six co-editor, 1989–1993: We were constantly running down Madonna stories then, and Liz Rosenberg [Madonna's publicist] was constantly shooting them down. At least once, we referred to her on the Page as "the Queen of Denial."

FLO ANTHONY, Page Six co-editor, 1984–1993: There was the time that José Canseco [then with the Oakland A's] showed up to Madonna's apartment. A restaurant publicist called me and said that José and Madonna had ordered food from one of his clients, and they got a picture of him going there.

JOANNA MOLLOY: George Rush brought a video camera to the party for Madonna's [1992] *Sex* book. Those cameras were pretty big at the time, so he had to hide it under an overcoat. At the party, Madonna had all these dioramas of live people having different kinds of sex. It was a sizzling video. He sold it to Steve Dunleavy, who was then at *A Current Affair*. George had been my plus-one. I was the one invited to the party. So Susan Crimp, a fierce British TV gossip reporter with *Hard Copy*, was mad because she had wanted the video. She ratted me out to Liz Rosenberg, who banned me from getting a copy of *Sex*. That was bad because, obviously, it was going to be the first, like, eight pages of the *New York Post* and the *Daily News* and every other tabloid the next day. Thank god, a friend at *New York* magazine let me come up there with a photographer to take pictures of their copy, because I would have been dead. [Metropolitan editor]

Richard Gooding said to me, "If you do not get a copy of the *Sex* book, you're fired." And he was my friend.

In early January 1993, the *Post*'s main competitor had a new owner, Mort Zuckerman.

JIM WILLSE: It turned out to be an auction—Conrad Black and Mort Zuckerman were the main contenders. It came down to who could strike agreements with the unions. Zuckerman was more successful. He also had to commit to building a new printing plant. So he got the sale. I supported Conrad Black and in retrospect, he would have been a bad choice. Mort sent a team of people from *U.S. News [& World Report]*, which he owned, to look at staff and recommend who should stay. A lot of people were let go. He said, "We're going to review editor candidates, including you." I took myself out of the running. The paper went into bankruptcy, came out with a new owner, and a much healthier financial setup with the unions.

With Leon Black no longer interested in becoming a white knight, the *Post* needed to find a savior fast.

PETER KALIKOW, owner, 1988–1993: Mort Zuckerman's partner, Fred Drasner, called Dan [Cremins] and says, "We want to buy the *Post*." Mort calls and we talk. First the pleasantries, and then he goes, "Why should I buy the paper? You're going to close anyway." I said, "That's probably true, but you've got two problems. One, Murdoch comes back, or two, I get a schlemiel to buy the paper." It turned out I got both. I wasn't nasty, but I said, "You can take the paper if you guarantee to pay all my obligations": pension obligations, which were four to five million—that was an exaggerated number—and all my legal fees, which were considerable. He didn't do it. I'm quite sure that on his list of "oh shit" moments, that's one of them. I always liked Mort, but he bought the wrong paper. So, this guy Steve Hoffenberg comes in. I don't remember who pulled him in, but they were people I had real respect for. I said to my guys Dan [Cremins] and Rick [Nasti], the first thing this guy's got to do for me to even see him is, I want a check for $6 million. And that's what I got.

MARK KRIEGEL, sports columnist, 1991–1993: We go up to the publisher's office—Lou Colasuonno, and might have been Richard Gooding, [Mike] McAlary. We're sitting up there waiting. I could actually feel the beat of my heart. We're literally waiting for a stay of execution. All of a sudden someone says, There's this guy Hoffenberg. He wants to buy the paper. Cindy [Adams] pipes up. "Steven Hoffenberg! I know him." Of course she does. In that moment, it went from doom to hope. Someone tells Cindy: get on the phone with him right now. She does. We went from walking to the gallows to "Hoffenberg will save us," in, like, a minute.

PETER KALIKOW: We were sort of closing down the paper that Sunday, and rest in peace, this is why I loved Mario Cuomo [then in his third term as New York's governor]. That whole weekend he was on the phone with me like ten times a day trying to help us out knowing that [Albany reporter] Fred Dicker beat the shit out of him. That's the kind of good guy he was.

AMY PAGNOZZI: My last fun night at the *Post* was the night Cindy Adams saved the paper. She was on the phone trying to get backers. I picked her up and carried her around the newsroom. I was pretty strong, and she's just a little thing. She's only five-foot-two. She just did not give up. She made one phone call after another trying to wring money out of people.

CINDY ADAMS, gossip columnist, 1981–current: The *Post* was going to fold over a weekend if they didn't have something like $6 million. Howard Rubenstein and I realized that nobody had the powers and the Rolodexes and the smarts that we did. I remember very well that I was not well. I had a terrible, heavy head cold, I could barely breathe. Howard was in his home, I was in mine in bed, and we were on the phone. We said, we have to find somebody who has $6 million. This is a weekend. This was before the coming of the billionaires. It was still a lot of money. We had to have the money by Monday. So, me, not well, went through my Rolodex, and Howard was going through his, and we both came up with Steven Hoffenberg, who was not number-one quality. But number-one quality doesn't have $6 million in their couch. He came up with the amount of money. He saved the paper, and then he went away for twenty years.

Several years later, Hoffenberg, who ran Towers Financial, a bill collection firm, would be sentenced to twenty years in prison after pleading guilty to charges connected to a $460 million Ponzi scheme. To add another layer of intrigue: Jeffrey Epstein worked for Hoffenberg—the same Jeffrey Epstein who was found hanged in a New York jail in 2019 while awaiting trial on charges that he had sexually abused and possibly trafficked dozens of girls, allegedly with the help of Robert Maxwell's daughter Ghislaine. Hoffenberg would claim Epstein masterminded the Ponzi scheme, but Epstein was never charged, and at the time Hoffenberg attempted to buy the *Post*, Epstein had not yet appeared on the radar of the New York media. Hoffenberg had. In addition to civil suits filed against him in numerous states, the Securities and Exchange Commission was already investigating Towers Financial. Newsroom wags dubbed the *Post*'s imposing new sort-of owner (technically he was a court-appointed "manager") "Bugsy" and "Repo Man."

STEVE HOFFENBERG, aspiring owner, 1993: It was a question of the *Post* going out of business or going to the *Daily News*, and there were some supporters. Politically, Governor Mario Cuomo wanted the *Post* to have an independent voice, and he and [limousine mogul and political gadfly] Bill Fugazy were instrumental in what I did, as well as Cindy Adams. They asked repeatedly if I would consider bailing out the circumstances of the foreclosure on the delinquent taxes for withholding by Peter Kalikow. We put up much more than [the reported] $2.5 million. I believe I put up at that point in time over $10 million and signed for $100 million.

JOANNA MOLLOY: I actually had Hoffenberg sign my computer with a magic marker that he would not destroy the *Post* and he would not lay off everybody. He signed it.

STEVE HOFFENBERG: Jeffrey Epstein was on the sidelines coaching me on the *New York Post* acquisition. He felt the profile was good if it could be turned around with the unions and he had a close relationship with [parking lot magnate] Abraham Hirschfeld and his daughter, Rachel Hirschfeld.

MICHAEL SHAIN, television editor, 1978–1993, 1996–2013: Three of us were assigned to do a story on Hoffenberg. In which we were told: no holds barred. It was one of the very few times I was ever in Mrs. Schiff's office, because that's where he was. I remember saying to myself, I'm being invited to jump overboard here. I'm not going to do a no-holds-barred story on the publisher. But I do remember realizing that he was a crook. I also realized that he loved where he was. He loved being the publisher. I kept saying to people, "There's nothing here to steal. The paper is bereft—there's no money. This guy's going to steal *for* us."

They would say, no, no, he's dishonest, he takes money from the old people, he's got a phone scam, all this other stuff.

CHARLIE CARILLO, reporter, columnist, 1978–1993: Hoffenberg with his press pass was like the kid who visits the police station. They give him a badge and a whistle, and they let him walk around. He really wanted to be a newspaperman.

> The biggest theft during the fraught weeks after Kalikow turned the paper over to Hoffenberg was committed by Mort Zuckerman, who lured three of the *Post*'s top editors—Editor Lou Colasuonno, Metropolitan Editor Richard Gooding, and Jimmy Lynch, a managing editor, along with columnist Mike McAlary—to the *News*. Other reporters and editors followed.

MILTON GOLDSTEIN, copy editor, 1974–current: At one point, Lou said to the staff, "We'll be okay, we'll survive. Watch me. I'm the canary in the coal mine." A week later, the canary flew out of the cage. They were opportunists, and I couldn't blame them. I took vacation days to do a week's tryout at the *News*. They wanted to hire me, but I asked them to wait a bit to see how things played out at the *Post*. I, too, was trying to keep a foot elsewhere in case they brought out the big padlock.

MYRON RUSHETZKY, head city desk assistant, 1974–1989, 1991–2013: I was at Maguire's with a bunch of Posties, and in the back were Mike McAlary and Richard Gooding. Gooding wandered down the bar to say hello to us. He stuck his hand out and I refused to shake. He ended up going back to McAlary and the other folks he was with. McAlary strolled down to the front of the bar and stuck out his hand. Obviously, Richard had told him that I would not shake it, and I did not. Down the road, we reconciled, if that's the right word. But at that moment, these were our leaders—the captains of our boat. They were supposed to go down with the ship, but like rats, they were the first ones to jump.

RICHARD GOODING, metropolitan editor, 1976–1993: I do not remember that, but it could be true. They definitely thought we were traitors. We all thought the *Post* was dead, that it didn't have a chance. Lou didn't want to go to the *News* alone. He knew he'd need some support down the line. We rationalized that if we went to the *News*, when the *Post* closed, we could hire as many people that we could get away with hiring. Then the *Post* didn't close.

DAN AQUILANTE, chief music critic, 1980–2012: Hoffenberg gave us this feeling that things were going to change. He threw us a party at Windows on the World at the top of the World Trade Center to boost staff morale. I understand he never paid for it.

JIM PRATT, copy editor, 1990–2013: There were a couple of people at the paper who used to create *Post* memorabilia, things like T-shirts and buttons. Mort Zuckerman was doing all he could to kill the *Post*, and they came up with these big yellow buttons with black all-caps type that read "Fuck the Zuck." When Hoffenberg got the *Post*, he threw a big party at Windows on the World. It was a great party with spectacular food and drink—no expense spared because he wasn't paying with his real money, obviously. I had the button, and I offered it to him. He said, "Oh, great!" He was going to put it on his lapel but one of his assistants stopped him, and said, "No, no, no, don't do that"—because there were photographers all around. She was very nervous that he would get a photo taken of him with his "Fuck the Zuck" button.

JERRY ENGEL, photographer, 1958–1993: I worked for Hoffenberg after the *Post*. Everything was rented with him. He didn't own anything. When he had a kid, I said, "Is that a rent-a-kid?"

In February, the SEC froze Hoffenberg and Towers Financial's assets just days before the judge overseeing Kalikow's Chapter 11 filing approved the sale of the *Post*. (In addition to his personal bankruptcy, Kalikow also put the *Post* into Chapter 11.) In short order, Hoffenberg came up with a new financial partner, real estate investor and parking lot magnate Abe Hirschfeld, and a new executive editor, Pete Hamill—choices that would usher in weeks of chaos at the *Post*. Hoffenberg and Hirschfeld soon fell out, and on March 12, Kalikow struck a deal with Hirschfeld that gave him control of the *Post*. Although Hamill briefly stabilized the newsroom, Hirschfeld fired him. He then brought in Wilbert "Bill" Tatum, an owner of the *New York Amsterdam News*, which served the city's Black communities, as editor, and, as part of a heated press conference on Sunday, March 14, announced that he was merging the two papers. The *Post* did not publish on March 15, a day that brought the firing of fourteen managers, including David Seifman, Eric Breindel, and Fred Dicker, and fifty-one Newspaper Guild members, until the union convinced him to take back all but one.

DAVID SEIFMAN, City Hall bureau chief, political editor, 1973–2019: I had dealt with Abe [Hirschfeld] before. At one point, he opened something called the Vertical Club. On East 61st Street. It was this super fancy gym. Before Equinox, he had a vision of a fancy gym. There was some complaint. Either he was underpaying or there was some safety issue. I call Abe, and he says, "Why don't you come over here and take a look." He gives me a tour of the club. At the end of the tour, I go into this office where his wife is. He said, "Do you have any more questions?" "No, thanks, Abe, you told me what I needed to know." Then his wife opens a drawer in the desk. They have all these little perfume or cream samples. I don't know if they got them in hotels or what. She says, "Why don't you take a few?" I said, "No, that's okay." Then Abe chimes in. I said, "Abe, I'm fine, thank you." It was the lowest-level attempted bribe you've ever seen.

MARK KRIEGEL: If you really looked at Hirschfeld's face, you expected something merry or at least ironic, like an old Borscht Belt comedian, but there was something malignant and humorless about him. He was an evil prick.

JIM NOLAN, reporter, 1986–1993: Hirschfeld wanted Pete to run his wife's poetry in the paper.

TERRY GOLWAY, sports copy editor, 1987–1992: The news people were in an uproar because Hirschfeld had fired Pete [Hamill]. They're having rallies, and there was really no representation from the sports department that I can remember. On the copy desk, we were talking about, what should we do? And one of my colleagues whose name escapes me said, "Pete Hamill is a celebrity. Pete Hamill is a novelist. He doesn't like it here after three months, he's going to quit and go write a couple more novels. If I lose my job, I'm going to be pumping gas." There was some wisdom in that. The feeling was, frankly, that Pete had newsroom credibility, but they saw him more as a celebrity editor other than someone like a Frank Devine—a Murdochian who was a newspaper guy. They were very skeptical of him, and that's exactly what happened. Pete had no real commitment to the *New York Post*.

FRED DICKER, Albany bureau chief, 1982–2016: I along with a bunch of others got a letter saying, "Thanks for your service and you're fired." [Bill] Tatum knew me and didn't like me. I also was high profile and I was management, so I wasn't in the union.

MILTON GOLDSTEIN: After Hirschfeld fired Hamill, Gerard Bray became the editor. Hirschfeld told Bray, fire X number of people. Bray said, "I'm not going to do it. I quit." Whoever took over for him—I think it was Steve Bumbaca—started going down the list of Guild people, "One, two, fired; one, two, fired." I was one of those fired, and I remember coming in that day. I knew what had happened, but when I got to the door, the security guard said, "Eh, go up." He had the list, but it was semi-controlled chaos.

FRANK DiGIACOMO: The Friday night that Hirschfeld fired Hamill, there was a massive snowstorm. The next day, I decided to go down to 210 and bring home my Rolodex and anything else valuable in case the *Post* shut down. Hirschfeld and Tatum come through the office, which was virtually empty where the Page Six department was. I remember Abe had on the kind of rubber boots my mother made me wear when I was a kid, with those cheap metal buckles that spring open. When they walked past me, I said, "Mr. Hirschfeld, I think it was a mistake to fire Pete Hamill. He had galvanized the staff." Abe did not like that. "Where will you be in thirty years when Pete Hamill is dead!" he yelled. Then he said, "What is your name?" When I came in the next Monday, I learned that I was one of the Guild members who had been fired, and I was the only one Hirschfeld refused to hire back because of my "insubordination." I met with Harry Leykis and some other Guild reps, and they told me they'd continue to pay me through some union fund. So, I kept coming in to work. There was a way to get into the newsroom that bypassed the security desk. It led to a locked door and I would wait there until Tim McDarrah let me in.

MILTON GOLDSTEIN: Hirschfeld held a press conference in Dolly Schiff's old office where he brought in Wilbert Tatum to be the new editor. In some quarters, he was known as a Black racist. He hated the *Post*, and he hated David Seifman. For some reason they let everybody go up. So [art director] Dennis Wickman, and [*Post* copy chief] Barry Gross and I said, "Let's go up." They let us right in. There are cameras there—NY1 and others—and some reporter asks, "Why'd you fire Hamill?" and Hirschfeld says, "I didn't!"—I can't do a Yiddish accent—but he says, "I didn't. I didn't fire Hamill!" and Barry and Steve Cuozzo start yelling from the edges. NY1 and the other cameras turned and got them yelling.

CHARLIE CARILLO: I was there the Sunday that Hirschfeld and Bill Tatum tried to make the announcement that they were coming together, with Marc Kalech yelling, "You fired Pete Hamill!" I remember being in that room. It was so entertaining—just insane. Then Hirschfeld gave us all those crossword puzzle [print] neckties. Paul Tharp burned one in front of the paper. It didn't really burn. It melted. It was some kind of Dacron.

> In the wake of the March 14 press conference, the paper's managing editor Marc Kalech hatched a revolt. The news pages and Page Six column of the following day's paper would be devoted to pillorying Hirschfeld, Tatum, and even Peter Kalikow for allowing the paper to fall into such destructive hands. On March 16, the *Post*'s wood carried no headline. The illustration of Alexander Hamilton that was part of the paper's logo had been blown up and occupied the entire front page. A single tear fell from his right eye. A photo on page three showed Hirschfeld spitting on a *Miami Herald* reporter. Beneath it ran the headline: "Who Is This Nut?"

ANDY SOLTIS, rewrite, editor, 1967–2014: The day of the staff revolt I was filling in for Hechtman as the lobster city editor. I had just gotten to the desk and was reading the proofs of the first edition when Maralyn Matlick called me. She said, "Did we get away with it?" I said, "Yeah, believe it or not." A few minutes later, I think it was Myron who called and said, "The publisher is on." I said, "The publisher?" He said, "Hirschfeld." I had no idea what I was going to say because, I mean, I could be sued for a gazillion dollars for what I was doing—for being peripherally in charge of this paper. Hirschfeld asked me, "Do we have a good newspaper tomorrow?" I said, "We have a very good newspaper tomorrow."

> The March 16 issue listed Pete Hamill as the paper's top editor, and he returned to run the paper until he was blocked by a bankruptcy court judge, who later reversed course and ruled that Hirschfeld and Hamill must work together. Upon his second return, Hamill ran the paper from the South Street Diner (formerly the Post Mortem bar) next door—in part, to protest the firings of Seifman, Breindel, Dicker, and others. A rally was staged outside the paper, and Governor Cuomo continued to search for a new owner. Amid the confusion and uncertainty, a glimmer of hope emerged.

DAVID SEIFMAN: At some point, either Hamill quits or he's fired and really has to go. So Hirschfeld, who has fired me, calls me. They're desperate for an editor and they're running down a checklist. He offers me the job. I said, "Abe, you want me to be the editor? You fired me." He said, "Vell, Dave, you were vun of the highest-paid employees." I said, "Abe, in your company, you have employees who make different salaries, right? Don't the employees at the top make more money than the other employees?" After he heard that, he hung up on me.

MARK KRIEGEL: The South Street Diner became like a nerve center in New York. There were TV cameras going in and out. Pete's making pronouncements and editorial decisions from there. Then we had this great rally. We had a flatbed truck. On the back of the flatbed was a microphone. So we had this rally to save the *Post*. I remember helping Norman Mailer up onto the bed of the truck so he could address the audience. I remember him saying, "Reporters should be able to tell their own lies, not the lies of their publisher."

MARSHA KRANES: I did not go to the diner with Pete Hamill to put out the paper. I doubt there were any women there. I loved Pete, but he was a man's man. He nurtured the talent of young men who were seeking careers in journalism. I really admired him and what he did, but I really felt excluded from the club.

CINDY ADAMS: At the rally, I remember sitting on the top of a *Post* delivery truck cab, my legs hanging down in front of the driver.

FRANK LOMONTE: They made T-shirts of that page one we ran of Alexander Hamilton with the tear. One of the Guild kids had it on when we were in bankruptcy court. Hirschfeld is talking to his attorney and his people in the audience there, and he says, "Kid, come over here" with his heavy Jewish accent. He says, "I want to buy this T-shirt" and the kid respectfully goes, "I'm sorry. It's not for sale." He goes back to where he was sitting. Hirschfeld turns around to his attorney and a friend. He says, "Watch me teach him how to do business. Kid, come back." The kid comes back, and Hirschfeld says, "I'm going to give you two hundred for that T-shirt." The kid says, "Are you saying to me you're going to give me two hundred dollars in cash right now for this T-shirt?" Hirschfeld says, "Yes, because it'll get my wife excited seeing it." He takes the T-shirt from the kid, runs out of the courtroom, and becomes Clark Kent. He comes back with the shirt on. The judge, Francis Conrad, says to Hirschfeld's attorney something like: "You better put a stop to this, or I will."

Amid the chaos, a familiar corporate name rang out. Rupert Murdoch exercised a clause inserted into the contract when he sold the paper to Kalikow in 1988.

FRANK LoMONTE: So everything quiets down; Hirschfeld gives the kid two hundred bucks, and that was pretty good. But it wasn't the best part. One of Mr. Murdoch's legal staff raises her hand and says to the judge, "I'm so-and-so, and News America declines to waive its right of first refusal to buy the paper." Everybody on our side of the room said, "Rupert's back in the game."

CINDY ADAMS: At one point, Rupert was talking to Governor Cuomo hourly. Rupert was calling Governor Cuomo, and Governor Cuomo was calling me because Governor Cuomo was saying, legally, what you can do, what you can't do. Rupert didn't know that Cuomo was talking to me every hour. He didn't know that. But it was Rupert to Mario to me.

FRED DICKER: Mario encouraged Murdoch to reacquire the paper. He even urged the federal court to allow Rupert to reacquire the *Post* in a bankruptcy proceeding.

RICHARD GOODING: Going to the *News* was the worst move I ever made. It certainly didn't help my career. Zuckerman was a fool. He changed his mind every day depending on who he had lunch with. The job itself was great, but it was a totally different atmosphere than the *Post*. I got used to it, but the *News* was a horrible place to work. People didn't like each other. And a lot of people looked down on [the top editors hired away from the *Post*]. They thought we were brought in to drag them down to the *Post*'s level, and a number of their so-called stars thought they really should be at the *New York Times*. I lasted three and a half years. Zuckerman got rid of Jimmy Lynch first, may he rest in peace. Then they got rid of Lou [Colasuonno]. Then Zuckerman brought back all the *News* editors. Arthur Browne was a smart guy, but he wanted his own metro editor. I don't blame him. He didn't really like me or that I was from the *Post* and Lou's guy. They didn't fire me, I resigned. I made a deal.

CHRIS POLICANO, City Hall reporter, 1994–1997: I have a theory about the *Daily News* and this is connected to the *New York Post* at the time. Mort Zuckerman doesn't know how little journalists make. He takes these guys from the *Post*—Gooding, Colasuonno, whatever—and he thinks he's going to pay these editors a lot of money and they're all going to have that *New York Post* hustle, that hunger and devil-may-care shit. He pays them money, makes them respectable, and like every other well-paid executive, they want to keep their jobs. They are so risk-averse that it totally defeats the purpose of getting the *Post* guys. Once you make a *Post* guy respectable, you've screwed up the whole thing.

ERIC FETTMANN: There's something about the *Post* mystique that the same people who can be so good in the atmosphere of the *Post*, can't replicate it elsewhere.

PETER KALIKOW: In many ways, Murdoch was the kind of guy you needed to run a place like the *Post*. Because he didn't give a shit what anybody said. He did what he wanted to do. He didn't care about people saying, you're crapping up the paper, nobody's going to read the paper anymore. He was probably right. I cared, and that was to my detriment.

MARK KRIEGEL: Years later, I got a tip that Hirschfeld was trying to murder a business partner. I was at the *Daily News*, I was writing a column—again for Pete [Hamill]—and we broke the story that the grand jury was investigating Hirschfeld. He sued me and the *News* saying I was biased against him from the time at the *Post*, but this story was right on. I can't say I wasn't happy about it because he was a prick. [Hirschfeld eventually served two years in jail for attempting to hire a hit man to take out his business partner.]

PETER KALIKOW: When I was a little kid my father had a card game with his friends, and all but one of them were war veterans. When you're a little kid you want to sit around and hear what they're saying because that's how little kids find out about the world, right? He had one friend who landed on D-Day plus one, June 7. Essentially he walked all the way to Czechoslovakia. I asked him, "What did you think about that?" His line was "If I knew how it came out, I'd have enjoyed it better. While I was there, I was scared shitless every day." That's what I say about the *Post*. If I knew how it came out, I would have had a better time. If you've got to pay 1,200 guys every Friday, that's fucking scary. But I'm glad I did it.

MARK KRIEGEL: The day that Murdoch came back [March 29, 1993], he was greeted like a conquering hero. It was a triumphant return. There was a sense that we were saved. I remember Pete [Hamill] telling me Murdoch offered him a column. No strings attached. Pete turned it down. But he was happy that the *Post* had been returned to a professional newspaperman, whatever his politics were.

JIM PRATT: When Murdoch came into the newsroom and spoke to us for the first time after he had reacquired the paper, I remember very clearly that he said, "I am not here as some fairy godmother." He made it very clear that it was not going to be all peaches and cream. He was going to be hard-nosed—and he was. It was a much more professional, solid place, and we knew that we were in for the long haul. We were going to fight against the *Daily News* and that as long as Murdoch was alive, we would prevail.

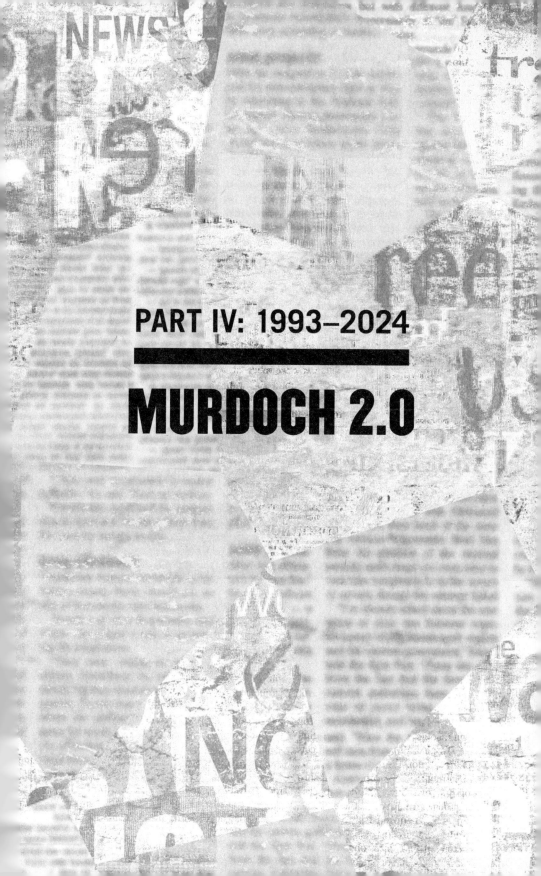

PART IV: 1993–2024

MURDOCH 2.0

25 | RUPERT'S RETURN

Union Strike-Out,
South Street Move-Out,
Chinese Takeout

epurchasing the *New York Post* may not have been a financially sound decision, but Rupert Murdoch was a newspaperman, and he did not want to see the foundation of his American media empire die an ignoble death after being stripped and swindled by a couple of mountebanks. His return to 210 South Street was partly an illusion, however. The takeover did not become official until months later, with skids and stops along the way. The paper even closed for a day or two as the craft unions tried to play hardball and the federal government waffled over granting Murdoch a permanent waiver allowing him to own a TV station and a newspaper in the same market. Without that and union concessions, Murdoch said, the *Post* held no allure. The union with the least clout—the Newspaper Guild, representing news, clerical, advertising, and circulation employees—balked at what Murdoch 2.0 was asking its members to relinquish, including job security and severance, which, at the *Post*, was the equivalent of a pension.

PAUL THARP, reporter, columnist, 1982–2014: Rupert comes in as a savior, and everybody applauds him. Everything seems to be okay. And then the Newspaper Guild—Harry Leykis and a couple of bomb-throwing radical types—say, we want more money now because he's a multimillionaire. They started demanding to have negotiations even before he'd taken the paper out of bankruptcy. He had put out a helping hand, paid off some stuff, and got paychecks going again. I said, "Holy cow, you people are nuts. When you're in bankruptcy, they don't have to honor any employment agreements, contracts, or anything. That's what bankruptcy is for—to throw everything out and start fresh." They wouldn't believe me.

MARCY SOLTIS, copy editor, 1976–2014: Management wanted a onetime right to get rid of whoever they wanted. As a union, how can you agree to something like that?

DAN AQUILANTE, chief music critic, 1980–2012: When we went on strike, there was initially a kind of party atmosphere. But before the vote, I remember Don Mc-Donald, one of the older people in drama—a union guy—spoke vehemently and said, "Do not leave. Do not walk off your job. They won't let us back in if you do it."

JIM RUTENBERG, Page Six reporter, 1993: At that time, I would tell anyone that I'll spend my life at the *Post*. It was fucking heaven to me. I had been flat broke before getting the job there, but now I've got money in my pocket, and I'm spending it like crazy at the Lion's Head or whatever. I'm running around the city on these crazy great stories for the paper and Page Six. When the Guild members decide to go on strike [in October 1993], I'm not officially in the union yet. I finished my probation two days before, and I'm eligible to join the Guild the day before the strike. I say to Joe Nicholson, who was a big union guy, "What should I do?" He says, "Go home and call in sick." But I was concerned that I would be asked to cross the picket line. I'm fucking broke. I don't even have a bank account. As I'm walking out the door to go on strike, I fill out the union card, and as I'm about to hand it to Barry Lipton [head of the Newspaper Guild in New York], I'm changing my mind. I see that there's a five-dollar fee, and I see my out. I say, "Mr. Lipton, I don't have the five dollars, so I can't join the union right now." He goes, "I'll spot you." We go on strike.

> At first it appeared the craft unions and the drivers would back the Guild, but that support quickly evaporated. Only one combatant truly had power: Rupert Murdoch. In the 1980s, he had busted unions at his English newspapers, and he intended to do the same at the *Post*.

JIM RUTENBERG: That first night of the strike is seared in my mind. We're out underneath the FDR ramp that's over South Street. The truckers and the press-men have a deal with Murdoch, by the way, but the Guild doesn't. The truckers are on one side of South Street and the Guild is on the other, and I think the chant was "Don't cross!" This goes on for hours. There are helicopters overhead. Other press are there. There's this incredible tension because it's time for the first edition to go out, and the truckers have all walked into the building. People were getting really upset, like, "Fuck! They're going to break our line." The strike is going to fail on its first night. The truckers pull out the trucks, but they don't pick up the papers. Instead, they start driving around the building honking their horns. Everyone was cheering. We survived the first night.

PAUL THARP: Rupert was so pissed that he said, "I'm not going to take the *Post* out of bankruptcy court. I'm just going to let it die on the vine." They suspended publication for a few days. Jan Constantine, who was the general counsel for the *Post*, said to me, "Rupert's looking for a sign to keep the paper alive. Is there anything?" I go out and try to talk to [the strikers], and they throw rocks and paper cups at me. I talked to like ten people on the picket line, and no one wanted to help. That night, I'm at home with my wife and my two dogs. We're watching a report on the strike on the eleven o'clock news. I thought: a sign? Okay, I talked to my two dogs, I talked to my wife. That's three people. So, about a third of the thirteen people I talked to don't want the strike. It was not a lie. I was talking to two dogs, and they understood me. Of course, my wife went along. I write up, "Ad Hoc Committee to Save the *Post*"—whatever it was. I go down to the AP, which was in Rockefeller Center at the time, and get this bullshit story on the wires about how a third of the strikers want to go back to work. Rupert, the next day, started to sign the paperwork. I said, "Jan, did it work?" She said, "I guess it did." I guess he said, "Ah, the tabloid spirit is alive."

JAN CONSTANTINE, senior deputy counsel, News Corp, 1991–2005: I do remember this vaguely. I probably said Rupert has a decision to make and a lot of it hinges on what the unions are going to do. If they had continued to give him trouble, he would have pulled the plug. A lot of his advisers were telling him that buying the *Post* out of bankruptcy was crazy, but he loved the paper. It sounds like Paul did a great thing. He made a sign out of thin air.

ERIC FETTMANN, associate editorial page editor, columnist, 1976–1991, 1993–2019: I was in Pat Purcell's office—he was the publisher at that point—and he's on the phone with Murdoch and Murdoch says, "Shut the paper down. Fuck 'em, close it." He finally agreed to give them twenty-four hours. Purcell—and Howard Rubenstein played a big role in this, and Cardinal O'Connor—got to work first on George McDonald of the [New York Allied Printing Trades Council, which represented ten newspaper unions] and persuaded him that the paper is dead if you guys don't cross and with it go all the jobs. The next night the Allied and all the other unions agreed to cross the lines. When the drivers realized the rest of the Allied was walking, they came in; they may have been given a little something. The second night they were able to publish.

> When Murdoch returned, he immediately brought back a respected editor, Ken Chandler, who had left the *Post* in 1986 to take over Murdoch's *Boston Herald* and later worked on *A Current Affair*.

KEN CHANDLER, editor in chief, publisher, 1978–1986, 1993–2002: The Guild totally played into Murdoch's hands.

JIM RUTENBERG: To make it even worse, Murdoch sent this tanker truck to the building. They linked a hose to a nozzle on the side of the building, and we're like, what are they doing? Word goes out, it's Murdoch. He's taking the printer ink out. He's giving up. He's not going to buy the paper, and the paper is going to go under. That night, the drivers crossed the line and that was the end of the strike.

PAUL THARP: I don't recall that. It could have just been the mafia stealing the ink.

> In the aftermath of the strike, it became clear that few Guild members would return to the paper.

DAN AQUILANTE: Out of four hundred people who walked, about forty people got their jobs back after they were allowed to reapply. Don McDonald lost all his severance. He was planning on retiring to Rhode Island. He ended up selling his home in Rhode Island to make it. Many, many lives were destroyed.

KEN CHANDLER: We said, "There's a new regime here. We're operating leaner and meaner going forward." But the benefit package was great. We didn't bring back any of the union leadership. Murdoch wanted to restore the paper to what it should be, build the circulation, and make the paper exciting again.

JIM RUTENBERG: Marc Kalech called me the day after the strike to see how I'm doing. He's like, "Come back tomorrow." Then he said, "You're not in the union, are you?" I say, "I don't think so because I filled out a card but I didn't have the five dollars so the truth is I don't know." He says, "I'll call you back." That phone never fucking rang. I'm twenty-four. I'm scared now. I'm fucking broke again. I don't even have a bank account. But every time I came back to Manhattan from Brooklyn over the Manhattan Bridge on the D Train and we passed the *Post* sign, I said to myself: one day, I'm going to fucking kick their ass. I got hired as a stringer for Linda Stasi and A.J. Benza at the *Daily News* and I made it my business to wallop Page Six—to beat them on any story.

PAUL THARP: They got rid of a lot of dead wood. There were guys on the overnight writing crime thrillers or just sleeping.

Traumatized by what had happened, one *Post* employee ended his life.

DAN AQUILANTE: Mike Gruber was a composing room makeup editor for the financial desk. He was a good guy. Mike did not want to walk off, but he walked with everybody else. He ended up committing suicide. I believe he asphyxiated himself in his garage with his car. I don't think he did what he did because he lost his severance. I think it was because he believed he had lost his career. Had he not done what he did, he would have been brought back. I think they brought back every makeup editor. It was a very traumatic time.

Retaking the *Post* signaled a return to Murdoch's roots after a period of severe financial volatility. He had spent vast sums of borrowed money to expand his media empire, along the way making some questionable investments, including the $2.8 billion purchase of Triangle Publications in 1988, which brought *TV Guide*, *Seventeen*, the *Daily Racing Form*, and other publications into the media baron's fold. When interest rates rose during the early '90s recession, News Corp's debt ballooned to $8.7 billion, and Murdoch spent three white-knuckle months negotiating with his lenders to pull his company back from the financial brink.

MICHAEL WOLFF, author, *The Fall: The End of Fox News and the Murdoch Dynasty*: Murdoch's repurchase of the *Post* in 1993 after his financial meltdown in 1990 to '91 and his self-exile—when he moved himself and his family to LA to concentrate on movies and TV—was part of his effort to escape the entertainment business and get back to news. Hollywood to him was fake and trivial; newspapers, even tabloid newspapers—or especially tabloid newspapers—were real and soulful.

> Without relinquishing his liberal bona fides, Jack Newfield, who'd been brought to the *Post* by Peter Kalikow in 1991, found a way to survive in the new Murdoch era.

KEN CHANDLER: Jack was a great investigative reporter. He produced some great page ones for me. You knew when Jack did a story, it was solid. It might not have quite the right political twinge on it for the *Post*, but it was a solid story.

STU MARQUES, managing editor, news, 1993–2001: I hired Maggie Haberman as a copykid and then promoted her to reporter. Then I put her at City Hall and in politics. She did the rest. Her father was [*New York Times* columnist and Schiff-era *Post* reporter] Clyde Haberman, so she had that in her blood somewhere. She caught on really fast, and she impressed a lot of people. Jack Newfield was doing columns at the *Post* then, and I asked Jack to take her under his wing. They worked on the "Worst Landlords" series and stuff like that. He basically taught her the nuts and bolts of good reporting.

> Newfield even got along with Steve Dunleavy, who occasionally mentioned him in columns as "my liberal friend." Yes, after a lengthy stint on TV, Dunleavy returned to print, but not before inspiring Robert Downey Jr.'s tabloid TV reporter in *Natural Born Killers*.

KEN CHANDLER: How can I put this delicately? Dunleavy's appearance, the drinking was becoming visible. He was beginning to look very old and haggard. People at *A Current Affair* and at Channel Five were concerned. It eventually got to Rupert. We were going to a black-tie dinner in Midtown. Rupert said, "I'll give you a ride uptown." On the way there, he said, "I'm going to get rid of Dunleavy." I said, "Don't get rid of him, because I'm sure he still could write a good column for the *Post*." Murdoch said, "Ah, you don't want him back." I said, "I think it would be a great idea. He's still pretty popular, and he still has a great turn of phrase." So that's how Dunleavy finished up back at the *Post*. I was kind of surprised when Rupert said, "I have to get rid of him." He may have been talking imprecisely and meant, "Get rid of him off *A Current Affair* and move him somewhere else." But that's not what he said.

Alongside Dunleavy and a few other Murdoch loyalists, plus the small contingent of former Guild members, the *Post*'s editorial staff began to fill with fresh faces.

BOB HARDT, political reporter, 1993–2003: I go into my job interview. Marc Kalech goes through my clips. I have all these clips I'm proud of from the Associated Press, like something about the first attack on the World Trade Center in 1993. There's a story about the hot dog–eating contest in Coney Island. He looks through the clips and says, "I like your hot dog story." I thought, okay, well, I'm at the *Post.*

CHRIS RUDDY, investigative reporter, 1993–1995: I had done a couple of stories for a small publication called the *New York Guardian* that challenged the claims of the PBS documentary *Liberators: Fighting on Two Fronts in World War II* that two Black combat units had liberated Buchenwald and Dachau. My story was that the Black soldiers were extremely heroic guys, they just weren't there on the day of the liberation. PBS pulled its support for the film, and then the American Jewish Committee and others agreed that the filmmakers had engaged in revisionism. That got the attention of Rupert Murdoch.

BOB HARDT: In 1994, post-strike, I got to sit with this amazing group of people, including Steve Dunleavy, coming back for his second go-round at the *Post*; Jonathan Karl [now chief Washington correspondent for ABC News]; Bobby Kennedy's son Doug Kennedy; and Kyle Smith, who's now at the *National Review.*

DOUGLAS KENNEDY, reporter, 1993–1995: My uncle Teddy was delighted that I was working at the *New York Post* and, in fact, I think it brought Rupert and Teddy together. Teddy had to sign off on Rupert buying back the *Post.* And he did. I talked to him all the time. He loved it. He said, "Anybody who tells you not to work there, tell them to screw."

JONATHAN KARL, reporter, 1994–1996: I remember getting advice from Mort Kondracke. He was on *The McLaughlin Group* [a PBS program on politics] and he worked at the *New Republic*, where I spent a year when I got out of college. I told him I had an offer from the *New York Post.* He said, "That would be good. You'll only spend about a third of the time apologizing for where you work, whereas if you went to the *Washington Times*," which was then owned by the Moonies, "you'll spend half your time apologizing." I never spent any time apologizing for working at the *Post*. I'm very proud of what I did there.

FRED DICKER, Albany bureau chief, 1982–2016: After Murdoch reacquired the paper and I wrote some negative stuff about Mario, I remember Cindy Adams giving me a hard time: "He saved our paper. How can you do that?" I felt it was my job as a journalist to report factual stuff. If it was negative to Mario Cuomo, so be it.

GRETCHEN VIEHMANN, photo editor, 1993–2001: I was thirty-two when I got the top job, which, in a world of crusty old men, was unheard of. There was a generation of guys who had a very difficult time with the transition of the old world into the new. It was right at the birth of digital. They could barely deal with the idea of color, let alone the possibility of digital. I do remember, with the exception of Louis Liotta, most of them being really angry. They were bitter toward the younger photographers, like Charlie Wenzelberg. He was shooting full-time for the *Post* while going to NYU and he's now the [chief] photographer.

> Jerry Lisker, executive sports editor in the first Murdoch era, did not return to the *Post* after "The Boss" reacquired it. He died in March 1993 at age 54.

PHIL MUSHNICK, sportswriter, television, 1973–current: Lisker died young, and I think it's because he was always under these tanning beds. He was such a hoot. The day of his funeral, I wrote that he would tell people he was half Jewish, half American Indian, and half whatever you were.

> Greg Gallo, who had worked for Murdoch since the early days at the *Star*, returned to run sports.

BOB DECKER, sports editor, 1989–1994: When they made the announcement that Murdoch was being allowed to repurchase the paper, my first thought was, the paper is saved. My second thought was, I'm going to lose my job. Because he brings in his own top editors. It's all Murdoch people. And I was not a Murdoch people.

MYRON RUSHETZKY, head city desk assistant, 1974–1989, 1991–2013: On Bob [Decker's] last day, a wave of applause started in the sports department and followed him as he walked through the newsroom to the elevator.

GREG GALLO, executive sports editor, 1977–1989, 1994–2009: I brought [Steve] Serby back when I came back in '94. He was at the *News.* He was one of the lucky ones. I brought him back because he's good. A lot of them wanted to come back, and I shook that off. [The pilfering of sportswriters by the *News*] was a real war. They took a lot of shots at us—and we at them—but we rarely took their guys. They took our guys.

> Barely a month after Murdoch officially assumed ownership of the paper, Rudolph Giuliani was elected mayor of New York. He had made his name in the 1980s as the crusading US attorney for the Southern District of New York who supposedly destroyed the mob.

JERRY CAPECI, reporter, organized crime, 1966–1986: Every time you had an indictment of some mobster, or six mobsters or eight mobsters, or the hierarchy of a crime family, it was the end of the mob. I would point out that it really wasn't. The [Mafia] Commission case was supposed to be the end of the mob. Rudy Giuliani went to town on it and became a folk hero. It helped him get elected, but it didn't end the mob.

ERIC FETTMANN: Giuliani's election was a reaction to four years of David Dinkins and the idea that "they're" taking over the city. So the *Post*'s audience became the Giuliani voter—Koch voters before Dinkins, Giuliani voters after, and that was a sizable enough chunk.

DAVID SEIFMAN, City Hall bureau chief, political editor, 1973–2019: Rudy got along pretty well with the *Post.* They were on the same philosophical wavelength most of the time. Especially when it came to crime. But we were pretty critical of him when necessary.

CHRIS POLICANO, City Hall reporter, 1994–1997: On the day Giuliani announced his first budget, he does it himself and it's a masterful performance. I'm disagreeing with it personally but he's an interesting guy to watch—and he wasn't crazy yet. The *Post* photographer, Charles Wenzelberg, says, "I've got these great pictures. Giuliani's got paperclips holding up the cuff of his pants." I said, "Are you out of your mind?" He goes back to the office, and we all go back to Room Nine. A *New York Times* guy is doing a big take on cuts to social services. Somebody else is doing infrastructure. Later on, Seifman comes down and says, "I got a call from the desk. They've got these pictures of Giuliani's pant leg. They want a story." I said, "I've been working all day on the implications of the budget." He says, "They want a story about the paperclips." I go up to the press office, where Giuliani's press secretary Colleen Roche is beleaguered by all these reporters asking about numbers. I say, "I've got to ask you about the paperclips." She says, "What?" Sure enough, Giuliani had been in Brooklyn borough president Howard Golden's office earlier in the day and noticed that his cuff was undone. Golden gave him paperclips to hold up his cuff. I go to write and had this moment of inspiration. I call the fashion editor at *GQ*. He says, "No matter what else was on the mayor's schedule, he should have had time to go to his tailor." I used that line as the kicker, and the next day, the budget story is on page three with a huge picture of Giuliani's cuff and the paperclips with the quote. I thought, what the fuck am I doing with my life?

The *Post* under Peter Kalikow did not handle Bill Clinton with kid gloves during his presidential run and election in 1992. Under Murdoch, the paper's scrutiny of the forty-second president of the United States intensified.

KEN CHANDLER: The *Post* covered Bill Clinton with a critical eye. It was a foretaste of today's politics. The Clinton administration could do no wrong in the *New York Times* and the *Washington Post*. People got more critical later. But he got a free ride from the media for years.

Clinton gave the paper ample opportunity to exercise its penchant for nicknames, in all departments of the paper. Pat "Hondo" Hannigan, night sports editor, who also wrote a betting guide, came up with some that stuck.

DOMINICK MARRANO, chief paginator, 1971–2008: Even though Hondo was supposed to tell the reader what would be a good bet, he would also talk about "Peyronie" Bill Clinton. He gave him that name. [Paula Jones's 1994 sexual harassment lawsuit against Clinton led to speculation that Clinton suffered from Peyronie's disease, which causes the penis to curve.] He would talk about political things in this little paragraph or two that he would write. He got in trouble a few times, politically. That was Hondo.

RICHARD JOHNSON, Page Six editor, 1978–1990, 1993–2019: The nickname that we used for Monica Lewinsky—"the Portly Pepperpot"—wasn't me. Hondo came up with that.

STU MARQUES: The *Post* was the most fun paper I worked for, although occasionally you had to battle on the politics. During elections, there came a point where you lost control of the stories that, early on, you could get on page seven or eight or nine. They would end up back on twenty-nine. They would run the story, but they buried it.

> The tabloid wars of the 1980s didn't end in the '90s. Following the strikes that almost put them out of business, and the death of one adversary (the Times Mirror Company closed *New York Newsday* in 1995), the *Post* and the *Daily News* went at each other with renewed vigor, though on one sensitive matter, they actually cooperated.

RICHARD JOHNSON: I was at the *Daily News* about two years. My contract was ending. Mort Zuckerman basically told me that he didn't like me. I told Ken Chandler, "I'd love to work for the *Post* again. But I don't want to do Page Six. I've already done that." He gave me the whole, "Oh, but you were the best editor" blah blah. I went back and ran the column for about ten more years. I wouldn't have minded working in sports. It would have been great to cover the Knicks for a year or two.

JOANNA MOLLOY, Page Six co-editor, 1990–1993: At one point, Mort Zuckerman and Rupert Murdoch, through Howard Rubenstein, had a nonaggression pact. At the *News* [where Molloy worked then], we weren't allowed to write about Rupert. At the *Post*, they weren't allowed to write about Zuckerman. Howard over the years reminded us of this, literally calling it a nonaggression pact.

JONATHAN KARL: I was sent to Washington to investigate some of what Boston Properties [*Daily News* owner Mort Zuckerman's real estate investment trust] had built, like a Supreme Court annex, at a time when I think Mort and Rupert were going after each other. Within a few days I got called back. They said, "Don't worry about that. Put that on the back burner." I don't know if that was the beginning of the moratorium, or if it was paused. I just knew there were powers above me who would decide whether I continued with that story.

In the '80s, Page Six retained its place on the tabloid's sixth page. If, on a particularly newsy day, it was moved farther back in the paper, a banner redirected readers. That ended in the '90s.

KEN CHANDLER: I wanted to send a message that the *Post* was back, and we were serious about news coverage. I pushed Page Six back to page ten or twelve so there would be more hard news in the front of the paper. People in the newsroom were upset. But I don't recall anybody outside even noticing. It gave the paper a bit more gravitas at the front. Unless there was a really good piece of gossip; then we would disguise it as serious news and put it in the front.

JIM FARBER, former music critic, New York *Daily News*: I love the moment when I realized that Page Six was so known as a brand that it no longer had to appear on the actual sixth page. It could be on any page and still have that Page Six magic. So, in my mind, this meant that Page Six could not be contained by physical space. It was in its way transcendent. A friend of mine said: "Oh my god, Page Six has gone rogue." He said, "It is now such a thing that it no longer has to obey the laws of physics."

KEN CHANDLER: Rupert said to me one day, "I don't know any of these people they write about on Page Six. I don't recognize their names." Because it's a younger generation. He said, "I think it was good when Neal Travis used to do it." I said, "Why don't you bring Neal back, and he can write a column for the old farts, and Page Six can write for the younger readers?" He did that, and Neal came back and wrote this column [which ran opposite Page Six]. I don't want to be uncharitable, but he phoned it in. It served its purpose though, because Rupert recognized the boldfaced names in Neal's column.

RICHARD JOHNSON: Gossip item about the pope? On Page Six? I'd read it. Also, I used to love to run pictures of dogs or cats. The perfect Page Six item, like with any news story, involves sex, money, and violence. So, if you can get all three into one item—plus the pope and a dog.

KEN CHANDLER: I was approached by a lawyer or an agent or whatever, representing Liz Smith. This is because she had a column in *Newsday*, but at that point *Newsday* had stopped publishing its New York City edition. She wanted an outlet in the city. Initially I was skeptical. I thought, I don't see that Murdoch would want to pay that sort of money for a column that's also appearing in *Newsday*, even though it's only outside the city. To my surprise, he was amenable. It was 1995, something like that. We brought her on, and Cindy Adams got word of this and went absolutely batshit crazy. How could I do this? Didn't I know that Cindy was a much better columnist than Liz Smith? Liz Smith just phoned it in. On and on and on and on. We got in this huge negotiation, eventually resolved by me promising that I would always put Cindy's column ahead of Liz Smith's in the paper. If Liz Smith is on page ten, Cindy would be on page eight. That kind of satisfied her—not really, but peace was declared.

GRETCHEN VIEHMANN: The photographers liked Cindy because she was self-deprecating. If you ran into her in the ladies room, you'd be like, "Hey, Cindy," and she'd be at the mirror with the makeup. She'd say, "I look like my own ass." Which is a line that I've used many, many times.

> With much of Murdoch's empire headquartered at 1211 Sixth Avenue (no one calls it Avenue of the Americas except, occasionally, the US Postal Service), in 1995 he moved the *Post* there as well. No longer would the paper be created and printed in the same building. Editorial and other staff left the funk and grit of 210 South Street—and the secrets it held—for a forty-five-story limestone and glass tower in Midtown across from Rockefeller Center.

KEN CHANDLER: It was pragmatic more than anything else. The building downtown was dilapidated, and it was a pain in the ass for him to have to go all the way downtown when most of what he was doing was in Midtown. Rupert wanted everybody to be under one roof, and Fox News was going to be uptown.

LAURA HARRIS, director of information services, 1994–2018: At 210 South Street, you could go up on the roof and smoke a cigarette, which some of the editors and I used to do. And you could open the windows. It was funky and great. And it was dirty. Physically dirty. My hands and my clothes always had newsprint on them. When we moved to Midtown, it became very corporate.

RICHARD JOHNSON: All of a sudden there was human resources. I had never even heard of human resources before.

MICHAEL RIEDEL, theater columnist, 1998–2020: I remember the great Annie Aquilina *was* human resources. That's all it was. Now you have teams of people who work in human resources. But when I joined the *Post*, it was Annie Aquilina sitting in this office with old stacks of papers and newspapers going back thirty years. When I was filling out my forms, the first thing Annie said was, "We pay for rehab once. After that, you're on your own."

MACKENZIE DAWSON, books editor, 2005–2023: At one point, the *Post* was using a new expense system. We all had to be on a conference call as someone from the software company walked us through the process. It was tedious, and not always straightforward. About forty minutes into the call, Annie Aquilina had a question for this very corporate person. "Sometimes our reporters talk to strippers to get tips, and they have to pay them," she said, making the call 250 percent more interesting. "Would that be 'general editorial,' the strippers?" The person leading the call was at a loss for words.

PATRICIA JACOBS, fashion writer, columnist, 1978–1993: As a tabloid, it lost its flavor. It joined everybody else. It drank from the Kool-Aid.

PETER TOCCO, sports makeup, 1970–2013: I worked Saturday mornings early at 1211. Rupert Murdoch would come from, I guess, his apartment, at like 10:30, and he'd walk around the city room. Then he'd go over to sports. They had this clothing door, where you hang up your coats and stuff. On this door, there were all the headlines where people made a mistake, something like, "win fifty pairs of tickets" and what they really mean is win two of fifty tickets. Some of the stuff was pretty humorous. He would find his way there pretty much every Saturday. He wore an old sweater that had holes in it. He'd look around like, "This is my paper," and he was happy, or he missed it. More like he missed it.

MILTON GOLDSTEIN, copy editor, 1974–current: When we moved up to Sixth Avenue, this one executive, using the facilities budget, built a little apartment for himself in an unused office. On some floor on Sixth Avenue. Nobody else had to sign off on it. I was told later it was illegal according to zoning. You couldn't build an apartment in a Sixth Avenue office building like that. They finally found out and sacked him.

KEN CHANDLER: He built this office and had it specially ventilated, so he could smoke cigars. It was a no-smoking building. People would see him drinking at Langan's [the Midtown bar that replaced downtown haunts like Mutchie's and the Post Mortem] till one o'clock in the morning. And then he'd be at work the next day. They'd say, "How do you manage that?" Because he had an apartment at 1211 that nobody knew about.

STU MARQUES: The offices at 1211, they were nicer. I don't know if "corporate" is the right word but, yeah, it certainly had a more serious, staid look and feel. But the paper didn't change. The surroundings changed.

MARSHA KRANES, rewrite, editor, 1974–2005: I had an investigations team. Kirsten Danis, who is now at the *Times*, was on it, Allen Salkin was on it. Allen jumped into the Hudson River. People were saying the river was polluted so I assigned him to investigate. I didn't ask him to jump in, but he did!

MARK STAMEY, reporter, 1993–2006: I heard about the crash of TWA Flight 800 and headed out to Center Moriches [Long Island]. I could see it on the horizon, but I couldn't get to it. So I found some guy with a cabin cruiser. We went right to it. The water was burning. A helicopter flew over and dropped parachute flares to illuminate the scene. It was a huge area. We thought we'd rescue people but there was not much left. The seats were floating. All the seat belts were buckled. But there were no people in them. The next day, [officials] cordoned off five miles on the surface and a thousand feet of airspace. I kept an inflatable Zodiac with a gas engine in the trunk of my car. I tried to get out there with it and got stopped. So, I'm driving back along the Southern State Parkway pulling my hair out, and I see a grass runway. There's a Cessna 172 sitting there. So I knocked and said: "Can you get me out there?" He said, "I can't. I had a heart bypass, but I can still give lessons." I said, "Meet your new student." I reported the story from flying over it, and I expensed it. I ended up getting my private pilot's license and my expenses paid.

MICHAEL RIEDEL: The *Post* was great with expense accounts, they never nickel-and-dimed me. The only time I got my expense account questioned, I took Elaine Stritch to Perry St restaurant. Elaine ordered three of everything. She said, "I'm diabetic and I could have an attack in the night so I need some food in the refrigerator." She says, "I'll have three poached lobster salads, and three spring pea soups" or something like that. One for here and two to go. It was a fancy restaurant so the bill was steep. I turned it in and [editor] Mackenzie Dawson said, "This is a really hefty expense account. What happened?" I said, "I took Elaine Stritch out and she ordered three of everything. What do you want me to do?" She thought it was so funny, she signed off on it.

DOUGLAS KENNEDY: There was a shooting in Queens. They made an *NYPD Blue* episode out of it. A guy had gone into a famous Chinese restaurant in Elmhurst, walked into the back, and shot the cashier in front of everyone. The cops cornered this guy in a parking lot and put seventy bullets in him. I was sent out on the story. I figured out the shooter's address, which was in a Chinese American neighborhood. Nobody talks in those neighborhoods. I asked like thirty people about this guy. As I'm leaving, I ask one more person, who said, "There was a guy that lived in the basement." It was a tight driveway. It was difficult to get by the car to get to the basement, so none of the cops had gone there. I slide past the car and get to the basement door, which was two inches open. I say, "Anybody here?" Somebody answered but they're not coming out. I open the door and I'm saying, "I'm sorry but I can't understand what you're saying. I'm from the *New York Post*. Did you know—?" I come around the corner, and I realize the guy is talking to me through a doorway that has an old telephone wire around the doorknob and around the lock. He's locked inside this room. Then I look down and there's a dead body—a guy shot in the head. The guy behind the door is still talking to me. Someone later described it as *Pulp Fiction*. This was actually the beginning of the story. It turned out to be a landlord-tenant dispute, and the cashier was the wife of the dead guy I was looking at. They were the landlords of these two guys living in the basement illegally. The shooter was one of them. Before the shooter had gone to the Chinese restaurant, he had fought with the landlord and killed him in that little hallway. There were bullet holes in the doorway through which I was talking to this other guy. [The killer] had locked [his fellow tenant] in that little room and shot through the door but missed. Then the shooter got in his car, went to the Chinese restaurant, and shot the landlord's wife. I call Stuart Marques, and I say, "Stuart, I'm here and I've got the dead guy and I've got another guy locked in this room." Stuart says, "Bring the live guy to the *Post* so nobody else gets him." The NYPD spokesman John Miller had to have a press conference and say that the *Post* found the body that the cops didn't find.

GRETCHEN VIEHMANN: Jack Newfield would always do stories like the "10 worst judges" or the "10 worst landlords." I used to dread those stories. We would have to do a *lot* of research. That's when the stakeouts happened. Staking out a judge was never easy. It was really hard to find out where they lived. Mike Pearl would always know where that judge liked to go to eat or he would know somebody who knew somebody. Steve Hirsch once got a garbage bag and put it over his head like you would if you didn't have a raincoat, but then he just hid in the garbage under a bunch of Christmas trees. It was either a "Worst landlord" or a "Worst judge" story. He basically disguised himself as garbage and got the shot. Hirsch would do anything.

MARSHA KRANES: I was doing rewrite with Ann Bollinger when she was covering the O.J. trial. On the wall, alongside where O.J. sat, there was a bunch of either plaques or diplomas, things in frames. I had a retired graphic artist friend who was watching the trial on Court TV, and she kept calling me, saying, "I'm going crazy. All these picture frames are crooked on the wall. It's bothering me. Can you get them to straighten out the frames?" I said, "Are you crazy?" Ann called about five minutes later, and I said, "I have a request. You don't have to do anything about it but listen to what my friend wants somebody to do." Anyhow, ten minutes later I get a call from my friend Shirley: "Marsha, they straightened out the frames."

GRETCHEN VIEHMANN: There was a homeless guy around Times Square. We were up at 1211 at that point. This was when you could still just walk into the newsroom. He came in and told us he kept seeing mice all over the doughnuts in the window at Dunkin' Donuts in Times Square. [Photo assignment editor] Vern Shibla and I got him a disposable camera. This is pre-digital. The homeless guy took the pictures and brought the film in. They ended up being great pictures of mice all over the doughnuts. That was the wood. We kept that wood going for days and days and days. [Future Pulitzer Prize winner Maggie Haberman did some of the reporting.]

KEN CHANDLER: We had great pictures through the window at night, with the mice scampering around, eating the doughnuts.

GRETCHEN VIEHMANN: David Letterman picked it up. He thought it was the funniest thing in the world, so he did a whole big thing about it on air. If I'm not mistaken, he, too, obsessed over it for days and days. That's how I met my husband. He's a New Yorker, but he was living in England. He came over and was talking to a mutual friend and said, "That story about the mice and the doughnuts. It's just fucking amazing." My friend was like, "I know the person that did that." That's why we got introduced.

Post headlines have been part of the cultural conversation since the beginning of the Murdoch era, making appearances on *Saturday Night Live, 30 Rock,* and most of the late-night talk shows. Murdoch even voiced himself on *The Simpsons,* the long-running hit on his Fox network. The story of the doughnut-loving mice was not the first, or last, time David Letterman and his writers borrowed from the *Post.* One night he proclaimed "Top 10 Words Used in *New York Post* Headlines":

Co-Ed
Tot
Horror
Straphangers
Mom
Weirdos
Hizzoner
Torso
Herr Steinbrenner
Slayfest/Lotto (tie)

KEN CHANDLER: We loved it. It appealed to our egos, I guess.

GRETCHEN VIEHMANN: We had this absolutely horrific picture of Howard Stern from, I want to say, '94 or '95. It was taken by a photographer who got low. It's his Adam's apple and nostrils—before he had his nose job. I think part of the reason he had the nose job was that picture. It was absolutely the worst picture ever taken of Howard Stern. We ran it. He ranted about it on the radio. Every time Howard Stern was mentioned in the paper, we would run that same picture. Even if there was no good reason for it. It started to drive Howard Stern insane. Then he got my name, and they invited me on the show. Ken was like, "Don't do it. Don't go on there. They'll get you." Again, this was the naughtiness of the *Post.* It was comedy, that we would just run this picture. He knew we were doing it on purpose. Then it became a cat-and-mouse thing where we would find a reason to put it in the way back, in some tiny little thing in the TV listings. And he would find it. It was sport, it was just us playing. Ken Chandler was the ringleader on that one. He thought it was the funniest thing ever.

> Despite Murdoch's personal disregard for sports, he understood their importance to the *Post* and his media empire.

GREG GALLO: Before Game 7 of the '94 Stanley Cup finals. Marc Kalech came and said, "I've got the headline: IT'S OURS." With a big picture of the Stanley Cup on page one, and after fifty-four years, the Rangers finally give blue-shirt fans what they wanted. Kalech said, "All we need to do is get these papers on the ice. Do you have somebody who can do that?" I said, "Yeah." Doug Gould was a reporter covering the Islanders as a freelancer. But he knew the security people down behind the benches at the Garden. I said, "Doug, this is what we need you to do." They did up some dummy front pages, front and back pages. So the players could hold them up while they were skating around the ice after winning the cup. We had a designated drop-off point for the bundles of papers. He would carry them behind the bench, keep them there, not let any of the *Daily News* photographers know what was going on. We told our photographers: set it up, and then give these things out as soon as the final horn goes off if the Rangers have won. Dick Klayman [associate sports editor] and I were upstairs at the Garden. I was looking at Gould behind the benches and there he is. I see the bundles, we are all set, and sure enough, it was a tight game, but they win. We looked great the next day. Everybody is holding up the *Post* and the *Daily News* is scratching their you-know-what. The Rangers win, we win.

GEOFF REISS, former senior vice president, ESPN: Murdoch's not a fan, but it's misleading to suggest he's indifferent. He used sports in 1993 to make the Fox network. He dislodged NBC and got the rights to broadcast the NFL. That was *the* thing that allowed him to build the Fox network. Before that, it was just a bunch of loosely affiliated stations.

> Murdoch's money-losing New York newspaper proved its value when Fox News debuted in 1996 and the cable behemoth Time Warner refused to carry the chan-

nel in the crucial New York market. The dispute turned into a battle of the media titans as Rupert Murdoch faced off against Ted Turner, whose Turner Broadcasting (and CNN) had merged with Time Warner.

CHRIS RUDDY: When Fox News launched they had problems because they couldn't get into New York City. Time Warner owned the whole franchise and they also owned CNN. Ted Turner was hell-bent on stopping that. Eric Breindel is the guy that got Rudy to go and put Fox on a public access channel. That broke the blockade and Fox News got on all the other systems. Had they not had the *New York Post*, and had Eric not been so aligned with Rudy I don't think they would have gotten that. Maybe Fox would have inevitably been a success but maybe not as early.

KELVIN MACKENZIE, night managing editor, 1978–1979: Murdoch campaigned against Time Warner using the *Post* and they buckled. A big headline on a successful bloody paper is a big political weapon.

MICHAEL SHAIN, television editor, 1978–1993, 1996–2013: Ken took me to a lunch with Roger Ailes pretty quickly after I got the television editor job. He had some flunky with him. Ailes talked the whole time and said that I had to get rid of the TV critic [at the *Post*]. One reason was that he had tried to start a *60 Minutes*–type show on Fox prime time and she had given it a bad review. She should have been fired because she was not supporting Mr. Murdoch. She should have been out there toeing the party line. Michele Greppi was the critic at the time. It was one of the reasons Ken wanted me to be TV editor, because she was in his office all the time saying how terrible the television section was, and he just wanted somebody to get rid of her. Basically, he hired me to get rid of Michele and the truth is, I did. Ailes spent twenty minutes on how much he hated Michele Greppi and he talked about how Fox was going to become a big part of American life and that we had a choice: we could get on board, or we could be in the opposition. It was a very chilly lunch. The footnote to the whole thing was that he didn't even know that I knew him from when I was a kid. When he was the producer of *The Mike Douglas Show*, he and his then-wife moved in down the street from us in suburban Philadelphia. In Media, Pennsylvania, of all places. I was in high school at the time, and I used to cut their lawn. I was the neighborhood kid who cut Roger Ailes's lawn. But I never ever wanted to tell him that story. First of all, he was like three wives down the road from that, and you never know what's going to happen in that kind of situation. And I didn't want to be familiar with him in any way. I didn't feel as if I needed to give him any succor. On Sixth Avenue, in those days, Fox was in the basement and the *Post* was on the tenth floor. After, as we're riding up in the elevator, I'll never forget Ken saying: he's not much of a newsman, but he's a hell of a propagandist.

KEN CHANDLER: Over the years, Roger told me he'd like a lot of people fired. I remember him calling me up in the newsroom one day about some story on page seventeen at the bottom of the page, and saying, "Hey, Chandler, are you running a roomful of communists out there?" I was fortunate because I didn't have to deal with the Fox PR department. If Roger had a complaint, he would call me directly, rather than have those thugs in the PR department do it. He always said what he said half-jokingly because he knew the *Post* had heavy Murdoch protection, so he wasn't necessarily going to win. He knew he wouldn't get all that far with the *Post*. But he felt obliged to go through the motions.

MICHAEL SHAIN: A couple of months later, Ken, who kept in touch with all his editors, took me out to lunch—just a how-are-things-going kind of thing. I said, "How's the paper doing?" The place where we were eating was right next door. He said, "We're still losing money, but not like them." He pointed at the wall that was between us and Fox News. He says, "They lose in a month what we lose in a year." So, he said, "I'm not worried about us."

JOE CONASON, former reporter, *The Village Voice*: I wrote a piece [for the *New Republic*] about Roger Ailes, the 1988 presidential campaign, and the Willie Horton ad [a 1988 TV commercial put out by supporters of George H. W. Bush's presidential campaign that played on fears of Black crime]. He was investigated by the Federal Elections Commission because of that story. They put him through the wringer. But somehow, he decided he liked me. I had been fair to him, I listened to his side, et cetera, et cetera. So he invited me to join Fox News when they were first creating the channel. I did an audition with Sean Hannity at a studio on the West Side. I kicked Sean's butt, which was one reason I didn't get the job. I never hear from Roger. Things move on. I see [Alan] Colmes has the job. I called again. Roger finally called me back. He says, "I'm really sorry about this. I fought for you. But you had too many enemies at the top of News Corp." I said, "What do you mean?" He alluded to Eric Breindel, who apparently hated me because I had mocked him on *The Morton Downey Jr. Show* [a combative syndicated talk show that is considered an early example of "trash TV"]. He and I appeared on the show together, and I had busted his chops. It was written about in *Spy* [magazine], which must have irritated him even more. Of course, Rupert hated me—he had tried to fire me [at the *Voice*]. The long and the short of it was I had made so many enemies at the *Post*, I could not get hired by the Fox News channel, where I assure you I would have been fired soon anyway, because Sean [Hannity] did not want me. Many years later, Ken Auletta did a big piece about Fox News and he revealed that they allowed Sean to pick the person he was going to debate. He picked Alan. He didn't want anyone who would have seriously debated him. They wanted a liberal, but a liberal with thick glasses.

CHRIS RUDDY: I was down in Washington and conservative media critic Reed Irvine told me some people were questioning Vince Foster's death. [The death of Foster, deputy counsel in the Clinton White House, was determined to have been a suicide.] They thought it was really bizarre that a White House aide would be going to Fort Marcy Park. I got approval to go to DC and talk to some of the police and paramedics. One of the paramedics thought it was—I quoted him in the paper—the oddest suicide he ever saw. There was little or no blood. The theory was either somebody killed him or that the body was moved. I always approached the story from the perspective that I didn't know what happened. I didn't say it was murder. I did say it should be treated as a homicide investigation because every suicide investigation should be treated as a homicide. I started this, people took tremendous interest. It played into the fact that on the night of Foster's death, two or three [White House aides allegedly] went into Foster's office and removed papers. There was a feeling it was a cover-up, and that led to one thing and another. The *Post* was pretty excited about me doing more stories as that went on. But the media goes on this jihad, saying it was just a conspiracy theory.

MARSHA KRANES: Ruddy kept pushing and pushing and pushing the Vince Foster story.

FRED DICKER: We used to laugh at Chris Ruddy at the *Post*. I believe he was fired by the *Post* because he was like a Bill and Hillary Clinton conspiracy nut, quote, unquote. When he left the *Post*, he started this Newsmax thing with the backing of a billionaire from Pittsburgh. Now I wouldn't be surprised if Chris Ruddy is worth a hundred million dollars. He's unbelievably successful. I mean, he owns Newsmax and he's a member of Mar-a-Lago.

CHRIS RUDDY: There was a tremendous amount of negative pressure at the *Post*. Some people say I was fired. It was a mutual departure because I knew they didn't really want to cover [the Vince Foster case], and I felt it should be further investigated. I didn't get fired and I was not upset with Murdoch. I figured, hey, he owns the newspaper. He can do whatever he damn pleases. I own a cyber media company now. If I don't want to cover something it doesn't mean I'm covering it up. In fact, with Murdoch's blessing, Eric Breindel called Richard Mellon Scaife and they recommended me for the position I took at [the Scaife-owned *Pittsburgh Tribune-Review*]. Other than my recent competition with Fox News, I've always had pretty good relations.

> The *Post* had long attracted a white-collar crowd, dating back to the days when it was the only paper to provide the final stock prices. In the late '90s, its appeal to that audience, which spent money on theater, restaurants, and nightclubs, increased as it stole a couple of columnists from the *Daily News* to target the same demographic: Michael Riedel, who wrote a gossipy theater column, and Keith Kelly, who covered media. The business section of the paper had been steadily improving throughout the decade, run by such editors as John Cassidy, who eventually decamped for the *New Yorker*, David Yelland, and Xana Antunes.

MICHAEL RIEDEL: Back in those days, the *Post* was a great outlet. Especially for someone like me, covering sort of a high-end business, because the *Post* was read by the most powerful people in New York City. You had the high end and the low end.

MICHAEL SHAIN: The business section became the fair-haired section of the *Post* in the early '90s. All of a sudden everybody on the street was reading what the *Post* had. Those were the days when John Cassidy was running it. Then Xana came in and was terrific.

KEN CHANDLER: Xana worked on a business section at the London *Evening Standard*, so she had a good understanding of what we wanted. The business section was successful because we focused on media, fashion, retail—stuff that gave the paper buzz.

KEITH KELLY, media columnist, 1998–2021: The business section was like the most favored nation. There's a sensibility that comes from covering business that general assignment reporters didn't have. I think Murdoch thought the business section was a little more sophisticated. They decided that a way to get attention is to cover media. So even though it was a small staff, they always had two people covering media, a columnist and a general assignment media reporter. I think Murdoch's theory was if we cover media in a fair, even-handed way, other publications will pay attention to us. And they did.

KEN CHANDLER: Donald Trump called me, and others, too, usually about stories in the business section. They weren't anti-him at all, but we would identify him as being worth whatever it was, $750 million, and he would say, "Don't you know I'm a billionaire, Ken? *B*. It begins with a *B*." It was always a fairly good-natured conversation. But I would say, "Donald, if you're a billionaire, can you provide us with some evidence?" "Yeah, sure." But he never did.

JAN CONSTANTINE, senior deputy counsel, News Corp, 1991–2005: Donald Trump sued us because he said the *Post* deflated his net worth. He said this was defamatory. That got thrown out pretty quickly, I think before we even had discovery.

JILL ABRAMSON, former executive editor, *The New York Times*: The *Post*'s business section was sometimes superior to ours. The real estate news was often superior to ours. I spent ten years at the *Wall Street Journal* before the *Times*, and those were two areas where I wanted to kick ass, so I paid attention to the *Post* coverage. Keith Kelly was pretty good. He broke news. I always took his calls.

NORMAN PEARLSTINE, former executive editor, *The Wall Street Journal*: The business news section was what I paid most attention to, and I thought—it's a cliché, but it's appropriate—that it punched above its weight. It was a small number of people, but in the places where they chose to be competitive, they were. Those tended to be media, law, real estate. The things that fueled New York.

Antunes so impressed her bosses that she rose to a top slot on the masthead in 1999 when editor Ken Chandler moved to the paper's business side, succeeding Marty Singerman as the *Post*'s publisher. Antunes's ascent would have been unheard of during Murdoch's first run as owner. For a time, she appeared to be the right leader for a reimagined newspaper as it approached a new century.

ERIC FETTMANN: Once Murdoch came back, it was much less of an old boys' club. At a certain point, there was a real concerted effort to diversify. To bring women up, to hire many more minorities. In the '90s and much more so in the next decade. Certainly, Xana did what she could to advance women.

Despite the growth of his empire, Murdoch made time for direct involvement in the *Post*'s political coverage when key races were in play, like Vice President Al Gore's battle with George W. Bush for the presidency and Hillary Clinton's run for New York's Senate seat.

STUART MARQUES: Rupert talked to Ken every day. The only time I saw him in the office regularly was during the five weeks that the Bush-Gore election [in 2000] went to the Supreme Court. He was in the office a lot then. He would talk to me and ask me who we had covering this and who's covering that. You know, "Don't forget to go after the Democrats, too." At one point, he gave me Karl Rove's cell phone number. I don't think I ever put it in my Rolodex.

When Hillary Clinton ran for the Senate in 2000, the *Post* would not back her, even though Murdoch hosted a fundraiser for her and one of his most popular columnists was in her corner—on paper at least.

BOB HARDT: The editorial board had a meeting with [Congressman] Rick Lazio [who ran against Hillary Clinton]. I was the reporter there to write it up as a news story, then the editorial board would inevitably endorse him. Lazio did not have a great interview and had not left a strong impression on the group. Murdoch was there for it. After Lazio leaves, Murdoch turns to them. There's, like, thirty seconds of silence, and he says, "What are we going to do?" Just like, wow, we have a dud of a candidate here. He's thinking, I need to endorse this guy, but I really don't want to. It was one of those great moments of candor.

They weren't going to endorse Hillary because it would go against the editorial brand of the paper. It just wasn't going to happen.

KEN CHANDLER: Cindy took me to a White House Christmas party as her guest. It must have been the last year that the Clintons were in the White House. Hillary at that point was thinking about running for the Senate. She was having these weekly or monthly lunches in New York with female reporters and columnists, to try and make friends with them and get their support. I guess that's how she became friendly with Cindy. At the White House Christmas party, you stand around for like an hour or so talking and drinking and nibbling hors d'oeuvres. Then you're ushered into this line where the president and the first lady shake hands with you, you move on, and suddenly you're out in the street and it's over. Cindy is ahead of me. She shakes hands with Bill Clinton first, and they chat a bit. Then I'm shaking Bill Clinton's hand. Cindy says to Bill, "This is the schmuck from the *New York Post* that gives you all the grief." His hand went limp and pulled away. The next move would have been for me to shake hands with Hillary, but she glared at me. I didn't even bother. I said to Cindy, "Did you have to do that?" She said, "I thought you'd like that."

> Some welcomed the version of the *Post* overseen by the first female editor promoted to the top job by Murdoch. Others, who had worked at the *Post* during the prior Murdoch era, felt the paper had lost some of its bite.

PHILIP MESSING, reporter, 1978–1991, 1994–2016: [The *Post*] was much more sedate, and it was much more tepid. It was like a rambunctious colt that had been gelded. I'm not saying the *Post* didn't have its moments, but this notion of—I hate to be a Debbie Downer, but when they wrote the story with the tear in Alexander Hamilton's eye, they were mourning something that didn't really exist except in their mind's eye. They took Dunleavy out of the seat of power. The paper was denuded of its vitality. It's like rock and roll. I mean in the '60s, things were one way. In the '70s, we still had rock and roll, but it wasn't quite the same. Janis wasn't singing. Hendrix wasn't playing.

26 | COL POT
A Brazen Editor, 9/11,
Anthrax in the Office

Editor Xana Antunes earned the respect, and even the affection, of her colleagues. She also oversaw an increase in average daily circulation at the *Post* from 434,000 in 1999 to more than 487,000 in 2001. But at that point, longtime rival the *Daily News* sold 734,000 copies on weekdays and Rupert Murdoch did not feel Antunes was delivering what he needed, in numbers or in tabloid pizzazz. With other editors at the paper as uncomfortable witnesses, he made his displeasure clear, sharply questioning Antunes's decisions about coverage. On April 23, 2001, she abruptly stepped down.

KEN CHANDLER, editor in chief, publisher, 1978–1986, 1993–2002: What happened was, Lachlan Murdoch [the elder of Murdoch's two sons] was brought in to oversee the *New York Post*, HarperCollins [the book publisher Murdoch's News Corp created in 1989 by merging two existing publishers], and the [supermarket coupon business]. Lachlan decided that he wanted to bring in his own generation, if you like, his own friends from Australia to run things. They fired the general manager, brought in someone from Australia. They got rid of the advertising director, brought in someone from Australia. Then along comes Col Allan.

GREGG BIRNBAUM, political editor, 1993–2010: Xana was certainly a competent editor. I don't mean to speak badly of her in any way, but given the change from

Xana to Col, which was a whole different kettle of fish, maybe I understand what Rupert was looking for: a bit more of the splash and the brashness and super self-confidence of a tabloid. Maybe what Xana lacked was a little bit of that special sauce.

MICHAEL SHAIN, television editor, 1978–1993, 1996–2013: Col ran meetings without ever looking at you. He would sit at his desk and look out the window and say the most vile things. It was a very imperial, imperious way of dealing, so that you knew who was boss.

KEN CHANDLER: Col was just a puppet of Lachlan's, that's all. He was doing what Lachlan told him to do.

COL ALLAN, editor in chief, 2001–2016; editorial adviser, 2019–2021: I had known Lachlan for ten years in Australia before I went to edit the *Post* in 2001. We were friends. If that makes me his hand puppet, so be it.

MILTON GOLDSTEIN, copy editor, 1974–current: Col Allan came in from the Sydney *Daily Telegraph*, the *New York Post* of Sydney, though the *Telegraph* was never as boisterous as the *Post*. One of the things he was known for in Sydney was . . . there was some survey in Australia that found that more than half of babies in a certain year were born out of wedlock. So his page one in the *Daily Telegraph* was A NATION OF BASTARDS.

WAYNE DARWEN, assistant managing editor, 1983–1987: Col would kill his grand-mother for a story. He's ruthless, brutal. I say it affectionately, but he's fucking crazy. He always has been. He was back when I knew him. But he's got what it takes to get that job done. If the boss told him to do a story, he's going to go. He'll do it full tilt. He's the ultimate axman. He's got all the qualities of a mob hitman. Murdoch likes that. Basically, a lot of his top guys—Dunleavy was the ultimate. You want a dirty job done, you get Dunleavy or Col Allan to do it.

GRETCHEN VIEHMANN, photo editor, 1993–2001: They used to call him Col Pot in the newsroom.

GARY GINSBERG, former executive vice president, News Corp: Col was on Rupert Mur-doch's speed dial. He really liked Col, he trusted Col, they shared a lot of sensibilities. They talked all the time and they very rarely differed on coverage. I think he really liked Col's populist flavor, his news judgment. He was part of the inner circle for the entire time I was there.

> At the *Daily Telegraph* in Sydney, Australia, Allan had been known to relieve himself in the sink in his office during editorial meetings. Some of his new colleagues greeted him with what they saw as a lighthearted gift.

AL GUART, federal court reporter, 1993–2004: It was like, I'm the top dog, so I'm going to mark my territory.

MARSHA KRANES, rewrite, editor, 1974–2005: When Col Allan came, they had done some research. I think Stu Marques, Marc Kalech, and Steve Cuozzo probably were part of this. They heard that in his office wherever he was coming from, he had a little urinal and during meetings he'd get up and use it. They bought one, either a urinal or I think it was a toilet, and they had it in his office when he arrived. They thought, he'll feel comfortable, it'll be a big joke we'll share with him.

STUART MARQUES, managing editor, news, 1993–2001: It was a small bathroom-sized sink. Col understood, and he was not happy about it.

JESSIE GRAHAM, reporter, 1999–2004: Oh, yeah, I didn't see it, but I heard about it. They called him "the sink pisser."

COL ALLAN: Ha. The sink. What is conveniently not reported is the sink [in Australia] was in a closet with a door in my office. But otherwise, guilty as charged. I was not amused. It was harmless. I should have enjoyed the joke.

> Two months later, Allan fired two of the *Post*'s managing editors, Stu Marques and Marc Kalech, along with liberal columnist Jack Newfield, associate metro editor Lisa Baird, who was battling breast cancer, and two other editorial staffers.

KEN CHANDLER: The prank sealed Stu's fate. But also, Murdoch thought Stu was a bit too left-wing for the paper.

STUART MARQUES: I don't think it was about the sink. Other people were fired who weren't involved. He wanted his own people in there.

AL GUART: Lisa Baird called me because she knew I knew a lot of lawyers. She wanted to buy a house before she died so her kids would have a home. I got her in touch with a lawyer I had done stories with over the years, Susan Chana Lask. She wrote a letter threatening to sue the *Post* and got a six-figure settlement for Lisa, who called to thank me.

SUSAN CHANA LASK, attorney: I successfully settled the Baird issue out of court with a letter citing facts and law supporting that she had a case against them for terminating her based on her cancer. Although I obtained a high six-figure settlement for her in a matter of months and she was so happy, it was a very sad case. I later learned she died of cancer soon after the settlement. [Baird died in October of 2001.]

FRANKIE EDOZIEN, City Hall reporter, 1993–2008: Col was kind to me, but I knew that he fired Lisa when she had cancer. That exacerbated her death. She died shortly after she left the paper. It makes me vomit to this day, that the weekend she died, there was conversation as to whether we should run an obit because people did not want to upset Col. She was a New York City journalism legend. *Newsday* ran an obit. There was back-and-forth and ultimately the *Post* ran three or four grafs. I remember one of the reporters almost in tears saying, "Why are we even having this conversation?"

KEN CHANDLER: Murdoch wanted to fire Jack Newfield in the worst possible way. I tried to defend and protect him for as long as I could. Eventually, all I could do was delay. Murdoch didn't trust him. He was a liberal. And I guess there was some background, something Jack had written in the *Village Voice* or somewhere, some underlying reason he hated Newfield, beyond the politics. I don't know what it was.

MICHAEL SHAIN: Col had cash register instincts for what people wanted to read. And for how stories were to be played. I learned a ton from him. But he was a miserable human being. He had no friends other than a few drinking buddies. He was insulting, abrasive, he was an asshole. I mean, a serious blue-ribbon, black-belt asshole. He was somebody you didn't talk to, you listened to. He had paid for one of those pay-per-view fights from Time Warner one Saturday night and the thing was over in a round and a half and he said, "I'm not paying for that. You call your friends at Time Warner and get it off my bill." That kind of nonsense that he would get you involved in.

CINDY ADAMS, gossip columnist, 1981–current: He was told to get rid of the dead wood and make the paper alive. So he made a lot of enemies. But he was smart. There's nobody who knows tabloid-ism like Col Allan.

Adams deftly navigated Allan's arrival, while Steve Dunleavy remained a carnival unto himself.

MICHAEL RIEDEL, theater columnist, 1998–2020: When Liz [Smith] was at the *Post* and Cindy was there, that was an uneasy relationship. This shows you the brilliance of Cindy. When Col Allan becomes editor in chief of the paper, he comes to town with his wife, Sharon. Liz expects Col to come to her to kiss her ring, which is not something Col Allan does. Knowing that Col Allan's wife is new to New York, Cindy arranges a series of lunches to introduce her to people like Barbara Walters, Katie Couric, all the fancy ladies of New York. What happens is Col gives Liz the boot and Cindy's still at the *Post*.

DEVLIN BARRETT, reporter, 1992–2002: There was no beat more fun than covering the Brooklyn courts in the '90s. They were wild. Dunleavy would show up for the big trials and write columns off them while I wrote the news story. We got along pretty well, but he did some shit that was insane. One day I'm covering the Abner Louima trial [Louima was brutalized by NYPD cops in 1997] and Dunleavy shows up in the courtroom with a shopping bag. You can hear the vodka bottles clinking. There's a press room at the federal courthouse. I said, "You can just leave your vodka bottles at my desk. It's fine." But he wanted to bring them with him. He didn't want them out of his sight, I guess. The whole day of testimony he would occasionally kick the bag, and you'd hear the vodka bottles clinking throughout the courtroom. This is federal court. It's not like state court where it's a little more loosey-goosey. Federal court is like church, man, and Dunleavy's vodka bottles are clinking away. The other thing is, he's sitting next to Jimmy Breslin, who is his own ball of wax. Breslin brought popcorn and starts eating the popcorn next to Dunleavy with his clinking vodka bottles. He's eating the popcorn with his mouth open, and it's really loud. So, these two very old-school, very I-do-what-I-want-and-the-world-can-adjust guys are putting on their own little sideshow in a really important police brutality trial. Everyone else in the room is dead serious and these guys are like, yep, I've got my popcorn, got my vodka, let's go.

BARBARA ROSS, political reporter, 1978–1985: I was in criminal court for the *Daily News*, and you could not sit anywhere near Dunleavy because he'd be inebriated by ten in the morning. But he was so amazing. I heard him dictate a column that was so on the money, so pointed, with punctuation and paragraphs. That part, it never left him. It's a tragedy that he was abusing himself, because he was quite good.

> The *Post*'s audacious tone was about to be dampened by events that irrevocably altered New York City life.

GRETCHEN VIEHMANN: I watched people that I loved get taken down by the culture Col encouraged. There was that sense of naughtiness, yes, but it had a meaner spirit. It was the worst aspects of the tabloid laid bare. I'd had enough. I was going to be the New York picture editor at the *New York Times*. I had to go through this horrible interview process, over weeks and weeks. I think the *Times* wanted to make sure they weren't getting some loudmouthed tabloid, snappy person. I proved I wasn't, but it was an arduous process. And then my fiancé and I took a month or so off over the summer, because I was meant to be starting in September 2001. You can see where I'm going with this. We went to Mexico and ended up living there for five years. But that first month, I thought, I've had it with newspapers, I'm tired. You don't realize how tired you are till you stop. I called the *Times* and said, "I'm not going to take the job after all." They were like, nobody says no to the *New York Times*, especially not somebody from the *Post*. My first day on the job would have been September 10, 2001. Later a friend said, "You would have had a Pulitzer." I'm like, "Yeah, but I have my sanity."

DAN MANGAN, reporter, rewrite, 2000–2013: The alarm went off, and I think CBS Radio had a report that a plane had hit one of the towers. I thought, this is going to fucking ruin the rest of my day because of some idiot in a propeller plane. Then I heard on the radio that another plane hit. I popped out of bed and called the city desk. Denise Buffa answered. I said, "Did you hear about this plane?" She goes, "Get down there." I went out to Second Avenue and started looking for a cab. I don't actually know why this woman stopped, but I waved down a Mazda Miata with the top down. I said, "Are you going downtown?" She goes, "Yeah, are you a reporter?" I said, "Yes. Can you drive me down toward the Trade Center?" She goes, "Yes." I got in the car, and she says,

"I'm in public relations. Can I pitch you a story for my company?" I was like, "Yeah, whatever. Here's my card." She drove me close to the Trade Center. I'm in touch with her to this day. On every anniversary, we write each other. I feel very confident that I am the only person in the past twenty, if not thirty years, that has hitchhiked in Manhattan and been picked up by a woman in a convertible at nine a.m.

GREGG BIRNBAUM: It was an election day on 9/11—a big day for me and my staff. There was a four-way Democratic mayoral primary going on. I got to the office. We're seeing it on TV. The towers are burning. [Managing Editor] Joe Robinowitz said, "Wow, looks like they're gonna have to cancel election day." This was before the towers fell. I said to Joe, "What are you talking about? No one is canceling election day." I didn't really get what was going on. I was in shock.

DAVID SEIFMAN, City Hall bureau chief, political editor, 1973–2019: They locked the doors to City Hall. I was outside, but I noticed a trailer that the police department had set up on the side of City Hall. I ran because the towers had just fallen, and I could see the debris coming at me. It was like a science fiction movie. I ran into the trailer, which luck would have it, had all sorts of filters. There were about a dozen of us. There were cops and City Hall personnel. They asked for all our names. I said, "What do you need our names for?" He said—this was a lieutenant or captain talking—"In case we don't make it out."

DEVLIN BARRETT: From the moment the second plane hit, I knew it had to be Al Qaeda because for most of 2001, I had sat in federal court in lower Manhattan and listened to all this testimony about how much bin Laden liked attacks with planes. [Four bin Laden associates were tried on charges related to the bombing of two US embassies in Africa in 1998.] At the time, it was interesting, but obviously, I didn't have some notion that, well, that means he's going to fly planes into buildings in the next three months. But as soon as it happened, it felt like, it's gotta be him.

DAN MANGAN: The buildings were on fire. I didn't have the experience that most other people had that day, which was seeing this on TV. I didn't have that distance—that kind of perspective where you see the skyline shots. It was like I was at the bottom of a very deep fucking pool looking up. I'm on pay phones—I don't think my cell phone worked. I left the Millennium Hotel [near the towers], and the cops were saying, "You've got to move back." They said they were afraid of a third attack. They were afraid of gas. I was behind a pillar, so I wasn't looking right at the towers when I heard a crack. I knew exactly what it was. I knew it was the building snapping. I popped my head out and I saw the top of the tower buckle. I said . . . [struggles to maintain his composure] I said . . . It's okay. It's okay. I said in my head, I'll stand here and wait for the building to fall down. Then I'll go interview people.

MARK STAMEY, reporter, 1993–2006: As I'm getting on the subway, I heard one of the buildings collapse. I kept a folding bicycle in the car. I rode my bicycle down there and I got a couple of pictures. One of the images I have was of hundreds of women's high-heeled shoes along the Hudson River. They kicked them off so they could run. There were guys combing through the papers that had fallen to the ground when the buildings collapsed. They said they were looking for currency or anything else of value.

DAN MANGAN: I was going to say it was like something out of a movie but there's no movie like this. You were in a completely white dome because there was dust everywhere. You're walking through powder. It was September 11, but it looked like the middle of winter without the cold. I walked by St. Paul's Chapel and its graveyard. You could see the headstones sticking out of the dust and debris. It was like they'd been hit by a blizzard. But it wasn't snow.

GREGG BIRNBAUM: When the towers came down, the chaos and the shock was extraordinary. We didn't know what we were doing. The regular story conference, which was either at nine-thirty or ten, was delayed for an hour or two. When we finally held the meeting, I realized why it was delayed. What the editor in chief [Col Allan] had done during that time was to develop a plan—a very clear division of labor, and a very clear and understandable tasking of the editors. We came into the conference, completely bewildered. What are we doing? By the time we left, we all knew exactly what. There is no love lost between me and Col Allan, but I will give him this: he planned our mission. And it worked. He gave us clarity and a roadmap to our coverage. That was a powerful meeting and a real lesson in what you do in a time of crisis.

LISA MARSH, fashion/retail business reporter, 2000–2003: No one in the office knew that Dan Mangan and I were dating. I was calling him and calling him. At the time, he covered the Port Authority and transportation, so I figured they would need him down there ASAP. I'm thinking, okay, knowing him he's in the middle of it all. I'm standing in front of the bank of televisions in the newsroom, and they show the first tower coming down. I'm like, oh my god, he's there. He's going to be dead. This is awful. At that point [crying] I kind of lost it. I fell to the floor. Everyone was like, "Lisa, are you okay? What's happening?" I was like, "No, no, I'm fine." Fifteen minutes later, he finds a phone, and he calls the office. He says, "Call my sister. Tell her I'm okay. Tell her you're the contact." His sister worked at a store with one of Dan's high school friends, who picked up the phone first. I said, "It's Dan's girlfriend." She says, "Dan doesn't have a girlfriend." I'm like, "Well, I'm Dan's girlfriend." "Danny has a girlfriend?" "Yeah, I'm the one that's telling you he's alive, and if you have any questions, call me." It was just ridiculous—"Danny has a girlfriend?"

DEVLIN BARRETT: So, I'm taking these feeds from the reporters, and at the same time—especially after the first tower fell—the family members of our reporters started calling in asking us to make sure their person was alive. You know, one thousand percent understandable, but for a lot of them, I couldn't give them an answer because after the first tower falls, the phones are really hard to work. Calling out is virtually impossible. I'm calling the phones of all the people I know are there, like Dan Mangan and Jessie Graham, and I'm getting nothing. Every now and then, one of them can get through to me, and I remember having this crazy phone call with, I don't know whether it was Dan or Jessie, but one of our reporters had gotten a Dutch tourist to call the newsroom. He got through to me, and he says, "I'm with your reporter, so-and-so. Can you please do me a favor? Can you call my wife in Holland and tell her I'm alive?" I was like, "Absolutely."

DAN MANGAN: I was going to different buildings and trying to talk to people. I saw Mary Altaffer, a photographer from the *Post*. She had an N95 mask on. She said, "You should leave. This is all asbestos."

JESSIE GRAHAM: God, this is so frigging fuzzy. It must be a PTSD thing. I remember at some point that I called, and I was like, please call my mom and tell her that I'm okay. I was there all night at Ground Zero. I ended up with all these volunteers very near the pile, not wearing a mask. I just wanted to be there, and I started interviewing people. I went home at like 3:00 a.m. And then I just kept going back to Ground Zero and doing stories from there.

DEVLIN BARRETT: I think I'd already put the first version of the extra to bed when [photographer] Don Halasy walks into the newsroom. He clearly had been down there [at Ground Zero] because he was covered head to foot with white dust. That was the moment where I actually felt like, oh, fuck, this is so much worse than my writing reflects. Because Don looks like he nearly died, and he's—emotionally and physically—a zombie at that point. [According to the *Post*'s 2014 obituary of Halasy, when the second tower fell, he was buried under a pile of debris, clawed his way out, then dug out his camera.] My immediate thought was, we can't send him back down there. But I'm not his boss. Knowing Don, he went back down, but I remember at the time thinking, holy crap—that guy can't go back down there.

KEN CHANDLER: Manhattan was effectively cordoned off that day, after 9/11. So the issue for us was how we would get papers distributed in the morning, and for a while, it was hard to get newspaper trucks, because they were trucks, and therefore police thought that they might be bombs—it was hard to get them into Manhattan. We had to negotiate with City Hall, and for a while we set up a staging area at, I think it was at Yonkers Raceway, then they would come in a convoy into the city to deliver the papers. After we moved [uptown] in 1995, the *Post* was still printed at South Street. I think the last time we printed at South Street was the day of 9/11. We'd already decided we needed to build a new plant. We'd actually built the plant in the South Bronx. It was undergoing tests. We were moving slowly. Then you had 9/11 where nobody could access downtown. So it forced us to move everything.

DEVLIN BARRETT: I want to say Jessie [Graham] stayed at the Ground Zero space, for at least a month—a crazy amount of time. The same thing with Don Halasy. I remember thinking, it's good to have these people who know this space, but we've got to get them out of there. It's going to break their brains. It seemed to me we were all very highly motivated and devoted to telling this as well as we possibly could. But it was also breaking our brains in different ways.

DAN MANGAN: I went into the office once, days later, and they didn't know what to do with me because I was a little bit frazzled. Then I went back down there for two weeks.

MARK STAMEY: I'm scared to death. They kept sending us there. They did not issue any [safety gear]. You knew it obviously. You printed it. You were warned. And you kept sending people down there.

DEVLIN BARRETT: This isn't a defense of management, but a lot of people were flying blind in the early days. I'm very sympathetic to the first week of decisions. Everything after that, I feel like, you've got to be careful and you've got to take care of your people. After the eleven days of rewrite that I did, they said, "Go back to federal court." Federal court is where the suspects are, in theory, going to be arrested and charged or brought to trial on this stuff. I worked downtown from that point on, and it was awful. The fires burned until, I think, December. I was ten blocks away, and it smelled awful. All of downtown smelled terrible. I hope Mark is enrolled in the WTC health program. I never did, mostly because I had to cover it, and I always felt, well, if I enroll in it, I can't cover this anymore.

COL ALLAN: I have no memory of a safety gear issue during 9/11. I can only say our reporters and all the staff were magnificent during what was surely the biggest story of our lifetimes.

MARK STAMEY: Giuliani comes out and says, go about your business. Right there, a tip-off. I had worked in construction at the time the towers were built and asbestos was considered safe then. I took a sample of the dust and brought it to a state lab. It was certified thirteen percent chrysotile asbestos [the major commercial form of asbestos, which can cause cancer]. I believe my story came out on the fourteenth and nothing happened. I took the report and the gorgeous Russian woman in whose apartment I had taken the sample, and I sent a box of Godiva chocolates to [New York congressman] Jerry Nadler. The chocolates got me past the receptionist. He took a look at the woman and a look at the report and launched an investigation into the EPA. [Then-administrator Christine Todd Whitman had said the air at Ground Zero was safe to breathe.] He also got the World Trade Center Health Registry started.

ROBERT GOTTHEIM, chief of staff for Jerrold Nadler: Representative Nadler formed the Ground Zero Elected Officials task force on September 14, 2001. I can't confirm any of what [Stamey] says. And it frankly is not believable. Showing up with a box of chocolate would not get you into our office and I doubt that happened.

The city did cancel the primary election on September 11. Michael Bloomberg emerged as the GOP candidate, but there was still no consensus on who his Democratic opponent would be. The two leading contenders faced a runoff before the general election on November 6.

DAVID SEIFMAN: We're dealing with 9/11. Mark Green emerges as a Democratic candidate. Mark Green, at the time, was progressive. Still is, I'm sure. He's gone through this pretty tough primary with [Fernando] Ferrer. After the runoff, he antagonizes Freddy Ferrer and his supporters [and does not get Ferrer's endorsement]. That gives Bloomberg an opening, which he grabbed. If the election hadn't been postponed because of 9/11, I'm convinced Mark Green would have won. But once 9/11 happened, Bloomberg exploited the risks and promoted the idea that "we need a businessman." I think 9/11 changed the equation completely. He, of course, ended up spending $75 million. That's in run number one. He barely gets in, even with that. Here's the *Post*, getting ready for the Mark Green administration with everyone else. Now we've got this guy who, even if he isn't a real Republican, ran on the Republican line. And he's certainly much closer to the *Post*'s philosophy than Mark Green. As a result, the *Post* kind of embraced him. And Bloomberg's no dope. He saw a newspaper with potential to agree with him on many of the issues. So, despite some significant flubs along the way, Bloomberg did pull the city out of 9/11. People forget what it was like.

DAN MANGAN: Shortly after September 11, they had a memorial event at Yankee Stadium on a Sunday. They said, "You're going to do the news story. Dunleavy is going to do the column. He's across the street. Pick him up and then go to Yankee Stadium." Across the street was understood to be Langan's. It's like ten in the morning, and Dunleavy's standing at the end of the empty bar drinking a beer, as you do Sunday morning if you're Steve Dunleavy. I tell him, "I'm going up to Yankee Stadium with you. Are you ready?" He goes, "Yeah, mate, just let me finish my beer." I'm getting a little anxious. When he's ready, he says, "Are we going to get a cab?" I said, "We'll get there faster if we take the D train," which was right there on the corner. We get to the subway station and the D is not running. I'm like, "Fuck, let's get a cab." He goes, "I don't have any money." I said, "Don't worry, I've got money." This was before cabs took credit cards. I flag down a cab, and as soon as Dunleavy gets settled, he turns to me and goes, "Why do you have money?" I'm like, "I normally carry around cash just in case I need to buy something. Don't you carry around money?" He goes, "No, my wife gives me an allowance every week. I get it on Monday, and it's gone by that night. Then I'm out of money the rest of the week."

MARSHA KRANES: After 9/11, it was amazing how much more cooperative people were all over the country when you called and said you were from the *New York Post*. I guess it was like that for any New York paper, even calling about something totally unrelated: "I hear there's been a shooting in your church. Can you tell me anything?" They'd say, "Oh, how are you? Is everybody okay?" Then cops, everybody, was so much more cooperative and talkative when you called them, for about a year or so after that.

DEVLIN BARRETT: A big part of my mindset at that time was, this is the biggest, most important story I will ever cover. The politics of it seemed so beside the point. As a New Yorker, I felt, this is the worst thing that's ever happened, hands down. I do remember having a bunch of conversations with the bosses about, when does September 11 come off the wood? If it had been the Devlin Barrett *Post*, I would have kept wooding with it until well into 2002 and maybe 2003. My 9/11 woods streak would have just been endless. Because to me, there was nothing that was ever going to be as important as this.

> A month after the attacks, the *Post* and other media outlets became part of the story as envelopes containing white powder were mailed to the newsroom.

KEN CHANDLER: In those days, we got letters to the editor by email. That was already the norm. Still, people would send letters by snail mail, and they would come in those plastic bins from the post office. I guess there was a whole bin sitting at the feet of the secretary in the editorial department, and she hadn't gotten around to opening them because probably they had enough coming by email to fill the column. She eventually opened them, and one had white powder in it. The whole building had to be evacuated, we had to have the hazmat people in to clean the place up. I think there were at least three people who got anthrax at the *Post*. We did a page one with one of them, Johanna Huden, giving the finger [which was infected and wrapped in a bandage. The wood was ANTHRAX THIS].

GREGG BIRNBAUM: I was on the subway going to work. Johanna Huden was on the same train. We started talking. She said, "Look at my finger. My finger is turning black. There's something wrong. I'm gonna have to go to the doctor today." She must have been very worried to bring it up to me on the subway out of the blue. We weren't really that close, just colleagues. It turns out, she was infected with anthrax. Later, when I saw the handwriting of the sender and what the envelopes looked like, I believe I had come across one of those envelopes and thrown it in the garbage.

KEN CHANDLER: I was sitting on the dais at the Al Smith dinner next to Roger Ailes. We'd had this white powder delivered to the *Post* and to Fox News. We didn't know what it was. We were waiting for the test to come back. Roger was particularly nervous the whole evening. At one point, he whispered to me, "You see that waiter? I don't like the look of him. I don't trust him with serving my food." The waiter looked a little Middle Eastern, but he could have been Hispanic for all Roger knew. During an intermission, Bernie Kerik, who was the police commissioner, came over to both of us and says, "We just got the test results back. That was anthrax." Roger says, "That's it. I'm going back to 1211. I'm going to have to tell the troops." He got up and walked out of the hotel. I got on the cell phone to call the office. Lachlan was in a bar in the Chinese restaurant at the back of 1211, drinking with Col Allan. I got patched through. I said, "Lachlan, we just got the test results, and it's confirmed that it's anthrax." He said, "Don't say anything. Don't tell anybody." I said, "Okay, but just to let you know, Roger Ailes is on his way back to the Fox newsroom." Lachlan was like, "What the fuck! I told him not to say anything! Fuck!" He hangs up on me. I thought, this is too good to miss. I leave, and I walk back to 1211. I go into the lobby, and I said to the guy there, "Did you see Roger Ailes?" He said, "Yeah, he's downstairs." They had a big newsroom in the basement. I go down there, and I missed it, but apparently, there had been this huge screaming match in front of everybody between Roger and Lachlan. With Lachlan ordering Ailes not to say anything. I go upstairs to tell the people at the *Post* what's happening. There's maybe a dozen people in the newsroom, it's like eleven o'clock at night. I call them over and say, "I just want to let you know that the test results came back positive for anthrax, but there's nothing to be alarmed at. We'll have medical support for anybody who needs it." Eventually I leave. I'm driving home to Westchester and on the West Side Highway, the phone rings. It's Roger. He says, "I'm out of here. I'm done. I can't work in this place any longer." I said, "Why not?" He said, "I worked for presidents of the United States. I've never been spoken to by anybody like that." Meaning Lachlan. "I'm not going to put up with that. I'm done." So I'm like, "Maybe you want to sleep on it and see how you feel in the morning. Maybe talk to Rupert," who I think was on the West Coast. Then, for several days, Roger would call me and say, "I'm leaving, I can't stay here." He was quite a drama queen when he put his mind to it. Then, eventually I guess, he did talk to Rupert and Rupert told Lachlan he had to apologize to Roger.

GARY GINSBERG: I remember being in Ken Chandler's office the morning after it broke. There was a gaggle of press in front of 1211, and Chandler and I and a few others met with Lachlan. Lachlan went out and did a press conference in front of the building to answer questions. I remember how well he did under a lot of pressure, handling all the questions. He had had a tough night the night before—the fight he had with Roger Ailes has been well documented. Everybody heard about it. But he went out the next morning and was really poised and articulate and represented the paper really well.

KEN CHANDLER: People were nervous. Some people wouldn't buy the paper because they thought there might be anthrax on the newsprint.

MICHAEL RIEDEL: The way they protected us from the anthrax was, the day after it happened, they put up a plastic wrapper with blue tape separating where Johanna [Huden]'s desk was from the rest, and then throughout the day, the tape would peel away and the thing was gradually falling apart. So I don't think we were that protected from the anthrax.

MARCY SOLTIS, copy editor, 1976–2014: People from the CDC were coming in and they'd have these meetings in the city room. They'd start talking about pores and spores and say, "Hey, that rhymes." The basic message was that "if the anthrax was a problem, you would be dead by now," which I didn't find terribly reassuring. Then they put up what looked like a shower curtain to block off the area where the anthrax letter was found.

MICHAEL RIEDEL: I remember a story about Jesse Angelo when he was, I guess, city editor. He was trying to tell everybody not to worry about anthrax. So he picked up a computer keyboard and he licked it in front of everybody. When they did tests on the keyboards, they found anthrax all over them.

MARCY SOLTIS: I think it was Dan Aquilante who took one of the rubber gloves they had been distributing to us, drew eyes on it, and inflated it. It became the mascot known as Thraxy, the anthrax chicken. And Thraxy was in this photo that was taken of all the features people by this shower curtain. It was sort of scary because people didn't know how this stuff traveled. Were there still spores that could get into our pores?

> Lachlan Murdoch waited until 2002 before taking his place at the top of the *Post*'s masthead.

KEN CHANDLER: Lachlan decides that he really wants to run the *Post* as publisher and pushes me out.

GREGG BIRNBAUM: Ken was a super editor. He got state news. He got politics. He loved politics. And I found him to be a very decent person. I liked having him at the helm of the *Post*.

KEN CHANDLER: Lachlan fired me himself. He was very nervous. One of the reasons why he was nervous was that it was six weeks before I was getting married, and I'd actually invited him to the wedding. I'm pleased to tell you that he didn't show up. It was the usual bullshit that I've used a million times myself: "Time for a change. You being publisher is not really working out so great. I think we need to go in a new direction." It was like, "Pack up and leave now." That same day I went down to see Rupert, and he said, "I'm very sorry it's ending like this. If I had another newspaper"—because by then they'd sold the *Chicago Sun-Times* and the *Boston Herald*—"I would love you to stay and work, but I don't have anything really to offer you," which was bullshit as well. Honestly, I think I wasn't completely upset about this. I had the best time being editor of the *New York Post*, but I knew I wasn't such a great publisher. I really wasn't into dealing with the circulation department, ad revenues, and union negotiations with printers. So I wasn't all that happy doing the job of publisher. When they came and said it was over, I was like, "Okay. I think it's probably a good time to leave. I had a good run." They were generous, so I really had no complaints about that.

STUART MARQUES: After I left, after Chandler was gone, and Col Allan came in, the *Post* moved much more to the right and—I'm trying to find the right words—they were less coy about it.

27 | TWENTY-FIRST-CENTURY BREAKDOWN

Gephardt Gaffe, Digital Fumbles, Page Six Potboiler

With Col Allan firmly in control, the *Post* began what was arguably the most hard-knuckled era of its modern existence, one that apparently appealed to readers. In 2007, the paper's average weekday circulation had climbed to almost 725,000—its peak through 2024. Provocative headlines like BIMBO SUMMIT, which accompanied a 2006 front-page photo of Lindsay Lohan, Britney Spears, and Paris Hilton together in a car, or WELL HUNG, which heralded the 2006 unveiling of the portrait of Bill Clinton destined for the National Portrait Gallery, alternated with ruthless reads of the day's news. The tabloid's cold-blooded confidence mirrored its patriarch's global success and power. Murdoch's net worth was more than $5 billion; wars in Iraq and Afghanistan fueled Fox News' ratings dominance; and ownership of the *Wall Street Journal*, which Murdoch had long coveted, was in his sights. But the competition was more brutal than ever. In addition to the *Post*'s print competitors, the decade saw the emergence of a series of websites, such as Gawker in 2002 and Radar Online in 2003, that peddled their own brand of instantly published snark while covering many of the same subjects that the *Post* once owned: celebrities, media, real estate, and restaurants. They joined the print dailies in the hunt for scandal and missteps at the *Post*, and the *Post* did not disappoint. The paper's louche office culture and loose ethics were due for a reckoning.

COL ALLAN, editor in chief, 2001–2016; editorial adviser, 2019–2021: I happen to believe in grudges. I happen to believe in getting square. I'm not one of these guys who likes to turn the other cheek and walk away. People fuck me, I'm going to fuck them. It's as simple as that. This is not small-town Tennessee here.

FRED DICKER, Albany bureau chief, 1982–2016: Col was a very tough, difficult guy. He did not have any warmth. He had an angry style. He didn't schmooze with you on the phone. He was right to the point, to the point of harshness. He didn't like journalists, other than maybe himself, getting attention from other media. I used to be invited to be on national shows a lot, especially when Hillary Clinton was running for the Senate and then for president. While I eventually was able to get him to agree to let me do some appearances, he was always reticent about that.

MACKENZIE DAWSON, books editor, 2005–2023: The news meetings were often pretty unpleasant. I used to present the features list every day, and when I was pregnant, toward the end of that pregnancy, I requested that another editor do the news meeting because I had read all this research about how babies can hear stuff on the outside before they're born. I remember thinking, I sure as hell don't want my unborn child hearing an angry Australian ranting. I don't want that to be his first perception of the world.

PETER GREEN, deputy business editor, 2005–2006: When I came in for my initial interview, Col's office was very dark. No lights are on, and there are three TVs tuned to CNN, Fox News, and the Food Network. I ask him, "Why the Food Network?" He says, "So I can fucking relax." He looks at my résumé. He says, "Ah, I see that you worked in Europe, you speak languages, and you covered these wars in Bosnia. You're CIA, right?" I didn't argue with him. Who would? He looks out the window. It's a corner office and you see Sixth Avenue with all the banks and hedge funds based there, and he says, "See all this money. Money is the porn of New York, and we're the pornographers."

JENNIFER FERMINO, reporter, 2001–2013: The joke was that the best kind of stories were RPI—rich people inconvenienced.

MICHAEL RIEDEL, theater columnist, 1998–2020: Right after Hurricane Sandy, half of Staten Island was underwater. In the morning meeting, Col is going down the list of stories and midway down, there's the story that Mayor Bloomberg wants the marathon to go on. He was taking the tactic that Giuliani did after September 11: we're not going to shut down, we're going to show the world we're still in business. It turns out they have two big generators for the tent for the media covering the marathon. Col yells, "Generators for the media? When the people of Staten Island are drowning? With no power? This is the front page tomorrow. We're gonna shut down that New York City Marathon." Boom, front page. That day, Bloomberg announced the New York Marathon would not go on. They weren't the kind of generators you would need in Staten Island, but that was Col putting these things together on the front page—the hurricane, the marathon, and the generators—and Bloomberg had to go back on his decision.

> While other news outlets treated the lead-up to the Iraq war with grim serious-ness, the *Post* found dark humor and a classic headline in France's and Germany's decisions not to get involved in the invasion.

GREGG BIRNBAUM, political editor, 1993–2010: The AXIS OF WEASEL wood was published before the invasion. France and Germany were opposing us at the UN. There was another wood around the same time on which they photo-shopped weasel faces on the UN representatives from some of the countries that voted against the war. AXIS OF WEASEL was such a good tabloid wood, we made T-shirts out of it. I wore one to the Chelsea Piers gym, and a bunch of French guys who were playing basketball went to management and told them to remove me or have me take off the T-shirt.

IAN SPIEGELMAN, Page Six reporter, 1999–2000, 2001–2004: Under Xana, but more so under Col, the *Post* was totally a Republican fucking shit rag. There were no right-wing extremists at the *Post* except for the editor in chief and a couple of lead editors of sections. That doesn't include features, fashion, anything involv-ing women. No one—*no one*—is Republican. Ignoring the shit that came from Fox News was a daily job. Everybody would get news from this little fat fuck from Fox who would come in with his little handful of papers saying, "Look at this story. Look at this story. Do this one." Everyone would have to find a way to politely say, "This is garbage" and not report it.

GREGG BIRNBAUM: Col wanted a military analyst who would write for the news pages about how the battle was proceeding. We got this guy, Harlan Ullman, famous in military circles for developing the shock-and-awe theory of war. Which is what the US was using. So Harlan was writing these columns. He was the biggest prick. You couldn't change a comma on this guy. He would go crazy yelling. Do you remember the DC Madam scandal? [Deborah Jeane Palfrey] was running basically the largest prostitution ring in Washington, catering to ambassadors, government officials, all these types of people. I don't think her black book has ever come out, but a couple of names did. One was Harlan Ullman. That was a wonderful day when I found out he was on that list.

> When the fighting began, the tabloid sent an unlikely correspondent.

GREGG BIRNBAUM: The *Post* embedded three reporters with the US troops. One was Jonathan Foreman, who was a film critic. Col Allan's idea was to bring a different perspective to the war than a regular reporter would. Jonathan agreed to go, and he ended up stumbling upon a massive story. The military unit that he was embedded with was bivouacking in one of Saddam Hussein's mansions, and a number of the soldiers were caught stealing money—hundreds of thousands of US dollars, hidden or left in the house, part of Saddam's riches. These soldiers were arrested. The funniest thing was, Jonathan was a film critic. He wasn't a journalistic writer. We asked him to write a story about what happened, and he filed something like forty inches of copy without a single quote. This is not critical of him, but we had to send him back to talk to people and get live quotes.

> Murdoch's success had taken him far away from the newspaper, but it had not dulled his desire to scoop the competition—which led to his involvement in one of the *Post*'s major gaffes in the aughts: On July 6, 2004, the paper's wood proclaimed Missouri congressman Richard Gephardt as presidential candidate John Kerry's pick for a running mate. KERRY'S CHOICE, as the wood proclaimed, was actually North Carolina senator John Edwards.

GREGG BIRNBAUM: I was the political editor at that point, but I was in London for a wedding. I arrived home in the late evening. [Political reporter] Debbie Orin was calling me. She said, "They told me they're making Gephardt the wood. He's the VP pick. They asked me to try and run this down." She said, "Gregg, I've spent a couple of hours calling everybody I know. Nobody knows a thing. The reason I'm calling you is, I'm asking for my name to be taken off the story, and I want to know that you will back me up on that." I told Debbie, "I will one hundred percent support you." Over time, it was pretty much established that it was a tip that came to Gary Ginsberg, who was a Democratic operative, and a News Corp guy. He was basically Rupert's liaison to the Democratic Party. It went from Gary to Rupert. I don't know if it was Rupert who called the desk or somebody else who called the desk that night and said, "I have the wood."

GARY GINSBERG, former executive vice president, News Corp: That is true. But I actually never spoke to Rupert, which is why I could deny it to the *New York Times*. I had gotten it from a source. I called Rupert to talk to him about it because he always liked political gossip. I never reached him. I left a message. Then we missed each other. I self-flagellated for a long time after that. I felt really bad for Rupert and I felt worse for Col. It was my mistake.

GEORGE KING, sportswriter, baseball, 1997–2020: In October 2006, the Tigers beat the Yankees in Detroit, and it ended their season. The *Daily News* early edition, or maybe it was the website, has it that Steinbrenner is going to fire [team manager] Joe Torre. Torre had won the World Series in '96, '98, '99, 2000 and came within an out or two of winning in 2001. This was the number one sports topic from the day the Yankees got beat in Detroit until two days later when Torre met with the press. I made a couple of calls, and that vibe didn't seem to be going through the whole organization. So I wrote that it's *not* happening. The night before that story ran, I got a call from Greg Gallo. He said, "Somebody upstairs wants to know if this is one hundred percent." Sometime before, they reported that Gephardt was going to be John Kerry's running mate, so I think it was about that. I said, "Yep, we're going with it." I drove to the press conference the next day and pulled into the parking lot at the same time as Torre. I didn't know if he was coming in to clean out his office. He rolls the window down and says, "Stop bothering me" with a smile on his face. I knew then that we were good.

> Political VIPs occasionally toured the newsroom at 1211—at their own risk, as Mayor Michael Bloomberg discovered.

JENNIFER FERMINO, reporter, 2001–2013: The *Post* had a complicated relationship with Bloomberg, The *Post* loves that Upper East Side, monied, philanthropist crowd. That's their base in a lot of ways. Bloomberg was part of that, and there was a level of respect for him. But they hated the nanny stuff. Bloomberg came in to meet with the editorial board, and they came upstairs with a photo of him giving them cupcakes. I had to write a story off the picture because Bloomberg had done all these health things. He banned trans fats and big sodas, and there was the salt thing and calorie counts. [He also banned smoking in bars and restaurants.] The *Post* thought that was just too much government intervention. We did this story about how Mayor Bloomberg brought fatty food to the *New York Post*. Didn't he know how many calories are in the cupcakes? He could have killed us! We did it like he had brought drugs in. The next day, his spokesperson, Stu Loeser, called me at seven a.m. I was asleep. He says, "Do you think you're funny?" I was like, "What do you mean?" He said, "It's a simple question. Do you think you're funny?" I said, "I don't know. I mean, I have my moments." He wasn't yelling at me. He was very calm. It was a real mind fuck. I'm a flack now, and sometimes the game is mental with reporters, and it was just to throw me off my game. But what can you say: they brought cupcakes in. They knew that the *Post* hated all the Nanny Bloomberg stuff. They walked into that one.

DAVID SEIFMAN, City Hall bureau chief, political editor, 1973–2019: I got the scoop that Bloomberg was going to run for a third term. This made the front page and a lot of people didn't believe it. They thought it was the *Post* trying to promote it or something. Eventually, of course, it was true. The *Times* picked it up. The guy who was, at the time, in Room Nine for the *Times*, Mike Barbaro, came over and said, "Someone gave that to you." I thought, "Well, yeah, that's how you get stories. People give you stories." He was so angry about that.

BILL KNAPP, political consultant: You could argue that the *Post* was instrumental in making the Giuliani and Bloomberg eras possible—nineteen years of progress in New York, that really helped turn the city around. The *Post* could legitimately wear that as a badge of honor.

> While intently following post-9/11 developments, the *Post* moved on to other news as well, including the post-presidency of Bill Clinton, who had decided it was better to keep his enemies close.

GARY GINSBERG: In 2001, or 2002, Rupert and I had gone up and seen Clinton at his office in Harlem and spent about three hours covering the world. Rupert, who had never met Clinton before, was dazzled by him. Afterward, Rupert said, "Let's invite him down to News Corp." So we had a lunch for him in one of our dining rooms. Somebody had the idea, let's do a tour of the newsroom after lunch. It was a little awkward only because of all the famous headlines hanging there. There were probably eight or nine headlines of various degrees of embarrassment to Clinton that were hanging on the wall. We were navigating the halls just to make sure he didn't see them and ruin the visit. Bill had moved to New York, and I think he wanted to have a good relationship with the *Post*, which had been a pretty constant irritation to him. He thought, why not meet the people who are directing the coverage and see if I can't put a human face to who I am? It worked to some extent. As I said, Murdoch was really taken by him. I think Col actually liked him, too. Col and I went later and had our own private meeting.

CHRIS WILSON, Page Six reporter, 2000–2006: Rupert and Clinton walked over to us. Rupert said, "This is Page Six. You know Richard [Johnson], don't you?" Richard shook his hand, and Clinton was kind of like, oh, you dirty dog! You guys are bad. He was having a little fun. You felt a presidential vibe, like, this is the big dog. This guy is pretty cool. He's rocking back on his heels and making light of the situation. Then, Richard handed him a copy of *Stuff* magazine that was laying on our cluttered desk with a woman in a bikini on it. He said, "You want to take this home?" Clinton said, "No, thanks."

> The early aughts ushered in the advent of branding—establishing one's brand, building one's brand, and marketing one's brand. The *Post*'s premier brand was Page Six. While new "It" girls rose and fell in its items, and publicists begged the column's reporters to run stories that contained incongruous plugs for liquor and fashion brands, the paper's powers attempted to build on the number one brand in gossip, which was now attracting the blue-chip ads that Peter Price and Valerie Salembier had worked so hard to bring in during the Kalikow days.

CHRIS WILSON: I've told people that I was the first person to write about Paris Hilton on Page Six. If I wasn't the first, I was one of the first. I covered her quite a bit in the early years because she was up and coming, and she was very accessible. She would call you. One time she called me and said, "I know I ran into you last night at the party but I'm actually grounded. I'm supposed to be staying at the Plaza for the night." I said, "No problem. I wasn't planning on noting your presence in the item but good to know. I hope you're not grounded for too long."

RICHARD JOHNSON, Page Six editor, 1978–1990, 1993–2019: I'm not embarrassed that we wrote about her. But there's not a sense of pride.

LISA MARSH, fashion/retail business reporter, 2000–2003: When I was there, we had a Paris Hilton moratorium for a while. Every once in a while they would put the kibosh on mentioning somebody unless there was a really great story.

RICHARD JOHNSON: I got the sense that Page Six's reputation was growing, the way they were promoting it, and the way they kept on adding space. I think I complained, occasionally, that, you know, you used to pay Neal Travis to fill the page opposite Page Six. And now you're asking me to do it for free.

CHRIS WILSON: The typical pitch would be something like: Ja Rule was spotted dancing at Conscience Point nightclub with Lindsay Lohan, while wearing Diesel jeans and sipping Svedka vodka. In one sentence you'd have three products. I'm like, "Don't you think it will be kind of obvious?"

RICHARD JOHNSON: As Page Six got bigger and bigger, they never consulted me about anything. But they did hire people. A lot of things didn't work out. I remember they did something that was supposed to be like TMZ but based in New York. But they didn't really get any good video. So why would you tune into this thing? I thought they were going to have more freelancers with cameras out there chasing celebrities around. That's what I would have told them to do. If they'd asked.

CHRIS WILSON: It was pre-algorithm, pre-traffic, pre-Google reports, so I could say to Richard, "I've got a scoop. Handsome Dick Manitoba [former frontman of punk band The Dictators] is dropping a new album." Richard would say, "Sounds good to me." He'd be working on a story about the archduke of Slovakia. We weren't beholden to traffic, so we could do high and low, uptown and downtown. Nowadays, it would be, who the fuck cares? Get me some Kardashian news.

GRAYDON CARTER, former editor, *Vanity Fair*; founder and co-editor, Air Mail: Of course it bothered me when I was on Page Six for some unflattering reason, but at the same time, I tried to take the advice I gave to other people who got upset over something about them on Page Six. I said, "Outside of this one story today, name one story on Page Six about anybody else you know, going back to when you started reading it." Nobody can. If there are ten stories on Page Six about you, like poor Alec Baldwin, that's going to stick. If there's one incident of you not holding the door open for somebody, that's not going to stick. Why fight with Page Six if there's no future in it?

ISAAC MIZRAHI, fashion designer: I know people who, even if it's a malicious item about them on Page Six, they send someone out to buy like twenty copies of the *Post.* There is something really wonderful about being on Page Six. You've arrived. It's like being in the *New York Times* crossword puzzle.

In the first decade of the 2000s, a surfeit of start-ups came online that exploded the original concept of Page Six. Whereas the column was an amalgamation of insider stories about New York, Washington, and Hollywood, these websites specialized. In addition to Gawker, which initially focused on media, Curbed covered real estate; Eater, the restaurant industry; TMZ, video mishaps of celebrities; Deadline Hollywood, the entertainment industry; Valleywag, the tech industry; Politico, obvious; and Deadspin, sports. (And that is hardly a comprehensive list.) The immediacy of the internet enabled these sites to break stories instantly—even if some of them were shabbily reported—which increasingly stole the thunder of print publications. But the *Post*, which had been in the gossip game for decades, initially held its own with a strong Wall Street–focused business section; Keith Kelly's Media Ink column; Michael Riedel's Broadway coverage; a top-notch sports section; mob coverage; and what was essentially the blueprint for the blogosphere, Page Six. Making the move to the internet would prove difficult for the *Post*.

KEITH KELLY, media columnist, 1998–2021: Col Allan hated Gawker. The bosses all hated it. I always thought part of the reason they hated it was because the Gawker people, at their inception, did what we did. And they did it faster. They also did it with lower journalistic standards. But they said, we're going to be very snarky. We're going to be very media-centric. They took the formula of Page Six gossip, and media coverage gossip, and melded it into a whole business. Eventually, they had to branch out because that's kind of a closed audience. But they did build a successful business, and media was their foundation.

RICHARD JOHNSON: Suddenly, a lot of celebrities who we used to write about are not getting publicists. They're doing their own press on the internet. And then everybody's getting it at the same time. It's like, you can't even write about it anymore, because it's not even gossip.

KEITH KELLY: When I was first there, in the '90s, it was no, no, no, don't put a story on the web. It has to go in the paper first. At some point, they realize that's not the way to do it; put it on the web as fast as you can. The print version almost became "the best of" yesterday's web version.

JARED STERN, Page Six reporter, Page Six Magazine editor, 1996–2003, 2004–2006: They really fucked up PageSix.com [which launched in 2008 and shut down three months later]. They spent a lot of money, and we had a big party at Guastavino's under the 59th Street Bridge. It was before social media became huge. I feel like it might have been James Murdoch's brainchild. I don't know why they shut it down. They were so ahead of the curve.

MICHAEL SHAIN, television editor, 1978–1993, 1996–2013: The one thing that's always escaped not just the *Post* but Murdoch altogether is digital. He has never once created anything in new media, and everything he's touched in new media has turned to shit, like MySpace. There's no reason in the world that TMZ should exist. There should have been a Page Six television show many years before that, that did what TMZ does. But he just never saw that. That's his biggest failing. At this point, to use a horse racing metaphor, they're just trying to run in the money. They're not even trying to get out in front of anything. He never saw the future. I can't blame him for that. There's a lot of us who didn't.

PETER GREEN: There was a lot of focus on the finance market and people in New York. [Business Editor] Dan Colarusso was fantastic at that. I said to him that he knew all the players in New York finance the way I used to know everyone on the Yankees—what position they played and what they did at last night's game. Keith Kelly covered the media like cops and robbers. What Keith could never do was meet a deadline. I gave him an alarm clock when he retired full-time from the *Post*. His wife thought it was the funniest thing, but he did not. Every Tuesday and Thursday, when Keith's copy was ready, we had a souvenir bell from the New York Stock Exchange, and we would ring it. Then all the copy editors would leap into action. We'd each take a piece of Keith's story and hope that we were able to chop it down to fit and still make sense. Keith had to be in the first edition because Rupert had to read it. The column was delivered to wherever Rupert was.

> Although Murdoch's attempts to establish a digital footprint fizzled, the *Post* was way ahead of the curve when it came to the buzzword that emerged in the tech world in the 2000s: disruption. Its news stories, editorials, and Page Six were dedicated to upending conventional wisdom and the status quo, whether through wiseass humor, outright mockery, investigative journalism, and sometimes, simply asking questions that other reporters were too polite—or afraid—to ask.

TARA PALMERI, City Hall/politics reporter, 2010–2015: Before the *Blue Valentine* premiere, we heard that Michelle Williams was hooking up on set with her co-star Ryan Gosling, for real, in between the sex scenes. I go up to her at the premiere, and I say, "Hi, Michelle, I write for Page Six. The sex scenes looked real. We heard that you guys were hooking up during that entire shoot." She freaked out and called over the publicist. They all were screaming at me. Everyone was having a meltdown, Michelle was yelling at me, asking me where I went to college and all this stuff. It was such a thing, and everyone said, "Oh, it's because of Heath Ledger. She's still so sensitive." The next thing I know I'm being cornered by Harvey Weinstein [the Weinstein Company distributed the film] at the Boom Boom Room at The Standard hotel, and he's like, "You cannot write about what she said to you." I said, "I'm going to write about it. She had a meltdown in the middle of the Boom Boom Room, and what are you going to do about it?" He was really bullying me. He's like, "I'm going to talk to Emily [Smith, then editor of Page Six]. I've got a better story for you guys anyway." Then he brings Ryan Gosling over to me, and I'm in total awe. I was so flustered I dropped my drink on him. I think, ultimately, we didn't run the story because Harvey did give Emily a better one.

MIKE VACCARO, lead sports columnist, 2002–current: When I went from the Newark *Star-Ledger* to the *Post*, I remember talking to [former New York Yankee] Bernie Williams and he said, "I'm going to be interested to see how your columns change." [Former New York Met] Mike Piazza's first reaction was, "Oh my god, are you going to work for Page Six?"

MARC BERMAN, sportswriter, basketball and tennis, 1997–current: Latrell Sprewell reported to training camp with a broken hand. No one knew how it had happened, and we broke the story that he did it on his yacht during a party. He broke his hand because of a fight. He threw a punch, missed, and hit a wall. He got a boxer's fracture. That story caused a lot of agita because he took us to court, but it was dismissed.

MIKE VACCARO: I was covering a Nets playoff series in Milwaukee. Gallo asked me to stay in Milwaukee and cover the Mets series that weekend. It was May and the Mets were already falling apart. I wrote a column on general manager Steve Phillips. He'd assembled a team of profoundly unlikable players, I would not write this now, but I wrote then that Mets fans aren't just mad, they want Steve Phillips's head on a pike and they want to put that pike on the Triborough Bridge. Back then, I'm surprised they didn't put a cartoon of Phillips's bloody head on a pike on the back page. That Saturday I reported to the ballpark in Milwaukee and Jay Horwitz, the PR director, said, "We might have a problem with Steve. He's gonna want to see you when you're in the clubhouse." I said, "That's fine." In those situations, I'm not looking for a fight. If you're going to rip them, you got to let them rip you back. Steve brings me into this empty office. He purposely kept the door open. He wanted the players to hear him air me out. He aired me out, and I took it. Then he went a bit farther than he should have. He said, "You made my wife cry. That's the worst part." Now, the backstory is that Steve Phillips was a serial adulterer. That had already been in the paper. He'd been suspended by the Mets because he just couldn't stay faithful to his wife for, like, more than ten minutes at a time. I said, "You know what, Steve? I'm not the only one in this room that has done that, am I?" As soon as I said it, here comes Steve Phillips, about ready to punch me in the jaw. Jay got in the middle and he dragged Steve out of there. I walked out, and I'm a little shaky, because you don't like it when somebody yells at you for five minutes straight, and Tom Glavine, Al Leiter, and a bunch of guys came over and said, "That was awesome." Phillips got fired about three weeks later.

KEITH KELLY: Whenever we would mention [New York Times Company chairman] Pinch Sulzberger, we would show him in a Mexican sombrero and a black eye. He was a victim of a mugging at some point in the '90s. So we sent a reporter to stake him out outside his house. He comes out. He turns and looks, boom, we get the picture. He had a big black eye. Anytime we mentioned him, we'd run the picture. We photoshopped in the sombrero when he took all that money from [Mexican business magnate] Carlos Slim.

JILL ABRAMSON, former executive editor, *The New York Times*: The *Post* bullies people. It certainly bullied Arthur [Sulzberger Jr., known to some as "Pinch"], which I thought was cruel and uncalled for and inaccurate and unfair. And they always ran that idiotic picture of him in the sombrero with a black eye. He had been hurt in an accident where someone on a bike hit him.

RICHARD KORNBERG, theater and dance publicist: One of the reasons *Hairspray* tried out in Seattle was Michael Riedel. Margo Lion, the producer, made the point that she wanted to be as far away from Michael as could be, because she wanted the show to be able to get its strength before he attacked it. Ultimately, when *Hairspray* was such a huge hit in Seattle and before it came to New York, Margo would say to me, "Do you think Michael would fly out to Seattle to see how wonderful *Hairspray* is?"

MICHAEL RIEDEL: I was on a tear against Bernadette Peters in *Gypsy*, this very Brechtian, Sam Mendes–directed version that was terrible. Bernadette was totally miscast in it and lost at sea. Arthur Laurents, the writer, hated it, and he wasn't speaking to Sam Mendes. Then, and I'm sure it was in direct response to all that I'd written, [*New York Times* theater critic] Ben Brantley gave the show an out-and-out rave review. I thought, "Hmm, well, that kind of abrogates my last four weeks of columns." But this is when the journalism gods give you a gift. The day Bernadette Peters got that rave review, she announced she was taking time off for vocal rest. We put her on the side of a milk carton: "Have you seen this woman?" We were back at it, going at it full tilt. Col loved that stuff. He loved wars, he loved feuds.

Page Six's popularity came with a cost. The column was at its most readable when it was taking down the rich, powerful, and famous, as well as the media establishment. This dynamic produced a number of enemies who waited for the column's reporters and its editor to stumble. The cascade of missteps began when Page Six reporter Ian Spiegelman gave a talk at the Learning Annex during which he described the column's fondness for vendetta, saying it was "a lot like being in a Mafia family." His remarks were recorded and later broadcast, which did not go over well with his superiors.

Scrutiny of Page Six escalated in 2006 when California business magnate and billionaire Ron Burkle—who had taken a number of hits in the column—accused one of its reporters, Jared Stern, of extortion by allegedly seeking Burkle's investment in a clothing company or a job as a media adviser in exchange for better treatment on the page. Recordings Burkle made of meetings with Stern—in one case, attended by an assistant US attorney and a federal agent—led to a federal investigation.

DAN MANGAN. reporter, rewrite, 2000–2013: I was going to leave for the afternoon and I walked by Lukas Alpert, a friend of mine who was also a rewrite guy. Lukas looked like somebody had shot his cat. He tells me about Jared. The FBI was there, and he was writing a story that there was this investigation into the possible extortion of Ron Burkle.

KEITH KELLY: Burkle, a friend of Bill Clinton's, said, "I'm getting shaken down by this guy." Burkle is influential, so the FBI says, "We'll set up a sting operation." In the sting operation, it appeared Burkle was trying to coax Stern into saying, "How much would it cost for maximum protection, $10,000?" Stern is like, "Yeah, I guess that probably would give you protection." He was agreeing to leading questions, so the FBI said, it doesn't look like there's anything we can make stand up in court. Knowing that the investigation had not officially been shut down, but the feds were not going to press charges, Burkle leaked it to the *Daily News*: "FBI is investigating." Jared was a fall guy because he didn't do the correct thing and say, "Nah, we can't take money from you." He didn't give the proper answers. It made Page Six look a little shady.

JARED STERN: The *Post* was pretty quick to throw me under the bus. I was a freelancer, so it was pretty easy to cut me loose and hope they weren't going to have any other scandals.

DAN MANGAN: The story about Richard and Jared explodes. It's a huge story, and the *Daily News* is going to town with it because they got the scoop. Among the many interesting things about the story was that the *Times* actually did a better job. The *Times* moved the ball. They broke stuff that suggested there was a pay-for-play situation.

CHRIS WILSON: It was totally misrepresented in the press, a way to punish Page Six for being the punisher and skewering the rest of the media for all those years. That's why it was on the front page of the *New York Times*, and the *Daily News* lost their minds.

KEITH KELLY: After the Page Six thing, the *Post* instituted a rule that you could not accept gifts worth more than $25. Maybe they had the rule before in the employee handbook, but nobody read it. I was pissed off because I had the scoop about Graydon Carter getting ready to step down from *Vanity Fair*. I called but he was away. It was a holiday weekend. Next thing I know there's a story in the *New York Times* with a photo of him at his home on Bank Street. I was cursing him out high and low. He sends me a bottle of really expensive single malt whiskey and says, "Sorry about the *Times*, I owe you one." I sent word that I could not accept a gift worth more than $25 so I would have to give the whiskey to the homeless.

> The *Times* and Deadline Hollywood also reported on deals that Richard Johnson and Page Six reporter Paula Froelich had with another frequent subject of the column, Harvey Weinstein, the co-founder of Miramax Films and later The Weinstein Company. According to Deadline, Johnson was attached to write a remake of the 2000 French comedy *Jet Set*. And in 2005, Miramax Books had published Froelich's *It! Nine Secrets of the Rich and Famous That Will Take You to the Top*. (A *Post* spokesman told the *Times* that Miramax had acquired the book at auction and that Froelich did not write about Weinstein.)

RICHARD JOHNSON: People would accuse me of having been poisoned by Harvey's influence because one time he gave me a movie and said, "You should write the screenplay." I took the thing home, watched it, and that was it. I never got a contract. I never got any money.

MICHAEL WOLFF, author, *The Fall: The End of Fox News and the Murdoch Dynasty*: At one point, I had written something negative about Harvey Weinstein, and Page Six took after me. It wasn't even that terrible what I had written. Maybe I called him fat. So, I called Richard, who I've certainly known and basically been friendly with, and said, "What's going on?" He said, "Don't underestimate the power of Harvey Weinstein on this page." Later, I kind of confronted Harvey and said, "What was that?" He said, "I totally own Richard."

JUDA ENGELMAYER, spokesman for Harvey Weinstein: Harvey *never* said he owned Page Six, and he never attacked Michael Wolff. If anything, Page Six owned Harvey, and Harvey would only use Page Six to promote something.

RICHARD JOHNSON: Michael Wolff is a fabulist, whose best fantasies star himself as a fearless truth-seeker.

> In early 2007, the US attorney decided not to bring charges against Jared Stern, and in March of that year, Stern filed a defamation suit against the *Daily News* and Burkle, among other parties. The lawsuit was dismissed, but not before the *Post* was embarrassed by its own hand when Page Six, in an attempt to get ahead of others covering the story, published an unsworn affidavit from Ian Spiegelman. The allegations included Richard Johnson taking a cash gift from a Manhattan restaurant owner and Col Allan accepting sexual favors at Scores, a Manhattan strip club.

IAN SPIEGELMAN: They did it to pull the teeth out of what Jared's lawyer was threatening.

COL ALLAN: The *Daily News* was having a field day and I believed we owed it to our readers to publish the truth about the episode. Richard was in error to accept money from a restaurant for Christmas drinks [for the Page Six staff]. He was disciplined just short of losing his job. As for me accepting favors from a sex club, it was a disgrace manufactured by the *Daily News* without the courage to publish. It hinged on a FBI wiretap of the so-called "Soccer Mom Madam" saying one of her clients was a "top editor" at the *Post*. The cowards at the *News* gave the story to the *New York Observer*, which published. I sent Jared Kushner [Donald Trump's son-in-law, then the *Observer*'s owner] a legal letter setting out that the tape was recorded in 1996 when I was working in Sydney! The *Observer* corrected this outrage, but of course the damage was done.

DAN MANGAN: The paper is sometimes tone deaf, and when they get called on either a mistake, a slip-up, or a problem with the way they're doing something, their reaction is not to step back, it's to punch back. They dig in.

> While the dot-com explosion led many media companies to move away from print, Murdoch's appetite for newspapers never waned.

KEITH KELLY: News Corp was trying to buy *Newsday* around the time they were trying to buy the *Wall Street Journal*. Sam Zell owned Tribune Media, which owned *Newsday* then. He kind of double-crossed us. This is around 2008. I'm trying to remember the price—I think $580 million. The *Post* said, "Could be a good fit. We could combine forces, sell ads to the city and suburbs." *Newsday* was much more vibrant then. The talks were very serious. But Sam Zell, double-crossing sleazebag, tells Mort Zuckerman, who says, "I'll match that." Zell says, "I have two offers. So now I gotta make a public disclosure and start an auction." The Dolans [who own Cablevision] lived on Long Island, and they revered *Newsday*. They said, "We'll offer $650 million." Zell probably thought Rupert was going to come back and top the offer. He didn't. The Dolans bought it. It was a fiasco. Probably one of the best deals Murdoch never made. As bad as MySpace was, this was as good. It balances out. [Murdoch bought MySpace in 2005 for $580 million and sold it in 2011 for $35 million.]

NORMAN PEARLSTINE, former executive editor, *The Wall Street Journal*: When [Murdoch] was trying to take over Dow Jones in 2006 or 2007—watching him then, it was masterful to see how many people he was talking to, how much information he was able to assemble. He was just trolling for information, and he knew I knew some of the people in the Bancroft family that controlled Dow Jones. He was a master chess player—what would it take to get the deal done?

JOHN WATERS, filmmaker: I actually think Murdoch made the London *Times* and the *Wall Street Journal* better. I know that's heresy to some. I read the editorials in the *Wall Street Journal* every day because I like to read how the smartest people that don't agree with me think. And if I want to read how the dumbest people think, I read the *Post*. Their editorials verge on Ed Anger, if you can remember him, he was the [*Weekly World News*'] most radical, ridiculous reporter. [*Post* columnist] Andrea Peyser falls within the Ed Anger category.

28 | POLITICS AS USUAL

Pols with Penis Problems, a Pussy Grabber Runs for President

The 2010s were en route to becoming a dystopian opera thanks in large part to one of the *Post*'s favorite characters, Donald Trump, who eventually won the editorial support of Rupert Murdoch and *Post* editor Col Allan. Trump had virtually disappeared from the front page of the *Post* starting in the summer of 2000 and didn't reappear until 2004, with the debut of his Mark Burnett–produced NBC TV show *The Apprentice* and his 2005 marriage to model Melania Knauss—which was attended by a number of *Post* staffers.

GEORGE RUSH, Page Six reporter, 1986–1993: Because Trump was so outrageous there were a lot of stories that you ran just because he was insulting, for instance, Rosie O'Donnell, who was a notorious liberal. But by the time I reached the *Daily News* in the 1990s, I remember Ed Kosner, our editor at the time, telling us he did not want to read Donald Trump stories. We should banish him to a desert island for a while. He would call, and nobody wanted to talk to him. It was, *not again*—who cares? We said, we will have to call you back. Then he discovered television, and that was a superior tool for his brand, where he reached a much larger audience.

ROGER STONE, political consultant and lobbyist: Trump first captures the tabloid culture and then pop culture. The thing that really puts him on the map is *The Apprentice*. The elites get the difference between entertainment and news, but to the average voter, it's all television. And Trump couldn't look any better.

500

He's perfectly lit. He's perfectly coiffed. He's perfectly made up. He's in the high-backed chair. He's acting decisively, the way they'd like their president to act. It's *The Apprentice* that brings him into a whole new stratosphere. People say, "Wow. If I were rich, that's how I'd want to live." You know, the limousines, the mansions, the jet planes. A huge part of this is aspirational.

MICHAEL SHAIN, television editor, 1978–1993, 1996–2013: We did a Sunday TV supplement for a while, and Trump was the cover of our first one. It was the season finale of the first year of *The Apprentice*. He was going to pick who was going to be the apprentice. I went to my neighborhood hardware store in Middle Village and bought an ax, which I gave to the photographer and said, "Trump is expecting you. Get me a picture of him wielding the ax, and that'll be the cover."

JENNIFER FERMINO, reporter, 2001–2013: I was the on-the-ground reporter outside of Mar-a-Lago when Trump married Melania, and inside the wedding were Cindy Adams, Richard Johnson, Col Allan, and I feel like even more people from the *Post*.

MICHAEL WOLFF, author, *The Fall: The End of Fox News and the Murdoch Dynasty*: Donald is a tabloid figure, and part of the reason Murdoch can't stand him is that he saw him as a tabloid figure. He had contempt for these people. He saw Trump as a clown. Murdoch is ultimately conservative in the more basic sense. He's very buttoned-down, not flamboyant. He thinks people should behave a certain way. If you're someone who is in charge, then you should behave like a businessman.

TARA PALMERI, City Hall/politics reporter, 2010–2015: I was at the Republican National Convention in 2012, and at that point, Col had said, "Enough stories about Donald Trump running for president." We had been writing about it all the time, and he was done with it. I was at the RNC, they had just nominated Mitt Romney, and Trump called me. He was like, "Write this down. I just met with John McCain, and he thinks I have a shot at the nomination." I was like, "What party?" I kind of gave him a little bit more 'tude than I would have normally. I said, "Mr. Trump, I'm sorry but we really can't write about this anymore because there's a nominee, and it's not going to happen." He never called me again after that. I always think about it. I was, like, twenty-six at the time, and I was like, you're not running, okay. Then lo and behold, four years later it really freaking happened.

As Trump's star rose for a second time, the paper soldiered on without two of its legends, who were also outsized characters in the ongoing novel that is New York: Steve "Street Dog" Dunleavy and Cindy Adams. Dunleavy retired in 2008.

KEN CHANDLER, editor in chief, publisher, 1978–1986, 1993–2002: It was great until Dunleavy started setting the office on fire. He would come back from Langan's, light a cigarette, and fall asleep. Right above his desk—smoke detector. Once they couldn't wake him up.

MARSHA KRANES, rewrite, editor, 1974–2005: At one point, I would come in around six or seven o'clock in the morning and be the first editor there. There'd be a couple of copykids answering phones. I walked in one morning and one of them came running over and said, "Marsha, Dunleavy. I think he's dead." She leads me over and he's sprawled face down on the floor. I said, "Steve. Steve." I tried to move him. She said, "He doesn't respond. Nothing." So I said, "Well, call 911." EMS comes running in, they look at him and say, "Oh, it's Dunleavy. That's okay. We know where to take him." They carried him across the street. He had a room behind the bar or in the bar across the street, at Langan's.

MACKENZIE DAWSON, books editor, 2005–2023: One night he had done his usual Dunleavy thing and come back to the newsroom after a night of drinking and vomited on Jesse Angelo's desk. I think Jesse was metro editor then. A new day rolls around, and people are giggling because they're like, what's Jesse's reaction going to be?

JESSE ANGELO, publisher and CEO, 1999–2019: It was mostly in the wastebasket, but a good amount on my desk. And he was passed out next to it, also on my desk. After I woke him and yelled at him, he went to the bathroom, put on some hairspray, and came out and told me he was going to federal court to cover something. I told him he could not represent the paper in the state he was in and sent him home. A half hour later, I was with Col going through the morning list and the phone rang—it was Myron saying, "Dunleavy for you." Dunleavy tried to apologize and said that, back in the day, it was actually a compliment—to which I yelled into the phone at the top of my lungs, "WHEN IN THE HISTORY OF JOURNALISM WAS IT A COMPLIMENT TO PUKE ON YOUR BOSS'S DESK!" And slammed the phone down.

In 2010, two years after Dunleavy's retirement, Cindy Adams's column disappeared from the paper as she battled a life-threatening health issue. That same year claimed both Yankees owner George Steinbrenner and Elaine's owner Elaine Kaufman.

DICK BELSKY, metropolitan editor, 1970–1989: Cindy almost died at one point. My understanding is that she had some health issue and didn't go to doctors or didn't believe in them. [Adams is, or was, a Christian Scientist. She did not respond to questions asking if she is still a member of the church.] One of her best friends is Judge Judy [Sheindlin], and she made Cindy go to a hospital. She was very sick for a long time.

CINDY ADAMS, gossip columnist, 1981–current: I left the paper for five months in 2010. I had an appendicitis thing, and it got infected. I was in surgery for a while. I was in the hospital. They said I wasn't going to make it. The day I came back home, I had IVs in my arm. I had nurses. I was a wreck. Joan Rivers came over and made me sit through a ninety-minute documentary on Joan Rivers. I said, "Joan, I just came out of the friggin' goddamn hospital. I'm dying." She says, "You've got to see the documentary." We sat in the kitchen and watched the documentary. I didn't work for five months. I was weak. I didn't care or have the energy. I certainly wasn't going to talk to PR people. I wasn't going to write. I didn't want to do it anymore. But Col Allan would never replace me. He told me of all the people who tried to take my place, who said, "I can write exactly the way Cindy can, and I'll be a lot cheaper." He said, "It doesn't make any difference. We're waiting until she comes back." Nobody else in the world would do that.

GEORGE KING, sportswriter, baseball, 1997–2020: When George Steinbrenner died it became a whole different deal from A to Z as far as the Yankee experience. When he was alive and you worked for the *Post*, when the Yankees just lost eight out of ten games, call George because nine times out of ten, he's going to give you the back page. If Alex Rodriguez or another superstar is not playing very well, call George. His son, Hal, who runs the Yankees now, is not that way.

FRANK DiGIACOMO, Page Six co-editor, 1989–1993: The deaths of Elaine Kaufman and Steinbrenner marked a generational shift. They were good friends—she once showed me the World Series ring that George had given her—and they both loved the press. They liked the power of whispering in some reporter's ear—with Steinbrenner it was more like bellowing—and a few days later, it's in the papers.

> Dunleavy died in 2019, at the age of eighty-one. "Steve Dunleavy was one of the greatest reporters of all time," Rupert Murdoch said in the *Post*'s obituary. "His passing is the end of a great era." Though Dunleavy often championed questionable, if not repugnant, people and causes (in his mind, no cop could do wrong, even those involved in the Abner Louima case), he had become a beloved figure in the city, a vestige of a long gone, heavily debauched era of newspapering. The *New York Times* and the *New Yorker* profiled him, and when Dunleavy retired, the headline on Ray Kerrison's column, splashed across two pages of a special tribute section in the *Post*, was "50 wild years of news and booze with the man who's the king of both."

GEORGE RUSH, Page Six reporter, 1986–1993: I wasn't at the *Post* during Dunleavy's last years there, but I gather that some thought he'd lost a step. I had a drink with [then–executive editor] Jesse Angelo around 2010. He lamented, "I don't know what's happened to him. I can write a Dunleavy column better than Dunleavy." After all his years of hell-raising, maybe the gray street dog was, understandably, a little tired. Or maybe the transition of newspapers from print to digital had left him dispirited.

BARBARA ROSS, political reporter, 1978–1985: It was amazing [that he lived as long as he did]. I think of all the other people that went earlier, like Mike McAlary and John Cotter, people who didn't make their fifties. Dunleavy was eighty-something.

DEVLIN BARRETT, reporter, 1992–2002: I always sort of weirdly respected the degree to which Dunleavy used to be a boss at the *Post*, and then came back and just worked as a writer. To me, that said something about his basic work ethic. For all his ego, in some ways he did not have much ego. Which is why I always tended to think of him as more of an actor than anything. He always seemed to me to be playing a role as far as he could take it.

CHARLIE CARILLO, reporter, columnist, 1978–1993: An editor from another paper who didn't care for Dunleavy's style once told me that if only Steve had some proper training when he was younger, he could really have been something. But he totally missed the point. Like they say, you don't put a saddle on a mustang. Steve ran long and hard, and his path was his own. He didn't die, he just wore out. And that's not a bad way to go.

Sexual misconduct became one of the running themes of the decade, ending the careers of two promising New York politicians: Hard-nosed governor Eliot Spitzer became caught up in a prostitution scandal and was alleged to have worn black dress socks while having sex (which he denied). New York congressman and mayoral candidate Anthony Weiner did prison time and was required to register as a sex offender after sexting a minor. FBI agents investigating emails on Weiner's laptop found messages between Weiner's wife, Huma Abedin, and Hillary Clinton that resulted in "the October Surprise," an FBI investigation just days before the 2016 presidential election, which was thought to have contributed to Clinton's loss. In addition to voluminous coverage, the scandals resulted in a bonanza of ribald *Post* front pages. The Spitzer woods included ELIOT'S BEST LAID PLAN, SOCK IT TO SPITZER, and HERE WE HO AGAIN! The Weiner woods (no pun intended) were endless: WEINER ROAST, WEINER EXPOSED, WEINER: I'LL STICK IT OUT, and OBAMA BEATS WEINER. Spitzer's replacement, David Paterson, who is legally blind, came in for a different type of dunning, and Mayor Michael Bloomberg's successor, Bill de Blasio, became a political piñata.

TARA PALMERI: I loved the Eliot Spitzer scandals. I loved the Anthony Weiner scandals. Keith Olbermann, Alec Baldwin . . . I would make a list of all the people the *Post* hated and keep it on my desk.

FRED DICKER, Albany bureau chief, 1982–2016: I wrote stories about what was called Troopergate, in which Spitzer was using state troopers to spy on Senate Majority Leader Joe Bruno. There were repeated stories that led to talk of impeachment, and led to a report that was extremely damaging to him that was put out by then–attorney general Andrew Cuomo. So Spitzer would be furious at the *Post*. He would call up editors, but all the things I wrote were true and he would back down. Then attention shifted to his prostitution scandal, and that was the end of him.

GARY GINSBERG, former executive vice president, News Corp: Rupert and I were flying back from Florida when the Spitzer news broke. We were sitting on the tarmac, and he called Col. He was like rubbing his hands together, going, "This is going to be one of the greatest headlines of all time." They had so much fun discussing options, [saying], let's keep close because this has got to be the headline of all headlines. He was pretty happy with it afterward. [The intitial wood was HO NO!] He had this whole thing with Col—it's all about the headline.

BILL KNAPP, political consultant: [Even before Weiner's sexting scandal], the *Post* was instrumental in driving Weiner out of the race for mayor when Bloomberg was running for reelection. We leaked constant stuff to the *Post* about all of Weiner's craziness—his not getting along with staff, his firing people, his romances, his vacations—all sorts of stuff. We just destroyed the guy through the *Post*. When the *Post* gets on to something, they get *on to* it.

> Governor Paterson initially thought the paper would deal with him evenhandedly, but he soon learned otherwise.

DAVID PATERSON, former governor of New York: When I first came in, Murdoch met with me. I think he really liked me, and I told him that oddly enough, we're going to wind up on the same side because we're going to have a huge budget deficit and the legislature doesn't want to fix it. The Democrats say tax the rich, and the Republicans say cut the budget. I was going to have to do both. I said, "I'm not going to make any friends up here and to whatever extent you could be supportive, I think I'm doing the right thing for the state," to which he agreed. This is mid-2008 into the end of 2008. But then in October, the *Post* writes an editorial headlined "Paterson's Eyes." After my secretary Charles O'Byrne had to resign for tax reasons, they said this was a severe blow to me because now there's no one to read to me. Actually, when I have my glasses on, I can read for a couple of minutes. I only see out of my right eye, and my vision is 20/400, but there were 200,000 people on the fucking payroll and they could all read. Then that December on *Saturday Night Live*, Fred Armisen does the famous imitation of me. Some of it I thought was funny, but what I didn't think was funny was equating a disability to stupidity. They had me falling down and holding maps upside down. By the way, I did hold a map upside down once. I don't think they knew about that, but it did happen. What *SNL* did was spark this chain reaction where everything was somehow connected to my vision, and I pretty much got a weekly dose of it from the *Post*. While they're doing all this, Murdoch calls and tells me he has a suggestion for who should fill the

Senate seat vacated by Hillary Clinton when she became secretary of state: Caroline Kennedy. I did not know when he called that his children [Murdoch's two daughters with his third wife, Wendi Deng] and her children had gone to the same school. There was a real friendship there. I thought, oh, we don't like Democrats until they become close friends. That totally surprised me.

GARY GINSBERG: Rupert had met Caroline a number of times when she was working at the New York City Department of Education. She was doing outreach. [Former schools chancellor and later, News Corp executive vice president] Joel Klein is a very close associate and friend of Rupert's, and Caroline was working with Joel. So we got to know her in that capacity. I think he was really impressed with her. So when she expressed interest in the US Senate seat, we did something in the paper to show support. I think we endorsed her. That was Rupert. It was going to be a Democrat so why not her? [After Kennedy removed herself from the running, Governor Paterson named Kirsten Gillibrand to replace Hillary Clinton.]

ERIC FETTMANN, associate editorial page editor, columnist, 1976–1991, 1993–2019: One of Col's favorite drinking buddies was Governor David Paterson.

DAVID PATERSON: I remember going to Elaine's with Col one night, and we must have been three or four drinks in, and I told him that I was going to commission an investigation of the state police because of some odd things that had happened there. Dicker was reporting on them, and he thought there should be one. Andrew Cuomo wanted to be the person to do the investigating. Finally I told them, "Okay, we'll do it." Allan calls the desk and changes the whole front page right in front of me. I was like, man, when I get buried, I don't want to be known as the former governor. I want to be known as the man who changed the front page of the *Post* at twelve o'clock in the morning.

FRED DICKER: The *Post* went after Paterson a great deal. I wound up getting him fined by the State Ethics Commission for accepting free tickets to the World Series at Yankee Stadium. I had to fight initially with Col to get it into print. He didn't think it was any big deal. On one level you could say, it's not a big deal. But for the governor of the state of New York to take freebies from the Yankees, when, in fact, the state has a critical role in granting tax exemptions and regulations and other things that the Yankees want, it's a significant story. Bottom line, Governor Paterson wound up getting fined [$62,125], including the price of the tickets. It was a huge story.

TARA PALMERI: De Blasio was a perpetual target. He was almost like a character in a cartoon. I had a good scoop about how he didn't have security clearance to get classified information from the federal government because of his trips to Nicaragua and his work with the Sandinistas.

DAVID SEIFMAN, City Hall bureau chief, political editor, 1973–2019: I have never seen a mayor who was so despised by so many people. I ran into people in progressive Brooklyn who hated de Blasio. I ran into people on the Upper East Side who hated him. I can't find one person that I've spoken to who has a good thing to say about him. This guy had everything going for him. He had an economy that was booming. He had people on his side. It's a progressive city. He's a progressive. He talked a good game. He just couldn't do much. He had so many opportunities that he missed.

> Despite the *Post*'s staunch conservatism, Murdoch was captivated by Barack Obama, and the paper did not support Donald Trump's claims that the forty-fourth president of the United States was not born in the United States. Yet in February 2009, barely a month into Obama's administration, the *Post* caused an uproar by publishing a cartoon by Sean Delonas that depicted a chimpanzee that had been shot by a policeman, who is telling his partner, "They'll have to find someone else to write the next stimulus bill." Although a rampaging chimpanzee was in the news at that time, the cartoon was interpreted as a racist depiction of Obama.

GARY GINSBERG: Rupert was definitely enchanted, definitely interested in Obama. He met him in June of 2008 at the request of Obama and [Obama adviser] David Axelrod. This was a month before he got the nomination, and then they talked on the phone a number of times. Rupert, I think, saw the advantages of having a relationship with a guy who was very likely to become the next president. He's done well befriending people in power.

SEAN DELONAS, Page Six cartoonist, 1990–2013: It was never meant to be Obama [in the cartoon]. The stimulus bill was supposed to be a badly written bill that was so stupid that even a crazed monkey could have written it. If that monkey represented anyone, it would have been Nancy Pelosi and Congress because they actually started the stimulus bill before Obama even took office. I was rushing through that cartoon because I was knocking out a lot of them for Col. With [previous editors] Lou Colasuonno and Ken Chandler, I would submit three cartoons a day. With Col Allan, I would submit eleven to thirteen cartoons a day. When I look back on it, I wish I could do that day over again. I did feel very bad about it the next day, but not because of Obama—because I didn't realize the woman that the chimpanzee attacked was so seriously hurt.

DAN AQUILANTE, chief music critic, 1980–2012: You have to understand that that cartoon, like everything in the *Post*, first went to the editor in chief, who made the selection. Then it went to a page editor, who placed it on Page Six. Then it went to the managing editor, Joe Robinowitz, who read every word in that paper every day, down to the Word Jumble and the movie clock listings. My understanding is that the only person who raised a red flag and said, "Hey, maybe we should do something about that," was one of the lower managing editors, Frank Zini.

SEAN DELONAS: After that cartoon came out, I was getting death threats—purely over Obama. Col wouldn't talk to me for four or five days. The police were at my house, and somebody mailed an envelope with powder to me. I was getting threats from the New Black Panther Party and the Nation of Islam. When Col did speak to me, it was on a speakerphone, so I'm assuming a lawyer was there. I think he was doing it to protect himself.

DAN MANGAN, reporter, rewrite, 2000–2013: You could hear people yelling outside. The phones were—it was like the bells at Notre Dame for hours.

> In an editorial, the tabloid issued an apology that nonetheless took a jab at "some in the media and in public life who have had differences with the *Post* in the past—and they see the incident as an opportunity for payback," as the editorial read. "To them, no apology is due. Sometimes a cartoon is just a cartoon— even as the opportunists seek to make it something else."

MARC BERMAN, sportswriter, basketball and tennis, 1997–current: There would have been a lot of great stories with Spike Lee. I knew him pretty well, riding the elevator to the concourses over the years and I did some stories with him, as the Knicks superfan. At some point, it was when LeBron snubbed the Knicks,

I was trying to get his reaction, and he said, "Marc, I really like you. But I can no longer talk to you on the record. Because you work for the *New York Post*." Maybe I tried two or three times later to try to convince him to do a story, and he just wouldn't do it. [Lee took part in protests over the Delonas cartoon.] He was actually telling athletes not to talk to the *New York Post*. It hurt.

The *Post*'s coverage of the man who would replace Obama in the White House stirred up a different kind of anger—from those who could not conceive of Donald Trump becoming president and chafed at the tabloid's validation of his candidacy, even if its reporting was initially ambivalent. The day after he declared his run on June 16, 2015, the wood blared TRUMP in gold lettering, above a photo of the White House. The subhead read: "Donald: I'll make White House mine." Although Col Allan was photographed wearing a "Make America Great Again" cap, Murdoch was not impressed, and that ambivalence showed on the *Post*'s front page. When Trump talked his way into trouble, claiming that GOP Senator John McCain, Vietnam veteran and POW camp survivor, was not a war hero, the wood declared DON VOYAGE! with a shark fin bearing down on a photoshopped image of the real estate developer and the subhead "Trump is toast after insult."

KEITH KELLY, media columnist, 1998–2021: It was weird in 2016 because they didn't endorse Trump in the general election. Yet they covered him shamelessly. They knew that he sold papers. So they would cover him. But they also knew Obama sold papers. They loved covering Obama. I think their calculation was that Trump was not qualified to be president, but he sure helps us sell papers.

CINDY ADAMS: Donald has been there for me for a thousand things. I lived next door to Jackie Kennedy for years on Fifth Avenue. When I moved in [to Doris Duke's former apartment on Park Avenue], Joey was fragile. He was not well. [Joey died in 1999.] I had nobody to help me. I had to buy the apartment with my own money. I had to furnish it. Donald understood that I was nervous and scared. He came in with his people to put in the alarm system for me. So he's been there for me. I've been there for him. I do not forget a friend. I am eternally loyal. Good or bad. Doesn't make any difference. Good or bad.

GARY GINSBERG: Rupert was friendly with Jared Kushner. Jared had reached out to Rupert when he bought the *New York Observer*, and then Ivanka became very good friends with Wendi. Rupert went to Ivanka and Jared's wedding.

MICHAEL WOLFF: When Ivanka tells Rupert that her father is going to run for president, he won't even entertain the idea. He says, "No, he's not. Don't bother me with this." Then Trump runs for president, and he's completely dismissive of it.

KEITH KELLY: I didn't mind Col going to Trump's wedding to Melania. Part of the way you get access is, you hobnob with the rich and powerful. I think Richard Johnson went to at least two of Trump's weddings. But the time Col was photographed in the newsroom wearing a MAGA hat was just bad. It bugged me.

SUSAN MULCAHY, Page Six editor, 1978–1985: A few months before Trump got the nomination, I wrote a piece for Politico about covering him in the '80s. I had devoted half a chapter to Trump's pathological lying in a book I wrote back then. Nothing had changed.

MICHAEL WOLFF: By May and June 2016, it's kind of clear that Trump's going to get the nomination. Murdoch goes to Ailes and says, tilt this to anyone but Trump—even Hillary. Ailes says it's the first time he's ever gotten a direct order on this.

Neither Col Allan nor Roger Ailes would finish the year at News Corp. Working at the *Post* had always required a thick skin. The place could be as combative and coarse as its headlines, but under Allan, some found it toxic. A number of staffers filed lawsuits—one of them digital editor in chief Michelle Gotthelf, who, in her 2023 filing, alleged years of "sex-based harassment" by Allan. After one particularly vicious run-in with him in 2016, she complained to HR. Soon after, Allan announced his retirement from the *Post*, which Gotthelf claimed was News Corp's effort to protect his reputation.

ERIC FETTMANN: Col cost the paper good talent. People left because of him. Like Gregg Birnbaum. Col had numerous fights with Michelle Gotthelf, which culminated in him taking [a list of potential news stories] at a meeting, ripping it up, and throwing it in her face. She decided she had enough so she went to human resources with a harassment complaint. Then Col decided to retire.

COL ALLAN, editor in chief, 2001–2016; editorial adviser, 2019–2021: I ripped up a Gotthelf list? I'm amazed it was only one. I had no idea [she] went to HR. Then or now. It was never raised with me by anyone. I asked Rupert to retire. I had been editing daily newspapers at that point—2016—for twenty-five years. I was exhausted.

TARA PALMERI: I had a great time at the *Post*, but I always went out on a story with a knot in my stomach, worried that if I didn't bring back the goods, I was dead to them. Jennifer Fermino used to say that our editors were our alcoholic parents. We all had this insane insecurity that we needed to be loved by all the editors up there. You had to be totally insecure, have a chip on your shoulder, or have mommy and daddy issues to truly succeed at the *Post*.

DAN AQUILANTE: Remember when I said I thought I could grow old at the *Post*? When I turned fifty-five, I retired. Unlike the days of Archer Winsten and Harriett Johnson, I was told that I had a problem with being in touch with what's happening now. I still feel now that I'm one of the more zeitgeisty people, but at the time, the trends I saw were totally ignored. I worked for people that didn't appreciate and didn't want anything to do with music, unless you could do a takedown on a star.

In July of that year, Roger Ailes, the Fox News chairman and CEO, was very publicly fired after he was accused of sexual harassment by on-air talent Gretchen Carlson and Megyn Kelly, among others. With the 2016 presidential election looming, Murdoch took control of Fox News, and Stephen Lynch, editor of the *Post*'s resurrected Sunday edition, succeeded Allan.

DAVID SEIFMAN: Before the 2016 election, I'm at my desk—I'm the political editor at that point—and [then–*Post* publisher] Jesse Angelo walks over to me and he says, "Do you think Trump can win?" So I'm thinking they're thinking of endorsing him. I say, "When it comes to Trump, I'm not going to predict anything." Because every prediction had been wrong up to that point. Hillary wrote him off as the guy she most wanted to run against. People said it was over when he gave that remark about women, "You grab them by the . . ." Everyone said, it's over, but the guy is still standing, and he's the front-runner. So I said I'm not going to predict. He asked me again. "Do you think he can win right now?" I said, "I would not bet that Trump is going to win." Every poll showed Hillary winning. She was acting as if she had already won. I surmised that they thought about endorsing him, seriously, and like most everyone else, didn't think he could win. That's strictly speculation. No one told me that, but newspapers like to go with winners.

CINDY ADAMS: The night Donald was elected president, around ten o'clock, before he went to the Hilton, I was in his office at Trump Tower. I'm there with Donald. This is history. He's standing. He never sat for hours. I was standing next to him. The two of us were the only two standing there. Behind us was Vice President Pence. There was Giuliani. There was Ivanka. There was Jared. And like twenty workers. Chris Christie was also standing off to the side. The only one standing with Donald in the middle of the room. Me. He said to me in my ear, "Do you remember what Roy [Cohn] said?" I said, "Yeah, I do." When Roy introduced me to Trump back in the 1970s, he said, "One day, this kid is going to own New York." Those were the only words Donald spoke to me the night he won. And the only words I spoke to him. I got chills just now when I said that.

CHRIS RUDDY, investigative reporter, 1993–1995: Trump still thinks the *Post* is very influential. Those old brands sit in his mind a lot more powerfully—the *National Enquirer, Sports Illustrated.* He thinks they're still big deals and the *New York Post* is still a big deal. It's still a player and it also is a conduit to Murdoch.

KEITH KELLY: My read on Murdoch over the years was that he did so much on gut instinct. Most of the time, that's much better than hiring McKinsey and paying millions of dollars to come up with these things.

ERIC FETTMANN: Murdoch was not a Trump partisan early on because he didn't think he could win, and he wanted a winner. We ended up endorsing him for the nomination, after he'd already clinched it. We endorsed him, saying, he has very serious faults, but we are sure that as a nominee, he will understand the gravity of his position and become more responsible. And that's why in November we did not endorse. Then, of course, Rupert became one in the long line of people who think, "I'm the one who can control Trump." Trump was calling him every day.

FRANK RICH, film critic, 1975–1977: Murdoch realized it was very much to his selfish advantage—his corporate advantage—to jump on the bandwagon and reap the rewards.

MACKENZIE DAWSON: All of a sudden this creature of New York—this creature almost of our own making—who had always been famous for calling up different departments at the *Post*, was running the country. So we were so much more in the news and in the spotlight.

> Murdoch was not about to sit on the sidelines during an administration led by a character that his tabloid had created—even if he thought Trump was "a fucking idiot," as Michael Wolff wrote in his 2018 book, *Fire and Fury*. With his son Lachlan Murdoch now the executive chairman of 21st Century Fox, Fox News commentator Sean Hannity counseling the president, and a roster of Trump-positive columnists at the *Post*—including political columnist Michael Goodwin and Cindy Adams—News Corp's brands got behind the president, for better or worse.

MICHAEL WOLFF: Removing Ailes from Fox News means they have no ballast there. Ailes was always very protective of anyone else's influence on the network. He would have pushed back against Trump. Rupert steps in. So Trump—basically the White House itself—is able to come in, and it's sending the message. Hannity and Trump are collaborating every night. So Murdoch is essentially, "What the fuck can I do?" At the same time, his whole family is erupting. James is like, no fucking way. Elisabeth is—the family is literally breaking up over Fox's support of Trump.

CHRIS RUDDY: Richard Johnson was a big Trump guy. I'm friends with Richard, and I brought him a couple of times to Mar-a-Lago. Trump is always extremely deferential and warm to Richard. He knows the play, although he'll always say, "The guy's a killer." Cindy Adams also had a close relationship with Trump. The story was that if Trump wasn't in the newspaper for three days, he'd call Cindy and say, "Tell everyone I was over at '21' last night" with whoever, and Cindy would deliver. I remember sitting with her once a couple of years ago, and she was going on about Trump's marriage, and how she knew all his secrets. I thought it was a little strange.

MARY TRUMP, niece of Donald Trump, author of *Too Much and Never Enough: How My Family Created the World's Most Dangerous Man*: The *Post* was the paper that gave him the most flattering or divorced-from-reality coverage. At the peak of the insanity of the '80s, his motto was, there's no such thing as bad news coverage. So, even if it was the *Daily News* with an unflattering cover, he was happy he was on it. Behind the scenes, I think he liked the *Post* because of people like Cindy Adams. She came out like a pit bull against me [after the publication of *Too Much and Never Enough*], which was amusing because I didn't realize she was still alive.

ANNA QUINDLEN, reporter 1974–1977: [Political columnist] Michael Goodwin seems to be a completely different person than the person I knew at the *New York Times*. He was a real middle-of-the-road reporter. I never had any sense that he had the kind of political bent that is evident in his *Post* column. It's so not evenhanded. Donald Trump used to say that he could shoot somebody, and he wouldn't get in trouble. If he did shoot somebody, Michael Goodwin would write about why it was the right thing to do. I'm just astonished at who he's become in print.

> The *Post*'s November 14, 2016, wood was the rare page one that did not use all caps to message its readers. "Don't be afraid," it read, the quote and cover photo from Trump's post-election interview with *60 Minutes*. The subhead: "Trump reassures divided nation in post-elect interview." Instead, four years of crises, two impeachments, and an administration that was a revolving door for key positions—including secretary of state, FBI director, chief of staff, and secretary of defense. The COVID pandemic and Black Lives Matter heightened the chaos.
>
> As it had during Trump's earlier period of tabloid deification, the controversies only emboldened him. As Trump's reelection campaign geared up, one of Murdoch's greatest hitmen reappeared in the *Post*'s newsroom in January 2019, ostensibly as a senior adviser. But it wasn't long before Col Allan was functioning as the tabloid's de facto editor in chief again.

WAYNE DARWEN, assistant managing editor, 1983–1987: Fox News does exactly what the *Post* does. It is still the same formula, and it hits that huge middle-America market, not the elitist places like LA where they're looking at the world through the bottom of a wine glass in a five-star restaurant. Fox News' audience is looking at the world through the bottom of a beer glass at the Post Mortem. Their influence is huge because it makes people feel like, oh, it's okay to support Trump. It emboldens them. It hugely validated Trump getting support. Murdoch, historically, is known for putting prime ministers in and out in Australia. So when the election was coming up, he called back Col Allan to break the knees of the opposition.

MACKENZIE DAWSON: When Col left in 2016, that was exactly the right time in terms of the national mood. Look, the *Post* was always a much rowdier place than most, but a lot of things were tolerated in the work world in general. It was a very different atmosphere. In the past six or seven years, there's been a lot more conversation about toxic work environments, what is tolerable and what is bullying. That's to say nothing of sexual harassment. I feel like Col left before that national conversation was being held, and a good thing, too, because when #MeToo emerged, I remember thinking again: oh my god, I always knew the way he treated people was unacceptable, but why didn't we ever say anything? And when he came back, I remember being astonished, along with many other staffers, thinking, are they seriously courting this amount of risk right now when he dodged the bullet the first time? It was like inviting the vampire back into the house.

NICK VEGA, reporter, tech, 2017–2021: When Col came back, there were other reporters there who were much more familiar with him than I was. And they were like, "Oh wow. What exactly is he coming here for? What is his title? What does this mean for our coverage? What does this mean for Steve Lynch [who became editor in chief of the print edition]? What does this mean for the direction of the paper?" I didn't fully grasp what the implications were.

MACKENZIE DAWSON: Michelle Gotthelf told me that she had some kind of behavioral clause put in his agreement that if he did anything unacceptable behavior-wise that he would be out of this newest arrangement. I don't know if that's true, but that's what she said, and I remember thinking, oh, now it feels like the women have the power. It felt like he had been defanged even though he hadn't been because, clearly, he was still there, and he was still being himself. [Gotthelf's lawsuit says that she renegotiated her contract to stipulate that under no circumstances would she report to Allan.]

COL ALLAN: A laughable untruth. The clauses in my contract were standard for any employee. If such nonsense were true, why was I asked to return to oversee the paper for two years and then offered a one-year extension? I have publicly and vigorously denied Gotthelf's claims. I do so again. For the record, I admitted no wrongdoing. It's all rather sad. [The lawsuit was settled in 2022.]

ERIC FETTMANN: Col mostly concerned himself with the print edition, and the political coverage. He made sure everything was loyal to Trump.

COL ALLAN: All I asked was that we be fair to Trump. Surely, that's our ethic.

ROGER STONE: I was not privy to their conversations, although I do know that Murdoch and Trump spoke uncommonly often during the reelection campaign. Was Murdoch giving Trump advice? To the extent that Trump takes advice. I was surprised because I don't think Murdoch is particularly a good friend. Nor do I think he's particularly Donald's enemy. I just think Murdoch is Murdoch. But Trump obviously regarded him as a supporter.

ERIC FETTMANN: The Trump reelection effort is a lot more significant than the election. In 2016, we were not Trump boosters. We did not endorse him in the general election. It was only after Trump reached out to Murdoch and began using him as a sounding board that the paper basically wound up in his pocket and became so deferential. There's a lot Trump did that the *Post* would support in any event, but what always got me was that whenever they would address something directly to him [in editorials], it was always, "Please, sir." It was like something out of Dickens, "Please, sir, I want some more." We had never been that deferential to any other political figure that I can think of.

MICHAEL RIEDEL, theater columnist, 1998–2020: There were a lot of people who I knew on Broadway—rich people—who were secretly on the side of some of the *Post*'s editorials. A lot of people supported the *Post* when it went after David Dinkins back in the day and supported Rudy Giuliani. But I know anecdotally that the *Post* going full tilt supporting Trump was a bridge too far for some.

MACKENZIE DAWSON: Some of the coverage was so over-the-top that it was hard to ignore, and yeah, people were not happy. I would also say that at that point, my job became harder in certain ways because there would be certain authors who would refuse to be covered in the *Post*. Even though it was good for them and our coverage would get their book sold. I think the entertainment desk had the same experience. That had always been true to a certain extent, but never to this extent. We were constantly having to convince people that our feature section is not political.

NICK VEGA: People in the office would message each other and be like, "Jesus, did you see the front page today?" Or "Oh my god, did you read that opinion piece that we ran?" And toward the very tail end of my time there, the *Post* had a good six-month stretch where it was doing just back-to-back-to-back embarrassing things. I would have friends and family sending me links. There's only so many times you can explain, "Hey, I have absolutely nothing to do with any of this. I read this in the paper the same way that you did."

CINDY ADAMS: Donald has a great sense of humor. He loves, loves, *loves* the United States of America, like I do. He made it. I don't care whether he's illegal. Or he's a thief. He made it. I love everybody who makes it.

ERIC FETTMANN: I think [executive editorial page editor] Mark Cunningham is doing what he thinks Murdoch would want and appreciate because [Cunningham] can't stand Trump, or at least he says he can't. There are people who kind of rationalize it away and not all that many who say, "I can't stand him, but I have no choice." Most political people generally find some way to rationalize what they're writing and doing.

Beginning in mid-October 2020, the *Post*'s woods were dominated by its coverage of emails found on a laptop left behind at a computer repair shop by Hunter Biden, the son of presidential candidate Joe Biden. According to the tabloid, the emails revealed that Hunter used his familial connections to profit from business deals in Ukraine and China. It also claimed that his father aided Hunter's efforts and may have profited from them, too. The laptop and its contents were initially ignored or dismissed as potential Russian disinformation by intelligence officials and much of the mainstream press; Twitter suspended the *Post*'s account over the reporting and Facebook suppressed its distribution. (To be fair, Rudy Giuliani, who said he had provided the hard drive contents to the tabloid, initially refused to share the data with other media outlets to allow independent verification.)

The *Post* went old-school on November 1, putting the death of actor Sean Connery on page one, then turned its full attention to the tight November 4 election. On the day after, the wood was NAILBITER, even though Fox News, before its cable news competition, had accurately called Biden as the winner of Arizona, angering Trump's camp and Fox viewers. Trump's biggest booster had sent the signal he had lost the election. Just days after the election, while Trump was claiming that the election had been stolen from him, Murdoch's remarks at an annual News Corp stockholders' meeting left little doubt as to where he stood. "It is crucial that conservatives play an active, forceful role in [the current American political] debate, but that will not happen if President Trump stays focused on the past," he said. "The past is the past, and the country is now in a contest to define the future." Col Allan, who announced his retirement a second time, was rewarded for his efforts with a hamburger dinner with the president in the Oval Office. In 2021, Murdoch named Keith Poole, deputy editor in chief of his London *Sun*, overall editor in chief of the *Post*.

JOHN WATERS, filmmaker: What was amazing to me was how they turned on Trump in one day! The order came down. One day.

KEITH KELLY: After the stolen election stuff, the *Post* was saying of Trump, you're going to damage your legacy. And then after January 6, it was, *what the hell?*

MICHAEL WOLFF: The whole Trump thing is probably the most painful stage of Rupert's career other than the near bankruptcy. He sold the [movie] business [to Disney in 2019] essentially because the family breaks up over Trump. Rupert, while at the same time he's controlling every outlet, he's also very responsive to whatever is working. So he hates Fox News, and it's really an incredible embarrassment, but to make so much money, what can he do?

TINA BROWN, former editor in chief, *The New Yorker*, *The Daily Beast*: Murdoch got what he wanted out of Trump. I don't think he considers backing Trump a mistake at all. He has dumped him, but not for reasons of moral conscience. Rupert lives in a world of winners and losers, and it is completely stark in that regard. He backs winners, and he dumps losers. To his mind Trump is looking like a loser right now. Rupert thinks Trump is just too much noise.

When Trump, who had moved to his home in Palm Beach, declared his 2024 run for the White House, the *Post* made its rejection of the former president crystal clear.

KEITH KELLY: "Florida Man Makes Announcement"—one of the funniest stories they have ever written. Absolutely brilliant. Page twenty-six.

29 | *POST*-MORTEM

arch 11, 2024, was Rupert Murdoch's ninety-third birthday. The communications empire he built, and the angry, divisive point of view many of his properties disseminate, now dominates our culture. The *New York Post* is its foundation. Without it, there would be no Fox News, no Newsmax, and arguably, no MSNBC, which employs similar strategies of outrage and omission, albeit from a progressive liberal perspective. Without the *Post*, reporters and segment producers at other media outlets would have to work a lot harder because the tabloid continues to churn up story angles, trends, and scoops that, as the previous chapters have shown, are often repackaged without crediting the original source. Critics contend that without the *Post*, journalism would be more trusted and trustworthy.

For some who worked at the paper in earlier decades, today's *Post* is a hollow version of its original self. Some of that judgment is generational, in the way that Baby Boomers think everything was better in the '60s and '70s. The internet, which has decimated print journalism in general and is now collecting the skulls of digital titles, also has much to do with the *Post*'s failings. The competition to break stories is relentless, and the need to drive traffic means Page Six leans heavily on items tied to reality television, while the *Post*'s digital operation blasts out stories involving grisly crimes, celebrity beefs, and the latest Hunter Biden news.

Then again, while debate continues over the ethics of releasing personal information on Biden's laptop, as well as the veracity of some of the data, its existence is not Russian propaganda. And Twitter and Facebook's decision to censure the tabloid's reporting challenges the notion that the *Post* is not as powerful a bully pulpit as it once was. Comments Donald Trump made in late 2023 suggest that he still pays close attention to the tabloid: "Since the *New York Post* went bad on Trump and they have gone bad, their numbers have fallen tremendously." In reality, Alliance for Audited Media (AAM) data shows that the tabloid's average circulation has grown by more than 100,000 since 2020 when it "went bad on Trump." But as Murdoch's history of throwing in with winners has shown, that could change.

As for the decades-long rivalry between the *Post* and the *Daily News*, Murdoch's tabloid is the clear winner. The *News*, now owned by the hedge fund Alden Global Capital, is a bare-bones operation without a physical newsroom. The last available AAM reports, from March 2024, put the *Post*'s combined print and digital average circulation at 510,077 for its Monday through Friday editions, and 517,735 for Sunday. The *News*' circulation: 92,927 and 115,114, respectively.

Ironically, it's the print version of the *Post*—where local and state political coverage, investigative stories, and the business section are not buried in some digital Siberia—that can still carry heat, especially when it reports on woke hypocrisy and wrongheaded political correctness. And because of its outrageous tone, the *Post* continues to act as a beacon to a particular demographic—the less anarchic, more corporate descendants of the punks who embraced the paper in the late 1970s; on August 13, 2018, Supreme, the über-trendy skateboard and streetwear brand, wrapped the print edition of the *Post* in a special ad. Regular readers could not find the paper that day as collectors and resellers hit newsstands and bodegas, buying every copy they could find.

Whether its print edition—or the *Post* at all—outlives Rupert Murdoch is a question that has swirled since the media baron hit his eighties. When the inevitable happens, the consensus is that the surviving members of Murdoch's family—whose internecine dramas partly inspired the hit HBO series *Succession*—and leadership at News Corp will either eliminate the *Post*'s print edition or close or sell the paper.

If the *Post* does not survive, what will be its legacy? We asked that question of those interviewed for the book, as well as for final thoughts they had about the tabloid. Here is a small sample:

GAY TALESE, author, *The Kingdom and the Power: Behind the Scenes at* **The New York Times:** *The Institution That Influences the World*: Rupert Murdoch has never had proper respect paid to what he has done. I've never met the man, but I greatly respect him.

MACKENZIE DAWSON, books editor, 2005–2023: What makes me the saddest is that the New York part of the *New York Post* has been downplayed as it has become a global digital brand. You can see it especially on Page Six. Page Six used to do such an amazing job of creating these creatures of the *Post*; these fantastic New York socialites who probably weren't well known outside of New York, but to readers of Page Six, you followed the whole narrative. It was just such a fun thing to read, and I feel like now it's just the Kardashians. It's not special and it has nothing to do with New York. I'm a big opera lover and I always felt like the *Post* covered New York like it was an opera. It didn't matter what your department was. Everything was about the highs and lows of the human experience.

DAVID NG, associate managing editor, 1980–1993: What was it that Murray Kempton once said of Rupert Murdoch? I think he called Rupert Murdoch the Long John Silver of the Staten Island Ferry. There was something to be said about that. We were the good bad guys of journalism, and it was a lot of fun.

MICHAEL SHAIN, television editor, 1978–1993, 1996–2013: It's the hub of Murdoch's American operation. The *Post* was a social phenomenon that made everything else possible.

ROBERTA BRANDES GRATZ, reporter, 1963–1978: Murdoch's purchase of the *New York Post* began the change of newspapers nationwide. He legitimized an unreliable journalism. And he made it okay for others to do so. I've always felt that things began to change all over the place after him, and it's been downhill ever since.

TINA BROWN, former editor in chief, *The New Yorker, The Daily Beast*: The *Post* still has power. Rupert enjoys having that power. And he knows it works for him. Without the *Post*, he would be just another rich guy. The *Post* gives him that edge.

REV. DR. C. VERNON MASON, civil rights activist: A paper that has the history that the *New York Post* has, you have a responsibility to the public good, the public safety, and the welfare of humanity. You cannot be embracing stuff that is destructive. I'm not talking about ideology now. I'm talking about violence. If you don't recognize that, you are as complicit and guilty as the people who do it. When I look at the history of the [*Post*'s] founding and the good people who worked there, and what it has turned into, and the damage that it is doing, I say: What is the purpose? What I see is profit and power. I don't know how Rupert Murdoch sleeps at night.

GARY GINSBERG, former executive vice president, News Corp: Rupert loves the playfulness and mischievousness of the paper. He loves that it punches well beyond its financial weight, for sure. The fact that the company is willing to tolerate losses every year is testament to the *Post*'s nonmonetary value. I think every shareholder understood that investing with Rupert meant you were investing in certain properties that just weren't going to make money, but had value, and the *Post* was a given. Its value was so much greater than the de minimis loss that it represented on the balance sheet. For a paper that saw declining circulation, newsstand sales, et cetera throughout the time I was there, it still maintained its primacy in New York journalism. It could direct or move sentiment through the way it presented the news, its willingness to take risks, how colorful its coverage was, and how powerful its columnists were. What also drove Rupert was having that kind of influence over a city that he really cared about.

WARREN HOGE, metropolitan editor, 1966–1976: The *New York Post* is an embarrassment for its politics.

DICK BELSKY, metropolitan editor, 1970–1989: One great thing about the *Post* is that it has an identity, and that identity really comes from Murdoch. When you say "the *Post*," you think Rupert Murdoch. How many other papers can you say that about?

JIM FARBER, former music critic, New York *Daily News*: The *New York Post* is a state of mind. I mean, it's a sensibility. It's iconic. It's a piece of conceptual art. You can't take it at face value. I hope people don't. It never occurred to me that people could take the politics seriously.

AMY PAGNOZZI, reporter, columnist, 1979–1993: Did Rupert Murdoch accelerate the cheapening of the collective consciousness? Obviously. Is he a negative force in the world? Totally. On a number of occasions, I wrote poorly about my own paper while I was working there, but looking back now, I wonder if I did enough, whether I was collaborating just by being there.

CANDICE BERGEN, actress: I start every day at the kitchen counter with a mug that says "Tired-ass Honky Ho" filled with coffee, and a pristine copy of that morning's *New York Post*. I have taken some heat about reading a rag religiously, and I can honestly say, I don't care. It helps get my brain back among the living. Helps me compute tiny events. Even though I never know the names of anyone in it, I love Page Six. I love it all. Every grisly, tragic story. It starts my day.

ANNA QUINDLEN, reporter, 1974–1977: I read it every day, and most of the so-called intelligentsia and one-percenters of New York I know read it every day. Do I set my watch by it? Absolutely not. I read a piece about the president or the governor or the mayor, and I think, okay, maybe, but it's in the *Post*. One of the reasons I read it is because there are interesting people writing there, like Michael Goodwin. I'm astonished at virtually everything they produce, but I feel like it's a point of view that is important for me to understand and allow for. I'm always trying to get a 360 view.

JOHN WATERS, filmmaker: Everybody I know in show business reads it. Some people say, "How can you read that?"—people who refuse to read it and are haughty about it. Lots of liberals. I'm a liberal, but not that kind of liberal.

CHARLIE CARILLO, reporter, columnist, 1978–1993: Everything now is so loud. In New York, you put on the morning shows, with the overtalk and the yelling. That definitely traces back in a lot of ways to the *Post*. Everybody's turned into a carnival barker.

HARRY SHEARER, humorist, actor, co-star of *This Is Spinal Tap*: I think the idea of a feisty, darkly humorous, but still striving to be accurate tabloid newspaper has always been a good idea. It's rarely done well. Certain aspects of that are done well by the *Post*—that is to say, the headlines and the archness of some of the attitude. But it labors under a certain burden of being owned by a guy who doesn't give a fuck.

FRANK RICH, film critic, 1975–1977: [Murdoch] is so determined to leave his mark on America that he's willing at any given moment to suck up to everyone from Ed Koch and Hillary Clinton to Donald Trump. And he was a better businessman than many of his progenitors in America. He was very savvy in terms of building things, including Fox Entertainment and the broadcast network before there was Fox News. I don't think it ever would have occurred to [William Randolph] Hearst to try and then succeed at buying an establishment organ as old-school as the *Wall Street Journal*. Murdoch has been fearless in that sense. His organs from Fox News to the *Post* are often bullying, mean, and bigoted, but he does have a fearlessness as a businessman. He has incredibly thick skin, and his fearlessness stops him from any kind of self-censorship, frees him of any kind of moral or ethical guidance. And it can take horrible forms like the phone-hacking scandal in England, including preying on a family whose child had been killed; to more subtle stuff like assuring the apparently quite gullible Bancroft family that controls would be put in place so that when he bought the *Journal*, he would uphold the same standards. And then of course, he did whatever the hell he wanted.

JILL ABRAMSON, former executive editor, *The New York Times*: You can find a causal connection between the tabloid pulse and the ascendancy of clickbait on the web—grab you by the throat and get your attention, sometimes with a misleading but irresistible headline. I think that comes from papers like the *Post*.

CINDY ADAMS, gossip columnist, 1981–current: Some version of the *Post* will continue because it's the bully pulpit. I also know that you can't have dinner in the Hamptons if you haven't read the *Post*, because there's nothing else to talk about.

GREGG BIRNBAUM, political editor, 1993–2010: For a lot of people in the media world, a tabloid background is a stain. That is so wrong and so unfortunate. I've worked at many different publications, CNN, NBC News, Politico, the *Miami Herald*, which has won something like twenty-three Pulitzer Prizes, and the reporters at the *Post* will stack up against the reporters at any of those places.

JOE CONASON, former reporter, *The Village Voice*: The *Post*'s legacy lives on in Fox News in some ways—that sort of freewheeling, "don't care too much about the facts, we know who our friends and enemies are" style of journalism imported into this country. It has definitely had an impact on how things are done here, largely negative. But Page Six is fun. I don't want to sound like I have a stick up my ass about this stuff. They were creative and fun in some ways. I disagreed with a lot of their purposes and prejudices. The other problem was that the editorial policy of the *Post* encouraged racial divisions in the city. It stigmatized African American and Latino politicians, and those who represented the aspirations of those communities. They were viewed with suspicion by white people already, and the *Post* encouraged that.

HARRY SHEARER: It was the tip of the spear of Limbaugh, Drudge, all of that—they came in the wake of and followed the lead of the *Post*. The fact that it happened, and happens, in the country's largest liberal city says there's a market for it in the rest of the country.

CHRIS RUDDY, investigative reporter, 1993–1995: Newsmax is a legacy of the *New York Post*.

BILL BIGELOW, city desk assistant, 1975–1979: Without Rupert Murdoch and the *New York Post*, there's no Fox News. And without Fox News, in my estimation, there's no Donald Trump. And without Donald Trump, we don't have all those people dead from COVID.

ANNA QUINDLEN: I'll be really interested to see where the two sons wind up when their father dies. Will either of them be inclined to change Fox News, given how old its demographic is? Will either of them be inclined to change the *Post*, given that they do have a perch in New York City which is, in some ways, second to none? If I were the next generation, I would be inclined to modify—not to emulate CNN or the *New York Times*, but perhaps to be less crazed.

FRANK RICH: Murdoch is a comparable figure with [Condé Nast owner] Si Newhouse, who held on to newspapers and magazines—operating them at full tilt—way past when he should have. And then once he was gone came the reckoning. If I had to guess, the moment Rupert dies, I wouldn't be shocked to see the *Post* go or get sold off for peanuts or whatever.

CHRIS RUDDY: I've estimated that, in all the years that Rupert has owned the *Post*, he's amassed at least a billion dollars in cash lost. In real money, that's probably two or three billion if he had invested that same money somewhere else. It's an amazing amount. I think it was probably helpful in getting his start in the entertainment business. I also think he felt that the *Post* was giving him a tremendous amount of political leverage and influence that maybe he used to the benefit of his other media properties in Europe and Australia. And if you look at Fox News, which was one of the last great gems of his empire, it throws off a billion-plus dollars in revenue a year.

CHARLES LACHMAN, reporter, 1981–1988: It's ultimately a story of a triumph of an idea. Sometimes they blow it, but on any given day it's entertaining, it's enlightening, and I think they put out a great product. And the fact that it's been in business since 1801, I would say they finally got it right.

SALVATORE "SAMMY THE BULL" GRAVANO, Gambino crime family underboss: The *Post* has got the balls enough to come out with things about Hunter Biden and get shut down by big tech. And they do it over and over again. I give them kudos for that. They're not letting nobody bully them. I liked that they're going after the truth. They don't give a fuck what you do or say.

ERIC FETTMANN, associate editorial page editor, columnist, 1976–1991, 1993–2019: The *Post* is alive certainly as long as Rupert is alive, and I think it's also true of Lachlan. He may not romanticize it as much. I think he understands the product. He's committed to the *Post* brand.

TONY MANCINI, reporter, 1958–1978: They do still break some pretty good stories. I just have a sour taste in my mouth. You know the old saying about no self-respecting fish would be caught dead wrapped in a copy of the *New York Post*? I told that to my students [at Brooklyn College]. They don't get it because they don't remember a time when people wrapped fish in newspapers.

JOANNE WASSERMAN, reporter, 1977–1986: I spent seven years as a reporter at the *Post*. Then, I was at the *News* for twenty-six years. But my memories from the *Post* are so much more vivid and dramatic. I mean, I met my husband at the *Daily News* and I finally got to do real journalism, but it was not as much fun, as loud, or as exciting.

RAMONA GARNES, copy editor, 1978–1990, 2000–2004: I'm talking out of my hat here, but I look at what Fox News has done to this country, and I say, it's the Brits getting the US back for having a revolution and declaring independence. They're gonna make us sorry we kicked King George to the curb.

JIM FARBER: The legacy of the *Post*? Pure evil. And I mean that as a compliment.

KENNY MORAN, sportswriter, outdoor sports and skiing, 1972–2013: The legacy will be Rupert Murdoch, not Dolly Schiff or anyone before.

COL ALLAN, editor in chief, 2001–2016; editorial adviser, 2019-2021: It's a work in progress. Much history has yet to be written.

CINDY ADAMS: You have enough from me. Be kind, or I will find you.

-30-

POST *POST*

Former *Post* staffers have gone on to a wide array of jobs. Some remained, or remain, in the media, and some of those have distinguished themselves with Pulitzer Prizes and other accomplishments. Of those people we interviewed—excluding those who are still at the paper or who retired upon leaving—here are highlights of their post-*Post* careers.

AIDA ALVAREZ, reporter, 1973–1977, became a TV journalist, an investment banker, and the first Hispanic woman to serve in a presidential cabinet, as the administrator of the Small Business Administration for Bill Clinton. She has also served on corporate boards, including Walmart and Hewlett-Packard.

JANE AMSTERDAM, executive editor, 1988–1989, eventually left journalism, adopted a son, started an antique charm and watch fob company, and became a competitive horse-drawn carriage driver.

JESSE ANGELO, publisher and CEO, 1999–2019, was global president of Vice Media and now runs his own company, Checker Media.

FLO ANTHONY, Page Six co-editor, 1984–1993, writes for the *New York Amsterdam News*, *amNewYork Metro*, and *Dan's Papers* and is a radio segment host.

HARVEY ARATON, sportswriter, basketball, 1977–1982, was a sportswriter for the *New York Times* for twenty-five years and has written nine books.

GEORGE ARZT, City Hall bureau chief, 1968–1986, was Ed Koch's press secretary, worked in TV news, and since 1995 has run his own communications firm.

DAVE BANKS, night managing editor, 1979–1981, worked for two Murdoch papers in Australia and at *The Sun* in London. He also worked for Murdoch competitors *The Mirror* in London and the *Daily News* in New York. He died in 2022.

DEVLIN BARRETT, reporter, 1992–2002, was part of *Washington Post* reporting teams that won Pulitzer Prizes in 2018 and 2022. He is also the author of *October Surprise: How the FBI Tried to Save Itself and Crashed an Election.*

DICK BELSKY, metropolitan editor, 1970–1989, is a former vice president at NBC Universal and former managing editor of the New York *Daily News.* He has written twenty-four mystery novels, including several set at newspapers.

CHERYL BENTSEN, feature writer, 1976–1977, freelanced for magazines and wrote the nonfiction book *Maasai Days.*

JOE BERGER, investigative reporter, 1971–1978, was a reporter and editor at the *New York Times* for thirty years and is the author of five books.

JAMI BERNARD, chief movie critic, 1978–1993, reviewed films for the New York *Daily News* and is now an author, book doctor, and headline writer for the *National Enquirer.*

BILL BIGELOW, city desk assistant, 1975–1979, is a Hollywood screenwriter.

GREGG BIRNBAUM, political editor, 1993–2010, worked as an editor, mostly covering politics, at CNN, Politico, NBC News, and the *Miami Herald.*

DOUG BLACKBURN, sportswriter, basketball, 1983, teaches newswriting at Florida A&M University.

ANN V. BOLLINGER, national correspondent, reporter, 1986–1999, taught journalism and digital media at Seton Hall University for eighteen years.

TIM BOXER, assistant to Earl Wilson, TV columnist, 1966–1986, is editor and publisher of 15minutesforever.com.

JAMES BRADY, creator of Page Six, 1977; Page Six editor, 1980–1982, wrote columns for *Ad Age, Parade, Crain's New York Business,* and *Forbes*; appeared regularly on television; and wrote many novels and nonfiction books. He died in 2009.

ROBERTA BRANDES GRATZ, reporter, 1963–1978, has written extensively about urban change, in periodicals and in six books. She also served on New York's Landmarks Preservation Commission; and, with Jane Jacobs, founded The Center for the Living City.

FRANK BRUNI, reporter, rewrite, 1988–1990, is a professor of journalism and public policy at Duke University and a contributing opinion writer for the *New York Times*, where he has also worked as an op-ed columnist, a White House correspondent, Rome bureau chief, and chief restaurant critic. He has written four *New York Times* bestsellers.

JERRY CAPECI, reporter, organized crime, 1966–1986, has written a weekly column about organized crime at ganglandnews.com since 1996, a column he previously wrote for the New York *Daily News.* He has also written six books.

CHARLIE CARILLO, reporter, columnist, 1978–1993, is a former producer at TV's *Inside Edition* and has written twelve novels.

KEN CHANDLER, editor in chief, publisher, 1978–1986,1993–2002, was editor in chief of the *Boston Herald* and is now executive editor of Newsmax media.

CLAUDIA COHEN, Page Six editor, 1977–1980, became a gossip column fixture herself upon marrying and divorcing (with an $80 million settlement) Ronald Perelman and dating then–US Senator Al D'Amato. She died in 2007.

JAN CONSTANTINE, senior deputy counsel, News Corp, 1991–2005 became general counsel for the Authors Guild, where she was extensively involved in the organization's landmark copyright infringement lawsuit against Google. She is now a partner at Constantine Cannon and sings with the MasterVoices chorus.

MARTHA COOPER, photographer, 1977–1980, earned international recognition for her photos of the graffiti scene in New York, published in the book *Subway Art.* She has also documented breakdancing and hip-hop, and is the subject of a 2019 documentary, *Martha: A Picture Story.*

WAYNE DARWEN, assistant managing editor, 1983–1987, is a TV writer and director.

HAL DAVIS, reporter, New York State Supreme Court, 1978–1993, worked as an editor at the *Dayton Daily News* and the *St. Paul Pioneer Press.*

LENORE DAVIS, photographer, 1980–1993, freelanced for the *New York Times* and CMP Publications.

MACKENZIE DAWSON, books editor, 2005–2023, covers books for The Free Press.

SEAN DELONAS, Page Six cartoonist, 1990–2013, worked as a syndicated cartoonist before trading ink and paper for paint and canvas. His political cartoons can be found in the permanent collections of the Library of Congress, the National Museum of American History, and the New-York Historical Society.

JOE DE MARIA, photographer, 1977–1993, freelanced for the *Post* after Murdoch broke the Newspaper Guild in 1993.

BOB DRURY, sports columnist, 1977–1984, was a reporter at *Newsday* and has written several nonfiction books.

FRANKIE EDOZIEN, City Hall reporter, 1993–2008, is director of New York University's program in Accra, Ghana, and the author of *Lives of Great Men: Living and Loving as an African Gay Man.*

JERRY ENGEL, photographer, 1958–1993, freelanced for the New York *Daily News* and other publications.

RICHARD ESPOSITO, reporter, 1982–1985, shared a 1992 Pulitzer Prize at *Newsday* and later worked at ABC News, where he won a Polk award for his investigation into CIA secret prisons. He recently completed a biography of Jimmy Breslin.

CYNTHIA FAGEN, reporter, 1976–1986, is a TV producer, co-host of *Killing Time The Podcast,* and, with James Patterson, co-author of *The House of Kennedy.*

PETER FEARON, reporter, 1980–1987, is a producer at *Inside Edition.*

JENNIFER FERMINO, reporter, 2001–2013, was City Hall bureau chief for the New York *Daily News* and is currently the vice president of communications and marketing at the New York Public Library.

DAVID FRANCE, reporter on tryout, 1985, is an author and filmmaker. His documentaries include *How to Survive a Plague,* about AIDS activism, which was nominated for an Oscar, and *Welcome to Chechnya,* winner of a Peabody and a BAFTA.

PETER FREIBERG, reporter, 1971–1978, wrote for the *Soho Weekly News, The Advocate,* and the *Washington Blade.*

RAMONA GARNES, copy editor, 1978–1990, 2000–2004, worked as a freelance copy editor, a nanny, and an administrator for Presbyterian missionaries.

LESLIE GEVIRTZ, reporter, rewrite, 1978–1988, was a reporter and editor at Thomson Reuters for more than twenty years, in New York, London, and Singapore.

HAL GOLDENBERG, photographer, 1979–1986, is chief dispatcher for a two-way radio public safety system for businesses and institutions.

MARIANNE GOLDSTEIN, assistant city editor, 1979–1993, was the editor of People.com and editorial director of United Feature Syndicate.

TERRY GOLWAY, sports copy editor, 1987–1992, is an author and historian whose most recent book is a biography of New York mayor Fiorello La Guardia. He also teaches US history and political science at the College of Staten Island.

RICHARD GOODING, metropolitan editor, 1976–1993, freelanced for *Star* magazine, *National Enquirer*, and *Vanity Fair* after leaving the New York *Daily News*.

JESSIE GRAHAM, reporter, 1999–2004, is an editor, producer, writer, and podcast consultant who has reported for NPR, BBC, and CBC programs and helped create and run the multimedia team at Human Rights Watch.

PETER GREEN, deputy business editor, 2005–2006, worked as a reporter for the *New York Times*, an editor and reporter at Bloomberg News, and a foreign affairs writer for The Messenger.

JOHN GRUBER, copy editor, 1971–1978, 1980–1985, was a sports copy editor at the New York *Daily News*.

AL GUART, federal court reporter, 1993–2004, produced stories for CBS News; owned the Catskill Mountain Lodge in Palenville, New York; and wrote *Beyond the Sphere: Encounters with the Divine*.

CLYDE HABERMAN, reporter, 1966–1977, has worked as a reporter, foreign correspondent, city columnist, and editorial writer during his more than forty years at the *New York Times* and was part of a team that won a Pulitzer Prize in 2009.

BOB HARDT, political reporter, 1993–2003, is political director at NY1.

THE VERY REV. GUY P. HAWTIN, investigations editor, 1979–1989, served as rector of Saint Stephens's Anglican Church in Timonium, Maryland, for thirty-three years. He died in 2022.

HENRY HECHT, sportswriter, baseball, 1969–1984, wrote columns for *Sports Illustrated* and *The National* and was a sports copy editor at *Newsday.* He has been tutoring high school students since 2005.

STEVE HOFFENBERG, aspiring owner, 1993, started a short-lived women's publication called *HER New York* after leaving the *Post*, but in 1997 was sentenced to twenty years in prison—plus a $1 million fine and $463 million in restitution—after pleading guilty to bilking investors out of $475 million through a Ponzi scheme. He died in 2022.

WARREN HOGE, metropolitan editor, 1966–1976, worked for more than thirty years at the *New York Times*, where he was a foreign correspondent, foreign news editor, and an assistant managing editor, among other assignments. He died in 2023.

PETER HONERKAMP, Page Six reporter, 1979–1980, owns the Stephen Talkhouse, a bar and music venue in Amagansett, New York. Paul McCartney, Jimmy Cliff, Paul Simon, and Patti Smith are among the artists who have performed there.

PATRICIA JACOBS, fashion writer, columnist, 1978–1993, freelanced for the *Post* until 2009 and is now PJ Cobbs, an artist who works mainly on silk.

RICHARD JOHNSON, Page Six editor, 1978–1990, 1993–2019, writes a gossip column for the New York *Daily News*.

KATHY KAHNG, assistant to the vice president of circulation, 1989–1991, worked for several business improvement districts in New York City; ran for a seat in the Putnam County, New York, legislature in 2023; and currently runs CityRax, a consulting firm for public space programs

ROBERT KALFUS, photographer, 1977–1993, 2002–2015, worked for the New York *Daily News*, the *New York Times*, the Bronx Borough President's office, and other clients in between his *Post* stints.

PETER KALIKOW, owner, 1988–1993, continues as president of the real estate firm HJ Kalikow & Co. He is also the former chairman of New York's Metropolitan Transportation Authority and a former commissioner of the Port Authority of New York and New Jersey.

JONATHAN KARL, reporter, 1994–1996, is chief Washington correspondent for ABC News; co-anchor of *This Week with George Stephanopoulos*; and author of three books about Donald Trump's presidency.

SETH KAUFMAN, Page Six reporter, 1989–1993, worked as editorial director and VP of merchandising at Barnes & Noble's ecommerce site and is a bestselling ghostwriter.

MICHAEL KAY, sportswriter, 1982–1988, has been the New York Yankees' play-by-play commentator for more than thirty years, on radio and TV. He also hosts a radio show for ESPN.

KEITH KELLY, media columnist, 1998–2021, is editor in chief of four local New York City newspapers, including *Our Town, Chelsea News*, and *West Side Spirit.*

DOUGLAS KENNEDY, reporter, 1993–1995, is a correspondent for Fox News.

JARED KOPEL, reporter, 1973–1978, is an attorney specializing in SEC investigations and securities litigation.

TOM KREUZER, editorial driver, 1972–1978, was a New York City firefighter for forty years, after *Post* reporter Joe Nicholson enouraged him to try out for the FDNY.

MARK KRIEGEL, sports columnist, 1991–1993, is a boxing analyst for ESPN, and author of a novel and three biographies of sports figures.

CHARLES LACHMAN, reporter, 1981–1988, is executive producer of *Inside Edition*, where he has worked since the show's 1989 launch. He has also written four nonfiction books.

CAROLE LEE, assistant to James Wechsler, photo syndication editor, 1963–1993, worked at the New York *Daily News*—on the city desk, on the editorial page, and as photo editor of the short-lived Sunday magazine.

DREW MACKENZIE, day news editor, 1979–1991, ran his own news agency, Drew's News, for twenty-five years, and authored or co-authored two books.

KELVIN MACKENZIE, night managing editor, 1978–1979, ran Rupert Murdoch's London *Sun* for more than a dozen years and later wrote a column for the paper. He was forced out in 2017 after comparing a British football player to a gorilla. In the 1990s, MacKenzie was managing director of LIVE TV in England, where programs included a "bouncing weather dwarf," who offered forecasts while jumping on a mini trampoline. MacKenzie also founded TalkSPORT, the UK's first commercial sports radio station. Rupert Murdoch's News Corp acquired its parent company in 2016 for £220 million.

TONY MANCINI, reporter, 1958–1978, was director of the journalism program at Brooklyn College, where he taught for more than forty years. He has also written ten eight novels, including *Ashes*, published in 2023.

DAN MANGAN, reporter, rewrite, 2000–2013, is a reporter at CNBC who focuses on politics.

STUART MARQUES, managing editor, news, 1993–2001, worked as managing editor, news, at the New York *Daily News* and opened his own communications company before retiring.

LISA MARSH, fashion/retail business reporter, 2000–2003, is a content creator and author of four books, including *The House of Klein: Fashion, Controversy, and a Business Obsession.*

DIANA MAYCHICK, entertainment writer, 1978–1989, reviewed films for the Bergen *Record* and restaurants for the *Indian River Press Journal.*

TIM MCDARRAH, reporter, Page Six co-editor, 1985–1993, conducted Save the Village tours in New York's Greenwich Village and ran the Art of Our Century gallery until his death in 2021.

BOB MERRILL, Page Six assistant, 1981–1982, is a jazz musician and bandleader and hosts a radio show in Palm Beach County.

PHILIP MESSING, reporter, 1978–1991, 1994–2016, writes freelance articles about crime and criminal justice and is the co-author of *Undisclosed Files of the Police: Cases from the Archives of the NYPD from 1845 to the Present.*

JOANNA MOLLOY, Page Six co-editor, 1990–1993, wrote the Rush & Molloy column for the New York *Daily News* with her husband, George Rush, and co-authored *The Greatest Beer Run Ever*, which was adapted for a 2022 film.

JIM MONES, drama editor, 1980–1987, became one of the first (if not the first) *Post* editorial employees to be hired by the *New York Times* after the end-of-the-Schiff-era exodus. He worked there for thirty-three years.

GREGG MORRIS, reporter, 1984–1988, teaches journalism at New York's Hunter College and is the author of two books.

PETER MOSES, reporter, 1984–1993, runs his own communications company.

MAURA MOYNIHAN, Page Six assistant, 1981–1983, led the effort to create the railroad station in Manhattan named after her father, US senator Daniel Patrick Moynihan. She also worked in Nepal for Radio Free Asia.

PAMELA NEWKIRK, reporter, 1988–1990, was part of a reporting team that won a Pulitzer Prize in 1992 at *Newsday* and is now a professor of journalism at New York University and the author of five books on different facets of the African American experience.

DAVID NG, associate managing editor, 1980–1993, was an editor at the *Star-Ledger* in New Jersey and executive editor of the *Daily News* in New York. He is now managing editor of the *Richmond Times-Dispatch* in Virginia.

DON NIZEN, vice president of circulation, 1989–1991, was a co-founder of the free daily newspaper *amNew York* (now *amNew York Metro*) and worked with controversial businessman and political donor Sheldon Adelson to start *Israel Hayom* (Israel Today), a Hebrew-language free daily published there.

JIM NOLAN: reporter, 1986–1993, was a reporter for the *Philadelphia Daily News* and the *Richmond Times-Dispatch*, and later served as press secretary for the mayor of Richmond, Virginia.

AMY PAGNOZZI, reporter, columnist, 1979–1993, wrote columns for the New York *Daily News* and the *Hartford Courant.*

TARA PALMERI, City Hall/politics reporter, 2010–2015, was a White House correspondent for ABC and is now senior political correspondent at Puck.

MARY PAPENFUSS, reporter, 1984–1993, was an editor at the New York *Daily News* and the *San Francisco Examiner*; staff writer at HuffPost; and is the author of three books.

ROCCO PARASCANDOLA, reporter, 1989–2001, is the police bureau chief at the New York *Daily News.*

JANE PERLEZ, reporter, 1972–1977, was a foreign correspondent for the *New York Times* for more than thirty years, most recently as Beijing bureau chief.

ESTHER PESSIN, reporter, rewrite 1988–1990, is co–executive producer of *Inside Edition.*

ELIZABETH POCHODA, Sunday book review editor, 1989, worked as an editor at the New York *Daily News, House & Garden, The Magazine Antiques*, and other publications.

CHRIS POLICANO, City Hall reporter, 1994–1997, is a veteran public relations professional, who, since leaving the *Post*, has worked in government, nonprofit, and labor sectors.

PETER PRICE, publisher, 1988–1989, recently funded a joint venture with the Columbia Business School to produce a series of online career courses.

JOYCE PURNICK, political reporter, 1970–1978, was a reporter, columnist, and editor at the *New York Times*, and the first woman to run the *Times'* Metropolitan section.

ANNA QUINDLEN, reporter, 1974–1977, won a Pulitzer Prize as a columnist for the *New York Times*, and has written twenty-one books, including ten novels.

REX REED, film critic, 1982–1986, is a film and theater critic at the *Observer* (formerly the *New York Observer*).

FRANK RICH, film critic, 1975–1977, was chief drama critic and a columnist for the *New York Times*, a writer at large for *New York* magazine, and executive producer of the HBO shows *Veep* and *Succession*. The latter focused on the ferocious rule of a powerful New York–based right-wing media mogul.

MICHAEL RIEDEL, theater columnist, 1998–2020, is a radio host and the author of two books about Broadway, *Razzle Dazzle* and *Singular Sensation*.

DAVID ROSENTHAL, reporter, desk editor, 1974–1977, has spent much of his career as an executive and editor at major book publishers, including Simon & Schuster and Random House.

FAIGI ROSENTHAL, assistant head librarian, 1978–1986, ran the library at the New York *Daily News* for twenty-two years.

BARBARA ROSS, political reporter, 1978–1985, covered politics and the courts for the New York *Daily News* for more than thirty years and was a Nieman Fellow at Harvard.

CHRIS RUDDY, investigative reporter, 1993–1995, is the founder and CEO of Newsmax.

GEORGE RUSH, Page Six reporter, 1986–1993, wrote the New York *Daily News'* Rush & Molloy column with his wife, Joanna Molloy, and is the author of three nonfiction books.

JIM RUTENBERG, Page Six reporter, 1993, is a writer at large for the *New York Times*, mostly covering politics and media, and was part of a team that won a Pulitzer Prize in 2018. He also co-wrote *The Murdochs: Empire of Influence*, a CNN miniseries.

VALERIE SALEMBIER, president, 1989–1990, is an executive coach and mentor at ExCo Leadership.

TONY SCHWARTZ, gossip columnist, 1976–1977, is founder and CEO of Leap Worldwide, a leadership development business, and author or co-author of several books, including Donald Trump's *The Art of the Deal* (which he now regrets) and *The Way We're Working Isn't Working.*

PAUL SCHWARTZMAN, reporter, 1989–1993, is a reporter at the *Washington Post* who specializes in political profiles.

ADAM SCULL, photographer, 1978–1981, 1985–1988, owns and operates wprnpublic radio.com, an independent web-only platform based in North Tampa, Florida.

CHARLES SENNOTT, reporter, 1988–1989, founded both the GlobalPost, the first web-based international news organization, and the GroundTruth Project, a nonprofit that supports journalists in underserved areas.

MICHAEL SHAIN, television editor, 1978–1993, 1996–2013, worked as an editor for weekly papers in Queens, including the *Queens Chronicle.*

MELANIE SHORIN, Page Six reporter, 1977, co-founded Narrative Trust, a multimedia oral history company.

STEPHEN SILVERMAN, entertainment writer, 1977–1988, was news editor of People .com for twenty years, and wrote thirteen books, including biographies of directors David Lean and Stanley Donen. He died in 2023.

PAT SMITH, night city editor, 1977–1989, spent nearly thirty years at Howard Rubenstein's communications firm, where he became a managing director.

RANDY SMITH, reporter, 1977–1980, was a reporter for the *Wall Street Journal,* where he was part of a group that won a 2002 Pulitzer Prize.

IAN SPIEGELMAN, Page Six reporter, 1999–2000, 2001–2004, has written two novels, and authored or co-authored four nonfiction books. He was also Gawker's first weekend editor.

MARK STAMEY, reporter, 1993–2006, worked briefly as a reporter for the New York *Daily News.* He is writing a memoir about his adventures in journalism.

NED STEELE, reporter, rewrite, 1977–1980, was Liz Holtzman's press secretary when she was Brooklyn DA, and later worked at Howard J. Rubenstein Associates. He currently edits the Brooklyn Technical High School alumni magazine.

RICHARD STEIER, City Hall reporter, 1989–1993, was head editor of *The Chief-Leader*, which covers New York's civil servants and organized labor.

JARED STERN, Page Six reporter, Page Six Magazine Editor, 1996–2003, 2004–2006, is a freelance writer.

PAT SULLIVAN, reporter, night editor, 1972–1980, had a long career at ABC News.

DONNIE SUTHERLAND, city desk assistant, 1978–1988, was a freelance writer and is now an environmental activist and organic farmer in Massachusetts.

PAUL THARP, reporter and columnist, 1982–2014, kept his press pass after taking a buyout at the *Post* and started City News Report NY, an online tabloid. When it shut down during the pandemic, he started a nonprofit.

LINDSY VAN GELDER, feature writer, 1968–1977, freelanced for a variety of publications and for eighteen years was chief writer for *Allure*.

PETER VECSEY, columnist, basketball, 1977–1991, 1994–2012, hosts a podcast for the National Basketball Retired Players Association.

NICK VEGA, reporter, tech, 2017–2021, is a pop culture reporter for CNBC.

GRETCHEN VIEHMANN, photo editor, 1993–2001, was photo editor at the New York *Daily News* and is now head of Documentary and Editorial Photography at Falmouth University in England.

JOYCE WADLER, feature writer, 1974–1977, was a staff reporter at the *New York Times* and wrote a humor column for the paper.

JOANNE WASSERMAN, reporter, 1977–1986, is executive editor of The 74 Media, a nonprofit news site that covers K–12 education.

SUSAN WELCHMAN, photo editor, 1977–1979, worked at *National Geographic* for thirty-five years, retiring as senior photo editor in 2015.

CHRIS WILSON, Page Six reporter, 2000–2006, is a travel and lifestyle writer and digital director at Maxim.

BOB YOUNG, photo editor, 1978–1986, was a producer of *A Current Affair* and co-creator of *Inside Edition*.

ACKNOWLEDGMENTS

The writers would like to thank:

The 240+ people who agreed to be interviewed for *Paper of Wreckage*. Without their observations and memories, there would be no book.

Peter Borland at Atria Books, for accepting the proposal to publish *Paper of Wreckage*; for responding so positively to the first (and other) drafts; for his overall enthusiasm and encouragement; and for his outstanding editorial guidance and close reading of the book throughout the publication process. Also at Atria, thanks to Sean deLone, Ryan Conaty, Samantha Cohen, Dana Sloan, Liz Byer, Vanessa Silverio, Jane Herman, David Brown, Falon Kirby, and Dayna Johnson. Thank you, too, to Carolyn Levin, for her excellent counsel.

The staff of the main branch of the New York Public Library, especially the Rose Main Reading Room and the Vartan Gregorian Center for Research in the Humanities, and NYPL CEO Tony Marx. The research for this book began at the height of the COVID crisis, when the Schwarzman Building at 42nd Street and Fifth Avenue was forced to close for nearly a year. Working remotely, the librarians helped us enormously by sifting through *New York Post* microfilm and other primary sources. Everyone was helpful throughout the process; among those who were exceptionally so: Rebecca Federman, Paul Friedman, Miriam Gianni, Melanie Locay, and Elizabeth Rutigliano.

Myron Rushetzky, for his amazing memory and for the resources of his Post Nation email community. Eric Fettmann, for his knowledge of the *Post*'s history. George Arzt, Dick Belsky, Charlie Carillo, Jerry Capeci, Ken Chandler, and Greg Gallo, for fielding more than their fair share of queries. Erin Boudreau, for navigating circulation archives at the Alliance for Audited Media.

Susan Mulcahy would like to thank:

Frank DiGiacomo, for agreeing to collaborate on a project involving the *New York Post*—an institution about which we share strong feelings. Based on the superb job he did on the Page Six oral history for *Vanity Fair*, I knew he had the right sensibility—along with exceptional reporting and writing skills—to make this book sing.

Kate Johnson, my agent at Wolf Literary, and Sloan Harris at CAA, for being such enthusiastic boosters of this project.

Jane Perlez, for allowing us to quote from her notes and for introducing me to Barbara Demick, who in turn introduced me to the Center for Research in the Humanities and its Frederick Lewis Allen Room. I am grateful to have had a workspace there.

Russell Abdo, Matt Mulcahy, Betsy Pochoda, Michelle Stoneburn, and Jim Willse, for troubleshooting technical issues, reading parts of the manuscript, putting me in touch with interview subjects, and fact-checking knotty topics.

D'Arcy Hyde, for a painless author photo session.

Geoff Reiss, for reading and commenting on an early (massively long) draft of this book.

Dan Klores, for saying, "You know, the *Post* would make a good oral history," upon hearing old *New York Post* stories over lunch in 2019. Agreed!

Frank DiGiacomo would like to thank:

Susan Mulcahy, for her invitation to collaborate on this project. I have long admired her writing, her wit, and her meticulousness, drive, and doggedness as a reporter, and having worked closely with her to publish this book, only admire her more.

Kate Johnson and especially my amazing agent Sloan Harris, who has long been in my corner, spurring me on with inspiration, wisdom, and straight talk. He also introduced me to the word "flense." Sloan, thank you for your continued faith in me.

Patricia Clough and my son Antony DiGiacomo for their love and support long before I took on this project; my father and North Star, Frank Sr., and siblings Sam, Tony, Mary, Jena, and Natalie and their spouses, partners, and pets; my mother and greatest teacher, Barbara Ann; and my extraordinary godson

Anthony "Sam" DiGiacomo, who both passed while I was writing this book. I miss you and carry you in my heart. Thank you also to Gay Talese, David Hirshey, Sophia Tezel-Tzelepis, Steven Gaines, John Pelosi, Pete Asimakopoulos, Dolores P. Sullivan, Carl Criniti, Hannah Karp, Joe Levy, Ed Christman, Terry Moseley, Dror Nir, and Charles Herr, for their friendship, support, and encouragement. A shout-out also to Bonnie Burke, for the flattering book jacket photo. I am extremely fortunate to have worked for some of the finest editors in journalism: Graydon Carter, Susan Morrison—who took a chance on me when no one else would—Peter Kaplan, Bruce Handy, Lisa Chase, Eric Etheridge, and Richard Johnson. Much gratitude to you all. You have taught me so much. Finally, thank you to James Murphy and LCD Soundsystem, and Will Toledo and Car Seat Headrest, whose music inspired me when I needed it most.

INDEX